The Key to Kanji

A VISUAL HISTORY OF 1100 CHARACTERS

漢字絵解き

Noriko Kurosawa Williams

16 15 14 13 12 11 10   2 3 4 5 6 7 8 9 10

First edition 2010

Published by
Cheng & Tsui Company, Inc.
25 West Street
Boston, MA 02111-1213 USA
Phone (617) 988-2400
Fax (617) 426-3669
www.cheng-tsui.com
"Bringing Asia to the World"™

ISBN 978-0-88727-736-8

Illustrations: Ayako E.L. Williams

Library of Congress Cataloging-in-Publication Data

Williams, Noriko Kurosawa.
    The Key to kanji : a visual history of 1100 characters = Kanji etoki /
Noriko Kurosawa Williams. -- 1st ed.
        p. cm.
    Includes indexes.
    ISBN 978-0-88727-736-8
    1. Japanese language--Study and teaching (Secondary)--English
speakers. 2. Chinese characters--Etmyology--Dictionaries. I. Title.
II. Title: Kanji etoki.

PL519.W55 2010
495.6'11--dc22
                                2009075171

Printed in the United States of America

CONTENTS

Preface

The Key to Kanji: A Visual History of 1100 Characters has been prepared for students and teachers of the Japanese language at all levels. In the past, the field of Japanese language education did not fully appreciate the relationship between kanji form and the meaning of a kanji – which can often seem completely unrelated – and yet it can be explained in a logical and memorable way if we trace the development and formation of the kanji from ancient times to present usage. I hope that this new presentation of etymology-based explanations of 1100 kanji will help you to appreciate the essence of kanji as visual stories of meanings and that the insights you gain from studying this book will equip you with a powerful tool in expanding the horizon of your Japanese language study.

From the time when kanji 漢字 was adopted by the Japanese language from the Chinese, and even after the Japanese people developed their own phonetic letter systems of *katakana* and *hiragana*, kanji remained the kernel part of Japanese writing systems. For over a hundred years, since the twentieth century, a number of archaeological excavations of ancient sites in China have uncovered an abundance of artifacts with various ancient inscriptions on oracle bones, bronzes, and stones and writings on bamboo and wooden writing tablets and cloths. Thanks to the painstaking efforts by kanji scholars who undertook the task of deciphering these inscriptions, we are now able to glimpse at the mystery behind the birth of individual kanji. In this book, we will take advantage of the fruits of those labors and learn about the intrinsic connection between kanji form and meaning, giving us insight and facilitating our study.

A modern kanji can be viewed as a sort of skeleton of its ancient writing form. When ancient writing was created for rulers to communicate with their ancestral gods, the shape of the writings was a direct depiction of the image of its meaning. But when the writings came to be used by people and got standardized into more regulated shapes, the original shapes were reconfigured into certain sets of lines and curves. The flesh and muscle of the original depiction was shed and only the skeleton remained. It was no longer possible for us to see an immediate image of the

meaning in present-day kanji. As a result, learning kanji became dry rote-memorization without a clue to the connection between form and meaning. In this book, we restore the "flesh and muscle" of the images showing the original meaning in simple drawings. You will be able to see how the original meanings inspired ancient people to come up with ancient writing forms, which eventually became the shapes that we now use. This book gives you the missing link between kanji form and meaning.

How this approach started:

I have taught Japanese in an English-speaking country at the university and high school level for three decades. I have always believed that someone who lives outside a kanji environment should not be taught kanji in the same way Japanese school children would learn. Children in Japan learn new kanji with ample time and repetitious practice, reinforced by what they see in their family environments and daily lives. Outside Japan, young adults and adults who study the language do not have the benefits of their surroundings and tire quickly from simplistic and time-consuming exercises. Instead, I concluded they would benefit from an approach that enabled them to use more mature learning ability and reasoning. However, I could not find any materials that supported my idea.

Two decades ago I started to introduce kanji to my students with a brief account of their origins, pointing out that each form that they saw was not a shape composed of arbitrary lines but, in fact, an image conceived by ancient people. Invariably, in every class that I taught—whether the students were beginners, intermediate, or advanced and whether it was a university program or high school program—my students responded with keen curiosity and listened to my explanations intently, to an extent that I had

not seen with any other classroom activities. My students were quite intrigued when they learned that a seemingly complicated and strange shape had a story of its own, like a living creature. Such stories unexpectedly transported them to the imaginary life of an ancient civilization and, to their surprise, showed how it connected to modern times. Developing this kanji-learning approach took a lot of time over many years. The effects I observed in class and the progress of my students motivated me to continue with this unique approach.

Field-testing: "Illustrated Kanji Anatomy"

Several years ago, with the help of two people who enjoyed drawing and have a passion for studying kanji, I was able to combine my etymological explanations in English with some original artwork. I named these materials "Illustrated Kanji Anatomy" because each kanji was dissected into smaller meaningful units with some visual illustration.

The "Illustrated Kanji Anatomy" was first shared with my colleagues and friends in the Japanese language teaching field and then with a larger group of teachers. Between 2005 and 2009, "Illustrated Kanji Anatomy" that I prepared for users of a popular Japanese textbook was shared with over one hundred fifty teachers in Europe, Australia, New Zealand, Japan, Canada, and the United States. I also prepared "Illustrated Kanji Anatomy" that corresponded to other textbooks and custom kanji lists for interested teachers. In addition, I shared 580 kanji origins via a public website.

The largest group of requests for custom kanji lists came from university teachers in the United States. Here, studying kanji tends to get placed on the back burner. The constraints of classroom time and the emphasis on oral proficiency tend to overshadow reading and writing skills.

Many people sent me positive feedback and relayed how the materials were put to use in the classroom, and valuable comments from teachers and students provided me with more ideas on how to improve the materials. I was excited by statements from people in the United States and all over the world commenting on how they have benefited. What struck me the most was the consistency of comments on how my approach unlocked a difficult process to become enjoyable, stimulating, and accessible.

It is not unusual for a Japanese language teacher not to be fully aware that there is a direct connection between the meaning and kanji form, in a way that this book shows. And yet, if you look around Tokyo, Kyoto, Nara, or most other Japanese cities, you will almost certainly come across something that is a clever use of an ancient writing style called *tenji/tenkoku* (official-seal style). I could not help smiling at myself several years ago when I realized that not only the elegant plaque of a posh cookie shop in a historical town called Kamakura was written in that ancient writing style, but also, the noren cloth above the door of a little ramen noodle shop in my hometown had this ancient writing. The combination of modern and ancient is startling and wonderful to those who know what to look for. We sometimes miss the treasures that can be utilized in our kanji teaching. It has been a real pleasure to see that so many teachers have started to take notice of these hidden treasures. I hope you will join the ranks of such kanji enthusiasts.

The sources used for this book were taken from kanji dictionaries, calligraphy publications, books on kanji history and etymology, and even store name plaques that are scattered around towns in Japan.[1] Different views exist about which ancient kanji form is the prototype for a particular modern kanji. Naturally, these different views produce different accounts of a kanji's origin. As fascinating as these academic debates are, they are left to the world of kanji historians. The goal of this book is to give Japanese language students and teachers materials that can be put to use right away, with the confidence that the information provided is historically authentic and extensive enough to understand both familiar and new kanji.

Acknowledgements

My long-held wish to develop this kanji study/reference book would not have been realized without the help of a number of people over the years.

The illustration artwork was largely done by Ayako E. L. Williams, with the initial help of Hiromi Kishimizu. Ayako's extraordinary patience and willingness to contribute to this book allowed me to make countless revisions every time new reference sources came to my attention. With 1100 kanji, the process sometimes seemed endless.

Special thanks go to many people: Chiaki Sekido of *The Japan Times* for providing me (through their website) the opportunity to reach teachers who were interested in my approach; Masae Masuda for her calligraphy on the development of hiragana; Bryon Lee Brunkow for his help in my English manuscript; Chinami Lay for her painstaking work to catalogue the references; Chieko Miyama, Sachiko Aoshima, Kumiko Akikawa, and Yasuyo Tokuhiro for their personal interest and support; and S. Linn Williams for his unfailing faith in me and the publication of this book and for his constant encouragement over the years.

---

[1] The illustrations on kanji development and ancient writing forms were all drawn by our illustrators and myself for this book. Among the sources that we consulted, the works by Kenneth G. Henshall (1988), Shizuka Shirakawa (2004), Shuji Suzuki, et. al. (ed) (1976), Akiyasu Todo (ed) (1991), Katsumi Yamada (1976), and John Jing-hua Yin (2006) were inspiring and helpful in our preparation.

I also would like to express my appreciation to over a hundred fifty teachers of Japanese around the world who took notice of my approach and incorporated my materials into their teaching. I feel quite humbled by their overwhelmingly positive responses and encouraging comments. Personal communications over the last four years have been enjoyable, and I felt a real comradeship among all of us who are searching for the most effective way to teach kanji in the language we love.

It was my strong wish to bring these materials to the public outside Japan, and the production of this complex project involved working in two languages through thousands of graphic files, hundreds of odd pieces of kanji and old-style kanji that were not ordinarily found, phonetic guide work, and searches for special typefaces. I would like to express my sincere gratitude and admiration to the staff at Cheng and Tsui in Boston, Massachusetts, especially to Penny, Karin, Paige, Tracy, Sumanth, anonymous reviewers, and all others who at various stages of the production were thoroughly professional and made gallant and tireless efforts to understand my numerous requests and revisions, even those made after the production had begun.

I also would like to mention the contribution of my mother to this book in a profound way. As a child, whenever I asked her for quick help with an unfamiliar kanji in a book I was reading, she would respond—to my great annoyance at the time but my gratitude now—"*kanwa-jiten hiite goran* (look it up in the kanji dictionary)." I grudgingly complied because I wanted to continue reading. Decades later when I chose a profession, I realized the hidden trove of information in kanji dictionaries.

And last but not least, special thanks go to my current and former students, who without fully appreciating how much they were helping, guided me to improve earlier versions of the materials with their questions and responses—occasionally even their body language. Every giggle, smile, laugh, puzzled or surprised look, indignant reaction, pondering posture, and any other reaction that I glimpsed in the classroom became important feedback for me to continue working on this project. To them and to all students after them who use my book, I wish the feeling of love that I have myself for the Japanese language.

About the Author

Noriko Kurosawa Williams has taught Japanese at American University in Washington, D.C., since 2005. A native of Japan, she graduated from Keio University in Tokyo (B. A. in political science) and Georgetown University (M.S. and Ph. D. in linguistics). She has taught at Georgetown University, George Washington University, George Mason University, and Soka University of America. She has also taught at the high school level.

This book, *The Key to Kanji: A Visual History of 1100 Characters*, is the culmination of many years of classroom teaching experience, and was derived from her fascination with the fact that kanji are a window into the imagination of another era. Her earlier work, *Illustrated Kanji Anatomy*, was well received by teachers in the United States, Europe, Australia, and Japan.

Dr. Williams also developed a visual method for Japanese pronunciation practice, the "Visual Tonal Guide" (目で見る音調), and has made a freeware available on a language-learning software. She is the author of a memoir-essay – "Kitchin Kara Mita Nichibei-Kosho," published by Bungei Shunju in Tokyo.

Introduction

Before you begin the individual study of 1100 kanji, I recommend that you read the three chapters on the general history of kanji and related issues.

In Chapter 1 "The Historical Development of Kanji Forms," the historical development of the three major styles of ancient writings into modern writings is examined, looking at how the visible connection between a kanji writing and its meaning, which was obvious in ancient writing styles, faded away as the writings grew to be standardized into a more uniform style. This new style was solidified during the Han (漢) Dynasty, resulting in the writing style called *hanzi* (漢字 "the writing of the Han") or *kanji* in Japanese, and it has remained for the next two millennia.

In Chapter 2 "Kanji Formation Types and Dictionary Section Headers (*Bushu*)," the four types of kanji formation are discussed. Of the four types, phonetic-semantic composition formation is generally credited with creating a large majority of the kanji. Knowledge of the recurring components in phonetic-semantic kanji provides a powerful tool to expand one's kanji knowledge. For this reason, a table of all the 184 types of dictionary section headers called *bushu* that appear in our 1100 kanji is provided with its description and example kanji. These 184 section headers cover virtually all the kanji used in present-day publications in the Japanese language.

Chapter 3 "Development of Japanese Writing Systems" focuses on Japan, which did not have a writing system initially, and discusses how the writings that were born in China influenced the Japanese language, not only in its writing system but also its sound system and vocabulary. In addition, this chapter discusses how two phonetic letter systems of *katakana* and *hiragana* were developed from kanji for different purposes and in different ways, and eventually the writing system of the present-day style emerged.

Main Body
1100 Kanji—History, Meanings, and Use

In addition to providing the missing links between each kanji's form and meaning, *The Key to Kanji: A Visual History of 1100 Characters* also provides all aspects of kanji study—sound, form, meaning, section header, usage, and stroke order—that learners will need to have for a complete picture of kanji. Each of the 1100 kanji in this book contains the following information:

Sample Kanji Table for 分

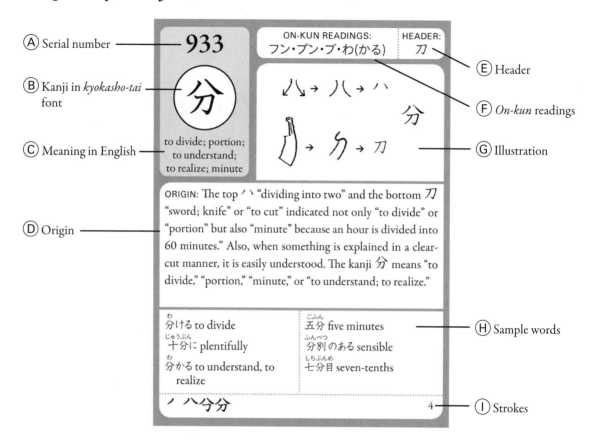

(A) Serial number

(B) Kanji in *kyokasho-tai* font

(C) Meaning in English

(D) Origin

(E) Header

(F) *On-kun* readings

(G) Illustration

(H) Sample words

(I) Strokes

(A) **Serial number (1 through 1100):** *The Key to Kanji* contains 1100 kanji that are numbered according to the "*on*-reading" of kanji, which are Chinese derivative pronunciations.

(B) **Kanji in *kyokasho-tai* font:** The *kyokasho-tai* "textbook style" typeface is the best approximation of an ideal handwriting style, which students are encouraged to emulate.

(C) **English definition:** The meanings of each kanji are given in English. Compound kanji words have different meanings, but it is helpful to know the core meaning of each individual kanji.

(D) **Origin:** The historical development of each kanji is explained in English. To clarify the delineation between ancient meanings and modern day mean-

ings, past tense is used to indicate historical uses while current tense is used to indicate present uses.

(E) **Header (dictionary section header):** A dictionary section header (*bushu*) found in traditional kanji dictionaries is provided for each kanji. *The Key to Kanji* includes 184 kanji section headers. A section header has sometimes been called a radical in English as well.

(F) ***On-kun* readings:** The *on*-reading (Chinese derivative pronunciation) is indicated in katakana, and the *kun*-reading (Japanese pronunciation) is indicated in hiragana.

(G) **Illustration:** Each kanji's historical development is illustrated in steps. A drawing of: (a) the image of the original meaning, (b) an ancient writing

form taken from the oracle-bone style, bronze-style, or seal-style, (c) the meaningful components of the kanji, and (d) the present-day kanji form.

(H) **Sample words:** An average of six frequently used words are chosen per kanji with *furigana* (Japanese phonetic guides) and meanings in English. There are approximately 6500 words in this book. Some of the words that are customarily written in a particular kanji, but not necessarily listed among its corresponding on-kun readings as described in (F), are also included.[1]

(I) **Strokes:** Each kanji's stroke order is fully illustrated in *kyokasho-tai* font in clear precise graphics. The total number of strokes is also provided.

Kanji selection

The total of 1100 kanji in *The Key to Kanji* includes all of the 1006 kanji on the educational kanji list (学習漢字), which is the list of kanji that the Japanese government requires textbook writers to introduce in primary school education in Japan. An additional 94 kanji are selected from the list of commonly-used kanji (*joyo-kanji* 常用漢字)[2]; these were chosen based on textbooks commonly used in the United States and linked to various proficiency test requirements in the United States and United Kingdom.[3]

---

[1] A kun-reading is essentially a matching up of an existing Japanese word with the kanji form of the same meaning. However, the use of kanji in some words may vary to some extent depending on the purpose or genre of writing or the individual writer's style.

[2] The commonly-used kanji list contains 1945 kanji, 1006 of which are designated as educational kanji. In 2010 a change is expected to include some additional kanji.

[3] With one or two exceptions, the book contains all the kanji introduced in the following materials: 377 kanji from *Japanese as Written Language* (Jorden and Noda 1995); 317 kanji from *Genki I & II* (Banno et al. 1999); 390 kanji from *Nakama 1 & 2* (Makino et. al. 1998 & 2000); 500 kanji from *Kihon Kanji 1 & 2* (Kano et. al. 1989); 410 kanji from the Advanced Placement Test in Japanese (College Board 2006) in the United States; and 600 kanji from the GCSE, AS and A2 kanji lists (Edexcel Foundation 2006) in the United Kingdom.

Indexes to search for kanji

Being able to locate kanji quickly and efficiently is crucial for a reference book. As noted in A, the 1100 kanji in *The Key to Kanji* are arranged in order of their *on*-reading (Index 1). We also provide five additional indexes for user navigation in the back of the book. The six indexes are as follows:

INDEX 1: Order of Appearance in *The Key to Kanji* (本書所収の漢字)

This is the list of the 1100 kanji arranged according to its on-reading (Chinese derivative pronunciation) in the order of the Japanese Syllabary, or the Table of Fifty Syllables (五十音図), which is a-i-u-e-o, ka-ki-ku-ke-ko, etc.

INDEX 2: On- and Kun-Readings: Japanese Syllabary Order (五十音順音訓読み)

This index lists all the on-readings and kun-readings (Japanese pronunciation) of the 1100 kanji in this book in the order of the Japanese Syllabary. Following convention, the on-reading is given in katakana and kun-reading in hiragana.

INDEX 3: On- and Kun-Readings in Romaji (ローマ字による音訓読み)

This index is for beginning students who may be using *romaji* (alphabetical rendition). Two types of romaji, the *kunrei* system and the Hepburn system, are included.

INDEX 4: Arranged by Total Number of Strokes (総画数による索引)

This index references the total number of strokes in a kanji. When the pronunciation is not known, you can count the total number of strokes and look it up in this index.

INDEX 5: **Arranged by Section Header** (部首による索引)

In the traditional kanji dictionaries, kanji are arranged according to a recurring part of the kanji called the section header or *bushu,* or sometimes known as the radical in English. This book contains 184 dictionary section headers. Look for the stroke number and you can quickly locate the kanji within a category of kanji. The arrangement of the section headers also follows convention.

INDEX 6: **Arranged by the Educational Kanji Designation** (学年別学習漢字)

This index is useful for heritage students and students who study kanji using textbooks that follow the grade designations from the Japanese government.

Benefits to Students and Teachers at All Levels

The Key to Kanji was written for students and teachers of the Japanese language at all levels. Here are some general thoughts for using this book.

If you are a beginner or a teacher of beginners, this book will serve as a reference accompanying your primary textbook. By using the pronunciation in the textbook as your guide, you can use the index to find the desired kanji.

First, read the explanation on what the kanji consists of and view the corresponding illustrations. After you understand the connection between the kanji's form and its meaning, write out the kanji in the stroke order shown. Keep in mind that the kanji is a result of a writing process that developed over more than three thousand years and the stroke order is a part of the tradition. Using the right stroke order will help you remember the kanji, and believe it or not, Japanese can usually tell from the writing if you did the strokes out of order. If you have more time, read through the sample words, and get accustomed to the idea that an individual kanji has more than one reading and meaning.

If you are an intermediate-level student or a teacher of intermediate-level students, you have probably studied nearly four hundred kanji already. Now you can learn new kanji in a new way and increase kanji knowledge and vocabulary at the same time.

Re-learn familiar kanji by carefully dissecting them into meaningful components. You will notice that those meaningful units reappear in other kanji that are related in meaning or pronunciation. They give you valuable building blocks for your intermediate-level study and beyond. Then, study sample words that use the kanji that you are studying. Learning to use a familiar kanji in different words is an effective way to increase the breadth of your vocabulary, which is an important goal of your study at the intermediate level.

If you are an advanced-level student or a teacher of advanced-level students, nearly all new vocabulary words that you will learn are compound kanji words. For that reason, knowledge of kanji is crucial to your progress in learning the Japanese language even if you are more interested in speaking than reading or writing.

Sit back, read through this book, and keep your mind open to this new approach to understanding kanji. Study the 184 section-header table carefully, and you will begin to realize that kanji and words that did not seem necessarily connected before are actually connected. Since the majority of kanji are formed by way of "phonetic-semantic composite formation," you have a powerful tool in deciphering a new unfamiliar kanji in its meaning and/or pronunciation to expand your kanji knowledge to all of the approximately 2000 kanji that are currently used in Japanese.

If you are studying for a proficiency test, such as the Japanese Language Proficiency Test, in addition to the suggestions above, it may be useful to keep in mind the following:

Many of the standardized proficiency tests require kanji recognition. This book's focus on the relationship between a kanji's form and meaning is helpful to preparing for these tests because you will be able to recognize the meaning of components of unfamiliar kanji. The 6500 sample words were chosen for its frequent use in Japanese newspapers (on-line media, in particular) and will be useful in expanding your vocabulary along with deepening your kanji study.

If you are a parent or a teacher of a student in a heritage Japanese language school or supplementary Japanese school (日本語補習校), this book is a good reading book for your student. A gap between fluent speaking skills and lower-level kanji knowledge can hinder further learning of compound words, which is essential in reaching adult-level proficiency. This book will fill that gap. The visual illustration that shows the origin of kanji in this book will motivate younger students to stay interested in kanji and maintain their efforts in Japanese language study. For any student, the visual can only aid in comprehension.

References

Arai, Kofu. 新井光風 1997年「古典の新技法 1 金文」二玄社 *Koten no shingihoo 1 – kinbun* [New technique for the classics 1—Bronze writing]. Kyoto: Nigensha, 1997.

Asahi Shimbun. 朝日新聞 2006年「最古の万葉仮名文，7世紀半ばの木簡に成立30年早まる」(2006年10月13日付) *Saiko no Man'yooganabun, nanaseiki-nakaba no mokkan ni seiritsu sanjuunen hayamaru* [A discovery of the mid-7th century wooden tablet dates the oldest Man'yoogana writing to be 30 years earlier]. *Asahi Shimbun* (Tokyo), October 13, 2006.

Atsuji, Tetsuji. 阿辻哲次 1989年「図説漢字の歴史普及版」大修館書店 *Zusetsu kanji no rekishi – hukyuuban* [Abridged illustrated history of kanji]. Tokyo: Taishukan Shoten, 1989.

Banno, Eri, Yutaka Ohno, Yoko Sakane & Chikako Shinagawa. 坂野永理・大野裕・坂根庸子・品川恭子 1999年「日本語初級げんきI」[Integrated Course in Elementary Japanese 1]. Tokyo: *The Japan Times,* 1999.

Banno, Eri, Yutaka Ohno, Yoko Sakane, Chikako Shinagawa & Kyoko Tokashiki. 坂野永理・大野裕・坂根庸子・品川恭子・渡嘉敷恭子1999年「日本語初級げんきII」[Integrated Course in Elementary Japanese 2]. Tokyo: *The Japan Times,* 1999.

College Board. *Japanese Language and Culture Course Description.* http://apcentral.collegeboard.com. Kanji List, pp. 7–9. New York: The College Board, 2006.

Edexcel. AS & GCE Kanji List. in *UA006790 – Specification – Edexcel AS/A GCE in Modern Foreign Languages (Arabic, Chinese, Japanese, Modern Greek):* Issue 3, pp. 30–36. London: Edexcel, 2006.

Fazzioli, Edoardo. *Chinese Calligraphy – from Pictograph to Ideogram: The History of 214 Essential Chinese/Japanese Characters.* New York: Abbeville Press, 1987.

Hatasa, Yukiko Abe, Kazumi Hatasa & Seiichi Makino. *NAKAMA – Japanese Communication, Culture, Context 2.* Boston: Houghton Mifflin Company, 2000.

Henshall, Kenneth G. *A Guide to Remembering Japanese Characters.* Vermont: Tuttle Publishing, 1988.

Ishikawa, Kyuyo (ed). 石川九楊編 1996年a「書の宇宙1 – 天への問いかけ・甲骨文・金文」二玄社 *Sho no uchuu 1 – Ten e no toikake – kookotsubun kinbun* [The world of calligraphy 1 – Vocative to the heavens – Oracle bone writing and bronze writing]. Kyoto: Nigensha, 1996a.

Ishikawa, Kyuyo (ed). 1996年b「書の宇宙2 – 人界へ降りた文字・石刻文」二玄社 *Sho no uchuu 2 – Jinkai e orita moji sekkokubun* [The world of calligraphy 2 – Secularization of writings – stone inscription writing]. Kyoto: Nigensha, 1996b.

Iyanaga, Teizo, et al. (eds). 弥永貞三他編 1974年「図説日本の歴史5貴族と武士」集英社 *Zusetsu nihon no rekishi 5 Kizoku to bushi* [Illustrated history of Japan – Aristocracy and warrior classes]. Tokyo: Shueisha, 1974.

Jorden, Eleanor Harz and Mari Noda. *Japanese: The Written Language 1 & 2 (Field Test Edition 1.0).* Boston: Cheng & Tsui Company, 1995.

Kano, Chieko, Yuri Shimizu, Hiroko Takenaka & Eriko Ishii. 加納知恵子・清水百合・竹中弘子・石井恵理子 1989年「基本漢字500 1 & 2」凡人社 [Basic Kanji 500. Vol. 1 & 2]. Tokyo: Bonjinsha, 1989.

Kawasaki, Tsuneyuki, et al. (eds). 川崎庸之他編 1974年「図説日本の歴史 4 平安の都」集英社 *Zusetsu nihon no rekishi 4 – Heian no miyako* [Illustrated history of Japan 4 – The capital of the Heian era]. Tokyo: Shueisha, 1974.

Makino, Seiichi, Yukiko Abe Hatasa & Kazumi Hatasa. *NAKAMA – Japanese Communication, Culture, Context 1*. Boston: Houghton Mifflin Company, 1998.

Ministry of Education, Culture, Sports, Science and Technology – Japan. 文部科学省1998年「新しい学習指導要領-別表学年別漢字配当表」*Atarashii gakushuu shidoo yooryoo beppyoo gakunen-betsu kanji haitoohyoo* [New curricular guidelines – Appendix: The table of kanji designation by grade level]. Tokyo: Ministry of Education, Culture, Sports, Science and Technology–Japan, 1998.

Onishi, Katsuya & Toru Miyamoto. 大西克也・宮本徹 2009年「アジアと漢字文化」（放送大学教材）放送大学教育振興会 *Ajia to kanjibunka – hoosoo daigaku kyoozai* [The kanji culture in Asia – Textbook for the Broadcasting University]. Tokyo: Hoso Daigaku Kyoiku Shinkokai, 2009.

Sasaki, Nobutsuna (ed). 佐佐木信綱編1954年「新訂新訓万葉集」岩波書店 *Shintei shinkun man'yooshuu*. [Revised new annotated Man'yoshu]. Tokyo: Iwanami Shoten, 1954.

Shirakara, Shizuka. 白川静 2004年「新訂字統」平凡社 *Shintei jitoo* [Revised Jitoo]. Tokyo: Heibonsha, 2004.

Shirakara, Shizuka. 2003年「常用字解」平凡社 *Joyo jikai* [Exposition of commonly-used kanji]. Tokyo: Heibonsha, 2003.

Suzuki, Shuji, Yoshiaki Takebe & Shizuo Mizukami (eds). 鈴木修次・武部良明・水上静夫 1976年「角川最新漢和辞典」角川書店 *Kadokawa saishin kanwa jiten* [Kadokawa new Chinese character dictionary]. Tokyo: Kadokawa Shoten, 1976.

Takeuchi, Rizo, et al. (eds). 竹内理三他編 1975年「図説日本の歴史3古代国家の繁栄」集英社 *Zusetsu nihon no rekishi 3 – Kodai kokkano han-ei* [Illustrated history of Japan 3 – Prosperity of the ancient nation]. Tokyo: Shueisha, 1975.

Todo, Akiyasu (ed). 藤堂明保監修 1991年「藤堂方式小学生版新訂漢字なりたち辞典」教育社 *Toodoo-hooshiki shoogakuseiban shintei kanji naritachi jiten* [Todo method kanji origin dictionary for elementary school students, revised edition]. Tokyo: Kyoikusha, 1991.

Tokuhiro, Yasuyo. 徳弘康代 2008年「日本語学習者のためのよく使う順漢字2100」三省堂 *Nihongo gakushuusha no tame no yoku tsukau-jun kanji 2100* [The 2100 kanji for Japanese language learners in the order of frequency]. Tokyo: Sanseido, 2008.

Tokyo National Museum & Asahi Shimbun (eds). 東京国立博物館・朝日新聞編 2007年 「中国国家博物館名品展―悠久の美」朝日新聞 [Prized Treasures of Chinese Art from the National Museum of China] Tokyo: *Asahi Shimbun,* 2007.

Williams, Noriko Kurosawa. ウィリアムズ憲子 2007年「語源の図説による漢字導入―漢字アナトミー」[The Kanji Anatomy—An etymological approach to kanji study]: Proceedings of *14th Princeton Japanese Pedagogy Forum.* Princeton, NJ: Princeton University, 2007.

Yamada, Katsumi. 山田勝美 1976年「漢字の語源」角川小辞典 1 角川書店 *Kanji no gogen – Kadokawa shoojiten 1* [The origin of kanji – Kadokawa little dictionary 1]. Tokyo: Kadokawa Shoten, 1976.

Yin, John Jing-hua. *Fundamental of Chinese Character.* New Haven, CT: Yale University Press, 2006.

The Historical Development of Kanji Forms

	STYLES	KANJI	MEDIUM	PURPOSES	TIME
ANCIENT FORMS	oracle–bone inscription	こうこつぶん 甲骨文	animal bones	to record communication between rulers and gods	Late Shang (Ing) 商・殷 (cir. 1300–1000 B.C.)
	bronze ware inscription	きんぶん 金文	bronze	same as above: later to commemorate events	Late Shang (Ing) 商・殷 (cir. 1300–1000 B.C.) and Zhou (Chow) 周 Dynasty (1045–256 B.C.)
	official-seal style	てんぶん 篆文 しょうてん (小篆)	bronze, stone	to spread ruler's policies throughout the country	Qin 秦 (221–206 B.C.)
MODERN FORMS	clerical style	れいしょ 隷書	bamboo tablets, paper and brush	to distribute and preserve large numbers of government documents and literature	Han 前漢・後漢 (202 B.C.–220 A.D.)
	grass style	そうしょ 草書	paper and brush	to be able to write a large number of characters faster	

THE DEVELOPMENT OF KANJI IN CHINA

The origin of the word *kanji* 漢字 (*Hanzi* in Chinese)

The word *kanji* is the Japanese pronunciation of the Chinese word *hanzi*, written as 漢字. *Hanzi* literally means the writing of the Han people (漢 /han/ in Chinese and /kan/ in Japanese; 字 /zi/ in Chinese and /ji/ in Japanese). During the Han Dynasty (202 B.C. to 220 A.D.), which is the longest-ruling dynasty in China, the ancient writing forms that had existed over a millennium for the ruling class as a means to communicate with the gods and demonstrate power over people came to be used as a means of communication among the popular class. The writing forms became more regulated, simpler forms over time and have remained virtually unchanged to the present day. We will have a brief overview of how present-day kanji developed from the forms used in ancient times in China.

Ancient Kanji Forms
A close relationship between a shape and its meaning

The Oracle-Bone Inscription (*Kookotsubun* 甲骨文)

The earliest writings in Chinese history were inscribed on fragments of the underside shells (plastron) of tortoise or shoulder bones of animals. Some of these have been found on archaeological sites of the later centuries of the Shang 商 (or Ing 殷) Dynasty around 1300 to 1000 B.C. The style of these earliest types of ancient writings is called *kookotsubun* 甲骨文 (literally, tortoise shell writing), or oracle-bone writing in English, as is more commonly known, because these writings were the recordings of divinations sought out by rulers.

In ancient times in China, a ruler was thought to be able to communicate with his ancestral god. A ruler would conduct a religious rite of divination to receive this god's will on important matters. In preparation for a divination, a small hole was drilled into a piece of or whole tortoise underside shell or a shoulder bone of another animal, and a thin wooden stick was placed in it. As the wooden stick burned, the tortoise shell became heated and cracks would appear. These lines made by the cracks were read as the revelation of a god's will. A ruler made decisions this way on such matters as when to begin a battle against an enemy, how to rule his people, or when to plant seedlings and harvest crops. An inscription was later made adjacent to those cracks with a sharp knife, recording how the oracle had been read and how the event actually turned out. This was the beginning of writing in Chinese history.

The oracle-bone writings were pictographs of life in ancient China. They depicted a person or people in various situations or relationships, animals and other aspects of nature, common objects, ideas, society, technology, and so on. Carving these pictographs with a sharp knife gave this style its characteristic thin straight lines.

It is only at the turn of the twentieth century when it came to be known that the mysterious carvings on old bones found in the fields of a village in Anyan were, in fact, the earliest writing of kanji, and that they were the precursors to the inscriptions found on ancient bronze ware. An often recited story is that the village people would crush these old animal bones with mysterious markings into powder and sell it as medicine with miraculous effects. The discovery of those writings lead to new discoveries of archaeological sites for the Shang Dynasty. It also became very important to understand how kanji originated prior to the bronze ware inscription style.

The Bronze Ware Inscription (*Kinbun* 金文)

The second oldest kanji type is seen in the inscriptions on the bronze vessels and other bronze artifacts from the Shang Dynasty and the succeeding Zhou Dynasty. The style is called *kinbun* 金文 (literally, metal writing), or the bronze ware inscription style in English.

During the Shang and Zhou Dynasties, large bronze vessels and other bronze objects were used in religious rites worshipping ancestral gods. The inscriptions were found on the inner walls of vessels so that only the ancestral gods could see them. This suggests that the writings were intended as means of communication by rulers or priests to the ancestral gods. Some vessels contained wine, food, grains, and other offerings. Some were used to cook sacrificial animals for offerings.

Later, inscriptions were made on the outside of bronze ware to chronicle important events, such as a victory in a battle. The expensive commemorative bronze ware was often given as rewards or awards with the intent to demonstrate the power and wealth of the givers. Writings were still exclusively used by the ruling class, but the sanctity that the writings previously had in earlier times had diminished and became secularized.

Making bronze ware required enormous wealth and resources because it involved not only the materials but also a large number of skilled workers with knowledge of casting technology. Only rulers with great power and resources could produce them. The process of making bronze ware was complex and took a long time.

The characteristics of the bronze ware inscriptions also reflect how they were made. The use of a clay mold made the inscribed lines of the writings thicker or bolder than those in the oracle-bone style. Because of their design and detail, the bronze ware vessels and other objects from these times have been treasured as art objects throughout history.

The Official Seal Style
(*Tenbun* 篆文)）

After several centuries of war among smaller independent states, the Emperor Shi Huangdi (始皇帝) unified the country and began a new dynasty, called the Qin (秦), in the third century B.C. Shi Huangdi carried out a number of new policies and measures for a newly centralized government. They included introducing a uniform legal system; banning the political philosophies that he viewed as opposing his centralized legalistic governing, such as Confucianism; unifying the system of weights and measures to be used throughout the country, introducing a new

national monetary system; and ordering a number of civil engineering projects, including the foundation of what would become the Great Wall of China. With extraordinary military skills, he expanded the empire ruthlessly and toured the country, leaving stone plaques, with inscriptions boasting of his power in many places.

During the preceding Warring States era, a number of different writing forms had existed or developed in the various regions. As part of his centralization of power, Shi Huangdi ordered the unification of these writing systems throughout the country. He adopted a style that was developed from the style used by his own people. This new style is called *tenbun* 篆文, or *official seal style* in English, because this writing style was used for official documents. This style is characterized by long cursive lines and each character being able to fit in a vertically oblong space, giving it refined elegance and uniformity. This dignified style was suitable for formal official inscriptions on stone such as Shi Huangdi's dictates and notice of the new unified measuring system which was sent out all around the country.

For its beauty, the Tenbun style is the longest-lasting style of kanji in Chinese history. Throughout its history, regardless of the dynasty, this official seal style was used by the imperial courts and government officials in their official seals as well as a signature seal in art work. In Japan today, this official seal style is still used for custom-made personal or corporate legal seals that are registered with the government.

The Common Characteristics of the Ancient Writings

The three ancient writing styles just reviewed have characteristics that are different from the later writing forms.

They are representational in that the graphic shapes are suggestive of the origin of each kanji. Let us look at the three ancient forms of the kanji 雨 "rain," 貝 "cowry (money shell)," and 元 "origin" and see how the three different styles progressed over nearly a millennium in Table 1.

TABLE 1 *Comparison of the Three Ancient Writing Styles*

STYLES	(A) ORACLE–BONE INSCRIPTION	(B) BRONZE WARE INSCRIPTION	(C) OFFICIAL SEAL STYLE	MODERN KANJI (KAI-STYLE)
MEANING	こうこつぶん 甲骨文	きんぶん 金文	てんぶん 篆文	かんじ かいしょ 漢字(楷書)
(1) RAIN				
(2) COWRY; MONEY SHELL				
(3) ORIGIN; HEAD				

(a) In the **oracle-bone inscription style,** in above column A, the forms are pictograms, the captured images of objects, items of nature, people, their relationships, ideas, and so on. The writing form for "rain" depicted water drops from a higher place which was shown in a line on top; the writing for "cowry or money shell" was a depiction of a cowry shell, which showed the side that had an opening; the writing for "origin or head" depicted a side view of a person standing where the head is shown above the neck, and below the neck, the body with an arm. The head is where one's mind originates, thus "origin." In the oracle-bone style, those shapes were still clear drawings.

(b) In the **bronze ware inscription style,** in above column B, the lines are thicker and bulkier and slightly less representational, yet it is not hard to see the origin of each character.

(c) By the time of the **official seal style** in above column (C), the thickness of the lines was more uniform. The forms for "rain" and "cowry or money shell" demonstrate a symmetry, and the form for "origin; head" shows better balance. The height is greater than the width, and the lines tend to be elongated in the lower half of the form reflecting balanced elegance with dignity. As a whole, the official seal style became more of an abstract writing form, yet we can still see the original meaning.

In all of the ancient writings, with some effort of imagination, it is not impossible for us, the people of modern times, to glimpse back to the original meaning. There is a strong visual connection between these ancient forms and the original meaning, which was lost when the next style, called the *reisho style* 隷書 "clerical style," came along. That signaled the end of the ancient writing systems.

Modern Kanji Forms
Two Millennia Unchanged

The Clerical-Style Kanji (*Reisho* 隷書)

The clerical style   During the Qin Dynasty, the official seal style was used for royal decrees inscribed in stone and important orders from the central government. The writing still embodied the meaning in a visual image and was aesthetically powerful and

pleasing. It is easy to imagine how people around the country were aware of the power of the new centralized ruling government. However, the unification of the country and centralization of power created increasing volumes of documents, and the officials and their clerks had to find a way to write faster in order to keep up with their ever increasing work load. Soon a more simplified style emerged during the Qin Dynasty. The new style called *reisho* 隷書 was said to have been invented by a lower-level clerk, who was also a prisoner. Thus it was called *reisho* 隷書 (literally, the writing of someone who does manual labor). This clerical-style writing became the norm in the succeeding Han Dynasty and was established as the common writing system of China that is used to this day. These writings over time came to be called *hanzi* 漢字—(writing of the Han) and kanji in Japan.

The characteristics of the clerical style are:

a) The lines are long and straight and the diagonal lines end with a sharp rise at the end.

b) The width of the oblong space is greater than the height, which is different from the official seal style. This was due to the common use of bamboo tablets for writing. When a brush crosses sideways against the grain of the bamboo, it requires a little pressure, and it is more likely to result in a longer stroke sideways.

c) The lines and the angles of bending were more uniform. For ease of people being able to recognize the shapes of kanji and recreating the same shapes themselves, it was necessary that lines become aligned with each other and shapes become geometric. As a result, the original connection between the image of meaning and the written form was diminished, and by and large, it became unrecognizable.

Writing was no longer the embodiment of people's prayers to the gods or a means to demonstrate the power of a ruler. Evolving away from the form itself, the message conveyed by the language became the most important purpose. Stripping away the symbolic uses, kanji became a writing system for communication among the people.

Writing Tools and Invention of Paper

Animal bones, bronze, stone   In the development of writing systems, the changes in the available writing surfaces and writing tools played important roles. In the earliest writing forms, such as the oracle-bone inscription, pieces of the collar bone of a cow or the plastron of a tortoise were excised using a sharp knife. Carving with a rather sharp object like a knife created thin straight lines in depicting images of the meaning. In the bronze ware inscription, an alloy of bronze was what the writings were left on and the means to create the writing was molded clay. This left the lines thicker and uneven and the shapes and sizes were not uniform. In the official seal style, a plaque of stone was the writing surface and the tool was a chisel. All of those required the resources of skilled artisans as well as special materials. Thus the person who actually made the writing and the person who spoke those words were quite different.

Other media was also being used in ancient times. Ink was made from the soot of burning pine chips or burning vegetable oil and brushes were made from animal hair. There were several writing surfaces available: silk cloth, wood and bamboo tablets, and paper. Silk cloth is made of filaments taken from silk worm cocoons. Silk had existed before cotton was introduced to China from the south. The technology of silk-raising was well-guarded by those who possessed

it, and silk cloth was scarce and expensive. It was only used for letters and special occasions by the nobles.

On the other hand, bamboo tablets were obtained more easily because bamboo grows in a large area of China. In the regions in the north and in the west where bamboo did not grow, wooden tablets were used. The wooden tablets were wider. In the early twentieth century, a series of explorations led by Westerners such as Aurel Stein and Sven Hedin discovered numerous such wooden and bamboo tablets and other important artifacts, which dated back to the Han Dynasty.

The way a bamboo tablet was made was that a piece of bamboo stalk was cut vertically into one- or two-inch wide strips. The surface was heated to force the resin to the surface, which made a rougher surface to write on and preserved the color better. Using an animal hair brush, they wrote on the surface of the bamboo tablets. The written bamboo or wooden tablets were laid flat and bound with strings to make a book. Even after paper began to be used, vertical lines were printed on it, not only as a writing guide, but to preserve the appearance of the old bamboo tablets.

The invention of paper was attributed to Ts'ai Lun in the early second century. He received strong support from the emperor to produce paper in quantity. This method involved hemp plants or tree bark being boiled in a lye solution to soften them and then pounded down into a flat surface of fibers using a mallet.

The invention of paper and an increased demand for a writing surface due to rising government use and intellectual activities coincided. Compared to the bulky bound bamboo or wood tablets, paper drastically reduced the physical volume of records and made them easier to transport. It became more easily available to intellectuals and literate people in general. The reduced volume, portability, and better access to a writing medium that paper provided all contributed to solidifying the contemporary reisho style as the form of writing to be used from then on.

The First Kanji Dictionary
Shuowen Jiezi: The first kanji dictionary compiled

As we will discuss in the next chapter, one of the most frequently used methods of making a new kanji is to juxtapose two different components, one of which represents the sound and the other the meaning. This is a very productive way to create a new kanji, and by the latter half of the Han Dynasty, the number of kanji on record amounted to almost ten thousand. The first scholarly kanji study was compiled in 100 A.D. and was called *Shuowen Jiezi* 説文解字. In *Shuowen Jiezi,* each kanji was given an explanation of its meaning based on the origin. To make the link between the clerical-style kanji form and its meaning, the author, Xu Shen, used the visual descriptiveness of the official seal style. *Shuowen Jiezi* became the foundation of kanji classification and the two major principles used remain the fundamental kanji classification to this day.

In classifying 9353 kanji, a principle called *bushu* 部首, 'section header,' was used. These sections are components that repeatedly appear in other kanji and share similar meanings. In *Shuowen Jiezi* there were 540 types of section headers.

Another principle that impacted kanji study throughout the history of kanji was the classification of kanji formations. The kanji were classified into six types of writings called *Rikusho* 六書. They are: a) pictograph b) indicative c) semantic composite d) phonetic-semantic composite e) transformation and f) borrowing. The last two types are in fact

not how a kanji was formed, but how it came to be used. With some modification, kanji dictionaries in modern times possess this same classification. The over nine thousand kanji entries in *Shuowen Jiezi* included variant forms. A variant form is a form that might be slightly different in part but still retains the same meaning.

Emergence of grass-style writing and reduced forms

As kanji came to be used by more people in quick informal communication, a style that was more suitable for rapid writing was sought. Unlike the ancient people, to whom writing was sacred communication with the gods or a demonstration of political power over subjects, the people in the Han period saw kanji as simply a means of written communication. Speed and clarity of the writing became important as people's lives became more complicated. A couple of changes took place to simplify kanji.

1) **grass-style writing** One was a new, more fluid writing style, called the grass-style *soosho* 草書, that emerged away from the more square and rigid clerical-style. In the grass-style, a quick move of a writing brush connects a few strokes together in a fluid manner, resulting in a reduction of the number of strokes producing a style that was more fluid. When kanji was introduced to Japan, this cursive style of writing played an important role in the development of Japanese phonetic letters called *hiragana* as discussed in Chapter 3.

2) **reduced forms** Another way of reducing the stroke number that took place during the Han Dynasty was seen in some recurring components. Earlier, even in ancient writings, a writing sometimes necessitated a depiction of a shape that was sideways into a vertical shape. A table and animals are some examples. A composite formation of new kanji that often placed two components next to each other further necessitated shrinking the size of the recurring components. Commonly used components such as the kanji 水 "water" was reduced to 氵 (called *sanzui*) and the kanji 人 "person" was reduced to 亻 (called *ninben*).

During the Han Dynasty, kanji reached a stage of final form and the fundamental shape of kanji did not change for the next two millennia except for some simplification in China. When kanji was introduced to Japan, the Japanese people adapted it to their oral language in its entirety. The kanji form, meaning, and sound all became part of the Japanese language. Before long the Japanese people started to devise two types of phonetic letter systems in order to express ideas in the Japanese language more freely while preserving kanji writing. There will be a brief overview of kanji in the Japanese language in Chapter 3.

CHAPTER 2

Kanji Formation Types &
Dictionary Section Headers

THE FOUR TYPES OF KANJI FORMATION

There are four different ways in which kanji are formed:

1. Pictographic Formation
2. Indicative Formation
3. Phonetic-Semantic Composite Formation
4. Semantic Composite Formation

In the first two types (pictographic formation and indicative formation), there is a one-on-one correspondence between a kanji's form and meaning. The other two types (phonetic-semantic composite formation and semantic composite formation) are ones in which two or more already existing forms were juxtaposed to form new kanji.

Pictographic Formation

A pictograph is a simple picture that represents meaning for the purpose of conveying a message to other people. In the history of kanji in China, the pictograph was the oldest form of writing. They were images expressed in linear drawings outlining an object, people, nature, matter, idea, animal, and others.

For example, in order to express "a moon," a crescent ☽ was depicted, which eventually became the kanji 月 "moon." In order to indicate the abstract meaning of "big," a person putting his arms out sideways with his two feet spread out to look as large as possible was sketched, as in 大, and it eventually became the kanji form 大 "big." For "water," a stream of running water was depicted, as in 巛, and it later changed to 水 "water." For ancient Chinese people, an elephant 象 was not something they had actually seen, but it did not stop them from making a pictograph, which eventually became the kanji 象. In a pictographic formation, a writing form corresponds to a meaning.

Indicative Formation

However, not everything can be expressed by a pictograph. Abstract concepts and numbers are among those ideas that required a different type of formation. This formation is used to describe a spatial relationship between two objects, usually viewed from a point of reference, and is called the indicative formation type.

For example, two opposing spatial notions "above" and "below" were indicated by pointing to the area above a reference line 上 or below 下 a reference line. The kanji that meant "above" was formed to be 上 and the kanji that meant "below" was formed to be 下, in which the emphasis by the pointer was added as a short stroke. The kanji for numbers, such as 一 "one," 二 "two," 三 "three," 十 "ten," 百 "hundred" are also in this category of formation.

There are some kanji that are more of a combination of a pictograph formation and an indicative formation. For example, the kanji 本 was formed by adding a short horizontal stroke on the lower end of a pictograph 木 "tree." The kanji 本 means "source or base" and it also means "book." The kanji 刃 "blade" was formed by putting an extra short stroke on the blade side of the pictograph of sword or 刀 "knife."

Phonetic-Semantic Composite Formation

This formation consists of two units, one of which bears the sound of the word (i. e., phonetic) while the other bears its meaning (i. e., semantic). This formation type is very productive because, in theory, by putting two already existing kanji together, a new kanji could be created and the kanji inventory could multiply. In fact, the majority of kanji belong to this formation category. 80 to 90 percent of kanji are said to belong to this formation type.

The kanji that has a recurring component called a *bushu* (dictionary section header) typically belongs in this category. A bushu carries the meaning and the remaining component (quite often on the right side) expresses the sound.

For example, take the sound /ki/. From a pictograph there existed kanji 己 which was pronounced /ki/.[1] The writing form 己 meant "self." Now, suppose there were three other words that had the same pronunciation /ki/: (a) the word that means "to record"; (b) the word that means "to get up"; and (c) the the word that means "to chronicle." This formation type could easily create three new kanji by using the sound of the existing kanji /ki/ and by bringing in another component that indicates the meaning of the new kanji:

記   For the word "a record or to record"—The meaning of "a record" or "to record" involved an oral tradition in ancient times, so the pictograph that means 言 "word" was juxtaposed with the pronunciation of /ki/. A new kanji 記 "to record" was created.

起   For the word "to get up"—The meaning "to get up" involves one getting up on his feet and moving. For this the kanji 走 "to run," which consisted of a person in running using feet, was a good candidate. The kanji 走 "to run" and the sound /ki/ were put together and a new kanji 起 "to get up" was created.

紀   For the word "to chronicle"—The meaning of "to chronicle" involves telling a long and linear story. The thread made from long continuous fibers from silk cocoons was a good candidate to

---

[1] For the discussion of the sounds in this book, comtemporary Japanese sounds are used.

represent this idea. The pictograph for thread 糸 and the sound /ki/ were put together and new kanji 紀 "to chronicle" was created.

Semantic Composite Formation

This is the formation type in which two or more components that were juxtaposed retain the meanings of both original components but create a new kanji with a new meaning.

Let us look at four examples:

休 To indicate the meaning "to rest," the kanji 人 "person," from 𠆢, a standing person viewed from the side, and 木 "tree," from a standing tree 🌳, were combined to indicate someone leaning against a tree resting, creating the kanji 休 "to rest."

取 The kanji 取 "to take, seize or catch" was formed by the two kanji 耳 "ear" and 又 "hand," signifying that when one holds someone or an animal by the ear, he is in control.

信 The kanji 信 "trust" is a semantic composite of the two kanji 人 "person" (亻) and 言 "word," signifying that a person's word is worthy of trust.

右 The kanji 右 "right side" is a semantic composite of two pictographs, the right hand ✋ and a mouth 👄. One carries food to the mouth using the right hand, thus indicating "right side."

Other Types of Kanji

Borrowed kanji

In addition to the four types of formation above, there are a small number of kanji whose current meanings have no relevance to the original meanings, but rather were "borrowed" from other already existing kanji. Since they were not formed anew, this type is usually excluded from the formation type discussion.

For instance, the kanji 無 "nothing" originally depicted a person who was dancing, possibly in a religious trance. However, when another kanji 舞 was created with two moving feet underneath, 舛, that one came to be used to mean "to dance." The meaning "nothing" was attached to the kanji that originally meant dance, but it had no relation to the origin of the kanji. Kanji that was "borrowed" from other kanji includes the ones for some numbers, such as 四 "four," 五 "five," 六 "six," 七 "seven," and other common ideas, such as 彼 "he" and 東 "east."

Kanji that originated in Japan

The kanji used in the Japanese writing systems almost all originated in China. There are a small number of kanji that were created in Japan and they are called *kokuji* 国字. For instance, the kanji 込 "to put in, include" was made up of the kanji 入 "to enter" and a 辶 "go-forward" on the lower left side. The kanji 国 "country" was made up of an enclosure to signify the land and a 玉 "crown jewel," which represented the ruler. (The original form for country 國 was also used.) The kanji 峠 "mountain path" was made up of three kanji, 山 "mountain," 上 "above," and 下 "below." It indicated a place on a mountain where one went up and down. The kanji that were originated in Japan are of semantic composite formation.

It is also worthwhile to note here that the question of which formation type particular kanji belongs to may differ depending on the kanji reference material. (Most reference materials follow the classification by the *Kangxi Zidian,* as explained below.) This is due to different scholarly interpretations of the ancient writing forms. Also, the ancient forms on the artifacts found at archaeological sites or even museums vary greatly depending on regions or eras.

BUSHU (SECTION HEADERS)

Most *bushu,* or section headers, originated as pictographs and reached the present-day forms with significantly reduced stroke numbers during the Han Dynasty. During this standardization of kanji when much of the visual relationship between the form and its meaning was lost, the bushu section headers also lost the visual connection between the form and its meaning.

Bushu and the *Kangxi Zidian* 康熙字典

The section header method of classifying kanji that Xu Shen had used in *Shuowen* in the early second century continued to be used in the eighteenth-century kanji dictionary, the *Kangxi Zidian* 康熙字典 (*Koki Jiten* in Japanese). The *Kangxi Zidian* kanji dictionary was compiled in 1716 under the order of Emperor Kangxi (1654–1722) and laid the foundation for present-day kanji dictionaries. This dictionary was quite large because the number of kanji had continued to increase, regardless of actual use. By the *Kangxi Zidian* dictionary, there were 49,000 known kanji including variant forms.

The *Kangxi Zidian* left two important legacies that still impact our use of kanji to this day. One is a reduction of the kanji section header bushu and the other is the Mincho-style typeface that was used in this dictionary.

Bushu Section Headers

The 540 section headers that were used in the beginning of the second century were reduced to 240 in this eighteenth century dictionary. Within the 240 kinds of section headers, the member kanji within each section were further divided according to the number of strokes that comprised the remaining components in each word. A user who is used to phonetic letters in alphabetical order may find the method of section headers cumbersome. More recently, some dictionaries in Japan arrange kanji in the on-reading for the use by a Japanese speaker as well. (A kanji with multiple on-readings requires an extra step or two to look up.) The advantage of the section header classification by shape is that it handles any difference in pronunciation among different dialects in China. It also allows the classification to be inclusive of any language that uses kanji, because it relates the form to the meaning. The cultural atmosphere of Qing Dynasty scholarly work was that of empiricism. The exposition of each kanji in the *Kangxi Zidian* included citations from classical studies.

Typeface for printing

The typeface known as 明朝 *mincho* style in modern printing came from the styles that were used in the *Kangxi Zidian.* It has the following characteristics:

a) Vertical lines are thicker than horizontal lines;

b) The four corners of an imaginary square for each kanji are fully utilized;

c) A horizontal line ends with a triangle-like shape.

Those characteristics allow a large number of kanji in a limited space, yet each remains legible. In modern printing, the *mincho* style is used in the majority of printed materials, such as newspapers, books, and computer software.

The 184 Dictionary Section Headers in This Book

For the 184 section headers that appear in the 1100 kanji in this book, please see *The 184 Section Headers* in *The Key to Kanji.*

#### CHAPTER 3

Development of Japanese Writing Systems

INFLUX OF KANJI TO JAPAN

Contacts with Chinese Culture

Early Contact with Kanji Via the Korean Peninsula

The history of the Japanese writing system began with contact from Chinese culture over many centuries. The earliest known official contact with China took place in 57 A.D., when the Han Chinese emperor gave a Japanese king a gold seal. This small gold seal was found in a farmer's field in northern Kyushu Island in the late eighteenth century. Chinese chronicles reflect that Japan was one of the neighboring countries which regularly paid courtesy visits to the Chinese court bearing gifts. This seal is believed to have been given on one of those occasions.

In the mid-sixth century, Buddhism was introduced to Japan from China via the Korean peninsula. Alongside that was the influx of kanji which was aided by the presence of ex-patriots from the Korean peninsula, who also had learned Chinese through their contacts with China. As the ruling classes of Japan became ardent believers of Buddhism

and adopted it as the national religion, a number of Buddhist temples were built around the country and the priests became educated. In the tradition of Buddhism, the practice of transcribing the *sutra* (Buddhism scriptures) word by word was encouraged and the nobles started to write in the Chinese language. The words from these Chinese-written sutra began to seep into people's lives as Buddhism spread in Japan.

The Cultural Envoys to China

Recognizing that China had advanced culture, the Japanese court wanted to learn more about their advanced legal, political, economic, and writing systems. From the beginning of the seventh century, the Japanese court sent official envoys to the Chinese court, first to the Sui Dynasty (581–618) and then to the Tang Dynasty (618–907). The members of the delegation also studied Chinese technology and culture, particularly the writing systems. A delegation had two to four hundred people in a fleet of three or four ships. These official visits lasted through the end of the ninth century, well after initial enthusiasm to

learn the new culture from China had died out. Books on political philosophy, law, technology, and literary works written in the Chinese language were brought back by those delegations. These books subsequently brought about permanent changes in the Japanese language in its sound systems and vocabulary and led to the creation of unique Japanese phonetic letters. All of this resulted in creating Japan's own writing system as well as influencing the language itself.

Two Kinds of Sounds Per Kanji— *On*-Reading and *Kun*-Reading

When Japanese people read books that had been brought back from China, they learned this new writing system in a tri-fold way: (a) the writing forms, i.e., kanji; (b) the Chinese pronunciations within the inventory of Japanese syllable sounds; and (c) the meaning. First, people almost faithfully copied the kanji forms and did not make any change at all (a). Secondly the Chinese sound of kanji pronounced in the Japanese syllable structure (b) was learned and was called the /*on*/ 音 sound reading. Further, people learned to associate their existing Japanese word with the kanji of the same meaning and read it as pronounced in Japanese. This reading was called the /*kun*/ 訓 "interpretation; meaning" reading (c). The words that had existed before the influence of the Chinese language are called *yamato-kotoba* "the language of Yamato," Yamato being the old name of Japan. As more Chinese words were learned and more yamato-kotoba were assigned to the Chinese kanji the Japanese language ended up with two sets of sounds per kanji, one in the Chinese on-reading and one in the Japanese kun-reading.

For example, when they learned the kanji 見 "see" along with the writing form, they learned to read this as /*ken*/ in the on-reading by approximating the Chinese sound. In addition, they also learned to associate

this kanji with their own word /*mi-ru*/ that meant "see" in the kun-reading.

Multiple Chinese-Derived Sounds for Certain Kanji

Taking in words from another language over many centuries creates discontinuities because a spoken language changes over time in pronunciation and vocabulary in the original language. This also happened to the Chinese language and the Japanese people. The dialect of Chinese language during Japan's earlier contacts was different from that of the Chinese language spoken by the people of the Tang Dynasty, which was called *kan-on* "sound of the Han people," the language of the people in power in China at the time. Efforts were made to correct the older pronunciation so that it matched the kan-on. For example, a Chinese linguist was brought in by Japanese Emperor Jito (645–703) for this very reason. Later Emperor Kammu (737–806) designated the kan-on to be the "correct" reading and tried to eliminate the older sound, an earlier Chinese dialect called *go-on*. From that time on, the on-reading of kanji became that of kan-on and to this day the Japanese pronunciation of kanji is based on kan-on. At the same time, some of the older go-on readings also survived because some of the words had already taken root in the lives of Japanese people, particularly the words related to Buddhism and daily life. This resulted in two kinds of Chinese-derived on-readings for some kanji.

Moreover, over time, other pronunciations from different regions were brought into the Japanese language. The distinction among those different on-readings is not something a Japanese speaker thinks about. Nonetheless, in the course of study of Japanese as a foreign language, a learner may be puzzled at the fact that it is not always the case that the on-reading he or she has learned can be applied to another word.

For example, look at the kanji 九, which means "nine," or *kokonotu* in yamato-kotoba, i.e., the kun-reading. After people learned the translated *kokonotu*, they also learned to pronounce this as /ku/, as in /ku-nin/ "nine people," in the earlier dialect of the Chinese go-on. Then, in the Heian period a newer pronunciation, /kyuu/, was brought back from China, such as in *kyuu-nin* "nine people," as the kan-on. The pronunciation of /kyuu/ was then made the "official" pronunciation, thus adding another on-reading to the Japanese vocabulary.

Take another example: the kanji 行 "to go; to carry out." The yamato-kotoba is *i-ku*, or the phonetic variant, *yu-ku*. That is the kun-reading. The first Chinese sound introduced in go-on was *gyoo*, as in *gyooji* 行事 "event" and *ichi-gyoo* 一行 "one line." in go-on. The second reading was *koo* in kan-on, as in *ikkoo* 一行 "one traveling group." The third reading, introduced in the Kamakura period (1192–1333) by the zen sects of Buddhism, was /an/ in words such as *angya* 行脚 "pilgrimage" and *andon* 行燈 "lamp." Now we have four (or five) different readings for one kanji 行: /i-ku

(or *yu-ku*)/ for the kun-reading, and the on-reading sounds /koo/, /gyoo/, and /an/, depending on the word. For this reason it is very important to study kanji in the context of words.

From the first contact with Chinese culture, the Japanese people eagerly took in what they lacked, including the writing system. When an oral language adopts the writing system of another unrelated language, one way to do so would be to adopt the writing system only and discard the words that come with it. The Japanese language did otherwise. They also adopted new words that came with the writing, with some adjustment in pronunciation, to create a totally new set of vocabulary directly from the Chinese language. In doing so, the Japanese language was enriched by doubling the vocabulary to express one thing in at least two ways.

Nonetheless, although Chinese words were adopted into the Japanese language, there was another movement in history to keep the Japanese language intact while still using the writing system of the Chinese language.

DEVELOPMENT OF HIRAGANA & KATAKANA FROM KANJI

Man'yoo-gana (Man'yoo Letters) The Phonetic Use of Kanji

In Buddhist practice the people made handwritten copies of Buddhist sutras written in Chinese. They also started to write for themselves, mostly in the Chinese word order. For example, political and legal records were written in kanji in the Chinese word order. After awhile, a new use of kanji appeared. That was to use kanji for its phonetic value only, discarding the meaning that was attached to it. Numerous wooden tablets with those phonetically used kanji

have been found at the archaeological sites of seventh-century through tenth-century Japan. A wooden tablet found at an archaeological site in Osaka, written with the phonetic use of kanji, is said to be the oldest find, from 652 A.D., so far.[1] A phonetic letter means a unit of writing that represents a sound only, without carrying a meaning. Alphabets are a good example of phonetic letters. The phonetic use of kanji was a little more complicated.

---

[1] 皮留久佐乃皮斯米之刀斯 is read as /harukusa no hajime no toshi/ (*Asahi Shimbun* 2006).

For example, the kanji 遅 "late" was used for its Chinese sound /chi/ and 波 "wave" was used for its Chinese sound /ha/. With these two kanji, the Japanese four-syllable yamato-kotoba word *chichi-haha* "father and mother; parents" was written as 遅遅波波.[2] A modern Japanese reader, who instinctively associates the kanji with its literal meaning, would interpret this as "late-late-wave-wave" and treat it as nonsensical. However, at that time, the meaning of the kanji was generally discarded, and the kanji was used solely for its pronunciation. The choice of kanji for a particular syllable was not uniform, and many different kanji were used to indicate the same syllable. For example, the syllable /chi/ was written not only as 遅, but also 知 or 千 or 地, all of which have the Chinese sound of /chi/.

The use of kanji in Chinese language was called *mana* 真名 "true name; true calling." This new phonetic use of a form is called *kana* 仮名 "temporary name." The first Japanese chronicle, *Kojiki* in the early eighth century, was written with this phonetically used kanji. *Kojiki* was an orally transmitted epic by an oratory historian, and was written in the Japanese word order using both Chinese *on*-sound words and Japanese yamato-kotoba.

The phonetic use of kanji was also used in the compilation of the first comprehensive anthology of Japanese poetry, called *Man'yooshuu* 萬葉集 "Anthology of Ten Thousand Leaves," in the mid-eighth century. Because the *Man'yooshuu* anthology became the foundation of Japanese poetry and literature, the phonetic use of kanji is called *man'yoo-gana* "phonetic letters of *Man'yooshuu*." The anthology not only has

the songs of the people at that time, but also included those created as early as the sixth century.

Katakana
The Tradition of Reading Classical Chinese

In order to be able to import advanced culture from China, the aristocrats, intellectuals, and the Buddhist priests had to read books on political philosophies, technology, Buddhist doctrines, and other subjects, plus the great literary works written in classical Chinese. They were interested in reading the texts, often in the classical language, but had little interest in Chinese as a living, spoken language. What is written in classical Chinese is called *kanbun* 漢文.

They had to overcome the different grammatical structures such as word order, inflections of verbs and adjectives, and grammatical particles. The Chinese language does not have grammatical inflections or particles. To fill in what was missing, Japanese readers wrote some notes on the side of the texts. Sometimes the pronunciation in the Chinese on-reading or Japanese kun-reading was also added on the side as well. Writing notes between the lines in a limited space necessitated devising a way to write in a less complex form and with only a small part of the kanji. These abbreviated phonetic letters were called *katakana* "piece-like temporary name" because only a part of a kanji was used.

For instance, for the syllable /a/, the left half of the kanji 阿 was taken away and a katakana phonetic letter ア was created. For the syllable /i/, the right side of the kanji 以 was taken away to make a katakana phonetic letter イ. Katakana enabled a Japanese reader to read kanbun as if it was written in Japanese. Table 1 *The Development of Katakana from Kanji* shows how the currently used 46 basic katakana were developed from kanji.

---

[2] There were some instances of semantic use, i.e., the use of kanji for its meaning. The word /chichihaha/ was also written as 父母 "father-mother" in *Man'yooshuu* (Sasaki (ed) 1954).

TABLE 1 *The Development of Katakana from Kanji*

	Roma-ji	Original kanji	Pieces taken	Kata-kana		Roma-ji	Original kanji	Pieces taken	Kata-kana		Roma-ji	Original kanji	Pieces taken	Kata-kana
1	a	阿	阿	ア	16	ta	多	多	タ	31	ma	万末	万末	マ
2	i	伊	伊	イ	17	chi/ti	千	千	チ	32	mi	三	三	ミ
3	u	宇	宇	ウ	18	tsu/tu	川	川	ツ	33	mu	牟	牟	ム
4	e	江	江	エ	19	te	天	天	テ	34	me	米女	米女	メ
5	o	於	於	オ	20	to	止	止	ト	35	mo	毛	毛	モ
6	ka	加	加	カ	21	na	奈	奈	ナ	36	ya	也	也	ヤ
7	ki	幾	幾	キ	22	ni	仁	仁	ニ	37	yu	由	由	ユ
8	ku	久	久	ク	23	nu	奴	奴	ヌ	38	yo	與	與	ヨ
9	ke	介	介	ケ	24	ne	禰	禰	ネ	39	ra	良	良	ラ
10	ko	己	己	コ	25	no	乃	乃	ノ	40	ri	利	利	リ
11	sa	散	散	サ	26	ha	八	八	ハ	41	ru	流	流	ル
12	shi/si	之	之	シ	27	hi	比	比	ヒ	42	re	礼	礼	レ
13	su	須	須	ス	28	fu/hu	不	不	フ	43	ro	呂	呂	ロ
14	se	世	世	セ	29	he	部	部	ヘ	44	wa	和	和	ワ
15	so	曽	曽	ソ	30	ho	保	保	ホ	45	(w)o	乎	乎	ヲ
										46	n/N	尓	尓	ン

Hiragana
The Birth of Japanese Phonetic Letters from Grass-Style Kanji

The Heian period (794–1185) was the time during which the influence of Chinese culture became less overt while the indigenous Japanese culture flourished in unique ways in many areas. Amidst that growth in Japanese culture, something new evolved in the writing system. The kanji-based phonetic letters, man'yoo-gana, had a one syllable per kanji correspondence. It takes time to write out a kanji of many straight line strokes for just one syllable. As the knowledge of kanji became more prevalent and more people started to use kanji for frequent or private communications, the need to write quickly and informally arose. In the Han Dynasty in China, the grass style was born for the same reason out of the clerical style of writing, and it was also imported to Japan. In the early Heian period, phonetically-used kanji man'yoo-gana began to be written in grass-style writing. However, in order to use kanji as phonetic letters, even a fast-writing version of grass-style was not enough. The grass-style writing was further reduced to an even simpler form—the third type of phonetic letters, called *hiragana* 平仮名 "simple temporary name."

For instance, the six-stroke kanji 安 that was used to indicate the syllable /a/ in kanji-based man'yoo-gana had been reduced to 𛀙 in a grass style, in which the top three strokes were coalesced into one and the bottom three strokes into two. The Japanese people further refined it into a more fluid-style あ in hiragana. The five-stroke kanji 以 was written as 𛀆 in a grass style and was further coalesced into two curved lines い in hiragana. Since multiple kanji were used

for the same phonetic letter in man'yoo-gana, earlier times saw hiragana that came from different kanji as well, and it was some time before hiragana became standardized to correlate with one form per syllable.

By creating hiragana, the Japanese language came to have kanji and two sets of phonetic writing systems. The two phonetic letters differ in how they were formed. Katakana was made from a part of kanji and retains the angular characteristics of kanji whereas hiragana was made out of a whole kanji written in a cursive style with rounder characteristics. Table 2 *The Development of Hiragana* shows how the currently used 46 basic hiragana on the hiragana syllable chart came about from the kanji. (Other old hiragana such as ゐ/(w)i/ and ゑ/(w)e/ are not shown.)

Hiragana gave writers of the Japanese language a freedom to write sentences as spoken in Japanese grammar. Writing in classical Chinese was still considered to be superior, and men of positions and culture were expected to write in kanji. Poetry and chronicles were also written in the classical Chinese style. Hiragana was viewed to be sufficient for private letters and for use by women. In this cultural tradition, a number of great literary works were produced by women authors using hiragana from this period. These include the oldest novel, *Tale of Genji,* written by Lady Murasaki (Murasaki Shikibu), *The Pillow Book Essay* by her contemporary Lady Sei (Sei Shonagon), and other novels and essays. Also, travel chronicles were written by women who served in the imperial courts of the Heian period. The abundance of literary works by Heian court women and a number of anthologies of Heian period poetry using hiragana attests to how it was able to free up the literary creativity in these authors.

TABLE 2 *The Development of Hiragana*

	Romaji	Kanji	Grass-style to Hiragana			Hiragana in Print	
1.	a	安	お	お	あ	あ	あ
2.	i	以	以	以	い	い	い
3.	u	宇	宇	う	う	う	う
4.	e	衣	え	え	え	え	え
5.	o	於	お	お	お	お	お
6.	ka	加	か	か	か	か	か
7.	ki	幾	幾	武	き	き	き
8.	ku	久	久	く	く	く	く
9.	ke	計	計	け	け	け	け
10.	ko	己	己	こ	こ	こ	こ
11.	sa	左	を	さ	さ	さ	さ
12.	shi/si	之	え	し	し	し	し
13.	su	寸	寸	す	す	す	す
14.	se	世	世	せ	せ	せ	せ
15.	so	曽	そ	そ	そ	そ	そ
16.	ta	太	太	た	た	た	た
17.	chi/ti	知	お	ち	ち	ち	ち
18.	tsu/tu	川	つ	つ	つ	つ	つ
19.	te	天	て	て	て	て	て
20.	to	止	止	と	と	と	と
21.	na	奈	奈	な	な	な	な
22.	ni	仁	に	に	に	に	に
23.	nu	奴	ぬ	ぬ	ぬ	ぬ	ぬ
24.	ne	彌	袮	ね	ね	ね	ね
25.	no	乃	乃	の	の	の	の
26.	ha	波	波	は	は	は	は
27.	hi	比	比	ひ	ひ	ひ	ひ
28.	hu/fu	不	ふ	ふ	ふ	ふ	ふ
29.	he	部	へ	へ	へ	へ	へ
30.	ho	保	保	ほ	ほ	ほ	ほ
31.	ma	末	末	ま	ま	ま	ま
32.	mi	美	美	み	み	み	み
33.	mu	武	む	む	む	む	む
34.	me	女	め	め	め	め	め
35.	mo	毛	も	も	も	も	も
36.	ya	也	や	や	や	や	や
37.	yu	由	ゆ	ゆ	ゆ	ゆ	ゆ
38.	yo	与	よ	よ	よ	よ	よ
39.	ra	良	良	ら	ら	ら	ら
40.	ri	利	利	り	り	り	り
41.	ru	留	る	る	る	る	る
42.	re	礼	礼	れ	れ	れ	れ
43.	ro	呂	ろ	ろ	ろ	ろ	ろ
44.	wa	和	和	わ	わ	わ	わ
45.	wo	遠	遠	を	を	を	を
46.	n/N	无	ん	ん	ん	ん	ん

Calligraphy by Masae Masuda

Wakan-Konkoobun—Present-Day Style
The Merged-Style of Japanese and Chinese

Each of the two sets of phonetic letters, hiragana and katakana, contributed to create the way in which we write the Japanese language today. Katakana enabled Japanese readers to translate classical Chinese into Japanese by adding the missing pieces, such as grammatical particles and predicate inflections, while preserving Japanese word order. *Kango* "Chinese words" (often a kanji compound) was preserved in the Japanese language without being broken down to follow Japanese grammar, and they were used primarily as nouns or nouns that convert into verbs. Sometimes katakana was written in the main texts between the kango, which helped readers understand the contents better.

Hiragana enabled the Japanese writers to write in Japanese using the yamato-kotoba freely. When the two styles combined, a new style emerged. This is called *wakan konkoobun* 和漢混淆文 "Japanese-Chinese Merged Writing." In wakan konkoobun, a Japanese sentence written in hiragana is punctuated by frequent use of kango within, giving it a masculine rhythmic sound. Compared to yamato-kotoba, which may consist of several mono-syllables, a Chinese syllable is almost invariably pronounced in two Japanese syllables. As a result Chinese compounds of two or four kanji give a more regular rhythm to the Japanese language. This characteristic was skillfully used in war chronicles, such as *The Tale of Heike,* and *Hojoki, an essay on hermit life,* which had an undertone of the impermanency or transiency of life, as taught in Buddhism.

Since the initial contact with Chinese language and throughout a few centuries after that, people's struggles to try to find a way to write Japanese using the writing system of another language finally found an answer. The new writing style they found was directly derived from a merger of the Japanese language and Chinese characters and vocabulary. It became the standard of the present-day writing system of the Japanese.

The remnants of the historical development of the three writing systems are very much evident in present-day writing in such terms as *okuri-gana* "kana after kanji" and *furigana* "kana for phonetic guide." Okuri-gana is hiragana that you put after kanji to show grammatical conjugations. It is a device to fill in the difference between the two grammars of Chinese and Japanese. For important grammatical particles, such as a subject, object, direction, and topic, using hiragana in a different way allows particles to stand out more within a sentence. We also benefit from furigana. Furigana is a handy phonetic guide that is placed generally in hiragana by the side or on top of a difficult kanji. Katakana is primarily used for foreign loan words in written text. More recently, katakana has gained the use of being an eye-catching device in advertisements and print media. It is certainly true that the Japanese have figured out a comprehensive system in retaining the best of both spoken Japanese and written Chinese.

The 184 Dictionary Section Headers
in *The Key to Kanji*

This table lists all the 184 dictionary section headers that appear in the 1100 kanji in *The Key to Kanji,* as well as in the nearly 2000 kanji used in Japan. Because these are recurring components that make up a majority of kanji, studying this table is an effective way to increase your kanji knowledge.

SECTION HEADER: The 184 types of currently used section headers are arranged according to the number of strokes.

NAMES: The names, except for a small number of them, are listed for reference purposes.

ENGLISH MEANING: A brief explanation of a section header's origin.

DICTIONARY ENTRY KANJI: Kanji that are conventionally classified as a member of that particular section header.

RELATED KANJI: Kanji that are listed elsewhere but contain the same component.

	SECTION HEADER	NAME	ENGLISH MEANING	DICTIONARY ENTRY KANJI	RELATED KANJI
			1-STROKE SECTION HEADERS		
1	一	いち	A single sideways stroke signifying 'one,' 'horizontal line,' 'ground level,' etc.	一丁七万丈三上下不世丘両	普譜否兵並
2	丨	たてぼう	A single vertical line in the middle.	中巨	引仲忠
3	丶	てん	A short diagonal dot, signifying a flame on a lit holder.	丸主	住往注柱駐
4	丿	はらいぼう	A longer diagonal stroke was a part of a person.	久乗	及級吸
5	乙 乚	おつにょう	Something bent or to stroke down something to straighten it.	九乱乳	札雑染礼究
6	亅	はねぼう	This stroke goes straight down and has a hook to the left. It has no particular meaning.	予事	序庁野預
			2-STROKE SECTION HEADERS		
7	二	に	Two sideways strokes signifying 'two.'	二互五	語仁
8	亠	なべぶた	The pot lid-like shape was merely used for a classification and had no particular meaning of its own.	亡交京率	液校稿郊卒夜恋裏忙忘壇停
9	人 亻	にんべん	A standing man viewed from the side, which was the etymology of a kanji 人, pertaining to a person or an act that he does.	人化仁仏仕他付代以仮仲件任休伝似位低住佐体何作使例供価便係保信修俳俵個倍候借値偉停健側備催傷働像僕億優	荷貨液宿縮夜
10	入 𠆢	ひとやね	A cover over goods or a person. Due to its similarity to kanji 人, this is traditionally placed in the section header 'person' (#9 人).	今介令会余全倉命舎	合捨拾除余創念輪領論冷
11	儿	にんにょう or ひとあし	A person with an emphasis on his legs, signifying a person standing or in motion.	元兄充兆先光免児	完祝税説洗続脱統逃読売晩勉焼党

12	入	いりやね	A movement to enter a structure.	入	込
13	八	はちがしら	a) A motion to divide a space into two, signifying 'to divide.' b) When used at the bottom, it often indicated two hands held upward.	八公六共兵具典	沿供松真選分粉
14	冂	けいがまえ	An outline of a structure or a square shape.	内円冊再	講構同銅納
15	冖	わかんむり	The shape was used merely for a classification and had no particular meaning of its own.	写	運軍揮
16	冫	にすい	Cracks in ice, signifying something icy cold.	冬冷	寒
17	几	つくえ or きにょう	A table. Due to similarity, 凡 was placed in the same category here.	凡処	机
18	凵	かんにょう or うけばこ	An open box inside of which something is placed.	出画	脳
19	刀	かたな	A sword or knife, which signified an act of cutting something.	刀刃分切初券	喫潔召招昭照紹解貧粉辺留貿
20	刂	りっとう	A sword or knife, which signified an act of cutting something. This form is used on the right side of kanji only.	刊列判別利到制刷刻則前剣副割創劇	列例型製制測側班輸
21	力	ちから	Physical strength, strenuous work, or power. Two different ancient forms are: a) a strong hand with muscles showing; and b) a plow used in fields for strenuous farming work.	力功加助努労効勇勉動務勝募勢勤	賀協筋男働幼
22	勹	つつみがまえ	Two different origins for this shape are: a) a hand wrapping around something, signifying 'to wrap; to surround'; b) bending one's body low to show humility.	包	句均胸敬驚警的
23	匕	さじ	A person sitting viewed from the side. It signifies a "sitting person."	北	貨皆階疑比指死態老背化
24	匚匸	かくしがまえ or はこがまえ	The two different shapes that signified "a place to hide" are in the category of present-day classification.	区医	
25	十	じゅう	Ten sticks bundled up, signifying 'ten' or 'full.'	十千午半卒協南博	計汁準針率判戦
26	卩	ふしづくり	A person bending over, signifying a show of humility or listening to an order.	印危即卵	御迎節命令(令)領冷
27	厂	がんだれ	A cliff, under which there was a fountain, rock, fire, etc.	厚原	圧灰願歴
28	厶		This shape is a reduced form from various shapes such as a worm, a plow, or simply used to replace a complicated component.	去参	強法広鉱始私治公松窓怠台態仏払弁法
29	又	また	One of several shapes that depicted a right hand and is used for an act involving a hand.	又及友反収取受	極緊経径軽寝度努怒髪抜板版飯報
30	⺈		A hand from above or a person bending over something.	争	久危負

			3-STROKE SECTION HEADERS			
31	口	くちへん	There are a number of sources for this small square, among which are: a) an open mouth, signifying "to speak" or "to eat"; b) an object or box; c) a hole or window in a wall.	口古句召可台史右号司各合吉同名后向君否吸吹告周味呼命和品員唱商問善喜喫器	歌荷賀局極始治召招昭照紹尋操息知鳴絡略臨路惑損絹別保部
32	口	くにがまえ	An oblong shape that encircles another component, signifying an encampment of something.	四回因団困囲図固国園	
33	土	つちへん	A pile of dirt neatly packed in a triangular shape with an emphasis stroke. The practice of soil formed in a triangular shape is still seen in ground-breaking ceremonies in Japan.	土圧在地坂均垂型城域基堂報場塩境墓増	経径軽座社赤等特陸法陸達報
34	士	し	An ax or weapon carried by a warrior placed upside down in a ceremony, signifying a warrior or male person.	士声売	志仕誌装続読
35	夂	すいにょう	A footprint facing backward, signifying moving backwards or retreating.	変夏	各格額閣客後降終処麦複腹復優絡略路愛
36	夕	ゆう	Having one stroke in the middle as contrasted to two strokes in a moon 月, it depicted a dim moon in the early hours of evening, which signified "early evening." It is also used to indicate a piece of meat or flesh.	夕外多夜夢	液名隣
37	大	だい	A person stretching his arms and legs to make himself big, signifying "large; big; grand." It is also used for "person."	大天太夫央失奇奏奥奮	英映恩器模類突美
38	女	おんな	A woman sitting with her hands crossed in front of her, a graceful posture. It is used in many kanji that pertains to a woman.	女好妹妻姉始姓委姿娘婚婦	桜接努怒要
39	子子	こ	A baby with wiggling arms is used to indicate a child or offspring.	子字存季学孫孝	教厚好浮遊乳
40	宀	うかんむり	A house with a roof and walls came to signify "house" or "something under a roof."	宅宇守安完宗官宙定宝実客宣室宮害家容宿寄密富寒寝察察	案憲
41	寸	すん	Finger pointing at the wrist where one's pulse was taken. The distance between the hand and that point is an inch so the kanji signified "a little."	寸寺対専射将尊尋導	詩時待持謝村団等討得特博付府符
42	小	小さい	A piece of wood being chipped away into smaller pieces, signifying smallness.	小少	秒歩省京涼就
43	尢	だいのまげじ	An unclear origin. Among the views are a bent arm that signified an act of beckoning or a dog.	就	
44	尸	しかばね	a) A person in a slumped position; and b) a roof.	尺局居届屋展属層	駅昼訳遅殿
45	山	やまへん	Mountain ranges, signifying mountains.	山岩岸島	催炭密
46	巛川	かわ	Flowing water, or a river, which flows smoothly or around a bend.	川州	災順
47	工	こう	A skillfully crafted work which has two pieces of wood boards held together by a pole.	工左差	佐功攻式試尋
48	己	き	A snake on the verge of straightening itself, or awareness of oneself when he gets up.	己巻	紀記起選配
49	巾	はばへん	A piece of cloth hanging on a pole, signifying a cloth, curtain, or something that drapes.	市布希師席帯帰帳常幕	掃婦綿

50	干	かん		A two-forked thrusting weapon fortified at the joint. Many of the dictionary entry kanji were placed for its similarity in shape.	干平年幸幹	刊岸
51	幺	いとがしら		In contrast to 糸 "thread," this indicated short threads, signifying that it does not have a full length or strength.	幼	後
52	广	まだれ		A house which has one side open.	庁広床序底店府度座庫庭康	席渡糖
53	廴	えんにょう		A crossroad, in which the bottom stroke extends, signifying an extension of something.	延建	健誕庭
54	廾	にじゅうあし		Two hands upwards holding up something.	弁	算鼻
55	弋	しきがまえ		A marking with a stake.	式	試貸代武
56	弓	ゆみへん		A double curvature bow, used for something that gets pulled to stretch like a bow.	弓引弟弱張強	第
57	ヨ 彑	よ		a) A hand; b) a piece of rod that gets chipped away.		当帰急寝尋雪掃婦緑録
58	彡	さんづくり		Three neatly drawn strokes, signifying a pretty pattern.	形	修顔髪
59	彳	ぎょうにんべん		The left half of a crossroad, signifying "a way to go" or "a way in which one conducts."	役彼往径待律後徒従得御復徳	行術街衛
60	丷		A segment of a current kanji form.		並兼	前
61	⺌		A segment of a current kanji form.		単巣営厳	学
62	⺍	さかさしょう	A segment of a current kanji form.		当党	堂
63	忄	りっしんべん		An anatomical shape of a heart. It had an artery coming downward. 忄 was used on the left side of a kanji.	忙快性悔情慣	
64	扌才	てへん		A hand, used on the left side of kanji. 才 was also placed in this header for its similarity to a hand.	才打払批技投折抜押担招拝拡拾持指捨掃授採探接推提揮損操	
65	氵	さんずい		Running water or liquid, used on the left side of a kanji.	汁汚池決汽河油治沿泊法波泣注泳洋洗活派流浅浮浴海消液涼深混清済減渡温測港湖湯満源準漁演漢潔潮激	酒染落
66	犭	けものへん		A dog, or an animal in general. When used on the left side, 犭 was usually used.	犯独狭	
67	艹 艸	くさかんむり		Two plants growing in the ground. Traditionally this section header has been classified as having six strokes (from 艸) or four strokes from ⺿.	花芸芽若苦英茶草荷菜落葉著蒸蔵薬	猫漢募墓暮幕夢模
68	辶 辵 辶	しんにゅう		A foot going beyond a crossroad, signifying moving forward. The older form 辵 (7 strokes) is reduced to 辶. Another form 辶 was also used in some kanji until recently.	辺込迎近返述迷追退送逃逆通速造連週進遅遊運過道達違遠適選遺	
69	阝邑	おおざと (on right side)		When used on the right side of a kanji, it signified a village. The current form comes from the old form 邑, which indicated land and people.	郊郡部郵郷都	
70	阝阜	こざとへん (on left side)		When used on the left side, it signified a boundary or higher area. Its old form was 阜, which indicated a pile of dirt, or an earthen wall.	防降限陛院除陸険陽隊階際障隣	

4-STROKE SECTION HEADERS					
71	心	こころ	An anatomical shape of a heart with chambers. 心 was used at the bottom of a kanji whereas 忄 was used on the left side of a kanji.	心必志忘応忠念怒思息急恋恐恩息悪悲惑想意愛感態憲	誌窓総認優
72	戈	ほこづくり	A halberd, used in kanji that pertains to war or threatening situations.	成我戦	越域感機城盛誠惑歳識織職
73	戸	とかんむり	A door.	戸所	編
74	手	て	One of several shapes of a hand (a right hand).	手承挙	材財閉
75	支	しにょう or えだにょう	A hand holding a twig, signifying holding something firmly.	支	技枝
76	攵 攴	ぼくづくり	A hand holding a stick, signifying a motion of pounding and also action or work in general.	改攻放政故救敗教散敬数整敵	激厳牧枚務
77	文	ぶん	Layered collars, which made a beautiful shape like a writing.	文	
78	斤	おのづくり	An ax, signifying something to cut.	断新	近質所折
79	方	ほうへん or かたへん	A plow with a long handle or a flag pole for a clan.	方旅族旗	放防遊
80	日	ひへん	A sun, signifying a "light" and "brightness or warmth" created by the sun.	日旧早明易昔星映春昨昭是昼時晩普景晴暑暖暗暮暴曜	指者借諸緒早得盟模量別普譜
81	曰	いわく	This group has little in common. They were chosen for its shape. 曰 depicted a sound coming out of a mouth, signifying to say.	曲更書最	層
82	月	つきへん	a) A crescent moon; b) a boat.	月服朗望朝期	湖前明盟潮
83	月 肉	にくづき	A piece of meat or flesh that shows tendons, signifying a part of the body. When used in this meaning, 月 is generally placed on the left side or at the bottom.	肉肥有育肺胃背胸能脈脱脳腸腹臓	筋骨散勝消態豚輸然燃
84	木	きへん	A standing tree with the roots firmly in the ground, signifying a tree or a product of a tree.	木未末本札机材村束条来東松板林枚果枝染柱査栄校株根格案桜梅械棒森植検業極楽構様標模権横樹橋機	禁困採菜殺集床新深染想操相探箱保味薬葉歴練妹
85	欠	あくび	A man yawning with his mouth open wide, signifying a lack of air or inhaling.	欠次欲歌	飲姿資吹
86	止	とめへん	A footprint of a left foot with a big toe having a more prominent shape.	止正武歩歳歴	歯
87	歹	がつへん or かばねへん	A decapitated head with hair attached that occurred in a war. It also signified a dead body.	死残	列例
88	殳	ほこづくり or るまた	A spear-like weapon or tool in a hand, signifying "to hit with a tool."	段殺殿	穀設投役
89	母	はは	A nursing mother.	母毎毒	海悔梅
90	比	ひ	Two people sitting next to each other, signifying "people lined up."	比	混批皆陛階
91	毛	け	Long hair of an animal.	毛	

92	氏	し	A ladle or spoon with a big handle for a clan's feast.	氏民	婚紙低底
93	气	きがまえ	Rising steam.	気	
94	水 氺	したみず	Running water.	水氷永求泉	救球線暴様 緑録康
95	火	ひへん	A burning fire.	火灯灰災炭焼煙燃	秋談畑
96	灬	れっか or れんが	A burning fire. When a fire is used at the bottom, 灬 is used.	点為無然照熟熱	黒蒸燃
97	父	ちち	A hand holding a stone, signifying a father or stern figure.	父	
98	片	かたべん	A half of a tree shape, signifying a piece.	片版	
99	牛 牜	うしへん	A cow's head with two big horns, signifying a cow or animal in general.	牛牧物特	解
100	犬	いぬ	A dog, or signifying an animal in general.	犬状	然燃
101	王 玉	たま・おう	a) Three jewels strung together; b) A powerful ax, a symbol of power, king.	玉王班現球理環	皇国聖全程 宝望
102	ネ	しめすへん	An altar, or religious activity. Used on the left side of kanji.	礼社祖祝神福	視
103	耂	おいかんむり	A long-haired old man with a walking stick, signifying old.	老考者	教孝暑緒 署都

5-STROKE SECTION HEADERS					
104	生	せい	Leaves growing out of soil, signifying life or living.	生産	性姓星
105	用	よう	A fence, behind which sacrificial animals are kept.	用	通
106	田	たへん	The traditional classification includes: a) 田 depiction of rice paddies; b) 申 lightening in the sky taken as a god's message; c) 由 liquid dripping out of a gourd.	田由申男町界畑留 略番異	思猫鼻勇油 笛富副福奮 届神
107	疋	ひきへん	A line and a footprint, signifying stopping in one place or just a foot.	疑	定提題是延
108	白	しろ	An acorn, inside of which is white. It signified white. A few came from a reduced form of 百 or 自.	白百的皆皇	習泉願原線 泊綿
109	疒	やまいだれ	A sick person on a raised bed, signifying sick. (A bed is the left side and a sick person is at the top.)	疲病痛	
110	癶	はつがしら	A quick move. One jumped quickly and landed with two feet apart.	発登	
111	皮	かわ	A hand pulling an animal out of its fur, signifying skin.	皮	波破疲
112	皿	さら	A plate or dish.	皿益盛盟	塩
113	目	めへん	An eye placed vertically.	目直相省看県真眠 眼着	算植想値箱
114	矢	やへん	An arrow.	矢知短	疑族候
115	石	いしへん	A rock under a cliff, signifying a stone, rock.	石砂研破確磁	岩

#	Kanji	Reading	Description	Examples	Examples 2
116	示	しめす	An altar table or religious activity. This is used when the meaning of "altar table" is used at the bottom of kanji, whereas ネ (#102) is used when it is on the left side.	示票祭禁	際察祭宗票標
117	禾	のぎへん	A rice or grain plant. The name comes from the hard awn of a barley plant called *nogi* in Japanese.	私秋科秒秘移程税種稿穀積穫	季利和誘
118	穴	あなかんむり	A house and a motion of dividing something or digging, signifying "a hole."	穴究空突窓	
119	立	たつへん	A standing person.	立章童競	位泣境障新接翌部
120	罒 网	あみがしら	a) A depiction of a casting 网 had its form reduced 罒; b) A watchful eye 目 placed sideways in some kanji.	罪置署	環憲夢徳買
121	ネ	ころもへん	A clothing collar. When used on the left side, it is written as ネ.	複補	初
	氺		Please see #94 氺.		

6-STROKE SECTION HEADERS					
122	竹	たけかんむり	Two stalks of bamboo with narrow pointed leaves that hang downward. Bamboo was useful material in living, craft, writing, and building.	竹笑笛符第筆等筋答策算管箱節築簡	
123	米	こめへん	Rice grain scattered in all directions, signifying grains in general.	米粉料精糖	奥断番迷隣類
124	糸	いとへん	Thin silk filaments being pulled out of silkworm cocoons or a skein of threads, used to pertain to a line that connects things, or continuity.	糸系紀約紅納純紙級素索細紹終組経結絡給統絵絶絹続綿緊総緑緒線編練縦縮績織	係孫潔
125	羽 羽	はね	Two wings of a bird.	羽翌習	曜
126	羊	ひつじへん	A sheep was valued for its versatility, warm wool, tasty food (lamb and mutton), and its beautiful appearance, and is used to signify something desirable.	羊美群義	鮮議洋養様遅
127	耒	すきへん or らいすき	A plow and rows of plowed soil. Only one kanji is currently used.	耕	
128	耳	みみへん	An ear, signifying to listen.	耳聖聞職	厳取最
129	自		A nose, the center of one's face, embodying a person. It signified oneself.	自	息鼻
130	至		An arrow hitting the ground, signifying to come to an end.	至	屋室到
131	臼	うす	A mortar.	興	
132	舌	したへん	A tongue.	舌	活辞乱話
133	舟	ふねへん	A boat.	航船	
134	艮	こんづくり or ねづくり	a) An eye and looking backwards; b) a basket and running water; c) food in a dish.	良	眼根郷限退娘朗即節
135	色	いろ	A man and a woman bending forward, signifying a love affair.	色	絶
136	虫	むしへん	Three worms indicated a worm for the kanji.	虫蚕	強風独

137	血	ち	A bowl which is filled with animal blood for religious rites, signifying blood.	血衆	
138	行	ゆきがまえ	A crossroad, signifying going beyond a crossroad. It is also used for one's conduct.	行術街衛	
139	衣	ころも	A clothing collar, signifying clothes in general.	衣表裁装裏製	遠園表
140	西 両	にし	a) A woman's hips with both hands placed on her waist. The waist is in the center of one's body, thus it signified "essential"; b) A basket.	西要	煙価票標

7-STROKE SECTION HEADERS					
141	見	みる	An eye with legs or to look at.	見規視覚覧親観	現
142	臣	しん	An eye viewed sideways or a subject who kept a watchful eye.	臣臨	緊蔵臓覧
143	角	つの	A pointed horn.	角解	
144	言	ごんべん	A needle with a handle for tattooing (for religious ceremony, punishment of criminals, etc.) and a mouth. Together they signified "to speak clearly and sharply."	言計討訓記訪設許訳証評詞試詩話誌認誕誘語誠誤説読誰課調談論諸講謝識警議護	信
145	谷	たに	Mountain ranges and an opening in between, signifying valley.	谷	容欲浴
146	豆	まめ	A raised bowl to offer food and drinks in religious rites.	豆豊	短頭登矢豆
147	豕	いのこへん	A wild boar or a pig. It also encompasses an elephant or other animals.	豚象	劇像隊家
148	貝	かい	a) A beautiful rare cowry shell from the southern sea used for money; b) A pot that was used for cooking sacrificial animals in religious rites.	貝負財貧貨貴貯貴買貸費貿賀賃資賛賞質贈	遺慣責積績則測側損員
149	赤	あか	A variant of 大 'large' and a variant of 火 'fire,' signifying the color of burning fire, or 'red.'	赤	
150	走	そうにょう	A running man and a footprint, signifying a man running or an act that pertains to the use of feet.	走起越	徒
151	足	あし	A knee cap and a footprint, indicating a foot or a leg.	足路	
152	身	み	A pregnant woman viewed sideways. The kanji that contains this pertains to a physical feature.	身	射謝
153	車	くるま	A chariot used in a battle with two wheels. The current form 車 depicted a platform with two wheels connected at an axel.	車軍転軽輪輸	運庫連
154	辛	つらい	A tattooing needle which had an ink reservoir and a handle.	辞	
155	辰	たつ	A clam with a feeler extended. Clam shells were used as tools for weeding in the field. It pertains to agriculture, or is used for its sound.	農	震
156	酉	とりへん	A large wine vase.	配酒酸	
157	里	さとへん	Rice paddies and a pile of dirt. An area of land where field work takes place signifies a hamlet.	里重野量	動働童裏

#	Header	Reading	Description		
158	麦 麥	むぎ	The old form 麥 had a wheat plant on the top and a backward foot underneath, signifying a plant heavy with grains and drooping over. It means "wheat plant."	麦	
	辵		Please see #68 辶.		
	阝 邑	おおざと	Please see #69 阝・邑.		

			8-STROKE SECTION HEADERS		
159	金 釒	かねへん	A mine in which pieces of metal glisten in the ground. The kanji containing this generally pertains to a mineral or a metal object.	金針鉄鉱銀銅銭鋼録鏡	
160	長	ながい	A long-haired old man, signifying old age or chief.	長	帳張髪
161	門	もんがまえ	Closed double doors hiding things from plain sight or keeping others out, or a gate.	門閉開間関閣	聞問簡
162	隹	ふるとり	A bird, which has feathers, an ability to take off, or may get caught by man.	集雑離難	獲確観権護催準進推誰曜
163	雨	あめかんむり	Rain drops falling from the heavens, signifying rain or other atmospheric phenomenon.	雨雪雲電震	
164	青 靑	あお	Leaves above ground and a well, signifying fresh, blue.	青静	情精晴
165	非	ひ	Two wings of a bird on opposite sides, signifying "not" or negation.	非	悲俳
166	食	しょくへん	Some food in a dish with a cover, signifying to eat; food. When used on the left, contains one stroke fewer than the kanji 食.	飯飲飼館	
	阝阜	こざと	Please see #70 阝・阜.		

			9-STROKE SECTION HEADERS		
167	面	めん	An enwrapped face, signifying mask or face.	面	
168	革	かわへん	An animal hide with a head still attached, signifying stretched hide.	革	
169	音	おと	A tattoo needle and a mouth with something inside, signifying a word that is not clear, that is sound.	音	暗意億職識織
170	頁	おおがい	A person with a formal headdress, signifying a head or something at the top.	頂順預領頭題額顔願類	
171	風	かぜ	A sail that catches the wind and an imaginary sacred animal such as a dragon or a phoenix bird inside, that was believed to control wind.	風	
172	飛	とぶ	A bird flying with its wings spread, signifying to fly. The kanji 飛 means "to fly."	飛	
173	食	しょく	Some food in a dish with a cover, signifying to eat; food.	食養	
174	首	くび	Two origins for a neck: a) A head with hair and a nose in the middle; b) An eye and an eyebrow.	首	道導

	**10-STROKE SECTION HEADERS**
175	馬	うまへん		A horse with a mane and four legs emphasized.	馬駅駐験驚	
176	骨	ほねへん		Bone joints and a piece of meat or animal flesh 月, signifying bones that were covered by flesh.	骨	
177	高	たかい		A tall watch tower.	高	稿
178	髟	かみがしら		A stooping elderly person and his long flowing hair emphasized, signifying "hair."	髪	
	**11-STROKE SECTION HEADERS**
179	黄黄	き		A flaming arrow whose bright yellow light illuminated all directions.	黄	横
180	魚	うお		A fish with a head, scaled body, and fins.	魚鮮	漁
181	黒黒	くろ		A grill with soot over a fire, signifying black.	黒	
182	鳥	とりへん		A bird.	鳥鳴	
	**12-STROKE SECTION HEADER**
183	歯	は		The top, 'footprint (to stay in one place)' and the bottom, 'two rows of teeth in a mouth,' together signifying tooth.	歯	
	**14-STROKE SECTION HEADER**
184	鼻	はなへん		A nose and a present on a table signified something noticeable, which is a nose.	鼻	

1	ON-KUN READINGS: アイ・まな	HEADER: 心

愛
love

ORIGIN: The ancient form had a form that signified a "person kneeling down to eat," 心 "heart" and 夂 "dragging feet" that pull one back. Together they described a state in which one's heart was filled with an emotion and it was hard to move on, that is, "love." The kanji 愛 means "love."

あい
愛 love
あいじょう
愛情 affection
れんあい
恋愛 love

あいしょう
愛称 nickname
あいちゃく
愛着 emotional attachment
あいよう
愛用する to use regularly

一 ノ ビ ヴ 心 心 心 心 心 愛 愛 愛 愛   13

2	ON-KUN READINGS: アク・オ・わる(い)・あ(しき)	HEADER: 心

悪
bad; ill; evil

ORIGIN: The top of the older form 惡 had 亞 "hollow in the ground," indicating something "suppressed." The bottom 心 depicted an anatomical shape of a heart, signifying "heart" or "feelings." Together they indicated "bad feelings that were suppressed" or simply "bad" or "evil." The kanji 悪 means "bad or ill."

わる
悪い bad
あく
悪 evil
けんおかん
嫌悪感 abhorrence

さいあく
最悪 the worst
あくい
悪意 ill-intention
あくよう
悪用 misuse

一 ニ 三 亓 亓 亜 亜 悪 悪 悪 悪   11

37

3	ON-KUN READINGS: アツ	HEADER: 土

圧
to press; pressure

ORIGIN: The old form 壓 consisted of 厂 "smothering cover," 日 "bone joint," and 月 "meat or flesh" of 犬 "dog or animal," which indicated sweet meat. After eating sweet meat, one feels full and a pressure in one's stomach. 土 "soil" added the meaning of pushing down. The reduced current form 圧 means "to press" or "pressure."

あつりょく
圧力 pressure
きあつ
気圧 atmospheric pressure
けつあつ
血圧 blood pressure

よくあつてき
抑圧的 oppressive
圧する to weigh on
あっとうてき
圧倒的 overwhelming

一 厂 厂 圧 圧   5

4	ON-KUN READINGS: アン・やす(い)	HEADER: 宀

安
secure; peaceful;
inexpensive; cheap

ORIGIN: The combination of 宀 "house" and 女 "woman" resting at home indicated "safety or at ease." Inexpensive things are less stressful to buy; hence, another meaning was "inexpensive." The kanji 安 means "secure" or "peaceful" and also "inexpensive, cheap."

やす
安い inexpensive, cheap
あんか
安価 reasonably priced
かくやす
格安な moderately priced,
   bargain priced

あんしん
安心する to feel relieved
ふあん
不安な anxious
あんぜん
安全 safe

丶 宀 宀 安 安 安   6

5

ON-KUN READINGS: アン・くら(い)

HEADER: 日

暗

dark; unclear

ORIGIN: This kanji consisted of 日 "sun" and 音 "a sharp needle and something inside a mouth." When people try to speak with something in their mouths, their words often come out garbled or "unclear." The two forms combine to indicate "sun not clearly seen," and thus the kanji 暗 means "dark; unclear."

暗い dark
明暗 light and darkness
暗示 hint

暗記する to learn by heart
暗号 secret code; password
暗黙の内に tacitly

｜ 冂 日 日 日' 日立 日立 日产 昨 昨 暗 暗 暗 13

6

ON-KUN READINGS: アン

HEADER: 木

案

plan; proposed idea

ORIGIN: On the top 宀 "house" and 女 "woman" indicated "secure and peaceful," here used phonetically. The bottom 木 "wood" indicated a "desk." One thinks of a plan at a desk. The kanji 案 means "proposed idea" or "plan."

案 proposal
案内する to show around
案内所 information desk

案外と contrary to what is expected
提案する to propose
名案 brilliant idea

﹅ ﹅ 宀 宀 安 安 安 宰 案 案 10

7

ON-KUN READINGS: イ・もっ(て)

HEADER: 人

以

starting point; by means of

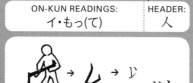

ORIGIN: The left side depicted a "plow" and the right side a "hand." A plow is a tool used at the start of work in the field. The kanji 以 means "by means of" or "starting point."

三人以上 three people or more
以下 below, less than
以内 within

以外 other than
以前 before
以後 thereafter

｜ 乚 以 以 以 5

8

ON-KUN READINGS: イ・くらい

HEADER: イ

位

rank; place; approximately

ORIGIN: This kanji consisted of イ a "standing person viewed sideways" and 立 a "person standing, facing front." Together they indicated a place or approximate area where one stood, according to his rank, before a ruler or in a ceremony. The kanji 位 means "rank, place" or "approximately."

位 rank
どの 位 how much
第一位 first place

位置 location
地位 position
各位 everyone [honorific]

ノ イ イ' 仁 伫 位 位 7

38

9

ON-KUN READINGS: イ・えら(い)

HEADER: イ

偉

grand; illustrious

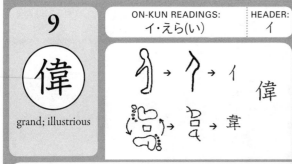

ORIGIN: The left side イ was a "person." The right side 韋 depicted two feet facing opposite one another, signifying different directions, here phonetically used to indicate "being different." Someone who is different and stands out because of his extraordinary quality is treated with respect. The kanji 偉 means "grand; illustrious."

えら
偉い illustrious
いだい
偉大な great, illustrious
いじん
偉人 great man

いぎょう
偉業 great work
いじょうふ
偉丈夫 tall well-built man

ノイイ'イ'佇佇佇偉偉偉偉偉   12

10

ON-KUN READINGS: イ・かこ(む)

HEADER: □

囲

enclosure; to surround

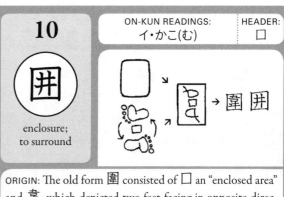

ORIGIN: The old form 圍 consisted of □ an "enclosed area" and 韋, which depicted two feet facing in opposite directions, walking in a circle. Together they indicated to encircle or to surround. The inside is now reduced to 井 (from 韋); the kanji 囲 means "to surround" or "enclosure."

かこ
囲む to surround
とり かこ
取り囲む to encircle
しゅうい
周囲 surrounding

ほうい
包囲される to be seized
ふんいき
雰囲気 atmosphere
はんい
範囲 scope, sphere

｜ 冂 冂 月 用 囲 囲   7

11

ON-KUN READINGS: イ・ゆだ(ねる)

HEADER: 女

委

to entrust; pliant

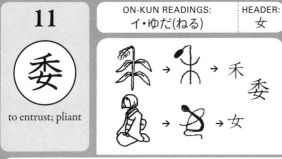

ORIGIN: The top 禾 was a pictograph of a rice plant drooping under the weight of ripening grain. The bottom 女 was a pliant posture of a woman. Being pliant and flexible gave the meaning of leaving a decision to others. The kanji 委 means "to entrust" or "pliant."

ゆだ
委ねる to entrust
いいんかい
委員会 committee
いにんじょう
委任状 proxy

いいん
委員 committee member
いさい
委細 the details
いたく
委託する to trust

一 二 千 禾 禾 秃 委 委   8

12

ON-KUN READINGS: イ

HEADER: 心

意

meaning; intention; mind

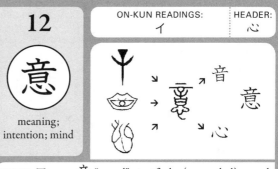

ORIGIN: The top 音 "sound" signified a (nonverbal) sound because something inside a mouth prevented what was said from becoming a word. The bottom 心 was an anatomical heart, signifying feelings. Together they indicated thought and feelings that were kept inside one's heart. The kanji 意 means "meaning," "intention," or "mind."

いみ
意味 meaning
いけん
意見 opinion
いがい
意外に unexpectedly

ちゅうい
注意 attention, heed
いとてき
意図的に intentionally
みんい
民意 popular sentiment, the will of the people

` 亠 十 立 产 斉 音 音 音 意 意 意   13

13

ON-KUN READINGS: イ・エキ・やさ(しい)・やす(い)

HEADER: 日

易

easy; to change; fortune telling

ORIGIN: The ancient form was a pictograph of a lizard with a big head and rays of the sun (彡). A lizard can change the color of its skin instantly. One's future also changes constantly, and it is also used for fortune telling. The kanji 易 means "easy," "to change," or "fortune telling."

易しい easy
貿易 trade
書き易い easy to write

易者 fortune teller
平易 plain
不易 unchanged

一 冂 冃 日 日 旦 昜 易 易   8

14

ON-KUN READINGS: イ・ため・な(す)

HEADER: 灬

為

to do; deed; purpose; sake

ORIGIN: In the old form 爲, the top was a "hand from above" and the bottom was an "elephant," which indicated "to handle an elephant by hand." Elephant was dropped from the meaning, and the form came to mean "to handle; to do something" or "deed." The kanji 為 means "to do," "deed," "sake" or "purpose."

Xの為に for X, because of X
人為的 artificial
行為 deed, behavior exchange

為政者 ruler, political leaders
作為的 deliberately

丶 ソ 艹 为 为 為 為 為 為   9

40

15

ON-KUN READINGS: イ・こと(なる)

HEADER: 田

異

different; to differ

ORIGIN: The top 田 was a mask of a god in a votive dance or play. The bottom 共 depicted two hands holding up the mask. By putting a mask on, one becomes a different person, or a character in a play. The kanji 異 means "different; to differ."

異なった different
異国 foreign country
異論 objection, different view

驚異の amazing
異色の novel
異例の exceptional

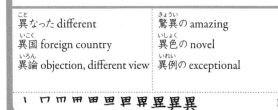

一 冂 冂 用 田 田 田 甼 里 異 異   11

16

ON-KUN READINGS: イ・うつ(る)

HEADER: 禾

移

to transfer; to move

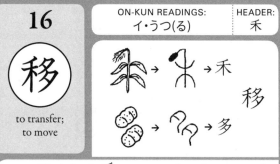

ORIGIN: The left side 禾 was a rice plant drooping under the weight of the grain. The right side 多 was two pieces of meat, suggesting "many," but here was used phonetically to mean "to move." Together the two forms indicated the swaying action of rice plants blown in wind. The kanji 移 means "to move; to transfer."

移る to move
移動 moving
移転 moving, relocation

移住する to migrate, to relocate
移民 immigrant
推移 transition

一 二 千 千 禾 禾 秒 秽 移 移 移   11

17

ON-KUN READINGS: イ **HEADER:** 月

胃

the stomach

ORIGIN: The top 田 depicted pieces of food in stomach, and the bottom 月 depicted flesh of a body. 月 is also used in a number of kanji that pertain to body parts. The kanji 胃 means "stomach."

胃 stomach	胃癌 stomach cancer
胃腸 the stomach and intestines	胃炎 gastritis
胃袋 stomach	健胃剤 peptic

｀ 冂 口 田 田 甲 胃 胃 胃 胃　9

18

ON-KUN READINGS: イ・ころも・きぬ **HEADER:** 衣

衣

clothes

ORIGIN: The ancient form depicted the collar and front portion of clothes, indicating clothes in general. The kanji 衣 means "clothes." When it is used as a recurring component, it is written ネ, as in 複 "duplicate" and 補 "to complement."

衣服 clothes	衣装 costume
衣 robe, coating, batter	衣食 food and clothes
衣替え change clothes for the season	羽衣 robe of feathers; celestial robe

｀ 亠 ナ 亢 卞 衣　6

41

19

ON-KUN READINGS: イ・ちが(う) **HEADER:** ⻌

違

to differ; wrong

ORIGIN: The upper right 韋 consisted of two feet facing in the opposite direction away from an area, 口, indicating "to move away." The lower left ⻌ came from a foot in the crossroad, indicating "to move forward." Together they signified "going in the opposite direction" (thus "being different; wrong"). The kanji 違 means "to differ" or "wrong."

違う different	駐車違反 parking violation
相違 difference	間違っている is wrong
行き違い miss each other on the road	違和感 sense of incompatibility

丿 ㇖ 土 ヰ 井 岸 岸 韋 韋 韋 違 違 違　13

20

ON-KUN READINGS: イ・ユイ **HEADER:** ⻌

遺

to leave; to bequeath

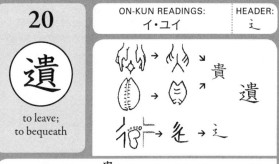

ORIGIN: The right top 貴 had two hands holding something precious and 貝 "cowry" that was used as currency, indicating "valuables." The old form 辵 of ⻌, was "foot inside a crossroad," which signified "moving forward." Together they indicated something precious that one left after he or she had moved on. The kanji 遺 means "to leave, bequeath."

遺跡 historical site	遺作 posthumous work
遺言 will	遺族 the bereaved family
遺産 inheritance, legacy	遺書 written will

丿 冂 口 中 虫 虫 毒 書 貴 貴 貴 遺 遺　15

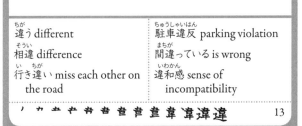

21

ON-KUN READINGS: イ
HEADER: 匸

医
medicine

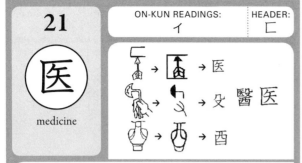

ORIGIN: The old form 醫 consisted of 医 "arrow hidden inside," 殳 "hand holding a bent arrow," signifying "attack," and 酉 "wine jar" used for medicinal purposes. Together they indicated an act of healing by hand a wound with medicinal plants from a jar. The kanji, now simplified only to 医, means "medicine."

いしゃ
医者 medical doctor
やすかわいいん
安川医院 Dr. Yasukawa's clinic
いがく
医学 medical science

いりょうひ
医療費 medical expenses
じゅうい
獣医 veterinarian
しゅじい
主治医 primary care physician

一 ア ア チ 至 至 医　　7

22

ON-KUN READINGS: イキ
HEADER: 土

域
area; limits

ORIGIN: The left side 土 indicated "pile of dirt neatly packed in a triangle shape," signifying "ground." The right side 或 consisted of 戈, a "halberd," 口 a "land marked" by 一 "boundary." Together they indicated a piece of land with a boundary that one protects. The kanji 域 indicates "area; limits."

ちいき
地域 area
くいき
区域 the limits, zone
いき
域 area, scope

りゅういき
流域 basin of river
せいいき
聖域 sacred precincts
りょういき
領域 domain

一 十 土 坊 圹 圹 坷 域 域 域　　11

23

ON-KUN READINGS: イク・そだ(つ)・はぐく(む)
HEADER: 月

育
to bring up;
to raise a child

ORIGIN: The top part was a baby with its head downward as it is being born; the bottom 月 was a pictograph of flesh of a body (a variant of 肉). The birth of a child entails raising him/her. The kanji 育 means "to bring up" or "to raise a child."

きょういく
教育 education
そだ
育てる to raise
いくじ
育児 childbearing

ほいくえん
保育園 day nursery, preschool
たいいく
体育 physical education
いくせい
育成する to foster

' 亠 亠 夳 夳 育 育 育　　8

24

ON-KUN READINGS: イチ・イツ・ひと(つ)
HEADER: 一

一
one; single; first

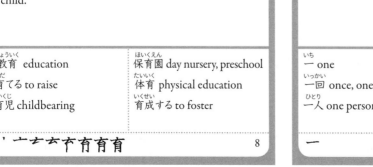

ORIGIN: The ancient form depicted a single extended finger or a stick of wood, which signified the number "one." The kanji 一 means "one; single; first."

いち
一 one
いっかい
一回 once, one time
ひとり
一人 one person

ついたち
一日 first day of the month
いちばん
一番 the first, most
とういつ
統一 unification

一　　1

42

25

ON-KUN READINGS: イン・しるし

HEADER: 卩

印

sign; seal; symbol; India

ORIGIN: The left side depicted a hand from above. The right side 卩 depicted a person bending his or her body with pressure from above. Together they indicated pressing someone down to kneel. One also presses a seal down with a hand. The kanji 印 means "seal; sign; symbol." It is also phonetically used to indicate India.

消印 postmark
印刷する to print
目印 landmark

印 seal, mark
印鑑 seal
封印する to seal

´ ｲ ｆ Ｅ 印 印   6

26

ON-KUN READINGS: イン

HEADER: 口

員

member of group; official

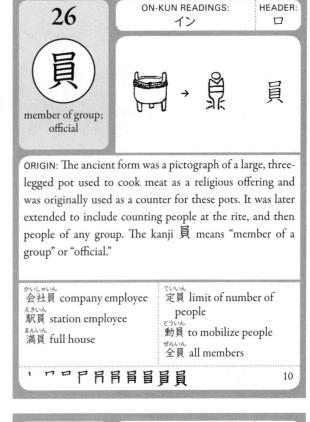

ORIGIN: The ancient form was a pictograph of a large, three-legged pot used to cook meat as a religious offering and was originally used as a counter for these pots. It was later extended to include counting people at the rite, and then people of any group. The kanji 員 means "member of a group" or "official."

会社員 company employee
駅員 station employee
満員 full house

定員 limit of number of people
動員 to mobilize people
全員 all members

丨 冂 冂 冃 冃 目 冒 冒 員 員   10

27

ON-KUN READINGS: イン・よ(る)・ちな(む)

HEADER: 囗

因

to depend on; to be caused by

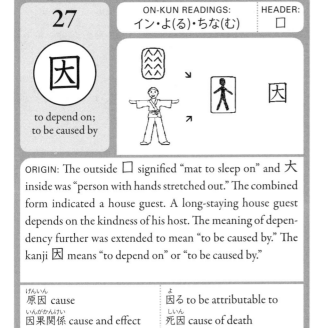

ORIGIN: The outside 囗 signified "mat to sleep on" and 大 inside was "person with hands stretched out." The combined form indicated a house guest. A long-staying house guest depends on the kindness of his host. The meaning of dependency further was extended to mean "to be caused by." The kanji 因 means "to depend on" or "to be caused by."

原因 cause
因果関係 cause and effect
起因する to originate in

因る to be attributable to
死因 cause of death
因みに incidentally

丨 冂 冂 囝 因 因   6

28

ON-KUN READINGS: イン・ひ(く)

HEADER: 弓

引

to pull

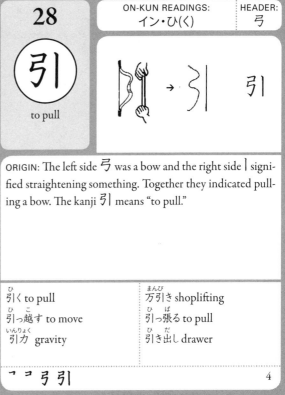

ORIGIN: The left side 弓 was a bow and the right side 丨 signified straightening something. Together they indicated pulling a bow. The kanji 引 means "to pull."

引く to pull
引っ越す to move
引力 gravity

万引き shoplifting
引っ張る to pull
引き出し drawer

フ ヨ 弓 引   4

29

ON-KUN READINGS: イン・の(む)　HEADER: 食

飲

to drink;
to swallow

ORIGIN: The current form 食 "to eat" replaced the depiction of a wine jar in the old form (not shown here). The right side 欠 depicted a person with a mouth wide open. Together they meant to put something in the mouth, or "to swallow; drink." The kanji 飲 means "to drink; to swallow."

の
飲む to drink, to swallow
の　く
飲み食い eating and drinking
いんしょくてん
飲食店 restaurant

の　もの
飲み物 drink, beverage
いんしゅ うんてん
飲酒運転 drunken driving
いんようすい
飲用水 drinking water

ノ　ハ　ヘ　今　今　今　食　食　食　飲　飲　飲　12

30

ON-KUN READINGS: イン　HEADER: 阝

院

a large public
house; institution

ORIGIN: The left side 阝 signified an earthen wall surrounding a house. The right side 完 showed that 元 "man" was entirely wrapped in 宀 "house." Together they meant a large house surrounded by a big wall. The kanji 院 means "large public house; institution."

びょういん
病院 hospital
だいがくいん
大学院 graduate school
にゅういん
入院 hospitalization

かいん
下院 House of
Representatives (U.S.),
the lower house
がくいん
学院 academy

’　彐　阝　阝’　阝’　阝　阼　阼　院　院　10

31

ON-KUN READINGS: ウ・ユウ・みぎ　HEADER: 口

右

right side

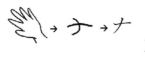

ORIGIN: The first two strokes indicated a right hand and the bottom 口 was a mouth. The right hand is used to bring food to the mouth. The kanji 右 means "right side." (Note that the first stroke is the slanted one.)

みぎ
右 right
みぎて
右手 right hand
みぎがわ
右側 the right side

さゆう
左右 both sides
うせつ
右折 right turn
うは
右派 conservative faction

ノ　ナ　オ　右　右　5

32

ON-KUN READINGS: ウ　HEADER: 宀

宇

roof; space (outer
space)

ORIGIN: The top 宀 came from the depiction of a house with a roof, and the bottom 于 was derived from 丂 "twisted or bent weed or shape." Together they indicated a large, slanted roof that covers a large space or open area. The kanji 宇 means "roof; space (outer space)."

うちゅう
宇宙 space

’　宀　宀　宇　宇　6

44

33

ON-KUN READINGS: ウ・は・はね **HEADER:** 羽

羽
wing; feather

ORIGIN: A pictograph of two wings indicated "wings" or "bird." It is also used as the counter for birds. The kanji 羽 means "wing; feather."

羽 feather, wing
三羽 three birds
羽毛 down, feather, plume

羽二重 thin glossy silk
羽化 emergence, eclosion, hatching
羽目 plight

一 ヨ ヨ 羽 羽 羽　6

34

ON-KUN READINGS: ウ・あま・あめ **HEADER:** 雨

雨
rain

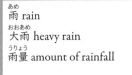

ORIGIN: The ancient form was a pictograph of raindrops falling from a cloud. The ancient people might have viewed the sky as a dome. When used as a recurring component, the form signifies meteorological phenomena, including thunder 雷, snow 雪, and cloud 雲. The kanji 雨 means "rain."

雨 rain
大雨 heavy rain
雨量 amount of rainfall

雨宿り taking shelter from the rain
春雨 light spring rain
小雨 light rain, drizzle

一 厂 厂 币 币 雨 雨 雨　8

45

35

ON-KUN READINGS: ウン・はこ(ぶ) **HEADER:** 辶

運
to transport; luck

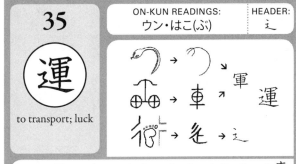

ORIGIN: The right top had 冖 "snake circling" and 車 "vehicle." In a battle, soldiers circle military vehicles. Thus, 軍 indicates "military." The bottom part 辶, formerly 辵 ("crossroad" and "foot"), indicated "moving forward." The kanji 運 means "to transport." It also means "luck," which is something that may come around.

運動 exercise, campaign
運転する to operate, to drive
運ぶ to transport

運 luck
運送する to transport
気運 opportunity

一 冖 冖 冖 冃 冒 宣 宣 軍 軍 運 運　12

36

ON-KUN READINGS: ウン・くも **HEADER:** 雨

雲
cloud

ORIGIN: The top 雨 depicted rainfall from the sky, which the ancient people might have believed to be in a dome shape. The bottom 云 depicted vapors rising or forming a thunderhead. Together they indicated a cloud. The kanji 雲 means "cloud."

雲 cloud
雲行き movement of the clouds, situation
雨雲 rain cloud

雲隠れする to vanish
雲間 break in the clouds
雲泥の差 as different as night and day, polar opposite

一 厂 厂 币 雨 雨 雨 雨 雪 雲 雲 雲　12

37

ON-KUN READINGS: エイ・いとな(む)　**HEADER:** ⺌

to conduct (business); barracks

ORIGIN: The old form 營 had ⼍ "cover" with two 火 "fire or torch" and 呂 "joined rooms," indicating an encampment surrounded by torches, or "military barracks." It also meant "to conduct," because affairs were negotiated in a barracks. Now simplified to 営, it means "to conduct (business)" or "barracks."

けいえいがく 経営学 business administration study
けいえい 経営 management
いとな 営む to run (business)

えいぎょうちゅう 営業中 "open" (for business)
こうえい 公営 publicly run
じんえい 陣営 warring camp

、 ゛ ⺌ ⺍ 𫝆 𫞁 営 営 営 営 営 営　12

38

ON-KUN READINGS: エイ・うつ(る)・は(える)　**HEADER:** 日

映

to be imaged; to be reflected

ORIGIN: The left side 日 was a "sun." The right side 央 highlighted the neck of a man, which is in the center of a man's body, and it signified "center." In the combined form, the sun projects the outline of a man casting his shadow, signifying "to reflect the difference between light and shadow." The kanji 映 means "to be imaged; to be reflected."

えいが 映画 movie
はんえい 反映する to reflect
うつ 映る to be mirrored

じょうえいちゅう 上映中 film now showing
映える to look attractive
ほうえい 放映 broadcasting

丨 冂 日 日 日 旫 旫 映 映　9

39

ON-KUN READINGS: エイ・さか(える)・は(える)　**HEADER:** 木

prosperity; to flourish

ORIGIN: The old form 榮 had two 火 "fire" or "torch" that illuminated a large area, signifying "to flourish." The bottom 木 is a tree. In the combined form, "flourishing plants" signified "prosperity." The top is now reduced, and the current kanji 栄 means "prosperity; to flourish."

えいよう 栄養 nutrition
はんえい 繁栄 prosperity
さか 栄える to prosper

こうえい 光栄だ to feel honored
みえ 見栄 vanity
は 栄えある glorious, honorable

、 ゛ ⺌ ⺍ 𫝆 学 学 栄 栄　9

40

ON-KUN READINGS: エイ・なが(い)　**HEADER:** 水

永

long time

ORIGIN: This was a pictograph of water flowing in a main stream of a river that split into smaller channels. A given amount of water takes a longer time to run through a smaller stream. The kanji 永 means "long time."

えいえん 永遠に eternally
えいきゅう 永久 eternal
えいみん 永眠する to pass away, rest in peace

なが 永い long (time)
えいじゅう 永住 permanent residence
えいきゅうし 永久歯 permanent tooth

` 丬 永 永 永　5

46

41

ON-KUN READINGS: エイ・およ(ぐ) | HEADER: 氵

泳

to swim

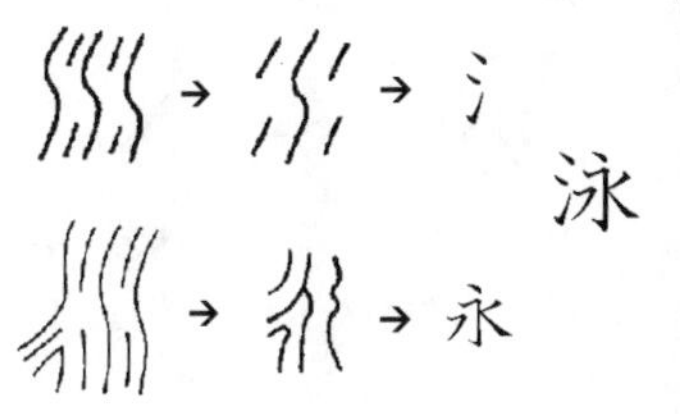

ORIGIN: The left side 氵 was "water" and the right side 永 depicted tributaries, narrow long streams of water, which signified "long (time)." Together they indicated "staying in water for a long time" or "to swim." The kanji 泳 means "to swim."

- 泳ぐ (およ) to swim
- 水泳 (すいえい) swimming
- 泳ぎ方 (およ かた) how to swim
- 平泳ぎ (ひらおよ) the breast stroke
- 背泳 (はいえい) back strokes
- 力泳 (りきえい) powerful swim

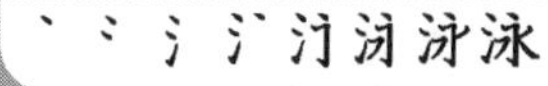
8

42

ON-KUN READINGS: エイ | HEADER: 艹

英

excellent; English

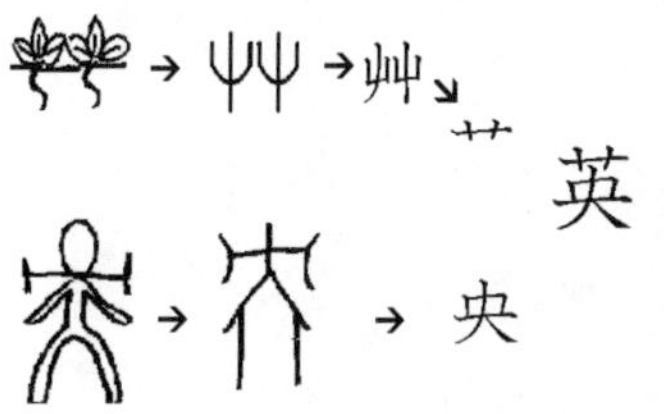

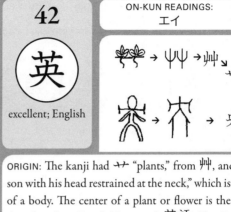

ORIGIN: The kanji had 艹 "plants," from 艸, and 央 "person with his head restrained at the neck," which is the center of a body. The center of a plant or flower is the best part, therefore "excellent." The word 英語 "the English language" comes from the Chinese pronunciation. The kanji 英 means "excellent" or "English."

- 英語 (えいご) the English language
- 英国 (えいこく) England
- 英和辞典 (えいわじてん) English–Japanese dictionary
- 英訳 (えいやく) English translation
- 英雄 (えいゆう) hero
- 英断 (えいだん) decisive decision, drastic measure

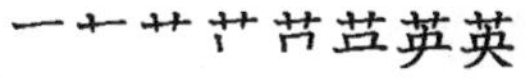
8

43

ON-KUN READINGS: エイ | HEADER: 行

衛

to guard

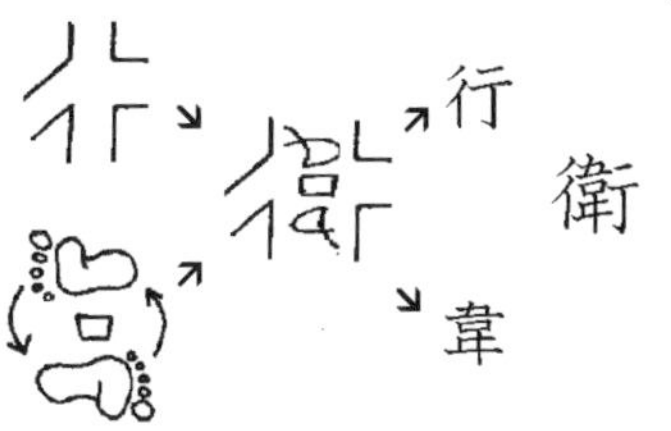

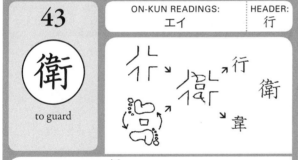

ORIGIN: The outside 行 was derived from a crossroad, indicating "to go." The middle part 韋 depicted two feet facing in opposite directions, indicating walking around an area in a circle, or patrolling. Together they indicated patrolling an area to protect it. The kanji 衛 means "to guard."

- 人工衛星 (じんこうえいせい) satellite
- 衛生 (えいせい) hygiene, sanitation
- 自衛隊 (じえいたい) Self-Defense Forces
- 防衛 (ぼうえい) defense
- 護衛 (ごえい) guard
- 衛兵 (えいへい) sentinel

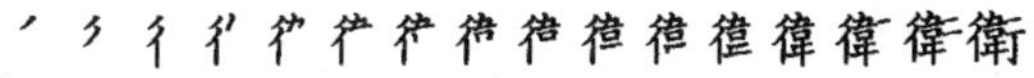
16

44

ON-KUN READINGS: エキ | HEADER: 氵

液

liquid

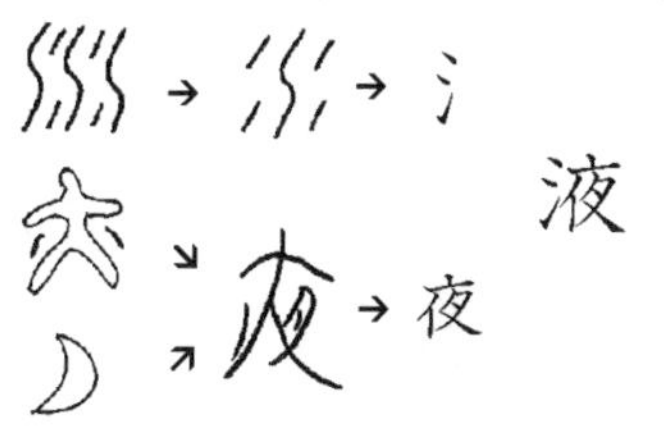

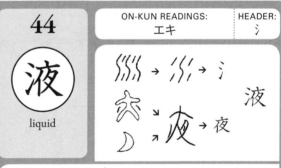

ORIGIN: The left side 氵 was water or "waterlike liquid." The ancient form of 夜 consisted of a person standing with a moon on one side and pointing to the other side for a repeat appearance. Here the form for moon is used phonetically indicating "to repeat," because the moon appears again every night. A liquid drips repeatedly. The kanji 液 means "liquid."

- 液 (えき) solution
- 液体 (えきたい) liquid
- 溶液 (ようえき) solution
- 血液 (けつえき) blood
- 液化する (えきか) to liquefy
- 乳液 (にゅうえき) milky lotion, milky liquid

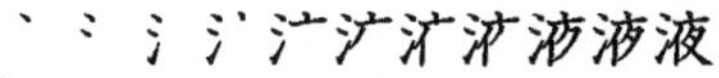
11

45

益

gain; profit

ORIGIN: The ancient form was a pictograph of water that was overflowing from a 皿 "dish" (viewed from the side), meaning "to replenish; to make full." The kanji 益 means "gain; profit."

利益 gain, profit
益 gain, profit
損益 profit and loss

収益 profit
ご利益 divine favor
公益の public benefit

`、 丷 丷 产 犬 犬 谷 谷 益 益`　10

46

駅

train station

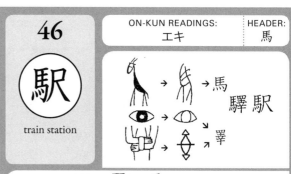

ORIGIN: The old form 驛 had 馬 "horse" and 罒 "watchful eye" over 幸 "type of hand shackle used to chain prisoners together." It was further extended to mean a succession of activities by officials. Together the forms indicated one of a series of stations where imperial messengers changed horses, and thus the kanji 駅 means "train station."

駅 railway station
東京駅 Tokyo Station
駅ビル building adjacent to the station

各駅停車 local trains
駅弁 box lunch at station
駅伝 long-distance relay

`1 Γ ΓΓ Ff Ff 馬 馬 馬 馬 馬 駅 駅 駅 駅`　14

47

越

to cross; to go over

ORIGIN: The left side comes from 走 "to run," with a person running hurriedly and a foot. The right depicted a halberd or weapon, here used phonetically to mean "to cross." Together they indicated someone running to cross over. The kanji 越 means "to cross; to go over."

引越し move of (residence)
年越し New Year's Eve
越える to cross, to go across

越境 crossing over a boundary
優越感 superiority complex
繰越金 balance forward

`一 十 土 ㄐ ㄐ 走 走 赴 走 越 越 越`　12

48

円

round; Japanese yen

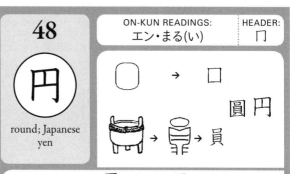

ORIGIN: The old form 圓 had a circle 囗 and a round-footed pot 員. Both expressed roundness, hence "harmony." The association with Japanese yen comes from the round shape of old coins. Now the much simpler 円 is used instead. The kanji 円 means "round" or "Japanese yen."

円 Japanese yen, circle
四百円 four hundred yen
円満な harmonious

円い round
半円 semi-circular
円滑に smoothly

`丿 冂 冂 円`　4

48

49

ON-KUN READINGS: エン・その

HEADER: 口

園

park; spacious garden

ORIGIN: Inside 口, "enclosure," is 袁, which was used phonetically to indicate "distance or roomy." (袁 came from a deceased person, clothed for departing on a long journey.) A spacious enclosure is a garden. The kanji 園 means "park; spacious garden."

こうえん
公園 park
にゅうえんりょう
入園料 park admission fee
ようちえん
幼稚園 kindergarten

どうぶつえん
動物園 zoo
ていえん
庭園 large garden
はなぞの
花園 flower garden

｜ 冂 冂 門 門 門 周 周 周 園 園 園 園　13

50

ON-KUN READINGS: エン・の(ばす)

HEADER: 廴

延

to extend; to postpone

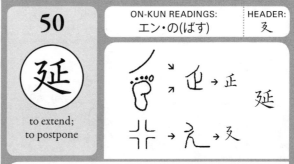

ORIGIN: The first stroke ノ over 止 "foot" signified that one extended one's walking. The lower left 廴, derived from the left half of a crossroad with the lower side stretched, also meaning a road extending. Together they indicated "one walks farther," or "to extend the time, or to postpone." The kanji 延 means "to extend" or "to postpone."

えんき
延期 postponement
の
延ばす to extend, to
　　postpone
うてんじゅんえん
雨天順延 postponement

until rain stops
えんたいきん
延滞金 overdue fee or fine
えんちょう
延長 extension

一 丆 千 正 正 延 延 延　8

51

ON-KUN READINGS: エン・そ(う)

HEADER: 氵

沿

to go alongside

ORIGIN: The ancient form consisted of 氵 "water," 八 "water splitting into two streams," and 口 "hollow." It depicted parallel streams running along a hollow. The kanji 沿 means "to go alongside."

えんがん
沿岸 coast, shore
えんせん
沿線 along the railway
そ
Xに沿って along X

えんかく
沿革 history
えんどう
沿道 along the route

丶 丶 氵 氵 氵 沪 沿 沿 沿　8

52

ON-KUN READINGS: エン

HEADER: 氵

演

to extend; to perform

ORIGIN: The left side 氵 "water" and the right side 寅, with 宀 "house" and an arrow with two hands, indicated "stretching out with two hands." Together they meant something that ran for a long time, like water. Because a performance of music, theater, or speech extends for a period of time, the kanji 演 means "to extend" or "to perform."

えん
演じる to perform
きょうえんしゃ
共演者 co-actor
こうえん
公演 public performance

えんぎ
演技 acting
えんそう
演奏 musical performance
しゅえん
主演 leading role

丶 丶 氵 氵 沪 沪 沪 沪 沪 演 演 演 演 演　14

53

ON-KUN READINGS: エン・けむ(い)・けむり

HEADER: 火

煙
smoke

ORIGIN: The left side 火 was a fire. The right side was used phonetically to mean "to block" the view or breathing; that is what smoke does. The kanji 煙 means "smoke."

けむり
煙 smoke
きんえん
禁煙 no smoking
えんがい
煙害 smoke pollution

けむ
煙たい smoky
えんとつ
煙突 chimney
きつえんしつ
喫煙室 smoking room

丶 ハ ツ 火 灯 灯 炉 炉 炉 炉 炉 煙 煙 　13

54

ON-KUN READINGS: エン・オン・とお(い)

HEADER: 辶

遠
distant; far

ORIGIN: The upper right 袁 consisted of 土 (from 止 "footprint"), 口 "jewelry," and 衣 "clothes," that signified a deceased dressed in clothes to depart on a long journey, hence "distance." The lower left 辶 indicated "to move on." The combined form meant "a long way" or "far." The kanji 遠 means "far; distant."

とお
遠い far, distant
えんりょ
遠慮 reserve, diffidence,
　　restraints
とおまわ
遠回り a detour

えんきょり
遠距離 long distance
ほどとお
程遠い far from
えんそく
遠足 excursion

一 十 土 キ 吉 吉 声 寺 幸 袁 袁 遠 遠 　13

55

ON-KUN READINGS: エン・しお

HEADER: 土

塩
salt

ORIGIN: The old form 鹽 had 監, which consisted of 臣 "downcast eye" and a person over 皿 "basin" watching or looking at a reflection, and 鹵, which depicted a salt farm viewed from above, where the dots show salts. The current reduced form 塩 means "salt."

しお
塩 salt
しおあじ
塩味 salty taste
えんぶん
塩分 portion of salt
えんそ
塩素 chlorine

しおから
塩辛い salty
てしお
手塩にかける to care for
　　with one's own hands,
　　to nurture

一 十 土 圵 坫 圹 圹 圹 塩 塩 塩 塩 塩 　13

56

ON-KUN READINGS: オ・きたな(い)・けが(らわしい)・よご(す)

HEADER: 氵

汚
dirty; soiled

ORIGIN: The left side 氵 was "water" and the right side 亐 depicted "hollow." Together they indicated water collected in a hollow, which was dirty. The kanji 汚 means "dirty; soiled."

きたな
汚い dirty, soiled
よご
汚れている to be dirty, soiled
おしょく
汚職 bribery, corruption

おすい
汚水 sewage
おてん
汚点 flaw
けが
汚らわしい loathsome

丶 丶 氵 沪 汚 汚 　6

57

ON-KUN READINGS: オウ | HEADER: 大

央

center; middle

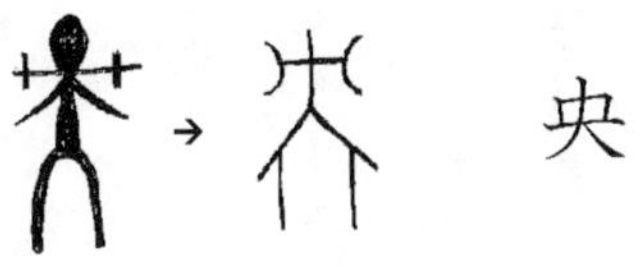

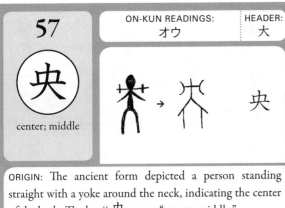

ORIGIN: The ancient form depicted a person standing straight with a yoke around the neck, indicating the center of the body. The kanji 央 means "center; middle."

- 中央 (ちゅうおう) center
- 中央出口 (ちゅうおうでぐち) central exit
- 震央 (しんおう) epicenter

丨 冂 口 央 央 — 5

58

ON-KUN READINGS: オウ・おく | HEADER: 大

奥

deep inside; honorific form for (someone's) wife

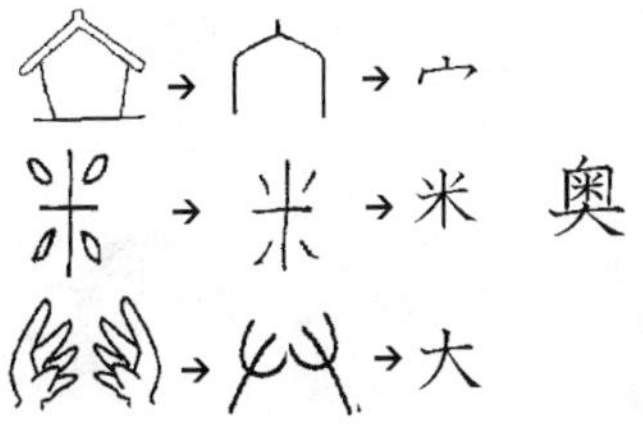

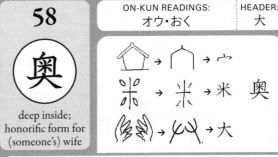

ORIGIN: The ancient form of 宀 "house," 米 "rice grains" inside, and two offering hands at the bottom indicated an area deep inside a house where rice was stored or offered at an altar. The kanji 奥 means "deep inside." A nobleman's wife stays in the back of a house; hence this kanji is also used for "wife" in an honorific form.

- 奥 (おく) back, deep inside
- 奥さん (おく) (someone's) wife
- 奥の方 (おく ほう) in the back
- 奥行き (おくゆ) depth
- 奥義 (おうぎ) secret principles
- 奥歯 (おくば) back tooth

丿 亻 冂 冂 冂 冋 冋 冏 冏 奥 奥 奥 — 12

59

ON-KUN READINGS: オウ・ゆ(く) | HEADER: 彳

往

to go; past

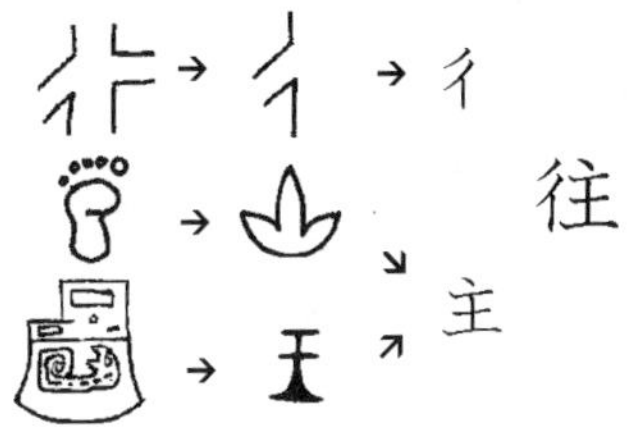

ORIGIN: The left side 彳 derived from the left side of a crossroad, and meant "to go." The right side of the ancient form was a foot above 王 "king" or "leader" with a weapon. Together they indicated to go ahead, led by a king on foot. It also meant something that had already gone by. The kanji 往 means "to go" or "past."

- 往来 (おうらい) traffic
- 往復切符 (おうふくきっぷ) round-trip ticket
- 往生 (おうじょう) in a tight place, death
- 右往左往 (うおうさおう) to rush about in confusion
- 往診 (おうしん) house call
- 既往症 (きおうしょう) past illness

丿 彡 彳 彳 彳 行 往 往 — 8

60

ON-KUN READINGS: オウ・こた(える) | HEADER: 心

応

to respond willingly

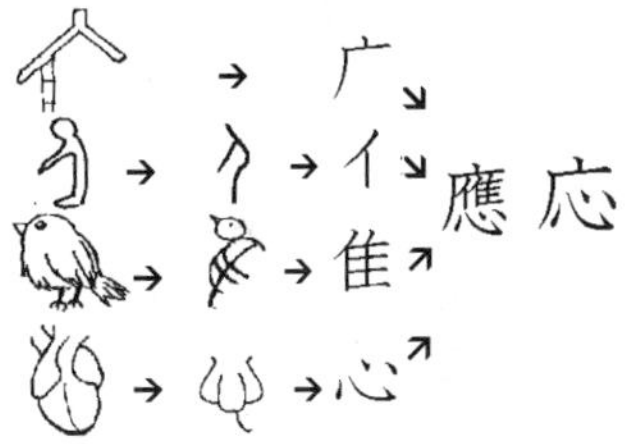

ORIGIN: The old form 應 had 广 "roof," 亻 "person," 隹 "bird," and 心 "heart." It signified that a person welcomed birds in his house, so the birds came willingly. Now simplified to 応, retaining a heart, the kanji means "to respond willingly."

- 応募する (おうぼ) to apply (for a job)
- 応じる (おう) to respond
- 応接間 (おうせつま) reception room, parlor
- 応える (こた) to respond
- 応急手当 (おうきゅうてあて) first aid
- 相応の (そうおう) befitting

丶 亠 广 广 応 応 応 — 7

61

ON-KUN READINGS:
オウ・お(す)

HEADER:
扌

押

to press; to push

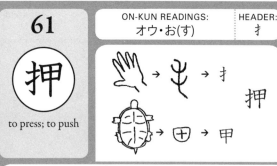

ORIGIN: The left side 扌 was a hand. The right side 甲 was a depiction of the underside of a tortoise, here used phonetically to indicate "to press." Together they indicated "to press a seal by hand." The kanji 押 means "to press; to push."

押す to push
後押し backing, support
押入れ closet

押しのける to push aside
押印 pressing a seal
押収 する to seize

一 十 扌 扌 扚 押 押 押 　　8

62

ON-KUN READINGS:
オウ・さくら

HEADER:
木

桜

cherry tree

ORIGIN: The old form 櫻 consisted of 木 "tree" and 嬰 "two shells over a woman," here used phonetically. (Shells were used for a woman's necklace, indicating surrounding or circling.) Now simplified to 桜, the kanji means 桜 "cherry tree."

桜 cherry tree
桜桃 cherry
八重桜 double-blossom cherry tree

夜桜 cherry-blossom viewing in the evening

一 十 オ 木 木 栄 栄 栄 桜 桜 桜 　　10

63

横

sideways; crooked

ON-KUN READINGS:
オウ・よこ

HEADER:
木

ORIGIN: The old form 橫 had 木 "tree or wood," and the right side had a fire arrow 廿 cast in the air, illuminating all sides with bright yellow light, used phonetically to indicate "sides." A wooden latch at a gate slides sideways, and the meaning of sideways extended to include "crooked." The kanji 横 means "sideways; crooked."

横 side
横断歩道 crosswalk
横切る to cross

横領 embezzlement
横柄 な arrogant
横転 する to roll sideways

一 十 オ 木 杧 栌 栌 栌 榯 榯 構 構 構 横 横 　　15

64

王

king

ON-KUN READINGS:
オウ

HEADER:
王

ORIGIN: The ancient form was a pictograph of a large ornamental ax which signified power, hence a "ruler." In later years, this kanji was often interpreted as a big person standing on the ground and stretching his or her arms and legs towards heaven. The kanji 王 means "king."

国王 king
王様 king
王国 kingdom

王者 monarch, champion
親王 imperial prince
王政 monarchy

一 丁 王 王 　　4

65

黄
yellow

ORIGIN: The ancient form had a fire and an arrow with a fire on top 廿, which had combustible materials in the middle. The flame of a fire arrow illuminated all directions with bright yellow light, as in the kanji for "sideways." This kanji 黄 means "yellow."

きいろ
黄色 yellow
おうごん
黄金 golden
たまご きみ
卵の黄身 egg yolk

らんおう
卵黄 egg yolk
きみどりいろ
黄緑色 light green

一 十 廿 芇 芇 芢 昔 苒 苗 黄 黄　11

66

億
hundred million

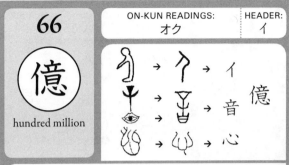

ORIGIN: This was a combination of イ "person" and 意 "thought kept inside one's heart," or "intent." (Please see kanji No. 12 意.) A hundred million was such a big number that it only existed in one's imagination. The kanji 億 means "hundred million."

ごおく
五億 five hundred million
おっくう
億劫な bothersome
おくまんちょうじゃ
億万長者 billionaire

ノ イ イ゙ 广 广 疒 产 佇 倍 倍 倍 億 億 億　15

67

屋
house; store

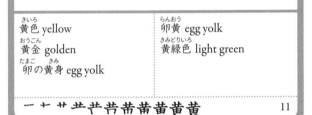

ORIGIN: The top part 尸 depicted a roof and the wall of a house. The bottom part 至 depicted an action in which an arrow hit the ground 土, indicating "to come to an end." Together they indicated a house in which one returned and relaxd. The kanji 屋 means "house; store."

ほんや
本屋 bookstore
へや
部屋 room
やね
屋根 roof

おくない
屋内プール indoor swimming
pool
ひらや
平屋 one-story house
やたい
屋台 booth

フ フ 尸 尸 尸 层 层 居 屋 屋　9

68

恩
favor;
indebtedness

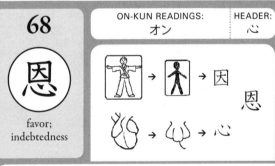

ORIGIN: The top 因 depicted a person 大 comfortably stretched out on a mattress 囗. The bottom 心 was a heart or feeling. Together they indicated someone who was under care or protection of someone else and thus feels indebted for the generosity. The kanji 恩 means "favor; indebtedness."

おん
恩 indebtedness
おんじん
恩人 benefactor, patron
おんがえ
恩返し repayment of a favor

おんしゃ
恩赦 amnesty
おんきゅう
恩給 pension
おんけい
恩恵 favor

丨 冂 冎 闩 闬 因 因 恩 恩 恩　10

69

ON-KUN READINGS: オン・あたた(かい)

HEADER: 氵

温
warm

ORIGIN: The ancient form had 氵 "water" and covered steamy hot water in a dish, signifying "warm." Together they indicated warmth that came from within. The kanji 温 means "warm."

きおん 気温 atmospheric temperature	ちきゅうおんだんか 地球温暖化 global warming
おんど 温度 temperature	おんしつ 温室 greenhouse; hot house
あたた 温める to warm	おんせん 温泉 hot spring

氵 氵 氵 氵 氵 氵 氵 氵 温 温 温 温   12

70

ON-KUN READINGS: オン・イン・おと・ね

HEADER: 音

音
sound

ORIGIN: The kanji 音 shares overlaps in etymology with that of 言 "words; to say." In 言, a tattoo needle and a mouth signified "to say clearly," whereas in 音 there was something inside the mouth, which prevented what was said from being meaningful, leaving it as a mere sound. The kanji 音 means "sound."

おんがく 音楽 music	ざつおん 雑音 noise
おと 音 sound	ぼいん 母音 vowel
はつおん 発音 pronunciation	ねいろ 音色 tone color, timbre

丶 亠 立 立 音 音 音 音 音   9

71

ON-KUN READINGS: カ・ゲ・お(ろす)・さ(がる)・くだ(る)・した・しも・もと

HEADER: 一

下
below; under; lower

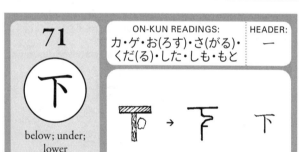

ORIGIN: The ancient form indicated an area under a line. The last short stroke in the current form emphasizes what was indicated. The kanji 下 means "below; under; lower."

した もと 下・下 below, under	げひん 下品な vulgar
くだ 下さる [Honorific] to give (to me)	ろうか 廊下 hallway
さ 下げる to lower	お 下ろす to lower, to bring down

一 丁 下   3

72

ON-KUN READINGS: カ・ケ・ば(ける)

HEADER: イ

化
to change

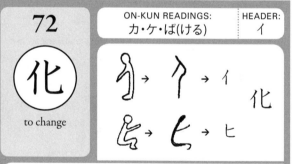

ORIGIN: The left part イ was a "person standing straight," whereas the right part ヒ was a "person sitting." A change of postures indicated a change of state. The kanji 化 means "to change."

ぶんか 文化 culture	ば お化け ghost
へんか 変化 change	けしょう 化粧する to put on makeup
かがく 化学 chemistry	あっか 悪化する to deteriorate

ノ イ イ 化   4

73

ON-KUN READINGS: カ・ケ・かり

HEADER: イ

仮

temporary; false

ORIGIN: The old form 假 consisted of イ "standing person" and the action of two hands taking precious metal out of a rock, which was used phonetically to indicate a mask. One puts a mask on to become something else, hence something "temporary" or "false." The right side was reduced to 反. The kanji 仮 means "temporary" or "false."

仮 temporary
仮面 mask
仮免許 temporary license

仮定 assumption
仮説 hypothesis
仮死 syncope

ノイイ仮仮仮 6

74

ON-KUN READINGS: カ・なに・なん

HEADER: イ

何

what

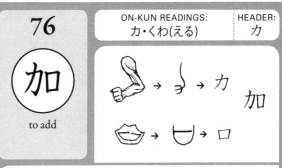

ORIGIN: Originally the depiction of a person who was carrying a load over his shoulder signified "to carry." When a new kanji meaning "to carry" was created as 荷, the original kanji came to be used to indicate "what" because of its sound. The kanji 何 means "what."

何 what
何人 how many people
何語 what language

何曜日 what day of the week
何日 what day
何月 what month

ノイイ仃仃何何 7

55

75

ON-KUN READINGS: カ・あたい

HEADER: イ

価

value; price

ORIGIN: The older form 價 has イ a "person" and a "lid or cover" over 貝 "cowry." Cowries were rare shells from the distant south and were used for trading as currency. A merchant hid his goods until the price or value went up. This kanji is now simplified as 価, meaning "value" or "price."

物価 good price
価値 value
価 value

定価 fixed price
小売価格 retail price
地価 land value

ノイイ仁仃価価価 8

76

ON-KUN READINGS: カ・くわ(える)

HEADER: カ

加

to add

ORIGIN: The left side 力 depicted a muscular arm showing strength. The right side 口 "mouth" or "words" signified that one adds strength by words. The original meaning of "words" came to be dropped, so the kanji 加 means "to add."

追加 addition
加える to add
参加する to participate in

加勢する to give support to
加速 acceleration
加工 process

フカカ加加 5

77

ON-KUN READINGS: カ・ベ(し)

HEADER: 口

可

possible; able

ORIGIN: The ancient form shown in the middle consisted of a bent shape, which signified "not straightaway," and 口 "mouth." When one speaks after some hesitation, it is a grudging approval, signifying something made possible. The meaning further extended to "able to do." The kanji 可 means "possible; able."

可能 possible, can
(かのう)
許可 permission
(きょか)
不可能 impossible
(ふかのう)

不可欠な indispensable
(ふかけつ)
可決する to pass a bill
(かけつ)
生半可な half-baked, superficial
(なまはんか)

一一一口可　5

78

ON-KUN READINGS: カ・ゲ・なつ

HEADER: 夂

夏

summer

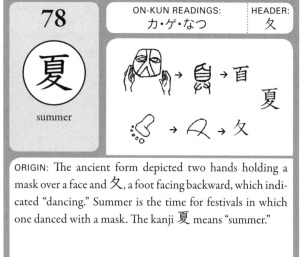

ORIGIN: The ancient form depicted two hands holding a mask over a face and 夂, a foot facing backward, which indicated "dancing." Summer is the time for festivals in which one danced with a mask. The kanji 夏 means "summer."

夏 summer
(なつ)
夏休み summer vacation
(なつやす)
夏至 the summer solstice
(げし)

初夏 early summer
(しょか)
夏場 during summer
(なつば)
真夏 midsummer
(まなつ)

一一一一一一百百夏夏　10

79

ON-KUN READINGS: カ・ケ・いえ・うち・や

HEADER: 宀

家

house; person

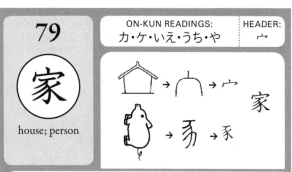

ORIGIN: The top 宀 was a house and 豕 was a pictograph of a pig, an important domesticated animal. Together they signified "to put valuable things, such as pigs, in a house, to protect them." It also refers to people who live inside the house. The kanji 家 means "house."

家・家 house, home
(いえ・うち)
家族 family members
(かぞく)
家庭 home
(かてい)
田中家 Tanaka family
(たなかけ)

一家 whole family
(いっか)
家主 landlord
(やぬし)
作家 writer
(さっか)

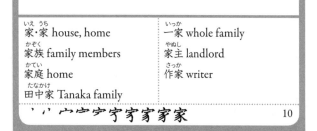　10

80

ON-KUN READINGS: カ

HEADER: 禾

科

section; category; to determine a penalty

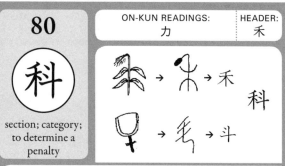

ORIGIN: The left side 禾 "rice plant with grain" and the right side 斗 "measuring ladle used for grain" indicated grains that were measured and sorted, suggesting classification. Penalty is something else measured as well. Authorities measured carefully the severity of criminal offenses and determined the penalty. The kanji 科 means "section; category" and "to determine a penalty."

科目 subject
(かもく)
科学 science
(かがく)
科する to impose a penalty
(か)

前科 criminal record
(ぜんか)
百科事典 encyclopedia
(ひゃっかじてん)
金科玉条 golden rule
(きんかぎょくじょう)

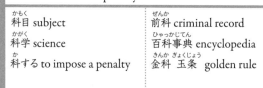　9

81

ON-KUN READINGS: カ・は(たす)

HEADER: 木

果

fruit; result; to perish

ORIGIN: The top 田 depicted fruits or nuts on a tree and the bottom 木 was a tree. The fruit of a tree signifies the result of an action, so the kanji 果 means "fruit" or "result" which can have many definitions, including "to perish."

果物 fruit
結果 result
成果 outcome

果実 fruit
果たす to fulfill
果てる to perish

丨 冂 冂 曰 旦 甲 果 果　8

82

ON-KUN READINGS: カ・うた

HEADER: 欠

歌

to sing; song

ORIGIN: 可 in 哥 on the left side depicted an angle and a mouth. A voice that does not come straight out sounds coarse. The right side 欠 was a person stooping forward with a gaping mouth. A person with a large open mouth trying to make sounds is singing! The kanji 歌 means "to sing" or "song."

歌 song
歌手 singer
歌う to sing

国歌 national anthem
歌謡曲 popular song
演歌 enka (popular Japanese ballad)

一 一 一 一 一 一 一 一 一 一 歌 歌 歌 歌　14

83

ON-KUN READINGS: カ・かわ

HEADER: シ

河

large river

ORIGIN: The left side シ is water. The right side 可 had a rock and a line that bent at a right angle, signifying something not straight. Together they indicated a big river that has many sharp turns before it reaches the sea. The kanji 河 means "large river."

河 river
河川 river
運河 canal

河岸 river bed
河口 river mouth
銀河 the galaxy, the Milky Way

丶 ニ シ 汀 汀 河 河 河　8

84

ON-KUN READINGS: カ・ひ・ほ

HEADER: 火

火

fire; Tuesday

ORIGIN: Originally, this was a pictograph of a fire with flames sparking. The kanji 火 means "fire." (When used as a recurring component at the bottom of kanji, it is often written 灬, as in 黒 "black," and 然 "naturally.") The kanji 火 is also used for Tuesday in Japanese.

火 fire
火曜日 Tuesday
花火 fireworks

火事 fire
火山 volcano
出火 outbreak of a fire

丶 丷 少 火　4

57

85

ON-KUN READINGS: カ・はな **HEADER:** 艹

花
flower

ORIGIN: The top 艹 depicted "plants." In 化, イ was a man standing straight, whereas the right part ヒ was a man sitting. A change of postures indicated a change of state. A flower changes its form from a bud to full bloom and eventually withers. The kanji 花 means "flower."

はな
花 flower
はなや
花屋 florist
はなみ
お花見 cherry blossom viewing

かふん
花粉 pollen
はなよめ
花嫁 bride
はなたば
花束 bouquet

一 十 艹 艹 荮 荮 花　7

86

ON-KUN READINGS: カ・に **HEADER:** 艹

荷
to bear; load;
luggage

ORIGIN: The top 艹 depicted "plants." イ is a person, and 可 came from a depiction of a man carrying a heavy load on his shoulder. The kanji 荷 means "to bear; to load" or "luggage."

にもつ
荷物 luggage
にづくり
荷造り packing
おもに
重荷 burden

しゅっか
出荷 shipping
にぐるま
荷車 wagon
しゅうか
集荷 collection of goods

一 十 艹 艹 荮 荮 荮 荷 荷 荷　10

87

ON-KUN READINGS: カ **HEADER:** 言

課
to assign; lesson;
section

ORIGIN: The left side 言 "word" and 果 "fruit" or "result" on the right together indicated a section of learning, or a lesson. It also meant a "section in a public or corporate organization" where assignments are carried out. The kanji 課 means "lesson; section" or "to assign."

だいろっか
第六課 Lesson Six
かもく
課目 subject
じんじか
人事課 personnel section

かちょう
課長 section manager
かだい
課題 theme, problem
かぜい
課税 taxation

丶 亠 亠 亖 言 言 言 言 訒 訒 訒 訒 評 課 課　15

88

ON-KUN READINGS: カ **HEADER:** 貝

貨
goods; money

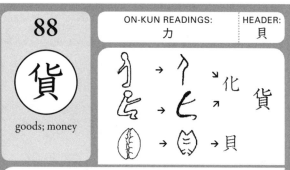

ORIGIN: The top 化 consisted of イ a person standing straight and ヒ a person sitting, signifying "change of state." The bottom 貝 was a rare shell (a cowry), which was used as currency. Together they indicated something that could change to money, or that could be changed with money. The kanji 貨 means "goods; money."

かもつ
貨物 cargo
ひゃっかてん
百貨店 department store
つうか
通貨 currency

こうか
硬貨 coin
ざっか
雑貨 general merchandise
がいか
外貨 foreign money

ノ イ イ 化 化 貨 貨 貨 貨 貨 貨　11

58

89

過

to pass through;
to make mistake;
excessively

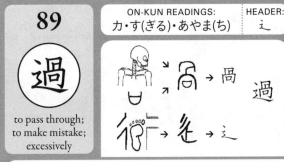

ORIGIN: The upper right 咼 "bones" was used phonetically.
The bottom 辶 indicated forward motion. The combined
form signified something going through easily, or "to go
excessively" (because it goes without a hitch). It also is used
for "to slip by" or an "error." The kanji 過 means "to pass
through," "to make a mistake," or "excessively."

食べ過ぎ overeating
過去 the past
通過 passage, transit

過ぎる to pass
寝過ごす to oversleep
過失 blunder, fault

｜ 冂 冎 咼 咼 咼 咼 咼 咼 渦 渦 過　　12

90

我

I; my; myself

ORIGIN: A pictograph of a halberd with decorative tassels
signified killing. The word "self" had the same sound; it was
borrowed phonetically and it has lost the original meaning.
The kanji 我 means "I; my; myself."

我 I, me
我々 we
我がまま selfishness

自我 self-awareness, ego
我慢 perseverance
我流 one's own way

ノ 二 千 手 我 我 我　　7

91

画

drawing; painting;
kanji stroke
counter

ORIGIN: The old form 畫 had a writing brush 聿, rice
paddies 田, and lines around 凵, signifying lines drawn
between partitioned rice paddies. Together they signified
one's drawing of a map or area, using a brush. The kanji
画 means "drawing; painting" and is also used for a stroke
counter for kanji.

映画 movie
計画 plan
画面 screen

五画 five strokes
漫画 manga comics
企画 planning

一 厂 厂 币 币 両 面 画 画　　8

92

芽

sprout; bud

ORIGIN: The top 艹 originated from 屮屮, which depicted
two plants growing with their roots in the ground. 牙 was
a pictograph of interlocking fangs. It depicted the way new
sprouts emerge. The kanji 芽 means "sprout; bud."

芽 sprout
発芽 sprouting
芽生える to sprout, to bud

新芽 new budding

一 ナ ナ 廾 芒 芽 芽 芽　　8

93

賀

to celebrate;
to congratulate;
auspicious occasion

ORIGIN: The top 加 means "to add." The bottom 貝 was a pictograph of a cowry, which was used as currency and thus also used to indicate "goods." When one congratulated someone, one added a present to the congratulatory words. The kanji 賀 means "to celebrate; to congratulate" or "auspicious occasion."

ねんがじょう
年賀状 New Year's greeting card
がしょう
賀正 New Year's celebration
しゅくがかい
祝賀会 celebration party

さんが
参賀 New Year's visit to the Imperial Palace

マ カ カ 加 加 加 如 智 智 智 賀 賀 賀　　12

94

介

to mediate; to help

ORIGIN: The ancient form depicted a person with armor in the front and back, signifying someone who is between two things or persons and mediates. The kanji 介 means "to mediate; to help."

しょうかい
紹介 introduction
かいご
介護 caretaking
ちゅうかいにん
仲介人 go-between, mediator

かいにゅう
介入 interference
せっかい
節介 meddling
やっかい
厄介な burdensome

ノ 人 介 介　　4

95

会

to meet; a meeting

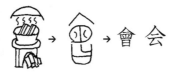

ORIGIN: The old form 會 has 亼 "lid or cover" and a pot for steaming rice. A steamer's lid fits the pot tightly. It was used phonetically to indicate "two things fit tightly." Now simplified to 会, which has 云 "to say," the kanji 会 signifies people getting together: "to meet" or "a meeting."

かいしゃ
会社 company, corporation
あ
会う to meet (someone)
えとく
会得する to understand, to master

しゃかい
社会 society
かいごう
会合 meeting, assembly
えしゃく
会釈 bowing

ノ 人 入 会 会 会　　6

96

解

to undo; to untie;
to solve

ORIGIN: The left side 角 was a pictograph of a pointed horn. On the right side, 刀 was a knife and 牛 was a cow. It indicated cutting a cow or its horns into parts or pieces. Undoing or loosening into parts also untangles a problem. The kanji 解 means "to untie; to undo" or "to solve."

かいけつ
解決 solution
と
解く to solve, to decipher
かい
解せない cannot understand, incomprehensible

どっかい
読解 reading comprehension
りかい
理解 understanding
かいしょう
解消する to dissolve

ノ 勹 勺 角 角 角 角 角 解 解 解 解 解　　13

97

ON-KUN READINGS: カイ・エ・まわ(る)

HEADER: 口

回

to rotate; time

ORIGIN: The ancient form depicted a rotational motion. This kanji is also used as a counter for "number of times." The kanji 回 means "to rotate" or "time."

さんかい
三回 three times
かいてん
回転する to revolve
まわ
回る to rotate

かいすうけん
回数券 multiple tickets
かいひ
回避 avoidance
じゅんかい
巡回する to make a round

一 冂 冂 冋 冋 回　6

98

ON-KUN READINGS: カイ・こころよ(い)

HEADER: 忄

快

pleasant; cheerful

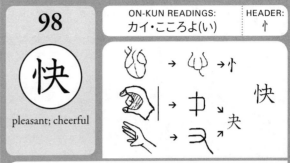

ORIGIN: The left 忄 was a variant of a heart 心. The right side 夬 depicted a U shape formed with a thumb and fingers, and another hand trying to clear the obstacle in the U area. Together they indicated a cheerful mood after something troublesome was removed. The kanji 快 means "pleasant; cheerful."

こころよ
快い pleasant
かいそく
快速 high speed, rapid service
かいてき
快適な comfortable

ぜんかい
全快 complete recovery (from illness)
けいかい
軽快に light-heartedly
ゆかい
愉快に delightfully, merrily

丶 丷 忄 忄 忙 快 快　7

99

ON-KUN READINGS: カイ・く(やむ)・くや(しい)

HEADER: 忄

悔

to regret; vexing

ORIGIN: The left side 忄 was the shape of a heart, indicating feelings. The right side 毎 "every," a nursing woman with lots of annoying hair accessories on her head, phonetically indicated "gloomy" or "dark." Together they indicated vexing feelings, or regret. The kanji 悔 means "vexing" or "to regret."

く
悔やむ to regret
こうかい
後悔 regret
く あらた
悔い改める to repent

く
悔い regret
く
お悔やみ words of condolence
くや
悔しい vexing

丶 丷 忄 忄 忄 忙 悔 悔 悔　9

100

ON-KUN READINGS: カイ・あらた(める)

HEADER: 攵

改

to renew; to change

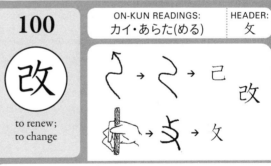

ORIGIN: The left side 己 depicted a motion in which crooked rope was trying to straighten itself. The right side 攵 came from a stick in a hand, which signified work or an action in general. Together they mean taking an action to correct. The kanji 改 means "to change" or "to renew."

かいさつぐち
改札口 ticket checkpoint
かいせい
改正 revision, amendment
あらた
改める to change, to alter, to modify

かいぜん
改善する to improve
かいていばん
改訂版 revised edition
かいちく
改築 remodeling

コ コ 己 己 改 改 改　7

61

101

ON-KUN READINGS:
カイ

HEADER:
木

械

machine; gadget

ORIGIN: The left side 木 is wood. The right side, 戒 "to admonish," had 戈 "lance" and 廾 "two hands," which indicated admonishing someone with a threatening weapon. Together they indicated a wooden tool to punish a criminal. The original meaning of punishment was dropped. The kanji 械 means "gadget; machine."

きかい
機械 machine
きかい
器械 instrument
てかせ
手械 handcuff

一 十 才 オ 朮 杖 栈 械 械 械   11

102

ON-KUN READINGS:
カイ・うみ

HEADER:
氵

海

ocean; sea; beach

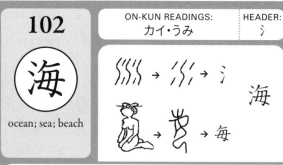

ORIGIN: The left side 氵 was "water." The right side 毎 "every," a nursing woman with lots of annoying hair accessories on her head, phonetically indicated "gloomy" or "dark." Vast, dark, unknown water that surrounds a country is an ocean. The kanji 海 means "ocean; sea; beach."

うみ
海 sea, beach
かいがい
海外 overseas
かいがいりょこう
海外旅行 overseas trip

にほんかい
日本海 the Sea of Japan
うみべ
海辺 beach
うなばら
海原 the ocean

丶 冫 氵 氵 汒 洭 海 海 海   9

103

ON-KUN READINGS:
カイ・はい

HEADER:
火

灰

ash

ORIGIN: The ancient form was a depiction of a hand over a fire. A person is removing by hand what is left after a fire dies out, which is ash. The kanji 灰 means "ash."

はい
灰 ash
はいざら
灰皿 ash tray
せっかい
石灰 lime

かざんばい
火山灰 volcano ashes
はいいろ
灰色 gray

一 厂 厂 厂 灰 灰   6

104

ON-KUN READINGS:
カイ

HEADER:
田

界

boundary; world

ORIGIN: In the ancient form, the top 田 depicted rice paddies or a boundary of land and the bottom 介 a soldier with a protective shield in front and on his back, signifying the distinction between inside and outside. What is inside boundaries is a world. The kanji 界 means "boundary" or "world."

せかい
世界 world
せかいいち
世界一 the best in the world
せかいじゅう
世界中 throughout the world

きょうかいせん
境界線 boundary
かいわい
界隈 neighborhood
しかい
視界 sight, visibility

丨 冂 田 田 田 界 界 界 界   9

62

105

ON-KUN READINGS: カイ・みな

HEADER: 白

皆

all; everybody

ORIGIN: In the top part 比, two people side by side signified "people lining up." The bottom 白 cames from 自 "self," which was a depiction of one's nose, hence "oneself" or "person." Together they indicated rows of people, thus all people. The kanji 皆 means "everybody; all."

皆 everyone
皆さん everyone
皆目 entirely

国民皆兵 universal conscription system
皆無 nothing, none
皆勤 perfect attendance

一 ト ト 比 比 比 皆 皆 皆   9

106

ON-KUN READINGS: カイ・エ

HEADER: 糸

絵

picture; drawing; painting

ORIGIN: In the old form 繪, 糸 on the left side was threads; 會 on the right side depicted a rice steamer with a stack of many steaming trays. Together they signified embroidery using many threads and cloth like layers of assorted steaming trays. Now simplified to 絵, the kanji 絵 means "painting; drawing" or "picture."

絵 painting, picture
絵画 painting
絵解き explanation by picture, illustration

絵葉書 post card
油絵 oil painting
絵本 picture book

く ⺈ 幺 幺 糸 糸 糸 給 絵 絵 絵   12

107

ON-KUN READINGS: カイ・ひら(く)・あ(ける)

HEADER: 門

開

to open; to begin

ORIGIN: The top part 門 was a pictograph of two doors that were closed, which signified hiding what was inside. Inside was 开 "two poles of equal length." Together 開 meant "to open the doors equally." The kanji 開 means "to open" or "to begin."

開く to open
開ける to open
開店時間 store-opening time

開閉 opening and closing
海開き the opening of a beach
開発 development

｜ 冂 冂 冂 門 門 門 門 門 開 開   12

108

ON-KUN READINGS: カイ

HEADER: 阝

階

step; story

ORIGIN: The left side 阝 was a terraced hill. The right side 皆, with 比 "two people side by side" and 白 from 自 "oneself;" indicated "rows (of people); every one." With a terraced hill, the kanji came to mean steps or gradation. The kanji 階 means "step; story."

階下 downstairs
階段 stairway
地階 basement

九階 nine stories, ninth floor
中二階 mezzanine floor

' ⻖ ⻖ ⻖ ⻖ ⻖ 階 階 階 階 階   12

63

109

ON-KUN READINGS:
かい

HEADER:
貝

貝
shell

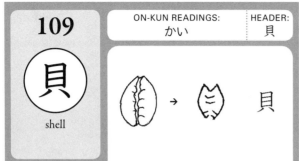

ORIGIN: The ancient form was a cowry (子安貝 in Japanese). The bottom two strokes might have been feelers. Rare shells such as cowries from the southern sea were used as currency for trade. The kanji 貝 means "shell." 貝 is used as a recurring component in kanji that deal with trading, money, or value, such as 買 "to buy" and 貧 "poor."

かい
貝 shell
しんじゅがい
真珠貝 pearl-oyster
かいがら
貝殻 shell; shellfish

こやすがい
子安貝 cowry
かいづか
貝塚 ancient shell heap
かいばしら
貝柱 shell ligament, scallop

｜ 冂 冃 月 貝 貝 貝   7

110

ON-KUN READINGS:
ガイ・ゲ・そと・ほか・はず(す)

HEADER:
夕

外
outside

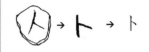

ORIGIN: The left side 夕 depicted a dim moon in the early evening (as contrasted to a moon 月) and 卜 depicted cracks that appeared on a baked tortoise shell or animal bone for divination. Another way of fortune-telling was to go outside and see the change of the moon. The kanji 外 means "outside."

そと
外 outside
ほか
外 others
がいこくじん　がいじん
外国人・外人 foreigner

かいがい
海外 overseas
ほか
その外 other than that
はず
外す to remove

ノ ク タ 列 外   5

111

ON-KUN READINGS:
ガイ

HEADER:
宀

害
to damage; a harm

ORIGIN: A big basket over a mouth signified preventing someone from using the mouth 口 to warn others of danger, or prayer that may result in harming something. The kanji 害 means "a harm" or "to damage."

がい
害 harm
むがい
無害 harmless
そんがい
損害 damage

ゆうがい
有害 poisonous
ひがいしゃ
被害者 victim
こうがい
公害 pollution

丶 宀 宀 宁 宇 宝 宔 害 害 害   10

112

ON-KUN READINGS:
ガイ・カイ・まち

HEADER:
行

街
town (with crisscrossing streets)

ORIGIN: The outside 行 was the kanji "to go" from a pictograph of a crossroad. The middle was two rounds of dirt stacked up neatly, signifying an area that people built. Together they indicated major streets that crisscrossed a town. The kanji 街 means "town (with crisscrossing streets)."

まち
街 town
しょうてんがい
商店街 shopping street
まちなか
街中 in the middle of the street

ちかがい
地下街 underground mall
まちかど
街角 street corner
かいどう
街道 road

ノ タ 彳 彳 彳 徍 徍 徍 徍 街 街 街   12

113

ON-KUN READINGS: カク・おのおの

HEADER: 口

各

each one; indivisual

ORIGIN: The top 夂 "foot coming down (with the toes on the bottom)" and 口 "rock" signified that a foot hit something hard and stopped. The action of stopping and then going one step at a time further indicated "individual." The kanji 各 means "each one."

かくじん
各人 each person
かくだいがく
各大学 each university
かっこく
各国 each country

おのおの
各々 each one of them, individually
かくかい
各界 various fields
かくろん
各論 treatise, particulars

ノ ク 夂 夂 各 各　6

114

ON-KUN READINGS: カク・ひろ(げる)

HEADER: 扌

拡

to spread; to widen

ORIGIN: The left side was "hand." The right side of the old form 廣 "wide" had 广 "house" and 黄 "fire rocket illuminating all four directions," hence a "large area." Together they indicated pushing by hand to widen an area. Now the right side is simplified to 広. The kanji 拡 means "to spread; to widen."

ひろ
拡げる to expand
かくだい
拡大 magnification, enlargement
かくちょう
拡張 expansion

かくせいき
拡声器 loudspeaker, megaphone
かくかくさん
核拡散 nuclear proliferation

一 十 扌 扌゛扩 扩 拡 拡　8

115

ON-KUN READINGS: カク・コウ

HEADER: 木

格

standing; class

ORIGIN: The left 木 was a tree, signifying something hard, and the right 各 indicated "individual." Together the combined form indicated the true core of a person, class, standing. The kanji 格 means "standing; class."

かく
格 standing, grade
かくあ
格上げ upgrading
ひんかく
品格 dignity, class

かっこう
格好 appearance
たいかく
体格 physique, build
ごうかく
合格 passing an examination

一 十 オ 木 杦 杦 柊 格 格 格　10

116

ON-KUN READINGS: カク・たし(か)

HEADER: 石

確

certain; firm

ORIGIN: The left side 石 was a rock. The right side depicted a crested bird that flew high (signified by a line over the bird), here used phonetically to mean "hard white quartz." The kanji 確 means "certain; firm."

たし
確かめる to confirm
たし
確かに for sure, certainly
せいかく
正確な precise

かくにん
確認 confirmation
かくじつ
確実に without doubt
めいかく
明確に clearly

一 丆 石 石 石 石 矿 矿 碏 碏 碏 確 確 確　15

65

117

ON-KUN READINGS: カク

HEADER: 禾

穀 (穫)

to harvest

ORIGIN: The left side 禾 was a pictograph of a rice plant drooping under the weight of the ripening grain. The right side was a bird and a hand, signifying to catch a bird by hand. Gathering crops by hand is a harvesting. The kanji 穫 means "to harvest."

しゅうかく
収穫する harvest

ノ ニ 千 禾 禾 禾 禾 禾 禾 禾 禾 禾 禾 禾 穫 穫 穫　18

118

ON-KUN READINGS: カク・おぼ(える)・さ(める)

HEADER: 見

覚

to realize; to wake; to memorize

ORIGIN: The old form 覺 had two adult hands to care, 爻 "to mingle" and 冖 "house," signifying a place for teaching. 見 was a person with an eye 目 emphasized. Together they meant the five senses mixing and becoming more aware. Now the top is reduced and the kanji 覚 means "to realize; to wake; to memorize."

おぼ
覚える to memorize
めざ　どけい
目覚まし時計 alarm clock
じかく
自覚する to be conscious of, aware

め　さ
目が覚める to wake up
かくご
覚悟 resolution, readiness
はっかく
発覚する to come out, to be detected

丶 丷 丷 丷 ⺍ 学 学 学 学 覚 覚 覚　12

119

ON-KUN READINGS: カク・つの・かど

HEADER: 角

角

horn; angle; corner

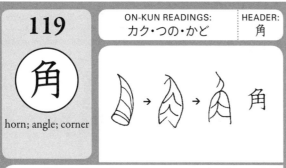

ORIGIN: The ancient form was a pictograph of a pointed horn. The kanji 角 means "horn; angle" or "corner."

かど
角 corner
しかく
四角い square shape
つの
角 horn

せっかく
折角 (in spite of) one's taking much trouble
よ　かど
四つ角 crossroad
しかく
死角 dead angle

ノ ク ヶ 角 角 角 角　7

120

ON-KUN READINGS: カク

HEADER: 門

閣

tall building; cabinet body

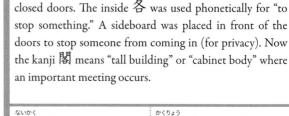
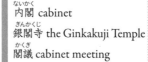

ORIGIN: The top 門 was derived from a pictograph of two closed doors. The inside 各 was used phonetically for "to stop something." A sideboard was placed in front of the doors to stop someone from coming in (for privacy). Now the kanji 閣 means "tall building" or "cabinet body" where an important meeting occurs.

ないかく
内閣 cabinet
ぎんかくじ
銀閣寺 the Ginkakuji Temple
かくぎ
閣議 cabinet meeting

かくりょう
閣僚 cabinet member
ろうかく
楼閣 tower
そかく
組閣 forming a cabinet

｜ ｢ ｢ ｢ ｢ 門 門 門 門 閃 閃 閣 閣 閣　14

121

革

leather; to renew
drastically

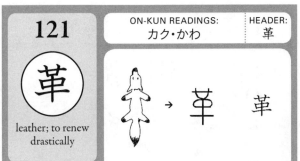

ORIGIN: The ancient form depicted an animal hide, with the head still attached, that was stretched to all directions. Because tanning changed a dead animal into a totally different shape, it was also used to mean "to renew drastically." This kanji was used for tanned leather goods without fur. The kanji 革 means "leather" or "to renew drastically."

かわ
革 leather
かわ
つり革 hand strap
かくめい
革命 revolution

かわば
革張り leathered
かくしんてき
革新的 innovative, reformist
かいかく
改革 reform

一十廾廾芦芦苦莒革　9

122

学

to study or learn

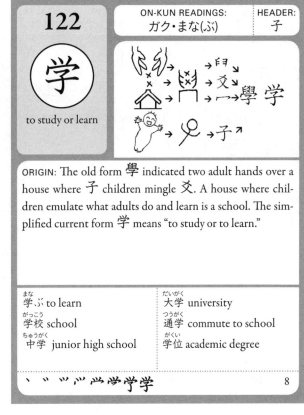

ORIGIN: The old form 學 indicated two adult hands over a house where 子 children mingle 爻. A house where children emulate what adults do and learn is a school. The simplified current form 学 means "to study or to learn."

まな
学ぶ to learn
がっこう
学校 school
ちゅうがく
中学 junior high school

だいがく
大学 university
つうがく
通学 commute to school
がくい
学位 academic degree

丶丷ツ宀学学学　8

⑥⑦

123

楽

happy, enjoyable;
comfortable;
without difficulty

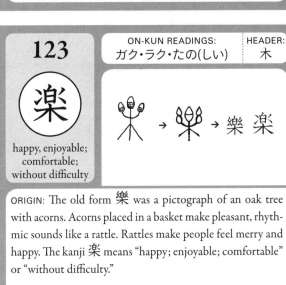

ORIGIN: The old form 樂 was a pictograph of an oak tree with acorns. Acorns placed in a basket make pleasant, rhythmic sounds like a rattle. Rattles make people feel merry and happy. The kanji 楽 means "happy; enjoyable; comfortable" or "without difficulty."

おんがく
音楽 music
らく
楽に easily, comfortably
たの
楽しみ enjoyment

こうらく
行楽 pleasure trip
らくらく
楽々と easily, effortlessly
がくふ
楽譜 sheet music

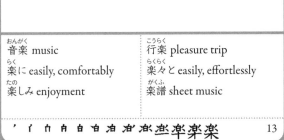
丶丨自自自泊泊泊楽楽楽　13

124

額

forehead;
sum of money;
frame

ORIGIN: 客 was used phonetically and 頁 depicted a head. Together they indicated a "forehead." It was also used for a writing that could be thought of as a prominent forehead—the headline of a plaque, the stated value of a bond or money, and the frame around a writing. The kanji 額 means "forehead; sum of money; frame."

ひたい
額 forehead
がく
額 sum of money, plaque
きんがく
金額 sum of money

がくぶち
額縁 frame
ていがくせい
定額制 set fee system
がくめん
額面 face value

丶丷宀宀安安客客客額額額額額額額　18

125

ON-KUN READINGS: カツ・わ(る)・さ(く)・わり
HEADER: リ

割

to divide;
to apportion

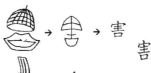

ORIGIN: The left side 害 had a basket over a mouth and signified "to stop (talking)." The right side リ is a variant of "sword." Together they indicated to cut decisively with a knife. The kanji 割 means "to divide; to apportion."

割る to divide
わりあい
割合に relatively
ぶんかつ
分割 division

わ　さん
割り算 division
さんわり
三割 30%
さ
割く to spare, to cleave

丶 宀 宀 宀 宀 中 宇 宝 害 害 割 割　12

126

ON-KUN READINGS: カツ・い(かす)
HEADER: シ

活

lively; life; activity

ORIGIN: The left side シ was water. The right side 舌 was used phonetically as the sound of water gushing, which indicated "lively activity" or "live." The kanji 活 means "lively; life; activity."

せいかつ
生活 (daily) life
かつどう
クラブ活動 club activity
かつやく
活躍 actively involved

かっぱつ
活発な active and lively
い
活きがいい fresh
かっき
活気 vigor

丶 丶 氵 汗 汗 汗 活 活　9

127

ON-KUN READINGS: かぶ
HEADER: 木

株

stump; share

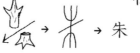

ORIGIN: The left side 木 was a tree or wood. The right side 朱 "red," here used phonetically, was derived from the fact that a tree stump is red. Together they meant a tree stump or stub. A share is part of an investment like a stump is part of a tree, and one expects a share to grow in value like a tree can grow from a stump. The kanji 株 means "stump; share."

かぶ
株 stump, share
かぶしきがいしゃ
株式会社 corporation
かぶぬし
株主 shareholder

かぶしきしじょう
株式市場 stock exchange
かぶや
株屋 stock broker
ふるかぶ
古株 old timer

一 十 才 才 木 杧 杧 杵 杵 株　10

128

ON-KUN READINGS: カン・さむ(い)
HEADER: 宀

寒

(to feel) cold

ORIGIN: The ancient form depicted a house 宀 over walls of bricks, to prevent cold air from coming in. Underneath were two hands 八 that blocked cold air, and ice 冫. Together they meant "to freeze" and then "(to feel) cold." The kanji 寒 means "(to feel) cold."

さむ
寒い cold (temperature)
さむけ
寒気 chill
ぼうかんふく
防寒服 clothes to protect against cold

はだざむ
肌寒い chilly
かんりゅう
寒流 cold current
かんそん
寒村 hamlet

丶 八 宀 宀 宀 宀 宙 実 実 寒 寒　12

68

129

ON-KUN READINGS:	HEADER:
カン	リ

刊

to publish

ORIGIN: The left side 干 was a pictograph of a spearlike forked weapon, but here it was used phonetically to indicate "to dry; to carve." The right side リ is a variant of "knife." One could carve writing on a piece of wood with a knife to make wood blocks, which were used for printing for circulation or publication. The kanji 刊 means "to publish."

ちょうかん 朝刊 morning paper
しゅうかんし 週刊誌 weekly magazine
かんこう 刊行する to publish

しんかんしょ 新刊書 newly published book
げっかん 月刊 monthly publication
きかんしょ 既刊書 previously published book

一 二 千 刊 刊　5

130

ON-KUN READINGS:	HEADER:
カン・まき・ま(く)	己

巻

to roll; volume
(of a book)

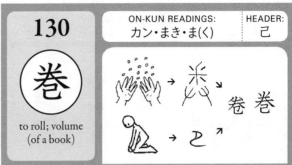

ORIGIN: In the old form 卷, the top was derived from two hands trying to make a rice ball and underneath was a person crouched. Together they signified "to roll." Formerly, a written document was rolled up in a scroll. The current form 巻 means "to roll" or "volume (of a book)."

だいにかん 第二巻 second volume
まきもの 巻物 scroll
のりまき 海苔巻き nori seaweed roll

あっかん 圧巻 the best of
まこ 巻き込まれる to get dragged into
まきがみ 巻紙 rolled paper

丶 ソ ツ 半 半 巻 巻 巻　9

131

ON-KUN READINGS:	HEADER:
カン	宀

完

perfect;
to complete

ORIGIN: The ancient form was 宀 "house" or "to completely surround," and 元 "person with an exaggerated head." A person completely surrounded by a house or a wall signified a meaning of "completeness." The kanji 完 means "to complete" or "perfect."

かんぜん 完全に perfectly
かんせい 完成 completed
みかん 未完の unfinished

かんぺき 完璧に perfectly
かんりょう 完了 complete end; finished
かんけつ 完結 completion

丶 宀 宀 宀 完 完　7

132

ON-KUN READINGS:	HEADER:
カン	宀

官

government
official; sense

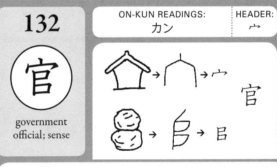

ORIGIN: The top 宀 was a pictograph of a house. Underneath it, two people or things signified "many." The term indicated many government officials in a building. Bureaucrats are to a government as senses are to a body, so, the term also came to mean "body senses." The kanji 官 means "government official" or "sense."

ちょうかん 長官 chief official
かんりょう 官僚 bureaucrat
かんり 官吏 government official

かんのう 官能 sensual
かんせい 官製 government-issued
かんりつ 官立 publicly supported

丶 宀 宀 宀 宀 官 官　8

69

133

ON-KUN READINGS: カン・ほ(す)・ひ(る)

HEADER: 干

干

to dry; to attack

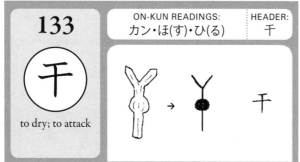

ORIGIN: The ancient form was a pictograph of a forked wood stick that was a spear or spike, indicating "to protect" or "to attack." The term came to be used for a phonetically similar word, "to dry." The kanji 干 means "to dry."

ほ
干す to dry, to air
ものほ
物干し clothes line
うめぼし
梅干 pickled plum

かんしょう
干渉 する to interfere, to meddle
ひもの
干物 dried fish
かんたくち
干拓地 reclaimed land

一二干　　3

134

ON-KUN READINGS: カン・みき

HEADER: 干

幹

trunk of a tree; main

ORIGIN: The left side and the top of the right side consisted of a sun, plants, and a banner, signifying the sun rising high. The right bottom 干 was a pictograph of a forked wood stick that was a spear, but here used phonetically. Together the kanji 幹 means "trunk of a tree" or "main."

みき
幹 trunk
かんじ
幹事 manager, secretary
かんせんどうろ
幹線道路 artery road

しゅかん
主幹 editor in chief
しんかんせん
新幹線 Shinkansen bullet train
かんぶ
幹部 leaders

一十士古古直卓乾乾幹幹幹　　13

135

ON-KUN READINGS: カン

HEADER: 心

感

to feel

 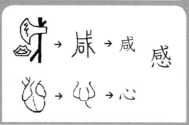

ORIGIN: The top 咸 was made up of 口 "mouth" and 戌 "spear" or "halberd," signifying to make someone be quiet with a threat of a weapon, or to keep the contents inside. The bottom 心 is a heart. Together they signified "to feel strongly inside." The kanji 感 means "to feel."

かん
感じる to feel
かんそう
感想 impression
かんじょう
感情 feeling

かんどう
感動 する to be moved
かんかく
感覚 sense
かんしん
感心 する to be impressed

丿厂厂厅后后咸咸咸咸感感感　　13

136

ON-KUN READINGS: カン・な(れる)

HEADER: 忄

慣

to become used to; to become acclimated

ORIGIN: The left side 忄 was a variant of a heart. The right side 貫 was "to string coins together," here used to mean "to accumulate." Together they indicated one's mind getting used to something. The kanji 慣 means "to become used to; to become acclimated."

しゅうかん
習慣 customs, habit
な
慣れる to be accustomed to
かんしゅう
慣習 tradition

かんようく
慣用句 idiomatic expression
かんこう
慣行 customs, traditions
かんせい
慣性 inertia

丶丷忄忄忄忙忊悍惯惯惯惯慣慣　　14

70

137

ON-KUN READINGS: カン

HEADER: 氵

漢

Chinese; man

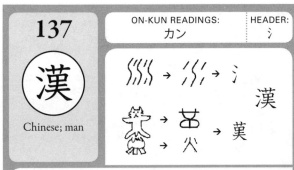

ORIGIN: The left side 氵 was water. The right side was an animal hide being dried over a fire, signifying "dryness." In China, the Han 漢 Dynasty originated in a dry river called 漢水. The post-ancient Chinese characters got solidified as the writing system of the Han and came to be called han-zi 漢字 "writing of the Han" (or kanji in Japanese). It also means a "man."

かんじ
漢字 kanji
かんご
漢語 Chinese word
かんわじてん
漢和辞典 Chinese character to Japanese language dictionary

かんぶん
漢文 classical Chinese language
たいしょくかん
大食漢 a man who eats a lot
もんがいかん
門外漢 outsider, layman

丶 氵 氵 氵 沽 沽 浩 浩 浩 漢 漢　13

138

ON-KUN READINGS: カン

HEADER: 王

環

circle; round

ORIGIN: The left side 王 was jewelry. The right side had an eye over jewelry 口 placed around the collar (variant of 衣) of the dead, dressed for a last journey. (An eye signified awakening again.) Together they indicated "to return" or roundness. The kanji 環 means "circle; round."

かんきょう
環境 environment
かんじょうせん
環状線 circular road, beltway

一 二 丁 王 王 玗 玗 玗 珊 珊 珊 環 環 環 環 環　17

(71)

139

ON-KUN READINGS: カン・み(る)

HEADER: 目

看

to watch closely; to gaze

ORIGIN: The hand 手 is above the eye 目. Together the term indicated "to see a distance with a hand above one's eye." The kanji 看 means "to watch closely; to gaze."

み
看る to see, to take care
かんごふ
看護婦 nurse
かんしゅ
看守 (prison) watch

かんばん
看板 sign-board
かんびょう
看病 nursing, tending to a sick person
かんか
看過する to overlook

一 二 三 手 手 看 看 看 看　9

140

ON-KUN READINGS: カン・くだ

HEADER: 竹

管

pipe; control

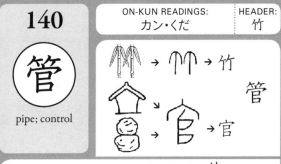

ORIGIN: The top was a pictograph of bamboo 竹. The sound of 官 indicated "to pierce through." Together they indicated a pierced bamboo stick for a musical instrument, such as a flute, or just a pipe. The kanji 管 means "pipe; control."

くだ
管 pipe
かんり
管理 control
すいどうかん
水道管 water pipe

けっかん
血管 blood vessel
いかん
移管 transfer of authority
くうこうかんせい
空港管制 air traffic control

丿 ㇒ 㣺 㣺 竹 竹 竹 竺 竺 笨 管 管 管 管　14

141

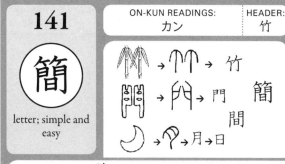

ON-KUN READINGS: カン
HEADER: 竹

簡

letter; simple and easy

ORIGIN: The top 竹 was "bamboo," which was used for writing brushes. The old form of 間 had "moon showing through an opening of a gate," or "small space." Together they indicated writing in a small space, such as a letter, which is simple and brief. The kanji 簡 means "letter" or "simple and easy."

かんたん
簡単な simple and easy
しょかん
書簡 letter, document
かんそか
簡素化 simplification

ちくかん
竹簡 bamboo tablet
かんい
簡易な plain
かんめい
簡明な concise

ノ ノ ケ ヤ ヤ 竹 竹 符 符 笞 笞 筲 筲 简 简 简 简 18

142

ON-KUN READINGS: カン・み(る)
HEADER: 見

観

to look over

ORIGIN: The left side of the old form 觀 was a big-eyed, crested bird like an owl, here giving the sound *kan* "to look around." The right side, from 目 "eye" and 儿 "person," indicated "to see." The kanji 観 means "to look over."

かんさつ
観察 observation
み
観る to look over
かんこうりょこう
観光旅行 sightseeing trip

しゅかんてき
主観的に subjectively
せいかん
静観 watchful waiting
らっかんてき
楽観的 optimistic

ノ ト ヒ チ ヂ 牟 牟 弁 弁 雀 雚 雚 雚 観 観 観 観 18

143

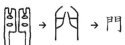

ON-KUN READINGS: カン・ケン・あいだ・ま
HEADER: 門

間

duration of time; between (spatially and temporally)

ORIGIN: The outside 門 was a pictograph of a two-door gate and the form 日 was originally 月 "moon." Together the term indicated "moon showing through an opening of a gate," or "distance between." The kanji 間 means "between" (spatially and temporally) and "duration of time."

あいだ
間 duration, between
じかん
時間 time, hour
ま
その間に while that, in the meantime

にんげん
人間 human being
か ま
貸し間 room to let
あいだがら
間柄 relationship

｜ ｢ ｢ ｢ ｢ ｢ 門門門門間間間 12

144

ON-KUN READINGS: カン・せき
HEADER: 門

関

relating; to connect; checkpoint

ORIGIN: The old kanji 關 had 門, the pictograph of two doors closed and two short threads tied together, which signified "to lock." Together they indicated "to lock a gate to control people coming in and out." The current form 関 means "relating," "to connect," or "checkpoint."

かんけい
関係 relationship
かん
関して concerning
ぜいかん
税関 customs house

せきしょ
関所 checkpoint
かか
関わる to pertain
げんかん
玄関 front entry

｜ ｢ ｢ ｢ ｢ ｢ 門門門門門門関関関 14

145

館

large building

ORIGIN: The left side 食 came from 皀 and depicted food in a bowl. The right side 官 came from a big house 宀 where many government officials and other people congregate. Together they indicated a large house where a lot of people gathered. The kanji 館 means "large building."

りょかん
旅館 Japanese-style inn
としょかん
図書館 library
えいがかん
映画館 movie theater

ほんかん
本館 main building
しんかん
新館 new building
やかた
館 large house

ノ 𠆢 𠂉 今 今 今 食 食 食 食' 食' 飠' 館 館 館 館 館 16

146

丸

round; circle; completely; a ship's name

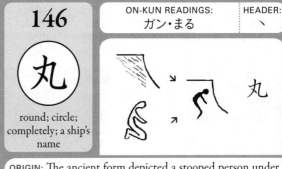

ORIGIN: The ancient form depicted a stooped person under a curved line. A person with a curved back signified roundness. The kanji 丸 means "round; circle" or "completely." 丸 is also used for a name for a ship, as in 氷川丸 "The Hikawa-maru."

まる
丸い round
ひ まる
日の丸 Japanese flag
まる こ
丸め込む to coax

まる
丸ごと in its entirety
まる
丸をつける to circle as correct
answer
だんがん
弾丸 bullet

ノ 九 丸 3

147

岸

cliff

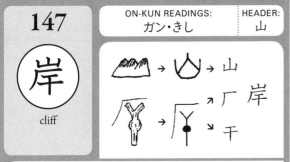

ORIGIN: The top was a mountain 山. The bottom had 厂 "cliff" and 干, which was used phonetically. The kanji 岸 means "cliff."

きし
岸 cliff
かわぎし
川岸 river bank
えんがん
沿岸 coastline

きしべ
岸辺 shore
む ぎし
向こう岸 the opposite bank
たいがん
対岸 opposite side of river

丶 屵 屵 屵 岩 岸 岸 岸 8

148

眼

eye

ORIGIN: In the ancient form the left side was an eye 目. The right side 艮 consisted of an eye and halted legs, signifying not able to move forward, thus staying in one place. Together they signified eyes that gaze at something. The kanji 眼 means "eye."

め まなこ
眼・眼 eye
りょうがん
両眼 both eyes
がんちゅう
眼中 に in one's eye

めがね
眼鏡 eye glasses
にくがん
肉眼 で with the naked eye
きんがん
近眼 near-sighted

｜ 冂 𦥑 日 目 目' 目7 目3 眼 眼 眼 11

149

ON-KUN READINGS: ガン・いわ
HEADER: 山

岩

rock; boulder

ORIGIN: A mountain 山 and a stone 石 made up the kanji for a mountain rock or boulder. The kanji 岩 means "rock; boulder."

いわ
岩 rock
がんせき
岩石 rock
いちまいいわ
一枚岩の monolithic

いわば
岩場 rocky area
いわはだ
岩肌 rock surface
いわや
岩屋 cave, cavern

｜ 山 屵 屵 屵 岩 岩 岩　8

150

ON-KUN READINGS: ガン・かお
HEADER: 頁

顔

face

ORIGIN: In the ancient form the left side 彦 had 文 "collar," 厂 "bluff; square," and 彡 "beautiful design," indicating "a man who has a well-defined, handsome forehead." The right side 頁 was a head. Together they indicated a part of a head that had pretty features. The kanji 顔 means "face."

かお
顔 face
かおいろ
顔色 facial color
かおみし
顔見知り acquaintance

かお
顔つき feature, expression
すがお
素顔 face with no makeup on
がんりょう
顔料 paints, pigment

｀ 亠 立 立 产 声 彦 彦 彦 彦 顔 顔 顔 顔 顔 顔 顔 顔　18

151

ON-KUN READINGS: ガン・ねが(う)
HEADER: 頁

願

to wish; prayer

ORIGIN: The left side 原 had 厂 "bluff" and 泉 "fountain in a crevice" or "the source of water"; it is used phonetically to indicate "source." The right side 頁 was a head. What flows out of one's head or mind is a wish. Together they meant "think profoundly" or "wish." The kanji 願 means "to wish" or "prayer."

ねが
お願い request, favor
ねが
願う to wish
がんしょ
願書 application document

ねんがん
念願 wish
がんぼう
願望 desire
がん
願をかける to make a vow

一 厂 厂 厂 庐 盾 盾 原 原 原 原 原 願 願 願 願 願 願 願　19

152

ON-KUN READINGS: キ・あぶ(ない)・あや(ぶむ)
HEADER: 厃

危

danger

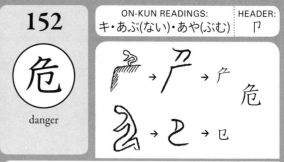

ORIGIN: In the ancient form the top depicted a person crouching 刀 over a cliff 厂 and the bottom 巳 was a bent person. A person on the edge of a cliff is in danger. The kanji 危 means "danger."

あぶ
危ない dangerous
きけん
危険 danger
あや
危うく nearly, almost

きき
危機 crisis
きがい
危害 harm
ききいっぱつ
危機一髪 hang by a hair

ノ ク 产 产 危 危　6

74

153

ON-KUN READINGS: キ・よろこ(ぶ)

HEADER: 口

喜

to feel pleased; happy

ORIGIN: The top depicted a bowl overflowing with food and the bottom 口 was a mouth. Together they indicated happiness at feasting. The kanji 喜 means "happy" or "to feel pleased; to rejoice."

よろこ
喜ぶ to feel pleased, to rejoice
よろこ
喜ばせる to please
かんき
歓喜 jubilation

ひきこもごも
悲喜交々 mingled feelings of joy and sorrow
きげき
喜劇 comedy
きどあいらく
喜怒哀楽 all feelings

一十士吉吉吉声声壴壴喜喜喜　12

154

ON-KUN READINGS: キ・うつわ

HEADER: 口

器

container

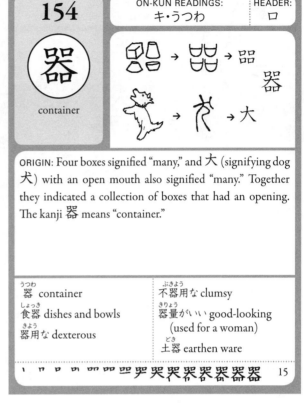

ORIGIN: Four boxes signified "many," and 大 (signifying dog 犬) with an open mouth also signified "many." Together they indicated a collection of boxes that had an opening. The kanji 器 means "container."

うつわ
器 container
しょっき
食器 dishes and bowls
きよう
器用な dexterous

ぶきよう
不器用な clumsy
きりょう
器量がいい good-looking (used for a woman)
どき
土器 earthen ware

丨口口口四吅哭哭哭器器器器　15

155

ON-KUN READINGS: キ・もと・もとい

HEADER: 土

基

foundation; base

ORIGIN: In the ancient form the top 其 was a pictograph of square sieve on a table or foundation, and the bottom 土 was dirt. Together they meant a square foundation. From that meaning, the kanji 基 means "foundation; base."

もと
基 base
きほんてき
基本的 fundamental
きそ
基礎 foundation

きじゅん
基準 standard
ききん
基金 fund
きち
基地 base

一十廿廿甘甘其其其基基　11

156

ON-KUN READINGS: キ

HEADER: 大

奇

strange; odd

ORIGIN: The ancient form consisted of 大 "a person standing tall" and 可, which was phonetically used to indicate "one-legged." Together they indicated a person who was standing on one leg; seeing such a person was unusual. The kanji 奇 means "strange; odd."

きみょう
奇妙 strange
きすう
奇数 odd number
すうき
数奇な adverse fortune

きせき
奇跡 miracle
きばつ
奇抜な novel, eccentric
きい
奇異な odd and strange

一ナ大太本奈奇奇　8

75

157

ON-KUN READINGS: キ・よ(る)

HEADER: 宀

寄

to be inclined to; to stop by

ORIGIN: Inside a house 宀 is 大 "person," and 可, which was phonetically used to indicate a "one-legged" person who needs to recline on something. In the combined form, the kanji 寄 means "to be inclined to" or "to stop by."

寄る to stop by, to depend
年寄り elderly person
寄付 donation

寄生動物 parasite
寄宿舎 residence hall
最寄の closest

`ゝ 宀 宀 宀 宆 宆 宆 寄 寄 寄` 11

158

ON-KUN READINGS: キ・ケ

HEADER: 巾

希

rare; wish

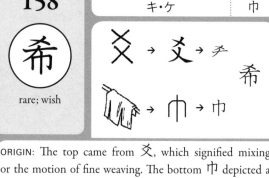

ORIGIN: The top came from 爻, which signified mixing or the motion of fine weaving. The bottom 巾 depicted a hanging cloth. Together they indicated that a tightly woven cloth rarely showed gaps; therefore the meaning became "rare" and also a "wish for that which is not ordinary." The kanji 希 means "rare" or "wish."

希望 wish
希少価値 value or worth due to scarcity
希代の unique

希有の unprecedented
希薄な rare, scarce

`ノ メ チ ヂ 齐 希 希` 7

159

ON-KUN READINGS: キ

HEADER: 扌

揮

to command; volatile

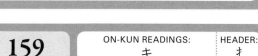

ORIGIN: The left side 扌 is a hand and the right side 軍 is military (soldiers surrounding a convoy). A military commander signals with his hand to charge, hence "to agitate; to wave a hand." From the meaning of "stirring up," it is also used for volatile matter. The kanji 揮 means "to command" or "volatile."

発揮 display
指揮者 musical conductor
指揮 command

揮発性の volatile
揮発油 benzine

`一 十 扌 扌 扌 扩 捊 挥 挥 揮 揮` 12

160

ON-KUN READINGS: キ・つくえ

HEADER: 木

机

desk

ORIGIN: The left side 木 "wood" and the right side 几 "table" indicated "wooden table." The kanji 机 means "desk."

机 desk
机上論 a mere theory, an academic theory
文机 writing desk

脇机 side table

`一 十 才 木 朹 机` 6

161

旗
flag

ORIGIN: The left side and the top of the right side was a flag on a pole. 其 on the right side was a pictograph of a square sieve on a table or foundation. Together they indicated a square flag. The kanji 旗 means "flag."

はた
旗 flag
こっき
国旗 national flag
きしゅ
旗手 standard-bearer

ぐんき
軍旗 the military colors
はんき
半旗 half-mast
はんき
反旗 the banner of revolt

' ー ゟ ガ ガ ゟ゙ ゟ゚ 扩 斿 斿 旗 旗 旗 旗　14

162

期
period; to expect

ORIGIN: The left side 其 indicated a demonstrative word "that" and the right side 月 indicated "moon." The waxing and waning of a moon signified a cycle of time, and further "what is foreseen or predictable." The kanji 期 means "period" or "to expect."

がっき
学期 school term
きたい
期待する to look forward to
きげん
期限 deadline

きまつしけん
期末試験 final exam
き
期す to expect
ていきてき
定期的 regularly

一 十 廾 甘 甘 苷 其 其 期 期 期 期　12

163

機
machine; loom; moment; chance

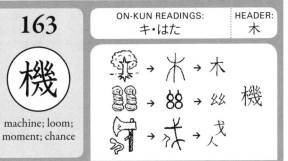

ORIGIN: 木 was "wood." The right side consisted of two 幺 "short threads" indicating small pieces and two 戈 "spears" adjacent to 人 "person." Together they indicated "wooden machine used to weave thread; loom." Works or a mechanism given by a god is a moment of fate or destiny. The kanji 機 means "machine; loom; moment; chance."

ひこうき
飛行機 airplane
せんたくき
洗濯機 washing machine
きかい
機械 machine

はたお
機織り weaving
とうきてき
投機的 on speculation
てんき
転機 turning point

一 十 才 木 杧 杧 杙 栏 栉 桦 機 機 機 機 機　16

164

帰
to go home; to return

ORIGIN: The old form 歸 had "two round piles of dirt" and "foot," signifying a round trip, and 帚 "broom." In ancient times, after a wedding the groom visited the bride's home before returning to his home with his new wife, who carried a broom. Now the left side is simplified to リ. The kanji 帰 means "to go home; to return."

かえ
帰る to return home
きか
帰化 naturalization
きのう
帰納 induction
きたく
帰宅 a return home

きこく
帰国 a return to one's own country
ふっき
復帰する to come back, to make a comeback, to be restored

丿 リ リ⁊ リヨ リヨ リヨ 帰 帰 帰 帰　10

165

ON-KUN READINGS: キ・ケ

HEADER: 气

気

air; spirit

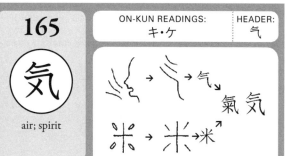

ORIGIN: In the old form 氣, 気 was a depiction of rising steam (or of one's breath) and 米 grains of rice scattered in all directions. Together they indicated "steam rising from cooked rice" and in turn meant "something in the air; spirits; unseen force." The current reduced form 気 means "air; spirit."

天気 (てんき) weather
気分・気持ち (きぶん・きもち) a feeling
空気 (くうき) air
気配 (けはい) sign, indication
気が付く (きづく) to notice
気前がいい (きまえがいい) generous

ノ ケ 气 気 気 気   6

166

ON-KUN READINGS: キ

HEADER: シ

汽

steam; vapor

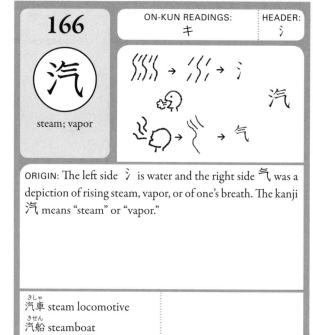

ORIGIN: The left side シ is water and the right side 气 was a depiction of rising steam, vapor, or of one's breath. The kanji 汽 means "steam" or "vapor."

汽車 (きしゃ) steam locomotive
汽船 (きせん) steamboat
汽笛 (きてき) (steam) whistle; siren

ヽ ゝ ミ シ シ 汽 汽   7

167

ON-KUN READINGS: キ

HEADER: 子

季

a quarter of a year; season

ORIGIN: The top 禾, "harvest," and the bottom 子, "child or offspring," signified the duration of time in which harvesting of crops is done—that is, three months. The kanji 季 means "quarter of a year," or "season."

季節 (きせつ) season
四季 (しき) four seasons
季語 (きご) season word (in haiku poem)
年季の入った (ねんきのはいった) experienced
雨季 (うき) rainy season
冬季 (とうき) winter

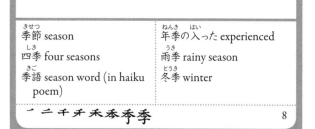

一 二 千 禾 禾 季 季 季   8

168

ON-KUN READINGS: キ

HEADER: 糸

紀

to begin; to chronicle; order

ORIGIN: The left side 糸 was thin, silk filaments being pulled out of silkworm cocoons, signifying threads. The right side 己 depicted a moment at which a crooked, long rope got straightened, here used phonetically. Together they indicated the beginning of a long continuous thread, or a travel journal. The kanji 紀 means "to begin" or "to chronicle" or "order."

紀元前 (きげんぜん) B.C., before the Common Era
ジュラ紀 (じゅらき) the Jurassic Period
紀行 (きこう) travel journal
紀元2000年 (きげんにせんねん) the year 2000 A.D.
二十世紀 (にじっせいき) twentieth century
風紀 (ふうき) public morals

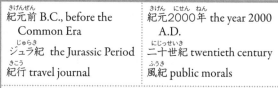

く 幺 幺 幺 糸 糸 紀 紀 紀   9

78

169

	ON-KUN READINGS:	HEADER:
	キ	見

規
standard

ORIGIN: In the ancient form the left side was a compass that one used to draw a circle. The right side 見 consisted of an "eye" and a "person," signifying "to see." Together they indicated someone looking at something using a tool to measure. The kanji 規 means "standard."

きそく
規則 rule
きてい
規定 regulation
じょうぎ
定規 ruler

きやく
規約 covenant
きせい
規制 regulation
しんきけいやく
新規契約 new contract

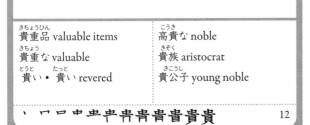
11

170

	ON-KUN READINGS:	HEADER:
	キ・しる(す)	言

記
to record

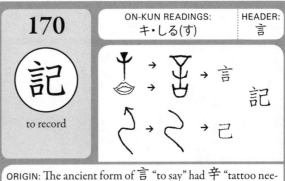

ORIGIN: The ancient form of 言 "to say" had 辛 "tattoo needle" and 口 "mouth," signifying "to express an idea sharply or to articulate with words." The right side 己 signified a crooked wire or a serpent on the verge of straightening itself, here used phonetically. Together they meant writing a long account, or recording. The kanji 記 means "to record."

にっき
日記 diary
きろく
記録 records
しる
記す to record

きおく
記憶 memory
きじ
記事 (journalistic) article
しょき
書記 recording secretary

`、 亠 亠 言 言 言 言 記 記 記`
10

79

171

	ON-KUN READINGS:	HEADER:
	キ・とうと(い)・たっと(い)	貝

貴
precious

ORIGIN: In the ancient form in the middle, the top had two hands holding something precious. The bottom 貝 was a cowry, a rare and beautiful shell from the southern region that was used as currency. Together they indicated "precious; high-ranking person." The kanji 貴 means "precious."

きちょうひん
貴重品 valuable items
きちょう
貴重な valuable
とうと　たっと
貴い・貴い revered

こうき
高貴な noble
きぞく
貴族 aristocrat
きこうし
貴公子 young noble

`、 口 口 中 虫 串 串 貴 貴 貴 貴 貴`
12

172

	ON-KUN READINGS:	HEADER:
	キ・お(きる)	走

起
to get up; to arise

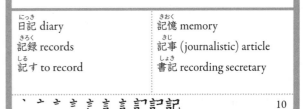

ORIGIN: In the ancient form the left side 走 had a person in motion and a foot, indicating an activity involving feet, or running. The right side 己 signified a crooked wire, or a serpent on the verge of straightening itself. Together they indicated a quick motion. The kanji 起 means "to get up; to arise."

お
起きる to get up
起きている to stay up
お
起こす to wake someone up

きしょうじかん
起床時間 time to get up
ほっきにん
発起人 initial organizer,
　proposer
きぎょうか
起業家 entrepreneur

`一 十 土 キ キ 走 走 起 起 起`
10

173

ON-KUN READINGS: ギ・わざ | HEADER: 扌

技

skill; work; deed

ORIGIN: The left side was a pictograph of a hand. The right side depicted a hand holding a bamboo stick 支, moving about with a "skillful hand." Together they indicated doing with two hands, or skills in general. The kanji 技 means "skill."

特技（とくぎ） special skill	技能（ぎのう） skill, ability
技術（ぎじゅつ） technology, skill	演技（えんぎ） acting
技（わざ） work, deed	国技（こくぎ） national sport, Sumo

一 十 扌 扌 扌 抄 技 7

174

ON-KUN READINGS: ギ・うたが(う) | HEADER: 疋

疑

to doubt

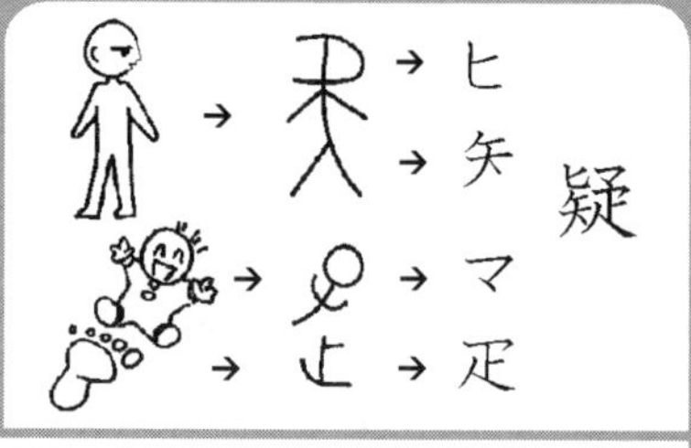

ORIGIN: The left side depicted a person with his or her head (匕) turning back. The right side consisted of the head of a child (マ) and a foot (疋), signifying halting steps. Not knowing what to do makes one doubtful. The kanji 疑 means "to doubt."

疑う（うたが） to doubt	懐疑的（かいぎてき） skeptical
疑問（ぎもん） a question	疑惑（ぎわく） a doubt, suspicion
質疑応答（しつぎおうとう） question and answer	半信半疑（はんしんはんぎ） half in doubt, incredulous

疑 14

175

ON-KUN READINGS: ギ・よし | HEADER: 羊

義

good; correct

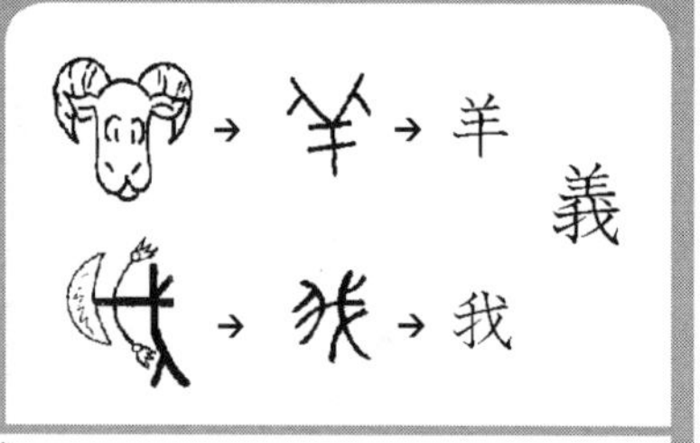

ORIGIN: The top 羊 came from a pictograph of a sheep, which was the embodiment of something good. The bottom 我, "halberd with rugged blade," was used to cut sheep, or just used phonetically. Together they came to mean "correct" or "right." The kanji 義 means "good" or "correct."

義（ぎ） correctness	名義人（めいぎにん） titleholder
大義（たいぎ） noble cause	義務（ぎむ） duty
義理（ぎり） obligation	義母（ぎぼ） mother-in-law

羊 羊 義 義 13

176

ON-KUN READINGS: ギ | HEADER: 言

議

to discuss

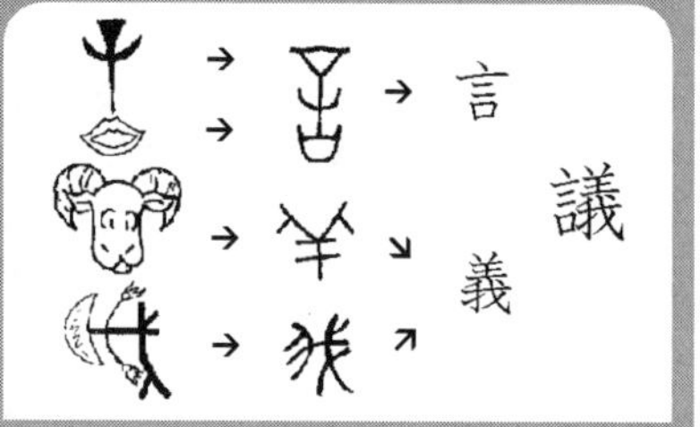

ORIGIN: The left side 言 was "to speak." The right side 義, used phonetically, had 羊 "sheep" (an embodiment of "goodness") and 我 "ragged-edged weapon." Together they indicated "discussing in search of the correct answer." The kanji 議 means "to discuss."

会議（かいぎ） meeting	議会（ぎかい） assembly
議題（ぎだい） agenda	不思議（ふしぎ） mystery
議論（ぎろん） argument	議長（ぎちょう） chairman, speaker

言 言 言 議 議 20

177

吉

good luck;
auspicious

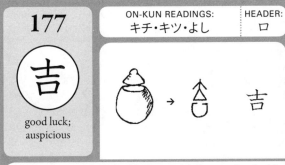

ORIGIN: A jar with a double-knotted lid secured valuable items. The form also came to indicate something auspicious or "good luck." The kanji 吉 means "good luck" or "auspicious."

吉報 good news
吉日 auspicious day
吉兆 good omen

大吉 great good luck (in *omikuji* "written oracle at a shrine")
不吉な ominous

一十士吉吉吉　6

178

喫

to swallow

ORIGIN: The left side 口 is a mouth. The right side 契 "contract" (a person carved with a knife, possibly a slave) was used phonetically. The kanji 喫 means "to swallow."

喫茶店 coffee house
喫煙所 smoking area
満喫する to eat and drink plentifully

丶口口口叶叶叶喫喫喫喫喫　12

179

客

guest; customer

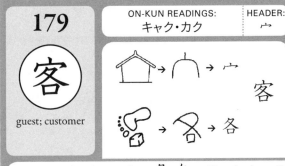

ORIGIN: Inside a house 宀 is 各. 夂, a "foot backward" (often signifying "not moving ahead"), and 口, a "rock," together indicated that someone hit something hard with a foot and stopped there. It signified a person from outside stopping at a house, or a guest. The kanji 客 means "guest" or "customer."

お客さん customer, guest
乗客 passenger
来客 visitor

客人 guest
客足が減る to lose a lot of customers
客観的 objectively

丶宀宀宀宮客客客　9

180

逆

opposite; reverse

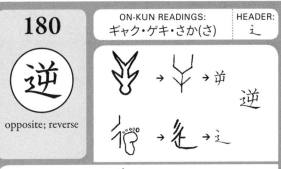

ORIGIN: The upper right 屰 depicted a person upside down. The bottom was the left half of a crossroad, signifying "to go forward." Together they indicated "to go backward" or "reverse." The kanji 逆 means "opposite; reverse."

逆 wrong side, reverse, wrong way
逆さま upside down
反逆 mutiny

逆転 reversal
逆立ち upside down
逆夢 dream or reverse reality

丶丷丷屰屰逆逆逆逆　9

181

ON-KUN READINGS: キュウ・おか

HEADER: 一

丘
hill

ORIGIN: The ancient form shown in the middle originally depicted a valley between two hills. Now the kanji 丘 means "hill."

<ruby>丘<rt>おか</rt></ruby> hill
<ruby>砂丘<rt>さきゅう</rt></ruby> dune
<ruby>丘陵<rt>きゅうりょう</rt></ruby> hill

ノイ仁斤丘　5

182

ON-KUN READINGS: キュウ・ク・ひさ(しい)

HEADER: ノ

久
long time; lasting

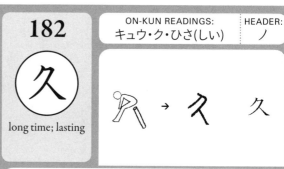

ORIGIN: The ancient form was a depiction of an old man with a stooped back, and an additional stroke pointing to his back to support him. Someone old has lived a long time. The kanji 久 means "long time" or "lasting."

<ruby>久<rt>ひさ</rt></ruby>しぶり after a long time
<ruby>永久<rt>えいきゅう</rt></ruby> eternity
<ruby>久々<rt>ひさびさ</rt></ruby>に after a long time

<ruby>久<rt>ひさ</rt></ruby>しく(〜ない) not for a long time
<ruby>持久力<rt>じきゅうりょく</rt></ruby> tenacity
<ruby>悠久<rt>ゆうきゅう</rt></ruby>なる eternal

ノ ク 久　3

183

ON-KUN READINGS: キュウ・やす(む)

HEADER: イ

休
to rest

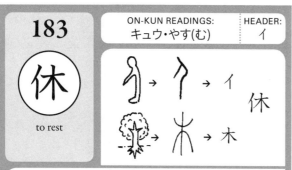

ORIGIN: The left side イ was a person standing, and the right side 木 was a tree. Together they signified a person resting in the shade of a tree. The kanji 休 means "to rest."

<ruby>休<rt>やす</rt></ruby>み rest, vacation
<ruby>休<rt>やす</rt></ruby>む to rest, to be absent
<ruby>夏休<rt>なつやす</rt></ruby>み summer vacation

<ruby>休日<rt>きゅうじつ</rt></ruby> holiday, a day closed
<ruby>休暇<rt>きゅうか</rt></ruby> vacation
<ruby>連休<rt>れんきゅう</rt></ruby> consecutive holiday, long weekend

ノイ仁什休休　6

184

ON-KUN READINGS: キュウ・およ(ぶ)

HEADER: 又

及
to reach; in addition

ORIGIN: The ancient form of 及 shown in the middle depicted a person with a hand of another person coming from behind, indicating being caught and pulled back. The kanji 及 means "to reach" and also "in addition."

<ruby>及<rt>およ</rt></ruby>び in addition
<ruby>及<rt>およ</rt></ruby>ぶ to reach, be equal
<ruby>波及<rt>はきゅう</rt></ruby>する to extend, to spread

<ruby>及第点<rt>きゅうだいてん</rt></ruby> passing score
<ruby>言及<rt>げんきゅう</rt></ruby>する to mention
<ruby>普及<rt>ふきゅう</rt></ruby>する to spread

ノ 乃 及　3

82

185

ON-KUN READINGS: キュウ・す(う)

HEADER: 口

吸

to suck

ORIGIN: The left side was 口 "mouth." The right side 及 depicted a person with a hand of another person reaching from behind, indicating being caught and pulled back. Using a mouth one sucks food or air in. The kanji 吸 means "to suck; to inhale."

吸う to inhale, to suck
吸い取る to absorb
吸収 absorption

呼吸 breathing
人工呼吸 artificial respiration
吸入器 inhaler

丨 口 口 叮 叭 吸 吸　　6

186

ON-KUN READINGS: キュウ・ク・グウ・みや

HEADER: 宀

宮

palace; prince

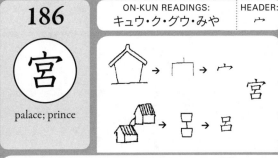

ORIGIN: The top 宀 is a house, and the bottom 呂 depicted houses or rooms connected. Together they indicated a big estate that had a number of houses within, that is a palace. The kanji 宮 means "palace" or "prince."

お宮 shrine
宮殿 palace
神宮 Shinto shrine
宮参り visit to a shrine

宮内庁 Imperial Household Agency
迷宮入り shrouded in mystery

丶 丷 宀 宀 宀 宀 宀 宮 宮　　10

83

187

ON-KUN READINGS: キュウ・ゆみ

HEADER: 弓

弓

bow

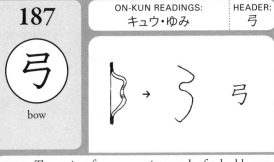

ORIGIN: The ancient form was a pictograph of a double curvature (recurved) bow. The kanji 弓 means "bow."

弓 bow
弓形 arch, arc
弓道 archery

洋弓 western bow
弓矢 bow and arrow

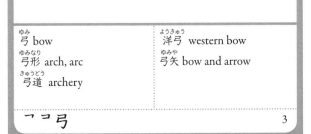
一 コ 弓　　3

188

ON-KUN READINGS: キュウ・いそ(ぐ)・せ(く)

HEADER: 心

急

to hurry; to rush

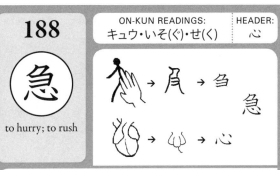

ORIGIN: The upper part ク was a person stooping over and ヨ was "hand," depicting a person chasing another person. The bottom 心 was a heart, or "feeling." Together they indicated a feeling of being rushed. The kanji 急 means "to hurry; to rush."

急ぐ to hurry, to rush
急行 express (train, bus)
特急 special express

急に suddenly, at short notice
早急に promptly
急場 emergency

丿 勹 刍 刍 刍 刍 急 急 急　　9

189

救

to rescue; to save

ON-KUN READINGS:
キュウ・すく(う)

HEADER:
攵

ORIGIN: The left side 求 depicted a pelt tied in the middle. Fur was highly sought-after and desirable. The right side 攵 was a depiction of a hand with a stick, signifying an action. Together they indicated an act of seeking something, or rescuing. The kanji 救 means "to rescue; to save."

救う to save, to rescue
救急車 ambulance vehicle
救命 saving life

救援活動 relief activity
救世主 savior
救い手 rescuer

一 十 寸 才 求 求 求 救 救 救 救　11

190

求

to seek; to request

ON-KUN READINGS:
キュウ・もと(める)

HEADER:
氺

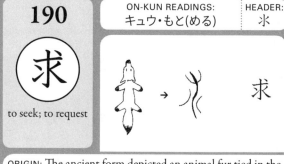

ORIGIN: The ancient form depicted an animal fur tied in the middle. A fur was essential to keep one warm in ancient days and thus was highly desirable and sought after. The kanji 求 means "to seek; to request."

求める to seek
求人広告 help wanted ad
追求する to pursue

求職 job hunting
要求 demand
求婚 marriage proposal

一 十 寸 才 求 求 求　7

191

泣

to cry

ON-KUN READINGS:
キュウ・な(く)

HEADER:
氵

ORIGIN: The left side 氵 is water; and 立, used phonetically, was abbreviated from the kanji 粒, "granule," which signified "tears." Together they indicated a person with tears, or crying quietly. The kanji 泣 means "to cry."

泣く to cry
泣き声 crying voice
泣き笑い tearful smile

泣き付く to implore
泣き言 complaint
号泣する to wail

丶 冫 氵 氵 汀 汁 泣 泣　8

192

球

ball; sphere

ON-KUN READINGS:
キュウ・たま

HEADER:
王

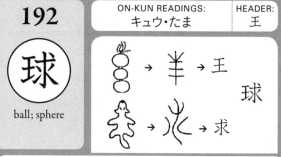

ORIGIN: The left side 王 was a pictograph of a beautiful jewel. The right side 求 was a depiction of fur pulled into the middle, making it a round shape, or "round." Together they meant something precious that was round. The kanji 球 means "ball; sphere."

地球 the earth
野球 baseball
球 ball

球場 stadium
卓球 Ping-Pong
気球 air balloon

一 丁 干 王 王 球 球 球 球 球 球　11

193

ON-KUN READINGS:	HEADER:
キュウ・きわ(める)	穴

究

to investigate thoroughly

ORIGIN: The top 穴 "hole" (from 宀 "house" and 八 "motion to divide") indicated thrusting through a house. The bottom 九 was a bent elbow trying to reach the end of a hole, to see what was there. Together they meant "to investigate further." The kanji 究 means "to investigate thoroughly to find the answer."

けんきゅう
研究 research
けんきゅうしつ
研究室 research office, professor's office
きゅうきょくてき
究極的 に ultimately

きわ
究める to investigate thoroughly
きゅうめい
究明 する to bring to light

`丶 ハ 宀 宀 究 究 究` 7

194

ON-KUN READINGS:	HEADER:
キュウ	糸

級

order; class

ORIGIN: The left side 糸 depicted thin silk filaments being pulled out of silkworm cocoons. The right side 及 depicted a person and someone behind, signifying an order. Together they signified weaving in order, a meaning that was extended to "class." The kanji 級 means "order" or "class."

こうきゅう
高級 high-class
どうきゅうせい
同級生 classmate
きゅうゆう
級友 classmate

にきゅう
二級 second grade level
とうきゅう
等級 grade
かいきゅう
階級 class, rank

`く 幺 幺 幺 糸 糸 紒 級 級` 9

195

ON-KUN READINGS:	HEADER:
キュウ・たま(う)	糸

給

to supply

ORIGIN: The left side 糸 was silk being pulled from silk cocoons. The right side has 亼 "to put a cover over" 口 a "hole," indicating "to meet." Together they meant to mend a hole with thread—and, further, to provide what is missing. The kanji 給 means "to supply."

げっきゅう
月給 monthly wage
きゅうりょう
給料 salary
じきゅうはっぴゃくえん
時給八百円 hourly wage of 800 yen

たま
給わる to be given [humble verb form]
きゅうすい
給水 water supply
しょうきゅう
昇給 salary raise

`く 幺 幺 幺 糸 糸 糸 給 給 給 給` 12

196

ON-KUN READINGS:	HEADER:
キュウ・ふる(い)	日

旧

old (not age)

ORIGIN: The old form 舊 consisted of a crested bird (such as a type of owl) at the top and 臼 a mortar that had a hole. Together they indicated "old," a meaning reinforced by the phonetic use of the bottom portion. Now drastically reduced, the kanji 旧 means "old." (This kanji is not used for one's age.)

ふる
旧い old
しんきゅう
新旧 new and old
ふっきゅうさぎょう
復旧作業 work to restore the old condition

きゅうしき
旧式 old style
きゅうゆう
旧友 old friend
きゅうこう
旧交 old friendship

`丨 丨丨 丨丨丨 旧 旧` 5

197

ON-KUN READINGS: ギュウ・うし   **HEADER:** 牛

牛

a cow

ORIGIN: 牛 was a pictograph of a cow's head with two horns. The kanji 牛 means "cow." Cows were early domesticated animals; this form is also used in a number of kanji representing things or matter in general, as in 物 "good," 件 "case; matter."

牛 cow (うし)
牛肉 beef (ぎゅうにく)
水牛 water buffalo (すいぎゅう)

牛歩 extremely slow walk (ぎゅうほ)
闘牛 bullfight (とうぎゅう)
牛耳を執る to take control (ぎゅうじ を と る)

ノ 一 二 牛   4

198

ON-KUN READINGS: キョ・コ・さ(る)   **HEADER:** ム

去

to leave; past

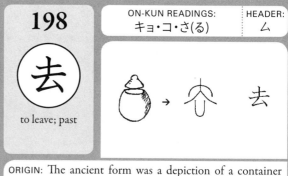

ORIGIN: The ancient form was a depiction of a container with a double lid. This double lid signified security, which further indicated "storing things for safekeeping while one goes away and leaves a place behind." The kanji 去 means "to leave" or "past."

去年 last year (きょねん)
過去 past (かこ)
去る to leave (さ る)

消去 deletion (しょうきょ)
死去 death (しきょ)
去来する to recur (きょらい)

一 十 土 去 去   5

199

ON-KUN READINGS: キョ・い(る)・お(る)   **HEADER:** 尸

居

to exist; to reside

ORIGIN: The top originally was the posture of squatting. The bottom 古 which came from "skull" signified something hard and immobile. Together they indicated that one stays in one place. The kanji 居 means "to exist" or "to reside."

居る・居る to exist (い・お る)
住居 dwelling (じゅうきょ)
居住者 resident (きょじゅうしゃ)

居間 living room (いま)
居留守を使う to pretend to be absent (いるす つか)

フ ヲ 尸 戸 戸 居 居 居   8

200

ON-KUN READINGS: キョ   **HEADER:** ｜

巨

huge

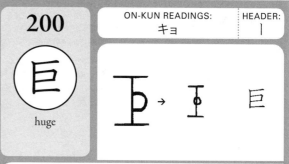

ORIGIN: The ancient form shown in the middle depicted a large, rectangular ruler (carpenter's square) with a handle in the middle. The kanji 巨 means "huge."

巨人 giant (きょじん)
巨大な huge (きょだい)
巨額 enormous amount of money (きょがく)

巨漢 big fellow (きょかん)
巨万の富 vast wealth (きょまん とみ)
巨船 large ship (きょせん)

｜ 匚 匚 巨 巨   5

201

ON-KUN READINGS: キョ・あ(げる)

HEADER: 手

挙

to raise hand; to conduct

ORIGIN: The top of the old form 擧 had four hands around an interlocked shape, signifying "to cooperate." The bottom 手 was also a hand. Four hands cooperatively raising something also had the meaning "to carry out." The kanji 挙 means "to raise one or both hands; to conduct."

せんきょ
選挙 election
きょしゅ
挙手 a show of hands
あ
挙げる to lift up

いっきょ
一挙に at a stroke
いっか　あ
一家を挙げて the whole family
たいきょ
大挙して in great force

、 ゛ ゛゛ ゛゛ ゛゛゛ 兴 ﬁ 兴兴 挙　　10

202

ON-KUN READINGS: キョ・ゆる(す)

HEADER: 言

許

to forgive; to grant

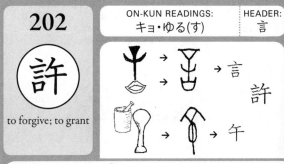

ORIGIN: The left side 言 meant "words" or "to say" and the right side 午 depicted a "mortar," here used phonetically to indicate "to forgive." The kanji 許 means "to forgive; to grant."

きょか
許可 permit
ゆる
許す to forgive
うんてんめんきょしょう
運転免許証 driver's license

とっきょ
特許 patent
きょようはんい
許容範囲 approved limit
いいなずけ
許婚 fiancee

、 ゛ ゛ 言 言 言 言 訁 訁 許許　　11

203

ON-KUN READINGS: ギョ・リョウ・あさ(る)

HEADER: シ

漁

to fish

ORIGIN: The left side was water and the right side 魚 was a pictograph of a fish (with a head, scaled body, and fins). The kanji 漁 means "to fish."

りょう
漁 fishing
ぎょぎょう
漁業 fishery
りょうし
漁師 fisherman

たいりょう
大漁 good haul of fish
ぎょせん
漁船 fishing boat
ふりょう
不漁 poor haul

、 ﹅ シ シ シ 汋 沩 漁 漁 漁 漁 漁 漁 漁　　14

204

ON-KUN READINGS: ギョ・さかな・うお

HEADER: 魚

魚

fish

ORIGIN: The ancient form was a pictograph of a fish (with a head, scaled body, and fins). The kanji 魚 means "fish."

さかな
魚 fish
さかなや
魚屋 fishmonger
きんぎょ
金魚 goldfish

うおがし
魚河岸 fish market
がいらいぎょ
外来魚 foreign fish
ねったいぎょ
熱帯魚 tropical fish

ノ ⺈ ⺈ 丹 甪 角 甪 魚 魚 魚 魚　　11

87

205

京
capital

ON-KUN READINGS: キョウ・ケイ・みやこ

HEADER: 亠

ORIGIN: The top 亠 was a roof; 口 was a house; and the bottom indicated a hill. The houses on a sunny hilltop were protected from floods or enemy attack and belonged to the most powerful people in the land. A place where the powerful people live is the capital. The kanji 京 means "capital."

とうきょう
東京 Tokyo
きょうと
京都 Kyoto
きょう みやこ
京の都 (old) Kyoto

じょうきょう
上京 する to go/come up to Tokyo
けいはんしん
京阪神 Kyoto-Osaka-Kobe
きょうふう
京風 Kyoto-style

`′ 一 亠 古 古 宁 京 京` 8

206

供

to offer;
accompaniment;
together

ON-KUN READINGS: キョウ・ク・そな(える)・とも

HEADER: イ

ORIGIN: The left side イ "person" and the right side 共 "two hands holding up something" together indicated "to offer." They also meant "to accompany." The kanji 供 means "to offer; accompaniment; together." It is commonly used for 子供 "child," indicating the hands of parents holding a child.

こども
子供 child
そな
供える to offer
ていきょう
提供 する to sponsor, to offer

とも
お供 accompanying person
くもつ
供物 offering at alter
じきょう
自供 confession

`ノ イ 仁 什 什 供 供 供` 8

207

競
to compete

ON-KUN READINGS: キョウ・ケイ・きそ(う)・せ(る)

HEADER: 立

ORIGIN: In the ancient form each of the top two shapes shared the origin 言 "to speak." Two people exchanging words sharply signified "to argue." The bottom was also two sets of legs 儿. Combined, they indicated two adversaries "to race" or "to compete." The kanji 競 means "to compete."

きょうそう
競争 competition
きそ
競う to compete
きょうばい
競売 auction

けいば
競馬 horse race
こぜ あ
小競り合い skirmish
せ
競り auction

`′ 一 十 立 立 产 音 音 音 音 竞 竞 竞 竞 竞 竞 竞 競 競 競` 20

208

共
together

ON-KUN READINGS: キョウ・とも

HEADER: 八

ORIGIN: The ancient form depicted a person holding something with two hands, signifying "both" or "together." The kanji 共 means "together."

とも
共に together
きょうどう
共同で jointly
きょうかん
共感 sympathy

きょうつう
共通 common
きょうさんしゅぎ
共産主義 communism
はんきょう
反共 anti-communism

`一 十 廿 甘 共 共` 6

209

協

to cooperate

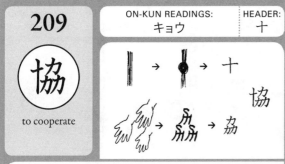

ORIGIN: The left side 十 indicated bundling ten into one. The right side had three strong hands. Together they indicated that many people did something together. The kanji 協 means "to cooperate."

きょうりょく
協力 cooperation
きょうかい
協会 association
のうきょう
農協 agricultural co-op

だきょう
妥協 compromise
きょうちょう
協調 cooperation
きょうてい
協定 agreement

一　十　忖　忖　協　協　協　協　8

210

境

boundary

ORIGIN: The left side 土 was "mound of soil." The right side 竟 consists of 音 "sound; music," and 儿 "person's legs," phonetically used to signify an "end of singing." Combined, they indicated the end of one's land. The kanji 境 means "boundary."

かんきょう
環境 environment
こっきょう
国境 country boundary
さかい
境 boundary

きょうかいせん
境界線 boundary
けいだい
境内 the grounds (of a temple)
しんきょう
心境 state of mind

一　十　址　址　垃　垃　垃　培　培　堷　堷　境　14

211

強

strong; to force

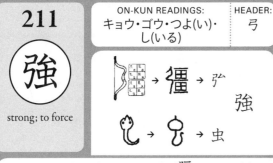

ORIGIN: The ancient form consisted of 彊 "re-curved fortified bow" to indicate "large; strong" and 虫 "worm." The worm in this instance would have been a hard shell worm such as a beetle. The kanji 彊 was eventually reduced to 弓 "bow" and ム (no particular meaning). Now the meaning "worm" has been dropped, and the kanji 強 means "strong; force."

つよ
強い strong
べんきょう
勉強 study
ごういん
強引に forcibly

きょうりょく
強力な powerful
し
強いる to compel, to force
きょうか
強化する to strengthen

フ　弓　弓　弘　弦　弦　強　強　強　11

212

恐

to fear

ORIGIN: The top consisted of a tool and a person's hands holding something in prayer, signifying "fear of god." The bottom 心 was a heart. The meaning of god was dropped. The kanji 恐 means "to fear."

おそ
恐ろしい frightening
おそ
恐れる to fear
きょうふ
恐怖 fear

きょうこう
恐慌 panic
きょうりゅう
恐竜 dinosaur
きょうしゅく
恐縮 to be much obliged for

一　丁　工　卫　巩　巩　巩　恐　恐　恐　10

213

ON-KUN READINGS: キョウ・おし(える)・おそ(わる)

HEADER: 攵

教

to teach; religious teaching

ORIGIN: The old form 敎 had 爻 "to mix or interact" and 子 "child" on the left. The right side was 攵 "motion or activity" (from "hand pounding something with a stick"). Together they signified an interaction in which adults teach a child. It also included religious teaching. The kanji 教 means "to teach" and "religious teaching."

おし
教える to teach
きょうしつ
教室 classroom
きょういく
教育 education

ぶっきょう
仏教 Buddhism
しゅうきょう
宗教 religion
おそ
教わる to be taught

一 十 土 屮 耂 耂 孝 孝 孝 教 教   11

214

ON-KUN READINGS: キョウ・はし

HEADER: 木

橋

bridge

ORIGIN: The left side 木 was wood and the right side 喬 shares the same origin as the kanji 高 "high; tall," except for one bent stroke on top that signified a hanging bridge. Together they meant a wooden bridge that sagged in the middle. The kanji 橋 means "bridge."

はし
橋 bridge
ほどうきょう
歩道橋 pedestrian bridge
てっきょう
鉄橋 railroad bridge

はしわた
橋渡しする to mediate
りっきょう
陸橋 overpass
まるきばし
丸木橋 log bridge

一 十 オ 木 杧 杧 杧 柞 柞 橋 橋 橋 橋 橋 橋 橋   16

215

ON-KUN READINGS: キョウ・せま(い)・せば(める)

HEADER: 犭

狭

narrow

ORIGIN: The left side 犭 came from a depiction of a dog or animal. The right side 夾 indicated a person between two people, indicating "narrow." Together they meant a road that was very narrow for a person to pass, such as an animal trail. The kanji 狭 means "narrow."

せま
狭い narrow, cramped
きょうりょう
狭量な narrow-minded
ところせま
所狭しと overcrowding

せまくる
狭苦しい cramped
てぜま
手狭な cramped

ノ オ 犭 犭 犭 狆 狆 狭 狭   9

216

ON-KUN READINGS: キョウ・むね・むな

HEADER: 月

胸

chest

ORIGIN: The left side 月 depicted flesh of a body. The right side 匈 showed a person embracing something 勹. 凵 inside was an empty container, signifying lungs. Together they indicated "chest; heart." The kanji 胸 means "chest."

むね
胸 chest
きょうちゅう
胸中 inside one's heart
どきょう
度胸 courage, nerve

むなさわ
胸騒ぎ uneasiness
きょうぞう
胸像 bust of a statue
きょうい
胸囲 girth of the chest

丿 丨 月 月 肝 肑 肑 胸 胸 胸   10

90

217

ON-KUN READINGS: キョウ・コウ・おこ(す)

HEADER: 臼

興

to raise; to start

ORIGIN: The ancient form of this kanji, shown in the middle, consisted of as many as four hands. The middle 同 meant "same" Together they indicated that many people lent hands to start or raise something. The kanji 興 means "to raise; to start."

きょうみ
興味 interest
おこ
興す to start
きょう
興ずる to amuse oneself

そっきょう
即興 impromptu
こうぎょう
興行 public entertainment
しんこうとし
新興都市 boom town

｀ ｆ ｆ ｆ 月 月 月 門 門 門 門 門 門 興 興 興　16

218

ON-KUN READINGS: キョウ・ゴウ

HEADER: 阝

郷

hometown; village

ORIGIN: Of the three parts, the left and the right both mean 邑 a village (an area and people). The middle part was taken from the middle part of a kanji 郷 that depicted two people eating a meal. Together they indicated a hometown. The kanji 郷 means a "village" where many people live, or "hometown."

ふるさと
故郷 hometown
こきょう
故郷 hometown
きょうど
郷土 homeland

ごうし
郷士 squire
ぼうきょう　ねん
望郷の念 nostalgia
ざいごうぐんじん
在郷軍人 ex-service man

｀ ｇ ｇ ｇ 纟 纟 纟 绵 郷 郷ˇ郷3郷　11

219

ON-KUN READINGS: キョウ・かがみ

HEADER: 金

鏡

mirror

ORIGIN: The left side 金 was metal. The right side 竟 consisted of 音 "sound; music" and 儿 "person," and was used phonetically to indicate "scene" or "shape." It indicated a metal that reflects the shape of a person. The kanji 鏡 means "mirror."

かがみ
鏡 mirror
てかがみ
手鏡 hand mirror
めがね
眼鏡 eye glasses

むしめがね
虫眼鏡 magnifying glass
そうがんきょう
双眼鏡 binocular
ぼうえんきょう
望遠鏡 telescope

ノ ハ ハ 今 今 牟 余 金 金ˋ鈩鈩鈩鈩鈩鈩鈩鏡鏡鏡　19

220

ON-KUN READINGS: キョウ・おどろ(く)

HEADER: 馬

驚

to be startled

ORIGIN: The top 敬 "respect" consisted of a person bent low to pray with a sheep head, and 攵 "to strike," and was used phonetically. The bottom, 馬 "horse," is an animal that gets startled easily. Together they originally indicated a horse getting startled. With the meaning of horse dropped, the kanji 驚 means "to be startled."

おどろ
驚く to be surprised
きょうい
驚異の amazing
きょうたん
驚嘆 wonder, admiration

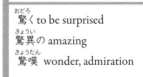

一 艹 艹 艹 芍 芍 苟 苟 岁 岁 岁 敬 敬 敬 敬 敬 敬 警 驚 驚 驚 驚 驚　22

91

221

ON-KUN READINGS:	HEADER:
ギョウ・ゴウ・わざ	木

業

(hard) work; skills

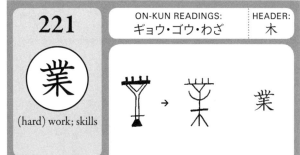

ORIGIN: The ancient form shown in the middle depicted a large stand for musical instruments, with a base and a top, and a number of hooks for hanging instruments. Because of the intricacy of musical instruments, the meaning extended to "skill" and "job." The kanji 業 means "(hard) work" and "skills (to be able to do complex work)."

じゅぎょう 授業 class instruction	じぎょう 事業 business
こうぎょう 工業 industry	きぎょう 企業 corporation
ごう 業 karma	じごうじとく 自業自得 consequence of own act

| 丶 丷 丷 些 丵 丵 丵 嶰 堂 堂 業 業 | 13 |

222

ON-KUN READINGS:	HEADER:
キョク	尸

局

section;
circumstances;
government agency

ORIGIN: The two forms on the left and the middle are the ancient forms that showed two hooks facing each other with a small square inside, indicating a part or section of a job. The kanji also was used to indicate circumstances, as might occur in a government office. The kanji 局 means "section; circumstances" or "government agency."

ゆうびんきょく 郵便局 post office	じきょく 時局 the situation, war time
けっきょく 結局 in the end	とうきょく 当局 authority
きょくばん 局番 telephone number prefix	たいきょく 大局 general situation

| 𠃌 𠃌 尸 尸 局 局 局 | 7 |

223

ON-KUN READINGS:	HEADER:
キョク・ま(がる)	日

曲

musical tune;
to bend

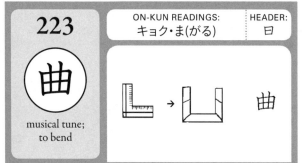

ORIGIN: The ancient form was a pictograph of a ruler that was bent. A musical composition also has a contour, so it came to signify a piece of music. The kanji 曲 means "to bend; a musical tune."

きょく 曲 (music) piece	わいきょく 歪曲 distortion
きょくせん 曲線 curved line	きょくげい 曲芸 stunt
ま 曲がる to bend, to turn	さっきょく 作曲 music composition

| 丨 冂 曱 曲 曲 曲 | 6 |

224

ON-KUN READINGS:	HEADER:
キョク・ゴク・きわ(める)	木

極

extreme;
to culminate

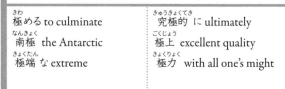

ORIGIN: The left side 木 was a tree, and the right side depicted a person stuck in a narrow space between two lines. A hand 又 on the right was also pushing the person into a small area 口. Together they signified something reaching an extreme. The kanji 極 means "extreme" or "to culminate."

きわ 極める to culminate	きゅうきょくてき 究極的 に ultimately
なんきょく 南極 the Antarctic	ごくじょう 極上 excellent quality
きょくたん 極端 な extreme	きょくりょく 極力 with all one's might

| 一 十 才 木 朽 朽 柯 柯 柯 極 極 極 | 12 |

225

玉
jewel

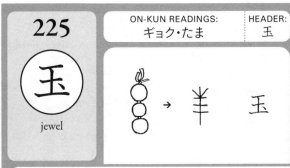

ORIGIN: The ancient form in the middle was a depiction of milky-colored jewels strung together. The kanji 玉 means "jewel." When used as a recurring component, it is written 王, as in 理 "logic" and 球 "ball."

百円玉 hundred-yen coin
玉 ball
玉手箱 a treasure box

玉座 throne
水玉 polka dot
目玉焼き sunny-side up

一 丁 干 王 玉   5

226

勤
to work hard

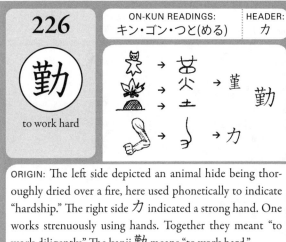

ORIGIN: The left side depicted an animal hide being thoroughly dried over a fire, here used phonetically to indicate "hardship." The right side 力 indicated a strong hand. One works strenuously using hands. Together they meant "to work diligently." The kanji 勤 means "to work hard."

通勤する to commute to work
勤めている to be employed
勤務先 place of employment

勤勉 な diligent
勤労 labor, service
出勤する to attend work

一 十 廿 艹 芇 苗 芹 苩 堇 菫 勤 勤   12

227

均
even; average

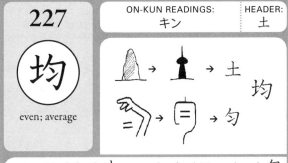

ORIGIN: The left side 土 was a pile of soil. The right side 勹 signified "to surround," and the last two strokes 冫 signified two equal things. Together they indicated even ground, or even. The kanji 均 means "even" or "average."

平均 average
均一 な uniform quality
均質 な uniform quality

均等に evenly
均分 equally divided

一 十 土 圵 圴 均 均   7

228

禁
to forbid

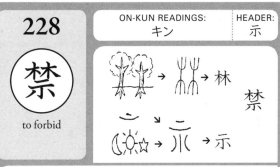

ORIGIN: The top 林 was a forest where gods were believed to live, hence a place that was sacred and forbidden to enter. The bottom 示 consisted of an altar table used in ancestral worship with a moon, sun, and star. Together they indicated "forbidden" by a god. The kanji 禁 means "to forbid."

禁じる to prohibit
禁止 prohibition
禁物 a taboo thing

禁煙 smoking not allowed
厳禁 strictly forbidden
禁句 taboo phrase

一 十 才 才 木 村 材 林 林 梦 梦 禁 禁   13

229

ON-KUN READINGS: キン・すじ

HEADER: 竹

筋

muscle; line; plot; reason

ORIGIN: The top 竹 was bamboo, indicating something wiry or fibrous. The bottom 肋 "limb" came from flesh (月) and muscles in a strong hand (力). A bundle of fiber-like tissues in a body are muscles. What goes throughout a story is a plot. The kanji 筋 means "muscle; line; reason; plot."

きんにく
筋肉 muscle
すじ
筋 muscle, tendon, story
すじがき
筋書き synopsis, outline

すじ　とお
筋の通らない unreasonable
すじちがい
筋違いに diagonally
ちすじ
血筋 blood, lineage

ノ ト ヒ ゲ ゲ 竹 竹 笠 笠 笠 筋 筋　12

230

ON-KUN READINGS: キン

HEADER: 糸

緊

tight

ORIGIN: The top 臣 an "eye staring closely" and 又 "hand" indicated "wise" or something very important. The bottom 糸 was a pictograph of thin silk threads being pulled out of silkworm cocoons. Together they indicated threads tangled tightly. The kanji 緊 means "tight."

きんちょう
緊張 tension
きんきゅうれんらくさき
緊急連絡先 emergency
　　contact
きんぱく
緊迫した strained, tense

きんしゅくざいせい
緊縮財政 tightening
　　finance policy
きんみつ
緊密 extremely close

一 厂 厂 戸 戸 臣 臣 臤 臤 堅 堅 堅 緊 緊 緊　15

231

ON-KUN READINGS: キン・ちか(い)

HEADER: 辶

近

near; close

ORIGIN: The upper right 斤 was a pictograph of an ax. The left bottom 辶, formerly 辵, was the left side of a crossroad and a foot; it signified "to go forward." The kanji 近 signified an ax coming close (to cut.) The kanji 近 means "close; near."

ちか
近い near
きんじょ
近所 neighborhood
さいきん
最近 recently

せっきん
接近する to move in close to
ふきん
付近 vicinity
みぢか
身近な close, familiar

ノ ナ ヂ 斤 沂 沂 近 近　7

232

ON-KUN READINGS: キン・コン・かね・かな

HEADER: 金

金

gold; metal; Friday

ORIGIN: The top part 个 meant "to collect things under a cover." The bottom depicted gold nuggets or other precious metal hidden underground. When used as a part of a kanji, it means "metal." It is also used to indicate Friday in Japanese. The kanji 金 means "gold; metal; Friday."

きんようび
金曜日 Friday
かね
お金 money
きん
金 gold

かねもち
金持 a rich person
ちょきん
貯金する to save money in
　　a bank
かなもの
金物 hardware

ノ 人 今 今 全 全 余 命 金　8

94

233

ON-KUN READINGS: ギン

HEADER: 金

銀
silver

ORIGIN: 金 "metal" had 亼 "to collect things under one cover" and "precious metal hidden in the ground." 艮 depicted an eye and twisted legs, indicating someone turning back to re-examine something. Together they indicated carefully re-examining and picking precious silver from among the metals of lesser value. The kanji 銀 means "silver."

ぎんこう
銀行 bank
ぎん
銀 silver
すいぎん
水銀 mercury

ぎんまく
銀幕 silver screen, movie
screen
ぎんか
銀貨 silver coin
ぎんいろ
銀色 silver-color

ノ ハ ハ 亼 牟 牟 余 金 釘 釘 釘 鉗 鉗 銀　14

234

ON-KUN READINGS: ク・キュウ・ここの(つ)

HEADER: 乙

九
nine

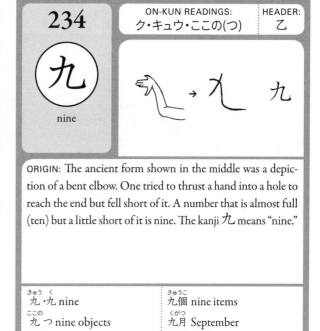

ORIGIN: The ancient form shown in the middle was a depiction of a bent elbow. One tried to thrust a hand into a hole to reach the end but fell short of it. A number that is almost full (ten) but a little short of it is nine. The kanji 九 means "nine."

きゅう く
九・九 nine
ここの
九 つ nine objects
ここのか
九日 nine days, ninth day

きゅうこ
九個 nine items
くがつ
九月 September
じゅっちゅうはっく
十中八九 nine out of ten,
more or less

ノ 九　2

235

ON-KUN READINGS: ク

HEADER: 口

句
phrase

ORIGIN: The ancient form shown in the middle depicted 口 a mouth (words) inside quotation marks, indicating a group of words. The kanji 句 means "phrase."

もんく
文句 complain
はいく
俳句 haiku poem
くとうてん
句読点 punctuation (。and
、)

くてん
句点 period, full stop
せっく
節句 festival
じく
字句 words and phrases

ノ ク 勹 句 句　5

236

ON-KUN READINGS: ク

HEADER: 匸

区
section; ward

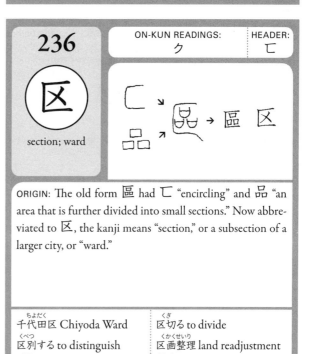

ORIGIN: The old form 區 had 匸 "encircling" and 品 "an area that is further divided into small sections." Now abbreviated to 区, the kanji means "section," or a subsection of a larger city, or "ward."

ちよだく
千代田区 Chiyoda Ward
くべつ
区別する to distinguish
ちく
地区 section of an area

くぎ
区切る to divide
くかくせいり
区画整理 land readjustment
がっく
学区 school district

一 フ ヌ 区　4

95

237

ク・にが(い)・くる(しい) ++

苦
bitter; painful

ORIGIN: The top ++ was a reduced form of 艸 "plants," and the sound of 古 in the bottom was the same as the word "bitter." Together they indicated a plant that tastes bitter. The kanji 苦 means "bitter; painful."

苦労 hardship
苦しい hard, painful
苦い bitter

苦心する to take pains
苦手な is weak in
苦笑い forced smile

一 十 艹 艹 井 芋 苦 苦 苦   8

238

グ・そな(わる) 八

具
to equip; tool; equipment; filling

ORIGIN: The top 目 came from a round pot containing food in a religious rite; the bottom showed two hands holding the pot. Together they indicated "to offer something with both hands" and, further, "to provide." It also is used for what is inside the pot, or filling. The kanji 具 means "to equip" or "equipment; tool."

道具 tool
具体的に concretely
具 filling (in food)

金具 hardware
器具 appliance
具象画 representational painting

一 几 日 日 目 目 具 具   8

239

クウ・から・そら・あ(く) 穴

空
sky; empty

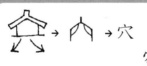

ORIGIN: The top 穴 "hole" indicated "open space under a roof" and the bottom 工 "craft" came from a depiction of two boards pieced together skillfully. When you pierce a board, the piercing leaves a hole, an empty space. A sky is an empty space. The kanji 空 means "sky" or "empty."

空 sky
空港 airport
空手 naked fist, karate

空く to become vacant
空 empty
空前 unprecedented

' ' 宀 宀 空 空 空 空   8

240

クン・きみ 口

君
lord; suffix for male name

ORIGIN: The top 尹 depicted a hand balancing a long bar that connected heaven and the earth, which signified ruling. A person who rules with words, 口 "mouth," is a lord. The kanji 君 means "lord." The term is also used in addressing a male person who is one's peer or junior.

石田君 Mr. Ishida
君 you
君主 head of a state

主君 master
君が代 Kimigayo, Japanese national anthem
君臨する to reign over

フ ヲ ヲ 尹 尹 君 君   7

96

241

ON-KUN READINGS: クン

HEADER: 言

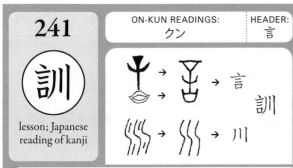

訓

lesson; Japanese reading of kanji

ORIGIN: The ancient form had 言 "to speak clearly and sharply" and 川 "river (flowing water)." Together the combined form indicated "to explain difficult matters with ease; to teach." When kanji was introduced to Japan, its Japanese meaning was kept as kun sound for kanji. The kanji 訓 means "lesson" or "Japanese meaning (reading) of kanji."

きょうくん
教訓 teachings, lesson
くんれん
訓練 training
かくん
家訓 family precept

おんくん
音訓 Chinese and Japanese sounds of kanji
くんどく
訓読 Japanese reading of kanji
くんわ
訓話 instructive lesson, moral

丶 亠 亠 言 言 言 訓 訓 訓   10

242

ON-KUN READINGS: グン・む(れる)・むら(がる)

HEADER: 羊

群

group; throng; herd

ORIGIN: The left side 君 "lord" consisted of 尹 "a hand balancing a long bar that connected heaven and the earth," which signified "to govern," and words 口. The right side 羊 was a sheep. Sheep stay in a herd. Together the forms indicated a group of animals or people. The kanji 群 means "group; throng" or "herd."

む
群れ herd
ぐんしゅう
群衆 crowd
たいぐん
大群 large herd

むら
群がる to crowd
ぐんとう
群島 archipelago
ぐんらく
群落 colony

コ ヨ ヨ 尹 尹 君 君 君 君' 群 群 群 群   13

243

ON-KUN READINGS: グン・いくさ

HEADER: 車

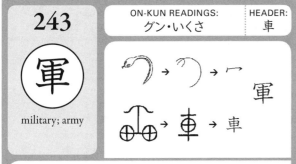

軍

military; army

ORIGIN: The top 冖 came from a depiction of a round serpent, indicating "to surround." Underneath, 車 was a part of a two-wheeled chariot viewed from above, and signifying vehicles. In a battle, the soldiers circled around military vehicles. The combined form indicated "military." The kanji 軍 means "army; military."

ぐんたい
軍隊 an armed forces, military
かいぐん
海軍 navy
ぐんじん
軍人 military personnel

りくぐん
陸軍 army
ぐんばい
軍配 an umpire's fan in sumo
ぐんぷく
軍服 military uniform

丶 冖 冖 冖 冒 冒 宣 宣 軍   9

244

ON-KUN READINGS: グン・こおり

HEADER: 阝

郡

district; county

ORIGIN: The left 君 "lord" consisted of 尹 "a hand balancing a long bar that connected heaven and the earth," which signified "to govern" and words 口. The old form 邑 of the right side, now 阝, consisted of an area where people gather, signifying a village. The kanji 郡 means "district" or "county."

ぐん
郡 county
ぐんし
郡市 county and city
ぐんけんせいど
郡県制度 county-prefecture system

コ ヨ ヨ 尹 尹 君 君 君' 君阝 郡   10

97

245

involvement;
person in charge;
relationship

ON-KUN READINGS:
ケイ・かか(わる)

HEADER:
イ

ORIGIN: The ancient form had イ "person" and 系 "thread" with an additional stroke at the top. The additional stroke signified that the threads were connecting to other threads or to people. Together they signified a relationship, or a person's involvement. The kanji 係 means "involvement," "person in charge," or "relationship."

係り person in charge
かんけい
関係 relationship
かか
係わる to be involved

うけつけがかり
受付係 receptionist
かかりいん
係員 person in charge
けいそう
係争 dispute

ノ イ 亻 亻 仵 俘 係 係 係   9

246

兄

older brother;
male elder

ON-KUN READINGS:
ケイ・キョウ・あに

HEADER:
儿

ORIGIN: In the ancient form shown in the middle the top part 口 signified a mouth (associated with speaking), or a large head. The bottom part 儿 was a man or older male child crouching in prayer. The kanji 兄 means "older brother" or a "male elder person."

あに
兄 older brother
にい
お兄さん older brother
きょうだい
兄弟 brothers, siblings

ふけい
父兄 parents (of students)
ちょうけい
長兄 oldest brother
じっけい
実兄 one's own older brother

丨 口 口 尸 兄   5

247

型

mold; pattern

ON-KUN READINGS:
ケイ・かた

HEADER:
土

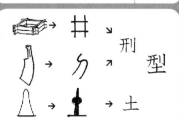

ORIGIN: The top 刑 consisted of a "well" or a "square shape" and "sword." The bottom was a mound of dirt. Together they indicated a mold or pattern to put dirt in. The kanji 型 means "mold; pattern."

かた
型 form, pattern
ぶんけい
文型 sentence pattern
かた
型にはまった grooved

かた と
型を取る to make a mold
おおがた
大型 large-scale
しんがた
新型 new model

一 二 テ 开 刑 刑 型 型 型   9

248

形

shape

ON-KUN READINGS:
ケイ・ギョウ・かたち・かた

HEADER:
彡

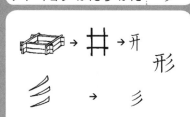

ORIGIN: The left side came from a square 井 (the shape of a well frame), and the right side 彡 signified "beautiful design." Together they indicated a frame that has various shapes. The kanji 形 means "shape."

かたち
形 shape
さんかっけい
三角形 triangle
にんぎょう
人形 doll

ぎょうそう
形相 facial expression
かたみ
形見 memento
ちけい
地形 topography

一 二 テ 开 形 形 形   7

249

ON-KUN READINGS: ケイ

HEADER: 彳

径

narrow, straight path

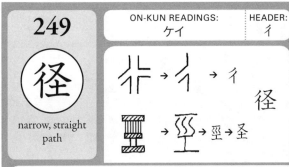

ORIGIN: The old form had 彳, the left half of a crossroad, signifying "to go," and 巛 "the warp on a loom that runs from the top to the ground 土." Together they indicated a narrow, straight path. Now 巛 has been replaced by 又. The kanji 径 means "narrow, straight path."

ちょっけい
直径 diameter
はんけい
半径 radius
こうけい
口径 caliber (of a firearm)

しょうけい
小径 a lane, path

ノ ク 彳 彳 彳 径 径 径　8

250

ON-KUN READINGS: ケイ・うやま(う)

HEADER: 攵

敬

to respect; to revere

ORIGIN: The left side depicted a person wearing a sheep's head bending low to show humility. (The sheep's head could have been used in a religious rite in which sheep were offered.) The right side 攵 depicted a hand moving a stick, signifying an action in general. The combined form indicated "to act humbly." The kanji 敬 means "to respect; to revere."

うやま
敬う to respect
けいご
敬語 polite expression
そんけい
尊敬 respect
けいれい
敬礼 salutation

けいい　　　あらわ
敬意を表す to express a respect
しっけい
失敬する to be impolite, to steal

一 艹 艹 艹 艻 芍 苟 苟 荀 苟 苟 苟 敬　12

251

ON-KUN READINGS: ケイ・ケ

HEADER: 日

景

fine view; scene

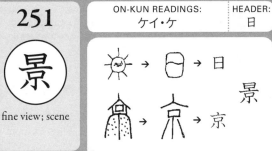

ORIGIN: The top 日 was a pictograph of "sun," and the bottom 京 came from a depiction of a house on a sunny hilltop. Together they indicated a scene in which an object was clearly seen under a bright sun. The meaning evolved to "view." The kanji 景 means "fine view" or "scene."

けしき
景色 scenery
ふうけい
風景 scenery
はいけい
背景 background

けいき
景気 business conditions, liveliness
けいひん
景品 premium, a giveaway
やけい
夜景 night scenery

丨 冂 日 日 日 昌 早 呆 景 景 景 景　12

252

ON-KUN READINGS: ケイ

HEADER: 糸

系

lineage; system

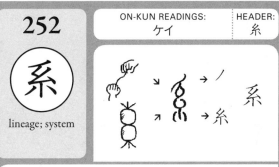

ORIGIN: In the ancient form shown the second from the left the first stroke signified an act of putting two skeins of thread together by a hand, making one continuous, long thread. It signified things tied together continuously, and it came to mean one's family lineage. It also means "system." The kanji 系 means "lineage."

にっけいじん
日系人 person of Japanese descent
けい
ブルー系 blue shade
けいとう
系統 lineage, system

ちょっけい
直系 direct descendant
たいけい
体系 outline, system
たいようけい
太陽系 the solar system

一 ノ 至 玄 系 系 系　7

99

253

ON-KUN READINGS: ケイ・キョウ・へ(る)・た(つ)

HEADER: 糸

経

to go straight; longitude; teaching of Buddha

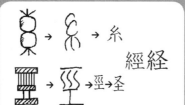

ORIGIN: The old form 經 had 糸 "threads" and 巛 "the warp on a loom" in which threads run from the top to the ground 土. Together they indicated "to pass or go straight." It also means the teaching of Buddha. Now 巛 is simplified to 又. The kanji 経 means "to go straight; to pass through," or "teaching of Buddha; longitude."

けいけん 経験 experience	きょう お経 Buddhist sutra
けいざい 経済 economy	へ 経る to elapse, to pass
けいれき 経歴 (personal) history	にっけいへいきん 日経平均 Nikkei index

く ㄥ ㄠ ㄠ 糸 糸 紀 約 経 経 経   11

254

ON-KUN READINGS: ケイ・はか(る)

HEADER: 言

計

to measure; to count

ORIGIN: The left side 言 consisted of a needle and a mouth, which indicated "to say words clearly and sharply," or "to say," or "word." The right side 十 signified a bundle of ten. One counts aloud by tens. The kanji 計 means "to measure; to count."

とけい 時計 clock, watch	けいさん 計算 calculation
けいかく 計画 plan	ごうけい 合計 sum
かいけい 会計 accounting	せいけい 生計 livelihood

丶 ㆍ ㆍ 言 言 言 言 計   9

255

ON-KUN READINGS: ケイ

HEADER: 言

警

to alarm; to warn

ORIGIN: The top, 敬 "respect," consisted of a person with a sheep's head, humbly bending low, and 攵 a hand holding a stick, which signifies an action in general, and was used phonetically. The bottom 言 indicates "word." Together the kanji 警 means "to alarm; to warn."

けいさつ 警察 police	けいび 警備 security, guard
けいほう 警報 alarm	けいかい 警戒 precaution
けいこく 警告 warning notice	けいかんたい 警官隊 police force

一 十 艹 艹 芍 芍 荀 荀 荀 荀 敬 敬 敬 警 警 警 警 警   19

256

ON-KUN READINGS: ケイ・かる(い)・かろ(やか)

HEADER: 車

軽

light

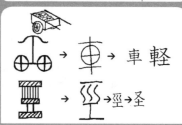

ORIGIN: The old form 輕 had a cart 車 on the left, and 巛 "the warp" on a loom that runs from the top to the ground 土, signifying "something going vertically." Together they meant a lightly armored chariot. Now somewhat simplified, the kanji 軽 means "light."

かる 軽い light	けいりょう 軽量 lightweight
かるがる 軽々と easily	かろ 軽やか airy
かるがる 軽々しく imprudently	けいそつ 軽率な careless

一 ㇆ 厅 币 百 亘 車 車 軒 軽 軽 軽   12

257

芸

art; skill

ORIGIN: In the old form 藝 the top was two plants; in the middle the plant is tended by someone carefully with two hands; and the bottom depicted something pushing upward. Together they indicated a person tending a plant. The current form is reduced to the top and the bottom. The kanji 芸 means "art; skill."

芸 art, skill
芸術 fine arts
手芸 handcrafting

園芸 horticultural
芸能人 show business people, entertainers
工芸 industrial craft

一十艹艹艹芸芸芸　7

258

迎

to welcome

ORIGIN: The right top depicted two people bowing to each other. The bottom ⻌, formerly 辵, was the left side of a crossroad and a foot, which signified "to go forward." Combined, they indicated the act of welcoming someone. The kanji 迎 means "to welcome."

歓迎 welcome
送迎バス shuttle bus
迎えに行く to go to pick up someone

出迎え coming out to welcome
迎合する to chime in with
迎春 Happy New Year

' ⺀ 4 印 印 迎 迎　7

101

259

劇

a drama; intensely

ORIGIN: The ancient form consisted of two animals, 虍 "tiger" and 豕 "pig" placed vertically, and 刂 "sword." Actors who wear an animal head act strenuously. It indicated that one does something intensely or acts in a militant swordplay. The kanji 劇 means "drama" or "intensely." (Many depictions were drawn vertically because of a narrow bamboo tablet.)

劇 play
劇場 theater
劇薬 powerful medicine; violent poison

劇的な dramatic
悲劇的な tragedic
歌劇 opera

' ⼘ ⼘ 广 声 声 声 虍 虏 虏 虏 豦 豦 劇　15

260

激

intense; agitated; violent

ORIGIN: The left side 氵 was water and the right side depicted that something white 白 was thrown to the four winds 方 by hand 攵. Splashing water signified something being agitated or violently thrown. The kanji 激 means "intense; agitated; violent."

激しい violent
感激 deeply touched
過激な extreme

激励する to encourage, to cheer up
激安 extremely cheap
激戦 fierce fight

' ⺀ 氵 氵 氵 沪 沪 沪 渹 渹 湧 激 激　16

261

ON-KUN READINGS: ケツ・か(ける)

HEADER: 欠

欠 to lack

ORIGIN: The ancient form depicted a person crouching with a mouth wide open, gasping for air (due to lack of oxygen), or exhaling (after which one lacks air). The kanji 欠 means "to lack."

けっせき 欠席 absent	けってん 欠点 weak point
か 欠けている to be chipped	ほけつ 補欠 an alternate, filling a vacancy
か 欠く to miss, to lack, to be short of	けついん 欠員 opening for position

ノ ケ ケ 欠   4

262

ON-KUN READINGS: ケツ・き(める)

HEADER: 氵

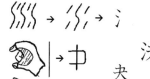

決 to decide; to do decisively

ORIGIN: The ancient form had 氵 "water" and 夬 "archer's glove" and "hand." (It protects the area between the thumb and the finger, where the archer holds a notched arrow.) When the archer decides to release the arrow, it flows like water. When a deadlock is broken, a decision is made rapidly. The kanji 決 means "to do decisively; to decide."

き 決める to decide	かいけつ 解決 solution
けってい 決定する to decide	たいけつ 対決 confrontation
けっしん 決心する to decide one's mind	けつい 決意 determination

ヽ ヽ 氵 氵 江 決 決   7

263

ON-KUN READINGS: ケツ・いさぎよ(い)

HEADER: 氵

潔 pure; brave

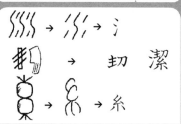

ORIGIN: The left side 氵 was water. On the right side the top indicated engraving with a knife; and the bottom 糸 was thread, which was used phonetically to signify "to mark up clearly." Together they indicated to cleanse or purify with water. The kanji 潔 means "pure; brave."

いさぎよ 潔い gallant, heroic	じゅんけつ 純潔 pure
せいけつ 清潔 cleanliness, hygiene	ふけつ 不潔 unsanitary
けっぱく 潔白 innocent	せいれんけっぱく 清廉潔白 integrity

ヽ ヽ 氵 氵 汢 洁 清 津 潔 潔 潔 潔 潔   15

264

ON-KUN READINGS: ケツ・あな

HEADER: 穴

穴 hole

ORIGIN: The top 宀 was a house and 八 underneath signified dividing something into two, or digging the ground or a wall to make a hole. Together they indicated digging a hole to make a dwelling. The kanji 穴 means "hole."

あな 穴 hole	あなば 穴場 good place known to a few people
あな ほら穴 cave	ほけつ ほ 墓穴を掘る to dig one's own grave
あなう 穴埋めする to cover a deficiency	

ヽ ハ 宀 宀 穴   5

102

265

ON-KUN READINGS: ケツ・むす(ぶ)・ゆ(う)

HEADER: 糸

結

to tie; to end

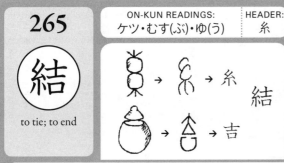

ORIGIN: The left side 糸 was a pictograph of thin silk filaments being pulled out of silkworm cocoons. The right side 吉 depicted a jar with a tight lid. Together they meant binding a jar tightly with thread. The kanji 結 means "to tie" or "to end."

けっこん
結婚 marriage
けつろん
結論 conclusion
けっか
結果 result

むす
結ぶ to tie
かみ ゆ
髪を結う to fix hair
ゆいのう
結納 betrothal gift

く 纟 纟 纟 糸 糸 糸 糸 結 結 結 結   12

266

ON-KUN READINGS: ケツ・ち

HEADER: 血

血

blood

ORIGIN: The ancient form (the second and the third forms) depicted a bowl of animal blood as an offering in a religious rite. The first stroke in the current form emphasized the contents rather than the container. The kanji 血 means "blood." (In contrast, the kanji 皿 means "plate.")

ち
血 blood
はなち
鼻血 nose bleeding
しゅっけつ
出血 bleeding

けつえき
血液 blood
けつえんかんけい
血縁関係 blood
  relationship
けっきさか
血気盛んな hot-blooded

ノ イ 白 血 血 血   6

267

ON-KUN READINGS: ゲツ・ガツ・つき

HEADER: 月

月

moon; month;
Monday

ORIGIN: The ancient form was the shape of a crescent moon. The kanji 月 means "moon; month." The kanji 月 is also used to indicate Monday in Japanese.

げつようび
月曜日 Monday
つき
月 month
にがつ
二月 February

さんかげつ
三ヶ月 for three months
まいつき
毎月 every month
つきぎ
月決め monthly

丿 几 月 月   4

268

ON-KUN READINGS: ケン

HEADER: イ

件

case; matter

ORIGIN: The left side イ was a person, and the right side 牛 depicted a cow's head. A cow was sometimes used to signify all things and matters, as used in the left side of the kanji 物 "thing; stuff." Together they indicated a person counting cows in a herd or counting cases. The kanji 件 means "case; matter."

けん
その件 the matter being
  discussed
じけん
事件 incident
じょうけん
条件 condition

あんけん
案件 matter, case
けんすう
件数 number of cases
じんけんひ
人件費 personal
  expenditures

ノ イ イ 仁 仁 件   6

103

269

ON-KUN READINGS: ケン・すこ(やか)

HEADER: イ

健

healthy

ORIGIN: The left side イ was a person. The right side 聿 depicted a hand holding a brush straight up to write. The lower left 廴 was the bottom half of a crossroad with one end extended, indicating "to extend." Together they indicated a healthy person standing straight. The kanji 健 means "healthy."

けんこう
健康 health
すこ
健やかに in good health
ほけんじょ
保健所 public heath office

けんぜん
健全 な wholesome
けんきゃく
健脚 good walker
けんざい
健在 する to be well

ノ イ 忄 忄 仱 仴 佇 侓 律 倠 健 健

11

270

ON-KUN READINGS: ケン・か(ねる)

HEADER: 八

兼

to do two things
at one time;
concurrent

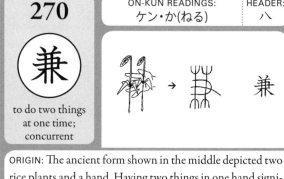

ORIGIN: The ancient form shown in the middle depicted two rice plants and a hand. Having two things in one hand signified "to do two things concurrently." The kanji 兼 means "to do two things at one time," or "concurrent."

か
兼ねる to double as
けんよう
兼用 serve both purposes
か
し兼ねる cannot, be hard to do

けんむ
兼務 additional post
きが
気兼ね constraint, difference
さいしょくけんび
才色兼備 having wit and
beauty

丶 丷 亼 半 当 当 単 兼 兼 兼

10

271

ON-KUN READINGS: ケン

HEADER: 刀

券

ticket

ORIGIN: The old form 劵 had three hands together (an open palm and two holding something upward), with 刀 "sword; knife" to make notches. Together they indicated a notched tally for a pledge or contract in business. Such a tally allowed one to pass into a meeting or membership. The kanji 券 means "ticket."

じょうしゃけん
乗車券 passenger ticket
けん
券 ticket
にゅうじょうけん
入場券 admission ticket

こうくうけん
航空券 airline ticket
しょうひんけん
商品券 gift certificate
りょけん
旅券 passport

丶 丷 丷 半 半 券 券 券

8

272

ON-KUN READINGS: ケン・つるぎ

HEADER: リ

剣

sword

ORIGIN: The old form on the left side 僉 depicted two goods and two people under a cover (亼), signifying that many things and people were gathered in one place. Here it was phonetically used to indicate "pointed." The right side リ is a variant of 刀 "sword." The kanji 剣 means "sword."

けん
剣 sword
しんけん
真剣 な earnest; serious
つるぎ
剣 sword

けんどう
剣道 Japanese
swordsmanship
けんじゅつ
剣術 swordsmanship
たんけん
短剣 dagger

ノ 𠆢 𠆢 亽 合 合 刍 刍 剣 剣

10

104

273

ON-KUN READINGS: ケン・コン・た(てる) | HEADER: 廴

建

to erect a building

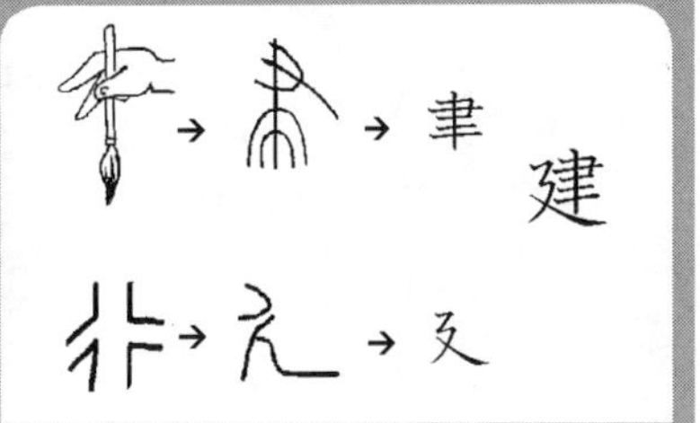

ORIGIN: The upper right 聿 depicted a hand holding a writing brush straight up, which signified "straight up." The lower bottom part 廴 comes from the lower half of a crossroad, which is stretching, signifying "to extend." Together the kanji 建 means "to erect a building."

建物（たてもの） building	建築（けんちく） architecture
建てる（た） to build	再建（さいけん） rebuilding
二階建て（にかいだ） two-story house	建立（こんりゅう） する to raise a temple

建 9

274

ON-KUN READINGS: ケン | HEADER: 心

憲

constitution; important law

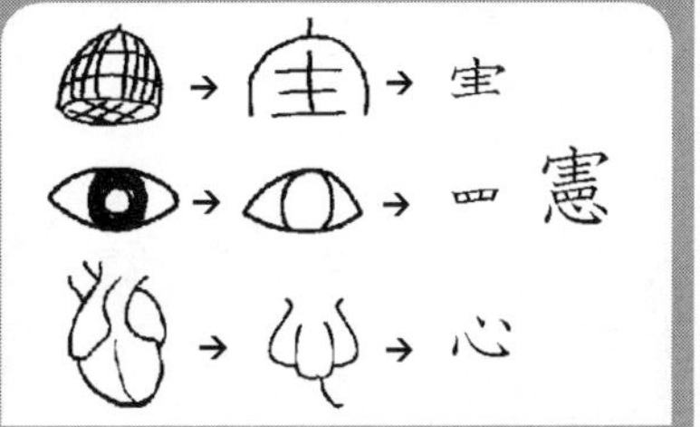

ORIGIN: The ancient form consisted of a basket covering an eye 罒, and a mind 心 at the bottom. Putting a cover over one's eyes signified something with power to restrain oneself from committing a bad action. A heart indicates that one is mindful of abiding an important law, such as a constitution. The kanji 憲 means "constitution; important law."

憲法（けんぽう） constitution	憲兵（けんぺい） military police (MP)
立憲（りっけん） constitutionalism	違憲（いけん） unconstitutional
憲法違反（けんぽういはん） breach of the constitution	官憲（かんけん） police authority

憲 16

275

ON-KUN READINGS: ケン | HEADER: 木

検

to examine; to inspect

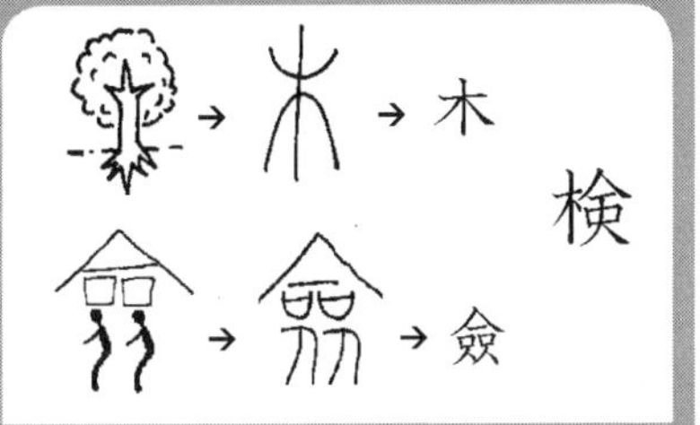

ORIGIN: The left side 木 was "wood." The old form 僉 on the right side depicted two goods and two people under a cover (亼), signifying that many things and people are gathered in one place. Officials checked the wood tallies used as records of goods. The kanji 検 means "to examine; to inspect."

検査（けんさ） inspection	検診（けんしん） physical checkup
検定試験（けんていしけん） license examination	検察官（けんさつかん） prosecutor
検疫（けんえき） quarantine	検眼（けんがん） eye exam

一 十 才 木 検 12

276

ON-KUN READINGS: ケン・ゴン | HEADER: 木

権

right; power; authority

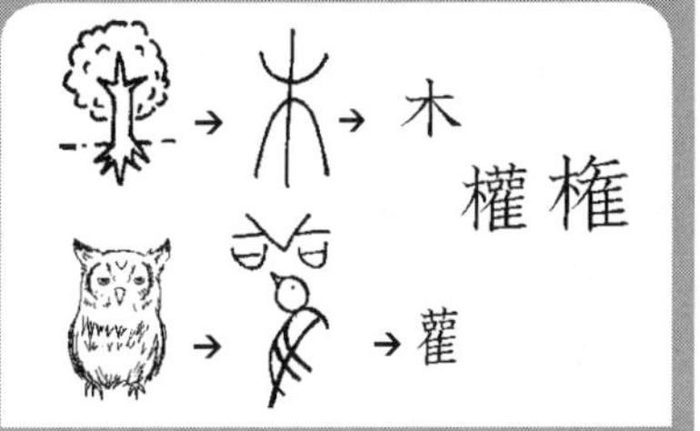

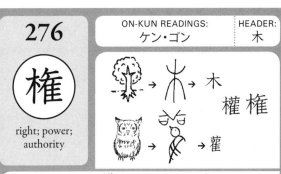

ORIGIN: The old form 權 consisted of wood 木 and a crested bird, here only used phonetically, to indicate "scale" or "to weigh to see a balance." Weighing was done by an authority. The kanji 権 means "right; power; authority."

権利（けんり） right	投票権（とうひょうけん） voting right
実権（じっけん） real power	権力（けんりょく） power
人権（じんけん） human right	市民権（しみんけん） citizenship

一 十 才 木 権 15

277

ON-KUN READINGS: ケン・いぬ

HEADER: 犬

犬
dog

ORIGIN: The ancient form was a depiction of a dog standing on its hind legs barking. The kanji 犬 means "dog." When used as a recurring component it is written 犭 to signify animals in general, as in 狩 "to hunt" and 狭 "narrow" (like an animal trail).

犬 dog
あきたけん
秋田犬 Akita breed
ばんけん
番犬 watchdog

いぬごや
犬小屋 dog house; kennel
けんえん　なか
犬猿の仲 hate each other
いぬじ
犬死にする to die in vain

一 ナ 大 犬　　　　4

278

ON-KUN READINGS: ケン・と(ぐ)

HEADER: 石

研
to hone;
to sharpen by
grinding

ORIGIN: The left side 石 signified rocks or stones under a cliff. The right side originally had two sticks of equal length. Together they indicated using stones to grind the sticks to an equal length, or "to hone or refine." The kanji 研 means "to hone; to sharpen by grinding."

けんきゅう
研究 research
と
研ぐ to sharpen (knife)
けんきゅうしょ
研究所 research institute

けんきゅうしつ
研究室 research lab,
professor's office

一 丁 丆 石 石 石 研 研　　　　9

279

ON-KUN READINGS: ケン・きぬ

HEADER: 糸

絹
silk

ORIGIN: The left side 糸 was a pictograph of thin silk threads being pulled out of silkworm cocoons. The right side 口 had a round worm or silkworm, and 月 signified flesh. Together they indicated the thread that a silkworm produced. The kanji 絹 means "silk."

きぬ
絹 silk
きぬどうふ
絹豆腐 fine-textured tofu
きぬじ
絹地 silk cloth

じんけん
人絹 rayon, artificial silk

く 幺 幺 幺 弁 糸 糸 紀 約 絹 絹 絹 絹　　　　13

280

ON-KUN READINGS: ケン

HEADER: 目

県
jurisdiction under a
national government;
prefecture

ORIGIN: The left side of the old form had a head hanging upside down for execution. The right side 系 indicated a continuous line, or rope. Together they signified an official in a large jurisdiction who had enough authority to execute a criminal. Now abbreviated, the kanji 県 means "prefecture; jurisdiction under a national government."

けん
県 prefecture
かながわけん
神奈川県 Kanagawa
　Prefecture
けんかい
県会 prefectural assembly

けんみん
県民 residents of a prefecture

一 П Ħ Ħ 目 但 県 県 県　　　　9

106

281

ON-KUN READINGS: ケン・み(る)

HEADER: 見

見

to see; watch; look

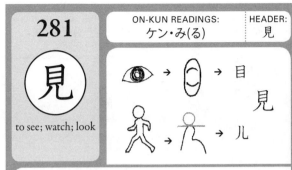

ORIGIN: The top part 目 depicted an eye, and the bottom 儿 depicted a person standing, or one's legs. Together they indicated a person looking at something. The kanji 見 means "to see; look; watch."

見る to see, to look at
発見する to discover
見物客 spectator

拝見する [humble] to view
見当がつく to have a rough idea of
見本 sample

丨 冂 冂 目 目 目 見   7

282

ON-KUN READINGS: ケン・けわ(しい)

HEADER: 阝

険

danger

ORIGIN: The left side 阝 signified dirt raised high, or terrain. The old form 僉 of the right side was used phonetically. Together they indicated mountainous terrain, which is dangerous. The kanji 険 means "danger."

危険 danger
険しい steep
保険 insurance

険悪な critical, gloomy
冒険 adventure
陰険な underhand, crafty

' 了 阝 阝' 阝ヘ 阝ヘ 阝合 阝合 険 険   11

283

ON-KUN READINGS: ケン・ゲン

HEADER: 馬

験

to examine

ORIGIN: The old form 驗 had 馬 "horse," and 僉, which had 亼 "gathering goods in one place" and 从 "many people." People gathered horses to examine and grade them. Now reduced a little, the kanji 験 means "to examine."

経験 experience
体験 personal experience
試験 examination

実験 experiment
受験生 person taking the exam, applicant
修験者 an ascetic

丨 厂 厂 匚 馬 馬 馬 馬 馬 馬 駖 駖 駖 駖 験 験   18

284

ON-KUN READINGS: ゲン・ガン・もと

HEADER: 儿

元

origin; source

ORIGIN: The ancient form depicted a person in motion; the head was enlarged for emphasis. The head is the most important part of a body or a place from which many things start. The kanji 元 means "head; origin; source."

元気 cheerful, healthy
元 formerly, origin
お中元 mid-year gift

元日 January first
紀元2007年 2007 A.D.
元手 funds

一 二 テ 元   4

107

285

ON-KUN READINGS: ゲン・はら

HEADER: 厂

原

field; meadow; original; source

ORIGIN: The top 厂 indicated a cliff. The part underneath came from 泉, a fountain. Together they depicted a fountain of water running from a cliff. It indicated a place or "field" from which water springs, and further, "its source." The kanji 原 means "field; meadow" or "source; original."

のはら
野原 field
げんいん
原因 cause
げんしりょく
原子力 atomic power

げんばく
原爆 atomic bomb
げんご
原語 original language
げんゆ
原油 crude oil

一 厂 厂 厂 匠 盾 盾 原 原 原   10

286

ON-KUN READINGS: ゲン・ゴン・おごそ(か)・きび(しい)

HEADER: ⺌

厳

strict; solemn

ORIGIN: The ancient form had three mouths 口 (used phonetically) and cliff 厂. Underneath, 敢 was a kanji that signified two hands grabbing hair and was used phonetically to indicate "hole." Together they originally meant "large boulder," but a new kanji 巌 was developed that meant "boulder" and the kanji 厳 came to be used to mean "strict; solemn."

きび
厳しい strict, difficult
げんかく
厳格な stringent
いげん
威厳 dignity

おごそ
厳かな solemn
げんじゅう
厳重に strictly, sternly
げんぷ
厳父 strict father

丶 丶 丷 丷 ⺍ 严 严 严 严 严 䓔 厳 厳 厳 厳 厳 厳   17

287

ON-KUN READINGS: ゲン・へ(る)

HEADER: 氵

減

to reduce

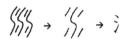
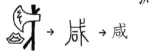

ORIGIN: The left 氵 is "water" and the right had 咸, which consisted of "halberd or weapon" and "mouth"; combined, they indicated "shutting someone's mouth up with a threat of a weapon." Throwing water on that threat could have been viewed as reducing the effect. The kanji 減 means "to reduce."

へ
減る to reduce
げんしょう
減少 reduction
かげん
加減する to make allowances for, to adjust

あじかげん
味加減 taste
めべ
目減り incremental loss (in weight)
はんげん
半減 reduced to half

丶 丶 氵 氵 氵 沪 沪 沪 沪 減 減 減   12

288

ON-KUN READINGS: ゲン・みなもと

HEADER: 氵

源

source; origin

ORIGIN: The left side 氵 was water. The right side 原 depicted a water fountain from which water ran from, signifying "source" of water. The kanji is now used to indicate source of many various things. The kanji 源 means "source; origin."

みなもと
源 source, origin
しげん
資源 natural resources
でんげん
電源 electric outlet

すいげん
水源 riverbed
ごげん
語源 origin of a word
こんげんてき
根源的 fundamental

丶 丶 氵 氵 沪 沪 沪 沪 沪 源 源 源 源   13

289

ON-KUN READINGS: ゲン・あらわ（れる）

HEADER: 王

現

to appear

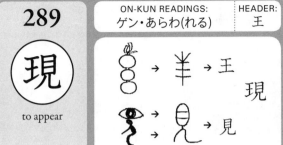

ORIGIN: The left side 王 was jewels strung together. The right side 見 had an eye and a person bent a little, signifying "to see." Combined, they indicated jewelry, such as a necklace, becoming visible, and "to become visible; appear" in general. The kanji 現 means "to appear."

げんざい
現在 at the moment, presently
あらわ
現れる to emerge
げんじつてき
現実的 realistic

しゅつげん
出現 emergence
げんだい
現代 modern times
げんきん
現金 cash

一 T 千 王 刋 珇 珇 珇 珇 現 現　　11

290

ON-KUN READINGS: ゲン・ゴン・い（う）・こと

HEADER: 言

言

words; to say

ORIGIN: The top "tattooing needle with a handle" was used for religious ceremonies and punishment of criminals, and signified "sharp." With the bottom 口 "mouth" the kanji indicated "to speak clearly." The kanji 言 means "words" or "to say." When used as a recurring component, it pertains to language, as in 話 "talk" and 語 "word."

ことば
言葉 words
い
言う to say, to speak
ひとこと
一言 a few words

げんご
言語 language
でんごん
伝言 message
はつげん
発言する to speak out

、 亠 亠 言 言 言 言　　7

291

ON-KUN READINGS: ゲン・かぎ（る）

HEADER: 阝

限

to limit

ORIGIN: The left side 阝 signified an earthen wall surrounding the house, or "boundary." The right side 艮 was an eye with halted legs, signifying the inability to move forward. Together they indicated marking of a boundary, or limit. The kanji 限 means "to limit."

かぎ
Xとは限らない not necessarily X
じょうげん
上限 upper limit
げんど
限度 limit

げんかい
限界 boundary, bounds, limits
せいげん
制限 restriction
げんてい
限定 limited

' 了 阝 阝 阝 阝 阝 限 限 限　　9

292

ON-KUN READINGS: コ

HEADER: イ

個

individual; general counter

ORIGIN: The left side イ was a person. The right side 固 had 囗 "an enclosure," and 古 "old," which came from a hard skull. Together they indicated a single solid object. The kanji 個 means "individual." It is also used as a general counter for objects.

さんこ
三個 three items
こじん
個人 individual
こべつ
個別に individually separately

ここ
個々に individually
こせい
個性 personal character
こてん
個展 one-man exhibit

ノ イ イ 们 们 们 個 個 個 個　　10

109

293

ON-KUN READINGS: コ・ふる(い)・いにしえ

HEADER: ロ

古

old (thing)

ORIGIN: One view of this kanji is that it was a skull-like mask that represented ancestral gods. Another view is that it was a depiction of an old skull whose pronunciation was the same as that of a word meaning "old." The kanji 古 means "old (thing)."

古い old
こだい
古代 the ancient times
ちゅうこ
中古 secondhand

古都 old
こてん
古典 classics
ここん
古今 now and the past

一十十古古　5

294

ON-KUN READINGS: コ・よ(ぶ)

HEADER: ロ

呼

to call out; to exhale

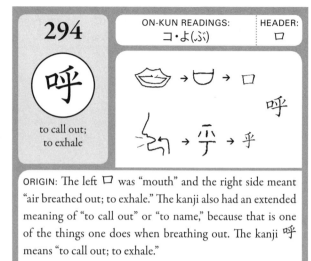

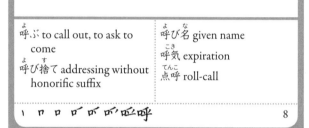

ORIGIN: The left 口 was "mouth" and the right side meant "air breathed out; to exhale." The kanji also had an extended meaning of "to call out" or "to name," because that is one of the things one does when breathing out. The kanji 呼 means "to call out; to exhale."

よ
呼ぶ to call out, to ask to come
よ　す
呼び捨て addressing without honorific suffix

よ　な
呼び名 given name
こき
呼気 expiration
てんこ
点呼 roll-call

ー ㇉ 口 口' 叮 虴 虴 呼　8

295

ON-KUN READINGS: コ・かた(い)

HEADER: 口

固

solid; firm

ORIGIN: Inside 口 "enclosure" was 古, which phonetically signified "hard; firm." It indicated a fortress wall serving as protection, or something hard. The kanji 固 means "solid; firm."

かた
固い hard
こたい
固体 solid body
がんこ
頑固な stubborn

けんご
堅固な steady, firm
こてい
固定する to fix
こじ
固辞する to decline firmly

｜ ㄇ ㄇ 円 円 固 固 固　8

296

ON-KUN READINGS: コ・キ・おのれ

HEADER: 己

己

self

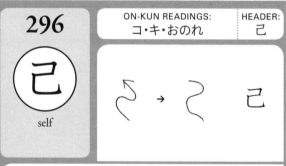

ORIGIN: The ancient form depicted the moment at which a crooked rope or a serpent became straight, or the moment at which a person with slouching posture straightened up. The consciousness of those acts leads to awareness of oneself. The kanji 己 means "self."

じこ
自己 self
りこてき
利己的 selfish, self-centered
ちき
知己 intimate friend

じこりゅう
自己流 one's own style
こっきしん
克己心 spirit of self-control

㇀ コ 己　3

297

庫

warehouse; storage

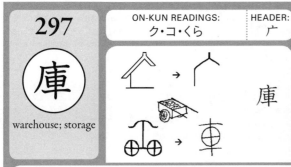

ORIGIN: The top 广 was a pictograph of a house whose one side does not have a wall. 車 was a pictograph of a long-shafted, two-wheeled chariot viewed from above. It indicated a place where vehicles and armor were kept, a warehouse, or a storage area. The kanji 庫 means "warehouse; storage."

車庫 car garage
文庫本 paperback book
倉庫 warehouse

在庫 stockpile
在庫切れ out of stock
金庫 a safe

、一广广广庐庐庐庫庫 　　10

298

戸

a door; household

ORIGIN: The ancient form was a pictograph of a door. A house where a family lives has a door. From this it also means "household." The kanji 戸 means a "door; household." (In contrast the kanji 門 had two doors in its ancient form.)

戸 door
戸締り locking a house
戸籍 family registry

一戸建て detached house
戸棚 cupboard
門戸開放 open-door policy

一ニラ戸 　　4

299

故

past; to cause

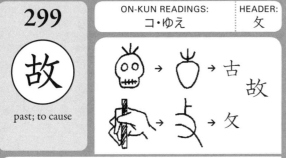

ORIGIN: The left side 古, meaning "old," originated from a skull. The right side 攵 depicted a hand holding a stick, indicating "motion," or "action" in general. Together they indicated "to cause something to become old." The kanji 故 means "to cause," or "past."

事故 accident
故人 deceased
それ故に consequently

故障 breakdown
縁故 connection
故意に deliberately

一十古古古古古故故 　　9

300

湖

lake

ORIGIN: The left 氵 was water. The right side 胡 was used phonetically to mean "large." A large pool of water is a lake. The kanji 湖 means "lake."

湖 lake
琵琶湖 Lake Biwa
湖水 lake water

湖畔 lake side

、、氵氵沽沽沽沽湖湖湖湖 　　12

301

ON-KUN READINGS:	HEADER:
ゴ・いつ(つ)	二

五
five

ORIGIN: One of the ancient forms had five lines to indicate "five." Another form had two lines, one at the top, one at the bottom, and a cross in between. When one counts to ten using one's fingers, five is the crossing point. The kanji 五 means "five."

五 five
いつ
五つ five items
いつか
五日 fifth day of the month

ごにん
五人 five people
ごがつ
五月 May
ごぶごぶ
五分五分 evenly divided

一 丁 五 五   4

302

ON-KUN READINGS:	HEADER:
ゴ・たが(い)	二

互
each other;
alternately

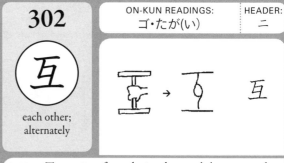

ORIGIN: The ancient form depicted a spool that was used to wind a string. The middle part indicated a place where a hand is placed. Winding two strings alternately signified "each other; mutual." The kanji 互 means "each other; alternately."

たが
お互い each other
そうご
相互 mutual
こうご
交互に alternately

ごかく
互角 evenly matched
ごけいてき
互恵的 reciprocal
ごじょ
互助 mutual aid

一 工 互 互   4

303

ON-KUN READINGS:	HEADER:
ゴ	十

午
noon

ORIGIN: The ancient form was a pictograph of a pestle for pounding steamed rice into cake. A pestle hits the center of a mortar, and symbolizes the middle of the day, noon. The kanji 午 means "noon."

ごぜん
午前 in the morning
ごぜんちゅう
午前中に before noon
ごご
午後 in the afternoon

しょうご
正午 noon time, midday
しごせん
子午線 the meridian line
ごすい
午睡 nap, siesta

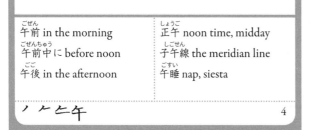
ノ 广 仁 午   4

304

ON-KUN READINGS:	HEADER:
ゴ・コウ・のち・あと・うし(ろ)・おく(れる)	彳

後
behind; later

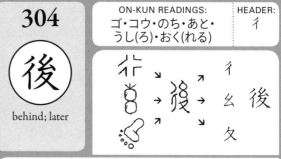

ORIGIN: The left side 彳 was "to go." The right side had 幺 "short threads," which further signified "smallness," and 夂 "a backward foot." Together they indicated a person with inverted feet moving with small steps, hence "behind" or to "delay." The kanji 後 means "behind; later."

うし
後ろ behind
あと
後で later
ごご
午後 afternoon

ご
その後 after that
こうはん
後半 second half
せんご
戦後 post war

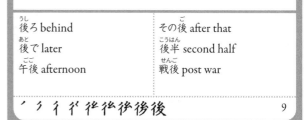
ノ ク 彳 彳 彳 彳 後 後 後   9

305

ON-KUN READINGS:	HEADER:
ゴ・ギョ・お・おん	彳

御

to control;
[honorific prefix]

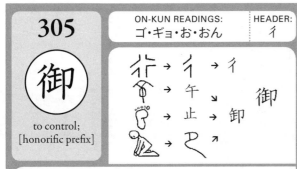

ORIGIN: The left side 彳 signified "to go" or "to act." The right side 卸, the depiction of "pestle," "footprint" and "kneeling," was used phonetically to indicate "to keep a horse." Together they indicated "to handle a horse" or "to control." Someone who controls or reigns the country was an emperor. This kanji was also used as an honorific prefix for a noun. The kanji 御 means "to control" or an honorific prefix.

御礼 token of gratitude
御主人 master, (someone's) husband
御中 messrs.

御する to handle, to control
制御する to control
御所 palace

丿 彳 彳 彳 彳 彳 件 件 件 徘 徘 御 御   12

306

ON-KUN READINGS:	HEADER:
ゴ・かた(る)	言

語

word; to talk

ORIGIN: The left side 言 consisted of a sharp tattooing needle 辛 and a mouth 口, signifying "to speak clearly." In 吾 on the right side, 五 signified "mixing" because two lines crossed and 口 "mouth" indicated "to speak." Together they indicated "to speak in response," then came to mean simply "to talk." The kanji 語 means "word" or "to talk."

日本語 the Japanese language
外国語 foreign language
単語 word

語学 language study
語句 word and phrase
語る to talk

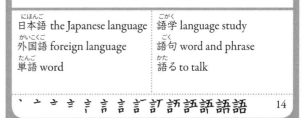

丶 丶 亠 亠 言 言 言 訂 訂 語 語 語 語   14

307

ON-KUN READINGS:	HEADER:
ゴ・あやま(る)	言

誤

to err; mistake

ORIGIN: The left side 言 was a combination of a sharp tattooing needle and a mouth 口, signifying "to speak clearly and sharply." The right side 呉 had a mouth next to a person, indicating that what was said was not the person's true thought or meaning. The kanji 誤 means "mistake" or "to err."

誤まった mistaken
誤解 misunderstanding
誤字 wrong letter or kanji

誤訳 mistranslation
誤報 erroneous report
時代錯誤 anachronism

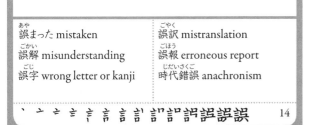

丶 丶 亠 亠 言 言 言 訂 訂 訳 誤 誤 誤 誤   14

308

ON-KUN READINGS:	HEADER:
ゴ	言

護

to protect

ORIGIN: The left side 言 consisted of a sharp tattooing needle 辛 and a mouth 口, signifying "to speak clearly." The right side was a crested bird with a hand, signifying "to catch in the hand." Together they indicated to speak sharply to protect something. The kanji 護 means "to protect."

保護 protection
護る to protect
護憲 safeguarding of the Constitution

護送 escort
護身術 art of self-defense
警護 guard

丶 丶 亠 亠 言 言 言 訂 訂 訂 護 護 護 護 護 護   20

309

ON-KUN READINGS: コウ・まじ(わる)・ま(ざる)・か(わす)

HEADER: 亠

交

to cross;
to intermingle

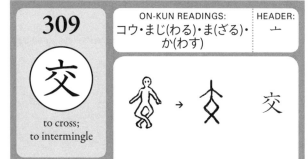

ORIGIN: In the ancient form a person with legs crossed signified crossing or mixing. The kanji 交 means "to cross; to intermingle."

交わる to mix
交ざる to mix
交差点 traffic intersection

交通違反 traffic violation
国際交流 international exchange
交わす to exchange

` 丶 亠 六 六 交 交 `   6

310

ON-KUN READINGS: コウ・そうろう

HEADER: イ

候

sign; to watch
for a chance

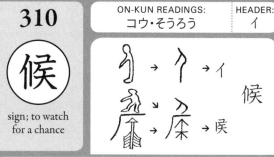

ORIGIN: In the ancient form the left side イ is a person. The right side had a person on top of a watch tower, where an arrow was hidden. It depicted an archer watching for a sign of an enemy approach. The kanji 候 means "to watch for a chance" or "sign."

気候 climate
天候 weather
候 the literary polite style of /aru/ or /iru/

測候所 meteorological station
兆候 indication, sign
立候補 candidacy

` ノ イ イ' イ' 伫 伫 伫 侯 候 候 `   10

311

ON-KUN READINGS: コウ・ひかり・ひか(る)

HEADER: 儿

光

light

ORIGIN: The ancient form depicted a burning fire, or a torch, above a person. A burning flame gives light. The kanji 光 means "light."

光 light
日光 sunlight
光線 ray

栄光 glory
蛍光灯 fluorescent light
脚光 spotlight

` ` 丨 ` 业 光 光 `   6

312

ON-KUN READINGS: コウ・ク・きみ・おおやけ

HEADER: 八

公

public

ORIGIN: The top 八 signified a motion of splitting something into two. The bottom ム was a bent elbow, indicating a claim of ownership, or private property (the same origin as the right side of 私 "I"). Breaking up private property meant making it public. The kanji 公 means "public."

公園 park
公立 publicly supported
公開 open to the public

公 public
公私 public and private
選挙公約 election pledge

` ノ 八 公 公 `   4

313

ON-KUN READINGS: コウ・ク　HEADER: 力

功

merit; achievement

ORIGIN: The left 工 was a pictograph of a tool made from two connected boards, signifying craft or skill. The right side was an arm, with flexing muscles to muster strength. Together they meant "skillful hand," "merit," or "achievement." The kanji 功 means "merit" or "achievement."

せいこう
成功 success
こう　そう
功を奏する take effect
ねんこうじょれつ
年功序列 seniority system

こうせき
功績 merits
こうざい
功罪 merits and demerits
くどく
功徳 pious act

一　丁　工　功　功　　5

314

ON-KUN READINGS: コウ・き(く)　HEADER: 力

効

having an effect

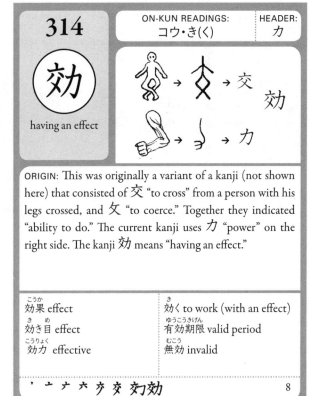

ORIGIN: This was originally a variant of a kanji (not shown here) that consisted of 交 "to cross" from a person with his legs crossed, and 攵 "to coerce." Together they indicated "ability to do." The current kanji uses 力 "power" on the right side. The kanji 効 means "having an effect."

こうか
効果 effect
きめ
効き目 effect
こうりょく
効力 effective

き
効く to work (with an effect)
ゆうこうきげん
有効期限 valid period
むこう
無効 invalid

`＇　亠　亠　六　�256　交　刻　効　　8`

315

ON-KUN READINGS: コウ・あつ(い)　HEADER: 厂

厚

thick

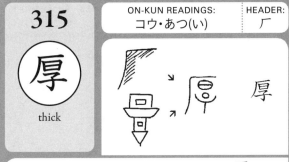

ORIGIN: The ancient form consisted of the top 厂, "cliff," and a tall watchtower that was upside down, here phonetically used. The concept of descending many stories of a tower was extended to indicate "substantial" or "thick." The kanji 厚 means "thick."

あつ
厚い thick
ぶあつ
分厚い thick
あつぎ
厚着 heavily clothed

てあつ
手厚い hospitable
おんこう
温厚 mild-mannered
あつ
厚かましい impudent

一　厂　厂　厂　戸　戸　厚　厚　厚　厚　　9

316

ON-KUN READINGS: コウ・ク・くち　HEADER: 口

口

mouth; opening

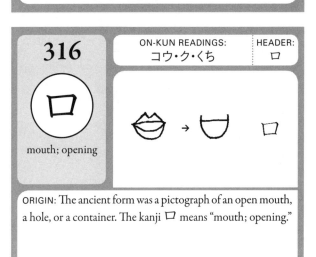

ORIGIN: The ancient form was a pictograph of an open mouth, a hole, or a container. The kanji 口 means "mouth; opening."

くち
口 mouth
でぐち
出口 exit
い　ぐち　いりぐち
入り口・入口 entrance

じんこう
人口 population
わるくち
悪口 foul mouth, slander
くちょう
口調 tone of voice

丨　口　口　　3

115

317

ON-KUN READINGS: コウ・む(こう)

HEADER: 口

向

to face; opposite

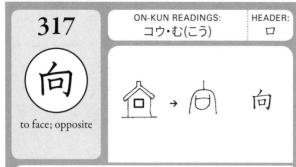

ORIGIN: The ancient form depicted a house with a window 口. The side that a window faces is the important side. The kanji 向 means "to face" or "opposite."

向く to face toward
向こう the other side
向上する to improve

上向き looking upward
向かい側 facing side
動向 tendency

ノイ 門向向向 6

318

ON-KUN READINGS: コウ・きさき

HEADER: 口

后

empress; queen consort

ORIGIN: In the ancient form the upper left signified a person, and 口 in the lower right signified a baby being born. A queen consort is someone who bears a child for her country's posterity. The kanji 后 means "empress; queen consort."

皇后 empress
后 queen consort
皇太后 empress dowager

ノ厂厂斤后后 6

319

ON-KUN READINGS: コウ・す(き)・この(む)

HEADER: 女

好

to be fond of; to like; desirable

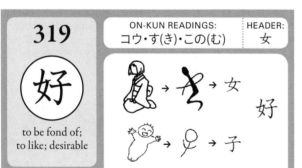

ORIGIN: The left side 女 "woman" and the right 子 "child" together indicated the tender way in which a woman cared for a child. It also meant "beautiful woman" or "desirable." The kanji 好 means "to be fond of; to like" or "desirable."

好き to be fond of
好み liking
好物 favorite food

好悪 partiality
好都合 convenient
好調 good condition

く タ 女 女 好好 6

320

ON-KUN READINGS: コウ

HEADER: 子

孝

filial responsibility

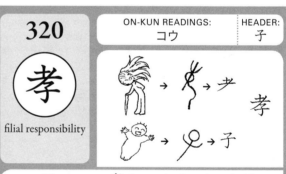

ORIGIN: The top part 耂 depicted a long-haired old man with a stooped back and a cane, indicating "old." The bottom 子 was a child. Together they showed a child supporting an elderly parent. The kanji 孝 means "filial responsibility."

親孝行 filial duty
孝行 devotion to parents
親不孝 act against filial duty

忠孝 loyalty and filial piety
孝女 filial daughter

一 十 土 耂 耂 孝 孝 7

321

ON-KUN READINGS: コウ・ク
HEADER: 工

工
craft

ORIGIN: One interpretation of this simple form is that it depicted a pole that connected two boards that had holes in the center, which requires skill to construct. Another is that it depicted a carpenter's tool. The kanji 工 means "craft."

こうじちゅう
工事中 under construction
くふう
工夫 plan, device
だいく
大工 carpenter

こうじょう
工場 factory
じんこう
人工の man-made
くめん
工面する to contrive

一丁工　3

322

ON-KUN READINGS: コウ・さち・しあわ(せ)・さいわ(い)
HEADER: 干

幸
good luck; happiness

ORIGIN: There were two ancient forms. One consisted of a person whose head was struck and another person who was upside down, which signified "to reverse a calamity." Another one depicted a handcuff with an inverted shape at the bottom, again indicating a reversal of misfortune. The kanji 幸 means "good luck; happiness."

しあわ
幸せな happy
さいわ
幸いに luckily
ふこう
不幸な unfortunate

こうふく
幸福 happiness
ぎょうこう
行幸 imperial visit
たこう
多幸 much happiness

一十土圭卉圭幸幸　8

117

323

ON-KUN READINGS: コウ・ひろ(い)
HEADER: 广

広
spacious; wide

ORIGIN: The old kanji 廣 consisted of 广 "house" and a variant of 黄 "yellow" that depicted a flaming arrow or rocket with combustible materials in the middle. A flame illuminated all four directions, hence a "wide" area. Now reduced, the kanji 広 means "spacious; wide."

ひろ
広い wide, spacious
ひろば
広場 public square
こうこく
広告 advertisement

ひろ
広める to broaden, extend
せびろ
背広 men's suits
ひろびろ
広々とした spacious

丶宀广広広　5

324

ON-KUN READINGS: コウ
HEADER: 广

康
healthy; peaceful

ORIGIN: The ancient form came from a depiction of two hands holding a pestle in the middle, indicating something solid in the middle. The bottom four strokes were scattered rice husks, which were hard and grooved. Together they indicated robust health and peace of mind that comes with it. The kanji 康 means "healthy; peaceful."

けんこう
健康 health
しょうこう　たも
小康を保つ to have a brief lull

丶宀广广庐庐唐庚庚康康　11

325

攻

to attack

ORIGIN: The left side 工 "to craft" (from piercing two holes in two boards) and 攵 "action in general" (a hand pounding a stick up and down) originally indicated "to produce military equipment." From this concept the kanji 攻 came to mean "to attack."

専攻 specialty in study
攻撃 attack
攻める to attack

攻防 attack and defense
攻略 capture, conquest
攻勢 the offensive

一 丁 工 丁 ヺ 攷 攻   7

326

更

again; further

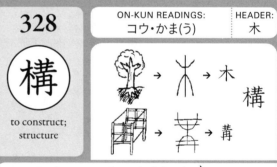

ORIGIN: The kanji originally consisted of 丙 "table," phonetically used here to indicate "to change"; it had a striking hand to indicate "to act; to coerce." Together they indicated "something goes further." The kanji 更 means "again" or "further."

変更 a change
更に furthermore
更新 renewal

今更 at this belated time, after so long a time
夜更け late into the night
更迭 shakeup, reshuffle

一 一 戸 戸 百 更 更   7

327

校

school; to check

ORIGIN: The left side 木 "tree" and 交 "a person with crossed legs" indicated a place to mingle. A school is a place where pupils and teachers mix. (Another interpretation of 校 is wooden shackles, a less congenial view of school.) The kanji also means "to check," because this is what teachers did at school. The kanji 校 means "school" or "to check."

学校 school
校門 school gate
下校する to return home from school

登校する to go to school
校庭 school yard
校正 proofreading

一 十 才 木 木 栌 栌 栌 核 校   10

328

構

to construct; structure

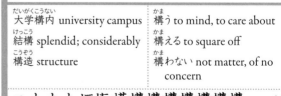

ORIGIN: In the ancient form the left side 木 was a tree or wood and the right side was a configuration made of timbers that had two identical sides. It depicted two balanced sides of a structure. The kanji 構 means "to construct a well-balanced structure" or "structure."

大学構内 university campus
結構 splendid; considerably
構造 structure

構う to mind, to care about
構える to square off
構わない not matter, of no concern

一 十 才 木 杧 杧 栐 栐 栐 栐 栐 構 構 構   14

118

329

ON-KUN READINGS: コウ・みなと
HEADER: 氵

港
port

ORIGIN: The left side 氵 was water. The right side 巷 "town" consisted of 共 "together" and 己 "person," indicating a place where a lot of people come and go. Together they indicated a waterfront where people come together, or a port. The kanji 港 means "port."

くうこう
空港 airport
みなと
港 port
こうべこう
神戸港 port of Kobe

みなとまち
港町 port town
ぎょこう
漁港 fishing port
ぐんこう
軍港 naval port

丶 丶 氵 氵 氵 氵 洪 洪 洪 港 港 12

330

ON-KUN READINGS: コウ・オウ
HEADER: 白

皇
emperor

ORIGIN: In the ancient form, the top came from a depiction of a nose, which signified "face" or "self," and the bottom 王 "king" came from an ornate weapon to signify the power of a king. Together they indicated a crown. The kanji 皇 means "emperor."

てんのう
天皇 (Japanese) emperor
こうてい
皇帝 emperor
こうしつ
皇室 imperial family

じょうこう
上皇 ex-emperor
こうぞく
皇族 imperial family
こうい
皇位 imperial throne

丿 丿 丿 白 白 白 自 皇 皇 9

331

ON-KUN READINGS: コウ
HEADER: 禾

稿
manuscript

ORIGIN: The left side 禾 was a pictograph of a rice plant drooping under the weight of the ripening grain. The right side 高 was used phonetically. Together they indicated straw. From the appearance of scattered straws this kanji was used to indicate quick writing or draft. The kanji 稿 means "manuscript."

げんこう
原稿 manuscript
そうこう
草稿 draft
とうこう
投稿する to contribute (an article)

げんこうようし
原稿用紙 squared manuscript paper
だっこう
脱稿 finish writing

丿 一 千 禾 禾 禾' 禾' 稿 稿 稿 稿 稿 稿 稿 15

332

ON-KUN READINGS: コウ・ク・べに・くれない
HEADER: 糸

紅
scarlet, red

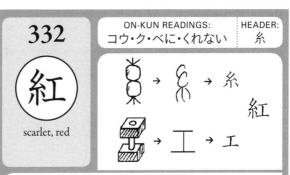

ORIGIN: In the ancient form the left side 糸 was a pictograph of thin silk threads being pulled out of silkworm cocoons. The right side was used phonetically. Together they indicated red cloth; the kanji 紅 means "red."

こうちゃ
紅茶 black tea
くちべに
口紅 lipstick
べに
紅 red
くれない
紅 red

しんく
深紅 scarlet
こうはく
紅白 red and white
こういってん
紅一点 one woman among men

く 幺 幺 幺 糸 糸 糸 紅 紅 9

119

333

ON-KUN READINGS: コウ・たがや(す)

HEADER: 耒

耕

to cultivate; to till

ORIGIN: In the ancient form the left side 耒 was a three-pronged plow, and the right side 井 was a square well. A field was divided into squares to till. The kanji 耕 means "to till; to cultivate."

たがや
耕す to cultivate, to till
きゅうこうち
休耕地 land laying fallow
こううんき
耕運機 tiller

のうこうせいかつ
農耕生活 farming life
こうさく
耕作する to farm, till
ひっこう
筆耕 copying, a scribe

一 二 三 三 丰 丰 耒 耒 耒 耕 耕 耕　10

334

ON-KUN READINGS: コウ・かんが(える)

HEADER: 耂

考

to think
(thoroughly)

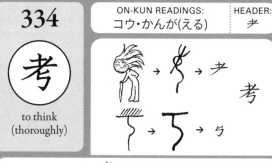

ORIGIN: The top part 耂 depicted an elderly stooped man with long hair blown in the wind—long hair signified being thoughtful. The bottom comes from 丂, which signified "bent; detour." Together they indicated a person who would ponder for a long time. The kanji 考 means "to think (thoroughly)."

かんが
考え thought
かんが
考える to think
かんが こ
考え込む to be lost in
　thought

しこう
思考 thinking, thought
こうこがく
考古学 archaeology
さんこうぶんけん
参考文献 references

一 十 土 耂 耂 考　6

335

ON-KUN READINGS: コウ

HEADER: 舟

航

to sail; to navigate

ORIGIN: The left 舟 is a boat and the right side 亢 depicted a long, straight neck and was used phonetically to indicate "straight." Together they indicated that a boat went straight forward. The kanji 航 means "to sail; to navigate."

こうくうがいしゃ
航空会社 airline company
こうかい
航海 voyage, navigation
しゅっこう
出航 ship leaving port

こうろ
航路 (sea) route
みっこう
密航 stowing away
なんこう
難航 stormy passage

' 丿 刀 丹 舟 舟 舟' 舶 舯 航 航　10

336

ON-KUN READINGS: コウ・ギョウ・アン・い(く)・
ゆ(く)・おこな(う)

HEADER: 行

行

to go; to carry out; to conduct business

ORIGIN: The ancient form was a pictograph of a crossroad, signifying "to go" beyond the crossroad. The meaning of going on also had the meaning of carrying out a task or business. The kanji 行 means "to go" or "to conduct business." The left half 彳 is used as a recurring component in a number of kanji that pertain to the meaning of "to go," as in 待 "to wait" and 後 "behind."

い ゆ
行く・行く to go
ぎんこう
銀行 bank
ぎょう
行 line
ゆくえ
行方 whereabouts

おこな
行う to conduct, to hold
　(an event)
ぎょうせい
行政 administration
じっこう
実行する to carry out

' 彳 彳 行 行 行　6

337

ON-KUN READINGS: コウ

HEADER: 言

講

to lecture

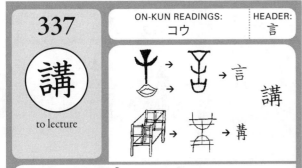

ORIGIN: The left side 言 came from two pictographs: a sharp tattoo needle 辛 and a mouth 口, signifying "to speak clearly and sharply." The right side was a pictograph of symmetrically built frames, signifying "well-balanced structure" but here used phonetically. The kanji 講 means "to lecture."

こうどう
講堂 lecture hall
こうぎ
講義 lecture
こうし
講師 lecturer

きゅうこう
休講 class cancelled
こうひょう
講評 review
ちょうこう
聴講 attendance at a lecture

`丶 一 亠 亖 言 言 言 計 計 詳 詳 講 講 講 講 講 講` 17

338

ON-KUN READINGS: コウ

HEADER: 阝

郊

suburbs

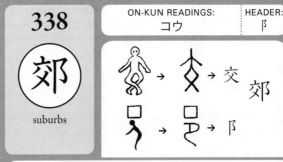

ORIGIN: The left side 交 depicted a person with his legs crossed, signifying "crossing or mixing." The right side 阝 signified a village (an area with people). Together they indicated a place where two villages meet, or outside the capital. The kanji 郊 means "suburbs."

こうがい
郊外 suburbs
きんこう
近郊 neighboring area

`丶 一 亠 六 方 交 交 郊 郊` 9

121

339

ON-KUN READINGS: コウ

HEADER: 金

鉱

ore

ORIGIN: In the old form 鑛, the left side 金 was metal, and the right side 廣, used phonetically, depicted a fire arrow illuminating a wide area with a yellow glow. Together they indicated a dispersed metal (a mineral or ore). The kanji 鉱 means "ore."

たんこう
炭鉱 coal mine
こうせき
鉱石 ore
こうざん
鉱山 mine

きんこう
金鉱 gold mine
こうみゃく
鉱脈 mineral vein
はいこう
廃鉱 abandoned mine

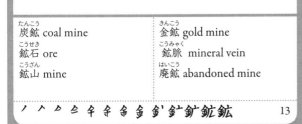

`丿 𠂉 𠂢 𠂢 年 余 金 金 金' 金广 釒广 鉱 鉱 鉱` 13

340

ON-KUN READINGS: コウ・はがね

HEADER: 金

鋼

steel

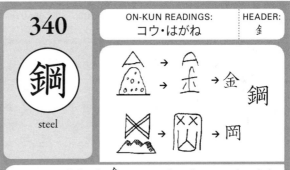

ORIGIN: The left side 金 was metal in the ground and the right side 岡, used phonetically, consisted of an iron mesh and hills that signified strong and hard. Together they indicated hard metal. The kanji 鋼 means "steel."

てっこう
鉄鋼 steel
はがね
鋼 hard metal
こうてつ
鋼鉄の steel

こうざい
鋼材 steel
こうばん
鋼板 steel plate
せいこうじょ
製鋼所 steel mill

`丿 𠂉 𠂢 𠂢 年 余 金 金 金 釘 釘 鋼 鋼 鋼 鋼 鋼` 16

341

ON-KUN READINGS: コウ・お(りる)・ふ(る)

HEADER: 阝

降

to fall from the sky; to step down

ORIGIN: The left side 阝 comes from a pile of dirt or a hill. The right side 夅 consisted of a right foot and a left foot, both of which faced downwards to signify "coming down." Together they indicated the motion of coming down from a high place to a lower place. The kanji 降 means "to fall from the sky" or "to step down."

お
降りる to get off
ふ
降る to fall from the sky
(rain, snow, etc.)
あめふ
雨降り rainfall

かこう
下降 decline
こうさん
降参する to surrender
こうふく
降服 surrender

｀ ３ 阝 阝 阝 阝 降 降 降 降　　10

342

ON-KUN READINGS: コウ・たか(い)

HEADER: 高

高

high; tall; expensive

ORIGIN: The old kanji 髙 was a pictograph of a tall watchtower. From that, it indicated "tall; high." Now slightly modified, 高 is used. The kanji 高 means "high; tall; expensive."

たか
高い high, tall, expensive
こうこう
高校 high school
こうこうせい
高校生 high school student

さいこう
最高 highest, maximum, best
けだか
気高い high-minded, noble
たかね
高値 high price

｀ 亠 亠 古 古 声 高 高 高 高　　10

343

ON-KUN READINGS: ゴウ

HEADER: 口

号

to call in a loud voice; number

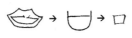

ORIGIN: In the ancient form the top 口 was a mouth and the bottom 丂 indicated something bent, signifying someone forcing his or her voice out of the throat (the passage of air is not straight) or to call out in a loud voice. One also counts things aloud. The kanji 号 means "to call in a loud voice" or a "number."

ばんごう
番号 number
だいよんごう
第四号 fourth one
こうつうしんごう
交通信号 traffic signal

ごうれい
号令 command
ろくごうしゃ
六号車 Car No. 6
ごうきゅう
号泣 wailing

１ 口 口 므 号　　5

344

ON-KUN READINGS: ゴウ・カッ・ガッ・あ(う)

HEADER: 口

合

(things) meet exactly

ORIGIN: The top 亼 was a cover and the bottom indicated a hole. Together they signified an action in which a cover and a hole met exactly. The kanji 合 means that "things meet exactly." (The kanji for "to meet someone" is 会う.)

あ
合う (things) to meet
かいごう
会合 meeting
ま あ
待ち合わせる to meet up

がてん
合点がいく That explains it.
かっせん
合戦 battle
ごうどう
合同で jointly

ノ 人 今 今 合 合　　6

122

345

ON-KUN READINGS: コク・きざ(む)

HEADER: 刂

刻

to cut into pieces; to carve; to tick away

ORIGIN: In the ancient form the left side 亥 was "wild boar or skeleton of an animal," which was phonetically used to indicate "carving an animal to the bone" or "engrave" on a hard surface. The right side 刂 was a "knife." Mincing time is similar to time ticking away. The kanji 刻 means "to mince" or "(time) to tick away."

時刻 time
遅刻する to be late
刻む to engrave; mince

刻々と every moment
深刻な serious
定刻 scheduled time

` 一 十 ナ 亥 亥 刻 刻`   8

346

ON-KUN READINGS: コク・つ(げる)

HEADER: 口

告

to proclaim; to inform

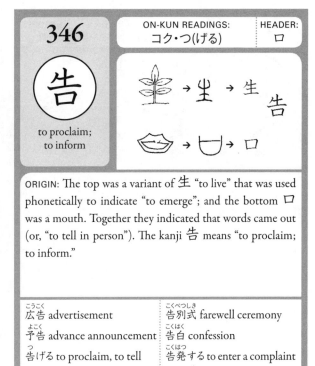

ORIGIN: The top was a variant of 生 "to live" that was used phonetically to indicate "to emerge"; and the bottom 口 was a mouth. Together they indicated that words came out (or, "to tell in person"). The kanji 告 means "to proclaim; to inform."

広告 advertisement
予告 advance announcement
告げる to proclaim, to tell

告別式 farewell ceremony
告白 confession
告発する to enter a complaint against

` ノ ヒ 牛 生 牛 告 告`   7

347

ON-KUN READINGS: コク・たに・や

HEADER: 谷

谷

valley

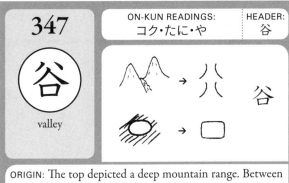

ORIGIN: The top depicted a deep mountain range. Between mountains there is a low area, an opening 口 into the mountains. The kanji 谷 means "valley."

谷 valley
谷間 ravine
渓谷 canyon

谷底 bottom of a ravine
谷川 mountain stream
峡谷 gorge, canyon

` ノ 八 グ 父 父 谷 谷`   7

348

ON-KUN READINGS: コク・くに

HEADER: 囗

国

country

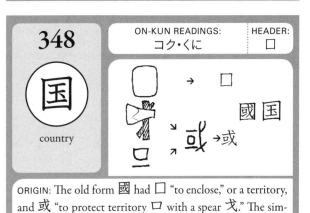

ORIGIN: The old form 國 had 囗 "to enclose," or a territory, and 或 "to protect territory 口 with a spear 戈." The simpler form used now is 国, where 玉 is a crown jewel. The kanji 国 means "country."

国 country
外国 abroad, foreign country
全国 throughout the country

中国 China
四国 Shikoku Island
国語 Japanese language

` 一 冂 冃 冃 用 国 国 国`   8

123

349

穀
grain

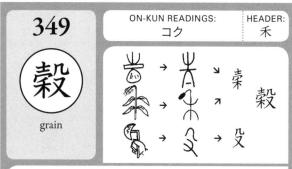

ORIGIN: The top left was a variant of a shell or husk, and the bottom is a rice plant. The right side 殳 consisted of an ax or a tool in hand, which signified "pounding; hitting." Together they indicated threshing grain hard, or grains. The kanji 穀 means "grain."

こくもつ
穀物 grain
だっこく
脱穀 threshing
ざっこく
雑穀 miscellaneous cereals

こくそう
穀倉 granary
ごこく
五穀 all kinds of grains

一 十 土 士 圭 圭 声 圭 幸 軎 軎 毃 殻 穀穀　14

350

黒
black

ORIGIN: The old form 黑 came from a chimney with black soot, viewed from the top, and a strong flame (炎) underneath. In the current form, the flame was replaced by 灬 "fire." The kanji 黒 means "black."

くろ
黒い black
しろくろ
白黒 black and white
こくばん
黒板 blackboard

くろぐろ
黒々と in deep black
あんこく
暗黒の dark, gloomy
くろまく
黒幕 the power behind the
　　scenes

丨 冂 冂 曰 甲 甲 里 黒 黒 黒 黒　11

351

骨
bone

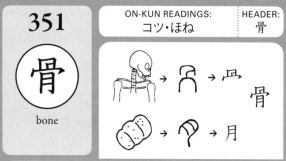

ORIGIN: The top meant a scalp and upper body bones connected by the vertebrae. The bottom 月 indicated flesh. Together they indicated bones with flesh attached. The kanji 骨 means "bone."

ほね
骨 bone
せぼね
背骨 backbone
がいこつ
骸骨 skeleton

ほねぐ
骨組み structure, frame
ほね お
骨を折る to take pains
せっこつ
接骨 bone-setting

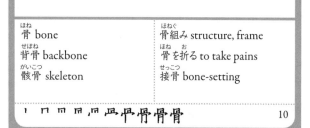

丨 冂 冂 冂 冎 冎 骨 骨 骨 骨　10

352

込
to be put in;
to be crowded

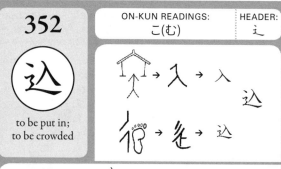

ORIGIN: The top part 入 was an arrow showing where to enter (an entrance). The bottom part 辶, formerly 辵, was the left side of a crossroad and a foot and signified "to go forward." The kanji 込 means "to be put in; be crowded." (This kanji was created in Japan; thus there is no on-reading.)

こ
込む to become crowded
ひとご
人込み throng, a crowded
　　place
こ あ
込み合う to become thronged

もう こ
申し込む to register, to apply
みこ
見込み prospect
か こ
駆け込む to dash into

ノ 入 入 込 込　5

353

ON-KUN READINGS: コン・キン・いま
HEADER: 人

今
now; present time

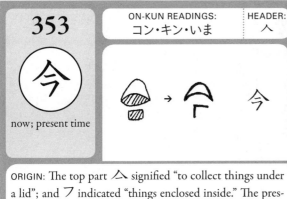

ORIGIN: The top part 亼 signified "to collect things under a lid"; and フ indicated "things enclosed inside." The present moment gets captured under a lid. The kanji 今 means "now; present time."

いま
今 now
きょう
今日 today
ことし
今年 this year

こんしゅう
今週 this week
こんど
今度 next time, this time
こんご
今後 from now on

ノ 人 今 今　　4

354

ON-KUN READINGS: コン・こま(る)
HEADER: 囗

困
in trouble

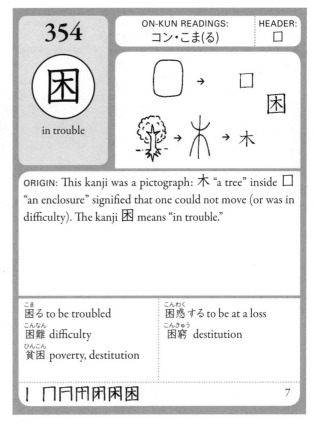

ORIGIN: This kanji was a pictograph: 木 "a tree" inside 囗 "an enclosure" signified that one could not move (or was in difficulty). The kanji 困 means "in trouble."

こま
困る to be troubled
こんなん
困難 difficulty
ひんこん
貧困 poverty, destitution

こんわく
困惑する to be at a loss
こんきゅう
困窮 destitution

｜ 冂 冂 用 困 困 困　　7

355

ON-KUN READINGS: コン
HEADER: 女

婚
marriage

ORIGIN: The left side 女 depicted a woman. The right side 昏 consisted of a sharp-edged ladle (also used for cutting food) and a sun, signifying "dusk." (The reason is unclear.) Wedding ceremonies were held at dusk in the ancient times. The kanji 婚 means "marriage."

こんやく
婚約 an engagement to marry
けっこん
結婚 marriage
けっこんしき
結婚式 wedding ceremony

こんれい
婚礼 wedding
しんこんふうふ
新婚夫婦 newlywed couple
りこん
離婚 divorce

乚 タ 女 女 奵 妖 娇 娇 婚 婚 婚　　11

356

ON-KUN READINGS: コン・ね
HEADER: 木

根
root

ORIGIN: 木 on the left is a tree or wood. 艮 on the right consisted of an eye and halted legs, possibly because the person saw something that prevented him or her from going forward. Thus the kanji indicated one who remains in one place. A tree root remains in the same place. The kanji 根 means "root."

き ね
木の根 tree root
ね
根っこ tree root
こんぽんてき
根本的な fundamental

ねづよ
根強い firmly rooted
こんぜつ
根絶する to eradicate
こんきょ
根拠 foundation, source

一 十 オ 木 村 村 村 柙 根 根 根　　10

357

ON-KUN READINGS:	HEADER:
コン・ま(ぜる)	シ

混

to mix

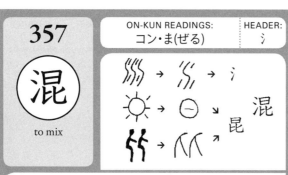

ORIGIN: The left side was "water." 昆 on the right side signified two (meaning many) people mingling under the sun, but this side was only used phonetically here to indicate the sound of water swirling. Water mixes easily with other things. The kanji 混 means "to mix."

ま
混ぜる to mix
こんざつ
混雑 congested, jammed
こんらん
混乱 confusion, disorder

こんどう
混同する to confuse
こんせん
混戦する to get entangled
こんよう
混用する to mingle

丶 亠 氵 氵 沪 沪 沪 沪 混 混 混   11

358

ON-KUN READINGS:	HEADER:
サ	イ

佐

to assist; assistant

ORIGIN: The left side イ is 人 "person," a side-view of a standing person. The right side 左 "left" originally had a left hand over 工 "crafted object." The left hand supports what the right hand does. Together they indicated someone who assisted others. The kanji 佐 means "to assist" or be an "assistant."

ほさ
補佐 assistance
たいさ
大佐 colonel

ノ イ イ 仁 佐 佐 佐   7

359

ON-KUN READINGS:	HEADER:
サ・ひだり	工

左

left

ORIGIN: This kanji had a left hand over 工 "crafted object." When making a craft, one uses the left hand to hold the object in place. The kanji 左 means "left." (Note that in 左 the first stroke is the horizontal one, whereas in 右 "right" the first stroke is the slanted one.)

ひだりがわ
左側 the left side
ひだりて
左手 left hand
さゆう
左右 left and right (both sides)

させつ
左折 left turn
ひだりきき
左利き left-handed
ひだりまえ
左前 financial difficulties

一 ナ 左 左 左   5

360

ON-KUN READINGS:	HEADER:
サ・さ(す)	工

差

difference

ORIGIN: The top depicted a rice plant with a ripe head. A slanted stroke signified a "left hand" and 工 was "craft," here used phonetically for the sound /sa/. Together they indicated uneven, differing heights of rice plants in the field. The kanji 差 means "difference."

こうさてん
交差点 traffic intersection
さ
差 difference (in number)
かくさ
格差 difference
さべつ
差別 discrimination

さ ひ
差し引き the balance
じさ
時差 time difference
じさ
時差ボケ jet lag

丶 丷 丷 主 主 差 差 差 差 差   10

126

361

査

to examine closely

ON-KUN READINGS: サ

HEADER: 木

ORIGIN: Originally (in China) this kanji indicated wood (木) placed in a stack (the bottom). But this kanji is not used in this meaning in Japanese now. This kanji was borrowed to mean "to examine closely." The kanji 査 means "to examine closely."

ちょうさ
調査 investigation
けんさ
検査 inspection
さしょう
査証 visa

さていがく
査定額 assessed amount
そうさ
捜査 search, investigation
じゅんさ
巡査 policeman

一十オ木木杏杏杏査　　9

362

砂

sand

ON-KUN READINGS: サ・シ・すな

HEADER: 石

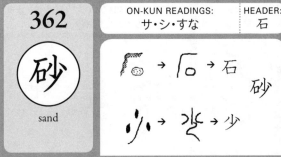

ORIGIN: 石 on the left indicated rocks under a cliff. 少 on the right indicated a wood stick being shaved into pieces, or "small." Together they indicated rocks broken into small pieces, that is, "sand." The kanji 砂 means "sand."

すな
砂 sand
どしゃぶり
土砂降り pouring rain
じゃりみち
砂利道 gravel road

さばく
砂漠 desert
すなやま
砂山 sand hill
どしゃ
土砂 dirt and sand

一ブ丆石石石砂砂砂　　9

363

座

to sit; seat

ON-KUN READINGS: ザ・すわ(る)

HEADER: 广

ORIGIN: This kanji depicted a scene under 广 "roof of a house"; two people faced each other sitting on the ground 土. It also signified a place where they sat or were sitting. The kanji 座 means "to sit" or "seat."

ざせき
座席 seating
すわ
座る to sit
ざぶとん
座布団 floor cushion (used for sitting)

ぎんこうこうざ
銀行口座 bank account
ざだんかい
座談会 table talk
ちゅうざ
中座する to leave in the middle

丶广广广広広座座座座　　10

364

催

to urge; to hold (an event)

ON-KUN READINGS: サイ・もよお(す)

HEADER: イ

ORIGIN: The left side イ "person" was a side view of a person standing. The right side 崔 consisted of 山 "mountain" and 隹 "pudgy small bird," here used phonetically to indicate "to urge strongly." The kanji 催 means "to urge" or "to hold an event."

かいさい
開催する to hold (event)
もよお
催す to hold (event)
もよお
催し event

さいそく
催促する to urge, to press
さいるいだん
催涙弾 tear gas bomb
さいみんじゅつ
催眠術 hypnotism

ノイイ仁伫伫伫伫伫佯催催催　　13

127

365

再

again

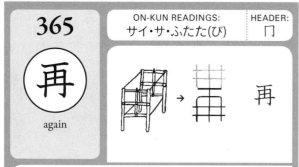

ORIGIN: The ancient form depicted a structure 冉 that is the same configuration in the front and in the back. (The first stroke signified a mirror image.) From that idea, the kanji 再 came to signify "again."

ふたた
再び again

さいかい
再会 meeting again

さいし
再試 re-examination

さいさん
再三 again and again

さいかい
再開 re-opening

さいげん
再現する to reenact

一 厂 厅 冃 再 再   6

366

最

the most

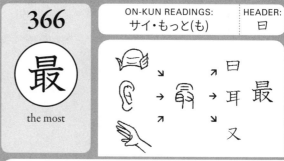

ORIGIN: The original meaning consisted of a warrior's helmet 冃 signifying "to attack" and an ear grabbed by a hand 取, signifying "to take." Together they indicated "to attack." How this form came to be used for the current meaning is not clear, but most likely it was simply borrowed. The kanji 最 means "the most."

さいきん
最近 lately

もっと
最も the most

さいしょ
最初 the first

さいあく
最悪 the worst

さいご
最後 the last

さいちゅう
最中 in the midst of

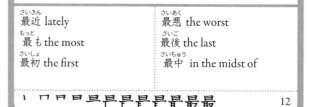

丨 冂 冃 日 旦 昌 昌 冔 冔 冔 最 最   12

367

妻

wife

ORIGIN: The ancient forms (the second and the third in the middle) depicted a bride, indicated by a woman wearing bridal hair ornaments, and a groom's hand in the middle showing that he took her as his wife. The kanji 妻 means "wife."

つま
妻 wife

ふさい
夫妻 husband and wife

さいし
妻子 wife and child

あいさい
愛妻 beloved wife

ぼうさい
亡妻 late wife

りょうさい
良妻 good wife

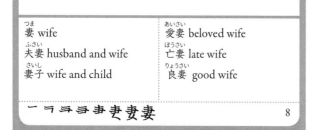

一 ラ ヨ 彐 妻 妻 妻 妻   8

368

才

talent; age counter

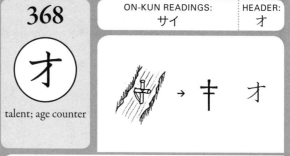

ORIGIN: The ancient form was a pictograph of a weir that blocked water flow. It came to be used to indicate timbers or materials in general. The kanji 才 means "talent," because one uses one's talent to build something. The kanji is also used for one's age in casual writing (the correct kanji is 歳).

さいのう
才能 talent

てんさい
天才 genius

じゅうきゅうさい
十九才 nineteen years old

さいえん
才媛 accomplished woman

さいかく
才覚 ready wit

きさい
鬼才 genius

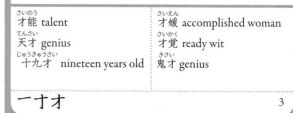

一 十 才   3

369

ON-KUN READINGS: サイ・と（る）

HEADER: 扌

採

to pick

ORIGIN: In the ancient form the left side 扌 was a hand. The right side 采 had ⺤ depicting a hand or fingers from above, and 木 "tree." Together this means the act of someone picking the fruits of a tree or plants by hand. The kanji 採 means "to pick."

採る to take
採用する to adopt, to employ
　(a person)
採決 ballot-taking

採光 lighting
採点 marking, scoring
採算が取れる to be profitable

一 十 才 才 才 才 扩 护 抖 採 採 採　11

370

ON-KUN READINGS: サイ・セイ・とし

HEADER: 止

歳

age; year

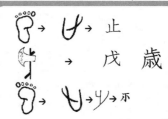

ORIGIN: The ancient form consisted of two "feet" 止・示 for "walking" and 戈 "weapon" in between for "a marking made with a sharp knife." Together they indicated that one walked back to the beginning. A passage of time brings you back to another beginning, or "one year." The kanji 歳 means "age; year."

十六歳 sixteen years old
歳末 end of a year
お歳暮 end-of-the-year gift

歳入 revenue
歳時記 glossary of seasonal
　terms
万歳 cheers, hurrahs

丨 ㇉ 止 止 芦 芦 芦 岸 岸 岸 歳 歳 歳　13

371

ON-KUN READINGS: サイ・す（む）

HEADER: 氵

済

to put in order

ORIGIN: In the old form 濟, the left side 氵 was water and the right side consisted of three things neatly lined up over a square, signifying neatness. Together they indicated regulating the amount of water. The kanji 済 means "to put in order."

経済 economy
経済学 economics
済ます to get through, to
　finish

決済 settlement of accounts
救済 relief
返済する to pay back

丶 冫 氵 汇 汸 浐 浐 済 済 済 済　11

372

ON-KUN READINGS: サイ・わざわ（い）

HEADER: 火

災

serious trouble;
calamity

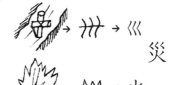

ORIGIN: The top 巛 was a weir to block a river, signifying flood, and the bottom 火 was a fire. Together they indicated a calamity. The kanji 災 means "serious trouble; calamity."

災害 calamity
火災 fire damage
災難 disaster, calamity

天災 natural calamity
災い calamity
人災 man-made disaster

く 巛 巛 巛 巛 災 災　7

129

373

ON-KUN READINGS: サイ・まつ(り)

HEADER: 示

祭

festival; to worship

ORIGIN: The ancient form consisted of 月 "meat," 又 "hand," and 示 "altar." Together they indicated that people offered, by hand, a purified, sacrificial animal on an altar for a religious rite. A festival was a celebration of a god. The kanji 祭 means "to worship" or "festival."

祭(まつ)り festival
祭日(さいじつ) holiday
祝祭日(しゅくさいじつ) holiday

大学祭(だいがくさい) college festival
感謝祭(かんしゃさい) Thanksgiving Day
祭壇(さいだん) altar

ノ ク タ タ 夗 夗 癶 祭 祭 祭   11

374

ON-KUN READINGS: サイ・ほそ(い)・こま(かい)

HEADER: 糸

細

slender; detail

ORIGIN: The left side 糸 was a pictograph of thin silk threads being pulled out of silkworm cocoons. In the ancient form, the right side was a depiction of a baby's head viewed from above. Together they indicated "small; slender; detail." The kanji 細 means "slender" or "detail."

細(ほそ)い thin
細(こま)かい minute, small
明細書(めいさいしょ) detailed account

詳細(しょうさい) details
細君(さいくん) wife [male speaker]
細長(ほそなが)い slender

く ㄠ ㄠ 幺 糸 糸 糸 紀 細 細 細   11

375

ON-KUN READINGS: サイ・な

HEADER: 艹

菜

vegetable; side dish

ORIGIN: The top 艹 "plant" is a simplified form of 艸 "plants." In 采, 爫 "fingers from above" and 木 "tree" indicated "picking with fingers." Together they indicated "leaf vegetable" or "vegetable" in general. The kanji 菜 means "vegetable" or "side dish" (food other than staple food).

野菜(やさい) vegetable
菜(な)っぱ leaf vegetable
白菜(はくさい) Chinese long cabbage

菜食主義者(さいしょくしゅぎしゃ) vegetarian
惣菜(そうざい) daily household cooking
山菜(さんさい) wild vegetable

一 十 艹 艹 艹 艹 苎 芝 菜 菜 菜   11

376

ON-KUN READINGS: サイ・さば(く)・た(つ)

HEADER: 衣

裁

to cut cloth; to make a decision in court

ORIGIN: The upper right side consisted of 十 "timber to make a weir" and 戈 "weapon," signifying "to cut." The lower left 衣 depicted a collar, or clothes in general. Together they indicated "to cut a cloth" and took on the extended meaning "to make a clear-cut decision" in court. The kanji 裁 means "to cut" or "to make a decision in court."

裁判(さいばん) justice, a trial
裁(さば)く to try (in court)
経済制裁(けいざいせいさい) economic sanction

洋裁(ようさい) Western-style sewing
体裁(ていさい) appearance
独裁(どくさい) dictatorship

一 十 土 キ 圭 圭 声 表 表 裁 裁 裁   12

130

377

際

occasion; contact;
edge of an area

ON-KUN READINGS: サイ・きわ

HEADER: 阝

ORIGIN: The left side 阝 was a pictograph of a dirt wall or boundary. The right side 祭 "festival" was used phonetically to indicate "to meet; to come in contact." Together they indicated a border between two areas. It is also used for a new phase or "occasion." The kanji 際 means "edge of an area; occasion" or "to contact."

国際的 international (こくさいてき)
実際に actually, in effect (じっさい)
その際 on that occasion (さい)

際どく narrowly (きわ)
窓際 windowside (まどぎわ)
手際 skill, cleverness (てぎわ)

 ノ 了 了 阝 阝 阝 阝 阝 阪 陘 陛 陉 際 際

14

378

在

to exist

ON-KUN READINGS: ザイ・あ(る)

HEADER: 土

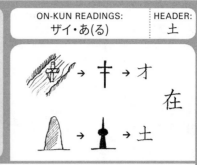

ORIGIN: The first three strokes came from 才, which was a weir that blocked water from flowing. Together with 土 "soil," it indicated that dirt blocked water flow and kept water in place. The sense of something in one place was extended to mean "to stay; to exist." The kanji 在 means "to exist."

現在 present time (げんざい)
在る to exist (あ)
存在 existence (そんざい)

実在 actual existence (じつざい)
在宅 be at home (ざいたく)
不在 absent from home (ふざい)

一ナ才右在在

6

379

材

timber; materials

ON-KUN READINGS: ザイ

HEADER: 木

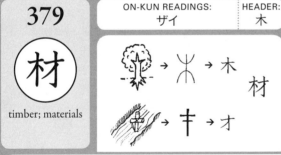

ORIGIN: The left side 木 was wood, and the right side 才 was a pictograph of a wooden weir that blocked water from flowing. Together they indicated timber or materials in general. The kanji 材 means "timber; materials."

材料 materials, ingredients (ざいりょう)
教材 teaching materials (きょうざい)
人材 capable person, good personnel (じんざい)

木材 timber (もくざい)
素材 materials (そざい)
題材 subject, theme (だいざい)

一十才オ木村材

7

380

罪

crime; sin

ON-KUN READINGS: ザイ・つみ

HEADER: 罒

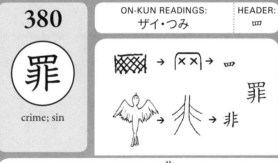

ORIGIN: The top 罒 is a net and 非 shows "going in the opposite direction" (wrong). A net over a wide area catches someone who went the wrong way. The kanji 罪 means "crime; sin."

罪 guilt, sin (つみ)
犯罪 crime (はんざい)
無罪 being not guilty, innocence (むざい)

有罪 being guilty (ゆうざい)
罪作りな cruel (つみつく)
謝罪 apology (しゃざい)

丶 冂 冂 罒 罒 罒 罪 罪 罪 罪 罪 罪 罪

13

131

381

財

fortune; finance

ON-KUN READINGS: ザイ・サイ

HEADER: 貝

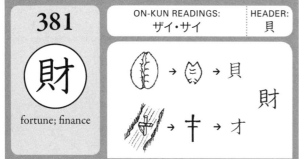

ORIGIN: The left side 貝 was a cowry that was used as currency, signifying trade or money. The right side 才 was a dam but here was used phonetically to signify "materials." Money and materials together make a fortune. The kanji 財 means "fortune; finance."

財産 property, assets
財政 financial policy
財務省 finance ministry

財布 wallet
財団 foundation, estate
財宝 treasure

丨 冂 冂 月 目 貝 貝 財 財　10

382

坂

slope; incline

ON-KUN READINGS: ハン・さか

HEADER: 土

ORIGIN: The left side 土 indicated a pile of neatly packed dirt. The right side 反 depicted an act in which one spread a cloth (but it draped back), here phonetically used. In walking up a slope, one feels that the body is being pulled back. The kanji 坂 means "slope; incline."

坂 slope
上り坂 upward slope
下り坂 downward slope

坂道 uphill road
男坂 steeper of the hills

一 十 土 圫 坂 坂 坂　7

383

作

to create; to make

ON-KUN READINGS: サク・サ・つく(る)

HEADER: イ

ORIGIN: The left side 亻 was a person. The right side 乍 depicted a tool, such as adze, chipping off pieces of wood. Together they indicated a person creating something from a raw material. The kanji 作 means "to create; to make."

作る to make
作文 written composition
作品 piece of work

創作 creation
作用 action
動作 movement, bearing

ノ イ イ 作 作 作 作　7

384

昨

past; last

ON-KUN READINGS: サク

HEADER: 日

ORIGIN: The left side 日 was the sun and the right side 乍 "to create" was used phonetically to indicate "to repeat." Together they indicated a day (or a time in general) that is repeated. The kanji 昨 means "past; last."

昨日 yesterday
一昨日 the day before yesterday
昨年 last year

一昨年 the year before last
昨晩 last night
昨今 recently

丨 冂 冂 日 旷 昨 昨 昨 昨　9

385

策

plan; policy

ORIGIN: The top 竹 was "bamboo" and the bottom 束 was a "thorny long stick" that was used to whip a horse. The bamboo tablets were used for records and plans. The kanji 策 means "plan" or "policy."

たいさく
対策 countermeasure
さく
策 plan, step
せいさく
政策 policy

かいけつさく
解決策 solution
きんさく
金策 raising money
さくし
策士 strategist, schemer

ノ ト ト ケ ケ ゲ 竹 竹 竹 笁 笁 笁 第 第 策　　12

386

索

rope; to search

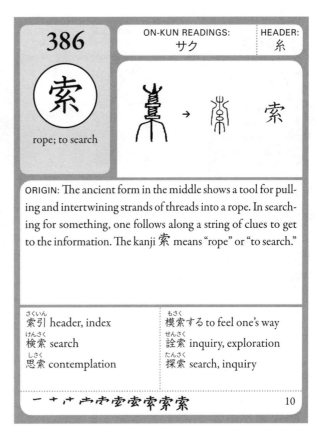

ORIGIN: The ancient form in the middle shows a tool for pulling and intertwining strands of threads into a rope. In searching for something, one follows along a string of clues to get to the information. The kanji 索 means "rope" or "to search."

さくいん
索引 header, index
けんさく
検索 search
しさく
思索 contemplation

もさく
模索する to feel one's way
せんさく
詮索 inquiry, exploration
たんさく
探索 search, inquiry

一 十 六 声 车 宏 宏 宏 索 索　　10

387

冊

volume (of books)

ORIGIN: The ancient form depicted a bundle of long wooden or bamboo tablets that were bound together as a record, or to make a bound book. Split bamboo sticks were singed to remove moisture and oil, and writing was more often done on the surface than on the inner side. The kanji 冊 means "volume" of books.

ごさつ
五冊 five (bound) books
しょうさっし
小冊子 booklet
たんざく
短冊 strip of paper for poem

さっすう
冊数 number of volumes
べっさつ
別冊 separate volume
ぶんさつ
分冊 separate volume

丨 冂 冂 冊 冊　　5

388

刷

to print; to renew

ORIGIN: The left side, a person and a cloth, indicated someone wiping his or her hands with a cloth. A knife 刂 shaved off the old writing on a wooden or bamboo tablet to be reused, signifying "to renew." Reusing a writing tablet over and over again would be equivalent to present-day printing. The kanji 刷 means "to print" or "to renew."

す
刷る to print
いんさつ
印刷 print
さっしん
刷新 renovation

ぞうさつ
増刷 additional printing
しゅくさつばん
縮刷版 reduced-size
　　edition
いろず
色刷り color print

フ コ ア ア 吊 吊 刷 刷　　8

133

389 察

ON-KUN READINGS: サツ

HEADER: 宀

to conjecture; to perceive; to look thoroughly

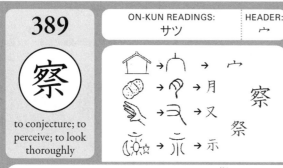

ORIGIN: The 宀 top was a house. Underneath, 祭 "festival or celebration of a god" consisted of 月 "meat for an offering," 又 "hand," and 示 "altar" signifying a hand purifying an offering. Inside a house of worship, people look for a god's will carefully and reflect on it. The kanji 察 means "to conjecture; to look thoroughly."

観察 observation
察する to perceive, to feel sympathy, to guess
察知する to perceive

推察 conjecture
診察 medical examination
洞察 insight

丶 丷 宀 宀 宀 宓 宓 宓 察 察 察 察 察 察　14

390 札

ON-KUN READINGS: サツ・ふだ

HEADER: 木

posted announcement; paper money

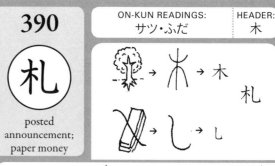

ORIGIN: The left side 木 was wood, and the right side 乚 indicated "pressing something down, or making flat." Together they meant a posted announcement written on a piece of wood. The kanji 札 means "posted announcement" or "paper money."

お札 bill, bank note
一万円札 10,000-yen note
札束 bundle of bank notes

札 tally, tag
切り札 trump
表札 house name plate

一 十 才 木 札　5

391 殺

ON-KUN READINGS: サツ・サイ・セツ・ころ(す)

HEADER: 殳

to kill; to reduce

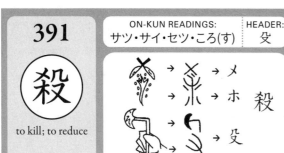

ORIGIN: The left side of the ancient form had メ a "scissors," and ホ "millet stalk." The right side 殳 had a weapon in a hand, indicating a fight or engaging in work. Together they signified to harvest and strip millet, or, further, to kill an animal, or to reduce. The simplified current form 殺 means "to kill; to reduce."

殺す to kill
殺人 murder
人殺し murder

相殺 set off, offset
殺菌 sterilization
毒殺 poisoning

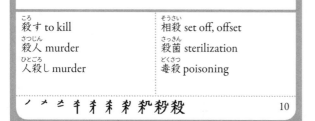 10

392 雑

ON-KUN READINGS: ザツ・ゾウ

HEADER: 隹

various; assorted

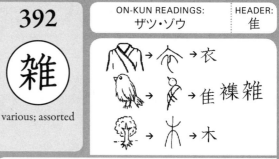

ORIGIN: The old form 襍 had ネ (衣) "clothes" and 集 "to gather" (隹 birds on 木 a tree). Together they indicated clothes made of various types of cloth, and in general meant "assorted; various." The current form 雑 has the bird on the right side. The kanji 雑 means "various; assorted."

雑誌 magazine
複雑な complicated
雑な careless

混雑 crowdedness
雑巾 dust cloth
雑煮 mochi soup (special New Year's dish)

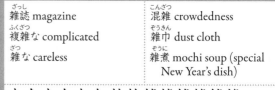 14

393

ON-KUN READINGS: さら

HEADER: 皿

皿

plate; flat dish

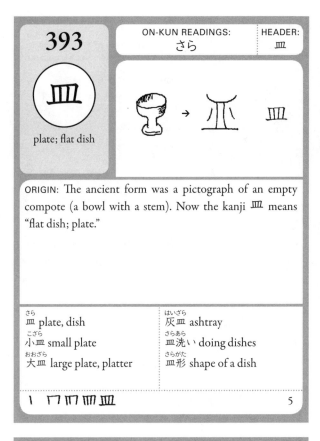

ORIGIN: The ancient form was a pictograph of an empty compote (a bowl with a stem). Now the kanji 皿 means "flat dish; plate."

さら
皿 plate, dish
こざら
小皿 small plate
おおざら
大皿 large plate, platter

はいざら
灰皿 ashtray
さらあら
皿洗い doing dishes
さらがた
皿形 shape of a dish

一 冂 冊 皿 皿   5

394

ON-KUN READINGS: サン・み・みっ(つ)

HEADER: 一

三

three; third

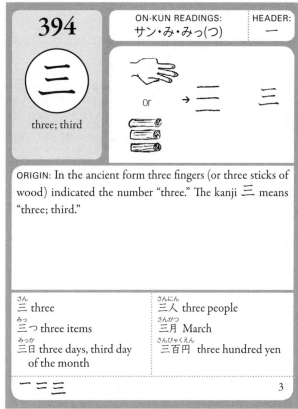

ORIGIN: In the ancient form three fingers (or three sticks of wood) indicated the number "three." The kanji 三 means "three; third."

さん
三 three
みっ
三つ three items
みっか
三日 three days, third day
  of the month

さんにん
三人 three people
さんがつ
三月 March
さんびゃくえん
三百円 three hundred yen

一 二 三   3

395

ON-KUN READINGS: サン・まい(る)

HEADER: ム

参

to come or go
[humble]; to visit
a temple or shrine

ORIGIN: The old form 參 depicted a woman who had three hair accessories ム on her head and was dressed in beautiful clothes (彡 "design"). Together they signified a woman visiting a temple or shrine. Now the top is abbreviated to one ム. The kanji 参 means "to come or go" (humble form) or "to visit a temple or shrine."

まい
参る [humble] to come, go
さんか
参加する to participate, join
はかまい
墓参り visit to a grave site

さんこう
参考にする to use as reference
さんどう
参道 shrine approach
しんざん
新参 newcomer

ㄥ ㅿ 쓰 쓰 夳 夅 参 参   8

396

ON-KUN READINGS: サン・やま

HEADER: 山

山

mountain

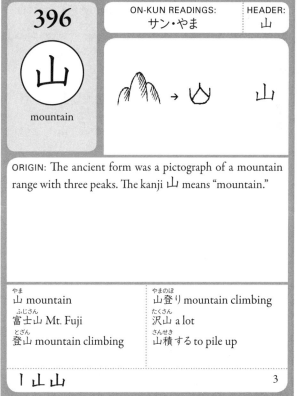

ORIGIN: The ancient form was a pictograph of a mountain range with three peaks. The kanji 山 means "mountain."

やま
山 mountain
ふじさん
富士山 Mt. Fuji
とざん
登山 mountain climbing

やまのぼ
山登り mountain climbing
たくさん
沢山 a lot
さんせき
山積する to pile up

｜ 山 山   3

397

ON-KUN READINGS: サン・ち(る)

HEADER: 攵

散

to disperse

ORIGIN: In the ancient form the left side consisted of hemp plants that were broken up for fiber, and 月 "meat" that were likewise cut into pieces. Together with 攵 "pounding action," it indicated the act of breaking into pieces and scattering. The kanji 散 means "to disperse."

散歩 a stroll (さんぽ)
散る to disperse, fall (ち)
分散 dispersion (ぶんさん)

散髪 haircut (さんばつ)
散々な merciless (さんさん)
解散 breakup (かいさん)

一 十 廿 廿 莊 莊 昔 昔 散 散 散   12

398

ON-KUN READINGS: サン・う(む)・うぶ

HEADER: 生

産

to give birth;
to produce

ORIGIN: In the ancient form, 文 "beautiful pattern" that a layer of collars formed and 厂 signified a handsome forehead, like a well-defined cliff. The bottom 生 is "birth." Together they indicated a birth of a beautiful child, or production of goods. The kanji 産 means "to give birth" or "to produce."

産む to give birth (う)
産み出す to create (う だ)
出産 childbirth, delivery (しゅっさん)

産業 industry (さんぎょう)
日本産 Japanese product (にほんさん)
倒産 bankruptcy (とうさん)

丶 亠 产 立 产 产 产 产 産 産   11

399

ON-KUN READINGS: サン

HEADER: 竹

算

to count

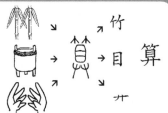

ORIGIN: The top 竹 was a pictograph of bamboo stalks. The bottom came from 具, which depicted two hands holding a pot. Bamboo sticks were used for counting. The kanji 算 means "to count."

計算 calculation (けいさん)
算数 arithmetic (さんすう)
暗算 mental calculation (あんざん)

足し算 addition (た さん)
引き算 subtraction (ひ さん)
打算的 calculating (ださんてき)

ノ 仁 仁 竹 竹 竹 竹 符 笪 筲 笪 算 算 算   14

400

ON-KUN READINGS: サン・かいこ

HEADER: 虫

蚕

silkworm

ORIGIN: In the old form 蠶, the upper part was used phonetically to indicate the action of burrowing, and the bottom had two 虫 worms. Silkworms burrow between mulberry leaves. From this idea, the kanji came to mean a silkworm and the simpler kanji 蚕 came to be used. The kanji 蚕 means "silkworm."

蚕 silkworm (かいこ)
養蚕 silkworm culture raising (ようさん)
蚕業 sericulture (さんぎょう)

一 二 チ 天 天 吞 吞 吞 蚕 蚕   10

401

ON-KUN READINGS:	HEADER:
サン	貝

贅

to assist favorably;
to praise

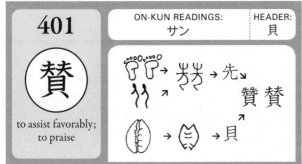

ORIGIN: The old form 贊 had two occurrences of the character 先 "two feet in a forward motion" and the bottom was a cowry, signifying money or goods. Together they indicated giving a present when meeting someone, which would presumably help the relationship. The kanji 賛 means "to assist favorably" or "to praise."

さんせい
賛成 する to support, to be in favor of
さんどう
賛同 する to support
じがじさん
自画自賛 self-admiration

さんびか
賛美歌 hymn
さんぴ
賛否 yes or no, approval or disapproval
らいさん
礼賛 praise, glorification

一 二 チ 夫 夫 夫 扶 扶 扶 替 替 替 替 賛 賛   15

402

ON-KUN READINGS:	HEADER:
サン・す(い)	酉

酸

sour; acid; oxygen

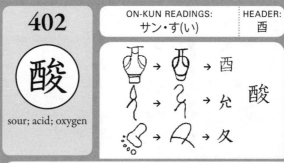

ORIGIN: The left side 酉 was a pictograph of a wine jar. In the right side 夋, the top signified a supple body and the bottom a backward foot, indicating a person who is slim and supple. Acid is believed to help to keep one's body supple. Fermented liquid like wine that tenderizes food is acid. The kanji 酸 means "acid" or "sour."

す
酸っぱい sour
さんせい
酸性 acidity
さんみ
酸味 sour taste

さんそ
酸素 oxygen
さんか
酸化 する to oxidize
さんけつ
酸欠 lack of oxygen

一 厂 厂 万 丙 酉 酉 酉 酚 酚 酸 酸 酸 酸   14

137

403

ON-KUN READINGS:	HEADER:
ザン・のこ(る)	歹

残

to remain; cruel

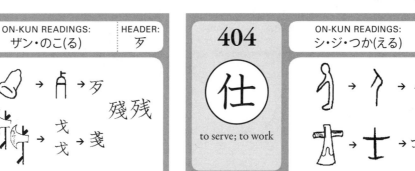

ORIGIN: The old form 殘 had 歹 "bones or death" and two 戈 "lances or halberds," which signified cutting (bones) into small pieces. Together they originally indicated to kill, cut, and leave the pieces, or remains. The kanji 残 means "to remain" or "to be cruel."

ざんねん
残念 な regrettable
のこ
残る to remain
むざん
無残 な atrocious

ざんだか
残高 the balance
ざんしょ
残暑 lingering heat of summer
なごり
名残 leave-taking, trace

一 ア 万 歹 歹 歼 歼 残 残 残   10

404

ON-KUN READINGS:	HEADER:
シ・ジ・つか(える)	イ

仕

to serve; to work

ORIGIN: The left side イ was "person." The right side, 士 "warrior," came from a weapon placed upside down during an audience or a ceremony, signifying a member of the warrior class, or standing upright. Together they indicated a man who stood upright to serve a master. The kanji 仕 means "to serve" or "to work."

しごと
仕事 job, work
しきた
仕来り tradition, a customary practice
つか
仕える to serve

しかた
仕方がない cannot be helped
ほうしかつどう
奉仕活動 volunteer activity
しおく
仕送りする to send allowance

ノ イ イ 什 仕   5

405

ON-KUN READINGS: シ・つか(う)

HEADER: イ

使

to use; servant

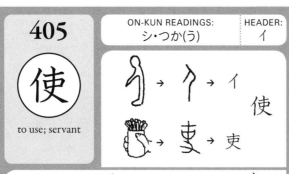

ORIGIN: The left side イ was a person. The right side 吏 was a hand holding a container of bamboo tallies that were used to count and record goods, or a hand of a government official who tallied. Together they indicated a person who worked (in general) and also the verb "to work." The kanji 使 means "to use" or "servant."

つか
使う to use
しょうちゅう
使用中 in use, occupied
たいし
大使 ambassador

しめい
使命 mission
しようりょう
使用料 fee to use
てんし
天使 angel

ノイ イ 仁 佢 侢 使使   8

406

ON-KUN READINGS: シ・つかさど(る)・つかさ

HEADER: ロ

司

to administer; official

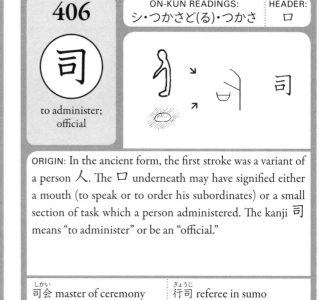

ORIGIN: In the ancient form, the first stroke was a variant of a person 人. The ロ underneath may have signified either a mouth (to speak or to order his subordinates) or a small section of task which a person administered. The kanji 司 means "to administer" or be an "official."

しかい
司会 master of ceremony
しほう
司法 judicature, administration of justice
つかさど
司る to take charge of

ぎょうじ
行司 referee in sumo
ししょ
司書 librarian
じょうし
上司 boss

フコ司司司   5

407

ON-KUN READINGS: シ

HEADER: ロ

史

history; to chronicle

ORIGIN: The ancient form was a depiction of a hand holding a container of bamboo sticks that were used to count, signifying counting and keeping records. A chronicle is a recorded history. The kanji 史 means "to chronicle" or "history."

れきし
歴史 history
にほんし
日本史 Japanese history
せかいし
世界史 world history

しじょう
史上 in history
しじつ
史実 historical facts
しせき
史跡 historical site

1 ロロ史史   5

408

ON-KUN READINGS: シ・よ・よん

HEADER: 囗

四

four

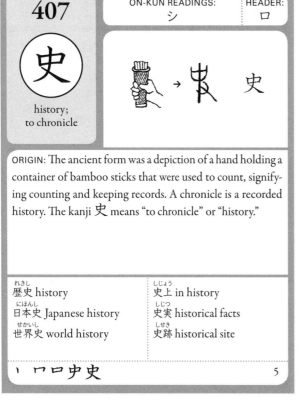

ORIGIN: The ancient form for "four" had four lines. The later form 四 consisted of 囗 "an area," and 八 "splitting up into half"; it was borrowed from another word that had the same sound. The kanji 四 means "four."

よん
四 four
よっ
四つ four items
よっか
四日 fourth day of the month, four days

よにん
四人 four people
しほう
四方 all directions
よもやまばなし
四方山話 chat about general topics

1 ロ 冂 四 四   5

409

ON-KUN READINGS: シ HEADER: 士

士
man; warrior

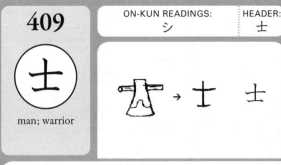

ORIGIN: The ancient form depicted an ax or a weapon placed with the blade down. During an audience or religious rite, having a weapon placed upside down by one's side signified a member of the warrior class. The kanji 士 means "man" or "warrior."

ぶし
武士 samurai
へいし
兵士 soldier
しぞく
士族 family of samurai ancestry

しき
士気 morale, fighting spirits
ぶんし
文士 literary person
りきし
力士 sumo wrestler

一十士　　3

410

ON-KUN READINGS: シ・はじ(める) HEADER: 女

始
to begin

ORIGIN: The left side 女 was woman. The right side 台 consisted of a plow ム and a mouth 口, here used phonetically for "to begin." Together they indicated a first-born daughter, but later the female meaning was dropped. The kanji 始 means "to begin."

はじ
始める to begin
かいし
開始する to begin
はじ
始めに in the beginning

しはつ
始発 first (train, bus) of day
てはじ
手始めに to begin with
しぎょうじかん
始業時間 beginning time

くゟ女女女女始始始始　　8

411

ON-KUN READINGS: シ・あね HEADER: 女

姉
older sister

ORIGIN: The left side 女 was a pictograph of a woman. The old form of 市 depicted a marking at the top of a vine stake, indicating a start. Together they indicated a first female person, such as a first-born daughter. The kanji 姉 means "older sister."

あね
姉 older sister
おね
お姉さん older sister
しまい
姉妹 sisters

あねご
姉御 bossy woman
あねむすめ
姉娘 elder daughter
あね　　にょうぼう
姉さん女房 wife who is older than husband

くゟ女女女女姉姉姉　　8

412

ON-KUN READINGS: シ・すがた HEADER: 女

姿
figure; form

ORIGIN: The top 次 means "to get ready" from 欠 a "person stooped to put two things (二) in order." The bottom 女 is a woman. Together they indicated a woman tidying herself up, or appearances in general. The kanji 姿 means "figure; form."

すがた
姿 figure, shape
ようし
容姿 appearances
うしろすがた
後姿 the appearance from the back

しせい
姿勢 posture
すがたみ
姿見 a full-length mirror
ゆうし
雄姿 gallant figure

丶冫丬次次姿姿　　9

139

413

ON-KUN READINGS: シ・ス・こ

HEADER: 子

子
child

ORIGIN: The ancient form of this kanji was a pictograph of an infant waving its arms. An infant is in a diaper (thus the two legs are not shown). The kanji 子 means "child."

子供 child
こども

男子学生 male student
だんしがくせい

女の子 girl
おんな こ

親子 parent and child
おやこ

弟子 disciple, student
でし

利子 interest
りし

フ了子　3

414

ON-KUN READINGS: シ・いち

HEADER: 巾

市
market; city; municipal

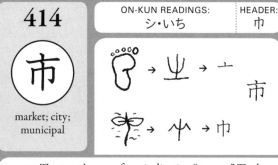

ORIGIN: The top 亠 was a foot, indicating "to stop." The bottom indicated balance (a water weed floating on water). 市 "market" is a place where many people stop walking to see the goods and negotiate prices. The kanji 市 means "market," "city," or "municipal."

市 city
し

京都市 Kyoto City
きょうとし

市長 mayor
しちょう

市場 market
いちば

株式市場 stock market
かぶしきしじょう

朝市 morning street market
あさいち

丶亠广市市　5

415

ON-KUN READINGS: シ・や

HEADER: 矢

矢
arrow

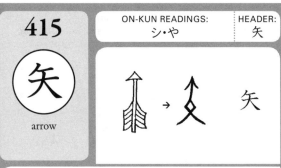

ORIGIN: The ancient form was a pictograph of an arrow. The kanji 矢 means "arrow."

弓矢 bow and arrow
ゆみや

矢 arrow
や

矢印 arrow
やじるし

毒矢 poisoned arrow
どくや

矢面 brunt of an attack
やおもて

一矢報いる to take a fling at
いっしむく

ノ 一 二 午 矢　5

416

ON-KUN READINGS: シ

HEADER: 巾

師
teacher; mentor; military unit

ORIGIN: The left side 𠂤 depicted a stack of dirt, or hill, or boundary. The right side was a banner. Together they signified a military division. A military division has a commander, who guides the soldiers. From this meaning it is also used for someone regarded as a mentor. The kanji 師 means "teacher; mentor" or "military unit."

教師 teacher
きょうし

牧師 pastor
ぼくし

師弟関係 teacher and
していかんけい
　student relationship

恩師 one's former teacher
おんし

師事する to study under
しじ

師団 military division
しだん

ノ 丨 斤 斤 自 自 卣 師師　10

140

417

ON-KUN READINGS: シ・こころざし・こころざ(す)

HEADER: 心

志

will; aspiration

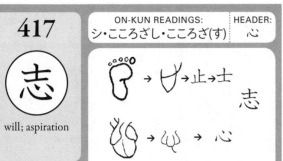

ORIGIN: The top 士 came from 止 "footprint," indicating "to go." The bottom 心 was a pictograph of a heart. Together, they indicated where one's heart wants to go—that is will, or ambition. The kanji 志 means "will" or "aspiration."

こころざし
志 aspiration
たいし
大志 ambition
しぼう
志望 desire, ambition

ゆうし
有志 volunteer
しがんへい
志願兵 volunteer (soldier)
しこう
志向 tendency

一十士士志志志 7

418

ON-KUN READINGS: シ・おも(う)

HEADER: 心

思

to think; thought

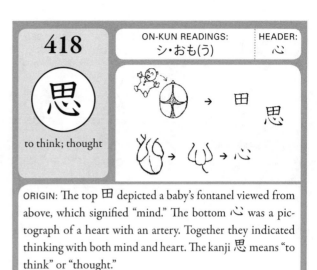

ORIGIN: The top 田 depicted a baby's fontanel viewed from above, which signified "mind." The bottom 心 was a pictograph of a heart with an artery. Together they indicated thinking with both mind and heart. The kanji 思 means "to think" or "thought."

おも
思う to think
おも で
思い出 memory
おも だ
思い出す to recollect
memory

しそう
思想 thought, ideology
しあん
思案する to consider

丨口口田田田思思思 9

419

ON-KUN READINGS: シ・ゆび・さ(す)

HEADER: 扌

指

finger

ORIGIN: The left side 扌 was a pictograph of a hand. The right side 旨 consisted of a small knife and a mouth with food inside. Together, they signified "tasty": using fingers to taste good food. The kanji 指 means "finger."

ゆび
指 finger
ゆびさき
指先 the tip of a finger
ゆびさ
指差す to point at

していせき
指定席 reserved seat
さしず
指図する to instruct, give
orders
ゆびわ
指輪 ring

一十扌扌扪扪指指指 9

420

ON-KUN READINGS: シ・ささ(える)

HEADER: 支

支

to support; branch

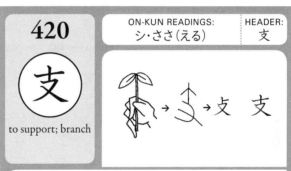

ORIGIN: The old form 攴 depicted a hand holding a bamboo stalk straight up, which signified "to support." A stalk also has branches, so it also indicated "branch." The kanji 支 means "branch" or "to support."

ささ
支える to support
しじ
支持 support
しえん
支援 support

しはいにん
支配人 manager
してん
支店 branch store
しぶ
支部 branch office, chapter

一十支支 4

141

421

ON-KUN READINGS: シ・えだ

HEADER: 木

枝

tree branch; bough

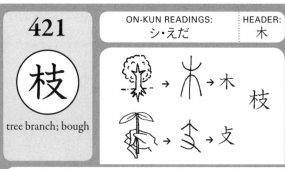

ORIGIN: The left side 木 is a tree or wood. The old form 支 depicted a hand holding a bamboo stalk straight up, which signified "to support" and branches. With the two sides combined, the kanji 枝 means "tree branch; bough."

枝 branch
枝先 the tip of a branch
小枝 twigs

枝分かれ branching out
枝葉末節 unimportant details
枝豆 green soy beans

一 十 オ 木 村 杙 杖 枝   8

422

ON-KUN READINGS: シ・と(める)

HEADER: 止

止

to stop

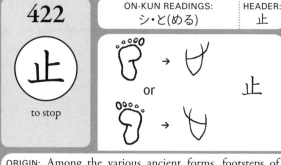

ORIGIN: Among the various ancient forms, footsteps of either right or left were found. (But only one foot! Both feet make up another kanji, 歩, "to walk.") A foot that stays in one place is stopped. The kanji 止 means "to stop."

止める to stop
止める to quit
中止する to cancel

取り止め cancellation
通行止め traffic closure
休止 stop, suspension

１ ト ト 止   4

423

ON-KUN READINGS: シ・し(ぬ)

HEADER: 歹

死

to die; death

ORIGIN: The left side 歹 was a variant of 骨 "bone." The right side depicted a person who pays respect to the deceased. In ancient times, a body was left outside to be weathered by exposure before a burial. The right side is now written as ヒ, a variant of "person." The kanji 死 means "to die" or "death."

死ぬ to die
病死 death due to an illness
死亡 death

必死で frantically
即死 instantaneous death
過労死 death due to overwork exhaustion

一 ア 万 歹 歼 死   6

424

ON-KUN READINGS: シ・うじ

HEADER: 氏

氏

surname

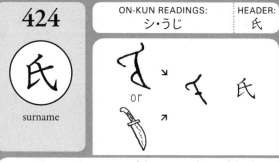

ORIGIN: One interpretation of the ancient form of this kanji is a flat spoon with a bent handle, which was borrowed to mean "particular noble family," on a hill. Another one is a short knife with a handle that was used to cut meat for a feast of a clan. 氏 indicated family lineage. The kanji 氏 means "surname."

山口氏 Mr. Yamaguchi
氏名 surname and given name
氏 lineage, blood

氏育ち family name and upbringing
氏神 patron saint
彼氏 he, boyfriend

丿 厂 氏 氏   4

425

ON-KUN READINGS: シ・わたくし **HEADER:** 禾

私

I; personal; private

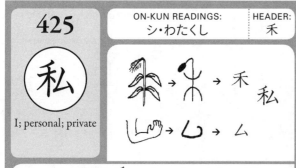

ORIGIN: The left side 禾 was "rice plants laden with crops" and the right side, 厶 "an arm bent to claim what belongs to oneself," signified an act of claiming one's personal property. The combined form indicated "private" or "pertaining to oneself." The kanji 私 means "I" or "private; personal."

私立大学 private university (しりつだいがく)
私用 personal errand (しよう)
公私 public and private (こうし)
私 I (わたし)

私的な personal (matter) (してき)
私物 personal property (しぶつ)
私費 private fund (しひ)

一二千禾禾私私 7

426

ON-KUN READINGS: シ・いと **HEADER:** 糸

糸

thread

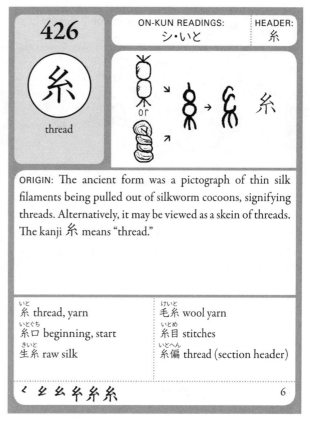

ORIGIN: The ancient form was a pictograph of thin silk filaments being pulled out of silkworm cocoons, signifying threads. Alternatively, it may be viewed as a skein of threads. The kanji 糸 means "thread."

糸 thread, yarn (いと)
糸口 beginning, start (いとぐち)
生糸 raw silk (きいと)

毛糸 wool yarn (けいと)
糸目 stitches (いとめ)
糸偏 thread (section header) (いとへん)

く纟纟纟糸糸 6

427

ON-KUN READINGS: シ・かみ **HEADER:** 糸

紙

paper

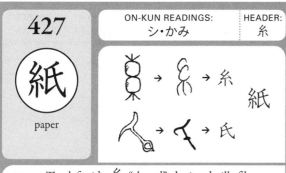

ORIGIN: The left side 糸 "thread" depicted silk filaments being pulled out of silkworm cocoons. The right side 氏 depicted a flat ladle, emphasizing flatness. Together they indicated a thin sheet of paper made of plant fibers. The kanji 紙 means "paper."

紙 paper (かみ)
色紙 colored paper (いろがみ)
手紙 letter (てがみ)

新聞紙 newspaper (paper) (しんぶんし)
紙切れ a piece of paper (かみきれ)
白紙に戻す to start afresh (はくし・もど)

く纟纟纟糸糸糸紙紙紙 10

428

ON-KUN READINGS: シ・いた(る) **HEADER:** 至

至

to reach an end

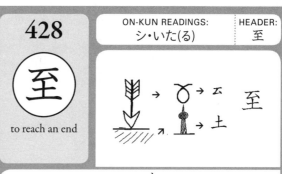

ORIGIN: An arrow hitting soil 土 does not have anywhere further to go. It reaches its target or the ground. The kanji 至 means "to reach an end."

至る to reach (いた)
夏至 the summer solstice (げし)
至急の urgent (しきゅう)

至上命令 supreme order (しじょうめいれい)
必至の inevitable (ひっし)
至難の extremely difficult (しなん)

一云云至至至 6

143

429

ON-KUN READINGS: シ
HEADER: 見

視
to gaze at

ORIGIN: The left side ネ originally depicted an altar where the moon, sun, and a star were worshipped with an offering on a table. Here the left side is used phonetically to mean "straight." The right side 見 depicted a large eye and a person, indicating someone looking straight at something. Together they form the kanji 視, "to gaze at."

視力 eyesight (しりょく)
近視 nearsighted (きんし)
視覚的 visual (しかくてき)

視点 viewpoint (してん)
直視する to look squarely (ちょくし)
無視する to ignore (むし)

丶 亅 ネ ネ ネ ネ 初 初 初 視 視 視　11

430

ON-KUN READINGS: シ
HEADER: 言

詞
part of speech; word; lyrics

ORIGIN: The left side 言 came from a needle 辛 and a mouth 口, signifying "to speak clearly and sharply." The right side 司 "to administer" was used phonetically. Together they indicated words that were connected, a part of speech, or lyrics of a song. The kanji 詞 means "word; part of speech; lyrics."

歌詞 lyrics (かし)
作詞者 lyricist (さくししゃ)
名詞 noun (めいし)

動詞 verb (どうし)
形容詞 adjective (けいようし)
助詞 particle (じょし)

丶 二 亠 亍 言 言 言 訂 訂 訶 詞 詞　12

431

ON-KUN READINGS: シ
HEADER: 言

詩
poetry

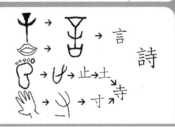

ORIGIN: The left side 言 came from a sharp needle 辛 and a mouth 口, signifying "to speak clearly and sharply." 寺 consisted of a foot and a hand holding something down. Together they indicated writing down words that express one's thoughts. The kanji 詩 means "poetry."

詩 poem (し)
詩人 poet (しじん)
詩歌 poetry (しいか)

詩集 collection of poems (ししゅう)
詩情 poetic sentiment (しじょう)
漢詩 classical Chinese poetry (かんし)

丶 二 亠 亍 言 言 言 訂 計 詰 詰 詩 詩　13

432

ON-KUN READINGS: シ・ため(す)・こころ(みる)
HEADER: 言

試
to test; trial

ORIGIN: The ancient forms in the middle consisted of 言 "to say," and 弋 "forked stick," and 工 "complicated craft." Together they signified that in testing an apprentice the examiner would tell the apprentice to make some craft. The kanji 試 means "to test" or "trial."

試験 examination (しけん)
入試 entrance examination (にゅうし)
試合 game, match (しあい)

試す to try, to attempt (ため)
試みる to try (こころ)
試しに on trial (ため)

丶 二 亠 亍 言 言 言 訂 訂 試 試 試　13

144

433

誌

magazine; journal

ON-KUN READINGS: シ

HEADER: 言

ORIGIN: The left side was 言 "word." The sound of the right side was 志 "to keep in one's heart" or "aspiration." Together, they indicated recording words—and, further, papers on which one writes down one's thoughts, or "magazine." The kanji 誌 means "magazine; journal."

雑誌 magazine
日誌 journal
週刊誌 weekly magazine

月刊誌 monthly magazine
文芸誌 literary magazine
地誌 topography

`丶 一 亠 言 言 言 言 計 計 試 試 誌 誌 誌` 14

434

資

resources; capital

ON-KUN READINGS: シ

HEADER: 貝

ORIGIN: The top 次 means "to get ready" from 欠, a person stooped over to put two (or many) things in order. The bottom 貝 was a cowry used for currency to buy goods. The combined form signified the goods that were to be used in the future. The kanji 資 means "resources; capital."

投資 investment
資料 data
資格 license, qualification

資本主義 capitalism
資金 fund
学資 education fund

`丶 冫 冫 汀 汀 次 次 済 済 资 資 資 資` 13

435

飼

to keep (animals)

ON-KUN READINGS: シ・か(う)

HEADER: 食

ORIGIN: The left side derived from 食 "food" (or "to eat"), and the right side 司 was used phonetically to indicate "to give"; combined, they signified feeding or rearing animals. The kanji 飼 means "to keep (animals)."

飼う to keep (an animal)
飼育 to raise (an animal)
飼料 animal feed

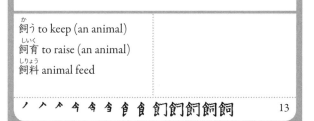
`丿 𠆢 𠆢 今 今 今 食 食 飼 飼 飼 飼 飼` 13

436

歯

tooth

ON-KUN READINGS: シ・は

HEADER: 止

ORIGIN: In the ancient form the top 止 was a footprint, indicating "to stay in one place." Inside 凵 "mouth" were two rows of teeth, a form that later was replaced by 米. Together the kanji combined to form the kanji 歯, "tooth."

歯 tooth
虫歯 decayed tooth, cavity
前歯 front tooth

歯科医 dentist
歯医者 dentist
歯痛・歯痛 tooth ache

`丨 ⺊ ⺊ 步 步 步 歯 歯 歯 歯 歯 歯` 12

437

ON-KUN READINGS:	HEADER:
ジ・ズ・こと	⼅

事

thing; matter

ORIGIN: The ancient form depicted a right hand holding a cylinder-shaped container with bamboo tallies, which were counted by a record-keeping official. The meaning was extended to indicate any job or any matter in general. The kanji 事 indicates "thing; matter."

こと
事 matter
ことがら
事柄 matter
ようじ
用事 errand

じじょう
事情 situation, circumstances
じけん
事件 incidence
じじ
時事 current affairs

一 一 一 写 写 写 写 事　　　8

438

ON-KUN READINGS:	HEADER:
ジ・に(る)	イ

似

to resemble; to take after

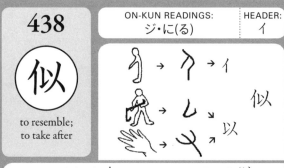

ORIGIN: The left side イ is a person. The right side 以 was a plow and a hand, signifying a farmer—here used phonetically to indicate "image." Together the kanji indicated someone who looked similar to another. The kanji 似 means "to resemble; to take after."

に
似ている to resemble
るいじ
類似する to resemble
にがお
似顔 portrait, likeness

ちちおやに
父親似 resemblance to one's father
そうじ
相似 similarity

ノ イ 化 化 化 似 似　　　7

439

ON-KUN READINGS:	HEADER:
ジ・二	儿

児

a very young child

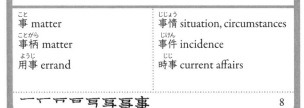

ORIGIN: The old form 兒 (as well as the ancient form shown in the middle) had a break in the top, signifying two tufts of hair on the head of a very young child. The bottom 儿 was legs, or a person standing. The kanji 児 means "a very young child."

じどう
児童 child
にゅうじ
乳児 infant
こじ
孤児 orphan

しょうにか
小児科 pediatrics
えんじ
園児 kindergarten pupil
さんさいじ
三歳児 three-year-old child

丨 丨丨 丨口 丨旧 丨日 旧 児　　　7

440

ON-KUN READINGS:	HEADER:
ジ・あざ	子

字

letter; writing

ORIGIN: The top 宀 signified a house, and the bottom 子 depicted a child. Children are born one after another in a house—and that idea signifies proliferation. Writing forms were also produced prolifically, similar to the birth of children. The kanji 字 means "letter; writing."

じ
字 letter, writing
かんじ
漢字 Chinese character, kanji
もじ
文字 letter, writing

すうじ
数字 numeral, number
あざ
字 a village section
じまく
字幕 subtitle

丶 丷 宀 字 字 字 字　　　6

146

441

ON-KUN READINGS: ジ・てら

HEADER: 寸

寺 temple

ORIGIN: The top 土, from 止 "footstep," was used phonetically and the bottom 寸 depicted a "hand". The combined form signified "to own; to hold." It was originally used to mean "government office" and then changed to "a temple" after a group of Buddhist monks started to occupy the building. The kanji 寺 means "temple."

寺 temple
寺院 temple
大德寺 Daitoku-ji Temple

寺子屋 old-style private school
山寺 temple in a mountain
寺社 temple and shrine

一 十 土 土 寺 寺

6

442

ON-KUN READINGS: ジ・も(つ)

HEADER: 扌

持 to hold something in hand; to possess

ORIGIN: The left side 扌 came from a pictograph of "a (left) hand." 寺 (土 from 止 "footstep" and 寸 "hand") originally indicated "to have in hand." Together they signified to hold something in hand. The kanji 持 means "to hold something in hand; to possess."

持つ to hold in one's hand
持っている to have, to own
持ってくる to bring

持参する to bring
持ち物 a belonging
持続する to sustain

一 十 扌 扫 担 持 持 持

9

443

ON-KUN READINGS: ジ・とき・と

HEADER: 日

時 time

ORIGIN: The left side 日 was a sun. 寺 is comprised of 土 (originally 止 "footstep") and 寸 "hands" or "a small amount." Together the forms signified sustaining time. The kanji 時 means "time."

時 time
時代 period, era
三時 three o'clock

時刻表 timetable
当時 at that time
瞬時 momentarily

1 日 日 日 旷 旷 旷 時 時 時

10

444

ON-KUN READINGS: ジ・シ・つ(ぐ)・つぎ

HEADER: 欠

次 next

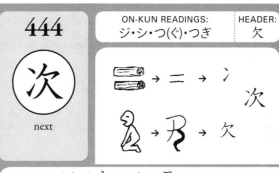

ORIGIN: The left side 冫 came from 二, which meant "to put things side by side." The right side 欠 was a person crouching with an open mouth to breathe deeply. A traveler, while resting, placed his belongings side by side for the next move. The kanji 次 means "next."

次に next
次の人 next person
次回 next time

目次 table of contents
次々に one after another
相次いで successively

ン ゝ 冫 汁 次 次

6

445

ON-KUN READINGS: ジ・チ・なお(す)・おさ(める)

HEADER: シ

治

to govern;
to control; to cure

ORIGIN: The left side シ was water. The right side 台 had a plow ム and a mouth 口, signifying communal, agrarian work. Together they indicated working together to control irrigation water or a flood. When one puts his illness under control, he is cured. The kanji 治 means "to govern," "to control," or "to cure."

なお
治る to recover from illness
せいじ
政治 politics
じち
自治 self-governance

おさ
治める to govern, to reign
ちあん
治安 public safety
ちりょう
治療 medical treatment, remedy

ヽ ゛ ⅰ 氵 沪 治 治 治 治　　8

446

ON-KUN READINGS: ジ

HEADER: 石

磁

magnet

ORIGIN: The left side 石 was a rock. The right side had grass and two short threads, signifying young, short grass multiplying profusely. Iron filings get pulled to a magnet and look like tiny seedlings of grass. The kanji 磁 means "magnet."

じしゃく
磁石 magnet
じば
磁場 magnetic field
でんじ
電磁 electromagnetic

とうじき
陶磁器 ceramic ware
じき
磁器 porcelain
せいじき
青磁器 celadon, porcelain

一 厂 T 石 石 石 石ᵗ 矿 矿 磁 磁 磁 磁 磁　　14

447

ON-KUN READINGS: ジ・シ・しめ(す)

HEADER: 示

示

to show;
to demonstrate

ORIGIN: In the ancient form the top was an offering on an altar. The bottom came from the moon, the sun, and a star, together indicating ancestor worship. An altar was where a god's will was shown; hence the kanji 示 means "to show; to demonstrate."

しめ
示す to show
けいじばん
掲示板 bulletin board
ひょうじ
表示する to indicate, to manifest

ていじ
提示する to present
じだん
示談 settlement out of court
あんじてき
暗示的 suggestive

一 二 亍 示 示　　5

448

ON-KUN READINGS: ジ・みみ

HEADER: 耳

耳

ear

ORIGIN: The ancient forms (the second and the third ones) were a pictograph of an ear. The kanji 耳 means "ear."

みみ
耳 ear
りょうみみ
両耳 both ears
じびか
耳鼻科 a nose and ear specialist

みみ　と お
耳が遠い hard of hearing
みみ　き
耳が聞えない deaf
そらみみ
空耳 mishearing

一 丁 下 下 耳 耳　　6

148

449

ON-KUN READINGS: シ・ジ・みずか(ら)・おのずか(ら)

HEADER: 自

自
oneself

ORIGIN: The ancient form was a stylized depiction of a nose. A nose is in the center of one's face. When one refers to oneself in Japan, one points to one's nose. The kanji 自 means "oneself."

自分で by oneself, on one's own
みずか
自ら on one's own
かくじ
各自 each

じどうしゃ
自動車 car, automobile
じてんしゃ
自転車 bicycle
じどうてき
自動的に automatically

' ｢ 冂 自 自 自　6

450

ON-KUN READINGS: ジ・や(める)

HEADER: 辛

辞
word; decline

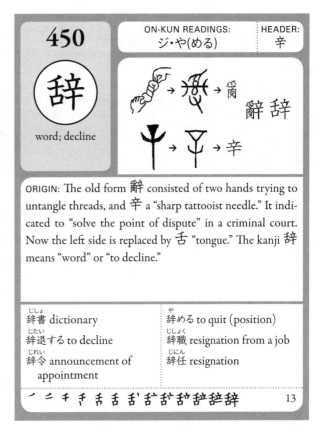

ORIGIN: The old form 辭 consisted of two hands trying to untangle threads, and 辛 a "sharp tattooist needle." It indicated to "solve the point of dispute" in a criminal court. Now the left side is replaced by 舌 "tongue." The kanji 辞 means "word" or "to decline."

じしょ
辞書 dictionary
じたい
辞退する to decline
じれい
辞令 announcement of appointment

や
辞める to quit (position)
じしょく
辞職 resignation from a job
じにん
辞任 resignation

一 二 千 千 舌 舌 舌' 舌＇舌辛 舌辛 辞辛 辞　13

149

451

ON-KUN READINGS: シキ

HEADER: 弋

式
ceremony; formula

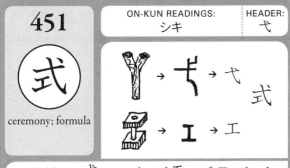

ORIGIN: The top 弋 was a stake and 工 a craft. Together they indicated a set way or format to make crafts, or a social setting such as a ceremony. The kanji 式 means "formula" or "ceremony."

しき
式 ceremony
そつぎょうしき
卒業式 graduation ceremony
わしき
和式 Japanese style

けいしき
形式 formality
せいしき
正式な formal
すうしき
数式 numerical formula

一 二 于 王 式 式　6

452

ON-KUN READINGS: シキ

HEADER: 言

識
knowledge; mark

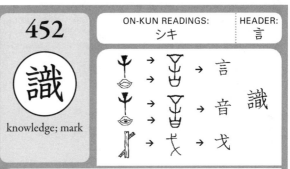

ORIGIN: The left side 言 came from a tattooist needle and 口 "mouth," signifying "to speak clearly and sharply." The right side had 戈 "pole posted in the ground" and 音 "sound," indicating "sign." Together they signified "to recognize differences with words and markings." The kanji 識 means "knowledge; mark."

じょうしき
常識 common sense
ちしき
知識 knowledge
ちしきじん
知識人 intellectuals

しきじりつ
識字率 literacy rate
しきべつ
識別する to discriminate
いしき
意識 consciousness

丶 亠 亠 言 言 言 言' 言＇諳 言立 諳 諳 諳 諳 識 識 識　19

453

	ON-KUN READINGS:	HEADER:
	シチ・なな・なの	一

七
seven

ORIGIN: The kanji 十 "ten" was cut in an odd way, not quite in the middle. Seven is an odd number that is more than a half but short of ten, which is full. The kanji 七 means "seven."

七・七 seven
七つ seven items
七日 seven days, seventh day of the month

七月 July
七夕 the Star Festival (July 7)
七面鳥 turkey

一七　　　　　　　　2

454

	ON-KUN READINGS:	HEADER:
	シツ・うしな(う)・う(せる)	大

失
to lose; to slip away

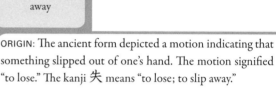

ORIGIN: The ancient form depicted a motion indicating that something slipped out of one's hand. The motion signified "to lose." The kanji 失 means "to lose; to slip away."

失礼 rudeness
失敗する to fail
失う to lose

失業者 jobless person, the unemployed
過失 fault
失恋 heartbroken

ノ ヒ 二 生 失　　　　　5

455

	ON-KUN READINGS:	HEADER:
	シツ・むろ	宀

室
room; cellar

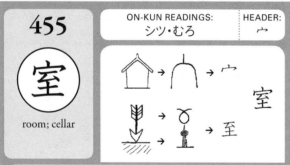

ORIGIN: The top part 宀 was a house. The bottom part 至 depicted an arrow reaching the ground 土 and not going any further, signifying "to hit an end." Together they indicated a room (because in a room, one cannot go beyond the walls or the ground). The kanji 室 means "room" or "cellar."

室内 indoors
室 cellar, greenhouse
和室 Japanese room

待合室 waiting room
在室 staying in one's room

`ノ 宀 宀 宀 宀 宀 室 室`　　　9

456

	ON-KUN READINGS:	HEADER:
	シツ・シチ・チ・ただ(す)	貝

質
contents; quality; to inquire

ORIGIN: The two tops 斤 were two ax heads, which were used as scale weights. The bottom 貝 was a cowry used as currency. Together they indicated goods or money whose values are weighed. The kanji 質 means "contents; quality" or "to inquire."

質問 question
性質 disposition, nature
人質 hostage

質屋 pawn shop
実質的な substantial
物質 material, substance

`ノ イ イ イ 斤 斤 斤 斤 質 質 質 質 質 質`　15

457

ON-KUN READINGS: ジツ・み・みの(る)

HEADER: 宀

実

real; fruit

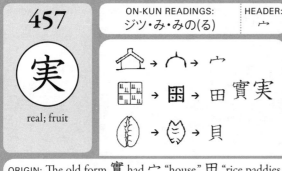

ORIGIN: The old form 實 had 宀 "house," 田 "rice paddies full of crops," indicating "fullness"; and 貝 "cowry" or "currency." Together they signified "filled with crops and treasures," or something of substance inside. Now simplified to 実, the kanji means "real" or "fruit."

実は as a matter of fact
現実的 realistic
木の実 nut

実物 actual thing
実感する to feel actually
実る to bear fruit

いハウ宀宇宇宇実実   8

458

ON-KUN READINGS: シャ

HEADER: 人

舎

house

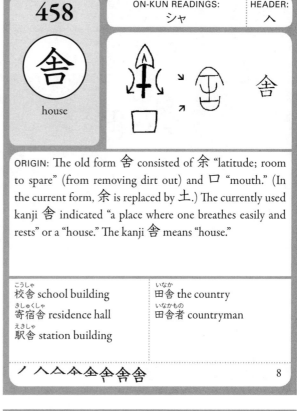

ORIGIN: The old form 舍 consisted of 余 "latitude; room to spare" (from removing dirt out) and 口 "mouth." (In the current form, 余 is replaced by 土.) The currently used kanji 舎 indicated "a place where one breathes easily and rests" or a "house." The kanji 舎 means "house."

校舎 school building
寄宿舎 residence hall
駅舎 station building

田舎 the country
田舎者 countryman

ノ人へ本全全舍舍舎   8

459

ON-KUN READINGS: シャ・うつ(す)

HEADER: 冖

写

to copy

ORIGIN: In the older form 寫 "a small bird in a house" was used phonetically to mean "to take it outside." The meaning of "transferring to somewhere else" was used for this kanji. Now simplified to 写, the kanji means "to copy."

写真 photograph
写す to copy
写し duplicate

描写 description, depiction
写生 sketching (of nature)
模写 reproduction

丶冖冖写写   5

460

ON-KUN READINGS: シャ・い(る)

HEADER: 寸

射

to shoot

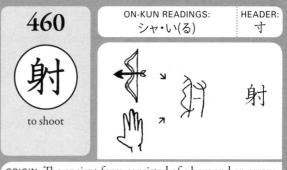

ORIGIN: The ancient form consisted of a bow and an arrow, and later 寸 "hand" was added to indicate "to shoot." The left side 身 (derived from a pregnant woman viewed sideways) in the current kanji is believed to be the result of miscopying the shape of a bow. The kanji 射 means "to shoot."

反射 reflection
発射 firing, launching
射る to shoot (an arrow)

射殺 to shoot to death
注射 injection
放射線 radiation

丶ィ竹竹自自身身射射   10

151

461

ON-KUN READINGS:	HEADER:
シャ・す(てる)	扌

捨

to throw away

ORIGIN: The old form was 捨. The left side was 扌 "hand." The right side 舍 was used phonetically to indicate "to put something down." Together the forms indicated a hand putting something down and leaving it there, or throwing away. The kanji 捨 means "to throw away."

捨てる to discard, to throw away
取捨選択する to pick a good one and discard a bad one

四捨五入 round-off
捨て身の desperate

一 十 扌 扌 扩 拧 扲 捨 捨 捨 捨 11

462

ON-KUN READINGS:	HEADER:
シャ・やしろ	ネ

社

shrine; company of people

ORIGIN: In the old form 社, 示 signified an altar table and the moon, the sun, and a star together. 土 was a mound of dirt. Together they indicated a shrine, and "congregation" or "company of people." The form ネ instead of 示 is used in the current form. The kanji 社 means "shrine" or "company of people."

神社 Shinto shrine
社内 inside a company
社員 company employee

社宅 company housing
社用 company business
社交 social intercourse

` ラ ネ ネ ネ 社 社 7

463

ON-KUN READINGS:	HEADER:
シャ・もの	耂

者

person

ORIGIN: Originally the top was a fire and the bottom a container, signifying "to bring things together to burn." This kanji was one of several variants such as 著 and 着. For phonetic similarity with the word that means "this" or "that," the kanji came to be used to point out someone. The kanji 者 means "person."

者 person
医者 medical doctor, physician
学者 scholar

悪者 villain
信者 believer, follower
記者 journalist, reporter

一 十 土 耂 耂 者 者 者 8

464

ON-KUN READINGS:	HEADER:
シャ・あやま(る)	言

謝

to apologize; to thank; to change

ORIGIN: The ancient form consisted of 言, "word," and 射 "a bow and arrow being pulled by a hand 寸." Like an arrow released from a bow, one feels a release of tension when one says words of apology or gratitude. It can also mean "to change." The kanji 謝 means "to apologize; to thank."

感謝 gratitude
謝る to apologize
謝罪 apology

謝礼 honorarium
月謝 monthly tuition
面会謝絶 no visitors allowed (for a patient)

` 亠 亠 亖 言 言 言 訁 訃 訂 訶 訥 謝 謝 謝 謝 17

465

車

wheel; vehicle

ON-KUN READINGS:	HEADER:
シャ・くるま	車

ORIGIN: The older of the two ancient forms (shown on the left) was a pictograph of a long-shafted, two-wheeled chariot with a load, viewed from above (shown on the top). The kanji 車 means "vehicle; wheel."

くるま
車 car, wheel
はっしゃ
発車する to depart (as in a vehicle)
ちゅうしゃ
駐車 parking

くるまざ
車座 sitting in a circle
しゃどう
車道 roadway
しゃそう
車窓 car/train window

一 ｢ 戸 百 甫 直 車   7

466

借

to borrow

ON-KUN READINGS:	HEADER:
シャク・か(りる)	イ

ORIGIN: The left side イ is a person. The right side 昔 comes from the sound meaning "repeating days." When something is borrowed, it changes hands to another person and then is returned to the owner, an action that is repeated between two people. The kanji 借 now means "to borrow."

か
借りる to borrow
しゃくや
借家 rented house
しゃっきん
借金 borrowing money, debt

はいしゃく
拝借する to borrow [humble-style]
しゃくよう
借用する to borrow
かしゃく
仮借ない relentless

ノ イ イ- イ# イ# イ# 佳 借 借 借   10

467

尺

scale; old Japanese foot

ON-KUN READINGS:	HEADER:
シャク	尸

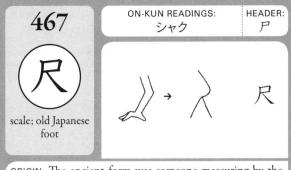

ORIGIN: The ancient form was someone measuring by the span between the thumb and the four fingers. That distance was used as a unit of measurement in China and one *shaku* 尺 was 22.5 cm (about 8.85 inches). In the Japanese measurement system one shaku was 30.3 cm (11.92 inches), or almost a foot. The kanji 尺 means a unit in the old measuring system or "scale."

しゃく
尺 the old Japanese foot
しゅくしゃく
縮尺 reduced scale
しゃくど
尺度 scale

まきじゃく
巻尺 measuring tape
しゃくはち
尺ハ (Japanese) shakuhachi flute

コ コ 尸 尺   4

468

若

young; if

ON-KUN READINGS:	HEADER:
ジャク・ニャク・わか(い)・も(しくは)	艹

ORIGIN: The ancient form depicted a young woman, or shrine maiden, with a supple body kneeling down and gently combing her hair. Both signified youth and suppleness. The form was also borrowed to mean "if." The kanji 若 means "young" or "if."

わか
若い young
わかもの
若者 young people
わかむき
若向きの fit for young people
も
若しくは or, otherwise

じゃっかん
若干の some, a few
も
若しや by any chance
じゃくはい
若輩 young man, green horn

一 十 艹 艺 芋 若 若 若   8

469

ON-KUN READINGS:	HEADER:
ジャク・よわ(い)	弓

弱 weak

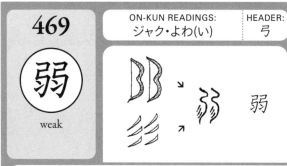

ORIGIN: The ancient form came from a depiction of two ornate bows (彡 "beautiful design"), signifying bows that were decorative but not strong. The kanji 弱 means "weak."

弱い weak
強弱 stress, rhythm
弱々しく feebly

弱点 weak point
病弱な sickly
弱み weak point

ヿ ㄱ 弓 弓 弓 弱 弱 弱 弱 弱   10

470

ON-KUN READINGS:	HEADER:
シュ・ス・ぬし・あるじ・おも	丶

主 master; main

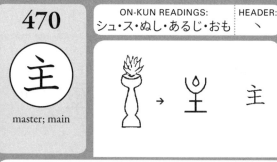

ORIGIN: The ancient form depicted a burning oil lamp. The top 丶 was a flame and 王 was an ornately decorated long-stem lamp that stood still. A master was someone who stayed in a place, whereas servants moved about working. The kanji 主 means "master" or "main."

主 proprietor
主人 master, husband
主婦 housewife

主に primarily
主要な principal, important
主義 doctrine, principle

丶 一 亠 二 主   5

471

ON-KUN READINGS:	HEADER:
シュ・と(る)	又

取 to take

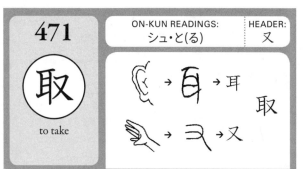

ORIGIN: The left side 耳 was a pictograph of an ear, and the right side 又 was a hand. Grabbing an animal by the ear usually gives you control. The kanji 取 means "to take; to get."

取る to take, to get
受け取る to receive
取材する to gather data, to interview

取り扱う to handle
手取り take-home pay
進取の progressive

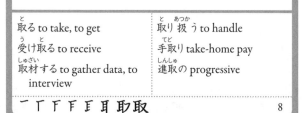

一 T F F E 耳 取 取   8

472

ON-KUN READINGS:	HEADER:
シュ・ス・かみ・まも(る)・も(り)	宀

守 to protect

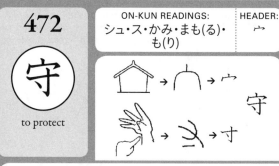

ORIGIN: The top part 宀 was a house, and the bottom part 寸 was a hand. With one's hand one protects a house and the people inside. The kanji 守 means "to protect."

守る to protect
留守 absence from a house
保守的 conservative

守衛 guard
子守 child care, baby sitter
見守る to watch over

丶 丷 宀 宀 守 守   6

473

ON-KUN READINGS: シュ・て・た

HEADER: 手

手

hand; person

ORIGIN: A pictograph of a right hand. The kanji 手 means "hand" and also "person," who uses a hand. There are a number of forms that also indicate hand, including, 又, as in 反, 扌, as in 持, 寸, as in 付, and ヨ as in 雪.

て
手 hand
じょうず
上手 skillful
みぎて
右手 right hand

うんてんしゅ
運転手 driver
てが
手書き handwritten
おおて
大手 a leading (company)

ー ニ 三手　　4

474

ON-KUN READINGS: シュ・たね

HEADER: 禾

種

seed; kind

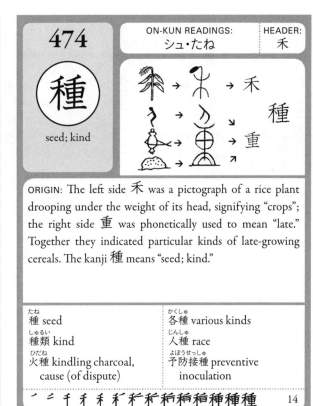

ORIGIN: The left side 禾 was a pictograph of a rice plant drooping under the weight of its head, signifying "crops"; the right side 重 was phonetically used to mean "late." Together they indicated particular kinds of late-growing cereals. The kanji 種 means "seed; kind."

たね
種 seed
しゅるい
種類 kind
ひだね
火種 kindling charcoal, cause (of dispute)

かくしゅ
各種 various kinds
じんしゅ
人種 race
よぼうせっしゅ
予防接種 preventive inoculation

ー ニ 千 千 禾 禾 秆 秆 秆 稻 稻 種 種 種　　14

475

ON-KUN READINGS: シュ・さけ・さか

HEADER: 酉

酒

Japanese sake; alcoholic drink

ORIGIN: The left side 氵 was water and the right side 酉 was a wine jar with a narrow neck. Together they indicated liquid in a wine jar. The kanji 酒 means "fermented or alcoholic drink" or "Japanese sake."

さけ
酒 alcoholic beverage
にほんしゅ
日本酒 Japanese sake
さかや
酒屋 liquor store

ようしゅ
洋酒 foreign wine or liquor
せいしゅ
清酒 refined sake
さかば
酒場 bar, saloon

　　10

476

ON-KUN READINGS: シュ・くび・こうべ

HEADER: 首

首

neck; chief; top

ORIGIN: There are two types of ancient forms, shown in (a) and (b) for this kanji. In (a), there is a head with hair and a nose in the middle. In (b) there is an eye and possibly an eyebrow. Both indicated a head or neck, and from that concept, it also means "chief." The kanji 首 means "neck" or "chief" or "top."

くび
首 neck
しゅしょう
首相 prime minister
とうしゅ
党首 head of a party

くび き
首を切る to fire (an employee)
くび
首になる to get fired
しゅい
首位 the top

丶 丷 ⺌ 产 产 首 首 首 首　　9

155

477

ON-KUN READINGS:	HEADER:
ジュ・う(ける)	又

受
to receive

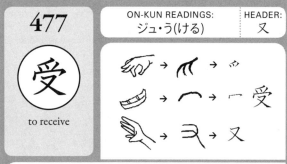

ORIGIN: In the ancient form the top 爪 was fingers, indicating a hand from above, and the bottom 又 was a hand from below. Together they depicted the act of one hand receiving something from another hand. The kanji 受 means "to receive."

受ける to receive	引き受ける to answer for, to be responsible for
受け取る to receive, to take delivery of	受診する to see a doctor
受験 taking an exam	受信する to receive a message

一 ⺈ ⺈ ⺤ ⺤ ⺤ 受 受　　8

478

ON-KUN READINGS:	HEADER:
ジュ・さず(ける)	扌

授
to bestow; to grant

ORIGIN: The kanji 授 consists of three hands: 扌 "hand," 爪 "hand picking something from above," and 又 "hand receiving from below." Together they indicated "to bestow or convey something." The kanji 授 means "to bestow; to grant."

授業 class instruction	伝授 personal instruction
授ける to grant; to instruct	授与 conferment, awarding
教授 professor	授産所 job training site

一 十 扌 扩 扩 扩 护 护 授 授　　11

479

ON-KUN READINGS:	HEADER:
ジュ・き	木

樹
tree; to establish

ORIGIN: The left side 木 was "tree." The middle depicted a feast but here is used phonetically to mean "to stand" (with 寸, "hand," on the right side). Together they indicated planting a tree and caring for it with one's hands to get it established. The kanji 樹 means "tree," or "to establish."

街路樹 roadside trees	樹液 tree sap
樹齢 age of a tree	果樹園 orchard
樹木 trees	樹立する to establish

一 十 才 木 村 村 村 村 村 樹 樹 樹 樹 樹 樹 樹　16

480

ON-KUN READINGS:	HEADER:
シュウ・おさ(める)	又

収
to collect; to store

ORIGIN: The left side 丩 depicted two strings twisted, signifying putting things together, and the right side 又 was a hand, which would have been used to put the things together. The kanji 収 means "to collect" or "to store."

収める to pay (fee)	月収 monthly income
収入 income	収益 earnings
回収する to recover (thing)	ゴミの収集 trash collection

丨 丩 収 収　　4

481

ON-KUN READINGS: シュウ・まわ(り)

HEADER: 口

周

around

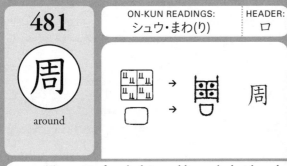

ORIGIN: The ancient form had rice paddies packed with seedlings and 口 a square lot underneath, signifying something "full; complete." From the meaning of something totally full, the form was also used to refer to the "entire circumference." The kanji 周 means "around."

まわ 周り surrounding	いっしゅう 一周 する to go around
しゅうい 周囲 circumference, surroundings	しゅうち 周知の well-known
しゅうへん 周辺 surrounding area	ごしゅうねん 五周年 five year anniversary

丿 刀 刀 円 円 円 周 周 周   8

482

ON-KUN READINGS: シュウ・ソウ・むね

HEADER: 宀

宗

religious belief of a group; head of group

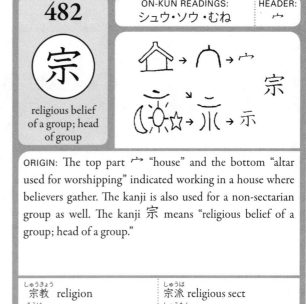

ORIGIN: The top part 宀 "house" and the bottom "altar used for worshipping" indicated working in a house where believers gather. The kanji is also used for a non-sectarian group as well. The kanji 宗 means "religious belief of a group; head of a group."

しゅうきょう 宗教 religion	しゅうは 宗派 religious sect
そうけ 宗家 the originator	しゅうもん 宗門 sect
かいしゅう 改宗 conversion to another religion	ぜんしゅう 禅宗 Zen sect

丶 宀 宀 宁 宇 宗 宗   8

483

ON-KUN READINGS: シュウ・ジュ・つ(く)

HEADER: 尤

就

to take up a job; to be completed

ORIGIN: The left side 京 was a house on a hilltop, a capital. The sound of 尤 "long, excellent" on the right side meant "to arrive." (Its origin is obscure.) Together they indicated an important person arriving to take up a position, or something becomes completed. The kanji 就 means "to take up a job; to be completed."

しゅうしょく 就職 する to become employed	ちい つ 地位に就く to take up a office
しゅうぎょうじかん 就業時間 working hours	じょうじゅ 成就 achievement, fulfillment
しゅうにん 就任 taking up an office	しゅうしんじかん 就寝時間 bedtime

丶 亠 亠 古 古 亨 京 京 京 就 就 就   12

484

ON-KUN READINGS: シュウ・す

HEADER: 川

州

sandbank; large area; state (in the United States)

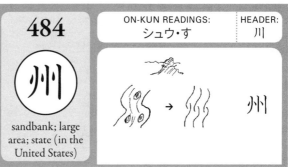

ORIGIN: The ancient form was a pictograph of a sandbank. The meaning was further extended to indicate a larger area and is also used to mean "state" in the United States. The kanji 州 means "sandbank," "large area," or "state."

きゅうしゅう 九州 Kyushu (island)	さんかくす 三角州 delta
ほんしゅう 本州 Honshu (island)	おうしゅう 欧州 Europe
しゅう テキサス州 the state of Texas	ごうしゅう 豪州 Australia

丶 丿 少 州 州 州   6

485

ON-KUN READINGS: シュウ・シュ・おさ(める)

HEADER: イ

修

to learn; to master

ORIGIN: The left side イ "person" with 丨 "water dripping on the back" and 攵 "action" indicated "to cleanse (body and soul)." The bottom 彡 on the right signified a "nice shape." Together they indicated "to master skills or knowledge." The kanji 修 means "to learn; to master."

修める to study, to pursue
けんしゅう
研修 training
しゅぎょう
修行 apprenticeship, ascetic practices

しゅうり
修理 repair
しゅうどういん
修道院 monastery
しゅうせい
修正 する to correct

ノ イ イ イ イ 伦 伦 修 修 修   10

486

ON-KUN READINGS: シュウ・ジュウ・ひろ(う)

HEADER: 扌

拾

to pick up; ten

ORIGIN: The left side 扌 "hand" and the right side 合 "to collect in one place and meet" suggested "to meet (pick up) something with one's hand." The kanji 拾 means "to pick up." This is also used as "ten."

拾う to pick up
しゅうとくぶつ
拾得物 lost-and-found item
ひろ もの
拾い物 a found object

いのちびろ
命拾い narrow escape
ひろ よ
拾い読み skimming through
じゅうまんえん
拾万円 a hundred thousand yen

一 扌 扌 扌 扒 扮 拾 拾 拾   9

487

ON-KUN READINGS: シュウ・あき

HEADER: 禾

秋

autumn; fall

ORIGIN: The left side, 禾 "grain plants drooping with the weight of ripe heads," signified harvest. The right side, 火 "fire," signified "to dry" or "to gather." Autumn is the season in which rice plants are harvested and aired to dry. The kanji 秋 means "autumn; fall."

あき
秋 autumn, fall
あきがっき
秋学期 fall school term
しゅうぶん ひ
秋分の日 autumnal equinox day

ばんしゅう
晩秋 late autumn
ばくしゅう
麦秋 early summer
あきば
秋晴れ clear, autumn day

ノ ニ 千 禾 禾 禾 禾' 秋 秋   9

488

ON-KUN READINGS: シュウ・お(わる)

HEADER: 糸

終

to end; to finish

ORIGIN: The left 糸 indicated "thread." The right side 冬 "winter" (the season when foods are stored, and the season of ice) is the end of a year. Together they indicated the end of a thread. The kanji 終 means "to end; to finish."

お
終わる to end
しゅうてん
終点 last stop, destination
さいしゅうび
最終日 the last day

しゅうじつ
終日 all day long
しゅうりょう
終了 end
しじゅう
始終 all the time

く 乡 幺 幺 糸 糸 糸' 終 終 終 終   11

158

489

to learn; learning
by repeating

ORIGIN: The top 羽 consists of two wings. The bottom 白 may originally have come from 自, here used phonetically to mean "repeatedly." Repeated flapping of wings signified a little bird learning to fly. The kanji 習 means "learning by repeating" or "to learn."

なら
習う to learn
れんしゅう
練習 practice
ふくしゅう
復習 refresh learning, study review

よしゅう
予習 study beforehand
しゅうじ
習字 calligraphy practice
なら
習い habit, custom

フ フ ヲ ヨ ヨ ヲ゛ヲ゛ 羽 羽 習 習 習   11

490

mass; many people

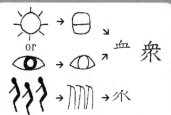

ORIGIN: There are two different ancient forms for the top, one with a sun and the other with an eye. The bottom was three people standing, indicating many people, or mass. The kanji 衆 means "many people; mass."

たいしゅう
大衆 mass (of people)
みんしゅう
民衆 people
しゅうぎいん
衆議院 the Lower House

うごう　しゅう
烏合の衆 mob
こうしゅう
公衆 the public
ちょうしゅう
聴衆 listeners

ノ イ 血 血 血 血 血 血 柔 衆 衆   12

491

week

ORIGIN: The upper right 周 indicated "around" phonetically. The lower left 辶, originally 辵 (the left half of a crossroad and a foot), indicated the motion of "going along a road." Together they indicated walking around the street. The kanji 週 is now used exclusively for "week," which is a cycle of days.

こんしゅう
今週 this week
らいしゅう
来週 next week
せんしゅう
先週 last week

しゅうまつ
週末 weekend
まいしゅう
毎週 every week
いっしゅうかん
一週間 one week

丿 刀 月 円 円 円 周 周 `周 调 週   11

492

to collect;
to gather; to
congregate

ORIGIN: The ancient form had three 隹 "birds" on top of 木 "tree," depicting three (signifying many) birds flocking on a tree. The kanji 集 means "to collect; to gather; to congregate."

あつ
集まる to gather
あつ
集める to collect
しゅうごうじかん
集合時間 meeting time

しゅうきん
集金 money collection
しゅうかい
集会 meeting
つど
集う to congregate

ノ イ イ゛ 作 竹 作 隹 隹 隹 隼 隼 集 集   12

493

住
to reside

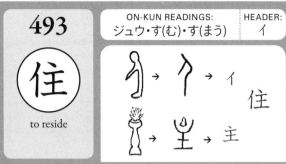

ORIGIN: The left イ was "person." The right 主 was "master," from a depiction of a burning oil lamp stand (as a master sits still). Together they indicated "where a master lives." The kanji 住 means "to reside."

す
住んでいる to reside
す
住まい residence
じゅうしょ
住所 address

じゅうみん
住民 resident
いじゅう
移住 migration
じゅうたくち
住宅地 residential area

ノイイ゙イ゙゙住住住　7

494

充
to fill

ORIGIN: The top part depicted a baby upside down, the way it is born. The bottom 儿 was legs. Together they indicated the changes that a baby goes through, from crawling to walking, as he or she grows, or fills out. The kanji 充 means "to fill."

じゅうぶん
充分 in full, enough
じゅうじつ
充実する to enrich
かくじゅう
拡充する to expand

じゅうけつ　め
充血した目 bloodshot eye
じゅうでん
充電する to recharge
ほじゅう
補充する to supplement

丶亠ㄊ去ㄊ充　6

495

十
ten; full

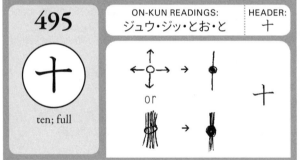

ORIGIN: There are two ancient forms: (a) Two lines crossing indicated all directions, signifying "full and complete." Alternatively, (b) in tallying, every ten sticks were tied together (marked with an emphatic dot). The kanji 十 means "ten" or "full."

じゅう
十 ten
とお
十 ten
とおか
十日 ten days, tenth day of the month

にじゅう
二十 twenty
じっぷん　じゅっぷん
十分・十分 ten minutes
じゅうぶん
十分に sufficiently

一十　2

496

従
to follow

ORIGIN: The left side イ "to go" from a crossroad was "to go further." The right side of the ancient form had two people, which became ソ, and a footprint, 疋. Together they indicated a person following in the footsteps of another. The kanji 従 means "to follow."

したが
従う to obey
じゅうじ
従事する to engage in work
じゅうぎょういん
従業員 worker, employee
ふくじゅう
服従 obedience

じゅうらい
従来 in the past
ついしょう
追従 flattery
ついじゅう
追従する to follow, to be servile to

ノ彳彳彳彳彳゙従従従従従　10

497

ON-KUN READINGS: ジュウ・しる
HEADER: 氵

汁
soup; liquid, juice

ORIGIN: The left side 氵 indicated "water" and the right side 十 "ten" was used phonetically to express "liquid." The kanji 汁 means "soup; liquid; juice."

しる
汁 soup
みそしる
味噌汁 *miso* (fermented bean paste) soup
かじゅう
果汁 fruit juice

しるこ
汁粉 sweet azuki bean soup
にくじゅう
肉汁 gravy
ぼくじゅう
墨汁 liquid ink

丶 氵 氵 汁 汁   5

498

ON-KUN READINGS: ジュウ・たて
HEADER: 糸

縦
vertical

ORIGIN: The left side 糸 was "threads." The right side 從 "to follow" had 彳 "to go" and "two people with a footprint," signifying that one person follows in the footstep of another. Together they indicated "a continuous line to follow," or "vertical." The kanji 縦 means "vertical."

じゅうだん
縦断する to cut vertically
たてが
縦書き vertical writing
じゅうおうむじん
縦横無尽 in all directions

たていと
縦糸 warp (as in weaving)
いちれつじゅうたい
一列縦隊 single file
じゅうそう
縦走 trek along a ridge

乡 幺 幺 糸 糸 糸 紗 絆 紗 絆 絆 絆 縦 縦   16

499

ON-KUN READINGS: ジュウ・チョウ・かさ(ねる)・おも(い)・え
HEADER: 里

重
heavy; layer

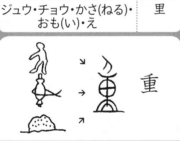

ORIGIN: The ancient form shows a man standing 壬, with a heavy bag (東 in the middle) on the ground 土. Together they indicated a person with a heavy load, or simply "heavy." The kanji also means "to overlap; layer." The kanji 重 means "heavy; layer."

おも おも
重い・重たい heavy
じゅうよう
重要な important
じゅうだい
重大な of great importance

ちょうほう
重宝な useful
かさ
重ねる to pile up
たいじゅう
体重 body weight

丿 一 亠 千 盲 盲 盲 重 重 重   9

500

ON-KUN READINGS: シュク・やど
HEADER: 宀

宿
inn

ORIGIN: Inside a house 宀 there is a person 亻 and a woven mat to sleep on 百. A place where people rest and sleep is an inn. The kanji 宿 means "inn."

やどや
宿屋 Japanese-style inn
げしゅく
下宿 boarding house
やど
宿 inn, place to stay overnight

のじゅく
野宿 camp out
やど
宿る to live, dwell, form
しゅくばまち
宿場町 an inn village

丶 宀 宀 宀 宀 宀 宿 宿 宿 宿   11

161

501

ON-KUN READINGS:	HEADER:
シュク・シュウ・いわ(う)	ネ

祝

to celebrate

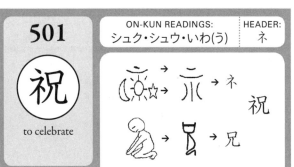

ORIGIN: The ancient form consisted of 示 "altar" and 兄 "person kneeling." Together they signified a priest chanting a prayer in front of an altar. A religious rite is a celebration of a god. The kanji 祝 means "to celebrate."

そつぎょういわい
卒業祝 graduation
celebration (gift)
いわ
祝う to celebrate
しゅくじつ
祝日 holiday

しゅうげん
祝言 wedding
しゅくふく
祝福 blessing
のりと
祝詞 Shinto prayer by priest

丶 ﾗ ｦ ｨ ﾈ 齐 初 祀 祝 祝　9

502

ON-KUN READINGS:	HEADER:
シュク・ちぢ(む)	糸

縮

to shrink;
to reduce

ORIGIN: The left side 糸 was threads, signifying continuity. The right side 宿 is a place where people rest and sleep, here used phonetically to indicate "to shrink." When the silk thread is pulled, the cocoon shrinks. The kanji 縮 means "to shrink; to reduce."

ちぢ
縮む to shrink
たんしゅく
短縮 curtailment
しゅくしゃく
縮尺 reduced scale

しゅくしょう
縮小 する to reduce
しゅくず
縮図 miniature copy, epitome
ぐんしゅく
軍縮 reduction of arms

乚 乼 幺 糸 糸 糸 糸 糸 紵 紵 紵 紵 紵 縮 縮 縮 縮 縮　17

503

ON-KUN READINGS:	HEADER:
ジュク・う(れる)	灬

熟

ripe; mature

ORIGIN: The top depicted a person bending forward to cook food with his hands. The bottom 灬 is a variant form of 火 "fire." Food is cooked to ready it for eating. The kanji 熟 means "ripe" or "mature."

じゅく
熟する to ripen
みじゅく
未熟な immature
じゅくれん
熟練 した skilled, experienced

う
熟れた ripe
じゅくご
熟語 idiom, Chinese
compound word
じゅくりょ
熟慮 careful consideration

丶 ﾗ ﾆ 六 古 古 吉 亨 享 享 郭 執 執 孰 孰 熟 熟　15

504

ON-KUN READINGS:	HEADER:
シュツ・スイ・で(る)・だ(す)	凵

出

to come out; to go
out; to appear; to
take out; to send out

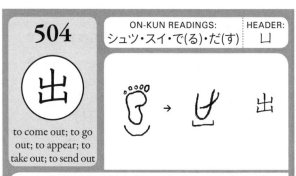

ORIGIN: The ancient form depicted a footprint above a line, or a foot in footwear, signifying "to go beyond a line" or "to go out." The kanji 出 means "to come out; to go out; to appear; to take out; to send out."

で
出る to come/go out
だ
出す to take/send out
でぐち
出口 an exit

がいしゅつちゅう
外出中 being out
しゅっせき
出席 attendance
ていしゅつ
提出する to submit

l 屮 屮 出 出　5

162

505

ON-KUN READINGS: ジュツ・すべ

HEADER: 行

術

methods; means

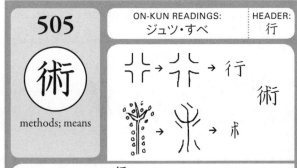

ORIGIN: The outside 行 was "to go" or "to conduct." The middle 朮 depicted a millet or rice plant with grains attached to it, signifying "to attach." Together they indicated the processes that people followed to do things, or "means or skills." The kanji 術 means "methods" or "means."

びじゅつ
美術 visual art
げいじゅつ
芸術 fine art
しゅじゅつ
手術 surgery

ぎじゅつ
技術 technology
まじゅつ
魔術 magic
いじゅつ
医術 medical art

ノ ク 彳 彳 犭 犳 衏 衏 術 術 術　11

506

ON-KUN READINGS: ジュツ・の(べる)

HEADER: 辶

述

to tell

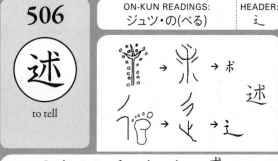

ORIGIN: In the ancient form the right top 朮 was grains of millet or rice sticking to one's hand, signifying "to stick to" or "to follow." The bottom left indicated "moving forward." Together they indicated "to follow" (what preceded) or "to reiterate." Now the meaning of "following" has been dropped. The kanji 述 now means "to tell."

の
述べる to state
じゅつご
述語 a predicate
ぜんじゅつ
前述の aforementioned

こうじゅつ
口述 dictation
きじゅつ
記述 description
きょうじゅつ
供述 statement

一 十 オ 木 术 朮 沭 述　8

507

ON-KUN READINGS: シュン・はる

HEADER: 日

春

spring

ORIGIN: In the ancient form a new growth of a mulberry tree and the sun indicated the season for new growth. The kanji 春 means "spring."

はる
春 spring
はるやす
春休み spring break
しゅんぶん ひ
春分の日 spring equinox
　　day

しんしゅん
新春 the New Year
はる
春めく to become spring-like
ししゅんき
思春期 (the age of) puberty,
　　adolescence

一 二 三 弐 夫 表 春 春 春　9

508

ON-KUN READINGS: ジュン

HEADER: 氵

準

standard; to apply correspondingly

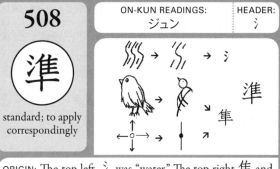

ORIGIN: The top left 氵 was "water." The top right 隹 and the bottom 十 made up the kanji 隼, phonetically used to indicate "leveling." The combined-form kanji 準 means "standard" or "to apply correspondingly."

ひょうじゅん
標準 standard
きじゅん
基準 standard
じゅん
準じる to apply
　　correspondingly

じゅんけっしょう
準決勝 semi-final
すいじゅん
水準 level
じゅんび
準備 preparation

丶 丶 冫 氵 汁 汁 浐 浐 淮 淮 淮 準 準　13

163

509

ON-KUN READINGS:	HEADER:
ジュン	糸

純
pure

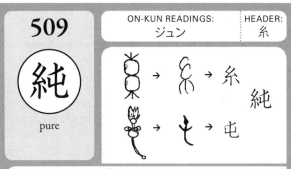

ORIGIN: The left side 糸 was a pictograph of thin silk threads being pulled out of silkworm cocoons. The right side 屯 depicted a silk tassel. Together they indicated a pure raw silk thread, a meaning that signified without impurity. The kanji 純 means "pure."

じゅんすい
純粋 な pure
じゅん
純 な pure
じゅんぱく
純白 な pure white

じゅんしん
純真 な naïve, pure
じゅんど
純度 purity
たんじゅん
単純 simple

く幺幺糸糸糸糸糸純純純　10

510

ON-KUN READINGS:	HEADER:
ジュン	頁

順
order; compliant

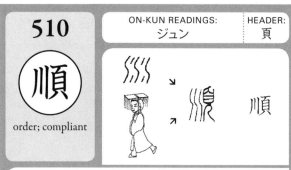

ORIGIN: In the ancient form the left 川 depicted a river and the right 頁 depicted a person with a head and a headdress or hat to show his rank. Together they indicated that one must follow along the course of the river, which gave the meaning of being "compliant" or "in an orderly manner." The kanji 順 means "compliant" or "order."

じゅんばん
順番 turn, order
じゅんじょ
順序 order
てじゅん
手順 order

じゅんちょう
順調 に smoothly
みちじゅん
道順 direction
じゅうじゅん
従順 な obedient

ノ リ 川 川 川 川 順 順 順 順 順 順　12

511

ON-KUN READINGS:	HEADER:
ショ・ところ	几

処
place; to manage;
to settle

ORIGIN: The ancient form of the old kanji 處 depicted a tiger, or a person with tiger fur, sitting on a table 几 with an emphasis on his feet 夂 resting. It signified "one stays in one place." One manages or settles the affairs of business while staying in one place. Now, the reduced form 処 is used. The kanji 処 means "place" or "to manage; to settle."

ところ
処 a place
しょり
処理 treatment
しょぶん
処分 する to throw away,
　punish

たいしょ
対処 する to handle
しょけい
処刑 execution
ぜんしょ
善処 to cope successfully

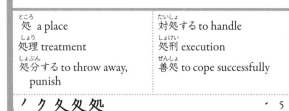
ノ ク 夂 処 処　5

512

ON-KUN READINGS:	HEADER:
ショ・うい・うぶ・ はじ(めて)・はつ・そ(める)	刀

初
for the first time;
to begin

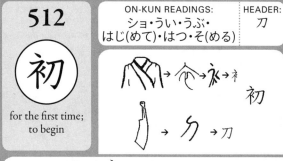

ORIGIN: The left side 衤 came from the collar of a piece of clothing, and the right side 刀 was "sword." Because the first step in making clothes is cutting cloth, the kanji 初, formed from the two characters, means "to begin" or "for the first time."

はじ
初めて for the first time
さいしょ
最初 は at the beginning
しょにち
初日 first day

ういうい
初々しい innocent, fresh
しょだい
初代 first generation
とうしょ
当初 the beginning

、 ラ ネ ネ ネ 初 初　7

513

ON-KUN READINGS: ショ・ところ

HEADER: 戸

所

place

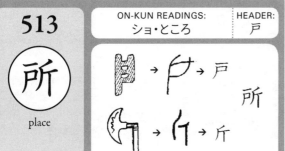

ORIGIN: The left 戸 was a door and the right side 斤 was an ax. Originally the left side 戸 "door" was used phonetically to indicate the sound of an ax, 斤 on the right side, chipping wood. The current use of "place" may have come from "a shop to make woodwork." The kanji 所 means "place."

じゅうしょ
住所 address
きんじょ
近所 neighborhood, vicinity
ばしょ
場所 place

だいどころ
台所 kitchen
しょてい
所定の prescribed, fixed
ちょうしょ
長所 merit, strong point

一 三 ヨ ヲ 戸 戸 所 所 所 　　8

514

ON-KUN READINGS: ショ・あつ(い)

HEADER: 日

暑

hot (atmosphere)

ORIGIN: The sun 日 was on the top. The bottom 者, originally a pictograph of a fire burning in a stove, indicated "to gather in one place to burn wood sticks." Like a fire in a stove, sunlight converges and gives heat. The kanji 暑 means "hot" (as in atmospheric temperature).

あつ
暑い hot (weather)
ざんしょ
残暑 lingering summer heat
む あつ
蒸し暑い hot and humid,
　muggy

しょちゅうみま
暑中見舞い mid-summer
　greeting letter
ひしょち
避暑地 summer resort
もうしょ
猛暑 extreme heat

丶 ㇆ ㄇ 日 旦 早 昇 昇 昇 暑 暑 暑 　　12

165

515

ON-KUN READINGS: ショ・チョ・お

HEADER: 糸

緒

rope; beginning

ORIGIN: The left side 糸 was "thread" or "continuity." The right side 者 was used phonetically to mean "beginning." Together they signified "the end of a knotted thread," or "beginning." The kanji 緒 means "beginning; rope."

いっしょ
一緒に together
じょうちょ
情緒 emotions, sentiment,
　atmosphere
ゆいしょ
由緒 pedigree, lineage

お
緒 rope
はなお
鼻緒 straps, thong (of
　sandals)
たんちょ
端緒 origin, beginning

く 幺 幺 幺 糸 糸 糸 紆 紵 紵 緖 緒 緒 緒 　　14

516

ON-KUN READINGS: ショ

HEADER: 罒

署

police station;
tax office

ORIGIN: The top 罒 was "a net" that cast over a wide area, and the bottom 者 phonetically indicated "to stick together." A government organization is like a net that is divided into divisions and sections. The police and the taxation office cover people thoroughly. The kanji 署 means "government office," or "police station," or "tax office" in particular.

けいさつしょ
警察署 police precinct
しょちょう
署長 chief of police
ぜいむしょ
税務署 tax office

じしょ
自署 signature
しょめい
署名 signature
しょうぼうしょ
消防署 fire department

丶 ㇆ ㄇ 罒 罒 罒 罒 署 署 署 署 署 署 　　13

517

ON-KUN READINGS: ショ・か(く) | HEADER: 日

書 to write

ORIGIN: The top part 聿 depicted a hand holding a writing brush upright. The sound of 日 (originally 者) was the same as that of "to copy." Together they indicated the act of writing using a brush. The kanji 書 means "to write."

書く to write (か)
図書館 library (としょかん)
葉書 postcard (はがき)
書類 document (しょるい)

清書 last clean copy (せいしょ)
書物 book (しょもつ)
辞書 dictionary (じしょ)

フ ㇮ ㇕ ㇕ 聿 聿 書 書 書 書   10

518

ON-KUN READINGS: ショ・もろ | HEADER: 言

諸 various; many

ORIGIN: The left side 言 was a sharp tattooist needle and a mouth 口, meaning "to speak clearly and sharply." The right side 者 was used phonetically to indicate "to gather." Together they indicated to gather many writings. The meaning of writing was dropped. The kanji 諸 means "various; many."

諸国 countries (しょこく)
諸君 all (male peers), gentlemen (しょくん)
諸々の various (もろもろ)

ハワイ諸島 the Hawaiian Islands (しょとう)
諸氏 all the people (しょし)
諸問題 various problems (しょもんだい)

丶 亠 亠 亖 言 言 言 計 計 訞 訞 諸 諸 諸 諸   15

519

ON-KUN READINGS: ジョ・たす(ける)・すけ | HEADER: 力

助 to help

ORIGIN: The left side depicted stacked layers of dirt. The right side 力 was flexing one's muscle to muster "strength." The kanji 助 means "to help" or "a help."

助ける to help (たす)
助かる to be helpful (たす)
助手 assistant (じょしゅ)

助手席 a front passenger seat (じょしゅせき)
助太刀 aid, backer (すけだち)
援助 financial support (えんじょ)

丨 冂 冃 月 且 助 助   7

520

ON-KUN READINGS: ジョ・ニョ・ニョウ・おんな・め | HEADER: 女

女 woman; feminine

ORIGIN: The ancient form depicted a woman kneeling with her arms crossed in front. The kanji 女 means "woman: or "feminine." The same origin of a pliant posture of a woman appears in 母 "mother," 毎 "every," 海 "sea," 毒 "poison," 妻 "wife," 安 "secure," 好 "favorable" and others.

女 woman, female (おんな)
女の子 girl (おんな・こ)
女性 woman (じょせい)

男女 man and woman (だんじょ)
女子学生 female student (じょしがくせい)
彼女 she, girlfriend (かのじょ)

く 女 女   3

166

521

ON-KUN READINGS: ジョ

HEADER: 广

序

order; beginning

ORIGIN: The top 广 was a roof over a house. Inside the house, 予 might also have depicted a motion in which a shuttle was going between two warps in weaving. This motion of weaving under a roof is orderly and the shuttle carried the beginning of a thread. The kanji 序 means "order; beginning."

順序 order
序列 order
序でに by the way, in passing
秩序 public order
序言 preface
序幕 prelude, opening act

' 亠 广 庐 庐 序 序   7

522

ON-KUN READINGS: ジョ・ジ・のぞ(く)

HEADER: 阝

除

to remove

ORIGIN: The left side 阝 signified an earthen wall surrounding the house, or a hill. The right side 余 consisted of a spade and 八 motion of digging, signifying making a space by removing dirt. Together they indicated removal of unwanted dirt. The kanji 除 means "to remove."

除く to remove
取り除く to remove
削除 deletion
除名 expulsion (from membership)
掃除機 vacuum cleaner
免除 waiving

' ３ 阝 阝 阝 阝 除 除 除 除   10

523

ON-KUN READINGS: ショウ・きず・いた(む)

HEADER: イ

傷

injury; wound

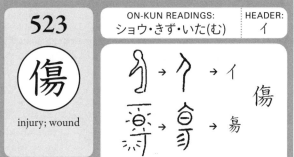

ORIGIN: The left side イ is a person and the right side was used phonetically to indicate "to injure." Together they indicated someone who was wounded. The kanji 傷 means "injury; wound."

傷 wound
負傷 injury
傷害 bodily harm
傷つく to hurt
傷口 cut
中傷 slander, defamation
火傷 burn

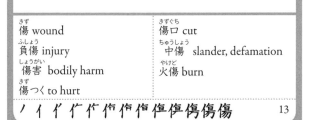
ノ イ イ 仁 仁 停 停 停 停 傷 傷 傷   13

524

ON-KUN READINGS: ショウ・か(つ)・まさ(る)

HEADER: 力

勝

to win; to gain; victory

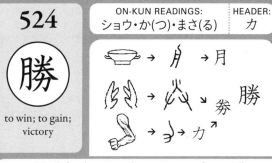

ORIGIN: The left side was a tub or container for an offering. The right side was two hands holding it up in prayer for a good harvest. Strength 力 was added to indicate an effort to gain. The kanji 勝 means "to win" or "to gain" or "victory."

勝つ to win
勝負 match, game
優勝 victory, championship
全勝 a sweeping victory
勝敗 result of a match
勝ち気な unyielding

丿 月 月 月 月 朋 朕 胖 胖 胖 勝 勝   12

167

525

ON-KUN READINGS: ショウ・め(す)

HEADER: 口

召

to summon;
to call; to wear

ORIGIN: The top of the ancient form has two different interpretations, "sword or knife," used only phonetically, and "person." Together with the bottom 口 "mouth," the kanji signified a nobleman summoning his servant to assist him to eat, put on clothes, and so on. The kanji 召 means "to summon" or "[honorific] to call; to wear."

召し上がる [honorific] to eat
召す to summon
和服を召す to wear Japanese-style clothes [honorific]

召集 する to convene

フ刀刀召召   5

526

ON-KUN READINGS: ショウ・あきな(い)

HEADER: 口

商

trade; commerce

ORIGIN: The ancient form consisted of a tattooing needle with a handle, a table, and 口 "mouth." The person who had the power to tattoo criminals also was the one who consulted the gods. When the meaning of god was dropped, the meaning of "consulting or talking to someone" remained. It came to signify a merchant negotiating the value of merchandise with a buyer. The kanji 商 means "trade; commerce."

商売 business, trade
商人 merchant
商社 general trading company

商う to trade
行商人 peddler
商戦 sales battle, trade war

`丶 亠 产 产 产 产 商 商 商`   11

527

ON-KUN READINGS: ショウ・とな(える)

HEADER: 口

唱

to recite; to sing
(energetically)

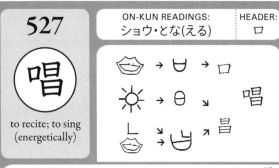

ORIGIN: The left side 口 is a mouth. The right side 昌 consisted of the bright sun and a voice coming out of the mouth; it was used phonetically to indicate something thriving. Together they indicated singing loudly. The kanji 唱 means "to recite" or "to sing (energetically)."

唱える to recite, to advocate
提唱 する to advocate
合唱 chorus

独唱 solo singing
唱歌 school song
唱和する to say in unison

`丨 丨 口 口 叮 叮 吧 唱 唱 唱`   11

528

ON-KUN READINGS: ショウ

HEADER: 寸

将

future; army
general

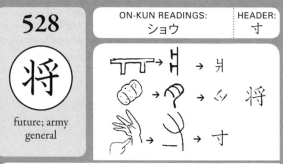

ORIGIN: The old form had 爿 "table with legs" on the left, and on the right, 月 "meat for an offering" and 寸 "hand." Together they indicated offering (by hand) meat on a table before a battle. A person who makes an offering for a future battle is a general. The current form of the kanji, 将, means "army general" or "future."

将来 future
大将 general
将軍 general, Shogunate

主将 team captain
武将 general, soldier
将校 commissioned officer

`丨 丬 丬 爿 将 将 将 将 将 将`   10

168

529

ON-KUN READINGS: ショウ・こ・ちい(さい)・お   HEADER: 小

小
small

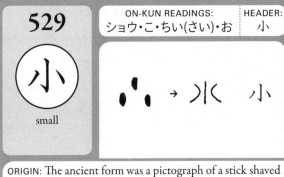

ORIGIN: The ancient form was a pictograph of a stick shaved into small pieces. The kanji 小 means "small."

ちい
小さい small, little
しょうがっこう
小学校 elementary school
ことり
小鳥 small bird

さいしょう
最小 the smallest
こさめ
小雨 drizzle
おがわ
小川 brook

丨 小 小   3

530

ON-KUN READINGS: ショウ・すく(ない)・すこ(し)   HEADER: 小

少
small amount

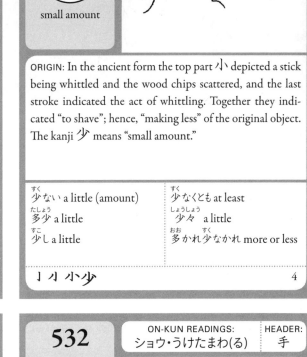

ORIGIN: In the ancient form the top part 小 depicted a stick being whittled and the wood chips scattered, and the last stroke indicated the act of whittling. Together they indicated "to shave"; hence, "making less" of the original object. The kanji 少 means "small amount."

すく
少ない a little (amount)
たしょう
多少 a little
すこ
少し a little

すく
少なくとも at least
しょうしょう
少々 a little
おお   すく
多かれ少なかれ more or less

丨 ⺌ 小 少   4

169

531

ON-KUN READINGS: ショウ・ゆか・とこ   HEADER: 广

床
floor; bed

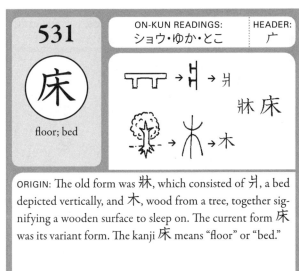

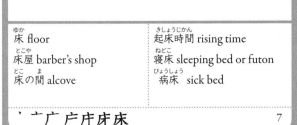

ORIGIN: The old form was 牀, which consisted of 爿, a bed depicted vertically, and 木, wood from a tree, together signifying a wooden surface to sleep on. The current form 床 was its variant form. The kanji 床 means "floor" or "bed."

ゆか
床 floor
とこや
床屋 barber's shop
とこ ま
床の間 alcove

きしょうじかん
起床時間 rising time
ねどこ
寝床 sleeping bed or futon
びょうしょう
病床 sick bed

丶 亠 广 广 庐 床 床   7

532

ON-KUN READINGS: ショウ・うけたまわ(る)   HEADER: 手

承
to receive;
to accept

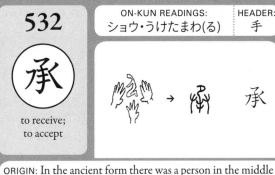

ORIGIN: In the ancient form there was a person in the middle crouching to show a humble act and on the side two hands were thrust out also to receive something humbly. Together they indicated an act of receiving humbly and accepting what was being said. The kanji 承 means "to receive; to accept."

しょうち
承知する to consent
うけたまわ
承る [humble] to
understand
りょうしょう
了承 consent

ふしょうぶしょう
不承不承 grudgingly,
reluctantly
しょうだく
承諾する to consent
けいしょう
継承する to succeed to

フ 了 了 手 手 承 承 承   8

533

ON-KUN READINGS:	HEADER:
ショウ・まね(く)	扌

招 to invite

ORIGIN: The left side 扌 was "hand." The right side 召 had a knife 刀 (used for the sound) and a mouth 口, signifying "to summon." Together they indicated "to beckon with a hand." The kanji 招 means "to invite."

まね
招く to invite
しょうたい
招待 invitation
しょうしゅう
招集 summon

しょうらい
招来する to bring about
しょうち
招致する to invite, bring

一 十 扌 扎 护 招 招 招　8

534

ON-KUN READINGS:	HEADER:
ショウ	日

昭 bright

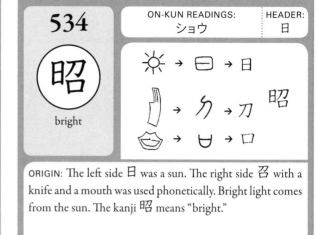

ORIGIN: The left side 日 was a sun. The right side 召 with a knife and a mouth was used phonetically. Bright light comes from the sun. The kanji 昭 means "bright."

しょうわ
昭和 Showa era (1926–1989)
しょうわにじゅうねん
昭和二十年 20th year of
　Showa (1945)

丨 冂 日 日 旷 叼 昭 昭 昭　9

535

ON-KUN READINGS:	HEADER:
ショウ・まつ	木

松 pine tree

ORIGIN: The left side 木 was a tree. The right side 公 was used phonetically to mean "to praise." A pine tree is an evergreen, grows tall, and has a graceful shape. For these qualities, it is considered to be an auspicious tree. The kanji 松 means "pine tree."

まつ
松 pine
しょうちくばい
松竹梅 pine-bamboo-plum
　(an auspicious arrangement)
まつばやし
松林 pine tree grove

まつば
松葉 pine needle
かどまつ
門松 gate decoration (for the
　New Year)
たいまつ
松明 a pine torch

一 十 オ 木 木 松 松 松　8

536

ON-KUN READINGS:	HEADER:
ショウ・け(す)・き(える)	氵

消 to disappear; to erase

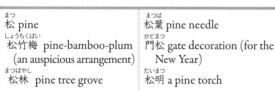

ORIGIN: The left side 氵 was "water." The older form of the right side 肖 had 小 "small" and 月 "flesh," signifying "shaving meat into small pieces." Together they indicated that something that is cut into small pieces disappears like water evaporates. The kanji 消 means "to disappear; to erase."

け
消す to erase
け
消しゴム eraser
き
消える to disappear

しょうかき
消火器 fire extinguisher
かいしょう
解消する to be dissolved
しょうか
消化 digestion

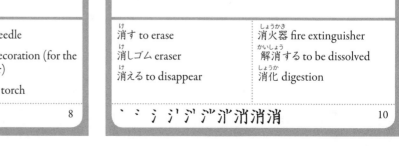　10

537	ON-KUN READINGS: ショウ・や(く)	HEADER: 火

焼
to burn

ORIGIN: In the old form 燒, the left side 火 was a fire, and the right side 堯 had three hills (土) and 儿 "person," signifying "high." Together they indicated a soaring fire, or "to burn." Now somewhat reduced to 焼, the kanji means "to burn."

焼く to burn
焼き増し duplicate print
全焼 total destruction by fire

焼香 incense-burning
焼き鳥 grilled chicken, yakitori
日焼け sunburn

丶 ヽ ⺌ 火 灯 灯 炉 炉 焼 焼 焼 焼   12

538	ON-KUN READINGS: ショウ・て(る)	HEADER: 灬

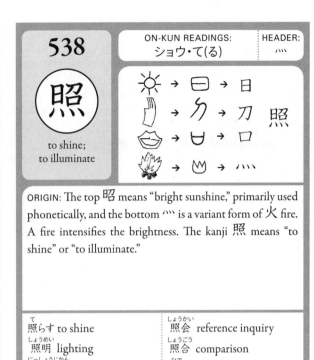

照
to shine;
to illuminate

ORIGIN: The top 昭 means "bright sunshine," primarily used phonetically, and the bottom 灬 is a variant form of 火 fire. A fire intensifies the brightness. The kanji 照 means "to shine" or "to illuminate."

照らす to shine
照明 lighting
日照時間 daylight time
参照 reference

照会 reference inquiry
照合 comparison
日照り drought

丨 冂 日 日 日' 日' 日ʼ 昭 昭 昭 照 照 照   13

539	ON-KUN READINGS: ショウ・セイ・かえり(みる)・はぶ(く)	HEADER: 目

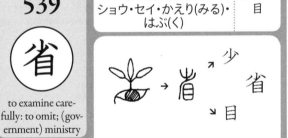

省
to examine carefully: to omit; (government) ministry

ORIGIN: The ancient form shown in the middle depicted a tree branch over an eye, possibly in a religious rite, which blocked one from seeing well. It means "to omit." The current form, 少 "little" and 目 "eye," was borrowed to mean "to examine carefully." A government ministry oversees affairs carefully. The kanji 省 means "to reflect; to omit" or "government ministry."

省みる to reflect
反省 reflection
省略 omission, abbreviation

外務省 Ministry of Foreign Affairs
自省 self-examination
省エネ energy saving

丿 亅 小 少 少 省 省 省 省   9

540	ON-KUN READINGS: ショウ	HEADER: 立

章
badge: chapter

ORIGIN: The ancient form depicted a tattooing needle with a handle that has an ink reserve in the middle. Beautifully done tattoos were something to show off or mark social class, thus "badge." The kanji form also signified something in increments, thus "chapter." The kanji 章 means "badge" and "chapters" of a book and movements in music.

第二章 Chapter Two
文章 writing
第一楽章 first movement (in music)

勲章 order, medal
記章 medal
腕章 arm-band

丶 亠 ㇄ 立 产 产 音 音 音 章 章   11

171

541

ON-KUN READINGS: ショウ・わら(う)・え(む)

HEADER: 竹

笑
to smile; to laugh

ORIGIN: The top 竹 is bamboo and the bottom 夭 depicted a supple body, or someone who was dancing. Together they indicated someone smiling easily. The kanji 笑 means "to smile; to laugh."

わら
笑う to laugh
わら ごえ
笑い声 laughter
え
ほほ笑む to smile

にがわら　くしょう
苦笑い・苦笑 forced smile
わら　もの
笑い物 object of ridicule
びしょう
微笑 faint smile

ノ ト ト メ メ 竹 竹 竺 竺 笁 笑　10

542

ON-KUN READINGS: ショウ

HEADER: 糸

紹
to introduce
(someone to
another)

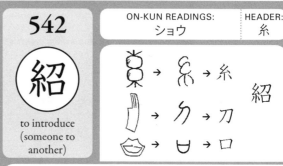

ORIGIN: The left side 糸 was threads, signifying continuity. The right side 召 "summon" was used phonetically. The combined form originally indicated "to connect thread or people" or "to succeed." The kanji 紹 means "to introduce (someone to another)."

しょうかい
紹介 introduction
しょうかいじょう
紹介状 letter of
introduction

く 纟 幺 幺 糸 糸 糸 紹 紹 紹 紹　11

543

ON-KUN READINGS: ショウ・あかし

HEADER: 言

証
to certify; proof

ORIGIN: The old kanji 證 consisted of 言 "word" and 登 "to climb" (癶 "two feet slightly apart" and 豆 "tall compote," both indicating to climb), which was used phonetically to mean "evidence." The combined form signified telling the truth, or giving testimony. Now a different kanji 証 is used, meaning "to certify" or "proof."

がくせいしょう
学生証 student ID
しょうめい
証明 proof
めんきょしょう
免許証 driver's license

ほしょう
保証 guarantee
しょうこ
証拠 evidence
ぎしょう
偽証 perjury

、 ㇒ 亠 言 言 言 言 訂 訂 評 証 証　12

544

ON-KUN READINGS: ショウ・ゾウ

HEADER: 豕

象
elephant;
to resemble

ORIGIN: The ancient form was a pictograph of an elephant with a long trunk, tusks, four legs, and a tail. An elephant is a huge animal with an unmistakable image. A strong image may be used as a point of reference in seeing other images. When two things have similar images, they "resemble" each other. The kanji 象 also means "to resemble."

たいしょう
対象 the object, the subject
ぞう
象 elephant
いんしょう
印象 impression

ぞうげ
象牙 ivory
しょうちょう
象徴 symbol
ちゅうしょうてき
抽象的 abstract

ノ ㇠ ㇠ ㅌ 呂 舁 舁 免 象 象 象 象　12

172

545

ON-KUN READINGS: ショウ

HEADER: 貝

賞

award

ORIGIN: The top 尚, a house with smoke rising from it, was used phonetically. The bottom 貝 was a cowry, which signified money or precious items. Together they indicated an award. The kanji 賞 means "award."

しょう 賞 prize	しょうきん 賞金 award money
じゅしょう 受賞 receiving an award	しょうひん 賞品 prize
おんがくかんしょう 音楽鑑賞 listening to music	しょうじょう 賞状 certificate of merit

丶 丷 丷 丷 尚 尚 尚 尚 尚 賞 賞 賞 賞 賞   15

546

ON-KUN READINGS: ショウ・さわ(る)

HEADER: 阝

障

to block; to hinder

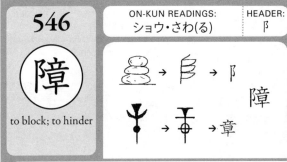

ORIGIN: The left side 阝 was an earthen wall made of piles of dirt. The right side 章 was used phonetically to indicate "to impede." Together they indicated blocking with a wall. The kanji 障 means "to hinder" or "to block."

しょうがい 障害 obstacle	さ さわ 差し障り hindrance
ししょう 支障 obstacle	しょうじ 障子 shoji screen
こしょう 故障 breakdown	からだ さわ 体に障る to be bad for one's health

フ ヲ ド ド ド ド ド 陪 陪 陪 陪 障 障 障   14

547

ON-KUN READINGS: ジョウ・ショウ・のぼ(る)・うえ・うわ・あ(がる)・かみ

HEADER: 一

上

top; above; to go up

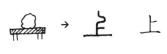

ORIGIN: The ancient form depicted a dot above a line, emphasizing a point in space. The kanji 上 means "above; top" or "to go up."

うえ 上 top, above	あ 上げる to give
のぼ 上る to climb, to go up	うわ 上着 outer wear
じょうげ 上下 top and bottom	じょうきょう 上京 coming up to Tokyo

丨 卜 上   3

548

ON-KUN READINGS: ジョウ・たけ

HEADER: 一

丈

length

ORIGIN: In the ancient form, the top came from a stick of wood 木 "tree; wood," and the bottom was a hand. Together they indicated a cane, which was used to measure length. One 丈 was approximately three meters. The kanji 丈 means "length." (The kanji for the original meaning of 丈 is now written as 杖 "cane.")

じょうぶ 丈夫な stout, strong	きじょう 気丈な tough-minded, courageous
だいじょうぶ 大丈夫な all right	
がんじょう 頑丈な stout, sturdy	たけ 丈 height, length
	せたけ 背丈 height

一 ナ 丈   3

173

549

ON-KUN READINGS: ジョウ・の(る) HEADER: ノ

乗
to ride; to get aboard

ORIGIN: The ancient form depicted a man 大 standing on a tree 木 with both feet firmly anchored to reach a high place. Now slightly reduced from 乘, the kanji 乗 means "to ride" or "to get aboard."

乗る to get aboard
乗車券 passenger ticket
乗り換える to transfer (transportation)

乗客 passenger
便乗 する to take advantage of
乗馬 horseback riding

一 二 三 千 丙 丙 乖 乗 乗   9

550

ON-KUN READINGS: ジョウ・しろ HEADER: 土

城
castle

ORIGIN: The left side 土 was "pile of dirt neatly forming a triangle shape." The right side 成 consisted of 戈 "halberd or weapon," and 丁 "nail," which signified "to hit." Together they referred to shoring up the soil against an attack, or making a castle. The kanji 城 means "castle."

城 castle
姫路城 Himeji Castle
城下町 castle town

城門 castle gate
城跡 castle ruin
古城 old castle

一 十 土 切 圹 圹 城 城 城   9

551

ON-KUN READINGS: ジョウ・ば HEADER: 土

場
place

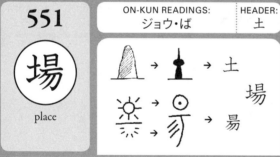

ORIGIN: The left side 土 was soil. The right side 昜 consisted of 日 "sun," the "motion of raising something high," and 彡 "sun rays." Together they signified "bright place" because the sun has risen, or "place" in general. The kanji 場 means "place."

場所 place
会場 venue
駐車場 parking lot

スキー場 ski resort
場面 situation
その場で on the spot

一 十 土 圹 圹 圹 坦 坦 埸 場 場 場   12

552

ON-KUN READINGS: ジョウ・とこ・つね HEADER: 巾

常
constant; always

ORIGIN: The top 尚 ("long" from a smoke rising long and high) was used phonetically to indicate the train (of an official's clothes). The bottom 巾 was a draped cloth. Because the length of the train was always the same, the kanji came to signify "always." The kanji 常 means "constant; always."

常に constantly
通常 usually
正常 normal

異常な extraordinary
常夏 tropics, everlasting summer
平常運転 regular operation

丷 丷 屵 屵 屵 常 常 常 常 常 常   11

174

553

ON-KUN READINGS: ジョウ・セイ・なさ(け)　**HEADER:** 忄

情

emotion; feelings

ORIGIN: The left 忄 is a variant of 心 "heart." The old form 青 consisted of 生 "new growth" or "fresh" and 丹 "clean water in a well," indicating clean freshness. One's feelings can be fresh and clean. The kanji 情 means "emotion; feelings."

ひょうじょう
表情 expressions
かんじょうてき
感情的 emotional
あいじょう
愛情 love

どうじょう
同情 sympathy
じつじょう
実情 real conditions
なさけ
情けない pitiful, deplorable

、忄忄忙忙忙情情情情　11

554

ON-KUN READINGS: ジョウ　**HEADER:** 木

条

line; clause

ORIGIN: In the old form 條, on the left was a person with dripping water on his back, and the right side was a hand holding a stick, signifying an action in general, and a purifying twig. Together they signified cleansing to purify. The kanji also indicated something long, such as a stripe or a line. The simpler form 条 means "line" or "clause."

じょうけん
条件 condition
かじょうがき
箇条書き itemized list
せいじょうき
星条旗 the Stars and Stripes

じょうやく
条約 treaty
じょうぶん
条文 article

ノ ク タ 久 冬 条 条　7

555

ON-KUN READINGS: ジョウ　**HEADER:** 犬

状

condition; letter

ORIGIN: The left side 爿 of the old form was a long table, that is, something flat. The right side 犬, "dog," has a slim shape. The kanji came to drop the "dog" meaning but kept "shape" or "condition." It also came to mean something that is written on a flat object, a letter. The kanji 状 means "condition" or "letter."

じょうたい
状態 condition
げんじょう
現状 present state
せんじょう
線状 linear

じょうきょう
状況 situation
きゅうじょう
窮状 distress, sad plight
めんじょう
免状 diploma

丬 丬 丬 丬 状 状 状　7

556

ON-KUN READINGS: ジョウ・む(す)　**HEADER:** 艹

蒸

steam

ORIGIN: The old form 艸 for the top 艹 was plant leaves and roots; the middle part 丞 had heat rising between two hands, which were throwing brushwood in a fire; and the bottom 灬 was a fire. Those three parts combine in the kanji 蒸, which means "steam."

む
蒸す to steam
蒸気 steam
む　あつ
蒸し暑い hot and humid, muggy

じょうはつ
蒸発 evaporation
じょうりゅうすい
蒸留水 distilled water
じょうきせん
蒸気船 steam boat

一 十 十 艹 艹 艹 芽 芽 茅 茅 蒸 蒸 蒸 蒸　13

175

557

ON-KUN READINGS: ショク・う(える)

HEADER: 木

植

to plant

ORIGIN: The left side 木 was "tree." The right side 直 was "straight" (from an eye looking straight at something). Together they indicated planting a tree straight up. The kanji 植 means "to plant."

植える to plant
植木 garden plant
田植え rice plant transplantation

植木鉢 planter, pot
植民地 colony
植物 plant, vegetation

一 十 才 木 木 杧 柿 枯 枯 柿 植 植　12

558

ON-KUN READINGS: ショク・シキ・お(る)

HEADER: 糸

織

to weave

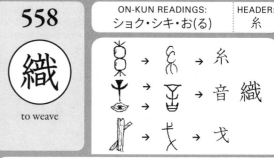

ORIGIN: The left side 糸 signified threads. The right side had 戈, a wooden pole posted in the ground for some intended meaning 音 ("sounds; meaning"), signifying a marking. The straight post is used to make a loom for weaving. The kanji 織 means "to weave."

織る to weave
織物 woven cloth
組織 organization

羽織 haori coat
羽織る to slip on, to put on
手織り hand-woven

く 幺 幺 幺 糸 糸 糸 絆 絆 絆 紵 絆 絆 絆 絆 織 織 織　18

559

ON-KUN READINGS: ショク

HEADER: 耳

職

job; employment

ORIGIN: The origin is obscure. One view is that the left was 耳 "ear," and that the middle and the right together signified "flag or notice on a stake." From that concept, the kanji indicated putting up a stake with a flag of one's trade. The kanji 職 means "employment; job."

職 job, employment
就職する to become employed
職業 occupation

求職活動 job hunting, job search
本職 primary job
職歴 job history

一 丅 丆 丆 ｢ 耳 耳 耵 耶 耵 耶 聆 聆 聯 聯 職 職　18

560

ON-KUN READINGS: ショク・シキ・いろ

HEADER: 色

色

color; amorous

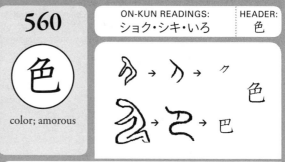

ORIGIN: The top ク "person" above 巴 another person who was kneeling down was a depiction of sex. Sexual passion heightens facial color, so the kanji also came to indicate "color." The kanji 色 means "color" or "amorous."

色 color
金色の golden
色々な various
顔色 facial color

特色 characteristics
物色する to hunt up
難色 reluctant
色事 love affair, an amour

ノ ク 冇 各 缶 色　6

176

561

ON-KUN READINGS: ショク・ジキ・た(べる)・く(う)

HEADER: 食

食
to eat

ORIGIN: In the ancient form the top part 亼 indicated "putting a lid over things"; under that was food in a compote, that is, a dish with a long stem (formerly 皀). The kanji 食 means "to eat." When used as a recurring component on the left side, the kanji is written as 飠 (one stroke fewer), as in 飲 "to drink."

た
食べる to eat
しょくじ
食事 meal
しょくどう
食堂 dining hall

ゆうしょく
夕食 evening meal
食べ過ぎる to eat too much
く
食う to eat, to bite, to live (by)

ノ 人 人 今 今 合 仐 仐 食 9

562

ON-KUN READINGS: シン

HEADER: イ

信
to believe; to trust;
letter

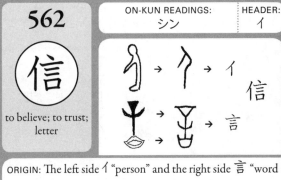

ORIGIN: The left side イ "person" and the right side 言 "word to say" indicated a person's true words. Together they meant to believe someone's words, and also correspondence. The kanji 信 means "to trust; to believe," or "letter."

しん
信じる to believe
しんよう
信用する to trust
じゅしん
受信 receipt of a message
かくしん
確信 conviction

はっしん
発信 sending
ししん
私信 private letter
おんしんふつう
音信不通 no correspondence

ノ イ 仁 仁 仁 仨 信 信 9

563

ON-KUN READINGS: シン・ね(る)

HEADER: 宀

寝
to sleep; to lie
down

ORIGIN: Originally it consisted of of 宀 "house" and the depiction of a "broom and purifying hand" for cleaning a shrine. Later on, 爿 was added to indicate a place to sleep. Together the combined form 寝 indicated "to sleep." Now the left side is slightly reduced, and the kanji 寝 means "to sleep; to lie down."

ね
寝る to go to bed
あさねぼう
朝寝坊 sleep late in the
morning
ひるね
昼寝 nap, siesta

はやねはやお
早寝早起き early rise, early
bed
ねごと
寝言 talking in one's sleep
ねぶくろ
寝袋 sleeping bag

丶 丷 宀 宀 宀 宀 宀 宇 宇 寝 寝 寝 13

564

ON-KUN READINGS: シン・こころ

HEADER: 心

心
heart; mind

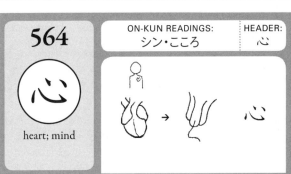

ORIGIN: The ancient form depicted the anatomical shape of the chambers of a heart and an artery, as the ancient people believed them to look. The kanji 心 means "heart; mind." (When used as a recurring component on the left side, a vertical form 忄 is used, as in 情 "feeling.")

こころ
心 heart
あんしん
安心する to feel relieved
しんぱい
心配する to worry
かんじん
肝心な vital

いごこち
居心地のよい cozy, snug
こころえ
心得 knowledge, preparation
しんがい
心外な unexpected,
regrettable

丶 心 心 心 4

177

565

ON-KUN READINGS: シン・あたら(しい)・あら(た)・にい

HEADER: 斤

新
new; fresh

ORIGIN: The left side was 立 "large needle" and 木 "wood." With the right side 斤 "ax," the kanji indicated cutting a tree down for firewood. Cutting a tree results in a fresh surface. The kanji 新 means "new; fresh." (For the original meaning, "firewood," a new form 薪 was created later.)

あたら
新しい new
あら
新た new, renewed
しんぶん
新聞 newspaper

しんぴん
新品 new item
しんにゅうせい
新入生 new student
さいしん
最新の the newest, latest

' ' ＋ ナ 立 立 辛 辛 亲 亲 新 新 新   13

566

ON-KUN READINGS: シン・もり

HEADER: 木

森
forest

ORIGIN: Three (signifying "many") trees 木 make a forest. The kanji 森 means "forest."

もり
森 forest, woods
しんりん
森林 forest
しんりんよく
森林浴 walk in the woods

しんかん
森閑とした still, silent

一 十 オ 木 木 本 杢 森 森 森 森 森   12

567

ON-KUN READINGS: シン・ふか(い)

HEADER: 氵

深
deep

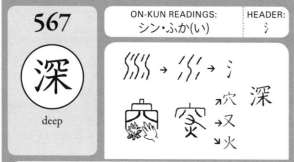

ORIGIN: The left side 氵 was "water." The right side depicted a hand looking for something in a deep hole by the light of a fire. Together the combined form signified "to look for something deep in water." The meaning of search was dropped from this kanji. The kanji 深 means "deep."

ふか
深い deep
ふか
深さ depth
いみぶか
意味深い meaningful
しんこく
深刻な grave

すいしんひゃく
水深百メートル depth of 100 meters
いみしんちょう
意味深長 full of meaning
ふかで
深手 severely wounded

 11

568

ON-KUN READINGS: シン・もう(す)

HEADER: 田

申
to say

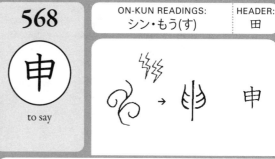

ORIGIN: The ancient form was a pictograph of a jagged bolt of lightning in the sky. Lightning was viewed as a god's will spoken. The meaning of "god" was dropped but the solemn meaning was somewhat retained. The kanji 申 means "to say" in a formal way, such as declaring in an official document, or talking to one's senior.

もう
申す to state
もう こ
申し込む to register
もう あ
申し上げる [humble] to say

しんこく
申告する to declare
しんせい
申請 application, filing

１ 口 日 日 申   5

569

真

truth; genuine

ORIGIN: In the older form 眞, the top ヒ was a fallen person. The middle and the bottom showed a person upside down. The original meaning was replaced by another kanji 顚. Instead this kanji was borrowed to mean "truth." Now written as 真, the kanji means "truth" or "genuine."

写真 photograph
真実 truth
真理 truth

真面目な serious, earnest
真空パック vacuum pack
真ん中 middle

一 十 广 市 古 肖 直 直 真 真　　10

570

神

god

ORIGIN: The left side 示 of the old form 神 was "altar table for ancestral worship," signified by the presence of the moon, the sun, and a star. The right side 申 "to say" depicted lightning bolts in the sky, which was then taken to mean a god's will spoken. The kanji 神 means "god."

神 god
神社 Shinto shrine
神道 Shinto

神々しい divine
神主 Shinto priest
神経質な highstrung, nervous

ヽ ラ ネ ネ ネ 礻 礻 神 神　　9

571

臣

subject; servant

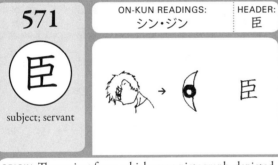

ORIGIN: The ancient form, which was a pictograph, depicted a watchful eye. A loyal subject keeps a watchful eye for his or her lord. The kanji 臣 means "subject" or "servant."

大臣 minister
臣下 subject
臣民 subject

総理大臣 prime minister
家臣 retainer
逆臣 traitor

丨 丆 卬 臣 臣 臣 臣　　7

572

親

parent; intimate

ORIGIN: The left side was 立 "needle" and 木 "wood," and the right side was 見 "to watch." Together they indicated "keeping an eye on wood while shaving it thinner." That meaning signified the intimacy with which family members know each other. The kanji 親 means "intimate" or "parent."

親 parent
両親 parents
親しい familiar, close

親友 close friend
親切な kind (as in a kind person)
親戚 relatives

亠 立 立 立 辛 辛 亲 亲 亲 親 親 親 親 親 親 親　　16

179

573

ON-KUN READINGS: シン・み　　HEADER: 身

身
body; flesh

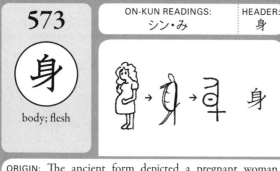

ORIGIN: The ancient form depicted a pregnant woman viewed from the side. The kanji 身 means "body; flesh."

身長 (one's) height
身 body, person
受け身 passive; passive voice (in grammar)

親身に with tender care
出身 to come from
身元 background, identity

ノ イ 竹 丹 丹 身 身　　7

574

ON-KUN READINGS: シン・すす(む)　　HEADER: 辶

進
to move forward

ORIGIN: The upper right 隹 originated from a pictograph of a little bird 辶, originally 辵 "left half of a crossroad and a foot," signified the motion of going along a road. The two parts combine in the kanji 進, which means "to move forward."

進む to move forward
進歩 progress
進学する to enter a higher school

行進 march, parade
進行中 in progress
進駐軍 occupation army

ノ イ イ イ イ 付 作 隹 准 准 進　　11

575

ON-KUN READINGS: シン・はり　　HEADER: 金

針
needle

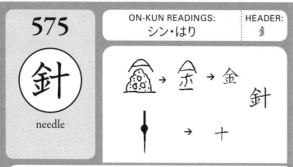
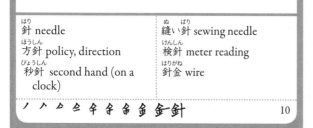

ORIGIN: The left side 金 was metal and the right side 十 was a needle with a thick middle. The combined form meant needle, and also something that shows the direction. The kanji 針 means "needle."

針 needle
方針 policy, direction
秒針 second hand (on a clock)

縫い針 sewing needle
検針 meter reading
針金 wire

ノ 人 人 人 牟 牟 牟 金 金 針　　10

576

ON-KUN READINGS: シン・ふる(える)　　HEADER: 雨

震
to tremble;
to shake

ORIGIN: The top 雨 depicted rain, which also signified something from the sky. The bottom 辰 depicted a clam extending a foot and signified "something moving." Thunder moves or shakes the air. The kanji 震 means "to shake or tremble."

震える to tremble
地震 earthquake
震度 seismic intensity

震災 earthquake damage
震源 the seismic center, epicenter

一 厂 戸 币 币 雨 雨 雨 雨 雩 雩 霄 霄 震 震 震　　15

577

ON-KUN READINGS: ジン・ニン・ひと・り
HEADER: 人

人 person

ORIGIN: The ancient form depicted a person standing slightly stooped, viewed from the side. The kanji 人 means "person." When used as a recurring component, the kanji pertains to something human and is written イ, as in 休 "to rest."

ひと
人 person
ひとり
一人 one person
にほんじん
日本人 Japanese person
おとな
大人 adult

にんげん
人間 human being
ひとで
人手 help, assistance, another's hand
じんこう
人口 population

ノ人

2

578

ON-KUN READINGS: ジン・ニ・ニン
HEADER: イ

仁 benevolent; virtuous

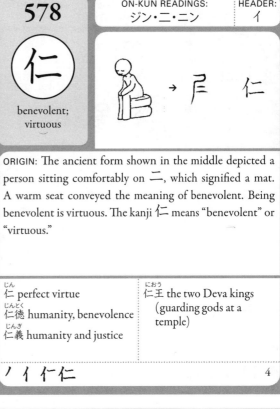

ORIGIN: The ancient form shown in the middle depicted a person sitting comfortably on 二, which signified a mat. A warm seat conveyed the meaning of benevolent. Being benevolent is virtuous. The kanji 仁 means "benevolent" or "virtuous."

じん
仁 perfect virtue
じんとく
仁徳 humanity, benevolence
じんぎ
仁義 humanity and justice

におう
仁王 the two Deva kings (guarding gods at a temple)

ノイ仁仁

4

579

ON-KUN READINGS: ジン・ニン・は
HEADER: 刀

刃 blade

ORIGIN: The ancient form depicted a blade of a sword 刀 in which the sharp cutting side pointed outward to emphasize the sharp edge. The kanji 刃 means "blade."

は
刃 blade
はもの
刃物 cutlery
つやきば
付け焼き刃 borrowed plumes, pretension

でばぼうちょう
出刃包丁 thick kitchen knife
はさき
刃先 tip of a blade
りょうば
両刃の double-edged

フ刀刃

3

580

ON-KUN READINGS: ジン・たず(ねる)
HEADER: 寸

尋 to inquire; to ask

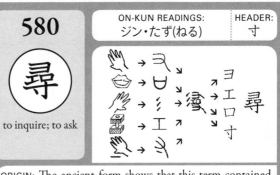

ORIGIN: The ancient form shows that this term contained three hands: a right hand ヨ (in 右), a left hand (in 左), and another hand (in 寸). Together they indicated the span between two stretched hands, which is also six feet (called *hiro* in Japanese.) One stretches his hands forward when seeking an answer. The kanji, now 尋, later came to mean "to inquire" or "to ask."

たず
尋ねる to ask
じんもん
尋問 interrogation
じんじょう
尋常 ordinary, common

ちひろ
千尋の fathomless

ヿ ⁊ ⁊ ⁊ ⁊ ⁊ ⁊ ⁊ ⁊ ⁊ 尋 尋

12

181

581

ON-KUN READINGS: ズ・ト・はか(る)

HEADER: 囗

図

drawing; to plan

ORIGIN: Formerly written as 圖, the kanji depicted a drawing that showed the location in a village of storage for grain. The present form uses a much-reduced form 図 and means "drawing" or "to plan."

ちず
地図 map
としょかん
図書館 library
ず
図 drawing

いと
意図 intention
ずうずう
図々しい impudent
はか
図らずも unintentionally

丨 冂 冋 冈 図 図 図　　　7

582

ON-KUN READINGS: スイ・ふ(く)

HEADER: 口

吹

to blow

ORIGIN: The left side 口 was a depiction of a mouth. The right side 欠 was a person crouching, with mouth open to breathe deeply. Together they indicated to blow air. The kanji 吹 means "to blow."

ふ
吹く to blow
すいそうがく
吹奏楽 wind instrument
　music
ふいちょう
吹聴 する to publicize

ふ よ
吹き寄せる to drift
ふ と
吹き飛ばす to blow away
ふ か
吹き替え voice-over

丿 ロ ロ ロ 吖 吹 吹　　　7

583

ON-KUN READINGS: スイ・た(れる)

HEADER: 土

垂

to hang down

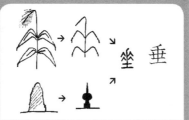

ORIGIN: The ancient form depicted plant leaves hanging down. The bottom 土 "soil" emphasized that the leaves reached the ground. Together they indicated a state of something hanging down. The kanji 垂 means "to hang down."

すいちょく
垂直 vertical
た
垂れる to hang down
た さ
垂れ下がる to hang down

垂線 plumb-line, perpendicular line

丿 一 二 千 千 垂 垂 垂　　　8

584

ON-KUN READINGS: スイ・お(す)

HEADER: 扌

推

to push forward;
to recommend;
to guess

ORIGIN: The left side 扌 was a hand. The right side 隹 was a depiction of a small pudgy bird, here used phonetically to mean "to thrust aside." Together they indicated a hand pushing something forward. The kanji 推 means "to push forward," "to recommend," or "to guess."

お
推す to recommend
すいしょう
推奨 する to recommend
すいせんじょう
推薦状 letter of
　recommendation

すいしん
推進する to propel
すいそく
推測 guess
すいりしょうせつ
推理小説 mystery novel

一 十 扌 扩 扩 扩 扩 拃 拃 推 推　　　11

585

ON-KUN READINGS: スイ・みず
HEADER: 水

水
water; Wednesday

ORIGIN: The ancient form depicted the flow of a river. The kanji 水 means "water." When it is used as a recurring component on the left side for "water" or "liquid," it is written 氵, as in 海 "ocean" and 酒 "sake." It is also used for "Wednesday."

水 water
水曜日 Wednesday
月水金 Monday–Wednesday–Friday

水泳 swimming
水道 water
水銀 mercury

丿 刁 才 水   4

586

ON-KUN READINGS: スウ・ス・かず・かぞ(える)
HEADER: 攵

数
number; to count

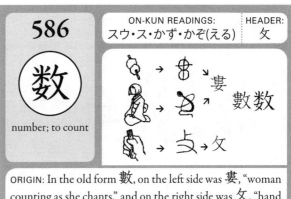

ORIGIN: In the old form 數, on the left side was 婁, "woman counting as she chants," and on the right side was 攵, "hand holding a stick pounding," signifying action in general. Together they indicated chanting while holding counting sticks. The kanji 数 means "number" or "to count."

数 number
数字 numeral, figure
数学 mathematics

多数決 decision by majority
数える to count
数珠つなぎ tying in a row

丶 ゛ ゛ ¥ ¥ ¥ ¥ 娄 娄 娄 娄 数 数   13

587

ON-KUN READINGS: スン
HEADER: 寸

寸
a little; an inch

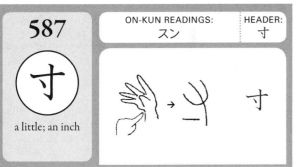

ORIGIN: The ancient form depicted a finger pointing at a wrist where one's pulse was taken. The distance between a hand and that point is an inch, so this portion signified "a little." The kanji 寸 means "a little," or "inch" in the old measuring system.

一寸 a moment
寸前 right before
寸劇 skit, short play
寸法 measurement

一寸先が見えない cannot see an inch ahead
寸分違わない absolutely identical

一 寸 寸   3

588

ON-KUN READINGS: セ・セイ・よ
HEADER: 一

世
a world; a generation

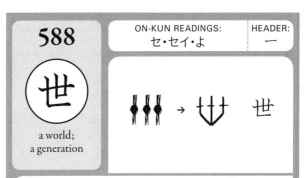

ORIGIN: The kanji 世 consisted of three tens 卅. A period of thirty years is a generation. Generations of people live together in the world. The kanji 世 means "world," or "a generation."

世界 world
世の中 the world, society
世間 world, people

二世 second generation
世話する to take care
世論・世論 public opinion

一 十 廿 廿 世   5

589

ON-KUN READINGS: ゼ・こ(れ) HEADER: 日

是
right; this

ORIGIN: The earlier ancient form (the second from the left) was a ladle or spoon, perhaps used to serve the food on an altar or at a banquet. A later form (the third form) consisted of a spoon and "just" (正). The kanji 是 indicates "just; proper," and is also used for the demonstrative word or pronoun "this."

是れ this
是非 by all means
是正する to correct, to improve

是認 approval
是非を問う to consider the rights and wrongs of a matter

｜ 口 日 日 旦 早 早 昻 是   9

590

ON-KUN READINGS: セイ HEADER: 刂

制
to put in order; to control

ORIGIN: The left side depicted a tree trunk having its limbs pruned, and the right side 刂 was a knife. Together they meant to prune a tree by removing unnecessary parts; the meaning extended to "put in order" (or a "system"). The kanji 制 means to "put in order; to control."

制度 system
政治体制 political system
制服 a uniform

交通規制 traffic control
制する to govern, control
制定 enactment, institution

丿 ﾉ 午 午 与 朱 制 制   8

591

ON-KUN READINGS: セイ・いきお(い) HEADER: 力

勢
vigor; power

ORIGIN: The top depicted a plant in soil being cared for by a person's hands. With strength 力 underneath, the term signified the vigor of growing. The kanji 勢 means "vigor" or "power."

勢い vigor
勢力 power
大勢 general tendency

大勢の人 many people
姿勢 posture
時勢 (trend of) the times

一 十 土 士 ｷ 赤 幸 幸 勃 執 執 勢 勢   13

592

ON-KUN READINGS: セイ・ショウ・かばね HEADER: 女

姓
surname; family name

ORIGIN: The left side 女 depicted a woman sitting with her hands crossed in front, and the right side 生 depicted growth of a plant, or "life." In the ancient matrilineal society, maternal family names were used. The kanji 姓 means "surname; family name."

姓名 full name
姓 surname
旧姓 maiden name

同姓同名 same full names
改姓 change of surname
百姓 peasant

く 女 女 女 妌 姓 姓 姓   8

184

593

ON-KUN READINGS: セイ・ショウ・さが

HEADER: 忄

性

innate nature; sex; gender

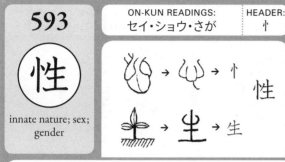

ORIGIN: The left side 忄 is a variant of 心 "heart," and the sound of the right side 生 means "pure; fresh." Together they indicated "the pure heart one is born with." The kanji 性 means "innate nature" or "sex; gender."

だんせい
男性 man
せい
性 sex, gender
せいかく
性格 character, personality
せいしつ
性質 attribute, nature

こんじょう
根性 guts
せいべつ
性別 gender distinction
せいのう
性能 efficiency

丶 丶 忄 忄 忙 忡 忡 性 性   8

594

ON-KUN READINGS: セイ・ジョウ・な(る)

HEADER: 戈

成

to become; to be completed

ORIGIN: The ancient form consisted of 戈 "a spear," which signified "tool," and the sound of 丁, which meant "pounding a nail into a flat surface." Together they indicated "to complete" or "something gets completed." The kanji 成 means "to become; to be completed."

せいこう
成功 success
なりたくうこう
成田空港 Tokyo Narita
    Airport
かんせい
完成 completion

な
成る to accomplish
な た
成り立ち origin
いくせい
育成する to rear, to foster

丿 厂 厅 成 成 成   6

595

ON-KUN READINGS: セイ・ショウ・まつりごと

HEADER: 攵

政

to govern justly; politics

 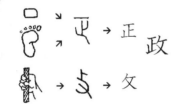

ORIGIN: The left side 正 "just" indicated soldiers walking to a town to conquer, which was seen as a just act. The right side 攵 is a hand holding a stick moving up and down, signifying an action in general. Together the combined form indicated the act of governing by mandate. The kanji 政 means "to govern justly," or "politics."

せいじ
政治 politics
あっせい
圧政 tyranny
せいけん
政権 political (administration) power

せいきょく
政局 political situation
せいへん
政変 coup d'etat
ぎょうせい
行政 administration

一 丁 千 正 正 正 政 政 政   9

596

ON-KUN READINGS: セイ・ととの(える)

HEADER: 攵

整

to set things in good order

ORIGIN: In the top, 束 was a bundle and 攵 was an action—thus the meaning was putting things together in a bundle. The bottom 正 was a line above a left footprint, moving in the right direction toward a goal. The kanji 整 means "to set things in good order."

ととの
整える to set in good order
せいり
整理 order
せいすう
整数 whole number

せいび
整備 complete adjustment
せいぜん
整然と in perfect order
きんせい と
均整の取れた well-
    proportioned

一 一 ㅜ 亘 申 束 束 束 敕 敕 敕 敕 整 整 整 整   16

185

597

ON-KUN READINGS: セイ・ショウ・ほし

HEADER: 日

星

star

ORIGIN: The ancient form had three 日 "sun," indicating "glistening"; and the bottom 生, used phonetically, meant "clear." Together they signified stars glistening in a clear sky. The kanji 星 means "star."

ほし
星 star, point, score, culprit
か ぼし
勝ち星 winning score
せいざ
星座 constellation

ほしぞら
星空 starry sky
りゅうせい
流星 shooting star
いくせいそう
幾星霜 many years

丨 冂 冃 日 尸 旦 甲 犀 星   9

598

ON-KUN READINGS: セイ・は(れる)

HEADER: 日

晴

clear sky

ORIGIN: The ancient form of the old form 晴 consisted of 日 "sun," 生 "lively growth of a plant," and 井 a "well", which signified fresh blue. Together the form signified a clear sky. Now 靑 is written as 青. The kanji 晴 means "clear sky."

は
晴れる to become clear
せいてん
晴天 clear sky
かいせい
快晴 clear day

にほんばれ
日本晴れ clear day
すば
素晴らしい splendid

丨 冂 冃 日 旷 旷 晴 晴 晴 晴 晴   12

599

ON-KUN READINGS: セイ・ショウ・ただ(しい)・まさ

HEADER: 止

正

just; correct; proper

ORIGIN: In the ancient forms, a box or a line signified a town surrounded by a wall, and a footprint signified advancing on foot. Together they indicated conquering a town, which was seen as a just act. The kanji 正 means "just; correct; proper."

しょうがつ
正月 New Year's Days
ただ
正しい correct, just
しょうじき
正直な honest

たいしょう
大正 Taisho era (1912–1926)
せいかい
正解 correct answer
ふせい
不正 injustice

一 丁 干 正 正   5

600

ON-KUN READINGS: セイ・ショウ・きよ(い)

HEADER: 氵

清

pure; clean

ORIGIN: The left side 氵 is water 水. On the right side, the old form had 生 "lively growth of a plant" and 井 "water in a well" (the dot emphasizes water). The kanji 清 means "pure; clean."

きよ
清い pure, clear, limpid
きよ
清らかな pure, clear
せいけつ
清潔な pure, clean

すがすが
清清しい invigorating
しみず
清水 spring water
せいそう
清掃 cleaning, scavenging

丶 氵 氵 汀 汢 洼 清 清 清 清 清   11

186

601

ON-KUN READINGS: セイ・ショウ・う(まれる)・い(きる)・は(える)・なま・き・お(う)

HEADER: 生

生

to live; life; person

ORIGIN: The ancient form depicted a plant just starting to sprout, indicating "to grow," or "life." A human being lives a life; the meaning included "person." The kanji 生 has come to mean not only "life" or "to live," but also "person."

せんせい
先生 teacher
う
生まれる to be born
い
生きる to live

なまにく
生肉 raw meat
いっしょう
一生 one's whole life
は
生える to sprout

ノ ┌ 屮 牛 生 5

602

ON-KUN READINGS: セイ・ジョウ・も(る)・さか(ん)

HEADER: 皿

盛

to thrive; prosperous

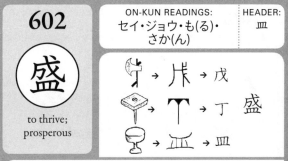

ORIGIN: The top 成 consisted of 戈, a spearlike weapon, indicating tools, and 丁 "to hit," and was used phonetically to indicate "to pile up." The bottom 皿 was a plate. Together they meant putting a heap of food on a plate, signifying thriving. The kanji 盛 means "to thrive" or "prosperous."

も
盛る to serve, to heap up
さか
盛んな thriving
はんじょう
繁盛 prosperous (business)

も あ
盛り上がる to liven up
ぜんせいき
全盛期 one's heyday
せいだい
盛大に with splendor

ノ 厂 厂 成 成 成 成 成 盛 盛 盛 11

603

ON-KUN READINGS: セイ・ショウ

HEADER: 米

精

pure; essence; details

ORIGIN: The left 米 was rice scattered in all directions. The old form 青 (not shown above) "fresh; blue" came from 生 "three leaves above the ground," signifying "fresh," and 丹 "clean water in a well." Removing tiny debris from small grains of rice is detailed work; what remains is the essence. The kanji 精 means "pure" or "essence; details."

せいいっぱい
精一杯 the best of one's ability
せいみつ
精密 precise
せいしん
精神 soul, spirit
せい だ
精を出す to work assiduously

せいつう
精通する to be well versed, knowledgeable
しょうじんりょうり
精進料理 vegetarian diet (originally for a Buddhist monk)

丶 丷 半 米 米 米 米 精 精 精 精 精 精 精 14

604

ON-KUN READINGS: ひじり・セイ

HEADER: 耳

聖

sage; sacred; saint

ORIGIN: The ancient form had 耳 "ear," that was emphasized by an elongated stroke, and 壬 "person standing" and 口 "mouth." Together the forms signified someone who could hear voices (including the words of gods) extraordinarily well and give advice. Such a person is knowledgeable and respected. The kanji 聖 means "sage," "saint," or "sacred."

せいじん
聖人 saint
せい
聖なる sacred
せいどう
聖堂 cathedral

ひじり
聖 saint
しんせい
神聖な sacred
せいしょ
聖書 the Bible

一 丁 丆 丆 耳 耳 耵 耵 耵 聖 聖 聖 聖 13

605

ON-KUN READINGS: セイ・ショウ・こえ・こわ

HEADER: 士

声

voice

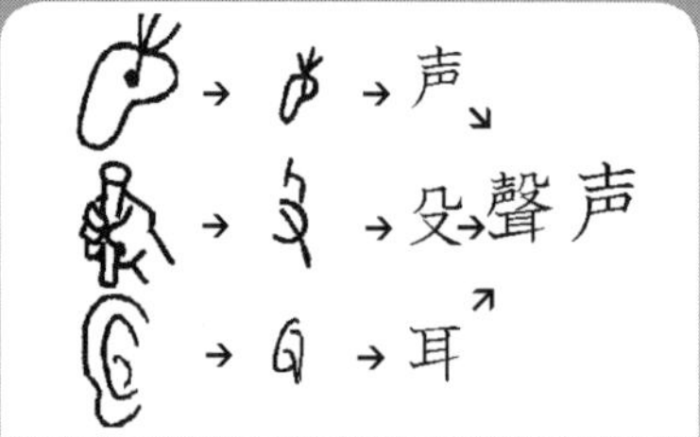

ORIGIN: The old form 聲 consisted of 声 "slate" (used as a musical instrument), 殳 "hit by hand with a stick," as a musical instrument is played, and 耳 "ear," to listen. Together, they meant banging a slate with a stick to make music that could be heard. The reduced kanji 声 means "voice."

- 声（こえ） voice
- 大声（おおごえ）で in a loud voice
- 四声（しせい） four tones in Chinese
- 声音（こわね） tone of voice
- 声望（せいぼう） reputation
- 声援（せいえん） cheering, support

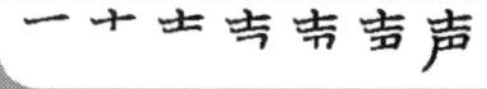

7

606

ON-KUN READINGS: セイ

HEADER: 衣

製

to manufacture

ORIGIN: The top 制 signified pruning a tree. The bottom 衣 depicted the folds of a collar, indicating clothes. Together they meant making clothes into a good fit using scissors, or simply to manufacture well. The kanji 製 means "to manufacture."

- 日本製（にほんせい） Japanese product
- 製作（せいさく） production
- 作製（さくせい） production
- 手製（てせい） handmade
- 製品（せいひん） (finished) product
- 私製（しせい）の privately made

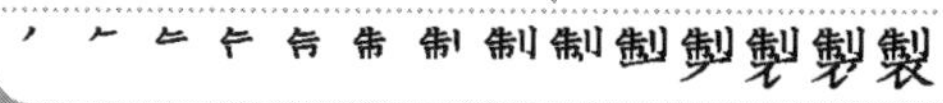

14

607

ON-KUN READINGS: セイ・サイ・にし

HEADER: 西

西

west

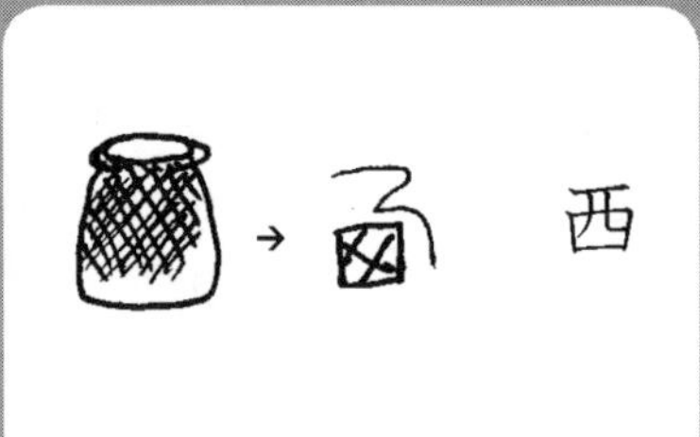

ORIGIN: The ancient form depicted a basket that was used to extract rice wine. The line on the right side indicated the sound of dripping. For an unknown reason, the kanji 西 took on its current meaning, "west."

- 西（にし） west
- 西口（にしぐち） west exit
- 東西（とうざい） east and west
- 関西（かんさい） the Kansai area
- 西部（せいぶ） the western region
- 西欧（せいおう） Western Europe

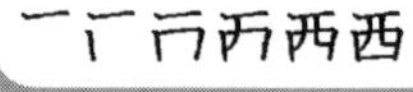

6

608

ON-KUN READINGS: セイ・まこと

HEADER: 言

誠

faithful; sincere

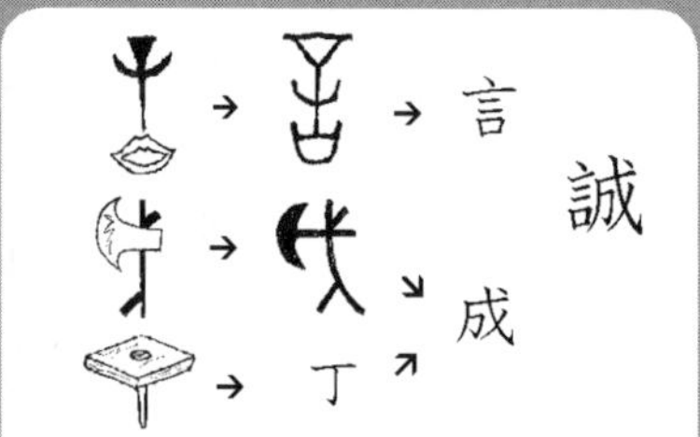

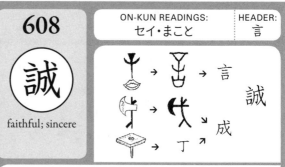

ORIGIN: The left side 言 was a needle and a mouth 口, signifying "to speak clearly" or "word." The right side 成 was used phonetically to indicate "to overlap each other." Together they indicated that words and actions are the same, or "sincere." The kanji 誠 means "faithful; sincere."

- 誠（まこと） sincerity, faithfulness
- 誠意（せいい） sincerity
- 忠誠（ちゅうせい） loyalty, allegiance
- 誠実（せいじつ）な sincere, faithful
- 至誠（しせい） one's true heart, devotion

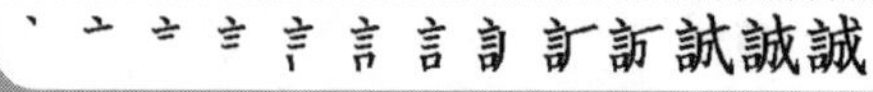

13

609

青

blue; fresh

ORIGIN: In the old form 青, the top part 生, which came from leaves above the ground, meant "fresh." The bottom part 丹 (now changed to 月) came from 井 (clean water in a well 井 was emphasized by a dot in the middle). The current kanji 青 means "fresh; blue."

あお
青 blue
せいねん
青年 young man
あおにさい
青二才 green youth, immature

せいしょうねん
青少年 youth
せいしゅん
青春 the bloom of youth
あおてんじょう
青天井の sky-rocketing

一 十 キ 主 キ 青 青 青　8

610

静

quiet; serene

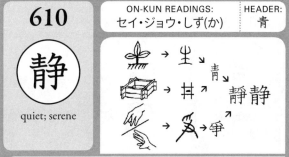

ORIGIN: In the old form 靜, the left side 青 (now written as 青) meant "blue and serene." The right side 爭 consisted of a hand coming from the top and one coming from the bottom, signifying fighting to grab something in the middle. Together the two sides indicated "quiet after a fight stops." The kanji 静 means "quiet; serene."

しず
静か quiet, serene
れいせい
冷静に calmly, cool-headedly
しず
静かさ tranquility

じょうみゃく
静脈 a vein
せいし
静止する to stand still
あんせい
安静にする to rest quietly in bed

一 十 キ 主 キ 青 青 青 青 靑 静 静 静 静　14

189

611

税

tax; levy

ORIGIN: The left side 禾 is a rice stalk, signifying "harvest." The right side of the old form 兌 consisted of 八 "to part in the middle" and 兄 "older brother or male member of family" (person with a big head). Together they indicated "to rid the head of a family of his harvest," that is, to levy a tax. The kanji 税 means "tax; levy."

ぜいきん
税金 tax
しょうひぜい
消費税 consumption tax
めんぜいひん
免税品 duty-free goods

かぜい
課税 taxation
かんぜい
関税 customs duties
だつぜい
脱税 tax evasion

一 二 千 禾 禾 禾 禾 秎 税 税 税 税　12

612

席

seat

ORIGIN: The two different ancient forms both had a "house" (广); the first one had a mat to sit on and the other a "cloth" (巾) for a floor cushion. Then the seating mat was replaced by a cooking pot, perhaps to signify seating in the comfort of home. The kanji 席 means "seat."

せき
席 seat
しゅっせき
出席 presence, attendance
けっせき
欠席 absence

きゃくせき
客席 audience, seating area
ざせき
座席 seat of a chair
せっけん
席巻 sweep over

' 亠 广 广 庐 庐 庐 席 席 席　10

613

ON-KUN READINGS:	HEADER:
セキ・シャク・むかし	日

昔

a long time ago; bygone days

ORIGIN: The top came from two lines indicating "to repeat." The bottom 日 was the sun, signifying the passage of time. Together they signified times that had been repeated. The kanji 昔 means "a long time ago; bygone days."

昔 old times, bygone days
昔々 once upon a time
昔話 story of the olden days

今昔 now and then
一昔 ten years
昔日 old days

一 十 廾 昔 芒 昔 昔 昔   8

614

ON-KUN READINGS:	HEADER:
セキ・シャク・コク・いし	石

石

stone; rock

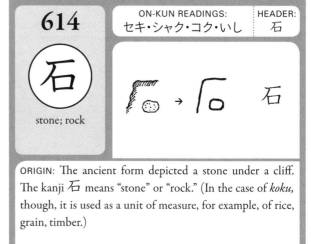

ORIGIN: The ancient form depicted a stone under a cliff. The kanji 石 means "stone" or "rock." (In the case of *koku,* though, it is used as a unit of measure, for example, of rice, grain, timber.)

石 rock, stone
化石 fossil
石鹸 soap

宝石 jewelry
小石 pebbles
一万石 10,000 *koku* of rice

一 ア イ 石 石   5

615

ON-KUN READINGS:	HEADER:
セキ・つ(もる)	禾

積

to pile; the product

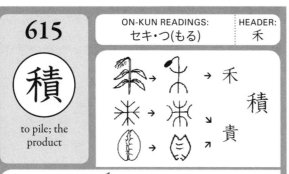

ORIGIN: The left side 禾 was a rice plant drooping under the weight of the crop. The right side, 責 "liability; responsibility"—phonetically used here—depicted a rugged, thorny shape above currency (貝). The kanji originally indicated tribute in the form of grains. Collected tributes would pile up. It also means "the product." The kanji 積 means "to pile."

積む to pile up
面積 area, measure
体積 volume

積もり intention, idea
積立金 reserve fund
積年の longstanding, of many years

丿 二 千 禾 禾 禾 秆 秆 秆 秸 秸 積 積 積 積 積   16

616

ON-KUN READINGS:	HEADER:
セキ	糸

績

to accumulate

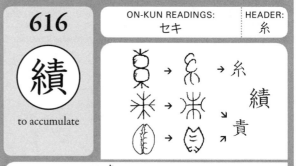

ORIGIN: The left side 糸 was "thin, silk threads pulled out of silkworm cocoons." The right side 責 indicated "liability; responsibility." The combined form originally indicated a tribute that was expected in the form of threads or woven cloth. The kanji 績 means "to accumulate" over time.

実績 past records
業績 achievement, business results
成績 result, grades

功績 distinguished services
紡績 spinning

   17

190

617

ON-KUN READINGS: セキ・せ(める)

HEADER: 貝

責

liability; to blame

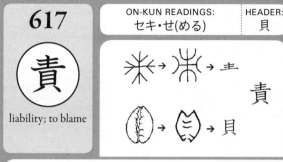

ORIGIN: In the ancient form the top depicted a rugged, thorny shape, and the bottom 貝 was a cowry, used as money in trade. The combined form was used to indicate tribute that people had to pay. From that, this form indicated something that is demanded. The kanji 責 means "liability" or "to blame."

責任 responsibility
責める to blame
引責 taking responsibility upon oneself
責務 obligation
自責の念 remorse
文責 responsibility for wording

一 十 キ 主 青 青 青 青 責 責 責   11

618

ON-KUN READINGS: セキ・シャク・あか

HEADER: 赤

赤

red

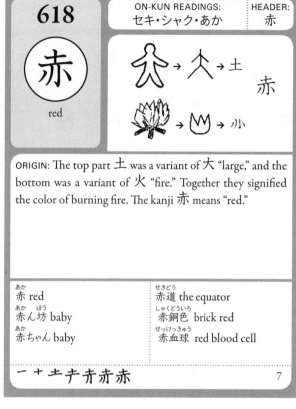

ORIGIN: The top part 土 was a variant of 大 "large," and the bottom was a variant of 火 "fire." Together they signified the color of burning fire. The kanji 赤 means "red."

赤 red
赤ん坊 baby
赤ちゃん baby
赤道 the equator
赤銅色 brick red
赤血球 red blood cell

一 十 土 ナ 亦 赤 赤   7

191

619

ON-KUN READINGS: セツ・サイ・き(る)

HEADER: 刀

切

to cut; serious; eanest

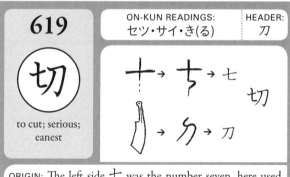

ORIGIN: The left side 七 was the number seven, here used phonetically for "cutting." The right side was 刀 "sword; knife." The use of a sword or knife creates a situation that one handles seriously. The kanji 切 means "to cut" or "serious; earnest.

切る to cut
親切な kind, good, obliging
切手 postal stamp
売り切れ sold out
大切な important, valued
一切 all, everything
切に earnestly, eagerly

一 七 切 切   4

620

ON-KUN READINGS: セツ・つ(ぐ)

HEADER: 扌

接

to contact

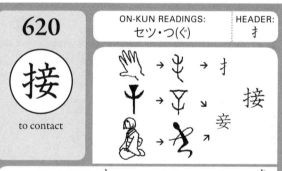

ORIGIN: The left side 扌 was a hand. On the right side 妾, 立 "tattoo needle" and 女 "woman" signified a tattooed woman—that is, a slave. A servant would have stayed close to do manual work; the meaning evolved to "close enough to contact." The kanji 接 means "to contact."

面接 interview
直接 direct
間接的 indirect
接する to meet in person, to contact
応接室 reception room
接近する to approach

一 十 扌 扌 扩 扩 护 护 接 接 接   11

621

ON-KUN READINGS: セツ・お(る)・おり

HEADER: 扌

折

to break; occasion

ORIGIN: The ancient form shown in the middle indicated that 扌 was in fact not "hand" but rather "grass; wood broken in two." The right side 斤 was an ax. Together the forms signified "to break." When a break happens, it creates a new occasion. The kanji 折 means "to break" or "occasion."

折る to bend; to break
右折 right turn
その折に on that occasion

屈折 refraction, bending
挫折 collapse, setback
折半する to divide in half

一 十 扌 扌 扌 折 折   7

622

ON-KUN READINGS: セツ・もう(ける)

HEADER: 言

設

to set up

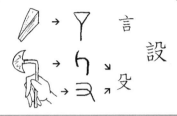

ORIGIN: The left side was "wedge," which was miscopied into 言 "word" later on. The right side 殳 was a weapon in hand, indicating "to fight," a general meaning that became "to engage in work." Together they indicated "to set up something following words (perhaps order)." The kanji 設 means "to set up."

設ける to set up
新設 new setup
設計 design

建設 construction
設定 setup
設備 equipment, installation

、 亠 亠 言 言 言 言 訳 設 設   11

623

ON-KUN READINGS: セツ・セチ・ふし

HEADER: 竹

節

section;
holiday; occasion;
moderation; tune

ORIGIN: The top 竹 "bamboo," which has distinct joints, and the bottom 即 "a person bending his knee to eat food" together signified "punctuation." Something that punctuates time was a "holiday" or an "occasion" and something that kept one's behavior from becoming in excess was "moderation." A flute made of a section of bamboo makes a tune. The kanji 節 means "section; joint; holiday; occasion; moderation tune."

季節 season
節 joint, tune
節度 moderation

関節 joint
節句 seasonal festival
浪花節 naniwa-bushi song

ノ ト ト ケ ケ 竹 竹 竺 竿 笞 節 節 節   13

624

ON-KUN READINGS: セツ・ゼイ・と(く)

HEADER: 言

説

to explain; opinion

ORIGIN: The left 言 had 辛 "needle," and 口 "mouth," signifying "to express an idea clearly" or "word." On the right side, in the old form 兌, 八 means to cut into two and 兄 was an "elder." Together they indicated a wise man who explained a difficult matter. The kanji 説 means "to explain" or "opinion."

説明 explanation
解説 commentary
遊説 canvassing tour, campaign

説 view, interpretation
説く to preach
口説く to persuade

、 亠 亠 言 言 言 言 訳 訳 説 説 説   14

625	ON-KUN READINGS: セツ・ゆき	HEADER: 雨

雪 snow

ORIGIN: The top 雨 depicted "rain; something that fell from the sky." The bottom ヨ came from 彗 "hand holding a broom to sweep" or "to cleanse." A snowfall blankets the earth as if cleansing everything on the ground. The kanji 雪 means "snow." (The broom has been dropped in the current form.)

ゆき 雪 snow
おおゆき 大雪 blizzard
ゆき 雪かき snow shoveling

しんせつ 新雪 new snow
なだれ 雪崩 avalanche
せつじょく 雪辱 vindicating one's honor

一一一一戸雨雨雨雪雪雪   11

626	ON-KUN READINGS: ゼツ・た(える)	HEADER: 糸

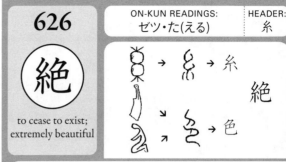

絶 to cease to exist; extremely beautiful

ORIGIN: The left side 糸 was "threads." The right side 色 "sword" and "bent body," used phonetically, indicated "to cut." The combined form indicated cutting threads. Because 色 means "color," thus it also gave the meaning of beautiful colored threads. The kanji 絶 means "to cease to exist" or "extremely beautiful."

ぜったい 絶対に absolutely
た 絶える to cease to exist
ぜっこう 絶交する to cut contact completely

ぜつぼうてき 絶望的 hopelessly, desperate
ぜっけい 絶景 very beautiful scenery
だんぜつ 断絶 extinction

く 幺 幺 糸 糸 糸 紀 紀 絶 絶   12

627	ON-KUN READINGS: ゼツ・した	HEADER: 舌

舌 tongue; speaking

ORIGIN: In the ancient form the top comes from a forked thrusting weapon, here used phonetically to mean "to thrust out," and the bottom is 口 "mouth." A tongue can move in and out of a mouth. The kanji 舌 means "tongue," and also "speaking."

した 舌 tongue
したた 舌足らずな insufficient (explanation)
したつづみ う 舌鼓を打つ to eat with gusto

べんぜつ た 弁舌が立つ to speak eloquently
どくぜつ 毒舌 speaking bitterly, stinging tongue

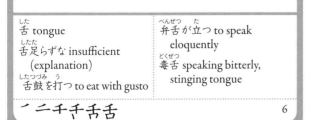

一 二 千 千 舌 舌   6

628	ON-KUN READINGS: セン・さき・ま(ず)	HEADER: 儿

先 ahead; to proceed; the past

ORIGIN: The top was a foot, and the bottom 儿 was the lower part of a person. The tip of the foot is the part of the body that is foremost when one walks. The kanji 先 means "ahead," "to proceed," or "the past" (that which has gone ahead).

せんせい 先生 teacher
せんしゅう 先週 last week
せんじつ 先日 a while ago, the other day

せんげつ 先月 last month
さき 先に ahead of
ゆうせんてき 優先的 by priority, preferential

ノ ト ⊢ 生 先 先   6

629

千
thousand

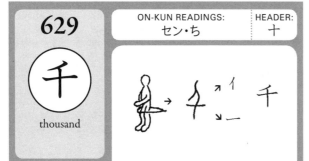

ORIGIN: The ancient form was a combination of a person 亻 and one 一. Soldiers were counted by the thousand, and divisions of troops were marked by a line. Hence the kanji depicted people coming together by the thousands. The kanji 千 means "thousand."

千 thousand
三千 three thousand
五千万円 fifty million yen

千代 thousand generations
千秋楽 closing day (in sumo, play)
千里眼 second sight

丿 一 千

3

630

宣
to state in public

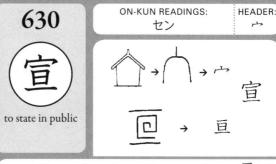

ORIGIN: The top 宀 is a house. The ancient form of 亘 had a coil between two lines, indicating an imperial room surrounded by boundaries. The words in a ceremony, and judicial decisions made in an imperial room, were proclaimed publicly. The kanji 宣 means "to state in public."

宣伝 advertisement
宣言 declaration
宣戦布告 proclamation of war

宣教師 missionary
宣誓 oath
宣下 imperial decree

丶 宀 宀 宁 宵 宫 宣 宣

9

631

専
specialty

ORIGIN: The old form 專 depicted silk threads from cocoons being reeled out by hand 寸 and converging into a single point for spinning. This signified "a point to converge" or "to specialize." Now slightly abbreviated to 専, the kanji 専 means "specialty."

専門 specialty
専攻 major (in academic field)
専制政治 autocracy

専用 exclusive use
専ら solely
専心して wholeheartedly

一 一 戸 百 百 亩 車 専 専

9

632

川
river

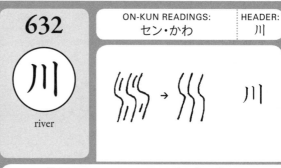

ORIGIN: Originating as a pictograph of a flowing river between two banks, the kanji 川 means "river."

川 river
天の川 the Milky Way
川岸 river bank

河川 river
川柳 satirical poem
川下 downstream

丿 丿丨 川

3

633

戦

war; to fight

ORIGIN: The left side 單 (the old form of 単) was a forked weapon in which the fork was emphasized and the right side 戈 was a halberd. The old form 戰 is now simplified. The kanji 戦 means "to fight" or "war."

せんそう
戦争 war
いくさ
戦 battle
たたか
戦う to fight

たいせん
対戦する to have a match
きょじんせん
巨人戦 Giants' game
せんりゃく
戦略 strategy

丶 丶 丷 ビ 兴 兴 単 単 単 戦 戦 戦　13

634

泉

fountain

ORIGIN: The ancient form was a pictograph of spring water running between rocks. The kanji 泉 means "fountain."

いずみ
泉 fountain
おんせん
温泉 hot spring, spa
せんすい
泉水 fountain water

かんけつせん
間欠泉 geyser
げんせんかぜい
源泉課税 taxation at the source

′ 亻 冂 冋 白 白 身 泉 泉　9

635

浅

shallow

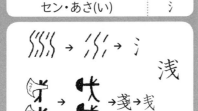

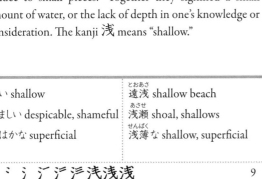

ORIGIN: The left side シ indicated water. The right side 戔 had two halberds, which signified "to cut away" or "to reduce to small pieces." Together they signified a small amount of water, or the lack of depth in one's knowledge or consideration. The kanji 浅 means "shallow."

あさ
浅い shallow
あさ
浅ましい despicable, shameful
あさ
浅はかな superficial

とおあさ
遠浅 shallow beach
あさせ
浅瀬 shoal, shallows
せんぱく
浅薄な shallow, superficial

丶 丶 氵 氵 汽 汽 浅 浅 浅　9

636

洗

to wash (with water)

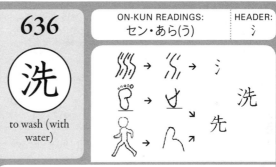

ORIGIN: The left side シ was water and the right side 先 consisted of a footprint and a person 儿, signifying "ahead" or "to proceed." (One's feet always move ahead of the body.) Combined, the two sides indicate to clean a foot with water. The meaning of foot was later dropped, so the kanji means "to wash."

あら
洗う to wash
てあら
お手洗い washroom
せんたくき せんたっき
洗濯機・洗濯機 washing machine

せんめんじょ
洗面所 washroom
すいせんべんじょ
水洗便所 a flush toilet
せんれい
洗礼 baptism

丶 丶 氵 氵 汗 浐 浐 洗 洗　9

195

637

ON-KUN READINGS: セン・し(み)・そ(める)

HEADER: 木

染
to dye

ORIGIN: The upper left side 氵 indicated "water"; the origin is the same as the kanji 水, which depicted a stream of water. The upper right 九 depicted a person who kept his eyes on fabric being dyed. Dyes were taken from the berries and bark of a tree 木. The forms combine in the kanji 染, which means "to dye."

そ
染める to dye
でんせんびょう
伝染病 contagious disease
おせん
汚染 contamination

せんしょくたい
染色体 chromosome
せんりょう
染料 dyes
かんせん
感染 infection

` ` 氵 氵 汈 氿 染 染 染   9

638

ON-KUN READINGS: セン

HEADER: 糸

線
line

ORIGIN: The left side 糸 was threads, signifying something "long and thin." The right side 泉 "fountain" was used phonetically to mean "slender." Together they indicated a thin thread, or line. The kanji 線 means "line."

せん
線 line
やまのてせん
山手線 Yamanote Line
にばんせん
二番線 track number two

かせん
下線 underline
だっせん
脱線 derailment
しゃせん
車線 lane

` ` 幺 幺 乍 糸 糸' 紣 紳 絼 緽 緽 線 線   15

639

ON-KUN READINGS: セン・ふね・ふな

HEADER: 舟

船
ship; boat

ORIGIN: The left side 舟 was "boat" and the right side indicated an action that moved along a hollowed-out area. A boat sails along with the flow of water. The kanji 船 means "ship; boat."

ふね
船 ship, boat
ふなびん
船便 by boat, by sea
こぶね
小船 little boat

ゆぶね
湯船 bathtub
ふなで
船出 embarkation
せんどう
船頭 ferryman, boatman

` 丿 刀 凢 舟 舟 舟 舯 船 船 船   11

640

ON-KUN READINGS: セン・えら(ぶ)

HEADER: 辶

選
to choose

ORIGIN: The top 巽 consisted of two people put forward by two hands, indicating "to select people." The bottom came from a footstep in a crossroad, signifying "go-forward." The kanji 選 means "to choose."

えら
選ぶ to select
せんきょ
選挙 election
せんしゅ
選手 athlete chosen to
   compete

とうせん
当選する to be elected
よせん
予選 preliminary heat
せんこう
選考 selection

` ` ` 巴 巴 巴 界 罪 罪 巽 巽 巽 選 選   15

196

641

銭

small change; coins

ORIGIN: The left side 金 was metal. The old form of the right side, 戔, had two sharp-edged halberds, indicating "to cut into small pieces." Together the two sides indicated small pieces of metal. The kanji 銭 means "coins" or "small change."

小銭 small change (of money)
きんせん
金銭 money
ごせん
五銭 five sen

せんとう
銭湯 public bath
ひぜに
日銭 daily cash income
ぜにかね
銭金 money

ノ 入 ム 二 牟 牟 余 金 金 釒 釒 銭 銭 銭 14

642

鮮

fresh

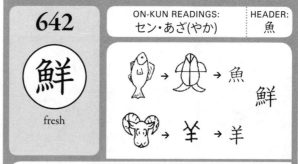

ORIGIN: The left side 魚 was a fish. The right side 羊 was sheep. Because sheep could be used for food or for wool, and were also attractive, the form for sheep was versatile enough to be used in various kanji to indicate 'fine or of desirable quality. The two sides together meant "fine fish," hence "fresh." The kanji 鮮 means "fresh."

しんせん
新鮮な fresh
あざ
鮮やか clear, vivid
せんめい
鮮明な distinct

せいせんやさい
生鮮野菜 fresh vegetables
きたちょうせん
北朝鮮 North Korea
せんど
鮮度 freshness

ノ ク ク 缶 缶 缶 魚 魚 魚 魚 魚 魚' 鮮 鮮 鮮 鮮 17

643

前

front; before

ORIGIN: The old form had 止 "footprint" and 月 "boat" to signify "moving forward." A 刂 "knife" was added to indicate "cutting the toenails," the foremost part of the body. Now the kanji 前 is used to mean "before" or "front."

まえ
前 before, front
ごぜんくじ
午前九時 9:00 A.M.
ごぜんちゅう
午前中 before noon, in the morning

にねんまえ
二年前に two years ago
こうえんまえ
公園前 in front of park
じぜん
事前に beforehand

丶 丷 ヴ 斿 斿 前 前 前 前 9

644

善

good deed

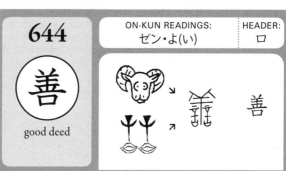

ORIGIN: In the ancient form, the top was derived from sheep 羊, signifying something good. (Sheep are good-looking, tasty, and useful for wool.) The bottom was derived from the two old forms of 言 "word." Together they indicated "good deed to be praised with words." The kanji 善 means "good deed."

ぜん
善 goodness
じぜん
慈善 charity
ぜんい
善意 goodwill

さいぜん
最善の the best
ぎぜんてき
偽善的 hypocritical
どくぜんてき
独善的 self-righteous

丶 丷 ゛ 兰 羊 羊 羊 羊 盖 盖 善 善 12

645

ON-KUN READINGS: ゼン・ネン・しか(し)

HEADER: 灬

然

naturally; yes

ORIGIN: The ancient form consisted of 月 "meat," 犬 "dog," and 灬, a variant of "fire" 火. Together they signified "to burn animal's meat." A new kanji 燃 was created for this meaning incorporating an additional form for fire 火. Then 然 came to be used phonetically to mean "naturally" or "yes."

ぜんぜん
全然〜ない not at all
しぜん
自然 nature
とうぜん
当然 justly

てんねん
天然 natural
しぜん
自然と spontaneously
しか
然り exactly so

ノ ク タ タ タ 쓨 然 然 然 然 然 然   12

646

ON-KUN READINGS: ゼン・すべ(て)・まった(く)

HEADER: 入

全

entire; all; perfect

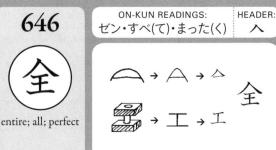
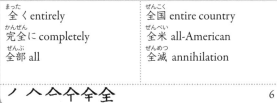

ORIGIN: The top part 亼 indicated "to collect things under one cover." The bottom 工 was a "craft." Together they indicated "collecting all the crafts completely," or just "complete," or "perfect." The kanji 全 means "all; entire; perfect."

まった
全く entirely
かんぜん
完全に completely
ぜんぶ
全部 all

ぜんこく
全国 entire country
ぜんべい
全米 all-American
ぜんめつ
全滅 annihilation

ノ 入 入 仐 仐 全 全   6

647

ON-KUN READINGS: ソ

HEADER: ネ

祖

ancestral

ORIGIN: The left side ネ (originally 示) depicted an altar; it was used in kanji that pertain to religious matters. The right side was a pile of stones, indicating a tombstone. Together they signified ancestral celebration. The kanji 祖 means "ancestral."

そふ
祖父 grandfather
そぼ
祖母 grandmother
せんぞ
先祖 ancestor (of family)

そせん
祖先 ancestor (of race)
そこく
祖国 one's own country
がんそ
元祖 originator

丶 ラ ネ ネ 礻 初 初 祖 祖   9

648

ON-KUN READINGS: ソ・ス

HEADER: 糸

素

crude; original

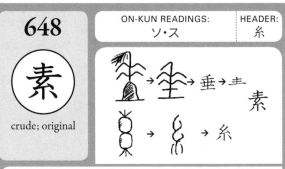

ORIGIN: The top form "to droop" came from the depiction of a rice plant hanging its heavy head, here used phonetically to indicate "soft." The bottom 糸 was thin silk threads being pulled out of silkworm cocoons. Together they indicated raw, unrefined threads. The kanji 素 means "crude; original."

かんそ
簡素 simple
すなお
素直な obedient, gentle
すあし
素足 barefoot

しろうと
素人 amateur
そぼく
素朴な simple, artless
すどお
素通り passing through

一 十 キ キ 主 主 妻 麦 素 素   10

649

組

group, to braid

ORIGIN: The left side 糸 depicted thin silk pulled from silkworm cocoons, signifying threads. The right side was a pile of stones, indicating ancestral tombstones. Together they meant to assemble threads one by one or "to braid," or what was put together, a group. The kanji 組 means "to braid" or "group."

くみ
組 class, group
そしき
組織 organization
く
組む to form a pair or group

ばんぐみ
番組 program
しく
仕組み mechanism
く　あ
組み合わせ combination

く　ㄑ　幺　幺　爷　糸　糸　糸′　糸′′　紵　組　組　　11

650

創

to cut; to create; wound

ORIGIN: The left side 倉 "storage" was used phonetically to indicate "to cut," and the right side リ was "knife." Together they indicated "to cut" or "to create" something new, or a "cut or wound." The kanji 創 means "to cut," "to create," or "wound."

つく
創る to create
そうぞう
創造 creation
どくそうてき
独創的な original, creative

そういくふう
創意工夫 ingenuity
そうししゃ
創始者 founder
そうしょう
創傷 knife wound

ノ　ㄥ　ㄈ　今　今　今　今　倉　倉　倉　創　　12

199

651

倉

storage; warehouse

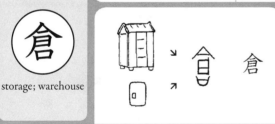

ORIGIN: The ancient form depicted a storage space for grain, with an opening for access, indicating that it was a structure where one could move grain or other crops in and out. The kanji 倉 means "storage; warehouse."

くら
倉 storage
そうこ
倉庫 warehouse
こくそうちたい
穀倉地帯 granary region

こめぐら
米倉 rice granary
むなぐら　つか
胸倉を掴む to seize by the
　　　　coat lapels

ノ　ㄥ　ㄈ　今　今　今　今　倉　倉　倉　　10

652

奏

to play (music); to report to a ruler

ORIGIN: The ancient form depicted a scene in which two hands offered a sacrificial animal to a god, signifying "to put words or music forth to a god or a higher being." The kanji 奏 means "to report to a ruler," or "to play (music)."

えんそう
演奏 musical performance
かな
奏でる to play music
どくそう
独奏 solo performance

じょうそう
上奏する to report to a ruler
ばんそう
伴奏 accompaniment
がっそう
合奏 musical ensemble

一　二　三　声　夫　表　春　奏　奏　　9

653

ON-KUN READINGS:	HEADER:
ソウ	尸

層

layer; class of
people

ORIGIN: The top depicted a roof and 曾, the old form of 曽 underneath, was a rice steamer. A food steamer has many layers so steam can circulate effectively. The meaning of layer also refers to people. The kanji 層 means "layer" or "class of people."

そう
層 layer
こうそう
高層ビル high-rise building
ひょうそうてき
表層的 superficial

ていしょとくしゃそう
低所得者層 low-income
people
ちそう
地層 stratum
さんそう
三層 three layers

一 フ フ コ コ コ コ コ 屉 屉 屉 層 層 層 層 14

654

ON-KUN READINGS:	HEADER:
ソウ・ソ・おも(う)	心

想

to contemplate;
to think

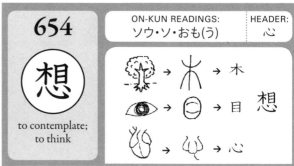

ORIGIN: The top had 木 "tree" and 目 "eye," signifying someone facing a tree. The bottom 心 was a pictograph of a heart. Together they indicated facing something in the heart. The kanji 想 means "to think; to contemplate."

そうぞう
想像 imagination
おも
想う to imagine, to
contemplate
かんそう
感想 impression

あいそ
愛想のいい sociable
りそう
理想 an ideal
れんそう
連想 association of ideas

一 十 オ 木 利 机 相 相 相 相 想 想 想 13

655

ON-KUN READINGS:	HEADER:
ソウ・は(く)	扌

掃

to sweep

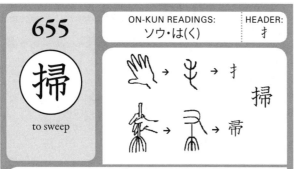

ORIGIN: The left side 扌 was "hand" and the right 帚 depicted a hand holding a broom, which signified "to sweep" or "to cleanse" a place of worship. The kanji 掃 means "to sweep."

そうじ
掃除 cleaning
は
掃く to sweep
せいそう
清掃 cleaning

いっそう
一掃する to sweep away, to
wipe out

一 十 扌 扌 扩 扫 扫 扫 掃 掃 掃 11

656

ON-KUN READINGS:	HEADER:
ソウ・あやつ(る)・みさお	扌

操

to operate; fidelity

ORIGIN: The left 扌 was a hand. The right had the mouths 品 of three birds perched on a tree 木, which indicated "noisy and busy." Together they meant doing something busily. It is also used for a way in which a person should behave, thus "chastity, faith." The kanji 操 means "to operate" and "fidelity."

たいそう
体操 physical exercises,
gymnastics
そうさ
操作 operation
そうぎょうじかん
操業時間 time in operation

あやつ
操る to operate, to
manipulate
せっそう
節操 integrity, chastity
じょうそう
情操 aesthetic sentiments

一 十 扌 扌 扩 护 护 护 押 捤 捤 捤 捤 操 操 操 16

200

657

ON-KUN READINGS: ソウ・サッ・はや(い)
HEADER: 日

早

early; quick

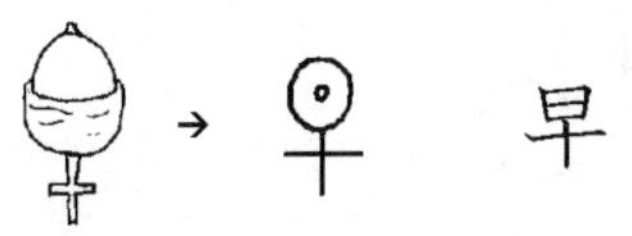

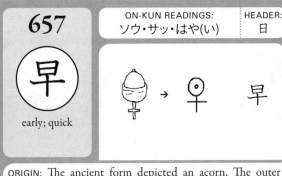

ORIGIN: The ancient form depicted an acorn. The outer shells were a source of black, or dark, dye. Because it is dark early in the morning before the sun rises, the kanji 早 means "early, quick."

- 早い (はや) early
- お早う (はよ) good morning
- 早速 (さっそく) at once
- 早退 (そうたい) leaving early
- 早朝 (そうちょう) early morning
- 早口 (はやくち) speaking quickly

丨 冂 日 日 旦 早 — 6

658

ON-KUN READINGS: ソウ・す
HEADER: ⺍

巣

(bird's) nest

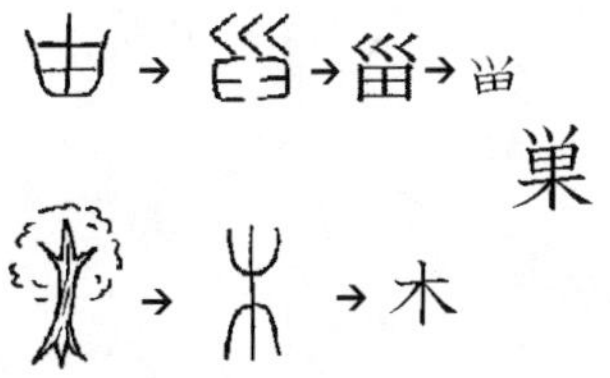

ORIGIN: The old form 巢 depicted 巛 "little heads of three chicks sticking out of a nest," which was on top of a tree 木. The kanji 巣 means "nest."

- 巣 (す) nest
- 巣立ち (すだ) leaving a nest
- 空き巣 (あ す) robbery in one's absence
- 病巣 (びょうそう) a lesion
- 巣箱 (すばこ) birdhouse

丶 丷 ⺍ 𭕄 当 当 当 当 単 巣 巣 — 11

659

ON-KUN READINGS: ソウ・あらそ(う)
HEADER: ⺈

争

to fight; dispute

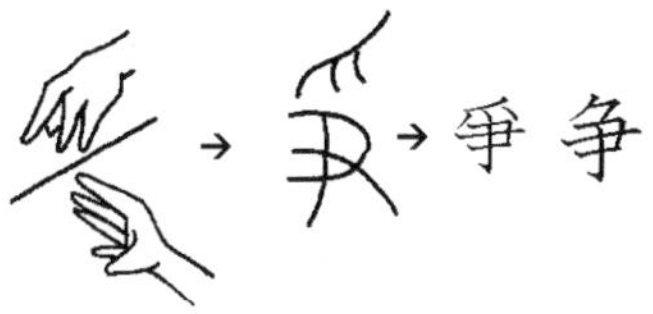

ORIGIN: The old form 爭 showed two hands, one coming from above and the other coming from below, fighting for something in between. Now the top ⺤ has been replaced by ⺈. The kanji means 争 "to fight; dispute."

- 争う (あらそ) to fight, to dispute
- 労働争議 (ろうどうそうぎ) labor dispute
- 論争 (ろんそう) controversy
- 紛争 (ふんそう) conflict, disturbance
- 争点 (そうてん) the point at issue
- 内争 (ないそう) internal conflict

ノ ⺈ ⺈ 刍 刍 争 — 6

660

ON-KUN READINGS: ソウ・ショウ・あい
HEADER: 目

相

mutual; state; minister

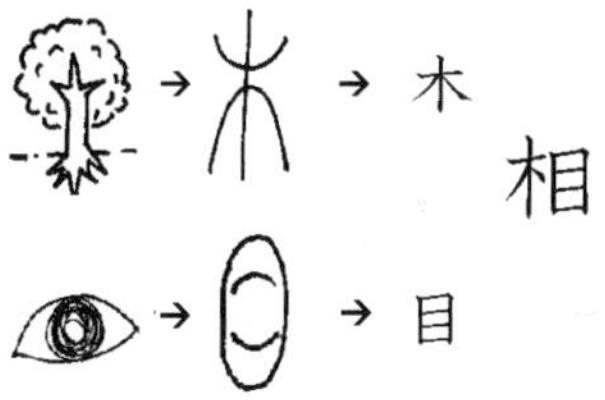

ORIGIN: The left side 木 was a tree and the right side 目 was "eye," which signified someone facing a tree. Combined, they suggested "observation" or the "state" of what was observed. At the same time, the tree faces the observer, making it "mutual." A government minister also closely watches a matter. The kanji 相 means "mutual" or "state" or "minister.'

- 相手 (あいて) opponent, partner
- 相談 (そうだん) consultation
- 外相 (がいしょう) foreign minister
- 相対する (あいたい) to confront
- 手相 (てそう) palm readings
- 相場 (そうば) market price, speculation

一 十 才 木 木 札 机 相 相 — 9

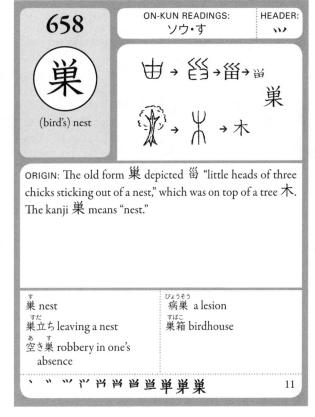

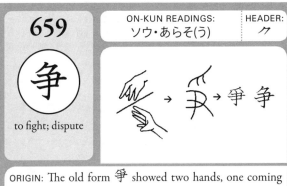

661

ON-KUN READINGS: ソウ・まど

HEADER: 穴

窓
window

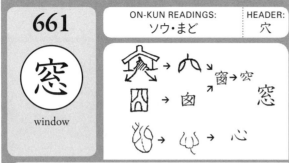

ORIGIN: The old form 窗 of this kanji depicted an opening in a house, that is, a window. Then, for reasons that are unclear, 心 "heart" was added underneath. Now simplified to 窓, the kanji means "window."

まど 窓 window	てんまど 天窓 skylight
まどぎわ 窓際 next to window	どうそうかい 同窓会 reunion (of
まどべ 窓辺 by the window	graduates), alumni
まどぐち 窓口 window, counter	association

`、ハ宀宀空空空空窓窓窓` 11

662

ON-KUN READINGS: ソウ・す(べる)・すべ(て)

HEADER: 糸

総
all; whole

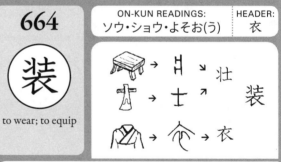

ORIGIN: The old form was 總. The left side 糸 was a pictograph of thin silk threads being pulled out of silkworm cocoons. The right side was used phonetically to mean "to get (threads) together in a bundle." Together they indicated a "putting things into one" or "all." The kanji 総 means "whole" or "all."

そう 総じて overall	すべ 総て all
そうかい 総会 general meeting	そうごう 総合 general, synthesis
そうむ 総務 general affairs, a	そうさい 総裁 president, governor
manager	

`く幺幺幺糸糸糸糸糸糸総総総総` 14

663

ON-KUN READINGS: ソウ・くさ

HEADER: 艹

草
grass; plant

ORIGIN: The older form 艸 of the top depicted two water plants floating in the water or two plants in the ground, which was simplified to 艹. The bottom 早 "early" was used for its sound. The kanji 草 means "grass; plant."

くさ 草 grass	ぞうり 草履 zori sandals
みちくさ 道草 detour	やくそう 薬草 medicinal herb
くさき 草木 plants and trees	そうしょ 草書 fast, grass-style writing

`一十卄芍芍芦芦苩草草` 9

664

ON-KUN READINGS: ソウ・ショウ・よそお(う)

HEADER: 衣

装
to wear; to equip

ORIGIN: The top 壮 consisted of a table and a soldier (signified by a weapon placed upright), indicating something "grand" or "manly." The bottom 衣 was "clothes." Together they indicated "to wear good clothes," or, by extension, "to equip" with something. The kanji 装 means "to wear" or "to equip."

ふくそう 服装 outfit	かそう 仮装 costume
よそお 装う to dress	ほうそうし 包装紙 wrapping paper
そうち 装置 installation	そうび 装備 equipment, gear
しょうぞく 装束 attire	

`丨丬丬丬壯壯壯壯芒芒芒装装装` 12

202

665

ソウ・はし(る) 走

走
to run

ORIGIN: The top 土 depicted a person running with arms up and down and head forward. The bottom was a footprint, which was somewhat stretched to indicate the long stride of a runner. The kanji 走 means "to run."

走る to run
徒競走 foot race
走行距離 mileage, distance covered to drive

走者 runner
師走 December

一 十 土 キ キ 走 走 7

666

ON-KUN READINGS: HEADER:
ソウ・おく(る) 辶

送
to send

ORIGIN: The upper right part depicted sending something with both hands. The ancient form of the bottom 辶 was the left half of a crossroad and a foot, signifying "to move forward." Together they indicated going to deliver something. The kanji 送 means "to send."

送る to send out
転送する to forward
送料 fee to send, shipping fee

放送局 broadcast station
見送る to see off, to postpone
送金 sending money

ヽ ヾ ヾ 乄 乄 关 关 送 送 9

203

667

ON-KUN READINGS: HEADER:
ゾウ イ

像
image; shape

ORIGIN: On the left イ is "person." The right side 象 was a pictograph of an elephant. The enormous size of an elephant and its odd shape imprinted a strong image in one's mind. Together they signified "image," or "shape," which are still the current meanings of the kanji 像.

肖像画 portrait
画像 visual image
映像 video footage, image

仏像 image of Buddha
実像 real-life image
現像 film development

ノ イ イ イ´ イ イ 俏 俏 倚 傍 傍 傍 像 像 14

668

ON-KUN READINGS: HEADER:
ゾウ・ま(す)・ふ(える) 土

増
to increase

ORIGIN: The left 土 was a neat pile of soil. The right side 曽 "rice steamer" was used phonetically to signify "to repeat." Together they indicated to add more soil. The kanji 増 means "to increase."

増す to increase
増加 an increase
増やす to increase

急増 sudden increase
増水 swelling (of a river)
増長する to grow presumptuous

一 十 土 ユ ヂ ザ 圹 坤 坤 増 増 増 増 14

669

ON-KUN READINGS: ゾウ
HEADER: 月

臓
organ; body part

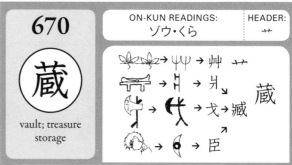

ORIGIN: The left side 月 came from 肉, a piece of meat or flesh with muscles, relating to a body. The right side 蔵 "storage" had a watchful eye of a protector (臣) with a halberd (戈). Together they indicated internal organs or body parts, which are protected within one's body. The kanji 臓 means "organ; body part."

しんぞう
心臓 heart
ないぞう
内臓 internal organ
ぞうきいしょく
臓器移植 organ transplant

ごぞうろっぷ
五臓六腑 the internal organs and bowels

丿 刀 月 月 月 月 旷 旷 腈 腈 臃 腈 腈 腈 臃 腈 臓 臓 臓 **19**

670

ON-KUN READINGS: ゾウ・くら
HEADER: 艹

蔵
vault; treasure storage

ORIGIN: The top 艹 is a grass radical originating from 艸 plants growing with the roots in the ground. Underneath was 臧, which had a halberd (戈) and a a watchful eye of a protector (臣), signifying "to protect." Combined, they indicated "to protect by hiding under grasses." The kanji 蔵 means "to store" or "storage."

くら
蔵 storage
ないぞうひん
内蔵品 internally equipped
ひぞう
秘蔵の treasure

くらい
お蔵入り storing into a vault
むじんぞう
無尽蔵 inexhaustible
じぞう
地蔵 jizo (guardian image)

一 十 艹 艹 产 芹 芹 芹 芹 芦 菧 蔵 蔵 蔵 蔵 **15**

671

ON-KUN READINGS: ゾウ・ソウ・おく(る)
HEADER: 貝

贈
to give a present

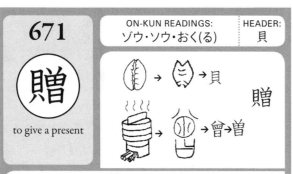

ORIGIN: The left side 貝 was a cowry, a rare shell that was used for currency. The right side 曽 came from 曾, which depicted a steamer with a stack of steaming trays, signifying "to add extras." Together they indicated "to give a valuable present." The kanji 贈 means "to give a present."

おく
贈る to give a present
おく もの
贈り物 present
ぞうとうひん
贈答品 present

ぞうてい
贈呈 presentation of gift
きぞう
寄贈 contribution
ぞうよぜい
贈与税 gift tax

丨 冂 冃 月 月 目 貝 貝 貝 貝' 貝' 貯 贈 贈 贈 贈 贈 贈 **18**

672

ON-KUN READINGS: ゾウ・つく(る)
HEADER: 辶

造
to create

ORIGIN: The ancient form consisted of a flat bowl on the left and 告 on the right, which was used phonetically to indicate "to reach." The left side was later replaced by 辶 "to go forward" and the new kanji 造 came to mean "to create."

つく
造る to create
そうぞう
創造 creation
せいぞうぎょう
製造業 manufacturing industry

ぞうか
造花 artificial flower
じんぞうこ
人造湖 man-made lake
もくぞう
木造 wooden structure

丿 ㇒ 艹 生 牛 告 告 告 浩 造 **10**

204

673

側

side; close by

ORIGIN: The left side 亻 was a person. The right side 則, which came from a tripod with a carving knife, symbolizing a tool used for inscription, was used phonetically to indicate "side." Together they indicated a person standing beside a tripod. The kanji 側 means "side" or "close by."

みぎがわ
右側 right side
したがわ
下側 below
む　がわ
向こう側 the other side

そっきん
側近 close associate
そば
側 side
えんがわ
縁側 veranda

ノ イ イ 们 们 但 但 但 倶 側 側   11

674

ON-KUN READINGS: | HEADER:
ソク | リ

則

rule; law

ORIGIN: The left side 貝 came from a three-legged pot that was used to cook offerings for an altar (it is not a cowry). The right side リ was a knife, signifying a tool "to inscribe." Characters were inscribed on the bronze pot to record important events. Those inscriptions became the rules to follow. The kanji 則 means "rule; law."

きそく
規則 regulation
がくそく
学則 school regulation
そく
則して in conformity with

ばっそく
罰則 punitive provisions
げんそく
原則として in principle
はんそく
反則 foul play

丨 冂 冂 月 月 貝 貝 貝 則   9

205

675

ON-KUN READINGS: | HEADER:
ソク | 卩

即

instant; to accede to (the throne)

ORIGIN: The left side depicted food, and the right side 卩 depicted a person taking a seat to eat. Combined, they meant "to take up something immediately," which extended to "instantly." The kanji 即 means "instant" or "to accede to (the throne)."

すなわ
即ち that is to say, exactly
そくざ
即座に promptly
そくせき
即席ラーメン precooked ramen noodles

そくい
即位 enthronement
そくばい
即売 spot sale
そくし
即死 instantaneous death

コ ヨ ヨ 彐 艮 即 即   7

676

ON-KUN READINGS: | HEADER:
ソク・いき | 心

息

to breathe; son

ORIGIN: In the ancient form the top 自 was a nose and the bottom 心 was a heart. One breathes through the nose, which moves oxygen to the heart, so the combined forms indicated "to breathe." Breathing deeply is a sign of life, which is perpetuated by the prosperity of a family. The kanji 息 means "to breathe; to increase" also "son."

いき
息 breath
むすこ
息子 son
いきぎ
息切れ out of breath
いきぬ
息抜き rest, relaxation

いき
ため息 a sigh
しそく
子息 [honorific] son
せいそく
生息する to inhabit

' 亻 宀 자 自 自 息 息 息   10

677

ON-KUN READINGS: ソク・たば

HEADER: 木

束

bundle; to be united

ORIGIN: The ancient form depicted a bundle of sticks tied tightly together in the middle. The kanji 束 means a "bundle" or "to be united" (such as people united for a cause).

約束 promise
束ねる to bundle
結束する to present a united front

花束 bouquet of flowers
束縛 yoke, restraint
拘束する to restrain

一丆丂百申束束   7

678

ON-KUN READINGS: ソク・はか(る)

HEADER: 氵

測

to measure

ORIGIN: The left side 氵 is "water." The right side 則 "rule" was used phonetically to indicate "to measure." Together they indicated measuring the depth of water, or measuring in general. The kanji 測 means "to measure."

観測 observation
測定 measurement
測る to measure
予測 forecast

目測 eye measurement
不測の unexpected
実測 actual measurement

丶丷氵氵沪沪沪沪沪測測測   12

679

ON-KUN READINGS: ソク・あし・た(りる)

HEADER: 足

足

leg; foot; to suffice; sufficient

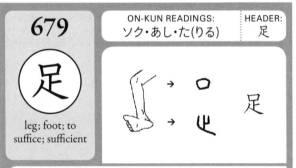

ORIGIN: The ancient form depicted a leg between the knee and the foot. The top part corresponded to the knee (口), and the bottom was the foot, which was somewhat stretched to indicate a motion. This form was also borrowed phonetically to indicate "to suffice" or "sufficient." The kanji 足 means "foot; leg," "to suffice," or "sufficient."

左足 left leg
足りない be short of
靴一足 a pair of shoes

不足 not sufficient, shortage
満ち足りた to be contented with
足首 ankle

丶口口尸尸足足   7

680

ON-KUN READINGS: ソク・はや(い)・すみ(やか)

HEADER: 辶

速

fast

ORIGIN: The upper right 束 "bundle" depicted a rope encircling twigs, but here it is used phonetically for "to be quick." The old form 辵 of 辶 (a foot on the left side of a crossroad) signified "moving forward." The combined form 速 means "fast."

速い fast
速度 speed
時速 speed per hour

快速電車 fast train
速達 express mail delivery
高速道路 highway, expressway

一丆丂百申束束束速速   10

206

681

ON-KUN READINGS:	HEADER:
ゾク	尸

属

to belong; same characteristic

ORIGIN: The old form 屬 suggests an animal mating. The top was the tail (尾) of a female animal, and the bottom 蜀 was a male animal. Mating results in producing an offspring with similar attributes. The kanji 属 means "to belong," or "same characteristic."

ぞく 属する to belong	せんぞく 専属 exclusive
しょぞく 所属 belonging to, affiliation	ふぞく 付属 being attached
ぞくせい 属性 generic character, attribution	きんぞく 金属 metal

¬¬尸尸尸尸尸尽尾属属属   12

682

ON-KUN READINGS:	HEADER:
ゾク	方

族

family; tribe

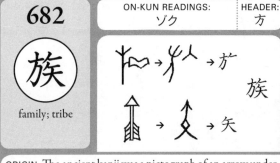

ORIGIN: The ancient kanji was a pictograph of an arrow under a clan's banner, which was tied to a crude pole. A clan moved along with its own banner in battle, signified by an arrow. The kanji 族 means "family" or "tribe (under one banner)."

いちぞく 一族 clan	しゅぞく 種族 tribe, race
みんぞく 民族 people, ethnic group	しんぞく 親族 family

どうぞくがいしゃ
同族会社 family-owned
    company
	ぞくぎいん
	族議員 special interest
	    politician

'一'方方方於於族族族   11

(207)

683

ON-KUN READINGS:	HEADER:
ゾク・つづ(く)	糸

続

to continue

ORIGIN: In the old form 續, the left side 糸 was threads, which signified continuity. On the right side, 士 was a foot, signifying "to walk"; 罒 was "net"; and 貝 was a cowry for trading. Together they indicated trading continuously. The kanji 続 means "to continue."

つづ 続く to continue	せつぞく 接続 connection
れんぞく 連続 continuation	ぞくはつ 続発 recurring occurrence
ぞくぞく 続々と one after another	そうぞく 相続 inheritance

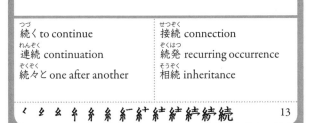
く幺幺幺糸糸糸糸紵続続続   13

684

ON-KUN READINGS:	HEADER:
ソツ	十

卒

soldier; to end; sudden

ORIGIN: The ancient form depicted clothes that had a marking or badge. Marked clothes were worn by slaves or soldiers. The ancient form has also been interpreted as clothes for the deceased, signifying an end. The kanji 卒 means "soldier," "to end," or "sudden."

そつぎょう 卒業 graduation	へいそつ 兵卒 soldier
だいがくそつ 大学卒 college graduate	そつぎょうしき 卒業式 graduation ceremony
そっとう 卒倒する to faint	

'一十广方交卒卒   8

685

ON-KUN READINGS: ゾン・ソン

HEADER: 子

存

to sustain; to know; to think [humble]

ORIGIN: The first three strokes came from 才, a weir that blocked water from flowing. The bottom right 子, used phonetically, indicated "to accumulate." Together they indicated "to pile up, to dam," that is, to create something solid. The kanji 存 means "to sustain; to exist." The kanji is also used as a humble form of "to think" or "to know."

そんざい
存在 existence
ぞん
存じている [humble] to know
ほぞん
保存する to preserve

せいぞん
生存 survival
きそん
既存の existing
ぞんぶん
存分に to one's heart's content

一ナオ存存存　6

686

ON-KUN READINGS: ソン・まご

HEADER: 子

孫

grandchild; offspring

ORIGIN: The left side 子 was a child, and the right side 系 was lineage (a skein of thread extended). Together they indicated a child in one's lineage. The kanji 孫 means "grandchild" or "offspring."

まご
孫 grandchild
しそん
子孫 descendant
まごむすめ
孫娘 granddaughter

そとまご・がいそん
外孫・外孫 daughter's child
ひまご・そうそん
曾孫・曾孫 great-grandchild

了子孑孑孫孫孫孫孫　10

687

ON-KUN READINGS: ソン・とうと(い)・たっと(い)

HEADER: 寸

尊

to revere; to respect

ORIGIN: The top part depicted a large wine vase, and the bottom 寸 was a hand (or two hands in some old forms). Together they indicated offering wine with both hands during worship. From that idea, the kanji 尊 came to mean "to revere," or "to respect."

とうと・たっと
尊い・尊い revered
そんけい
尊敬 respect
そんちょう
尊重する to think highly of

じそんしん
自尊心 self-respect
そんだい
尊大に haughtily
ほんぞん
本尊 principle image

丷丷丷丷酋酋酋酋尊尊　12

688

ON-KUN READINGS: ソン・そこ(なう)

HEADER: 扌

損

damaged; loss

ORIGIN: The left side 扌 was a hand, and the right side, 員, was a big, round tripod, here phonetically used to mean "to damage." Together they indicated something that was damaged or lost. The kanji 損 means "damaged" or "loss."

そん
損 loss
そんとく
損得 gain and loss
そんがい
損害 damage

はそん
破損する to damage
そんしつ
損失 loss
まるぞん
丸損 complete loss

一十才才扩护护捐捐損損損　13

208

689

ON-KUN READINGS:	HEADER:
ソン・むら	木

村 village

ORIGIN: The left side 木 is a tree and 寸 on the right side is a hand (used here for its sound). A place where one rests (a hand) is a place where there are trees. From that, the kanji 村 came to mean "village."

村 village
市町村 city, town, and village
農村 farm village

漁村 fishing village
村人 village people
村長 village mayor

一 十 オ 木 木 村 村　　7

690

ON-KUN READINGS:	HEADER:
タ・ほか	イ

他 others

ORIGIN: The left side イ was a person, and the right side 也 was a big-headed scorpion, signifying danger. Combined, they indicated a potentially dangerous person, or a person from outside the group. The kanji 他 means "others."

その他 others
他人 people outside one's family, outsiders
他に other than

他言する to tell other people
自他共に both oneself and others
他殺 murder

ノ イ 仼 仲 他　　5

691

ON-KUN READINGS:	HEADER:
タ・おお(い)	夕

多 many; a lot

ORIGIN: The ancient form has two different interpretations: 夕 was a pictograph of meat. Two of them together indicated "many, a lot." An alternative view is that 夕 was an early crescent moon, and many moons also indicated "many, a lot." The kanji 多 retains that meaning.

多い a lot
多少 some, a few, more or less
多分 probably

雑多な varied kinds
多様化 to become manifold; diversification
多難な full of difficulties

ノ ク タ タ 多 多　　6

692

ON-KUN READINGS:	HEADER:
タイ・タ・ふと(い)	大

太 big; thick; fat; peaceful

ORIGIN: One view is that the current form was simplified from the kanji 泰 "peaceful," which had depicted two hands saving a person from drowning in water. Another interpretation is that 太 comes from 夳, which meant "big" (double "big"). The kanji 太 means "peaceful" or "thick; fat; big."

太い thick
太平洋 the Pacific Ocean
太陽 the sun

図太い impudent
丸太 log
筆太に in bold strokes

一 ナ 大 太　　4

693

ダ・う(つ) | 扌

打

to hit; (making a compound word)

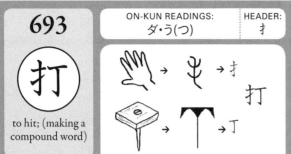

ORIGIN: The left side 扌 was a hand, and the right side 丁 was a pictograph of a nail. A hand hit a nail to pound it in. The kanji 打 means "to hit." The kanji 打 is also used to give a simple word an appearance of a compound word without adding any meaning.

打つ to hit
打ち明ける to confide
打ち合わせ meeting

打開する to break the deadlock
打者 hitter
打破 to abolish, break down

一 十 扌 打 打　　5

694

タイ・テイ・からだ | イ

体

body

ORIGIN: The old form 體 consisted of 骨 "upper body bones," 月 "flesh" and 豊 "plentiful harvest offered on an altar." Together they signified an entity with full bones and flesh—or an entire body, in contrast to limbs only. Now replaced by a totally different simpler form, the kanji 体 means "body."

体 body
身体 body
全体 whole

体育 physical education
体裁 appearance
正体 one's true colors

ノ イ 亻 仕 休 休 体　　7

695

タイ・ツイ | 寸

対

opposing; pair

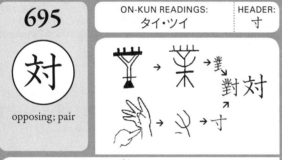

ORIGIN: In the old form 對 "notched stand to hang musical instruments" signified complexity. 寸 indicated a hand. Together they signified a hand balancing complex things, or a pair of things. The current reduced kanji form 対 means "opposing; pair."

絶対に absolutely
それに対して on the other hand
対応する to respond

対の in a pair
対比 comparison
対決 confrontation

ノ 亠 ナ 文 文 対 対　　7

696

タイ・おび・お(びる) | 巾

帯

belt; obi; sash; to carry on one's body

ORIGIN: The top part of the old form 帶 depicted a scene in which various decorations were hung, and the bottom part depicted a hanging cloth. Together they signified a long sash with various decorations. The kanji 帯 means "belt; obi; sash" or "to carry on one's body."

帯 belt
携帯電話 portable phone, cellular phone
一帯 whole area

工業地帯 industrial belt
連帯 solidarity
所帯 household, family

一 十 艹 芋 芦 芦 芹 芾 帯 帯　　10

697

タイ・ま(つ)

HEADER: 彳

待

to wait; to handle

ORIGIN: The left side 彳 was the left half of a crossroad, which signified "going." The right side 寺 "temple" consisted of 土 "footstep" and 寸 "hand" and meant "to hold in hand; to handle." Together they indicated someone waiting for the time to act. The kanji 待 means "to wait; to handle."

待つ to wait
招待 する to invite
待ち合わせる to meet up

待合室 waiting room
待遇 treatment
待望 の hoped-for

ノ ク イ ヂ 彳 待 待 待 待 待　9

698

ON-KUN READINGS:
タイ・なま(ける)・
おこた(る)

HEADER: 心

怠

lazy; to neglect

ORIGIN: The top part was ム "plow." The middle 口, "mouth," was used phonetically to mean "listless." The bottom 心 was the shape of a heart, signifying emotion. Combined, they indicated "lazy" or "to neglect," a meaning that remains for the current kanji 怠.

怠ける to be lazy, to neglect
怠慢 negligence
怠る to neglect

倦怠 fatigue, ennui
怠惰 idleness
怠け者 lazybones

ム ム ヤ 台 台 台 怠 怠 怠　9

699

ON-KUN READINGS:
タイ

HEADER: 心

態

appearance of one's intent or ability; demeanor

ORIGIN: The top 能 meant "ability" and the bottom 心 was a "heart." (The origin of 能 is unclear. The ancient form somewhat resembles a bear.) When one is able and determined to do something, that determination shows in one's demeanor. The kanji 態 means "appearance of one's intent or ability; demeanor."

態度 demeanor
実態 actual condition
旧態依然 remaining, unchanged

容態 one's condition
変態 abnormality
態勢 preparation, attitude

ム ム ケ 肖 肖 育 能 能 能 態 態 態 態　14

700

ON-KUN READINGS:
タイ・か(す)

HEADER: 貝

貸

to lend; to loan

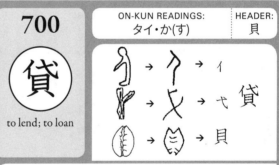

ORIGIN: The top 代 consisted of 亻 "person" and 弋 "stake." The same pronunciation also meant "to replace people," or "to change." The bottom 貝 depicted cowry shells used for trading. Combined, they signified money changing hands from one person to another. The kanji 貸 means "to lend; to loan."

貸す to lend
貸しビデオ rental video
貸し出し lending

貸家 house to let
賃貸 lease
貸与 loan, lending

ノ イ 亻 代 代 代 伐 伐 貸 貸 貸 貸　12

211

701

ON-KUN READINGS: タイ・しりぞ(く)
HEADER: ⻌

退

to retreat; to regress

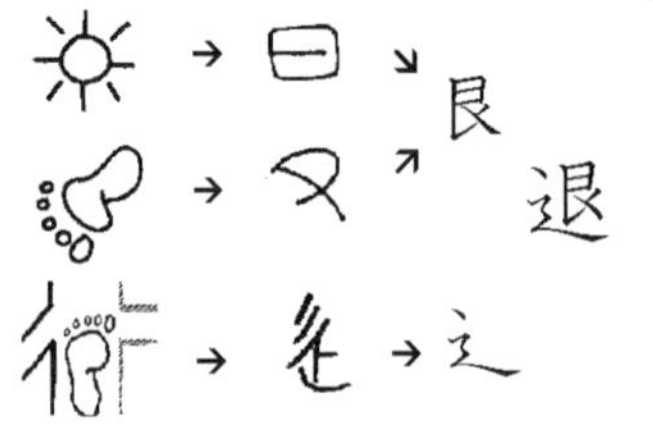

ORIGIN: In the ancient form, the upper right 艮 came from the sun and a backward foot, indicating that the sun was setting. The lower bottom ⻌ was "moving forward" (formerly ⻍, or 辵 "crossroad" and 止 "foot"). Combined, the kanji 退 means "to regress; to retreat."

引退(いんたい) retirement	後退(こうたい) recession, retreat, regression
退職(たいしょく) retirement from job	退治(たいじ) conquest, root out
退(しりぞ)く to recede	進退(しんたい) one's course of action

9

702

ON-KUN READINGS: タイ
HEADER: 阝

隊

band of people

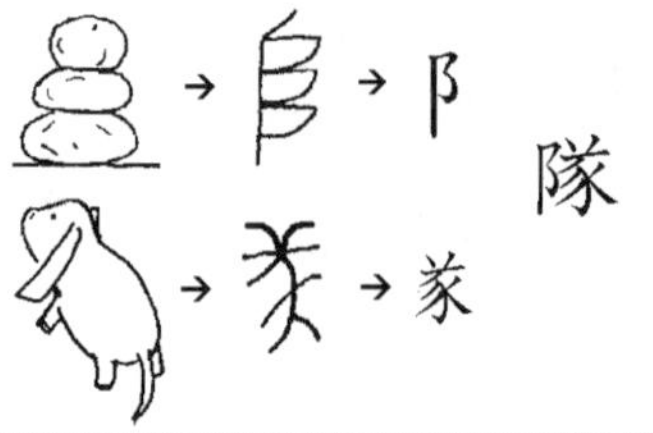

ORIGIN: In the ancient form, the left side 阝 was a dirt wall or a large hill. The right side depicted a pig or an animal with big ears; phonetically, it meant "to fall down fast." The combined form was also borrowed to mean a "group of people." The kanji 隊 means "band of people."

隊(たい) band	編隊(へんたい) formation
入隊(にゅうたい) enlistment	探検隊(たんけんたい) exploration party
隊商(たいしょう) caravan	楽隊(がくたい) musical band

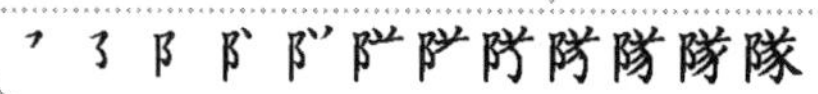
12

703

ON-KUN READINGS: ダイ・タイ・しろ・か(わる)・よ
HEADER: イ

代

(people) change; generations

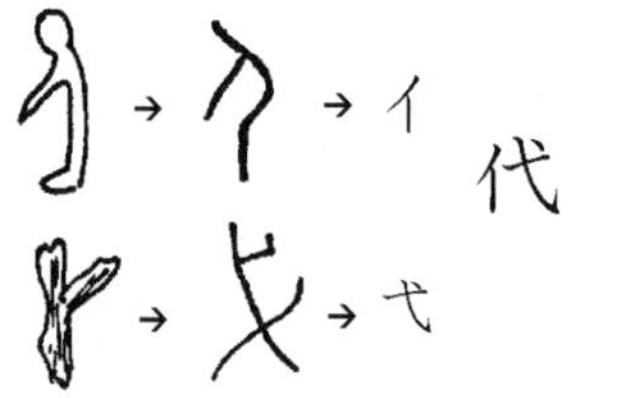

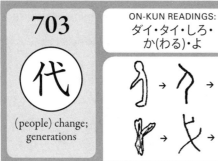

ORIGIN: The left side イ was "person." The right side 弋 depicted "something twisted," or "stake." Together they indicated people interacting with one another, or changing generations. The kanji 代 means "(people) change," and "generations."

時代(じだい) age, era	代(か)わる to change
1960年代(ねんだい) 1960s	代理(だいり) surrogate
代(か)わりに in place of, instead of	君(きみ)が代(よ) Japanese national anthem "Kimigayo"
交代(こうたい) a turn, shift	

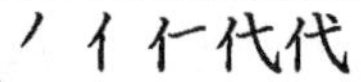
5

704

ON-KUN READINGS: ダイ・タイ
HEADER: ロ

台

platform

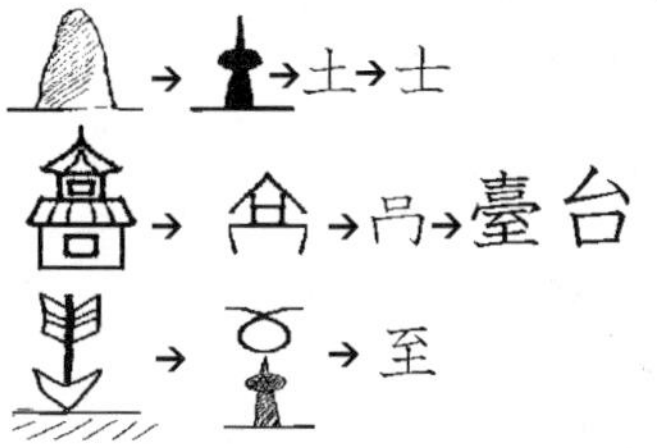

ORIGIN: The old form 臺 consisted of 土 "dirt," a part of 高 "tall house," and 至 "reach to the ground," which together indicated "platform that reaches." The much simpler current form 台 was borrowed phonetically to indicate the original meaning of 臺 and means "platform."

台(だい) platform	二台(にだい) two machines/cars
台所(だいどころ) kitchen	舞台(ぶたい) stage, platform
台風(たいふう) typhoon	台無(だいな)しになる to become spoiled, ruined

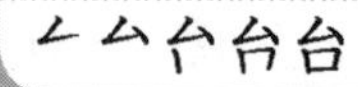
5

705

大

big, large, great, grand

ON-KUN READINGS: ダイ・タイ・おお(きい)

HEADER: 大

ORIGIN: The ancient form was a depiction of a person standing with arms and legs spread to look as large as possible. The kanji 大 means "big, large, great, grand."

おお
大きい large
だいがく
大学 university
たいさく
大作 masterpiece

おとな
大人 adult
だいがくいん
大学院 graduate school
ばくだい
莫大な colossal

一ナ大   3

706

第

order

ON-KUN READINGS: ダイ

HEADER: 竹

ORIGIN: This kanji consists of bamboo 竹 and a variant of 弟 "younger brother." The ancient form of 弟 depicted a marking on a stake indicating a point below, which in turn signified the lower rank of a young age. Combined they indicated "order," in which bamboo writing tablets were placed. The kanji 第 means "order."

だいさんか
第三課 Lesson Three
だいいちい
第一位 a first place
しだい
次第に gradually

だいいちいんしょう
第一印象 first impression
だいろっかん
第六感 sixth sense
だいいっせん
第一線 front line, leading

ノ ト ケ ヤ 竹 竹 笁 笁 竿 第 第   11

213

707

題

title; topic

ON-KUN READINGS: ダイ

HEADER: 頁

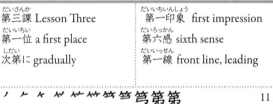

ORIGIN: The left side 是 ("this" or "to go straight") came from a ladle, but that meaning has no relationship to the current meaning. The right side 頁 was "head." The title comes at the head of a work. The kanji 題 means "title; topic."

だいもく
題目 title
しゅだい
主題 theme
だいじ
題字 writing of the title

めいだい
命題 proposition
だいめい
題名 title
むだい
無題 untitled

丨 冂 冃 日 旦 早 早 昇 是 是 是 趄 趄 題 題 題 題 題 題   18

708

宅

house

ON-KUN READINGS: タク

HEADER: 宀

ORIGIN: Under the roof of a house 宀 was モ "deeply rooted grass," signifying a place where one stays in one place for a long time (such as one's home). The kanji 宅 means "house."

たく
お宅 (your) house
じたく
自宅 one's own home
たっきゅうびん
宅急便 home delivery service

じゅうたく
住宅 housing
ざいたく
在宅 stay home
きたく
帰宅 return home

丶 宀 宀 宅 宅 宅   6

709

ON-KUN READINGS: タツ・たち

HEADER: 辶

達

to attain; to reach; plural suffix for people

ORIGIN: The top 土 was a variant of a person, and 羊 "sheep," an animal that gives birth easily. Together with the bottom 辶 "to go forward," the term indicated "things go smoothly." Because people do things together, it also was used to mean "people." The kanji 達 means "to reach; to attain." The kanji is also used as a plural suffix for people in the kun-reading.

友達 friend
友人達 friends
配達 delivery

お達者で stay in good health
達成する to reach
達人 expert

一 十 土 十 圭 圭 圭 幸 幸 達 達   12

710

ON-KUN READINGS: ダツ・ぬ(ぐ)

HEADER: 月

脱

to take off; to leave

ORIGIN: The left side 月 was "flesh of the body." The old form of the right side 兌 consisted of 八 "to cut something apart" and 兄 "elderly man." Combined, they described the state of the soul of a man in prayer: it puts his body in a trance. From this concept, the kanji 脱 has come to mean "to take off; to leave."

脱ぐ to take off (clothes)
脱出 to escape
脱皮する to cast off the skin

脱水 dehydration
脱する to free oneself from
脱字 omitted letter or character

丿 刀 月 月 月 月 胖 胖 脱 脱 脱   11

711

ON-KUN READINGS: だれ

HEADER: 言

誰

who

ORIGIN: In the ancient form 言 on the left side indicated "words" or "to speak" and the right side 隹 was a pictograph of a little bird. Originally the kanji was used to mean "to inquire." Over time the kanji 誰 came to be used for the interrogative word "who."

誰 who
誰か someone
誰もない no one

誰でも anyone

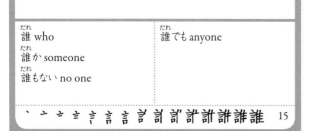
、 二 ニ 言 言 言 計 訂 訂 計 計 誰 誰 誰   15

712

ON-KUN READINGS: タン

HEADER: ⺍

単

simple; only

ORIGIN: The ancient form, which became 單, was a two-pronged thrusting weapon, with each prong wrapped for reinforcement or another type of weapon, a shield with two feather decorations on top. The meaning was lost entirely when it was borrowed to indicate the current meaning. The kanji 単 means "simple" or "single."

単語 word (in isolation)
単元 lesson unit
単身赴任 taking up post without one's family

単位 (credit) unit
単行本 a book, separate volume
単独 alone

、 ゛ ゛ ゛ ゛ 肖 肖 単 単   9

214

713

ON-KUN READINGS: タン・かつ(ぐ)・にな(う)　HEADER: 扌

担

to carry (a burden);
to bear

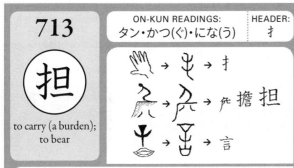

ORIGIN: The old form 擔 had 扌 "hand" and a person putting a heavy weight over a word (言), which was phonetically used to indicate "to carry a burden." Together they indicated carrying a burden in one's hand. Now the right side is replaced by 旦. The kanji 担 means "to carry (a burden); to bear."

担任 teacher in charge
たんにん
分担 sharing responsibility
ぶんたん
担う to carry on the shoulder
にな

負担 burden
ふたん
担当する to take charge of
たんとう
加担 assistance, participation
かたん

一 十 扌 扌 扣 扣 担 担　　8

714

ON-KUN READINGS: タン・さが(す)・さぐ(る)　HEADER: 扌

探

to search;
to look for

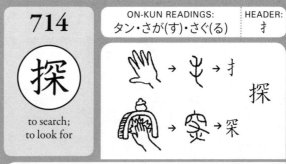

ORIGIN: The left side 扌 was a hand, and the right side depicted a hand searching for something by the light of a fire. The kanji 探 means "to search; to look for."

探す to search, look for
さが
探る to investigate
さぐ
探検 exploration
たんけん

探究心 inquiring mind
たんきゅうしん
探知 detection
たんち
探偵 detective
たんてい

一 十 扌 扌 扩 扩 押 押 押 探 探　　11

215

715

ON-KUN READINGS: タン・すみ　HEADER: 火

炭

charcoal; carbon

ORIGIN: The ancient form consisted of 山 "mountain," 厂 "cliff," and 火 "fire." Together they signified burning wood under a cliff (a dirt platform) to make charcoal. The kanji 炭 means "charcoal" or "carbon."

炭 charcoal
すみ
石炭 coal
せきたん
炭素 carbon
たんそ

二酸化炭素 carbon dioxide
にさんかたんそ
消し炭 cinders
け　ずみ
炭化する to carbonize
たんか

一 屮 屮 岸 岸 岸 炭 炭 炭　　9

716

ON-KUN READINGS: タン・みじか(い)　HEADER: 矢

短

short

ORIGIN: In ancient times, an arrow 矢 was used to measure length. The right side 豆 depicted a raised bowl and was used phonetically. The two items are short in height or length, and thus the kanji 短 means "short."

短い short
みじか
長短 length
ちょうたん
短期間 short period
たんきかん

短所 shortcoming
たんしょ
短命 short-lived life
たんめい
短針 hour [short] hand
たんしん

ノ ト ヒ 矢 矢 矢 短 短 短 短 短 短　　12

717

ON-KUN READINGS: タン **HEADER:** 言

誕
to be born

ORIGIN: The original meaning of 誕, "to prolong," was totally different from the current meaning. Because the sound of 延, "to extend" had the same sound as "to appear," the kanji 誕 came to be used as "to be born."

誕生日 birthday
誕生 birth
生誕百年記念 centennial anniversary (of the birth)

丶 亠 一 亖 言 言 言 訂 訂 訂 訂 証 証 誕 誕 15

718

ON-KUN READINGS: ダン・トン **HEADER:** 囗

団
a mass; group of people

ORIGIN: In the old form 團, a spinning spool 專 was inside an enclosure 囗. A hand at the bottom signified "round motion," or "round." Together they indicated things wrapped together, or a rounded mass. Now abbreviated to 団, the kanji 団 means "group of people; a mass."

布団 futon
座布団 a floor cushion
団体 organized group

集団 group, mass
劇団 theatrical company
団結する to be united

丨 冂 円 用 用 団 6

719

ON-KUN READINGS: ダン・た(つ)・ことわ(る) **HEADER:** 斤

断
to cut decisively

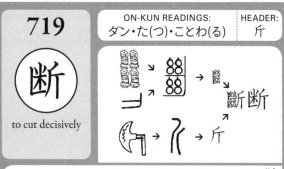

ORIGIN: In the ancient form the left side of the old form 斷 had four short skeins of thread in sections, and the right side was an ax that was ready to cut. Now the inside of the left side is reduced to 米. The kanji 断 means "to cut decisively."

断る to decline
断つ to cut
決断 determination

断水 suspension of water supply
断乎として resolutely
中断 interruption

丶 丷 丷 半 米 米 米 断 断 断 断 11

720

ON-KUN READINGS: ダン・あたた(かい) **HEADER:** 日

暖
warm

ORIGIN: The left 日 was the sun. The right side consisted of a hand from above and another hand from below, 又, pulling a round object, and it was used phonetically. Together they indicated "warmth that is created by the sun." The kanji 暖 means "warm."

暖かい warm
地球温暖化 global warming
暖房 heating

寒暖計 thermometer
暖冬 warm winter
暖炉 fireplace

丨 冂 月 日 日 日 日 日 日 日 日 日 暖 暖 13

721

ON-KUN READINGS: ダン

HEADER: 殳

段

step; paragraph; case

ORIGIN: The left side was "pile of stones laid" and the right side was "tool in hand." A blacksmith used tools in his hand and the stones laid on many levels to forge metal and to build a hearth. The kanji came to mean "steps" or a part of many layers or levels. A section of writing is "paragraph" and a part of a situation is "case." The kanji 段 means "step; paragraph; case."

七段 seventh step
階段 stairs
段階 steps

段々と gradually
普段の usual, every day
段落 paragraph

´ ｲ ｆ ｆ ｆ 阝 卽 段 段　9

722

ON-KUN READINGS: ダン・ナン・おとこ

HEADER: 田

男

man; male

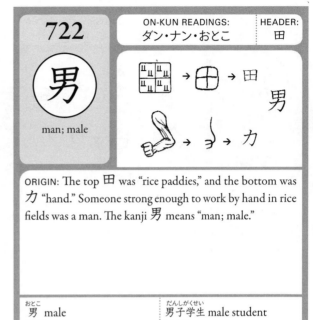

ORIGIN: The top 田 was "rice paddies," and the bottom was 力 "hand." Someone strong enough to work by hand in rice fields was a man. The kanji 男 means "man; male."

男 male
男性 man
男の子 boy

男子学生 male student
長男 first-born son
男女 men and women

｜ 冂 冂 甲 田 甲 男　7

723

ON-KUN READINGS: ダン

HEADER: 言

談

to talk

ORIGIN: The left side 言 indicated "to speak" or "word." The right side 炎 was abbreviated from three (signifying "many") fires burning strongly, and was used phonetically to mean "peacefully." Combined they meant "to talk softly." The kanji 談 means "to talk."

相談 consultation
会談 talk
雑談 idle small talk

談合 collusion in bidding price, consultation
談話 conversation
冗談 a joke

` 亠 亖 亖 言 言 言 言 訁 談 談 談 談 談 談　15

724

ON-KUN READINGS: チ・あたい・ね

HEADER: イ

値

value

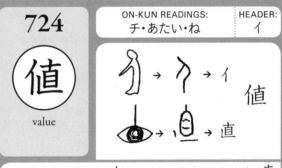

ORIGIN: The left side, イ "person," and the right side, 直 "straight" together indicated someone looking at a matter squarely to evaluate it. The kanji 値 means "value" or "price."

値段 price
値打ち value
安値 low price

値 value
値下げ lowering of price
数値 numerical value

ノ イ 亻 仁 什 佑 佑 値 値 値　10

725

ON-KUN READINGS: チ・し(る)

HEADER: 矢

知
to know;
knowledge

ORIGIN: The ancient form consisted of pictographs of an arrow 矢 and a mouth 口. Together they indicated speaking with the speed of an arrow. To do so, one must know what one is talking about, or to have knowledge. The kanji 知 means "to know" or "knowledge."

知っている to know
お知らせ a notice
知り合い acquaintance

知識 knowledge
知らんぷり nonchalance
知恵 wisdom

ノ 亡 二 チ 矢 矢 知 知　　8

726

ON-KUN READINGS: チ・ジ

HEADER: 土

地
ground; soil

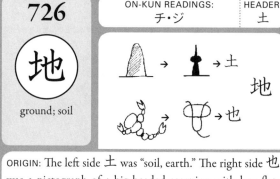

ORIGIN: The left side 土 was "soil, earth." The right side 也 was a pictograph of a big-headed scorpion with legs flattened, signifying something stretched flat. Together they indicated a space that was stretched flat, or land. The kanji 地 means "ground; soil."

地名 place name
大地 the earth
意地 temper, obstinancy

地主 landlord
地下水 ground water
地元 local, home

一 十 土 丣 地 地　　6

727

ON-KUN READINGS: チ・いけ

HEADER: 氵

池
pond

ORIGIN: The left side 氵 was "water," and the right side 也 was a big-headed scorpion with legs flattened, signifying something stretched flat. Combined, they indicated a pool of water that was spread flat. The kanji 池 means "pond."

池 pond
乾電池 dry cell, battery
貯水池 water reservoir

溜め池 irrigation pond
古池 old pond

丶 丶 氵 汁 沖 池　　6

728

ON-KUN READINGS: チ・お(く)

HEADER: 罒

置
to place; to leave

ORIGIN: The top 罒 was "net." The kanji 直 "straight" came from 目 "eye," facing something straight. Together they signified leaving a net straight up to catch birds. From that idea, the meaning extended to "to place something." The kanji 置 means "to place" or "to leave."

置く to place
装置 apparatus
設置する to install

置き去りにする to desert
買い置きする to hoard
倒置 inversion

丶 丿 冖 冖 罒 罒 罒 罒 罒 眉 置 置 置　　13

218

729

ON-KUN READINGS: チ・おそ(い)・おく(れる)　HEADER: ⻌

遅 — late; slow

ORIGIN: The upper-right part of the old form 遲 was a rhinoceros, an animal that moves slowly. The old form of the bottom, 辵, was the left half of a crossroad and a foot, signifying "to move forward." Now the kanji is somewhat simplified to 遅, which means "slow" or "late."

おそ
遅い late, slow
ちこく
遅刻する to be tardy
おく
遅れる to be late

おそ
遅まきながら belatedly
ちはい
遅配 delayed delivery
ちち
遅々として little progress

一 コ ヲ ア ア 戸 尸 屋 犀 犀 遅 遅　12

730

ON-KUN READINGS: チク・きず(く)　HEADER: 竹

築 — to build

ORIGIN: The top 竹 was bamboo stalks with leaves. The middle part had 工 "craft" and a person pounding the dirt with hands. The bottom part is 木 "tree, wood." One builds a house using bamboo and wood on a well-prepared foundation. The kanji 築 means "to build."

けんちく
建築 architecture
きず
築く to build
こうちく
構築する to construct

しんちく
新築 new construction
かいちく
改築 remodeling
ぞうちくこうじ
増築工事 expansion work

ノ ト ケ ケ ケケ ケケ ケケ ケケ 竺 竺 筑 筑 筑 築 築 築　16

219

731

ON-KUN READINGS: チク・たけ　HEADER: 竹

竹 — bamboo

ORIGIN: The ancient form was a pictograph of two bamboo stalks with narrow, pointed leaves which hang downwards. Bamboo was used for many things in ancient life, such as in crafts (箱笛算管), writing (筆答), building (築), and so forth. The kanji 竹 means "bamboo."

たけ
竹 bamboo
たけやぶ
竹藪 bamboo bush
たけ こ
竹の子 bamboo shoot

ちくば とも
竹馬の友 childhood friend
あおだけ
青竹 fresh bamboo
はちく いきお
破竹の勢い irresistible force

ノ ト ケ ケ ケケ 竹　6

732

ON-KUN READINGS: チャ・サ　HEADER: 艹

茶 — tea

ORIGIN: The older form 艸 of the top 艹 was plants. The bottom 余 came from a spade. A spade moves dirt to help make a room, which can be used to relax in, and 余 also had a sound that meant "bitter." Tea leaves are relaxing and also bitter. The kanji 茶 means "tea."

ちゃ
お茶 tea
こうちゃ
紅茶 black tea
りょくちゃ
緑茶 green tea

ちゃ
せん茶 (quality) green tea
きっさてん
喫茶店 coffee shop, cafe
さどう
茶道 the art of tea ceremony

一 十 艹 艹 艹 苎 苯 茶 茶　9

733

ON-KUN READINGS: チャク・ジャク・き(る)・つ(く)

HEADER: 目

着

to put (clothes) on; to arrive

ORIGIN: 着 was originally a variant of 著, which depicted putting used writing tablets into a stove, thus meant "to put in" or "writing." Later, 著 came to be used for writing and 着 was used for "to put (clothes) on" as well as "to arrive" because of the similar sound . The kanji 着 means "to put (clothes) on" and "to arrive."

着る to wear
着く to arrive
着物 kimono

二着 two pieces of clothing, second place in a race
六時着 arriving at six o'clock
着想 good idea, concept

 12

734

ON-KUN READINGS: チュウ・なか

HEADER: ｜

中

middle; center; inside; throughout

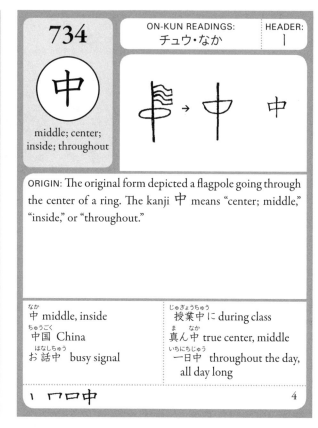

ORIGIN: The original form depicted a flagpole going through the center of a ring. The kanji 中 means "center; middle," "inside," or "throughout."

中 middle, inside
中国 China
お話中 busy signal

授業中に during class
真ん中 true center, middle
一日中 throughout the day, all day long

｜ 口 口 中 4

735

ON-KUN READINGS: チュウ・なか

HEADER: イ

仲

relationship

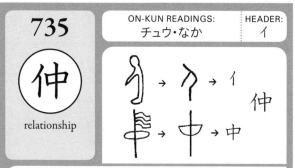

ORIGIN: The left side イ was "person" viewed from the side; and the right side 中 was "middle." Together they indicated something between people, that is, a relationship. The kanji 仲 means "relationship."

仲が良い be on good terms with
仲介 mediation
仲良く in harmony

仲良し close friend
不仲の on bad terms
仲人 go-between, matchmaker

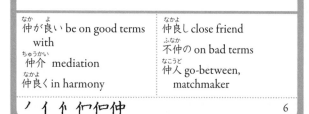 6

736

ON-KUN READINGS: チュウ

HEADER: 宀

宙

space; sky

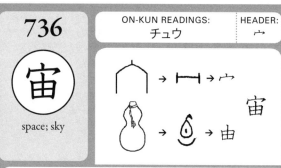

ORIGIN: The top 宀 was "roof" and the bottom 由 depicted an empty gourd. The dot in the middle in the ancient writing emphasized the emptiness inside. Combined, the top and bottom indicated an empty space under a roof. The kanji 宙 means "space; sky."

宇宙 universe
宙に浮く to float in the air
宙返り somersault

宙吊り hanging in midair

丶 宀 宀 宀 宙 宙 宙 8

220

737

忠
loyal

ORIGIN: The top 中 is middle or center, and the bottom 心 is an anatomical heart. What is in the middle of a heart is sincerity, or loyalty. The kanji 忠 means "loyal."

忠告 advice
忠実に faithfully
忠義な devoted

忠臣 loyal subject
忠節を尽くす to serve loyally

丶 口 口 中 史 忠 忠 忠　8

738

昼
daytime

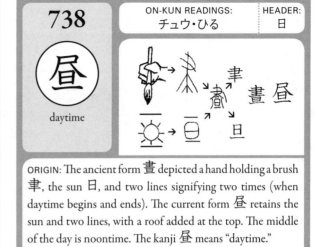
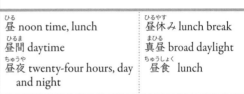

ORIGIN: The ancient form 晝 depicted a hand holding a brush 聿, the sun 日, and two lines signifying two times (when daytime begins and ends). The current form 昼 retains the sun and two lines, with a roof added at the top. The middle of the day is noontime. The kanji 昼 means "daytime."

昼 noon time, lunch
昼間 daytime
昼夜 twenty-four hours, day and night

昼休み lunch break
真昼 broad daylight
昼食 lunch

フ ㄱ 尸 尺 尺 尽 屄 昼 昼　9

739

柱
pillar; column

ORIGIN: In the ancient form the left side 木 was "wood," and the right side 主 was a "master." (A burning lamp stays in one place just as a master stays in one place to give an order.) Together they indicated the wood that did not move but was most important. The kanji 柱 means "column; pillar."

柱 pillar, column
電柱 electric pole
大黒柱 the central pillar of a house, breadwinner

柱時計 wall (grandfather) clock
火柱 pillar of fire flames
門柱 gate

一 十 才 木 术 村 村 柱 柱　9

740

注
to pour carefully;
to pay attention

ORIGIN: The left side 氵 was water or fluid. The right side 主 was a candle flame burning still. When one pours water or liquid carefully, one must stand still and pay close attention. The kanji 注 means "to pour carefully" or "to pay attention."

注文 an order
注意する to warn, to watch
注ぐ to pour

注目 する to pay attention to
注目を集める to attract attention
発注 placement of an order

丶 丶 氵 氵 汁 注 注 注　8

741

ON-KUN READINGS: チュウ・むし

HEADER: 虫

虫

worm; insect; bug

ORIGIN: The old form 蟲 was a depiction of three (signifying "many") coiled snakes or caterpillars. It indicated "small creatures," such as a "worm. Now an originally unrelated and yet abbreviated form 虫 is used. The kanji 虫 means "worm; insect; bug."

むし
虫 worm, insect, bug
がいちゅう
害虫 harmful insects
きせいちゅう
寄生虫 parasite

むしぼし
虫干し airing of stored
　　　clothing
けむし
毛虫 hairy caterpillar
さっちゅうざい
殺虫剤 insecticide

丨 口 口 中 虫 虫　　6

742

ON-KUN READINGS: チュウ

HEADER: 馬

駐

to park (a vehicle);
to stay in one place

ORIGIN: The left side 馬 was a horse and the right side, 主, "master," was someone who stays in one place. Together they indicated a place where a horse stops. The kanji 駐 means "to park" or "to stay in one place."

ちゅうしゃ
駐車 する to park a vehicle
ちゅうしゃじょう
駐車場 parking lot
ちゅうざいいん
駐在員 personnel who are
　　　assigned to stay

ちゅうりゅうぐん
駐留軍 occupation army
ちゅうにちたいし
駐日大使 ambassador to
　　　　Japan

丨 亻 厂 厂 厓 厓 馬 馬 馬 馬 馬 馬 駐 駐 駐 駐　15

743

ON-KUN READINGS: チョ・あらわ(す)・
いちじる(しい)

HEADER: 艹

著

to write;
conspicuous;
remarkable

ORIGIN: In the original kanji, the top was "bamboo," which was made into a writing tablet. The bottom 者 was used phonetically to indicate "to make something clear." The top was replaced by 艹 "grass," and the kanji 著 now means "to write" or "conspicuous; remarkable."

ちょしゃ
著者 author
あらわ
著す to author
ちょしょ
著書 book
ちょめい
著名な famous

いちじる
著しい conspicuous
けんちょ
顕著な conspicuous
めいちょ
名著 famous book

一 十 艹 艹 艹 芽 芽 芽 著 著 著　11

744

ON-KUN READINGS: チョ・た(める)・
たくわ(える)

HEADER: 貝

貯

to save money
or goods

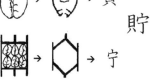

ORIGIN: In the ancient form the left side 貝 was a precious cowry used as money in trade and the right side depicted a frame or container to hold precious things such as cowry shells. The kanji 貯 means "to save money or goods."

ちょきん
貯金 money saved in a bank
ちょすいち
貯水池 reservoir
た
貯める to save (money)

ちょちく
貯蓄 saving
ちょぼくじょう
貯木場 lumberyard

丨 冂 冃 冃 目 貝 貝 貝 貯 貯 貯 貯 貯　12

222

745

ON-KUN READINGS: チョウ・テイ　HEADER: 一

丁
(square) block

ORIGIN: The ancient form was a pictograph of a nail. A nail is pounded in at a straight angle, so the kanji came to signify a straight angle or square. It is also used for a city block, and as a counter for small items. The kanji 丁 means "(square) block."

にちょうめ
二丁目 2-chome block (block used in street addresses)
よこちょう
横丁 side street
ちょうど
丁度 exactly

とうふいっちょう
豆腐一丁 one piece of tofu (bean curd)
ほうちょう
包丁 kitchen knife

一丁　　2

746

ON-KUN READINGS: チョウ・きざ(し)　HEADER: 儿

兆
sign; omen; trillion

ORIGIN: The ancient form was a pictograph of cracks on the underside of a baked tortoise shell. In divination, a piece of a tortoise shell or animal bone was heated, and the lines that appeared were read for the ruler to make a decision. This kanji was also borrowed for its sound to indicate trillion. The kanji 兆 means "sign; omen" or "trillion."

にちょうえん
二兆円 2 trillion yen
きざ
兆し sign, omen
ちょうこう
兆候 sign, omen

ぜんちょう
前兆 precursor
きっちょう
吉兆 good omen

ノ ノ ノ 兆 兆 兆　　6

747

ON-KUN READINGS: チョウ　HEADER: 巾

帳
drape; booklet

ORIGIN: The left side 巾 was a piece of cloth hanging on a pole. The right side 長 "long," used phonetically here, came from a stooped old man with long hair. Combined, they indicated "drape." It is also used for a bound booklet in the current writing. The kanji 帳 means "drape" or "booklet."

きちょうめん
几帳面な meticulous, methodical
てちょう
手帳 pocketbook
ちょうめん
帳面 notebook

きちょう
記帳 record keeping
つうちょう
通帳 passbook
ちょうぼ
帳簿 account book

丨 冂 巾 巾 帄 帄 帄 帄 帳 帳 帳　　11

748

ON-KUN READINGS: チョウ　HEADER: 广

庁
government agency

ORIGIN: The ancient form of the old form 廳 had 广 "roof of a house," 耳 "ear", 壬 "standing person", and 悳 "sincere heart." Together they indicated a place where government officials listened to what people had to say. Now the lower right side has been replaced by 丁 phonetically. The kanji 庁 means "government agency."

かんちょう
官庁 government agency
きしょうちょう
気象庁 meteorological agency
けんちょう
県庁 prefectural office

しちょうしゃ
市庁舎 city hall
けいしちょう
警視庁 metropolitan police
ちょうしゃ
庁舎 government building

丶 亠 广 庁 庁　　5

223

749

ON-KUN READINGS: チョウ・は(る)

HEADER: 弓

張

to stretch; to pull
to extend

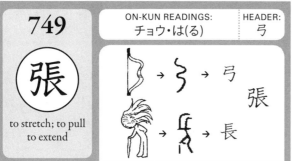

ORIGIN: The left side 弓 "bow" indicated something being pulled straight. The right side 長 depicted a stooped elderly man with long hair, with the general meaning "long." The kanji 張 means "to stretch; to pull to extend."

しゅっちょう
出張 する to go on a
business trip
ひ ば
引っ張る to pull
は き
張り切る to be enthusiastic

ちょうほんにん
張本人 the author of a plot,
(ring) leader
しゅちょう
主張 assertion, claim
こちょう
誇張 exaggeration

フ フ 弓 引 弨 弨 弨 弨 張 張 張   11

750

ON-KUN READINGS: チョウ・あさ・あした

HEADER: 月

朝

morning; court;
dynasty

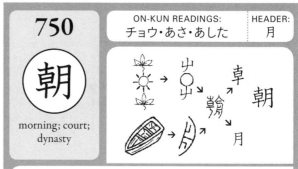

ORIGIN: The ancient form had the sun 日 rising from beyond a field of grass with a boat 月. Together they signified the time when a sun rises and a new tide comes in, "morning." Important business in the court included worshiping the sun; thus the kanji was used for "court" and "dynasty." The kanji 朝 means "morning" or "court; dynasty."

あさ
朝 morning
けさ
今朝 this morning
ちょうてい
朝廷 court
へいあんちょう
平安朝 Heian era

あさばん
朝晩 morning and night
おうちょう
王朝 the dynasty
ちょうしょく
朝食 breakfast

一 十 十 吉 吉 直 直 卓 卓 朝 朝 朝   12

751

ON-KUN READINGS: チョウ・しお

HEADER: シ

潮

tide; seawater

ORIGIN: The left side シ was "water." The right side, 朝 "morning," was derived from 日 "sun" rising through the grass along a river, signified by 月 "boat." Together they indicated a tide that comes as a morning starts. The kanji 潮 means "tide; seawater."

しおどき
潮時 chance to do;
opportunity
まんちょう
満潮 high tide
かんちょう
干潮 low tide

しおひがり
潮干狩り shell gathering
くろしお
黒潮 the Japan current

丶 冫 冫 氵 浐 浐 浐 浐 洁 淖 淖 潮 潮 潮 潮   15

752

ON-KUN READINGS: チョウ・まち

HEADER: 田

町

town

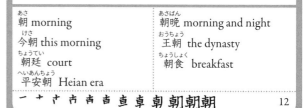
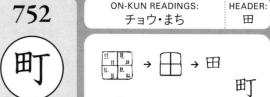

ORIGIN: In the ancient form the left side 田 was a pictograph of rice paddies with footpaths. The right side 丁 was "nail pounded in a straight angle," suggesting a junction of paths or "square block." Together they indicated land that had blocks of areas with footpaths. The kanji 町 means "town."

まち
町 town
ちょうないかい
町内会 neighborhood
association
まちなか
町中 the street

まちじゅう
町中 the entire town
とうきょう　　したまち
東京の下町 the Ueno and
Asakusa areas of Tokyo

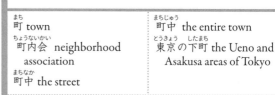

一 冂 冂 田 田 町 町   7

224

753

	ON-KUN READINGS:	HEADER:
	チョウ	月

腸
intestine

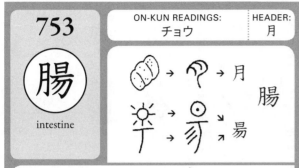

ORIGIN: The left side 月 came from 肉, a piece of meat or flesh with muscles, pertaining to parts of a body. The right side is phonetically used to mean "long." Intestine is a part of the body that is long. The kanji 腸 means "intestine."

だいちょう
大腸 large intestine
しょうちょう
小腸 small intestine
だんちょう　おも
断腸 の思い heartrending grief

もうちょう
盲腸 the appendix
ようちょう
羊腸 long, winding

丿 刀 月 月 肝 肥 肥 胛 腭 腭 腸 腸 腸　13

754

	ON-KUN READINGS:	HEADER:
	チョウ・しら(べる)・ととの(う)	言

調
to investigate; tune; condition

ORIGIN: The left side 言 signified "to express an idea sharply," or "word." The right side 周, used phonetically, indicated "thoroughly" or "harmony." Using words, one can investigate the state or condition of a matter. The kanji 調 means "to investigate; to arrange," "condition," or (from harmony) "tune."

しら
調べる to check
ちょうし
調子 condition
ちょうちょう
ト 長調 G major

しら
調べ tune
たいちょう
体調 health condition
ととの
調う to become prepared

、 亠 䒑 言 言 言 訂 訂 訂 調 調 調 調 調　15

755

	ON-KUN READINGS:	HEADER:
	チョウ・なが(い)	長

長
long; chief; principal

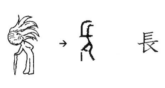

ORIGIN: The ancient form was a pictograph of an elderly person with long, flowing hair with a cane. An elderly person was also a tribal chief. The kanji 長 means "long" or "chief; principal."

なが
長い long
しゃちょう
社長 company president
しちょう
市長 mayor

ちょうろう
長老 elder, wise old person
ちょうじょ
長女 first-born daughter
ちょうじゅ
長寿 longevity

丨 ⻦ ⻢ ⻢ ⻣ 長 長 長　8

756

	ON-KUN READINGS:	HEADER:
	チョウ・いただ(く)・いただき	頁

頂
summit; to receive [humble]

ORIGIN: In the ancient form the left side 丁 was a nail with a flat top and the right side 頁 depicted a person who was wearing a headdress to show his rank. Together they indicated the top of a head. The form was also used to describe a deep bowing of a head. The kanji 頂 means "summit," or "to receive" in the humble-style verb *itadaku*.

いただ
頂く to receive [humble]
ちょうだい
頂戴 する to receive [humble]
ちょうてん
頂点 pinnacle

ちょうじょう
頂上 summit
やま　いただき
山の 頂 summit
とうちょう
登頂 to reach the summit

一 丁 厂 厂 厂 兩 頂 頂 頂 頂 頂　11

757

ON-KUN READINGS: チョウ・とり

HEADER: 鳥

鳥
bird

ORIGIN: The ancient form was a pictograph of a bird. The kanji 鳥 means "bird." (Another pictograph of a bird is 隹, which is mostly used for more abstract ideas, such as in 曜 "day of the week" and 難 "difficulty.")

鳥 bird (とり)
小鳥 small bird (ことり)
渡り鳥 migratory bird (わたりどり)

白鳥 swan (はくちょう)
鳥目 night-blindness (とりめ)
野鳥 wild bird (やちょう)

´ ｒ ｒ ｒ ｒ ｒ 自 鳥 鳥 鳥 鳥 鳥   11

758

ON-KUN READINGS: チョク・ジキ・なお(す)・す(ぐ)・ただ(ちに)・じか

HEADER: 目

直
straight; direct; to correct

ORIGIN: The top part had a straight line over an eye 目, indicating looking something straight in the eye. The lower left was added later to indicate "to straighten" phonetically. The kanji 直 means "straight; direct" or "to correct."

直す to fix (なお)
直に directly (じか)
直通 direct communication service (ちょくつう)

直ぐ immediately (す)
直談 する to negotiate personally (じきだん)
直感 で intuitively (ちょっかん)

一 十 ナ 方 盲 盲 盲 直   8

759

ON-KUN READINGS: チン

HEADER: 貝

賃
wages; fee; fare

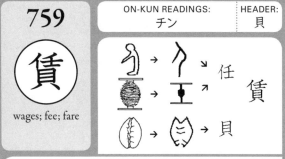
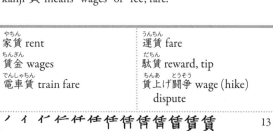

ORIGIN: The top 任 "to bear a burden" derived from a person having a burden (a full spool of thread). 貝 was a cowry, which was used as currency for trading. Together they referred to paying money to hire a person to do work, a meaning that was extended to money paid for fees. The kanji 賃 means "wages" or "fee; fare."

家賃 rent (やちん)
賃金 wages (ちんぎん)
電車賃 train fare (でんしゃちん)

運賃 fare (うんちん)
駄賃 reward, tip (だちん)
賃上げ闘争 wage (hike) dispute (ちんあげとうそう)

ノ イ イ 仁 仟 任 任 侏 侏 賃 賃 賃 賃   13

760

ON-KUN READINGS: ツイ・お(う)

HEADER: 辶

追
to follow; to chase; to pursue

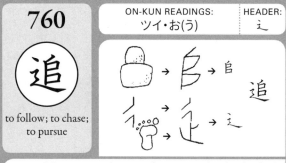
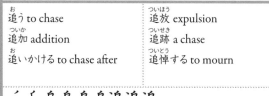

ORIGIN: The upper right came from mounds of soil, which was also used phonetically for the kanji that means "to follow." The bottom part 辶 meant "moving forward" (formerly 辵, or 彳 "crossroad" and 止 "foot"). Together they indicated to follow someone or to chase. The kanji 追 means "to follow; to chase; to pursue."

追う to chase (お)
追加 addition (ついか)
追いかける to chase after (お)

追放 expulsion (ついほう)
追跡 a chase (ついせき)
追悼 する to mourn (ついとう)

´ ｒ ｒ ｒ 自 自 追 追   9

226

761

ON-KUN READINGS:
ツウ・いた(い)

HEADER: 疒

痛
pain

ORIGIN: The upper left 疒 was a vertical depiction of a person lying on a bed, signifying someone sick. In 甬, the top マ was a person stamping down a stick through a board to get it through (用), which signified "to go through." Together they indicated "pain going through a body." The kanji 痛 means "pain."

いた
痛い painful
ずつう
頭痛 headache
ふくつう
腹痛 stomachache

つうかん
痛感する to take to heart
つうせつ
痛切に poignantly
いたで
痛手 damage

丶 亠 广 广 疒 疒 疒 疒 痛 痛 痛 痛　12

762

ON-KUN READINGS:
ツウ・ツ・とお(る)・かよ(う)

HEADER: 辶

通
to pass through;
to go through
smoothly

ORIGIN: The upper right 甬 (マ "person stamping on a stick to push it through a board 用") signified "to pass through." The bottom part 辶 meant "moving forward" (formerly 辵, or 彳 "crossroad" and 止 "foot"). The kanji 通 means "to go through smoothly; to pass through."

かよ
通う to commute
とお
通る to pass through
つうがく
通学する to commute to
　school

つう
通じる to be understood, to
　open up
こうつうじこ
交通事故 traffic accident
ふつう
不通 suspension of service

マ ア 阝 甬 甬 甬 甬 涌 通 通　10

763

ON-KUN READINGS:
テイ・ひく(い)

HEADER: イ

低
low; short in
stature

ORIGIN: The left side イ was "person." The right side 氐 signified a mound of soil, with the underline indicating the lowest point. Together they referred to a short person. The kanji 低 means "low" or "short in stature."

ひく
低い low
さいてい
最低 worst
ていか
低下 lowering

ていめい
低迷する to hang low
ていきあつ
低気圧 low pressure
ていとう
低頭 bowing low

ノ イ イ 仁 仟 低 低　7

764

ON-KUN READINGS:
テイ・と(める)

HEADER: イ

停
to stay and not
move

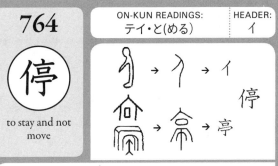

ORIGIN: The left side イ was "person," standing sideways. The right side 亭 was an inn or a house with a gated archway through which people come in. Together they indicated a person stopping and staying in one place. The kanji 停 means "to stay and not move."

かくえきていしゃ
各駅停車 local train
てい
バス停 bus stop
ていりゅうじょ
停留所 (bus) stop

ていし
停止 stoppage, suspension
ていせん
停戦 cease fire
ていでん
停電 power outage

ノ イ イ 仁 仁 侁 侁 停 停 停 停　11

227

765

ON-KUN READINGS: テイ・ジョウ・さだ(める) HEADER: 宀

定
to decide;
to be fixed

ORIGIN: In the ancient form, under 宀 "house" was 疋 "line over foot," signifying "to halt a step." Together they indicated "to stop one's feet in a house," and thus "stable; fixed." The kanji 定 means "to be fixed; to decide."

けってい 決定 decision
みてい 未定 decision yet to be made
さだ 定める to determine

よてい 予定 scheduled
あん じょう 案の定 as feared
じょうせき 定石 play by the book

丶丶宀宀宇宇定定   8

766

ON-KUN READINGS: テイ・そこ HEADER: 广

底
bottom

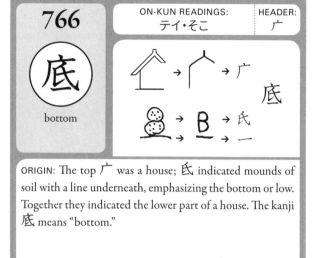
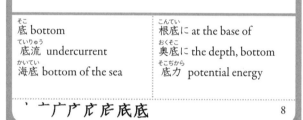

ORIGIN: The top 广 was a house; 氏 indicated mounds of soil with a line underneath, emphasizing the bottom or low. Together they indicated the lower part of a house. The kanji 底 means "bottom."

そこ 底 bottom
ていりゅう 底流 undercurrent
かいてい 海底 bottom of the sea

こんてい 根底に at the base of
おくそこ 奥底に the depth, bottom
そこちから 底力 potential energy

丶 亠广广庐底底底   8

767

ON-KUN READINGS: テイ・にわ HEADER: 广

庭
garden

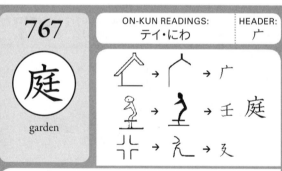

ORIGIN: 广 depicted a house with one side open, indicating a courtyard. 廷 consisted of 壬 "person standing on dirt," and 廴, "to extend" (lower part of 廴). The three ideas together—a person standing on the ground in a courtyard with a roof extending over it—suggested a courtyard garden. The kanji 庭 means "garden."

にわ 庭 garden
ていえん 庭園 garden
にわ 庭いじり gardening as pastime

にわし 庭師 gardener
うらにわ 裏庭 backyard
にわさき 庭先で in the garden

丶 亠广广庐庄庄庭庭   10

768

ON-KUN READINGS: テイ・ダイ・デ・おとうと HEADER: 弓

弟
younger brother

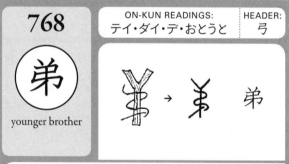

ORIGIN: A twine-wrapped stake had a marking at the lower end, indicating someone who was lower in order by age, that is, younger. The kanji 弟 means "younger brother."

おとうと 弟 younger brother
ぎてい 義弟 brother-in-law
でし 弟子 apprentice, disciple

ていまい 弟妹 younger siblings
してい 子弟 male children
いぼてい 異母弟 half-brother (younger)

丶 丷丷严弟弟弟   7

769

ON-KUN READINGS: テイ・さ(げる)

HEADER: 扌

提

to carry; to hold hands; commander

ORIGIN: The left side 扌 was a hand. The right side 是 derived from a ladle with a handle, but here used phonetically to indicate "to carry." Together they indicated "to carry by hand "or "to put something out," or "to hold each other's hand (in cooperation)." A commander symbolically uses a hand to lead. The kanji 提 means "to carry" or "to offer" or "commander."

ていきょう 提供 sponsor	ぜんてい 前提 premise
ていしゅつび 提出日 due date (to turn in)	ていけい 提携 tie-up, cooperation
てさ 手提げ handbag	ていとく 提督 admiral, commodore

一 十 扌 扌 押 押 押 押 押 押 提 提   12

770

ON-KUN READINGS: テイ・ほど

HEADER: 禾

程

extent; order

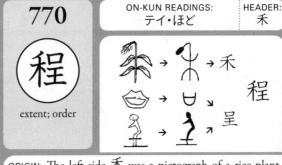

ORIGIN: The left side 禾 was a pictograph of a rice plant drooping under the weight of the crop. The right side 呈 (a mouth and a person standing on tiptoe) was used phonetically to indicate "straight." Together they indicated "to pile the rice plants neatly," but over time the kanji 程 came to mean "extent" or "order."

ていど 程度 degree	にってい 日程 itinerary
ほど 程 extent	こうてい 工程 manufacturing process
ほどほど 程々に in moderation	おんてい 音程 musical interval

丿 二 千 手 禾 禾 和 和 和 秆 程 程   12

771

ON-KUN READINGS: テキ・かたき

HEADER: 攵

敵

enemy

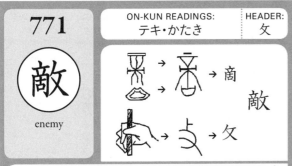

ORIGIN: Originally the left side was 啇, which had 帝 "emperor," a person unifying three lines, with 口 "words." The right side 攵 depicted the motion of hitting or pounding repeatedly with a stick. Together they indicated a person who faced an enemy. Now the kanji 敵 means "enemy."

てき 敵 enemy	しゅくてき 宿敵 archenemy
てきち 敵地 hostile territory	きょうてき 強敵 powerful rival
てきこく 敵国 enemy country	しょうばいがたき 商売敵 rivals in business

丶 亠 十 十 广 产 产 商 商 商 商 敵 敵 敵   15

772

ON-KUN READINGS: テキ・まと

HEADER: 白

的

target; having characteristics of

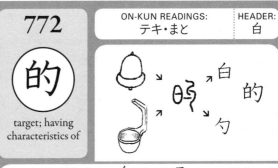

ORIGIN: The left side was 白 "white" (日 in some old forms) and the right side was 勺 "ladle scooping water." What was selected in the bright sun stood out and became a target. The kanji 的 means "target." When added to a noun, 的 can also mean "having characteristics of."

もくてき 目的 purpose	まと 的 target
にほんてき 日本的 having the characteristics of Japan	てきかく 的確に accurately
ちゅうしんてき 中心的な central	かがくてき 科学的 scientific

丶 丨 白 白 白 白 的 的   8

229

773

flute

ON-KUN READINGS: テキ・ふえ **HEADER:** 竹

ORIGIN: The top 竹 was a pictograph of bamboo stalks with leaves. The bottom 由 depicted liquid flowing out of a narrow mouth of a pot or an empty gourd. Air coming out of holes in bamboo stalks makes the sound of a flute. The kanji 笛 means "flute."

ふえ
笛 flute
くちぶえ
口笛 whistle
けいてき
警笛 alarm horn, warning whistle

きてき
汽笛 steam whistle, siren
よこぶえ
横笛 flute
こてきたい
鼓笛隊 drum and fife band

ノ ト ヶ ベ ベ 竹 竹 竹 竹 笛 笛 笛 笛　11

774

適

suitable

ON-KUN READINGS: テキ **HEADER:** 辶

ORIGIN: The old form had 啇, comprising 帝 "emperor," a person unifying three lines and 口 "mouth; words"—here used phonetically to indicate "going straight." The lower left indicated "moving forward." Combined, they indicated that going forward was appropriate. The kanji 適 means "suitable."

てきとう
適当な suitable
さいてき
最適な best suited
かいてき
快適な comfortable

かな
適う appropriate
てきせつ
適切な appropriate
てきにん
適任の competent

丶 亠 ヰ 啇 产 斉 咼 商 商 商 商 商 滴 適 適　14

775

鉄

iron

ON-KUN READINGS: テツ **HEADER:** 金

ORIGIN: The ancient form of the old form 鐵 had metal 金 on the left. The right side had 土 "to cut down a blockage," 呈 "straight," and 戈 "halberd," used phonetically to indicate "black." In the current reduced form, the right side has been replaced by 矢 "arrow." The kanji 鉄 means "iron."

ちかてつ
地下鉄 subway, underground trains
てつどう
鉄道 railroad, railway
てつ
鉄 iron

てっせい
鉄製 made of iron
てっそく
鉄則 iron rule
してつ
私鉄 private railroad

ノ ト ト ト ヒ 牛 牟 金 金 釘 針 鈝 鈝 鉄 鉄　13

776

典

law; code

ON-KUN READINGS: テン **HEADER:** 八

ORIGIN: The ancient form depicted a bundle of bamboo writing tablets placed on a table. In ancient times, treated bamboo and wood tablets were used to record important decrees or chronicles and were strung together as books. The kanji 典 means "code; law."

ひゃっかじてん
百科事典 encyclopedia
ほうてん
法典 code
じてん
辞典 dictionary

しゅってん
出典 the source (for quoting)
こてん
古典 classics
しきてん
式典 ceremony

丨 冂 曱 曲 曲 典 典 典　8

777	ON-KUN READINGS: テン・あま・あめ	HEADER: 大

天 heaven; sky

ORIGIN: The first stroke 一 originated from an emphasis on one's head, to indicate "top." Later the meaning shifted to what was above one's head. The kanji 天 means "heaven; sky." Note: The first stroke ("sky, heaven") is usually written longer than the second (one's hands).

てんごく 天国 heaven
うてん 雨天 rainy weather
あま かわ 天の川 Milky Way
せんてんてき 先天的 innate, congenital

ぎょうてん 仰天する to be stupefied
あまくだ 天下り former official taking up a position with influence

一二チ天　　4

778	ON-KUN READINGS: テン	HEADER: 尸

展 to extend; to exhibit

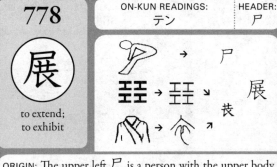

ORIGIN: The upper left 尸 is a person with the upper body bent forward, slumping somewhat. The middle was layers of bricks, indicating "to extend," and 衣 "clothes." Together they indicated clothes that are pressed flat with the weight of laid-out bricks. The kanji 展 means "to exhibit; to extend."

てんらんかい 展覧会 exhibition
てんかい 展開 development
はってん 発展 development

てんぼう 展望 outlook
しゃしんてん 写真展 photograph exhibit
びじゅつてん 美術展 art exhibit

一コ尸尸尸尸屈屈展展　　10

231

779	ON-KUN READINGS: テン・みせ	HEADER: 广

店 shop; store

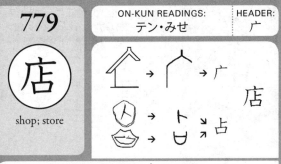

ORIGIN: Inside 广 "house" was 占 "divination." 卜 depicted lines that appear in a heated tortoise shell (or animal bones), and 口 "mouth" signified that the signs were read orally. Together they indicated a house where fortunes were told, and later a place where people would shop. The kanji 店 means "store; shop."

みせ 店 a store
かいてんじかん 開店時間 store's opening time
しょてん 書店 bookstore

てんとう 店頭 store front
しょうてんがい 商店街 rows of shops
みせばん 店番 a shop clerk

、一广广广店店店　　8

780	ON-KUN READINGS: テン・ころ(ぶ)	HEADER: 車

転 to roll

ORIGIN: In the old form 轉, 車 was a loaded cart with two wheels and 專 was a spinning spool and a hand, signifying "rolling." Now the right side is simplified to 云. The kanji 転 means "to roll."

うんてん 運転する to drive
ころ 転ぶ to fall
かいてん 回転ずし revolving sushi bar

ころ 転がる to roll over
てんそう 転送する to forward
てんきん 転勤 a transfer

一厂厂厂戸亘車車転転　　11

781

ON-KUN READINGS: テン・つ(ける)

HEADER: 灬

点

spot; dot

ORIGIN: In the old form 點, 黑 comes from a depiction of a chimney, signified by black soot and a fire. 占 on the right was a cracked turtle shell used for divination. Together they indicated a black marking for divination, which came to mean simply a spot or point. The kanji 点 means "spot; dot."

てん 点 score ひゃくてん 百点 a hundred points けってん 欠点 fault	てんか 点火 to light てんじ 点字 the Braille system げんてん 原点 the origin, starting point

丶 卜 卜 占 占 占 点 点 点　9

782

ON-KUN READINGS: デン・つた(える)

HEADER: イ

伝

to convey;
to transmit;
to hand down

ORIGIN: The old form 傳 had イ "person" and 專 "spinning spool with a hand," hence "rolling." Just as things roll from hand to hand, a message is conveyed from person to person. Now simplified to 伝, the kanji means "to convey; to transmit; to hand down."

でんごん 伝言 message つた 伝える to convey, to hand 　down でんとう 伝統 tradition	てつだ 手伝う to help せんでん 宣伝 advertisement いでん 遺伝 heredity

ノ イ 仁 仁 伝 伝　6

783

ON-KUN READINGS: デン・テン・との・どの

HEADER: 殳

殿

palace; lord; Mr.
[formal address]

ORIGIN: The left side was a person leaning forward (尸) on a stool (共). The right side 殳 was a weapon in hand, indicating slapping or hitting a buttock. Possibly derived from the concept of the seat of power or rule, the form was used for "a grand building; palace; lord." It is also used as a form of address for a male adult in a letter.

との 殿 lord とのさま 殿様 lord たなかどの 田中殿 Mr. Tanaka	ごてん 御殿 palace とのがた 殿方 gentleman しんでん 神殿 shrine, sanctuary

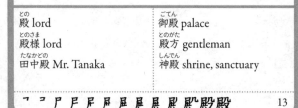

コ ア ア 尸 尸 屈 屏 屏 屏 屖 殿 殿 殿　13

784

ON-KUN READINGS: デン・た

HEADER: 田

田

rice paddies

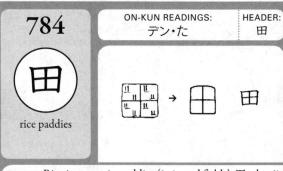

ORIGIN: Rice is grown in paddies (irrigated fields). The kanji 田 depicted levees (strips of raised land) between the paddies, which were also footpaths for farmers. The kanji 田 means "rice paddies."

た 田 rice paddies すいでん 水田 irrigated rice fields た 田んぼ irrigated rice paddies	でんえん 田園 pastoral; rural びでん 美田 fertile land でんや 田野 fields

丨 冂 田 田 田　5

785

ON-KUN READINGS: デン
HEADER: 雨

電

electricity;
extremely swift

ORIGIN: The ancient form consisted of 雨 "rain" and a variant of 申 "to say," which depicted lightning in the sky. Thunder and lightning were believed to be "God's words descending from heaven." Together they indicated the electrifying power of lightning, or extreme swiftness. The kanji 電 means "electricity" or "extremely swift."

でんどう
電動 electrically operated
はつでんじょ
発電所 power plant
でんぽう
電報 telegram

でんし
電子 electron
でんかせいひん
電化製品 electric appliances
でんりょく
電力 electric power

一个戶币币币雨雨雷雷雷雷電　13

786

ON-KUN READINGS: ト・いたず(らに)
HEADER: 彳

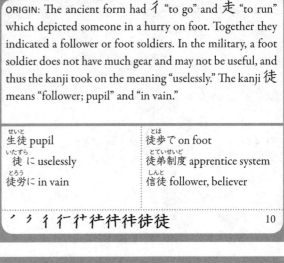

徒

follower; pupil;
in vain

ORIGIN: The ancient form had 彳 "to go" and 走 "to run" which depicted someone in a hurry on foot. Together they indicated a follower or foot soldiers. In the military, a foot soldier does not have much gear and may not be useful, and thus the kanji took on the meaning "uselessly." The kanji 徒 means "follower; pupil" and "in vain."

せいと
生徒 pupil
いたずら
徒 に uselessly
とろう
徒労に in vain

とほ
徒歩で on foot
とていせいど
徒弟制度 apprentice system
しんと
信徒 follower, believer

ノ彳彳彳彳彳彳彳徒徒　10

787

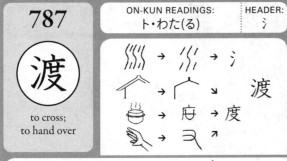

ON-KUN READINGS: ト・わた(る)
HEADER: 氵

渡

to cross;
to hand over

ORIGIN: The left side 氵 indicated water. 度 on the right originally indicated "measuring using the span of a hand"; here it was phonetically used to mean "to cross." Together they indicated "to go across a river" or "to cross." The kanji 渡 means "to cross; to hand over."

わた
渡る to cross
てわた
手渡す to hand out
とべい
渡米 travel to the United
　States

とおう
渡欧 travel to Europe
かとき
過渡期 transition period
とせい
渡世 living, occupation

丶丶氵氵沪沪沪沪沪渡渡渡　12

788

ON-KUN READINGS: トウ・ト・のぼ(る)
HEADER: 癶

登

to climb

ORIGIN: The top 癶 depicted two feet, indicating climbing feet. Underneath, 豆 was a pictograph of a tall container, whose sound signified "tall." Together they indicated climbing to a higher place. The kanji 登 means "to climb."

のぼ
登る to climb
とざん
登山 mountain climbing
とうこう
登校 going to school

とうじょう
登場 entrance
とうりゅうもん
登竜門 gateway to success
とうよう
登用 appointment

フフ가가癶癶癶癶癶登登登登　12

233

789

ON-KUN READINGS: ト・ツ・みやこ
HEADER: 阝

都

capital; many

ORIGIN: The left side 者 originally depicted firewood that's been gathered and was burning in a stove—but here it is phonetically used to indicate that "many things gather." The right side 阝 comes from 邑 "village" (land and people). A place where a lot of people gather to live is a capital. The kanji 都 means "capital" or "many."

みやこ
都 capital
つごう
都合 convenience
きょうと
京都 Kyoto

とかい
都会 big city
とか
都下 Tokyo metropolitan area
つど
その都度 every time

一 十 土 耂 者 者 者 者 者 者³ 都 都　11

790

ON-KUN READINGS: ド・つと(める)
HEADER: 力

努

to try hard

ORIGIN: In the top, 女 "woman" and 又 "hand" signified a female slave taken from enemies in a battle. With 力 "strength," added, the kanji indicated "working hard" or "making a tenacious effort." The kanji 努 means "to try hard."

どりょく
努力 efforts
つと
努める to endeavor

く タ 女 如 奴 努 努　7

791

ON-KUN READINGS: ド・ト・タク・たび
HEADER: 广

度

time; degree

ORIGIN: The ancient form was a combination of 庶 "commoner" (whose home had a pot of food over a fire) used phonetically, and 又 "hand." Because one measured something using a hand, the measurement units such as 寸 and 尺 came from a hand. The kanji 度 means "degree; time."

こんど
今度 this time
いちど
もう一度 once more
く たび
来る度に every time one comes

たびたび
度々 often, repeatedly
したく
支度 preparation
ひゃくど
百度 100 degrees

丶 广 广 广 庁 庐 度 度 度　9

792

ON-KUN READINGS: ド・ト・つち
HEADER: 土

土

soil; earth; Saturday

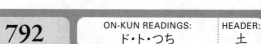 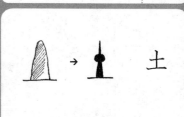

ORIGIN: The ancient form depicted a mound of soil on the ground. The first stroke is added for emphasis. The kanji 土 means "soil; earth." It is also used for "Saturday."

どようび
土曜日 Saturday
つち
土 dirt
とち
土地 land

どそく
土足 with one's shoes on
どにち
土日 Saturday and Sunday
こくど
国土 a nation's territory

一 十 土　3

793

ON-KUN READINGS: ド・ヌ・おこ(る)・いか(り)

HEADER: 心

怒
angry

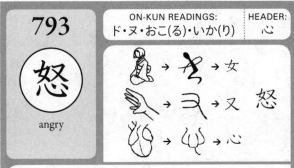

ORIGIN: The top part 奴 signified a slave who did manual work, which was strenuous or vigorous. With a heart 心 added, the kanji described an agitated state of mind. The kanji 怒 means "angry."

おこ
怒る to get angry
げきど
激怒 fury
いか
怒り anger, wrath

どせい
怒声 angry voice
どき
怒気 anger

く タ タ 如 奴 奴 怒 怒 怒　　9

794

ON-KUN READINGS: トウ

HEADER: ⺌

党
political party

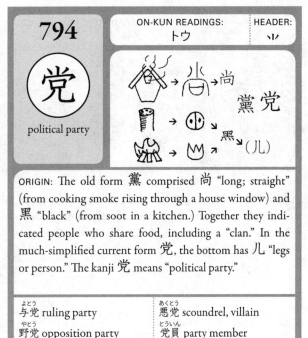

ORIGIN: The old form 黨 comprised 尚 "long; straight" (from cooking smoke rising through a house window) and 黑 "black" (from soot in a kitchen.) Together they indicated people who share food, including a "clan." In the much-simplified current form 党, the bottom has 儿 "legs or person." The kanji 党 means "political party."

よとう
与党 ruling party
やとう
野党 opposition party
とうは
党派 faction

あくとう
悪党 scoundrel, villain
とういん
党員 party member
ととう く
徒党を組む to form a league

⸝ ⸜ ⅋ ⅋ ⅋ ⅋ ⅋ 当 党 党　　10

795

ON-KUN READINGS: トウ・ふゆ

HEADER: 冫

冬
winter

ORIGIN: The top 夂 depicted food hanging on a string for winter storage. The bottom 冫 was a variant form of 氷 "ice." In winter people ate stored food, and outside it was icy and cold. The kanji 冬 means "winter."

ふゆ
冬 winter
ふゆやす
冬休み winter break
とうき
冬季 winter season

ふゆやま
冬山 winter mountain
えっとう
越冬する to pass a winter
とうみん
冬眠 hibernation

ノ ク ク 冬 冬　　5

796

ON-KUN READINGS: トウ・かたな

HEADER: 刀

刀
sword; knife

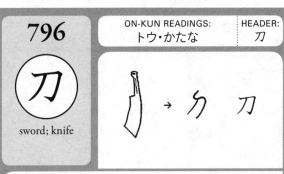

ORIGIN: The ancient form was a pictograph of a curved sword or knife. The kanji 刀 means "sword; knife." When it is used as a recurring component, the form 刂 is also used, as in 利.

かたな
刀 sword
こがたな
小刀 small knife
とうけん
刀剣 swords

しない
竹刀 bamboo sword
ぼくとう
木刀 wooden sword
たち
太刀 long sword

フ 刀　　2

235

797	ON-KUN READINGS: トウ・しま	HEADER: 山

島
island

嶋島

ORIGIN: The old form 嶋 came from 山 "mountain" and 鳥 "bird." Together they indicated "a little mountain on an island in a sea, where birds come to rest." In the current form, birds' feet 灬 was replaced by 山 mountain. The kanji 島 means "island."

しま
島 island
はんとう
半島 peninsula
にほんれっとう
日本列島 the Japanese islands

こじま
小島 small island
ことう
孤島 solitary island
しまぐに
島国 island country

´ ｨ ｢ ｦ ｦ 自 鳥 鳥 島 島   10

798	ON-KUN READINGS: トウ・な(げる)	HEADER: 扌

投
to throw

投

ORIGIN: The left side 扌 was a hand. The right side 殳 had a weapon in hand, indicating a fight, and also engaging in work. Together they indicated using a hand to throw something. The kanji 投 means "to throw."

な
投げる to throw, to cast
とうしょばこ
投書箱 suggestion box
とうしゅ
投手 pitcher (in a baseball game)

ほう な
放り投げる to toss
とう
投じる to throw
いきとうごう
意気投合する to get along well

一 十 扌 扌 扩 抄 投   7

799	ON-KUN READINGS: トウ・ひがし・あずま	HEADER: 木

東
east

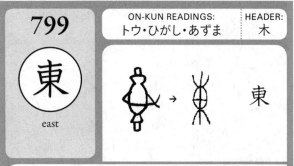

東

ORIGIN: The ancient form depicted a tied sack with a pole sticking out, indicating "to thrust through." The form was phonetically borrowed to mean "east." The kanji 東 means "east."

ひがし
東 east
とうきょう
東京 Tokyo
とうざい
東西 east and west

かんとう
関東 the Kanto region
きょくとう
極東 Far East
あずまや
東屋 arbor, gazebo

一 ｢ ｢ 戸 百 申 東 東   8

800	ON-KUN READINGS: トウ・ゆ	HEADER: 氵

湯
hot water;
hot bath

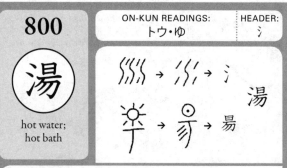

湯

ORIGIN: The left side 氵 was water, having the same origin as 水. The right side 昜 "to rise" was from 日 "sun" and a motion of raising something high, and 彡 "sun rays." Water rises as it is heated. In Japan 湯 also refers to a hot bath. The kanji 湯 means "hot water" or "hot bath."

ゆ
湯 hot water, bath
ねっとう
熱湯 boiling water
せんとう
銭湯 public bath house

ゆの
湯呑み teacup
ゆげ
湯気 steam
ゆぶね
湯船 bath tub

、 ｀ ｼ 氵 沪 沪 沪 沪 沪 湯 湯 湯   12

236

801

ON-KUN READINGS: トウ・ともしび・ひ **HEADER:** 火

灯

light; lamp; torch

ORIGIN: The old form 燈 consisted of 火 "fire" and 登 "to climb to a high place." A fire raised high is a torch or light. The current simplified form has replaced 登 with 丁. The kanji 灯 means "light; lamp; torch."

ひ
灯 torch, light
けいこうとう
蛍光灯 fluorescent light
がいとう
街灯 street light

とうゆ
灯油 kerosene
でんとう
電灯 (electric) light
しょうとうじかん
消灯時間 lights-out time

、 ゛ ゛ 灯 灯 灯   6

802

ON-KUN READINGS: トウ・あ(たる) **HEADER:** ⺌

当

to hit; just; right; this

ORIGIN: The ancient form of the old form 當 consisted of 尚 "appropriate" and 田 "rice paddies." The kanji signified "to divide up a field appropriately." Now abbreviated to 当, the kanji means "just; right," "to hit," or "this."

ほんとう
本当 truth
あ
当たる to hit (a target); to correspond to
とうぜん
当然 naturally, deservedly

てきとう
適当な suitable
とうぶん
当分 for the time being
とうしゃ
当社 our company, our firm

、 ⺌ ⺌ 当 当 当   6

803

ON-KUN READINGS: トウ・など・ひと(しい)・ら **HEADER:** 竹

等

equal; equivalent; and the like

ORIGIN: The top ⺮ (from 竹) was bamboo stalks with leaves. 寺 consisted of a halted foot and a measuring hand, here used phonetically to indicate "equal" or "and others; and the like." Bamboo tablets were strung together to form booklets; the space between them was equal. The kanji 等 means "equal; equivalent" or "and the like."

にとう
二等 second place
など
等 etc.
ひと
等しい equal
われら
我等 we

とうぶん
等分する to divide into equal parts
どうとう
同等 equal
とうしんだい
等身大 life-sized

丿 ㇇ ⺦ ⺦ 竹 竹 竹 等 等 竿 等 等   12

804

ON-KUN READINGS: トウ・こた(える) **HEADER:** 竹

答

to answer a question

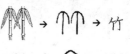

ORIGIN: The top ⺮ was "bamboo," used to make writing tablets. The bottom 合 was "to fit," from "cover fitting a hole"; it was also used for "answer." Together they indicated "to answer fittingly." The kanji 答 means "to answer a question."

こたえ
答 answer
とうあんようし
答案用紙 answer sheet
かいとう
回答 a reply, answer

もんどう
問答 question and answer
とうしん
答申 a report

丿 ㇇ ⺦ ⺦ 竹 竹 竹 答 答 答 答 答   12

237

805

ON-KUN READINGS: トウ

HEADER: 米

糖

sugar

ORIGIN: The left side 米 is rice, and the right side 唐 was phonetically used to indicate "dry heat." Combined, they referred to dry candy made of sweet rice. The kanji 糖 means "sugar."

さとう
砂糖 sugar
とうぶん
糖分 sugar content
とうにょうびょう
糖尿病 diabetes

せいとう
精糖 refined sugar
こなざとう
粉砂糖 powdered sugar
くろざとう
黒砂糖 brown sugar

丶 丷 丷 ㇒ 丬 米 米 米' 米' 米' 米' 米' 糖 糖 糖 糖   16

806

ON-KUN READINGS: トウ・す(べる)

HEADER: 糸

統

to unify

ORIGIN: The left side 糸 was "silk cocoons," from which long continuous filaments were pulled out. The right side 充, used phonetically here, depicted a change from a new-born to a person, or to fill (the body). Collecting things or people together into one is "to unify." The kanji 統 means "to unify."

とういつ
統一 unification
とうけい
統計 statistics
だいとうりょう
大統領 president

けっとう
血統 blood line
せいとう
正統 legitimate
とうそつ
統率する under the command

く 幺 幺 幺 糸 糸 糸' 紵 統 統 統 統   12

807

ON-KUN READINGS: トウ・いた(る)

HEADER: 刂

到

to reach an end

ORIGIN: The left part 至 "hitting an end" depicted an arrow reaching the ground 土, and thus unable to go any further. The ancient form (the third form from the left) shows a person instead of the sword shown in the current form. (Possibly the form was miscopied at one point in history!) The kanji 到 means "to reach an end."

とうちゃくじかん
到着時間 arrival time
とうてい
到底 by no means
よういしゅうとう
用意周到 prudent, careful

さっとう
殺到 to pour in
とうたつ
到達する to reach a
       destination
とうらい
到来 arrival

一 工 互 豆 至 至 到 到   8

808

ON-KUN READINGS: トウ・う(つ)

HEADER: 言

討

to attack; to inquire thoroughly

ORIGIN: The left side 言 came from a tattoo needle 辛 and a mouth 口, which signified "to speak clearly" or "words." The right side 寸 "hand" was used phonetically to indicate "to accuse." The kanji 討 means "to attack" or "to inquire thoroughly."

う
討つ to attack
けんとう
検討 examination
とうろん
討論 discussion

あだう
あだ討ち revenge
とうぎ
討議 discussion
とうばく
討幕 overthrow of the
       shogunate

丶 二 亠 三 言 言 言 言 討 討   10

809

豆

bean

ORIGIN: The ancient form was a pictograph of a raised bowl (for food and drink for religious rites). The origin of the use of this kanji for "bean" is not clear, but it may have been used phonetically or because wooden or clay beans for religious rites were placed inside such a container. The kanji 豆 means "bean."

まめ
豆 bean
まめ
豆まき bean throw
くろまめ
黒豆 black bean

だいず
大豆 soybean
あずき
小豆 azuki bean
にまめ
煮豆 boiled beans

一 厂 厂 亘 亘 豆 豆   7

810

逃

to run away

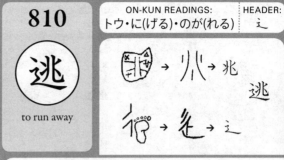

ORIGIN: The upper right 兆 was a crack on a heated tortoise shell or animal bone used for divination; here it was used phonetically to indicate "to jump out." The lower left came from a part of a crossroad and a foot and indicated "moving forward." The kanji 逃 means "to run away."

に だ
逃げ出す to run away
とうぼう
逃亡 escape, flight
とうひ
逃避 escape, flight

とうそう
逃走 escape, desertion
よに
夜逃げ flight by night

丿 丿 丬 兆 兆 兆 兆 逃 逃   9

811

頭

head; top; counter for a large animal

ORIGIN: The left side 豆 was a stemmed bowl, which signified something standing still, here used phonetically. The right side 頁 was a person with a headdress emphasized. The kanji 頭 means "head," or "top." It is also a counter for a large animal.

あたま
頭 head
ずつう
頭痛 headache
ずじょうちゅうい
頭上注意 watch overhead

あたま
頭ごなしに unsparingly
うし ごとう
(牛)五頭 five animals (cows)
せんとう
先頭 leading

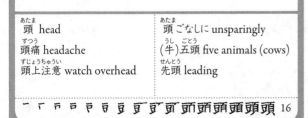

一 厂 厂 亘 亘 豆 豆 豆 豇 可 頭 頭 頭 頭 頭 頭   16

812

働

to work; to operate

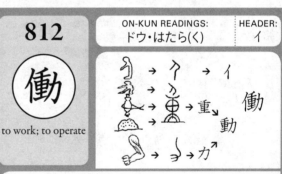

ORIGIN: This kanji originated in Japan. The three parts イ "person," 重 "heavy," and 力 "strength" made up the new kanji 働. It indicated that a person moves his or her body and applies strength, that is, works. The kanji 働 means "to work (for wages); to operate."

はたら
働く to work
ろうどうしゃ
労働者 laborer, worker
じつどうじかん
実働時間 actual working
    hours

かどう
稼働 in operation

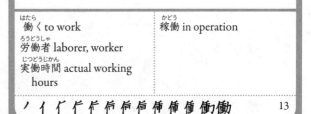

丿 イ イ 仁 仟 仟 伃 佰 俥 俥 働 働   13

239

813

ON-KUN READINGS: ドウ・うご(く)　　HEADER: 力

動

to move

ORIGIN: The left side 重 "heavy" was derived from a depiction of a person with a heavy load, standing on dirt. The right side was 力 "hand" or "strength." Together they indicated moving heavy items by hand. The kanji 動 means "to move."

動機 motive, motivation
どうき
運動 exercise
うんどう
動く to move
うご

動物 animal
どうぶつ
騒動 disturbance,
そうどう
　　commotion
不動産 real estate
ふどうさん

一 一 イ イ 育 育 重 重 重 動 動　11

814

ON-KUN READINGS: ドウ・おな(じ)　　HEADER: 口

同

same; the said

ORIGIN: The ancient form depicted a piece of wood with a hole through it. The openings on either side were the same diameter. The kanji 同 means "same." It is also used to refer to something that has been discussed as in "the said."

同じ same
おな
同情 sympathy
どうじょう
同時に at the same time
どうじ

共同 corporation
きょうどう
同じく likewise
おな
同校 the said school
どうこう

｜ 冂 冂 同 同 同　6

815

ON-KUN READINGS: ドウ　　HEADER: 土

堂

hall; grand
building

ORIGIN: The upper part comes from another kanji, 尚, a window from which air rises, signifying "high, rising." Underneath was 土, a mound of dirt. Together they indicated a tall building on a mound or an earthen platform. The kanji 堂 means "grand building" or "hall."

食堂 dining hall
しょくどう
堂々と splendidly
どうどう
正々堂々 fair and square
せいせいどうどう

堂々回り to go in circles
どうどうめぐ
母堂 mother [honorific]
ほどう
殿堂 palace
でんどう

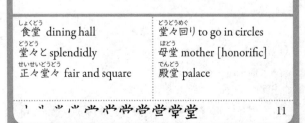　11

816

ON-KUN READINGS: ドウ・みちび(く)　　HEADER: 寸

導

to guide

ORIGIN: The top 道 "road" consisted of 首 "neck" or "head" and 辶 "to move forward." The bottom 寸 was "hand." Together they indicated a guiding hand to move forward. The kanji 導 means "to guide."

指導 guidance
しどう
導く to guide
みちび
導入 する to introduce
どうにゅう

先導 する to guide
せんどう
誘導 leading
ゆうどう
導火線 primer, fuse
どうかせん

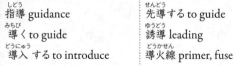　15

817

ON-KUN READINGS: ドウ・わらべ・わらわ
HEADER: 立

童
child

ORIGIN: The top 立 stood for 辛, a tattooing needle spearing the eyes of a slave. The bottom 里 stood for 東, which was used phonetically to indicate "to pierce." Together they originally indicated a male slave. Over time, the meaning changed to indicate someone who was not knowledgeable. The kanji 童 means "child."

じどう
児童 schoolchild
おおわらわ
大童 で in an extremely
　hurried way
わらべ
童 child

しんどう
神童 prodigy
どうしん
童心 innocence, naivety
どうよう
童謡 children's song

ノ 立 立 立 产 音 音 音 音 童 童 童　12

818

ON-KUN READINGS: ドウ・トウ・みち
HEADER: ⻌

道
road; street;
direction

ORIGIN: The top 首 was "head; chief," and the lower left ⻌ came from 辵, which was a left half of a crossroad, and a foot, signifying "to move forward." Together they indicated a way in which someone moves forward, facing ahead. The kanji 道 means "direction; road; street."

みち
道 street
とうかいどう
東海道 the Tokaido Road
ちかみち
近道 shortcut
どうろ
道路 road

ちかどう
地下道 underpass
どうり
道理 reason
どうり
道理 で indeed, that makes
　sense

ヽ ヽ ⺍ ⺍ 产 首 首 首 首 ⺌ 道 道 道　12

(241)

819

ON-KUN READINGS: ドウ
HEADER: 金

銅
copper

ORIGIN: The left 金 was metal. The right side 同 was a square board with a hole, signifying that the front and the back are the same, here used phonetically. It is easy to make a hole in a soft metal such as copper. The kanji 銅 means "copper."

どう
銅 copper
せいどうき
青銅器 bronze ware
どうざん
銅山 copper mine

どうぞう
銅像 bronze statue
ふんどう
分銅 weight
どうせん
銅線 copper wire

ノ ノ 人 ⺌ ⺌ 牟 牟 牟 金 釒 釒 釗 銅 銅 銅　14

820

ON-KUN READINGS: トク・う(る)・え(る)
HEADER: 彳

得
to gain

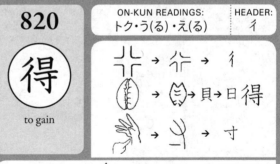

ORIGIN: The left side 彳 "to go" came from the left half of a crossroad. In the old form, the right side had 貝 "cowry" (then changed to 日), pertaining to money, and a hand 寸. Together they indicated going somewhere to earn money using one's hands. The kanji 得 means "to gain."

とく
得 gain, profit
え
得る・得る to obtain
とく
得する to gain, to profit

えとく
会得する to master
せっとく
説得する to persuade
とくい
得意 pride, strong point

ノ ク 彳 彳 彳 彳 徂 得 得 得 得　11

821

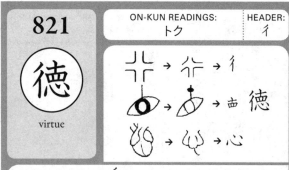

ON-KUN READINGS: トク
HEADER: 彳

徳
virtue

ORIGIN: The left side 彳 "to go" came from the left half of a crossroad and signified "doing; conduct." The right side had an eye that looked at something straight, and a heart, which signified honesty. Someone whose conduct is sincere is a virtuous person. The kanji 徳 means "virtue."

とく 徳 virtue
じんとく 人徳 virtue, merit
とくり・とっくり 徳利・徳利 sake bottle

びとく 美徳 virtue, merit
とくよう 徳用 economical
とくせい 徳性 moral character

ノ ク オ 彳 彳 彳 彳 徝 徝 徝 徳 徳 徳 徳 14

822

ON-KUN READINGS: トク
HEADER: 牛

特
special; noticeable

ORIGIN: The left side 牛 was "cow; bull." The right side 寺 originally indicated "to have in hand," and then later on, a "temple." How the current meaning evolved from that point is not clear. The kanji 特 means "special" or "noticeable."

とく 特に especially
とくべつ 特別 special
とくちょう 特徴 characteristics

とくばい 特売 sale
とくだい 特大 extra large
とくせい 特性 characteristics

ノ ソ 牛 牛 牛 牜 牜 牸 特 特 10

823

ON-KUN READINGS: ドク
HEADER: 毋

毒
poison

ORIGIN: The ancient form depicted a woman with many accessories in her hair for a festival. The form was phonetically borrowed and does not have a relevance to the current use of the kanji 毒, which means "poison." (Another explanation is that the top came from growing grass. Plants that harm are "poisonous.")

どく 毒 poison
ゆうどくぶつ 有毒物 poisonous substance
げどく 解毒 detoxification

どく 毒ガス poisonous gas
ちゅうどく 中毒 poisoning, intoxication
どくけ 毒消し antidote

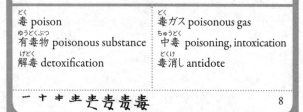
一 十 キ 主 丰 毒 毒 毒 毒 8

824

ON-KUN READINGS: ドク・ひと(り)
HEADER: 犭

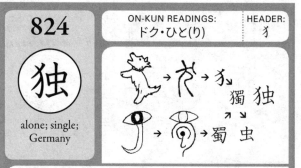

独
alone; single; Germany

ORIGIN: In the old form 獨, the left side 犭 came from a dog. The right side 蜀 was a big-eyed worm, or caterpillar, phonetically used to mean "to join together." Animals stay in a pack and, in contrast, the kanji 獨 indicated a single animal; and from that idea, the reduced kanji 独 came to mean "single" or "alone." The Japanese word for Germany ドイツ also uses this kanji (独逸).

ひと 独り alone
どくりつ 独立 independence
こどく 孤独 solitude

どくがく 独学 self education (without a teacher)
どくせん 独占 monopoly
どくしん 独身 single

ノ ろ オ 犭 犭 犭 独 独 独 9

242

825

読
to read

ORIGIN: The old form 讀 consisted of 言 "word" or "to speak" and 賣 "to sell," which had 士 "foot," 罒 "net," and 貝 "cowry" (currency for trade). Together they indicated that words flow one after another like goods in trade, signifying reading. The right side was replaced by 売, and the kanji 読 means "to read."

よ
読む to read
どくしょ
読書 book reading
よ　　もの
読み物 readings

おんどく
音読 reading aloud
おんよ
音読み Chinese sound of
　　　　kanji
どっかい
読解 reading comprehension

丶 亠 亠 言 言 言 言 計 計 計 詩 詩 読 読　14

826

突
to thrust;
to protrude

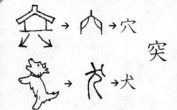

ORIGIN: The top 穴 indicated a hole in a roof. The ancient form of the bottom was 犬 "dog," here used phonetically to indicate "to thrust; to protrude." Together they indicated a hole in a roof, or a protruding chimney with smoke coming out. The kanji 突 means "to thrust; to protrude."

とつぜん
突然 sudden
つ　あ
突き当たり dead end
つ　で
突き出る to protrude

げきとつ
激突 crash
しょうとつじこ
衝突事故 accident involving
　　　　　a collision
とつにゅう
突入 する to plunge into

丶 宀 宀 宀 空 空 突 突　8

827

届
to reach; to deliver

ORIGIN: In the ancient form the top 尸 was a person with the upper body slumped forward and the bottom 由 came from a depiction of putting dirt in a hole. Together they indicated burying something deep in the ground. The kanji 届 means "to reach; to deliver."

とど
届く to reach
とど
届ける to deliver
とど
届け official notification

けっこんとどけ
結婚届 marriage registration
とど　　もの
届け物 a present, an article
　　　　to be delivered
けっせきとどけ
欠席届 report of absence

フ コ ヨ 尸 尸 屇 届 届 届　8

828

豚
pig

ORIGIN: The left side 月 came from 肉 "piece of meat or flesh with muscles." The right side 豕 depicted a wild boar or pig. The kanji 豚 means "pig."

ぶた
豚 pig
ぶたにく
豚肉 pork
とんじ
豚児 my son [humble]

ようとん
養豚 pig-farming
ぶたばこ
豚箱 police cell, lockup

丿 几 月 月 肝 肝 肝 豚 豚 豚 豚　11

829

ON-KUN READINGS: ダイ・ナイ・うち
HEADER: 冂

内
inside

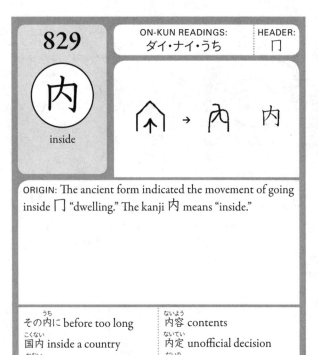

ORIGIN: The ancient form indicated the movement of going inside 冂 "dwelling." The kanji 内 means "inside."

その内に before too long
国内 inside a country
家内 my wife

内容 contents
内定 unofficial decision
内裏 palace

一 冂 内 内   4

830

ON-KUN READINGS: ナン・ナ・みなみ
HEADER: 十

南
south

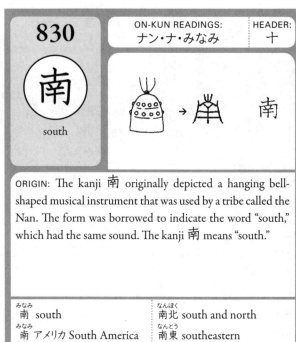

ORIGIN: The kanji 南 originally depicted a hanging bell-shaped musical instrument that was used by a tribe called the Nan. The form was borrowed to indicate the word "south," which had the same sound. The kanji 南 means "south."

南 south
南アメリカ South America
南極 the South Pole; Antarctica

南北 south and north
南東 southeastern
南部 the South

一 十 市 内 内 南 南 南 南   9

831

ON-KUN READINGS: ナン・かた(い)・むずか(しい)
HEADER: 隹

難
difficulty

ORIGIN: The left side showed an animal hide being dried over a fire. The right side 隹 depicted a small, pudgy bird. Together they signified the agony of a bird being roasted. The kanji 難 means "difficulty."

困難 difficulty
難しい difficult
読み難い hard to read

し難い difficult to do
難解な difficult to understand
難民 refugee

一 十 卝 廿 昔 昔 苩 莫 莫 堇 莫 勤 勤 難 難 難 難   18

832

ON-KUN READINGS: ニ・ふた(つ)
HEADER: 二

二
two; second; double

ORIGIN: The ancient form depicted two extended fingers (or two sticks of wood), which signified the number two. The kanji 二 means "two; double" or "second."

二 two
二つ two items
二人 two people

二日 two days, second day of the month
二月 February
無二の matchless

一 二   2

244

833

ON-KUN READINGS: ニク

HEADER: 肉

肉
meat

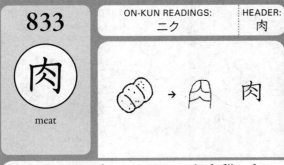

ORIGIN: The ancient form was a pictograph of a fillet of meat (or flesh of an animal) showing two tendons. The kanji 肉 means "meat." (When used as a recurring component pertaining to flesh or a part of the body, it is written as 月, as in 有, 背.)

にく 肉 meat	にくしん 肉親 blood relative
にくや 肉屋 butcher's shop	にくがん 肉眼 with naked eyes
にくたい 肉体 the flesh	にくせい 肉声 natural human voice

 6

834

ON-KUN READINGS: ニチ・ジツ・ひ・か

HEADER: 日

日
sun; day; date

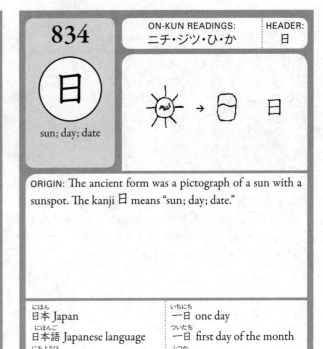

ORIGIN: The ancient form was a pictograph of a sun with a sunspot. The kanji 日 means "sun; day; date."

にほん 日本 Japan	いちにち 一日 one day
にほんご 日本語 Japanese language	ついたち 一日 first day of the month
にちようび 日曜日 Sunday	ふつか 二日 second day, two days
 どの日 which day	へいじつ 平日 weekday

１ 冂 冂 日 4

245

835

ON-KUN READINGS: ニュウ・ちち・ち

HEADER: し

乳
milk

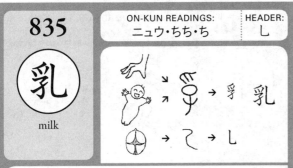

ORIGIN: The ancient form indicated that this kanji consisted of a hand above an infant whose fontanel was not yet closed, which signified the support of an infant who was still nursed and cared for. The kanji 乳 means "milk."

ちち 乳 milk	とうにゅう 豆乳 soy milk
うば 乳母 nursemaid	にゅうせいひん 乳製品 diary product
ぼにゅう 母乳 mother's milk	ふんにゅう 粉乳 powder milk, formula

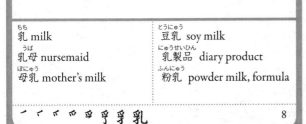 8

836

ON-KUN READINGS: ニュウ・はい(る)・い(れる)

HEADER: 入

入
to enter; entrance

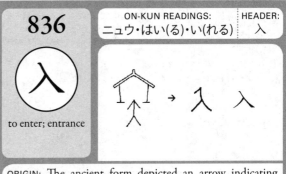

ORIGIN: The ancient form depicted an arrow indicating the entrance to a house. The kanji 入 means "to enter" or "entrance."

はい 入る to enter	い　ぐち 入り口 entrance
い 入れる to put in	にゅうがく 入学 entrance to a school
てい 手入れ tend, to take care	にゅうえんりょう 入園料 entrance fee

ノ 入 2

837

ON-KUN READINGS: ニン・まか(せる)

HEADER: イ

任

to take up
a burden;
responsibility

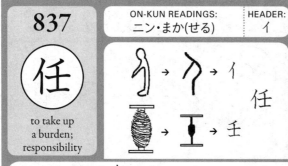

任

ORIGIN: The left side イ is a side view of a person standing. The right side 壬 depicted a spool of thread that is full in the middle. Combined, they signified a person who had a burden or is full of responsibility. The kanji 任 means "to take up a burden" or "responsibility."

まか
任せる to entrust
ふにん
赴任する to start for a new
　　post
にんめい
任命 appointment

ほうにんしゅぎ
放任主義 laissez-faire policy
しゅにん
主任 task manager
たいにん
大任 important duty

ノ イ イ 仁 任 任　　6

838

ON-KUN READINGS: ニン・みと(める)

HEADER: 言

認

to recognize

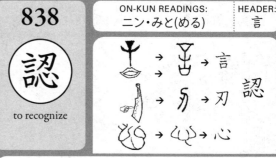

認

ORIGIN: The left side 言 was "word." The right side 忍 consisted of blade (a short stroke pointing out the sharp blade side of a knife 刀) and a heart, signifying "to endure." Together they indicated "to accept what is said." The kanji 認 means "to recognize."

かくにん
確認 confirmation
みと
認める to recognize
にんしき
認識する to recognize

みとめいん
認印 receipt stamp
しょうにん
承認 approval
ひにん
否認 denial

、 二 三 言 言 言 訂 訒 訒 認 認 認 認　　14

839

ON-KUN READINGS: ネツ・あつ(い)

HEADER: 灬

熱

heat; hot; fever

熱

ORIGIN: The upper part depicted a person tending plants on the ground carefully by hand. The bottom 灬 depicted a fire. Together they indicated a person tending a fire carefully. The kanji 熱 means "heat; fever" or "hot."

あつ
熱い hot
ねつ
熱 heat, fever
ねっしん
熱心に earnestly

じょうねつてき
情熱的 passionate
ねったい
熱帯 tropical
ねっぷう
熱風 hot blast

一 十 土 尹 夫 赱 幸 幸 刲 刲 執 執 執 熱 熱　　15

840

ON-KUN READINGS: ネン・とし

HEADER: 干

年

year

年

ORIGIN: The ancient form consisted of a rice-plant 禾 and a person bending his body forward a little, possibly to harvest the rice. The rice harvest happened once a year, so it signified a year's cycle. The kanji 年 means "year."

とし
年 year, one's age
ことし
今年 this year
にせんご ねん
2005年 the year 2005

ていねん
定年 retirement age
ねんきん
年金 pension, annuity
としよ
年寄り elderly person

ノ ヒ 七 仁 三 年　　6

246

841

念

to ponder; thought

ORIGIN: The top 亼 indicated a cover over something, signifying "to catch within," and the bottom 心 was a heart. Together they indicated something contained in the heart for a long time. The kanji 念 means "to ponder," or "thought."

ねん
念のために to make sure
だんねん
断念する to give up
ねんい
念入りに carefully

しんねん
信念 belief
しゅうねん
執念 obsession, tenacity
しつねん
失念 slip of memory

ノ 人 今 今 今 念 念 念　8

842

燃

to burn

ORIGIN: Originally, the right side 然 consisted of 月 "flesh; meat," 犬 "dog; animal," and 火 "fire"—together, roasting animal meat over a fire. But 然 came to be used as "nature"; and for the original meaning of "burning," 火 "fire" was added to the left. The kanji 燃 means "to burn."

も
燃える to burn
ねんりょう
燃料 fuel
かねんせい
可燃性 flammable

ねんしょう
燃焼 combustion
さいねん
再燃する to begin to burn
　again
ふねんせい
不燃性 nonflammable

丶 丷 少 火 火 灯 灯 炒 炒 燃 燃 燃 燃 燃 燃 燃　16

843

納

to pay (due); to store

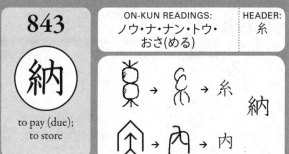

ORIGIN: The left side 糸 "thread" signified woven goods. The right side 内 was a house 冂 and the motion of putting something in it. Together they indicated storage, or paying a levy with woven fabrics. The kanji 納 means "to pay (due)" or "to store."

おさ
納める to pay (due)
のうにゅう
納入 purvey
すいとう
出納 revenues or
　expenditures

なっとく
納得 assent, understanding
なや
納屋 storage barn, shed
ゆいのう
結納 engagement to be
　married

乀 纟 纟 纟 纟 糸 糸 糸 糽 納 納　10

844

能

ability

ORIGIN: Searching the origin of this kanji leaves room for the imagination; scholars have suggested origins as various as a black bear or an insect in water. All agree, however, that the kanji 能 means "ability."

のうりょく
能力 ability
ゆうのう
有能な able
ぜんのう
全能 almighty

のう
能 Noh play
せいのう
性能 efficiency, performance
ほんのう
本能 instinct

乚 乄 亇 育 育 育 能 能 能 能　10

845

脳
brain

ORIGIN: The left side 月 from 肉 "flesh" pertains to parts of a body or organs. The right side of an earlier form 𡿺 had 巛 "hair" and a skull with a soft spot (viewed from above). Together they indicated "brain." Now the form has changed, and the kanji 脳 means "brain."

のう
脳 brain
せんのう
洗脳 brainwash
だいのう
大脳 cerebrum

のうひんけつ
脳貧血 cerebral anemia
のうり
脳裏 one's mind
のうは
脳波 brain waves

丿 刀 月 月 月 朊 肶 胪 胗 脳 脳　11

846

農
agricultural;
farming

ORIGIN: The top came from 田 "rice paddies," and the bottom 辰 depicted a clam extending a fleshy foot. Sharp pieces of shell were attached to a wood stick to make a tool to till the soil or for weeding. The kanji 農 means "farming" or "agricultural."

のうぎょう
農業 agriculture
のうか
農家 farmer
のうみん
農民 farmer

のうじょう
農場 ranch
のうふ
農夫 farmer
のうやく
農薬 agricultural chemical, pesticide

丶 冂 曰 而 曲 曲 芦 芦 芦 農 農 農 農　13

847

波
wave

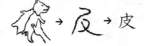

ORIGIN: The left side 氵 was derived from 水 "water." The right side 皮 "skin" was used phonetically to indicate "to move up and down." Together they indicated waves that move back and forth. The kanji 波 means "wave."

なみ
波 wave
はもん
波紋 ripple
つなみ
津波 tidal wave
なみの
波乗り surfing

たんぱ
短波 shortwave
おんぱ
音波 sound wave
はらん
波乱 turmoil

丶 丶 氵 氵 沪 沪 波 波　8

848

派
faction; to split;
to stand out

ORIGIN: The left side 氵 was water and the right side depicted tributaries, indicating something branching out into different groups. Separating oneself from the mainstream makes one stand out. The kanji 派 means "groups that originated from the same origin; faction" and "to split."

りっぱ
立派な splendid, impressive
はせいご
派生語 derived word
りゅうは
流派 school of art

とう　はばつ
党の派閥 party factions
とくはいん
特派員 correspondent
はで
派手な showy

丶 丶 氵 氵 沪 沪 泝 派 派　9

248

849

ON-KUN READINGS: ハ・やぶ(る)・やぶ(ける)
HEADER: 石

破
to break; to tear

ORIGIN: The left side 石 is a rock. The right side 皮, "an animal being skinned by hand," was used phonetically to indicate the sound of a rock being smashed. Together they indicated "to break." The kanji 破 means "to break; to tear."

やぶ
破る to break
やぶ
破ける to get torn
はかい
破壊 destruction

はれつ
破裂 explosion
とっぱ
突破する to break through
やぶ
破れかぶれ desperate

一 丆 石 石 石 矿 矿 矿 破 破　　10

850

ON-KUN READINGS: バ・うま・ま
HEADER: 馬

馬
horse

ORIGIN: The ancient form was a pictograph of a horse with its mane and four legs emphasized. The kanji 馬 means "horse."

うま
馬 horse
ばしゃ
馬車 horse-drawn carriage
もくば
木馬 wooden horse

うまの
馬乗り horseback riding
じょうば
乗馬 horseback riding
しゅつば
出馬 to run for office

｜ 丨 厂 厎 厍 馬 馬 馬 馬 馬　　10

851

ON-KUN READINGS: ハイ
HEADER: イ

俳
actor; amusement

ORIGIN: The left side イ was "person." The right side 非 depicted the two opposing wings of a bird. Two opposing wings are always apart; neither can be the other. From this the form came to mean "not; against." It also phonetically indicates "jester." An actor acts one character, and then another that is totally different. The kanji 俳 means "actor" or "amusement."

はいく
俳句 haiku poetry
はいゆう
俳優 actor
はいじん
俳人 haiku poet

ノ イ イ′ 付 付 俳 俳 俳 俳 俳　　10

852

ON-KUN READINGS: ハイ・おが(む)
HEADER: 扌

拝
to worship;
to revere; do
[humble]

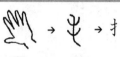

ORIGIN: The left side of the old form 拝 depicted a hand. The right side depicted a stalk with many flowers. Together they indicated an act of kneeling down to pick flowers, and, further, "to bow deeply to show respect." The form also serves to comprise humble-form words such as 拝見. The kanji 拝 means "to worship" or "to revere."

おが
拝む to pray to (with hands)
はいけん
拝見する [humble] to view
はいかん
拝観 viewing of religious
　icons

さんぱい
参拝 a visit to worship
はいしゃく
拝借する [humble] to
　borrow
れいはい
礼拝 worship service

一 十 扌 扌 扩 拝 拝 拝　　8

249

853

ON-KUN READINGS: ハイ・やぶ(れる)

HEADER: 攵

敗

to lose; to fail

ORIGIN: The left side 貝 was a cowry, a rare shell from the south, used as currency in trading. The right side 攵 depicted the motion of hitting or pounding repeatedly with a stick. Together they indicated damaging or breaking something valuable. The kanji 敗 means "to lose," or "to fail."

やぶ
敗れる to lose (a fight)
しっぱい
失敗 failure
ごしょうにはい
五勝二敗 five wins and two losses

はいぼく
敗北 complete loss
はいせん
敗戦 defeat, loss
はいしょく
敗色 signs of defeat

丨 冂 冃 冃 目 目 貝 貝 貯 敗 敗　　11

854

ON-KUN READINGS: ハイ・せ・せい・そむ(く)

HEADER: 月

背

back; height; betrayal

ORIGIN: The top 北 "north" depicted two people back to back. The bottom 月 has the same origin as the kanji 肉 "flesh." Showing one's back also signified betrayal. The kanji 背 means "back," "height," or "betrayal."

せなか
背中 one's back
せ　　たか
背の高さ one's height
はいしん
背信 betrayal

はいけい
背景 background
せの
背伸び standing on tiptoe
うわぜい
上背がある to be tall in stature

一 ナ オ 士 北 北 背 背 背　　9

855

ON-KUN READINGS: ハイ

HEADER: 月

肺

lung

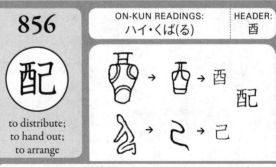

ORIGIN: In the ancient form the left side 月 "flesh" was a recurring component pertaining to a part of the body, and the right side, originally written differently, depicted the moment of a plant sprouting, a sign of life. Like a heart, a lung was considered to be vital for life. The right side has been replaced with 市. The kanji 肺 means "lung."

はい
肺 lung
はいえん
肺炎 pneumonia
はいかつりょう
肺活量 breathing capacity of the lungs

はいけっかく
肺結核 tuberculosis
かたはい
片肺 a lung

丿 刀 月 月 月' 肝 肝 肺 肺　　9

856

ON-KUN READINGS: ハイ・くば(る)

HEADER: 酉

配

to distribute; to hand out; to arrange

ORIGIN: The left side 酉 was a wine jar. The right side 己 was a person kneeling. Together they indicated a person tending a wine jar to pour wine or arranging things. The kanji 配 means "to distribute; to hand out; to arrange."

しんぱい
心配する to be worried about
はいたつ
配達 delivery
くば
配る to deal, deliver

たくはいびん
宅配便 home delivery service
てはい
手配 arrangement
ねんぱい
年配 elderly person

一 丆 冂 丙 丙 酉 酉 酉' 酉フ 配　　10

250

857

ON-KUN READINGS: バイ ・ イ

HEADER: イ

倍

to double;
to multiply

ORIGIN: The left side イ is "person," from a side view of a person standing. The right side 音 had the same origin as 否 and depicted a ripe fruit that was about to split. Splitting leads to multiplication. The kanji 倍 mean "to double," or "to multiply."

さんばい
三倍 three times
ばいぞう
倍増 double increase
ひといちばい
人一倍 more than usual

ばいりつ
倍率 magnifying power
ばいすう
倍数 multiple
ばいおん
倍音 harmonic

ノ イ イ´ 伫 伫 伫 伫 倍 倍 倍   10

858

ON-KUN READINGS: バイ ・ うめ

HEADER: 木

梅

plum

ORIGIN: The left side 木 is a "tree." The right side 毎 "every" has the meaning of fertility from the depiction of a nursing woman, similar to the origin of the kanji 母 "mother". The tart acidity of plums was effective for morning sickness. The kanji 梅 means "plum."

うめ き
梅の木 plum tree
うめぼし
梅干 pickled plum
つゆ ばいう
梅雨・梅雨 rainy season

にゅうばい
入梅 onset of rainy season
うめみ
梅見 plum flower viewing
はくばい
白梅 white plum

一 十 オ オ 材 材 梅 梅 梅   10

859

ON-KUN READINGS: バイ ・ か(う)

HEADER: 貝

買

to buy

ORIGIN: The top 罒 signified "net," and the bottom 貝 was a cowry, a rare shell from the southern coast, which was used for currency. Together they indicated a net full of shells that allows one to buy things. The kanji 買 means "to buy."

か
買う to buy
か もの
買い物 shopping
ばいばい
売買 trading

かいね
買値 purchase price
ばいしゅう
買収 acquisition, purchase
こうばいりょく
購買力 purchasing power

、 冖 冂 罒 罒 罒 罒 買 買 買 買 買   12

860

ON-KUN READINGS: バイ ・ う(る)

HEADER: 士

売

to sell

ORIGIN: The old form 賣 consisted of the top 士 "to go out" (originally from 出 "to go out"), 罒 "net," and 貝 "cowry" (a shell used for currency in trade). Together they indicated "going out to trade goods." The current kanji was reduced to 儿 "legs" at the bottom. The kanji 売 means "to sell."

う
売る to sell
売店 kiosk, selling booth
やすう
安売り a sale

はんばい
販売 selling, sales
とくばい
特売 special sale
ばいめい
売名 self-promotion

一 十 士 士 声 売 売   7

251

861

ON-KUN READINGS: ハク・バク

HEADER: 十

博
extensive

ORIGIN: The left side 十 "ten" signified "numerous." The right side depicted a young plant whose roots were protected, and also the hand that planted it in the ground, but here it was used phonetically to mean "spread." Together they indicated to spread plants on the ground, and, further, "breadth of knowledge." The kanji 博 means "extensive."

はくぶつかん
博物館 museum
はかせ・はくし
博士・博士 expert
ばんぱく
万博 (international) exposition

はくしき
博識 learned, knowledgeable
はくあい
博愛 philanthropy
とばく
賭博 gambling

一 十 十 忄 忄 忄 忄 忄 忄 博 博 博 博 12

862

ON-KUN READINGS: ハク・と(まる)

HEADER: 氵

泊
to stay a night

ORIGIN: The left side 氵 was "water" and the right side 白 gave the sound /haku/. The ancient form indicated calm water in which a boat could be anchored. The kanji 泊 means "to stay a night."

にはくみっか
二泊三日 two night–three day stay
と
泊まる to stay overnight
しゅくはく
宿泊 stay, lodge

がいはく
外泊する to sleep out
しゃちゅうはく
車中泊 a sleep on a train
ていはく
停泊 anchorage, mooring

丶 丶 氵 氵 泊 泊 泊 泊 8

863

ON-KUN READINGS: ハク・ビャク・しろ・しら

HEADER: 白

白
white

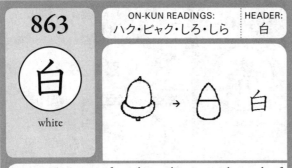

ORIGIN: The ancient form depicted an acorn, the inside of which was white. The kanji 白 means "white."

しろ
白い white
あおじろ
青白い pale
はくし
白紙 blank paper

じはく
自白 a confession
はくまい
白米 white polished rice
しらじら
白々しく shamelessly

ノ 亻 白 白 白 5

864

ON-KUN READINGS: バク・むぎ

HEADER: 麦

麦
barley plant

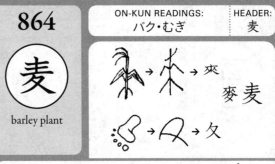

ORIGIN: Originally a barley plant was written as 來 (not shown here). There was a similar kanji 麥 with "foot" underneath, which signified "to come." Over the years the two forms became reversed in their use. 麥 is now reduced to the kanji 麦, and it means "barley plant." (來 is now reduced to 来, and it means "to come.")

むぎ
麦 barley; wheat
こむぎこ
小麦粉 wheat flour
ばくが
麦芽 malt

おおむぎ
大麦 barley
むぎめし
麦飯 rice boiled with barley
むぎちゃ
麦茶 roasted barley tea

一 十 キ 主 丰 麦 麦 7

252

865

ON-KUN READINGS: はこ

HEADER: 竹

箱

box

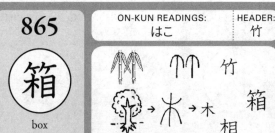

ORIGIN: The top ⺮, from 竹, was a pictograph of bamboo stalks. The bottom 相 had 目, an "eye" looking at 木 "tree" closely, signifying "to face each other." A horse carriage had two bamboo baskets on the sides facing each other to carry belongings. The kanji 箱 means "box."

はこ
箱 box
ほんばこ
本箱 bookcase
ししょばこ
私書箱 post office box

じゅうばこ
重箱 tier of food boxes
くすりばこ
薬箱 medicine box
はこにわ
箱庭 miniature garden

ノ ⺊ ⺊ ⺊ ⺮ 竹 竹 竺 笭 笋 筲 筲 箱 箱 箱 箱　15

866

ON-KUN READINGS: はたけ・はた

HEADER: 田

畑

agricultural field

ORIGIN: This kanji originated in Japan. The kanji 田 referred to irrigated rice paddies. Fields that were not irrigated would occasionally be burned to give the soil certain nutrients; 火 "fire" was added to indicate those fields. The kanji 畑 means "(agricultural) field."

はたけ
畑 field
たはた
田畑 rice paddies and fields
むぎばたけ
麦畑 wheat (barley) field

ちゃばたけ
茶畑 tea field
はたさく
畑作 (field) farming
だんだんばたけ
段々畑 terraced field

、 ⺍ 少 火 灯 炉 畑 畑 畑　9

867

ON-KUN READINGS: ハチ・や・やっつ・よう

HEADER: 八

八

eight; many

ORIGIN: The ancient form was two lines moving away from each other, or "splitting up." Four is eight divided in half. It also means many. The kanji 八 means "eight," or "many."

はち
八 eight
やっ
八つ eight items
はちにん
八人 eight people

ようか
八日 eight days, eighth day of the month
はちがつ
八月 August
はっせん
八千 eight thousand

ノ 八　2

868

ON-KUN READINGS: ハツ・ホッ・た(つ)

HEADER: 癶

発

to depart; sudden move

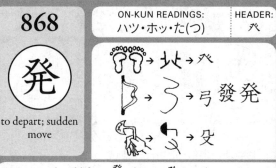

ORIGIN: In the old form 發, the top 癶 "quick move" signified someone jumping quickly and landing with feet apart. 弓 was a bow, and 殳 was a hand holding an ax, indicating a swift motion. Together they signified taking off quickly. Now reduced to 発, the kanji means "sudden move" or "to depart."

しゅっぱつ
出発 departure
ろくじはつ
六時発 departing at six o'clock
とうきょうはつ
東京発 originating from Tokyo

はっけん
発見 discovery
ほったん
発端 onset
じはつてき
自発的に voluntary, spontaneous

フ ⁊ ⁊ ⺀ 癶 癶 癶 発 発　9

253

869

ON-KUN READINGS: ハツ・かみ

HEADER: 髟

髪
hair

ORIGIN: The top 髟 consisted of 長 "long (hair)" and 彡 "beautiful shape." The bottom 友 originally 犮 ("to grow"), was used phonetically. Together they indicated "beautiful hair that keeps growing" or just "hair." The kanji 髪 means "hair."

髪 かみ hair
毛髪 もうはつ hair
白髪 しらが gray hair
黒髪 くろかみ black hair

髪型 かみがた hairstyle
理髪店 りはつてん barber shop
洗髪 せんぱつ washing hair, shampooing

丿 亻 亇 严 岸 肀 툰 髟 髟 髟 髟 髟 髟 髟 14

870

ON-KUN READINGS: バツ・ぬ(く)

HEADER: 扌

抜
to pull out;
to go above

ORIGIN: The old form 拔 consisted of 扌 "hand" and 犮 "to grow or pluck hair." The ancient form of 犮 looked like a dog and may be associated with fur. Combined, the two sides meant to pull a hair that kept on growing, or "to pull out by hand." What is pulled out may appear above other things. The current form has 友 on the right side. The kanji 抜 means "to pull out; to go above."

抜く ぬく to pull out; to pluck out
海抜 かいばつ above sea level
追い抜く おいぬく to outrun

切り抜き きりぬき clipping
抜粋 ばっすい an excerpt
抜群 ばつぐん outstanding, preeminence

一 十 扌 扌 扩 抜 抜 7

871

ON-KUN READINGS: ハン・バン

HEADER: 刂

判
to judge

ORIGIN: The left side 半 "half" was derived from a sacrificial cow 牛 split into half 八. The right side 刂 was a knife, which also indicated "to cut." Together they signified "to judge which half is correct," or simply "to judge." The kanji 判 means "to judge."

判断 はんだん judgment
審判 しんばん a judge
評判 ひょうばん reputation

裁判になる さいばん to be put on trial
判明する はんめい to become known
談判 だんぱん negotiation, bargaining

丶 丷 ソ 半 半 判 判 7

872

ON-KUN READINGS: ハン・なか(ば)

HEADER: 十

半
half; middle

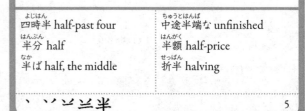

ORIGIN: This kanji consisted of two parts, 八 and 牛. 八 indicated a pushing motion to divide something into two. 牛 was a pictograph of a sacrificial cow's head in a religious rite. Together they meant "split a cow in half." The kanji 半 means "half; middle."

四時半 よじはん half-past four
半分 はんぶん half
半ば なかば half, the middle

中途半端な ちゅうとはんぱ unfinished
半額 はんがく half-price
折半 せっぱん halving

丶 丷 ソ 半 半 5

873

反

to oppose;
to reverse; cloth

ORIGIN: The ancient form depicted the motion of a hand pushing back a piece of "cloth," indicating "to push back; to roll back" or "to reverse." The term also means "to oppose." The kanji 反 means "to oppose; to reverse" or "cloth."

はんたい
反対 opposition, the reverse
はんそく
反則 violation of rule
そ　かえ
反り返る to warp

たんもの
反物 a roll of kimono cloth
はんかん
反感 dislike, ill feeling
はんしゃ
反射 reflection

一 厂 反 反　　4

874

板

board

ORIGIN: The left side 木 was a piece of wood from a tree. The right side 反 was the motion of a hand pushing back a draped cloth, here used phonetically to indicate "flat thing." Together they indicated a wooden board. The kanji 板 means "board."

いた
板 board
いた
まな板 cutting board
こくばん
黒板 blackboard

いたまえ
板前 Japanese chef
いため
板目 wood grain
へいばん
平板 な monotonous, dull

一 十 オ 木 朽 板 板 板　　8

255

875

版

printing block;
edition

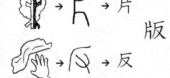

ORIGIN: The left side 片 was taken from half a tree, indicating "piece of wood." The right side 反 was the motion of a hand pushing back a draped cloth, here used phonetically to indicate "flat thing." Together they indicated a wood block for printing. The kanji 版 means "printing block," or "edition."

しゅっぱん
出版 publication
はんが
版画 woodblock print
とっぱんいんさつ
凸版印刷 relief printing

はんぎ
版木 wood block
はんけん
版権 copyright

丿 丬 爿 片 片 朽 版 版 版　　8

876

犯

crime; to violate

ORIGIN: The left side 犭 came from a depiction of a dog or animal. The right side depicted a person in a crouched position. Together they indicated an animal harming a person, or, simply "to harm" or "crime." The kanji 犯 means "crime" or "to violate."

おか
犯す to violate
はんざい
犯罪 crime
はんにん
犯人 culprit
はんこう
犯行 crime, offence

ぼうはん
防犯 crime prevention
きょうはん
共犯 conspiracy
せんぱん
戦犯 war criminal

丿 犭 犭 犴 犯　　5

877

班

small groups;
squad

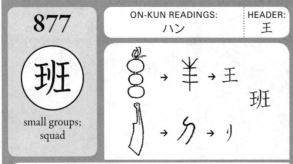

ORIGIN: Each of the 王 on either side depicted jewels strung together. Putting a sharp knife between jewels separates them into smaller pieces. Together they indicated a small group. The kanji 班 means "(to divide into) small groups" or "squads."

班 group, squad
班長 group leader
調査班 survey group

救護班 relief party

一 丁 王 王 丑 珏 珏 班 班 10

878

飯

meal

ORIGIN: 食 on the left consisted of a 亼 "cover" and eating bowl (formerly written as 皀), signifying "food" or "to eat." The right side 反 was used phonetically for the sound of /han/. The kanji 飯 means "meal."

ご飯 meal, cooked rice
朝ご飯 breakfast
炊飯器 rice cooker

晩飯 evening meal (male
　speaker)
夕飯 evening meal
冷や飯 cold rice, treated coldly

ノ 𠆢 𠆢 今 今 今 食 食 食 飯 飯 飯 12

879

晩

evening

ORIGIN: The left side 日 was "sun." The phonetically used right side 免 was a woman in labor, signifying "barely managing to do something." Together they indicated the time of the day when the sun goes down and one can barely see things. The kanji 晩 means "evening."

晩 evening
今晩 this evening
晩ご飯 evening meal

一晩中 throughout the
　night
晩成 late success
晩酌 evening drinking

丨 冂 日 日 日' 日⁷ 明 昭 晚 晚 晚 12

880

番

watch; turn; order

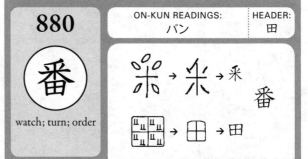

ORIGIN: The top 米 depicted threshed rice, in which the rice grains are scattered in all directions. The bottom 田 was rice paddies. Growing rice involves a set of ordered routines; from this concept, the form came to mean "turns; order." People took turns watching the fields. The kanji 番 means "turn," "order," or "watch."

番 watch, turn
一番 first place, most, best
交番 police box

非番 off-duty
番人 watch
番地 street number

一 ⺍ ⺍ 平 平 平 来 来 番 番 番 番 12

256

881

ON-KUN READINGS: ヒ・いな(む)

HEADER: 口

否

to deny; no

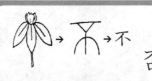

ORIGIN: The top 不 was a calyx of a flower, here used phonetically. The bottom 口 was a mouth to say "no." The kanji 否 means "to deny," or "no."

ひてい 否定 denial いな 否む to deny きょひけん 拒否権 a veto	あんぴ　と 安否を問う to inquire about 　 safety ひけつ 否決 voting down かひ 可否 yeas and nays

一フ不不否否   7

882

ON-KUN READINGS: ヒ・かれ・かの

HEADER: 彳

彼

he or she;
over there

ORIGIN: On the left, 彳 is "to go." On the right, 皮 "skin" was used phonetically to indicate "distance." Together they indicated "to move into the distance." This kanji also refers to a third person, or a direction away from the speaker or listener. The kanji 彼 means "over there," or "third person (he; she)."

かれ 彼 he, boyfriend かのじょ 彼女 she, girlfriend ひがん 彼岸 equinoctial week 　 (Buddhist service is held)	かなた 彼方 far distance

ノクイ彳彷彷彼彼   8

257

883

ON-KUN READINGS: ヒ・かな(しい)

HEADER: 心

悲

sad; sorrow

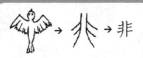

ORIGIN: The top 非 depicted two wings of a bird, which are always apart from each other. The sound /hi/ meant "sad." The bottom 心 is a heart. Together they signified sadness that tears one's heart apart. The kanji 悲 means "sad" or "sorrow."

かな 悲しい sad かな 悲しみ sorrow ひかんてき 悲観的 pessimistic	ひそう 悲壮な tragic ひれん 悲恋 tragic love ひがん 悲願 earnest wish or prayer

ノ丿丬ヺヺ扌非非非悲悲   12

884

ON-KUN READINGS: ヒ

HEADER: 扌

批

to disparage

ORIGIN: The ancient form consisted of 扌 "hand" and the form on the right that was used phonetically. (Even though the ancient form existed its origin is not clear.) Together they indicated "to hit hard by hand." The meaning of hitting hard became "to criticize." Now the right side uses 比 "to compare." The kanji 批 mean "to disparage."

ひひょう 批評 a critical review ひはん 批判する to criticize ひじゅん 批准する to ratify	

一十扌扌批批批   7

885

ON-KUN READINGS: ヒ・くら(べる)

HEADER: 比

比
to compare

ORIGIN: The ancient form depicted two people standing next to each other, facing the same direction. The kanji 比 means "to compare."

比べる to compare
比較 comparison
比率 ratio

比例する to be proportional
前年比 compared to the previous year
比重 specific gravity

一 ヒ と 比   4

886

ON-KUN READINGS: ヒ・つか(れる)

HEADER: 疒

疲
to get tired; fatigue

ORIGIN: The top 疒 depicted a person lying on a bed (shown vertically.) The inside 皮 "skin" was used for its sound. The combined form indicated physical fatigue. The kanji 疲 means "to get tired," or "fatigue."

疲れる to get tired
疲労 fatigue, exhaustion
疲弊 exhaustion, impoverishment

丶 亠 广 广 疒 疒 疒 疲 疲   10

887

ON-KUN READINGS: ヒ・かわ

HEADER: 皮

皮
skin

ORIGIN: The ancient form depicted a hand trying to get fur from an animal. This kanji refers to a softer skin or fur (as contrasted to 革, which refers to the thicker and stronger hide or leather). The kanji 皮 means "skin."

皮 skin, peel
皮むき peeler
皮膚 skin

皮肉 sarcasm
脱皮する to cast off the skin
皮相的 superficial

丿 厂 广 皮 皮   5

888

ON-KUN READINGS: ヒ・ひ(める)

HEADER: 禾

秘
to keep secret

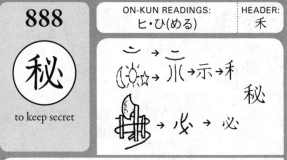

ORIGIN: The current form 秘 was a variant of the older form 祕, which consisted of 示 "altar" and 必 "without fail." Together they signified a sacred religious ceremony that was very secret. The current form 秘 means "to keep secret."

秘密 secret
秘書 secretary
極秘書類 confidential document

秘める to keep secret
秘話 an unknown episode
秘訣 key, knack

一 二 千 禾 禾 禾 秒 秘 秘 秘   10

258

889

ON-KUN READINGS: ヒ・こ(える) | HEADER: 月

肥

fat; corpulent; rich

ORIGIN: The left side 月 came from 肉, a piece of meat or flesh with muscles, pertaining to a part of the body. The right side 巴 was a corpulent person. The meaning of the combined form is used for person as well as soil. The kanji 肥 means "fat; corpulent; rich."

肥料 fertilizer
肥満 obese
肥えた fat, rich

肥沃な土地 rich soil
肥糧 animal feed
肥大 swelling

ノ 刀 月 月 肚 肥 肥 肥 肥   8

890

ON-KUN READINGS: ヒ・つい(やす) | HEADER: 貝

費

to spend

ORIGIN: The top 弗 was a loose string dividing something, but here used phonetically to indicate "nothing." The bottom 貝 was a cowry, a rare shell from the south used for currency. Together they indicated spending money until none was left. The kanji 費 means "to spend."

費用 cost
会費 membership fee
実費 actual cost

費やす to spend (money or time)
浪費 wasteful spending
消費 consumption

一 二 三 弓 弔 弗 弗 費 費 費 費 費   12

259

891

ON-KUN READINGS: ヒ・あら(ず) | HEADER: 非

非

what is not; not good

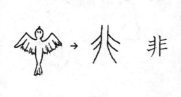

ORIGIN: The ancient form depicted two wings on opposite sides of a bird. The two wings of a bird never meet, a negation of ever meeting. From this, the kanji represents "not" or "negation" or "not good." The kanji 非 means "what is not."

非常口 emergency exit
非常事態 emergency
是非なく by force, unavoidably

非難 criticism, accusation
非礼 impolite
非情な unmerciful

ノ ナ ヲ ヺ 刦 非 非 非   8

892

ON-KUN READINGS: ヒ・と(ぶ) | HEADER: 飛

飛

to fly

ORIGIN: The ancient form was a pictograph of a bird flying with its wings spread. The kanji 飛 means "to fly."

飛行機 airplane
飛ぶ to fly
飛び出す to rush out

飛躍する to leap
突飛な erratic, extraordinary
飛語 rumor

乀 乁 飞 飞 飞 飛 飛 飛 飛   9

893

ON-KUN READINGS: ビ・そな(える)

HEADER: イ

備

to be prepared; to be equipped with

ORIGIN: The left side イ is from the kanji 人 "person," a side view of a person standing. The right side depicted a soldier carrying a quiver on his back, being well prepared to fight. From this idea, the kanji 備 came to mean "to be prepared; to be equipped with."

せつび
設備 equipment
そな
備える to be prepared, to be equipped with
びひん
備品 equipment

よびこう
予備校 preparatory school
ふび
不備 deficient
かんび
完備 completely furnished

ノ イ イ′ 伊 伊 俏 倄 倄 倄 備 備 備   12

894

ON-KUN READINGS: ビ・うつく(しい)

HEADER: 羊

美

beautiful

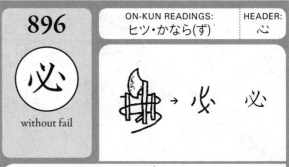

ORIGIN: The top came from sheep 羊. A sheep is attractive, and it provides wool and tasty meat. The top was used to mean something good, pretty, or tasty. The bottom 大 was a person. Together they indicated a beautiful or fine person. The kanji 美 means "beautiful."

びじん
美人 beauty
びじゅつ
美術 fine arts
かび
華美な gorgeous, gaudy

びか
美化 beautification
かんび
甘美な sweet, delicious
びじれいく
美辞麗句 flowery words

丶 丷 丷 丷 羊 羊 美 美   9

895

ON-KUN READINGS: ビ・はな

HEADER: 鼻

鼻

nose

ORIGIN: The top 自 "oneself" was a pictograph of a nose. Underneath it was 田 "present" placed on 廾 "table," but here the character is used phonetically to mean "noticeable." The nose is a noticeable feature on one's face. The kanji 鼻 means "nose."

はな
鼻 nose
はなち
鼻血 nose bleeding
はなうた
鼻歌 humming

はなお
鼻緒 sandal straps
びおん
鼻音 nasal sound
じびか
耳鼻科 ear and nose doctor

丶 亻 亣 冉 臽 自 自 島 島 鼻 畠 畠 鼻 鼻   14

896

ON-KUN READINGS: ヒツ・かなら(ず)

HEADER: 心

必

without fail

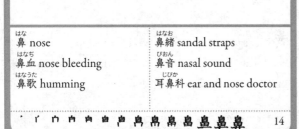

ORIGIN: The ancient form was 戈, a "lance strapped tightly between two poles," signifying the secure and safe storage of weapons. The meaning of security led to the current meaning of the kanji 必 "without fail."

かなら
必ず without fail
ひつよう
必要な necessary
ひつぜんてき
必然的に inevitably
ひつどくしょ
必読書 a must-read book

ひつじゅひん
必需品 necessities
ひっしゅうかもく
必修科目 required subject
かなら
必ずしも(〜ない) not necessarily

丶 丷 必 必 必   5

897

ON-KUN READINGS:	HEADER:
ヒツ・ふで	竹

筆
writing brush

ORIGIN: The top from 竹 "bamboo" was a pictograph of bamboo stalks with leaves. 聿 depicted a hand holding a brush. A writing brush typically had a bamboo handle. The kanji 筆 means "writing brush."

ふで
筆 brush
ひっしゃ
筆者 writer
もうひつ
毛筆 writing brush

えんぴつ
鉛筆 pencil
じきひつ
直筆 one's own handwriting
ひっせき
筆跡 penmanship

ノ ト ヶ ヶ 竺 竺 竺 竺 筜 筜 筜 筆   12

898

ON-KUN READINGS:	HEADER:
ヒャク	白

百
hundred

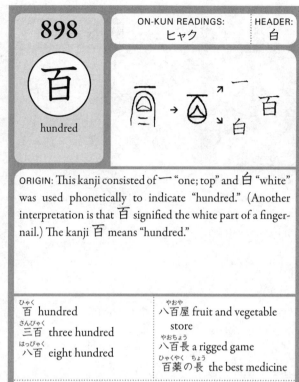

ORIGIN: This kanji consisted of 一 "one; top" and 白 "white" was used phonetically to indicate "hundred." (Another interpretation is that 百 signified the white part of a fingernail.) The kanji 百 means "hundred."

ひゃく
百 hundred
さんびゃく
三百 three hundred
はっぴゃく
八百 eight hundred

やおや
八百屋 fruit and vegetable
store
やおちょう
八百長 a rigged game
ひゃくやく ちょう
百薬の長 the best medicine

一 一 丆 百 百 百   6

899

ON-KUN READINGS:	HEADER:
ヒョウ・たわら	イ

俵
straw bag

ORIGIN: The ancient form consisted of イ (from the kanji 人 "person") and 表 "surface," which was used phonetically to indicate "lightly." In Japan a lightweight straw bag was used for rice. The kanji 俵 means "straw bag."

こめだわら
米俵 rice pack
どひょう
土俵 sumo wrestling arena
すみだわら
炭俵 charcoal pack

ノ イ 仁 什 件 件 伴 俵 俵 俵   10

900

ON-KUN READINGS:	HEADER:
ヒョウ	木

標
sign; mark

ORIGIN: The left side 木 was a tree or wood. The right side was 覀 "woman's slender waist" and 示 "fire." Together they indicated a wooden piece that is so light that it may blow away like sparks of a fire (or a small piece of a sign, or something to mark). The kanji 標 means "sign" or "mark."

もくひょう
目標 target, goal
ひょうほん
標本 specimen
ひょうてき
標的 target

ざひょう
座標 coordinates
ひょうご
標語 slogan
ひょうこう
標高 altitude

一 十 才 木 木 杧 杧 枦 桿 桿 桿 標 標 標 標   15

261

901

ON-KUN READINGS: ヒョウ・こおり・ひ

HEADER: 水

氷
ice

ORIGIN: The old form 氷 consisted of 冫, two strokes depicting lines that appeared as ice forms (as shown in the ancient form, second from the left), and 水 "water" on the right side. Now with one less stroke, the kanji 氷 means "ice."

こおり
氷 ice
ごおり
かき氷 shaved ice
ひょうてんか
氷点下 below freezing point
ひむろ
氷室 icehouse

ひょうが
氷河 iceberg
ひょうざん　いっかく
氷山の一角 small part of a larger problem, tip of the iceberg

㇀ ㇀ 氵 氺 氷　5

902

ON-KUN READINGS: ヒョウ

HEADER: 示

票
vote; ballot

ORIGIN: The top 覀 was derived from 要, a "woman's slender waist." The bottom 示 was derived from a fire. Together they indicated something so slight and light that it could blow away like sparks of a fire. A ballot is a lightweight piece of paper. The kanji 票 means "vote; ballot."

ひょう
票 vote
とうひょう
投票する to vote
でんぴょう
伝票 slip, ticket

かいひょう
開票 ballot counting
とうひょうりつ
投票率 voter turnout
ふどうひょう
浮動票 undecided votes

一 ⼂ 市 西 西 西 覀 票 票 票　11

903

ON-KUN READINGS: ヒョウ・おもて・あらわ(れる)

HEADER: 衣

表
surface; outside; front; to make public

ORIGIN: The ancient form shown in the middle depicted fur 毛 and clothes 衣. A fur coat was worn with the fur on the outside, which other people could see. The meaning of fur was dropped. The kanji 表 means "surface; outside; front" or "to make public."

はっぴょう
発表する to make a presentation
おもて
表 the right side; outside
あらわ
表れる to show

ひょうめん
表面 surface
ひょう
表 table
だいひょう
代表 chief representative

一 十 キ 丰 声 耂 表 表　8

904

ON-KUN READINGS: ヒョウ

HEADER: 言

評
to comment

ORIGIN: The left side 言 was from a tattoo needle 辛 and a mouth 口, signifying "to speak clearly and sharply." 平 on the right side depicted a water plant floating flat on water, signifying "flat; even." Together they indicated speaking evenly, or making a balanced comment. The kanji 評 means "to comment."

ひょうばん
評判 reputation
こうひょう
好評 favorable reaction
ひょうか
評価 estimation

ひょうろん
評論 criticism, review
ふひょう
不評 unpopular
ていひょう
定評のある having an established reputation

ヽ 亠 亠 言 言 言 言 訂 訌 評 評　12

905

病

illness; disease; sick

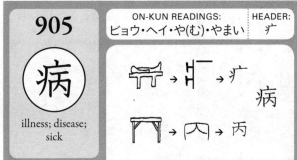

ORIGIN: In the ancient form, the top 疒 depicted someone (一 on the right) lying in bed (shown vertically). 丙 was a table, used phonetically to mean "to increase." Together they indicated a worsening illness. The kanji 病 means "illness; disease" or "sick."

やまい
病 illness
びょうき
病気 illness
きゅうびょう
急病 sudden illness

びょうにん
病人 patient, ill person
けびょう
仮病 feigned illness
しっぺい
疾病 disease

丶亠广广广疒疒病病病　10

906

秒

tiny; second

ORIGIN: The left side 禾 was a rice plant. The tip of the rice kernel was covered with tiny hard awn and they signified "a lot of minute pieces." The right side 少 phonetically was also used to indicate smaller pieces. Together they indicated something tiny. The form was also used to mean the smallest amount of time. The kanji 秒 means "extremely small" or "second."

びょう
秒 second
びょうよ
秒読み countdown
びょうそく
秒速 speed per second

びょうしん
秒針 second hand (on a clock)

丿二千禾禾利利秒秒　9

907

品

goods; grade; class

ORIGIN: The kanji 品 came from three boxes or three mouths, signifying many goods. Many goods have different qualities; the form also was used for different grades of goods, and class in general. The kanji 品 means "goods; grade; class."

しな
品 item
さくひん
作品 piece of work
じょうひん
上品 have class, refined

げひん
下品 low class
しなもの
品物 goods, item
ひん
品がいい graceful, elegant

丨口口口口口品品品　9

908

貧

poor

ORIGIN: The top 分 consisted of ハ "to divide" and 刀 "sword." 貝 was a cowry shell, which was precious and used as currency in trade. When one's money or goods are divided, one ends up poor. The kanji 貧 means "poor."

びんぼう
貧乏 poverty
まず
貧しい poor
ひんぷ
貧富 wealth and poverty

ひんこん
貧困 poverty, lack
ひんそう
貧相 shabby-looking
ひんけつ
貧血 anemia

丿八分分分谷谷谷貧貧貧　11

909

ON-KUN READINGS: フ・ブ

HEADER: 一

不

denial; not

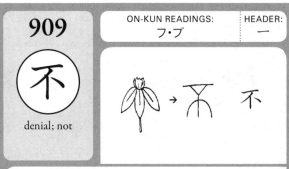

ORIGIN: The ancient form was a pictograph of the calyx of a flower, which is attached to the bud or petals on one end and to the stem on the other end. The sound of "to attach," /fu/, was similar to a word for denial and so its form was borrowed for that meaning. The kanji 不 means "denial" or "not."

不安な worried, apprehensive
不便 inconvenience
不幸な unfortunate

不利 disadvantage
不況 business slump
不和 discord, bad blood

一ブ不不   4

910

ON-KUN READINGS: フ・つ(く)

HEADER: イ

付

to attach; to issue

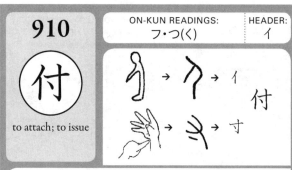

ORIGIN: The left イ "person" and the right 寸 "hand catching something" indicated putting a hand on someone from behind, or reaching out and giving out something, or an official issuing paper by hand. The kanji 付 means "to attach; to issue."

付ける to attach
気を付ける to pay attention
送付する to send out
寄付 donation

添付ファイル an attached file
日付 date
交付する to issue, grant

ノイイ付付   5

911

ON-KUN READINGS: フ・フウ・おっと

HEADER: 大

夫

man; husband

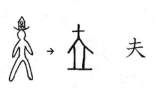

ORIGIN: One interpretation of the ancient form is that in ancient times, a man would wear an ornamental hairpin upon reaching adulthood. An alternative interpretation is that a single hairpin was worn by a bridegroom, whereas a bride wore three, 妻. Once used to signify a distinguished man, the kanji 夫 now means "man" or "husband."

夫 husband
夫婦 married couple
夫人 the wife of [honorific]

人夫 laborer
工夫する to devise
水夫 sailor

一二チ夫   4

912

ON-KUN READINGS: フ

HEADER: 女

婦

woman

ORIGIN: The left side 女 depicted a woman sitting with her hands crossed in front. The right side 帚 was a hand holding a broomstick, which signified "to cleanse; to purify." Together they indicated a woman who did domestic work, or a married woman. The meaning then extended to women in general. The kanji 婦 means "woman."

婦人 woman
主婦 housewife
夫婦 married couple

家政婦 housekeeper
新婦 bride
情婦 mistress

く タ 女 女' 女ヨ 女ヨ 女ヨ 婦 婦 婦   11

264

913

ON-KUN READINGS: フ・フウ・とみ・と(む)

HEADER: 宀

富
wealth

ORIGIN: The top 宀 was a house; underneath was a wide-mouthed container filled with food or rice wine. Together they signified a house that has containers filled with food and sake, that is, a wealthy household. The kanji 富 means "wealth."

とみ 富 wealth	と 富んだ abound with
ほうふ 豊富 abundance	ふごう 富豪 a person of wealth
ふゆうそう 富裕層 the affluent group of people	きょふ 巨富 huge fortune

丶 丷 宀 宀 宀 宀 宀 宮 宮 富 富 富　12

914

ON-KUN READINGS: フ・ぬの

HEADER: 巾

布
cloth; to spread

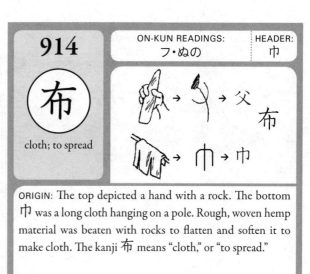

ORIGIN: The top depicted a hand with a rock. The bottom 巾 was a long cloth hanging on a pole. Rough, woven hemp material was beaten with rocks to flatten and soften it to make cloth. The kanji 布 means "cloth," or "to spread."

ぬの 布 cloth	ぶんぷ 分布 distribution, spread
もうふ 毛布 blanket	ふきょう 布教 missionary work
ふきん 布巾 dish cloth	ぬのじ 布地 fabric

ノ ナ オ 右 布　5

915

ON-KUN READINGS: フ

HEADER: 广

府
government; prefecture

ORIGIN: The top was 广 "roof" and the right bottom 付 "to issue" meant someone (亻) giving out a document by hand (寸). Together they indicated a place where official documents were stored or issued. It came to mean a place where a government was located. The kanji 府 means "government" or "prefecture."

おおさかふ 大阪府 Osaka-fu	しゅふ 首府 capital
せいふ 政府 government	がくふ 学府 seat of learning
ばくふ 幕府 *bakufu,* military government	そうりふ 総理府 general office of prime minister

丶 亠 广 广 疒 府 府 府　8

916

ON-KUN READINGS: フ

HEADER: 日

普
universal; ordinary

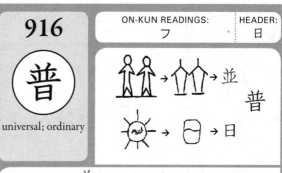

ORIGIN: The top 並 depicted two (signifying many) people standing side by side in a row, signifying something "spreading far and wide." The bottom 日 was sun illuminating everything. Together they indicated something that could be seen everywhere, thus not special. The kanji 普 means "universal," or "ordinary."

ふつう 普通 ordinary	ふきゅう 普及する to pervade
ふつうでんしゃ 普通電車 ordinary train	ふしん 普請する to build
ふへんてき 普遍的 universal	ふだんぎ 普段着 everyday clothes

丶 丷 丷 ᅭ ᅭ 並 並 普 普 普 普 普　12

265

917

ON-KUN READINGS: フ・う(かぶ)

HEADER: 氵

浮
to float

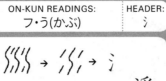

ORIGIN: The left side 氵 had the same origin as 水 "stream of water." The right side 孚 consisted of a hand from above grabbing a child. Together they indicated a hand keeping a child afloat in water. The kanji 浮 means "to float."

浮かぶ to float
浮き輪 flotation ring
浮遊物 floating objects

浮き沈み ups and downs
浮き世 transitory world, life
浮浪者 a tramp

丶 冫 氵 氵 浮 浮 浮 浮 浮 浮   10

918

ON-KUN READINGS: フ・ちち

HEADER: 父

父
father; paternal

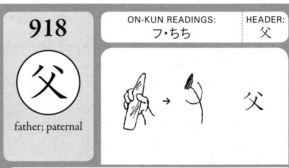

ORIGIN: The ancient form depicted a hand holding a stone ax to strike (same origin as 攵). It signified a stern figure. The kanji 父 means "father" or "paternal."

お父さん father
父 father
父親 father
伯父・叔父 uncle

祖父 grandfather
父兄 parents of students
義父 father-in-law

ノ ハ グ 父   4

919

ON-KUN READINGS: フ

HEADER: 竹

符
tag

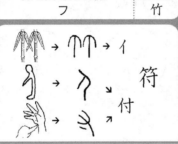

ORIGIN: The top 竹, from 竹, was bamboo stalks with leaves. The bottom 付, used phonetically here, had イ "person" and 寸 "hand" signifying a hand giving something to another person, or reaching out and touching. A letter was written on a bamboo tally. The kanji 符 means "tag."

切符 ticket
音符 musical note
符号 symbol

護符 charm, talisman
休止符 rest, pause
割符 tally, check

ノ 广 卜 什 竹 竹 符 符 符 符 符   11

920

ON-KUN READINGS: フ・ま(ける)・お(う)

HEADER: 貝

負
to lose; to owe; to bear

ORIGIN: The top ク was a person stooping over. 貝 was a cowry, a valuable shell used as currency. Together they indicated a person carrying valuable goods on his or her back, which signified bearing a heavy burden. Showing one's back indicated defeat or loss. The kanji 負 means "to lose; to owe" or "to bear."

負ける to lose
勝負 match, game
勝ち負け victory and defeat

負う to owe
負債 debt
背負う to shoulder

ノ ク ケ 负 台 角 自 負 負   9

266

921

ON-KUN READINGS: ブ・ム

HEADER: 止

武

warrior; military

ORIGIN: In the ancient form, the upper right side 戈 was a pictograph of a halberd; and the lower left 止 was a footprint. Together they indicated a person who advanced on foot with arms to fight, or "military" matters, as contrasted to "civil" matters. The kanji 武 means "warrior," or "military,"

武士 samurai warrior
武器 arms, weapons
文武 the sword and the pen

武力行使 use of armed forces
武装 armed
影武者 a general's double

一 二 干 于 正 正 武 武　　8

922

ON-KUN READINGS: ブ・ベ

HEADER: 阝

部

part; section

ORIGIN: The left side 音 was borrowed from the kanji that had the same sound as "to divide." The right side 阝 originally signified a village, consisting of land and people. Together they meant a part of a village, or a section in general. The kanji 部 means "part; section."

部屋 room
全部 entirely
部分 part
一部 part

学部 academic department
部下 a subordinate
内部 inside
部隊 a corps

' 亠 十 立 产 音 音 音' 部3 部　　11

923

ON-KUN READINGS: フウ・フ・かぜ・かざ

HEADER: 風

風

wind; manner; style

ORIGIN: The top ancient form had a dragon (here 虫) under a sail 几 that catches wind whereas the bottom one had a large imaginary sacred bird 鳳 with a "crown" crest, and a sail. Wind was believed to be caused by a dragon or sacred bird. The current kanji 風 kept the crown on top of 虫 in a stroke ノ, and is also used for abstract (invisible) concepts such as "manner; style."

風 wind
台風 typhoon
日本風・和風 Japanese style

風呂 bath
風邪 a cold
そんな風に in a manner like that

ノ 几 几 凡 凤 凨 風 風 風　　9

924

ON-KUN READINGS: フク

HEADER: 刂

副

to accompany; deputy

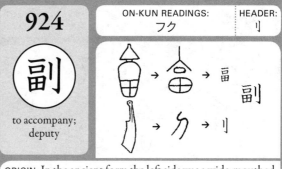

ORIGIN: In the ancient form the left side was a wide-mouthed container filled with food, signifying wealth. The right side was 刂 "knife." The combined form indicated something that was cut and placed next to the main thing. The kanji 副 means "to accompany" or "deputy."

副社長 vice president of a company
副業 side job
正副 original and duplicate

副える to attach
副作用 side effect
副産物 by-product

一 ー 戸 百 后 后 昌 畐 畐 副 副　　11

267

925

ON-KUN READINGS: フク

HEADER: 彳

復

again; to repeat

ORIGIN: The left side 彳 "to go" was the left half of a cross-road. The right side had two conjoined containers, one of which was upside down, signifying "double," and a foot facing backward, signifying going and returning, or a round trip. Together they indicated repeating something. The kanji 復 means "to repeat" or "again."

ふくしゅう
復習 review
かいふく
回復 recovery
おうふくきっぷ
往復切符 round-trip ticket

ふっかつ
復活する to revive
ふっこう
復興 reconstruction
ふくげん
復元 restoration

ノ ク 彳 彳 沪 沪 沪 沪 祏 復 復   12

926

ON-KUN READINGS: フク

HEADER: 月

服

clothes; to obey

ORIGIN: The left side 月 was "boat," which had two long sides. The right side 㕨 depicted a person being pushed down by another person's hand (又), signifying "to yield, to serve." Clothes, which have a front and a back, mold to a person's body, yielding to the shape of the body. The kanji 服 means "to obey" or "clothes."

ふく
服 clothes
ようふく
洋服 Western-style clothes
わふく
和服 Japanese-style clothes

ふくじゅう
服従する to be obedient
ふくよう
服用する to take medicine
くっぷく
屈服 submission

ノ 刀 月 月 肝 服 服 服   8

927

ON-KUN READINGS: フク

HEADER: ネ

福

fortune; good luck

  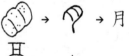

ORIGIN: The left side ネ from 示 was an altar for making an offering. The right side was a wide-mouthed container used to store sake and food, signifying wealth. Together they indicated food or sake that was offered to a god. With the religious meaning diminished, the kanji 福 still retains a certain focus on hope, with the meaning "fortune; good luck."

ふく
福 good luck
こうふく
幸福 happiness
ふくびき
福引 lottery

ふくし
福祉 welfare
ふくぶくろ
福袋 New Year's grab bag
ふくぶく
福々しい plump

丶 ラ ネ ネ 礻 祚 福 福 福 福 福 福   13

928

ON-KUN READINGS: フク・はら

HEADER: 月

腹

abdomen; belly

ORIGIN: The left side 月 came from 肉, a piece of meat or flesh with muscles, and pertains to parts of a body. The right side was used phonetically to indicate "thick." The abdomen is the thickest part of a person's body. The kanji 腹 means "abdomen; belly."

はら
腹 stomach
はらだ
腹立てる to get upset
ふくつう
腹痛 stomach ache

くうふく
空腹 hunger
ふくしん
腹心 trusted confidante
ふくぞう
腹蔵なく frank

ノ 刀 月 月 月 旷 胪 胪 胪 腹 腹 腹 腹   13

929

ON-KUN READINGS: フク

HEADER: ネ

複

to duplicate

ORIGIN: The left side ネ from the kanji 衣 signified clothes. On the right side were two conjoined containers, one of which was upside down, signifying "double," and a backward foot, indicating going and returning, and thus meaning "to repeat." Together they indicated two layers of clothes. Later, the meaning of clothes was dropped, so the kanji 複 means "to duplicate."

ふくせい
複製 copy
じゅうふく・ちょうふく
重複・重複 duplication, overlap
ふくすう
複数 multiple number

ふくがんてき
複眼的 from various angles
ふくしゃき
複写機 copier
ふくざつ
複雑な complicated

` ラ ネ ネ ネ ネ ネ ネ ネ ネ 複 複 複   14

930

ON-KUN READINGS: フツ・はら(う)

HEADER: 扌

払

to pay; to brush away

ORIGIN: The old form 拂 meant to disperse or deny by sweeping one's hand 扌. It also came to mean getting rid of a debt with a payment, or generally making a payment. As is the case with 仏 "Buddha," 弗 became simplified to ム. The kanji 払 means "to pay" or "to brush away."

はら
払う to pay
まえばら
前払い advance payment
あとばら
後払い pay afterwards

しはら
支払い payment
もんぜんばら
門前払い to turn a person away
ふっしょく
払拭する to wipe out

一 十 扌 払 払   5

269

931

ON-KUN READINGS: ブツ・ほとけ

HEADER: イ

仏

Buddha; France

ORIGIN: The right side 弗 of the old form meant to disperse or deny by sweeping one's hand, which has the sound /fu/. It was then borrowed to express the "bu/fu" sound in Buddha. It is also used to signify France, taking the first syllable /fu/ from the name written in kanji. The reduced current form 仏 means "Buddha" or "France."

ぶっきょう
仏教 Buddhism
ほとけ
仏 Buddha
べいえいふつ
米英仏 U.S.–U.K.–France

だいぶつ
大仏 Great Buddha image
じょうぶつ
成仏する to enter Nirvana

ノ イ 仏 仏   4

932

ON-KUN READINGS: ブツ・モツ・もの

HEADER: 牛

物

stuff; things

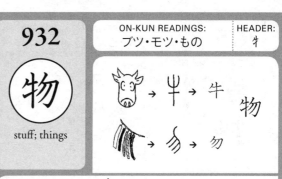

ORIGIN: The left part 牛 indicated a cow's head. The right side 勿 depicted a variety of streamers, signifying "assorted things." Combined, they indicated cows with different colorations. The meaning of cow was dropped, and the kanji 物 means "stuff" or "things."

もの
物 thing
た もの
食べ物 food
しなもの
品物 goods, item
どうぶつ
動物 animal

ぶっか
物価 price of goods
しょくもつ
食物 food
ものわか
物別れ breakdown of negotiations

ノ ヒ 牛 牛 牛 牜 物 物   8

933

ON-KUN READINGS: フン・プン・ブ・わ(かる)

HEADER: 刀

分

to divide; portion; to understand; to realize; minute

ORIGIN: The top ハ "dividing into two" and the bottom 刀 "sword; knife" or "to cut" indicated not only "to divide" or "portion" but also "minute" because an hour is divided into 60 minutes." Also, when something is explained in a clear-cut manner, it is easily understood. The kanji 分 means "to divide," "portion," "minute," or "to understand; to realize."

分ける to divide
十分に plentifully
分かる to understand, to realize

五分 five minutes
分別のある sensible
七分目 seven-tenths

ノ 八 分 分   4

934

ON-KUN READINGS: フン・ふる(う)

HEADER: 大

奮

to muster up strength; to be invigorated

ORIGIN: The ancient form consisted of 大 "big" and 隹 "pudgy small bird" on "rice paddies," giving the depiction of a bird flapping its wings, starting to take flight. The kanji 奮 means "to muster up strength; to be invigorated."

興奮 excitement
奮う to muster the courage
奮発する to make strenuous efforts

奮闘 to fight hard
発奮 be spirited
奮起 brace oneself for

一 ナ 六 六 卒 卒 卒 卒 奮 奮 奮 奮 奮 奮 奮 奮   16

935

ON-KUN READINGS: フン・こ・こな

HEADER: 米

粉

flour

ORIGIN: On the left 米 rice grains scatter in all directions. On the right in 分, which was used phonetically, ハ meant "to divide" and 刀 meant "knife." When rice and other grains are divided, that is, ground into powder, they make flour. The kanji 粉 means "flour."

粉 flour, powder
小麦粉 wheat flour
粉々に in pieces

粉末 powder
粉砕する to smash
花粉 pollen

丶 丷 业 并 米 米 米 粉 粉 粉   10

936

ON-KUN READINGS: ブン・モン・ふみ・あや

HEADER: 文

文

writing; letter; sentence; culture; civil; penny

ORIGIN: The ancient form depicted a beautifully overlaid collar and indicated writing that expressed careful thought, using intricate writing forms, thus leading to the meaning of "writing." The kanji 文 also represented what is produced by human wisdom and intellect, such as "culture; civilization; writing; fine arts; scholarship, etc." *Mon* was the smallest unit of money in olden days.

文 sentence
作文 (student's) essay, composition
文化 culture

文学 literature
英文 English writing
文句 complaint
一文無し penniless

丶 亠 ナ 文   4

937

ON-KUN READINGS: ブン・モン・き(く)

HEADER: 耳

聞

to listen; to hear; to ask

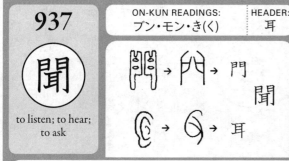

ORIGIN: The top 門 was a pictograph of two closed doors, which signified something unknown. Inside the 門, 耳 was also a pictograph of an ear, signifying listening to hear sounds. When one wants to know something, one listens for answers. The kanji 聞 means "to listen; to ask."

聞く to hear, ask
聞こえる to be audible
新聞 newspaper

見聞きする to see and hear
前代未聞 unheard of
聞き手 listener

丨 冂 冂 冃 冃 門 門 門 門 門 門 門 聞 聞 14

938

ON-KUN READINGS: ヘイ・ヒョウ・つわもの

HEADER: 八

兵

soldier

ORIGIN: The top depicted an ax or a weapon. The bottom depicted two hands. Together they indicated someone who fights with a weapon in his hand. The kanji 兵 means "soldier."

兵士 soldier
兵隊 soldier
派兵 sending troops

兵器 weapons
徴兵制度 the conscription system
兵役 military service

丿 亻 亇 斤 乒 乒 兵 7

271

939

ON-KUN READINGS: ヘイ・ビョウ・たい(ら)・ひら

HEADER: 干

平

flat; calm

ORIGIN: The ancient form depicted a water plant floating flat on the water. The form signified "flat" and described a state that was not extraordinary. The kanji 平 means "flat; calm."

平ら flat
平たい flat
平成 The Heisei Era (1989–)

平等 equality
平気 unconcerned
平行 parallel

一 丆 口 兀 平 5

940

ON-KUN READINGS: ヘイ・なみ・なら(べる)

HEADER: 丷

並

to line up; row; ordinary

ORIGIN: The old form 竝 came from a pictograph of two (signifying many) people standing side by side. It also meant something that spread sideways, hence "row." Since there are so many of them standing in a row, none of them is special. The kanji 並 means "to line up," "row," or "ordinary."

並みの ordinary
並ぶ to line up
並列 parallel

並立する to stand side by side
平日並み weekday average
人並に decently, like others

丶 丷 丷 二 並 並 並 並 8

941

ON-KUN READINGS: ヘイ・し(める)・と(じる)

HEADER: 門

閉

to close

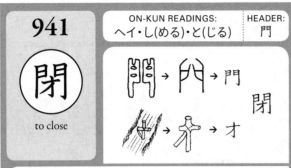

ORIGIN: In the ancient form the upper part 門 depicted two closed doors, and 才 was a pictograph of a weir blocking the flow of water. The kanji 閉 means "to close."

し
閉める to close
と
閉じる to close
へいてんじかん
閉店時間 a store's closing
time

かいへい
開閉 opening and closing
へいさ
閉鎖 closure
みっぺい
密閉 tightly shut

｜ 「 「 「 「 「 門 門 門 閉 閉 閉   11

942

ON-KUN READINGS: ヘイ

HEADER: 阝

陛

his or her majesty

ORIGIN: The left side 阝 was a pictograph of a dirt wall or a hill. The right side depicted two people standing next to each other, facing in the same direction, putting things in order. With the addition of 土 soil the kanji indicated stairs, specifically stairs in an imperial palace. The kanji 陛 means "his or her majesty."

へいか
陛下 his or her majesty
りょうへいか
両陛下 their majesties

' 了 阝 阝' 阡 陟 陛 陛 陛 陛   10

943

ON-KUN READINGS: ベイ・マイ・こめ

HEADER: 米

米

rice; America

米 → 米   米

ORIGIN: The ancient form was a depiction of rice scattered in all directions. In old times, America was written phonetically as 亜米利加; the stressed syllable /me/ became a reduced form, as in 米国. The kanji 米 means "rice" or "America."

こめ
米 rice
しんまい
新米 new crop of rice,
beginner
べいこく
米国 U.S.A.

しんべい
親米 pro-American
はんべいてき
反米的 anti-American
にちべいかんけい
日米関係 Japan–U.S.
relationship

丶 丷 丷 半 米 米   6

944

ON-KUN READINGS: ベツ・わか(れる)

HEADER: 刂

別

to separate

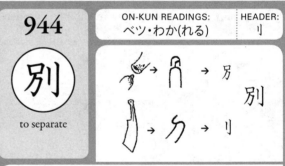

ORIGIN: In the ancient form the left side was a variant form of 骨 "bone." The right side 刂 was a knife. Together 別 indicated "to cut bones with a knife; to disassemble," and further indicated something separate. Now the kanji 別 means "to separate."

べつ
別に～ない not particularly
わか
別れる to separate
べつべつ
別々に separately

べつ
別にする to put separately
かくべつ
格別に exceptional
べつびん
別便 by separate mail

丨 冂 冂 号 另 別 別   7

945

ON-KUN READINGS: ヘン・か(わる)　HEADER: 夂

変

strange; extraordinary

ORIGIN: The old form 變 had two threads that couldn't be untangled even with the use of a knife. The bottom 夂 indicated an action in general. Together they signified a state that was not normal. In the current form, the top was replaced with 亦. The kanji 変 means "strange; extraordinary."

へん
変な strange
たいへん
大変な tough, hectic
へんか
変化 change, transition

か
変わる to change
へんどう
変動 fluctuation
こころが
心変わり change of mind

' 亠 ナ 亣 ホ 亦 麥 麥 変　9

946

ON-KUN READINGS: ヘン・かた　HEADER: 片

片

one side; piece

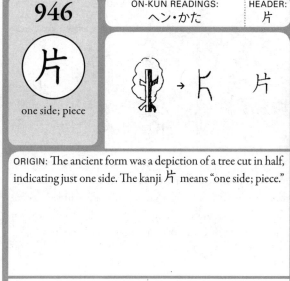

ORIGIN: The ancient form was a depiction of a tree cut in half, indicating just one side. The kanji 片 means "one side; piece."

かたほう
片方 one side
いっぺん
一片の of one piece
かた　ばし
片っ端から one by one

だんぺんてき
断片的な fragmental
かたとき
片時も even for a moment
かたて
片手 one hand

丿 丿' 广 片　4

947

ON-KUN READINGS: ヘン・あ(む)　HEADER: 糸

編

to arrange; to edit; to knit; book

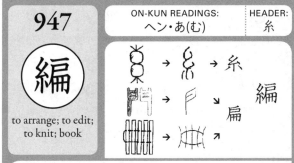

ORIGIN: The left side 糸 signified threads or strings. The right side 扁 consisted of a door and thin pieces of writing tablets that were bound with a string into books. Together the kanji 編 means "to arrange; to edit; to knit" or "book."

あ
編む to knit
あ　もの
編み物 knitting
へんしゅう
編集 editing

たんぺんしょうせつ
短編小説 short story
じゅうりょうへんせい
十両編成 ten-car train
へんきょく
編曲 music arrangement

く 幺 幺 糸 糸 糸 糸' 紀 紆 絈 絹 絹 絹 編 編　15

948

ON-KUN READINGS: ヘン・あた(り)・べ　HEADER: 辶

辺

around; peripheral; edge

ORIGIN: The ancient form of 邊 had 自 "nose" (or "self"); 丙 "square table," and 方 "four directions," signifying spreading to all directions. The bottom, 辶, was "to go forward." Together the kanji indicated the peripheral as opposed to the center (oneself). Now with the top replaced by 刀, the kanji 辺 means "peripheral" or "around."

へん
この辺 in the area, around here
あた
その辺り around there
しゅうへん
周辺 surrounding area

へんきょう
辺境 remote region
しんぺん
身辺 one's safety or affairs
みずべ
水辺 waterside

フ 刀 刀 辺 辺　5

273

949

ON-KUN READINGS: ヘン・かえ(す)

HEADER: 辶

返

to return

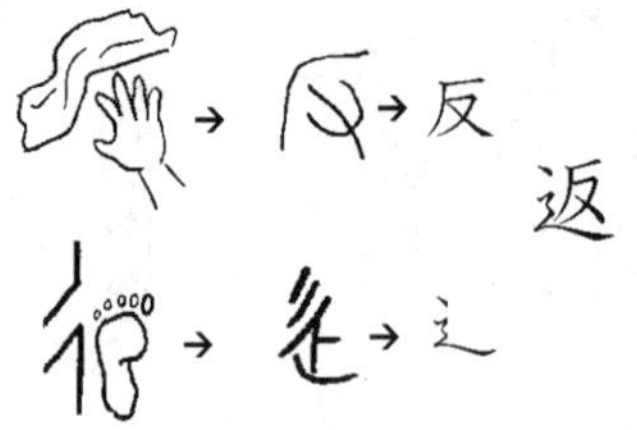

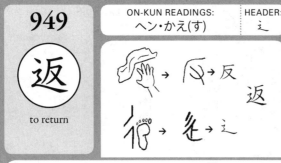

ORIGIN: In the ancient form the right top 反 depicted the motion of a hand pushing a cloth back. The bottom left 辶 came from 辵 "a foot in a crossroad" and signified "to go beyond" or "to move forward." Together they indicated to move something back. The kanji 返 means "to return."

- 返事 (へんじ) reply
- お返し (かえ) return gift
- 返信 (へんしん) reply letter
- 返品 (へんぴん) return of merchandise
- 返還 (へんかん) return
- 折り返し運転 (お かえ うんてん) shuttle service

一 厂 万 反 反 坂 返 — 7

950

ON-KUN READINGS: ベン・ビン・たよ(り)

HEADER: イ

便

service; convenient

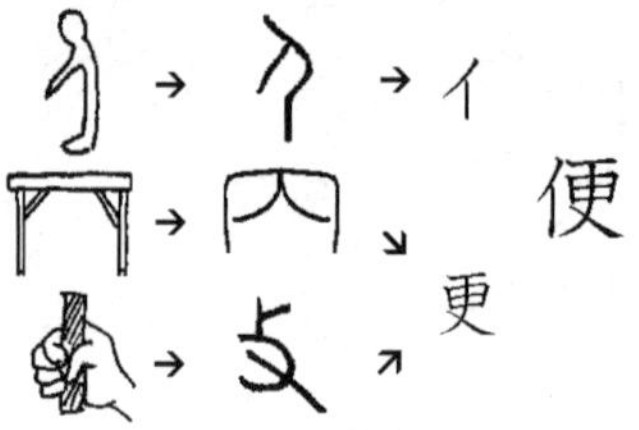

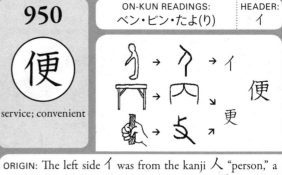

ORIGIN: The left side イ was from the kanji 人 "person," a side view of a person standing. The right side 更 consisted of a table and a tool in hand, here phonetically used to indicate "service." Together they indicated using a servant or having the convenience of a servant. The kanji 便 means "service" or "convenient."

- 便 (べん) convenience, stool
- 便利 (べんり) convenient, useful
- 不便 (ふべん) inconvenient
- 便所 (べんじょ) toilet
- 穏便に (おんびん) amicably, privately
- 宅配便 (たくはいびん) home delivery service
- 便り (たよ) letter

ノ イ 亻 仁 亻 佰 佰 俥 便 — 9

951

ON-KUN READINGS: ベン・つと(める)

HEADER: 力

勉

exerting oneself

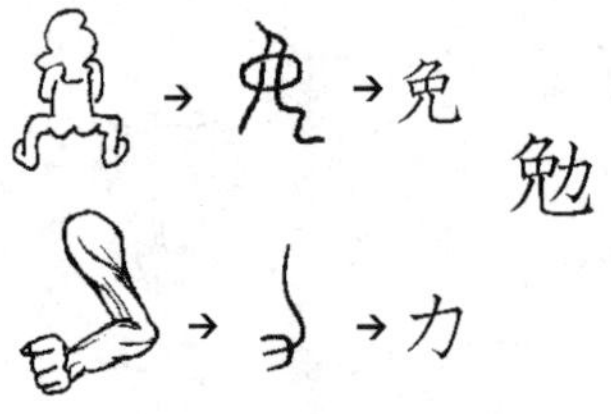

ORIGIN: The left side 免 depicted a woman straining in labor but eventually managing to give birth, signifying "something barely going through." The right side 力 signified strength or power. The kanji 勉 means "applying strength to try hard."

- 勉強する (べんきょう) to study, to sell at low price
- 勤勉な (きんべん) diligent
- 勉学 (べんがく) study
- 不勉強 (ふべんきょう) idle, not well studied

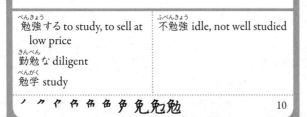

ノ ク ク 各 各 色 免 免 勉 勉 — 10

952

ON-KUN READINGS: ベン

HEADER: 廾

弁

speech; flower petal; valve

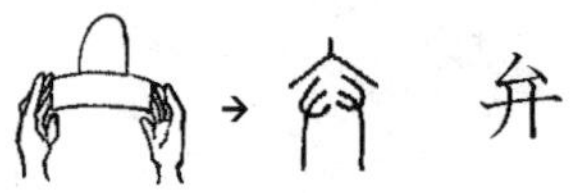

ORIGIN: The kanji 弁 depicted a man putting his hat over his head with both hands. This kanji 弁 came to be used for various meanings as a simplified form that had no relevance to its original meaning. These include (a) "speech" from "argue in court" 辯 and "dialect"; and (b) "flower petal" or "valve" from 瓣.

- 弁当 (べんとう) box lunch
- 弁解 (べんかい) excuse
- 弁護士 (べんごし) lawyer
- 関西弁 (かんさいべん) Kansai dialect
- 弁 (べん) valve
- 多弁 (たべん) talkative

ㄙ ム 厶 弁 弁 — 5

953

保
to keep

保

ORIGIN: The left side イ was a recurring component from the kanji 人 "person," a side view of a person standing. The right side was an infant wrapped in a blanket or diaper. Together they indicated that a person cares for, or keeps, a baby. The kanji 保 means "to keep."

保つ to hold
健康保険証 health insurance card
保温 keeping warm, thermal

保母 kindergarten teacher
保存 to preserve, keep
保管 custody, storage

ノ イ イ 仔 仔 仔 仔 仔 保保　9

954

歩
to walk; step

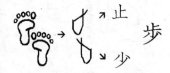

歩

ORIGIN: In the ancient form the top 止 depicted a left foot, and the bottom 少 depicted a right foot. One walks by moving the right foot and left foot alternately. The kanji 歩 means "step," or "to walk."

歩く to walk
散歩 walk
一歩 one step

歩道 sidewalk
歩む to walk
歩合で for a commission

1 上 止 止 歩 歩 歩 歩　8

275

955

補
to fill a gap; to compensate for

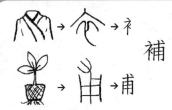

補

ORIGIN: The left side ネ was from 衣 "clothes," from layers of collars around a neckline. The right side 甫 was a young rice plant whose damaged roots were protected. Together they indicated mending clothes or filling a gap. The kanji 補 means "to fill a gap" or "to compensate for."

補う to complement
補給 replenishment
補足 supplementation

補欠 alternate
補充する to replenish
補助 assistance

` ラ オ ネ ネ ネ 袻 袻 袻 補補　12

956

募
to recruit people; to raise money

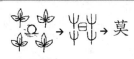

募

ORIGIN: The upper part 莫 "to disappear" was only used phonetically to indicate "to gather." The bottom 力 was flexing muscles, indicating strength. Together they indicated hands gathering people or money. The kanji 募 means "to recruit (people)" or "to raise money."

募る to collect
募集 recruitment, invitation
募金 fundraising

応募 application
公募 open application
急募 urgent recruit

一 十 艹 艹 苜 苜 苜 莫 莫 募募　12

957

ON-KUN READINGS:	HEADER:
ボ・はか	土

墓
tomb; grave

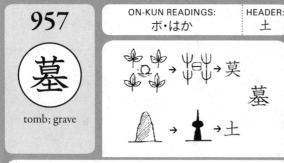

ORIGIN: The upper part, had a sun setting in overgrown grasses, which signified something disappearing. A tomb buries someone who has disappeared into the soil (土). The kanji 墓 means "tomb; grave."

はか 墓 tomb, grave
ぼち 墓地 cemetery
はかまい 墓参り・墓参 ぼさん visit to a cemetery

はかいし 墓石 gravestone
ぼしょ 墓所 burial ground
ぼぜん 墓前に in front of a tomb

一十艹艹艿芇苎苩莫莫墓墓墓　13

958

ON-KUN READINGS:	HEADER:
ボ・く(れる)	日

暮
sunset; end of a year

ORIGIN: The upper part 莫 had a sun setting in overgrown grasses, which signified something disappearing. Underneath is another sun. Together they indicated the time when the sun disappears, either at the end of the day or in winter (when the sun does not shine much). The kanji 暮 means "sunset" or "end of a year."

くれ 暮 end of a year
ゆうぐ 夕暮れ dusk
せいぼ お歳暮 end-of-year gift

ひぐ 日暮れ sunset
ぼしょく 暮色 twilight

一十艹艹艿芇苎苩莫莫募暮暮暮　14

959

ON-KUN READINGS:	HEADER:
ボ・はは	母

母
mother

ORIGIN: The ancient form was a pictograph of a nursing mother (with an exaggeration of the breasts, suggesting nursing and motherhood). The kanji 母 means "mother." (The two kanji 母 and 女 share a similar origin.)

かあ お母さん mother
母親 ははおや mother
ふぼ 父母 parents
そぼ 祖母 grandmother

ぼこく 母国 native country
ははかた 母方 maternal side
おもや 母屋 main house

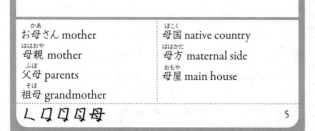　5

960

ON-KUN READINGS:	HEADER:
ホウ・つつ(む)	勹

包
to wrap

ORIGIN: The upper part 勹 depicted a person viewed sideways. Inside was a baby in a fetal position, the old form of which showed a head in 巳, instead of 己. Together they signified "to wrap around." The kanji 包 means "to wrap."

こづつみ 小包 small package, parcel
つつ 包む to wrap
ほうちょう 包丁 kitchen knife (from 庖丁)

つつ がみ 包み紙 wrapping paper
ほうたい 包帯 dressing, bandage
ほうかつてき 包括的 comprehensive

ノ勹勹匀包　5

961

ON-KUN READINGS: ホウ・むく(いる)
HEADER: 土

報

to report; to repay; to reward

ORIGIN: The ancient form had depicted handcuffs and a person kneeling pushed by a hand from behind, together indicating a criminal being punished for a crime. The punishment was reported to a higher authority. The left side 幸 has the meaning of "reversal of misfortune." The meaning of a criminal "to repay" for his crime also became reversed to mean "to reward." The kanji 報 means "to report; to repay; to reward."

報告 report
天気予報 weather forecast
報いる to reward, to repay

報復攻撃 retaliatory attack
報道 media, report
誤報 incorrect report

一 十 土 キ 去 去 圭 幸 幸 報 報 報 — 12

962

ON-KUN READINGS: ホウ・たから
HEADER: 宀

宝

treasure

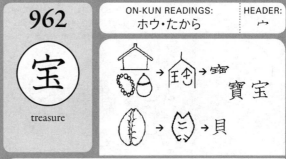

ORIGIN: The old form 寶 indicated that inside 宀 "house," there were 王 "jewelry," 缶 "container for valuable things," and 貝 "cowry," a rare shell used as currency. Together they indicated "treasure." Now reduced to a house with jewelry inside, the kanji 宝 still means "treasure."

宝物 treasure
宝くじ lottery
子宝 blessing of having a child

国宝 national treasure
宝物 highly prized treasure
家宝 heirloom

丶 丷 宀 宀 宀 宇 宝 宝 — 8

963

ON-KUN READINGS: ホウ・はな(す)
HEADER: 攵

放

to emit; to release

ORIGIN: The left side was 方 "four directions," and the right side was 攵, a hand pounding a stick, signifying an action in general. Together they showed an act of releasing something from constraint, freely into all directions. The kanji 放 means "to release" or "to emit."

放送 broadcasting
放す to release
開放する to release

見放す to abandon
放置する to neglect
放火 arson

丶 亠 方 方 扩 扩 放 放 — 8

964

ON-KUN READINGS: ホウ・かた
HEADER: 方

方

direction; a square; person [honorific]

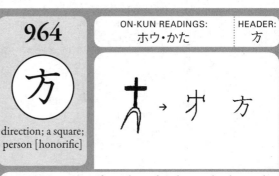

ORIGIN: The ancient form showed a plow with a long sideways handle. The handle and the top and bottom point to four directions; pulling something in four directions forms a square. Referring only to the direction in which someone is situated is a form of honorific expression. The kanji 方 means "direction; square; person [honorific]."

その方 [honorific] the person
その方 that choice
両方 both

方向 direction
先生方 [honorific] teachers
地方 locality

丶 亠 方 方 — 4

277

965

ON-KUN READINGS: ホウ・ハッ・ホッ・のり
HEADER: 氵

法
law

ORIGIN: In the old form 灋, 氵 was water and the right side indicated "to enclose," from an imaginary animal forced inside a tight-lidded container, 去. The kanji signified rules and laws that restrict people. Now the right side is reduced to the bottom 去. The kanji 法 means "law."

ほうほう
方法 method, means
ほうりつ
法律 law
いほう
違法 illegal

ほうりついはん
法律違反 illegal
ほうがい
法外な absurd
ほうじ
法事 Buddhist memorial service

丶 氵 氵 汁 洼 法法 8

966

ON-KUN READINGS: ホウ・おとず(れる)・たず(ねる)
HEADER: 言

訪
to visit

ORIGIN: 言 was a tattoo needle and a mouth 口, signifying "to speak clearly and sharply" or "word." 方 was a plow with a long sideways handle. The handles and the top and bottom pointed to four directions. People ask for directions when they visit a new place. The kanji 訪 means "to visit."

ほうもん
訪問 visit
おとず
訪れる to visit
ほうにち
訪日 visit to Japan

ほうべい
訪米 visit to the U.S.A.
らいほう
来訪 coming to visit

丶 亠 亠 言 言 言 訁 訪 訪訪 11

967

ON-KUN READINGS: ホウ・ゆた(か)
HEADER: 豆

豊
abundant; rich

ORIGIN: The old form 豐 came from the pictograph of stalks of broomcorn millet, freshly harvested, in a food container. It signified the abundance of harvest placed on an altar. Now the top part is somewhat reduced, and the kanji 豊 means "abundant; rich."

ゆた
豊かな rich
ゆた
豊かさ abundance
ほうふ
豊富 abundance

ほうさく
豊作 good harvest
ほうねん
豊年 a year of good harvest
ほうまん
豊満 plump, fleshy

丨 口 曲 曲 曲 曲 典 典 豊 豊 豊 豊 豊 13

968

ON-KUN READINGS: ボウ・モウ・な(くなる)・うしな(う)・ほろ(びる)
HEADER: 亠

亡
to pass away; to die

ORIGIN: The ancient form was a pictograph of a person disappearing behind a screen. One disappears when one dies. The kanji 亡 means "to pass away" or "to die."

な
亡くなる to pass away
しぼう
死亡 death
みぼうじん
未亡人 widow
ほろ
亡びる to fall, become extinct

ぼうれい
亡霊 departed spirit
めつぼう
滅亡 downfall
ぼうめい
亡命 defection, political asylum

丶 亠 亡 3

278

969

ON-KUN READINGS: ボウ・わす(れる)

HEADER: 心

忘
to forget

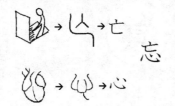

ORIGIN: The top 亡 depicted a person hidden behind a screen, signifying "to disappear," or "to lose." The bottom 心 is the anatomical shape of a heart with an artery. Together they indicated that a memory was lost. The kanji 忘 means "to forget."

わす
忘れる to forget
ぼうねんかい
忘年会 end-of-the-year party
わす　もの
忘れ物 lost-and-found item

ものわす
物忘れ slip of memory
けんぼうしょう
健忘症 forgetful
ぼうきゃく
忘却 oblivion, forgetfulness

丶 亠 亡 亡 忘 忘 忘　7

970

ON-KUN READINGS: ボウ・いそが(しい)

HEADER: 忄

忙
busy

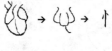

ORIGIN: The left 忄 was a variant of "heart," and the right side 亡 meant "disappear." Together they originally indicated the state of one being stupefied. Later the kanji came to be used to indicate the state that one was absent-minded because one was so busy. The kanji 忙 means "busy."

いそが
忙しい busy
たぼう
多忙 busyness
ぼうさつ
忙殺される to be swamped
　with work

ぼうちゅう
忙中 in the midst of a busy
　life

丶 丶 忄 忄 忙 忙　6

⟨279⟩

971

ON-KUN READINGS: ボウ・バク・あば(れる)・あば(く)

HEADER: 日

暴
to expose; violent

ORIGIN: The ancient form had 日 "sun," two hands, and 氺 "animal." It depicted an act using two hands to skin an animal for fur under the sun. Skinning an animal was a violent act and the carcass was left exposed to the sun. The kanji 暴 means "to expose," or "violent."

ぼうふうう
暴風雨 rainstorm
あば
暴れる to act violently
らんぼう
乱暴な violent
ぼうりょく
暴力 violence

あば
暴く to expose
ばくろ
暴露 exposure, debunking
ぼうどう
暴動 riot
ぼうらく
暴落 crash

丶 冂 冃 日 旦 早 昃 昃 昃 昃 暴 暴 暴 暴 暴　15

972

ON-KUN READINGS: ボウ・モウ・のぞ(む)

HEADER: 月

望
to wish; to overlook (view)

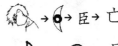

ORIGIN: The left top 亡 was originally 臣 "watchful eye"; the right top was 月 "moon." The bottom depicted a man standing on tiptoe, looking into the distance. The kanji 望 means "to look over (to view)" or "to wish."

きぼう
希望 hope
のぞ
望み a hope, a desire
しぼう
志望 a desire, a wish

ぜつぼうてき
絶望的 desperate, hopeless
しつぼう
失望する to feel disappointed
ほんもう
本望 long-cherished desire

丶 亠 亡 亡 亡 朌 胡 胡 朚 望 望 望　11

973

ON-KUN READINGS: ボウ

HEADER: 木

棒

club; pole

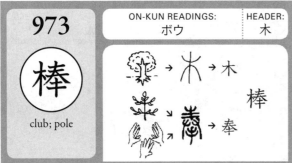

ORIGIN: The left side 木 was a tree. The right side 奉, "revere," used phonetically, depicted three (or many) hands holding a tree 丰, which was growing high, toward the gods. Together it indicated something that extended a long way. In Japan this kanji was also used for a partner who helped to bear the poles of of a palanquin (a covered litter). The kanji 棒 means "club; pole."

棒 stick
相棒 partner
棒読み reading without emotion
棒グラフ bar graph
丸太ん棒 log
泥棒 thief

一 十 十 木 术 村 柞 杼 棒 棒 棒 棒　12

974

ON-KUN READINGS: ボウ

HEADER: 貝

貿

to trade

ORIGIN: In the ancient form the top came depicted a bit in a horse's mouth viewed from the front and was used phonetically to indicate "to scheme." The bottom 貝 "cowry" signified "money." Together they meant to try to make a profit by moving merchandise, or to trade merchandize. The kanji 貿 means "to trade."

貿易 trade
貿易収支 trade balance
自由貿易 free trade
保護貿易 protective trade
貿易風 trade wind

′ ⺊ ⺍ 丿 ⺗ ⺗ 卯 留 貿 貿 貿 貿　12

975

ON-KUN READINGS: ボウ・ふせ(ぐ)

HEADER: 阝

防

to defend; to prevent

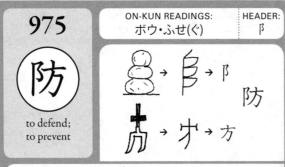

ORIGIN: The left side 阝 was an earthen wall that surrounded a house. The right side 方 signified four directions. Together they indicated defending all directions by building a wall. The kanji 防 means "to defend; to prevent."

防ぐ to protect
予防 prevention
防止 prevention
防御 defense
国防 national defense
消防団 fire brigade

⻖ ⻖ ⻖ ⻖ ⻖ 防 防　7

976

ON-KUN READINGS: ホク・きた

HEADER: 匕

北

north; to be defeated

ORIGIN: The ancient form depicted two people sitting back to back because their relationship was cold. It also indicated that two people were running away, showing their backs after losing a battle. The side opposite to the sunny south side is north. The kanji 北 means "north" or "to be defeated."

北 north
北米 North America
北海道 Hokkaido
東北地方 the Tohoku region
敗北 loss in a game or battle
北斗七星 the Big Dipper

一 十 キ 北 北　5

280

977

ON-KUN READINGS: ボク | HEADER: イ

僕

I [male speaker]; servant

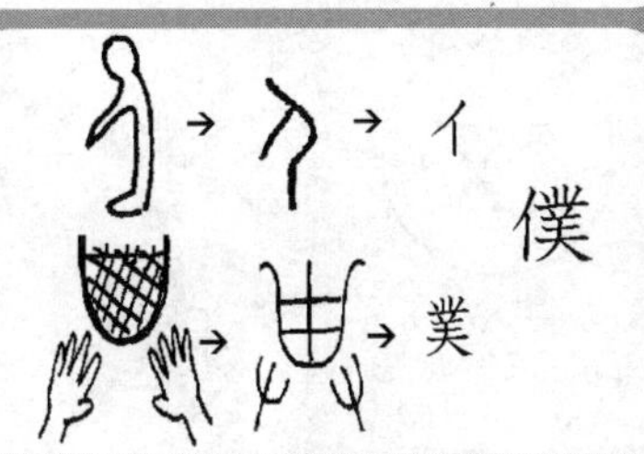

ORIGIN: The left side イ was a person. The right side depicted a basket held by two hands. Someone who held a basket was a servant or a low-level official. From the meaning of low rank, this form was also used by a male speaker when referring to himself in the humble style. The kanji 僕 means "servant" or "I" (when used by a male speaker).

僕 (ぼく) I (first person) [used by a male speaker]
公僕 (こうぼく) public servant
下僕 (げぼく) manservant

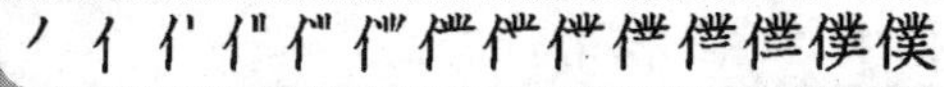
14

978

ON-KUN READINGS: ボク・まき | HEADER: 牜

牧

pasture

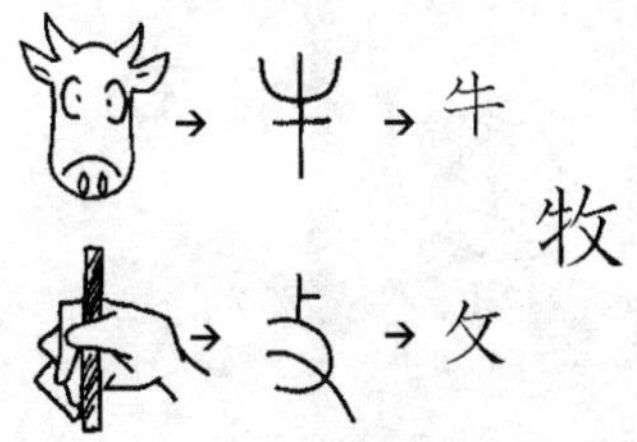

ORIGIN: The left side 牜 showed a cow's head with horns sticking out. The right side 攵 depicted the motion of hitting or pounding repeatedly with a stick, signifying an action or activity in general. Together they meant to herd cattle (or a place where cattle graze). The kanji 牧 means "pasture."

牧場 (ぼくじょう) ranch
牧草 (ぼくそう) pasture
牧師 (ぼくし) pastor
牧場 (まきば) pasture
放牧する (ほうぼく) to graze
牧歌的 (ぼっかてき) pastoral, idyllic

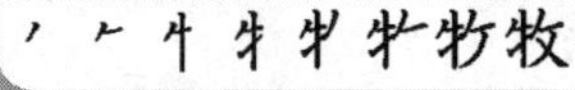
8

979

ON-KUN READINGS: ホン・もと | HEADER: 木

本

source; origin; book; counter for long object

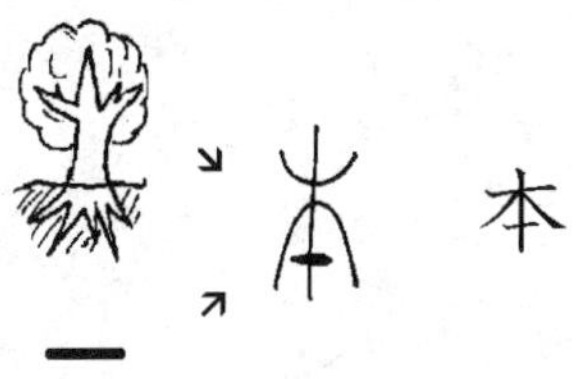

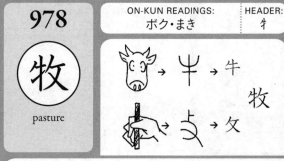

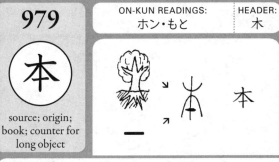

ORIGIN: The ancient form depicted a tree with its roots emphasized, where a tree originated. The kanji 本 means "source; origin; book (source of knowledge)." It is also used as a counter for a long object.

本 (ほん) book
本屋 (ほんや) bookstore
日本 (にほん) Japan
ペン三本 (さんぼん) three pens
本気 (ほんき) serious
本人 (ほんにん) the person himself or herself

一十才木本 5

980

ON-KUN READINGS: ボン・ハン | HEADER: 几

凡

covering all; ordinary

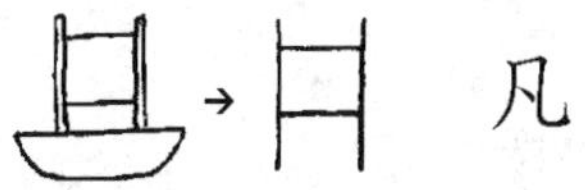

ORIGIN: The ancient form depicted a sail on a boat. The first two strokes are the same as those of 風 "wind." How it came to mean "all" or "ordinary" is unclear. The kanji 凡 means "covering all; ordinary."

平凡な (へいぼん) common
凡人 (ぼんじん) ordinary person
凡そ (およ) roughly
凡例 (はんれい) explanatory notes
非凡な (ひぼん) extraordinary
凡庸 (ぼんよう) mediocrity

ノ 几凡 3

981

ON-KUN READINGS: マイ・いもうと

HEADER: 女

妹

younger sister

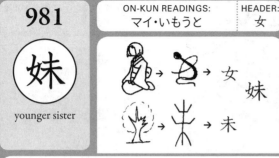

ORIGIN: The left side 女 was a woman sitting. In 未 on the right side, the short stroke at the top indicated that the top of a tree was yet to grow. A female person not fully grown is considered a younger sister. The kanji 妹 means "younger sister."

いもうと
妹 younger sister
しまい
姉妹 sisters
ていまい
弟妹 younger siblings

じつまい
実妹 real sister
ぎまい
義妹 sister-in-law

く タ 女 女 女 妹 妹 妹   8

982

ON-KUN READINGS: マイ

HEADER: 木

枚

counter for a flat, thin object such as paper or cloth

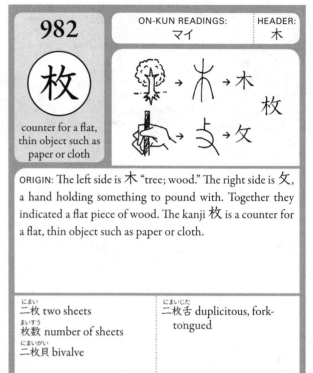

ORIGIN: The left side is 木 "tree; wood." The right side is 攵, a hand holding something to pound with. Together they indicated a flat piece of wood. The kanji 枚 is a counter for a flat, thin object such as paper or cloth.

にまい
二枚 two sheets
まいすう
枚数 number of sheets
にまいがい
二枚貝 bivalve

にまいじた
二枚舌 duplicitous, fork-tongued

一 十 オ オ 木 朴 杉 枚   8

983

ON-KUN READINGS: マイ・ごと

HEADER: 母

毎

every

ORIGIN: The ancient form, shown in the middle, was phonetically used to indicate "to work busily." It was also a variant form of "mother." A mother can bear children one after another, so the kanji signified repetition of the same event. The kanji 毎 means "every."

まいしゅう
毎週 every week
まいにち
毎日 every day
まいつき
毎月 every month

まいかい
毎回 every time
みっかごと
三日毎に every three days
まいとし
毎年 every year

ノ 𠂉 ト 匃 毎 毎   6

984

ON-KUN READINGS: バク・マク

HEADER: 巾

幕

curtain; drapery

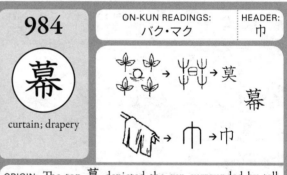

ORIGIN: The top 莫 depicted the sun surrounded by tall grasses that were making the sun invisible at sunset. Underneath was a hanging cloth. Together they indicated a cloth that hid something. The kanji 幕 means "curtain; drapery."

まく
幕 curtain
ばくまつ
幕末 the end of the Tokugawa era
じまく
字幕 subtitle

てんまく
天幕 tent, marquee
ぎんまく
銀幕 silver screen, movie
じょまくしき
除幕式 unveiling ceremony

一 十 艹 艹 莒 莒 苩 苩 草 莫 莫 幕 幕   13

985

ON-KUN READINGS:	HEADER:
また	又

又
again

ORIGIN: The ancient form was a pictograph of a right hand. This kanji was used for various meanings that use a hand, including a "right hand" and "to possess; to help; to repeat." The current meaning of the kanji 又 is "again."

又 again
又は alternatively
又聞き hearsay

又いとこ second cousin
又貸し sublease

フ又

2

986

ON-KUN READINGS:	HEADER:
マツ・バツ・すえ	木

末
end

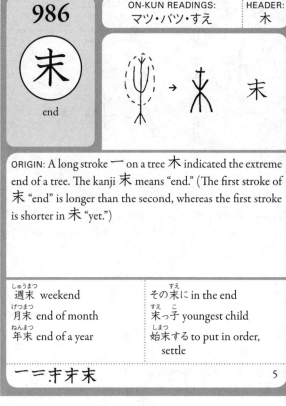

ORIGIN: A long stroke 一 on a tree 木 indicated the extreme end of a tree. The kanji 末 means "end." (The first stroke of 末 "end" is longer than the second, whereas the first stroke is shorter in 未 "yet.")

週末 weekend
月末 end of month
年末 end of a year

その末に in the end
末っ子 youngest child
始末する to put in order, settle

一二キ末末

5

283

987

ON-KUN READINGS:	HEADER:
マン・バン・よろず	一

万
ten thousand; all

ORIGIN: The original kanji 萬 came from a depiction of a scorpion, used phonetically. For a long time in Buddhism, the kanji 万 has been used as a variant of 卍 called *manji*, an ancient symbol of good fortune or happiness. It came to its current meaning phonetically. The kanji 万 means "ten thousand."

三万円 30,000 yen
百万人 a million people
万事 everything

万の all
万全の taking all possible measures
万歳 banzai cheer

一フ万

3

988

ON-KUN READINGS:	HEADER:
マン・み(ちる)	氵

満
full; to be filled

ORIGIN: In the old form 滿, 氵 was "water," and the right side depicted the conjoined halves of two dried gourds (phonetically, "full"). Together they indicated "to be filled with water." The kanji 満 means "full" or "to be filled."

満ちる to be filled with
満月 full moon
満員 full house

満員電車 jam-packed train
満足 satisfaction
不満 dissatisfaction

丶丶丶氵汀汁沸沸満満満満

12

989

ON-KUN READINGS: ミ・あじ
HEADER: 口

味
taste

ORIGIN: The ancient form had 口 "mouth" and 未 "yet" (from a tree 木 yet to grow.) The top stroke is short, meant to indicate that something is yet to grow. Similarly, tasting food in one's mouth is the process of trying to figure out what it is. It is yet to be determined. So, the kanji 味 means "taste."

味 taste
あじ

興味 interest
きょうみ

趣味 hobby
しゅみ

味方 ally
みかた

賞味期限 food expiration date
しょうみきげん

美味しい tasty
おい

ノ 口 口 ロー 旷 吽 昧 味   8

990

ON-KUN READINGS: ミ・ま（だ）・いま（だ）
HEADER: 木

未
yet

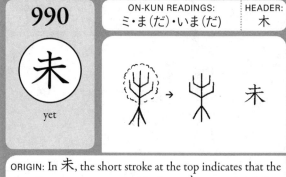

ORIGIN: In 未, the short stroke at the top indicates that the top of a tree is yet to grow. The kanji 未 means "yet." (On the other hand, the first stroke of 末 "end" is longer than the second, contrasting its meaning.)

未だに not yet
いま

未だ not yet
ま

未来 future
みらい

未開 primitive
みかい

未経験 inexperienced
みけいけん

未明 daybreak
みめい

一 二 キ 末 未   5

991

ON-KUN READINGS: ミツ
HEADER: 宀

密
dense; secret

ORIGIN: The top 宀 was a house (or sacred place). The middle part 必 depicted 戈 "lance" strapped tightly between two poles, stored away and closely fitted, thus "dense." The bottom, now 山, originally came from fire, which suggested the power of a secret ritual. The kanji 蜜 means "dense" or "secret."

秘密 secret
ひみつ

密かに secretly
ひそ

密談 secret talk
みつだん

密集した cramped
みっしゅう

密約 secret agreement
みつやく

密接な close
みっせつ

親密な intimate
しんみつ

丶 宀 宀 宀 宓 宓 宓 宓 宓 密 密   11

992

ON-KUN READINGS: ミャク
HEADER: 月

脈
vein; pulse

ORIGIN: The left side 月 came from 肉 "flesh with muscles" and pertains to a body part. The right side depicted tributaries, indicating things branching out into different groups. Together they indicated veins. The kanji 脈 means "vein," and has also come to mean "pulse."

脈 pulse
みゃく

山脈 mountain ranges
さんみゃく

動脈 artery
どうみゃく

人脈 network of personal contacts
じんみゃく

文脈 context
ぶんみゃく

脈動 pulsation
みゃくどう

丿 月 月 月 肝 胈 胈 脈 脈 脈   10

284

993

民
people

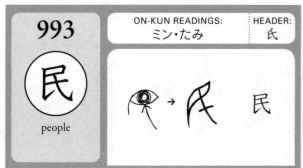

ORIGIN: The ancient form depicted an eye pierced with a needle to make someone blind, symbolizing someone who must do things against his or her will. It indicated "ordinary people" who do not see things or express their own judgment or view under a ruler. Now the kanji 民 just means "people."

国民 people
民主主義 democracy
市民 citizen

民 people
民宿 family-run inn
移民 immigrant, immigration

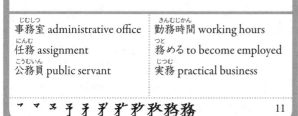
5

994

眠
to sleep

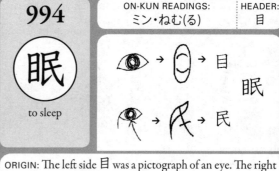

ORIGIN: The left side 目 was a pictograph of an eye. The right side 民 came from an eye pierced with a needle to blind it, indicating a slave, that is, someone who is ruled blindly. A closed eye is asleep. The kanji 眠 means "to sleep."

睡眠 sleep
眠る to sleep
仮眠を取る to take a nap

眠気 drowsiness
眠たい sleepy
不眠症 insomnia

｜ 冂 冂 𠃌 目 目' 目" 眠 眠 眠
10

285

995

務
to work on; duty; mission

ORIGIN: The left side was 矛 "halberd," a weapon or something that intimidated. The upper right side was 攵, which depicted repeated pounding with a stick, or an "action in general." The bottom right was 力, a "strong hand." Together they indicated that one was forced to work, or "duty; work." The kanji 務 means "to work," or "duty; mission."

事務室 administrative office
任務 assignment
公務員 public servant

勤務時間 working hours
務める to become employed
実務 practical business

フ マ ヌ 予 矛 矛 矛 矜 矜 務 務
11

996

夢
dream

ORIGIN: In the old form, the top depicted a medium, whose eyebrows were drawn on thick (signified by the top 艹), praying in a trance at an ancestral altar. The bottom 夕 indicated night. A dream was believed to be in a prayerful trance that happened at night. The kanji 夢 means "dream."

夢 dream
夢中で frantically, in a trance
悪夢 nightmare

正夢 dream that comes true

一 十 艹 芦 苧 苧 莳 莳 芦 芦 夢 夢 夢
13

997

nothing; to not exist

ON-KUN READINGS: ム・ブ・な(い)

HEADER: 灬

ORIGIN: The ancient form originally depicted a person dancing with heavily adorned long sleeves for a religious ceremony. It took on the meaning of a phonetically similar word, "nothing," and a new kanji, 舞 "dance," which incorporates 舛 "footsteps" at the bottom, was created for "to dance." The kanji 無 means "nothing" or "to not exist."

な 無い none	ぶなん 無難な cruel
むり 無理 unreasonable	むだ 無駄な wasteful
ぶじ 無事 safety	むしょく 無職 having no job

ノ ヶ 二 壬 缶 缶 毎 無 無 無 無 無　12

998

娘

daughter; young woman

ON-KUN READINGS: むすめ

HEADER: 女

ORIGIN: The left side 女 was a woman. The right side 良 depicted a process in which rice was washed in water to remove dust, thereby leaving only the best grains in the basket. The kanji 娘 means "daughter; young woman." (This was originally a reduced form for 嬢, as in お嬢さん.)

むすめ 娘 daughter	はこい むすめ 箱入り娘 a girl raised in a 　protective, good family
こむすめ 小娘 young girl	むすめごころ
まごむすめ 孫娘 granddaughter	娘心 girlish innocence

く タ タ 女 如 奻 娂 娘 娘 娘　10

999

名

name; reputation; pretext; people counter[honorific]

ON-KUN READINGS: メイ・ミョウ・な

HEADER: 口

ORIGIN: The ancient form was a pictograph of a crescent moon in the early evening 夕. A crescent moon at dusk is in a dim light. A mouth 口 symbolized someone calling someone's name to identify him or her at dusk. It is also used as an honorific counter for people. The kanji 名 means "name; reputation; pretext."

なまえ 名前 name	だいみょう 大名 feudal lord
ゆうめい 有名 famous	せいめい 姓名 surname and given 　name
しめい 氏名 full name	みょうじ 名字 family name

ノ ク タ 夕 名 名　6

1000

命

life; order

ON-KUN READINGS: メイ・ミョウ・いのち

HEADER: 人

ORIGIN: The top 亼 indicated gathering people in one place. In the bottom, 口 was a mouth, and 卩 depicted a person kneeling. Together they meant people gathered to hear the words of a superior or god—words that govern peoples' lives. The kanji 命 means "life; order."

いのち 命 life	しめい 使命 mission
めいれい 命令 order	めいにち 命日 the anniversary of 　someone's death
いっしょうけんめい 一生懸命に with all of one's strength	よめい 余命 remainder of one's life

ノ 人 亼 亼 合 合 合 命 命　8

1001

ON-KUN READINGS: メイ・ミョウ・あか(るい)・あ(く)・あき(らか)

HEADER: 日

明

bright; obvious; following; to become known

ORIGIN: The ancient form consisted of a window and a moon 月, indicating bright moonlight coming through a window. Later on, the left side was replaced by 日 "sun," for a bright light. The kanji 明 means "bright; clear; evident; following" or "to become known." A bright light brings out something in public, and makes it obvious. A new daybreak brings another day.

あか
明るい cheery, bright
あした・あす・みょうにち
明日・明日・明日 tomorrow
めいじ
明治 the Meiji Era (1968–1912)

せいめい
声明 declaration
明らかに clearly, obviously
ゆくえふめい
行方不明 missing, lost, unaccounted for

丨 冂 冃 日 日 明 明 明 明   8

1002

ON-KUN READINGS: メイ

HEADER: 皿

盟

promise; pledge; alliance

ORIGIN: The top 明 depicted moonlight coming in through a window at which an altar was placed. The bottom 皿 was an offering bowl filled with animal blood that was used in the rite of making a pledge (originally 血). Together they meant pledging or promising, or forming an alliance. The kanji 盟 means "pledge; promise; alliance."

こくさいれんめい
国際連盟 United Nations
どうめい
同盟 alliance
かめいこく
加盟国 member country

かめいてん
加盟店 member store
めいしゅ
盟主 leading power
めいやく
盟約 pledge, covenant

丨 冂 冃 日 日 明 明 明 明 盟 盟 盟 盟   13

287

1003

ON-KUN READINGS: メイ・まよ(う)

HEADER: 辶

迷

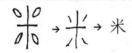

to get lost; to be perplexed

ORIGIN: The upper right 米 depicted rice grains scattered in all directions, here phonetically used to mean "too small to see." The bottom part 辶 indicated "forward-moving foot." Together they indicated losing one's way. The kanji 迷 means "to get lost; to be perplexed."

まよ
迷う to get lost
まいご
迷子 lost child
めいわく
迷惑 annoyance to others

めいろ
迷路 maze
ていめい
低迷 crawling low
めいそう
迷走 stray

丶 丷 丶 半 米 米 米 迷 迷   9

1004

ON-KUN READINGS: メイ・な(く)

HEADER: 鳥

鳴

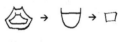

to chirp; making sound

ORIGIN: The left side 口 was a mouth. The right side 鳥 was a pictograph of a bird. The noise of a bird chirping also represented other sounds. The kanji 鳴 means "to chirp" or "making sound."

な
鳴く to chirp
きょうめい
共鳴 resonance
ひめい　あ
悲鳴を上げる to cry out

な　ものい
鳴り物入り with fanfare
らいめい
雷鳴 thunderbolt
めいどう
鳴動 rumbling

丨 口 口 口 叩 吖 吖 鸣 鸣 鳴 鳴 鳴 鳴 鳴   14

1005

ON-KUN READINGS: メン・まぬか(れる)

HEADER: 儿

免

to exempt from

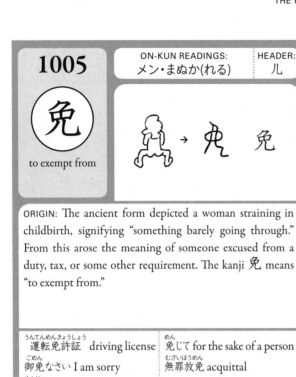

ORIGIN: The ancient form depicted a woman straining in childbirth, signifying "something barely going through." From this arose the meaning of someone excused from a duty, tax, or some other requirement. The kanji 免 means "to exempt from."

うんてんめんきょしょう
運転免許証 driving license
ごめん
御免なさい I am sorry
めんじょ
免除 exemption

めん
免じて for the sake of a person
むざいほうめん
無罪放免 acquittal

ノ ワ や 内 内 色 免 免　8

1006

ON-KUN READINGS: メン・わた

HEADER: 糸

綿

cotton

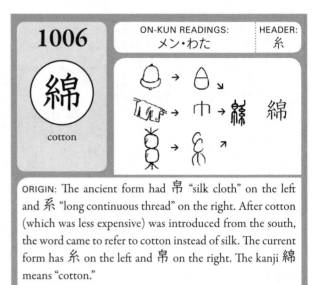

ORIGIN: The ancient form had 帛 "silk cloth" on the left and 系 "long continuous thread" on the right. After cotton (which was less expensive) was introduced from the south, the word came to refer to cotton instead of silk. The current form has 糸 on the left and 帛 on the right. The kanji 綿 means "cotton."

わた
綿 cotton
もめん
木綿 cotton
めんせいひん
綿製品 cotton product

めんか
綿花 raw cotton
だっしめん
脱脂綿 absorbent cotton
まわた
真綿 floss silk

く 幺 幺 糸 糸 糸 糸' 糸白 綿 綿 綿 綿 綿　14

1007

ON-KUN READINGS: メン・おも・おもて・つら

HEADER: 面

面

mask; face; phase; surface

ORIGIN: The ancient form highlighted the outline of a face, indicating a mask. Putting on a mask gives not only a new face to someone but also a new phase or surface to something. The kanji 面 means "mask; face; surface" or "phase."

めん
面 mask, aspect
おもしろ
面白い interesting, amusing
めんぼく
面目 honor, face

めんどう
面倒な troublesome
じめん
地面 the surface of the Earth
めんく
面食らう to be bewildered

一 ア 了 丙 而 而 面 面 面　9

1008

ON-KUN READINGS: ボ・モ

HEADER: 木

模

to model after

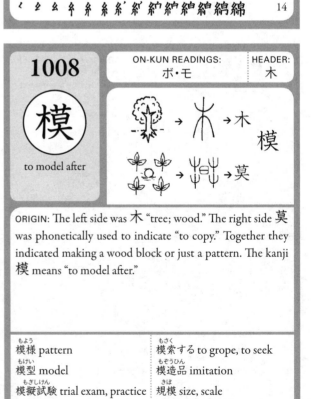

ORIGIN: The left side was 木 "tree; wood." The right side 莫 was phonetically used to indicate "to copy." Together they indicated making a wood block or just a pattern. The kanji 模 means "to model after."

もよう
模様 pattern
もけい
模型 model
もぎしけん
模擬試験 trial exam, practice exam

もさく
模索する to grope, to seek
もぞうひん
模造品 imitation
きぼ
規模 size, scale

一 十 才 オ オ 杧 杧 柞 柑 楂 槿 模 模　14

288

1009

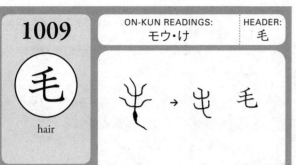

ON-KUN READINGS:
モウ・け

HEADER:
毛

毛
hair

ORIGIN: The ancient form was a pictograph of a tuft of fine hair. The kanji 毛 means "hair."

け
毛 hair
もうふ
毛布 blanket
かみ　け
髪の毛 hair
ようもう
羊毛 lamb's wool

じゅんもう
純毛 pure lamb's wool
ふもう
不毛 barren
うもう
羽毛 plume

丿 二 三毛   4

1010

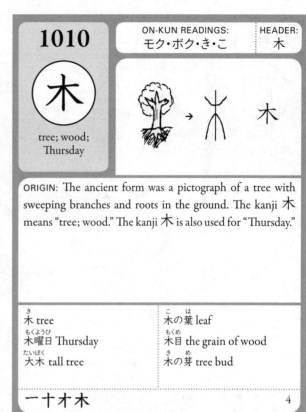

ON-KUN READINGS:
モク・ボク・き・こ

HEADER:
木

木
tree; wood;
Thursday

ORIGIN: The ancient form was a pictograph of a tree with sweeping branches and roots in the ground. The kanji 木 means "tree; wood." The kanji 木 is also used for "Thursday."

き
木 tree
もくようび
木曜日 Thursday
たいぼく
大木 tall tree

こ　は
木の葉 leaf
もくめ
木目 the grain of wood
き　め
木の芽 tree bud

一 十 才 木   4

(289)

1011

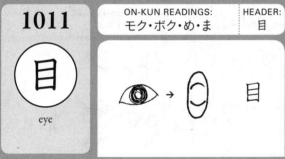

ON-KUN READINGS:
モク・ボク・め・ま

HEADER:
目

目
eye

ORIGIN: The ancient form was a pictograph of an eye. In addition to the meaning of "eye," the kanji 目 is used for various meanings, including "order" (三回目 "the third time"), "heading" (目次 "table of contents"), "experience" (大変な目 "terrible experience"), and "characteristics of" (小さ目 "smaller-sized").

め
目 eye
みっかめ
三日目 third day
めうえ
目上 one's senior
かいもく
皆目 altogether, utterly

めあ
目当て aim
だめ
駄目 no good
はやめ
早目に in good time
め　あ
目の当たり in one's presence

丨 冂 冂 月 目   5

1012

ON-KUN READINGS:
モン・と(い)・とん

HEADER:
口

問
to question;
to inquire

ORIGIN: In the ancient form the top 門 was a pictograph of two doors concealing what was inside. Inside, 口 "mouth" signified speaking. One asks about what is not seen or known. The kanji 問 means "to question; to inquire."

もんだい
問題 problem
しつもん
質問する to ask a question
がくもん
学問 scholarly studies

と
問い question
とんや
問屋 wholesale
ふもん　ふ
不問に付する to pass over the
matter

丨 冂 冂 冂 冂 冂冂 冂冂 冂冂 問 問 問   11

1013

ON-KUN READINGS: モン・かど | HEADER: 門

門

gate; doors

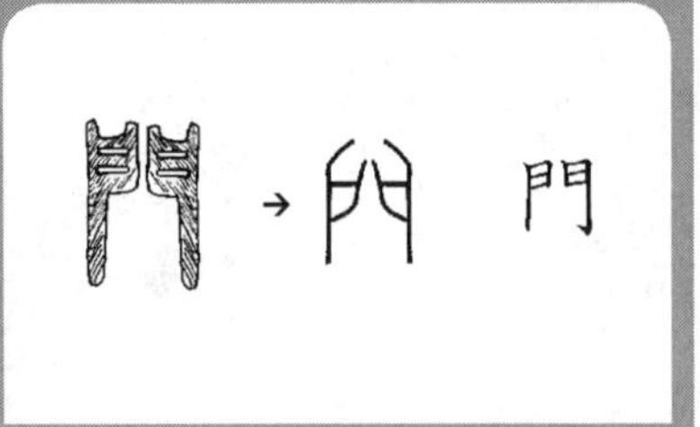

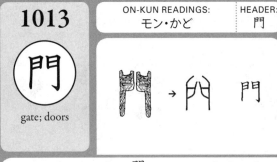

ORIGIN: In the ancient form, 門 was a pictograph of two doors concealing what is inside. The kanji 門 means "gate; doors."

門 (もん) gate	正門 (せいもん) front gate
専門 (せんもん) specialty, major	門ごとに (かど) at every house
門限 (もんげん) curfew time	お門違い (かどちが) barking up the wrong tree

8

1014

ON-KUN READINGS: ヤ・よる・よ | HEADER: 夕

夜

night

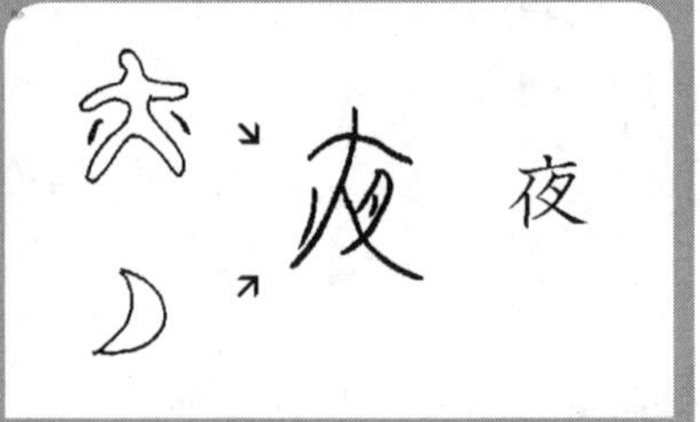

ORIGIN: The ancient form shown in the middle indicated that this kanji consisted of 大 "person" and 月 "moon," which was about to emerge from the side of the person. A moon comes out at night. The kanji 夜 means "night."

夜 (よる) night	徹夜 (てつや) sit up all night
今夜 (こんや) tonight	夜更かし (よふ) staying up late
夜中に (よなか) in the middle of the night	深夜 (しんや) a late night

8

1015

ON-KUN READINGS: ヤ・の | HEADER: 里

野

field; outside; outsider

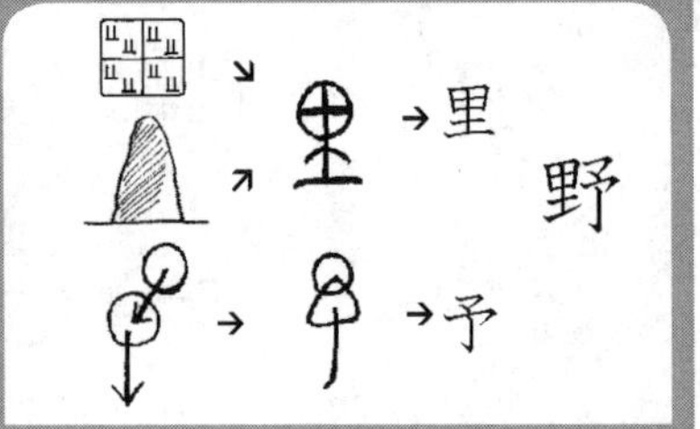

ORIGIN: The left side was 里 "village" (田 "rice paddies" plus 土 "mound of earth"), indicating a place people inhabited. The right side, 予 "advance," depicted something pushing another thing to make room. Both sides together indicated a spacious piece of land that was outside the main area. The kanji 野 means "field," or "outside; outsider."

野菜 (やさい) vegetables	野党 (やとう) opposition party
野球 (やきゅう) baseball	在野 (ざいや) people out of office
野原 (のはら) field	野生 (やせい) wild nature

11

1016

ON-KUN READINGS: ヤク・エキ | HEADER: 彳

役

role; service; war

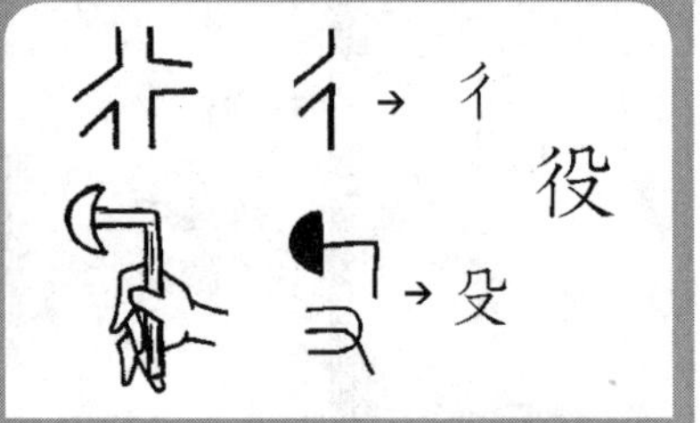

ORIGIN: The left side, 彳 "to go," came from the left half of a crossroad. The right side 殳 had a weapon in hand indicating a fight but also engagement in work. Together they indicated going to fight (or war), and, by extension, role or duty. The kanji 役 means "war," or "role; service."

役 (やく) role	役所 (やくしょ) government office
役目 (やくめ) role	使役動詞 (しえきどうし) causative verb
役 (えき) civil war	役に立つ (やく た) to make use of

7

1017

約

approximately;
to promise;
to shorten

ORIGIN: The left side, 糸 "silk filaments being pulled out of cocoons," meant "threads." On the right side, the bent shape of a ladle, 勺, looked like the loop of a thread, signifying a shortcut. When one tied a piece of yarn, it was a token of a promise as well. The kanji 約 means "to promise" or "shorten" or "approximately."

約一年 approximately a year
予約 reservation
約束 promise

要約 summary
契約 contract
節約 economization

く 乡 幺 糸 糸 糸 糸 約 約　　9

1018

薬

medicine;
pharmaceutical

ORIGIN: The old form 藥 had 艹 "plants" and 樂 "pleasant" or "soothing" (coming from acorns making pleasant rhythmic music), indicating medicinal herbs. The kanji 薬 means "medicine; pharmaceutical."

薬 medicine
薬屋 drug store, pharmacy
薬局 pharmacy

薬学 pharmacology
薬草 medicinal herb
薬味 condiment

一 十 艹 艹 艹 ヤ 节 肖 苩 苩 苅 濼 薬 薬 薬 薬　　16

1019

訳

reason; translation

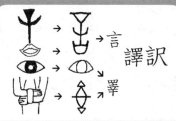

ORIGIN: The ancient form of the old form 譯 had 言 "word," an eye, and a handcuffed criminal, indicating a careful interrogation. Together they meant "to translate words one by one." Now the right side uses 尺 "to measure." The kanji 訳 means "translation; reason."

訳 translation
訳 reason, interpretation
英訳 English translation

申し訳ない I apologize for ~
内訳 breakdown
言い訳 excuse

、 亠 亠 言 言 言 訂 訂 訳 訳　　11

1020

油

oil

ORIGIN: The left side 氵 is "water" or liquid. The right side 由 depicted a gourd. When a gourd ripens and rots, its flesh becomes oily. Combined, the two sides of the kanji indicated an oil-like substance dripping from a small-mouthed container. The kanji 油 means "oil."

油 oil
石油 petroleum
油断する to be off one's guard

灯油 kerosene
原油 crude oil
油汚れ oily soil

、 ミ 氵 氵 汩 油 油 油　　8

1021

ON-KUN READINGS: ユ

HEADER: 車

to transport

ORIGIN: The left side was 車, a pictograph of a two-wheeled chariot, viewed from above. The right side, used phonetically, was a boat and a knife, signifying "to move" and "to remove." The combined form indicated moving goods on a chariot from one place to another. The kanji 輸 means "to transport."

ゆしゅつ
輸出 export
ゆにゅう
輸入 import
ゆそう
輸送 transport

ゆけつ
輸血 blood transfusion
うんゆ
運輸 transportation
みつゆ
密輸 smuggling, contraband

一 厂 厂 亓 亓 亘 車 軒 軒 軒 軒 輪 輪 輪 輪   16

1022

ON-KUN READINGS: ユウ・やさ(しい)・すぐ(れる)

HEADER: イ

actor; excellent; graceful

ORIGIN: The left side イ is "person," from a side view of a person standing. The right side 憂 depicted an actor with a mask on his face and his feet facing toward the viewer, signifying acting for an audience. An actor expresses emotions 心 and performs a slow ritual dance gracefully. The kanji 優 means "actor" or "excellent; graceful."

ゆうしゅう
優秀 excellence
やさ
優しい kind
はいゆう
俳優 actor
せいゆう
声優 voice-over actor

ゆうせん
優先 priority
ゆうが
優雅 elegance
ゆうえつかん
優越感 a sense of superiority

ノ イ イ゙ 仁 仵 仵 俏 俏 俏 俍 優 優 優 傷 傷 優   17

1023

ON-KUN READINGS: ユウ・いさ(ましい)

HEADER: 力

brave

ORIGIN: The top was 甬, depicting a person stamping his or her feet on a pole to put it through a board, here phonetically used to mean "to spurt." The bottom 力 was a strong hand. Bravery involves spurts of strength. The kanji 勇 means "brave."

ゆうき
勇気 courage
いさ
勇ましい gallant
ゆうかん
勇敢な brave

いさ あし
勇み足の rash, imprudent
いさ
勇んで valiantly
ゆうたい
勇退 voluntary resignation

一 マ マ マ 丙 甬 甬 甬 勇 勇   9

1024

ON-KUN READINGS: ユウ・とも

HEADER: 又

friend

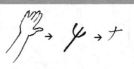

ORIGIN: The ancient form depicted two hands. Two hands coming together indicated togetherness and friendship. The kanji 友 means "friend."

とも
友 friend
ともだち
友達 friend
ゆうじん
友人 friend

しんゆう
親友 close friend
ゆうこうかんけい
友好関係 friendly
relationship
ゆうこうこく
友好国 ally

一 ナ 方 友   4

1025

有

to exist; to have

ON-KUN READINGS:
ユウ・ウ・あ(る)

HEADER:
月

ORIGIN: The ancient form had a right hand (as in the kanji 右 "right") above a piece of meat 月, from 肉 "meat." Together they signified meat in hand for an offering. Pointing out the offering by hand also declared its existence. The kanji 有 means "to have" and "to exist."

あ
有る to have, to exist
ゆうめい
有名な famous
ゆうりょうどうろ
有料道路 toll road

しょゆうしゃ
所有者 owner
うむ
有無 existence
ゆういぎ
有意義 meaningful

ノ ナ ナ 右 有 有   6

1026

由

reason; means; originated from

ON-KUN READINGS:
ユウ・ユイ・ユ・よし

HEADER:
田

ORIGIN: The original kanji depicted a gourd. When a gourd becomes ripe and rotten, its flesh liquefies and drips out. From the idea of something coming out, the meaning of this kanji came to be "cause" or "reason." The kanji 由 means "reason" or "means; originated from."

りゆう
理由 reason
じゆう
自由 freedom
ゆらい
由来 origin

よし
由 I hear that
けいゆ
経由 via, to go by way of
ゆえん
由縁 reason

丨 冂 巾 由 由   5

1027

誘

to invite; to induce; to lure

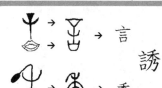

ON-KUN READINGS:
ユウ・さそ(う)

HEADER:
言

ORIGIN: The left side 言 signified "word." The right side 秀 depicted a plant with a flower on top, signifying a most beautiful time, and hence "excellence," here used phonetically. By using good words, one can induce others to act or lure them into something. The kanji 誘 means "to invite; to induce; to lure."

さそ
誘う to invite
ゆうわく
誘惑 temptation
ゆうはつ
誘発する to induce

ゆうかい
誘拐 abduction
ゆうち
誘致 to lure (company) to own locality

丶 亠 亠 言 言 言 訁 訁 訡 誘 誘 誘   14

1028

遊

to play; to have fun

ON-KUN READINGS:
ユウ・ユ・あそ(ぶ)

HEADER:
⻌

ORIGIN: The ancient form consisted of "flag pole with a banner" (now written in two separate components) and 子 "child" in water; the child moving about (like a waving flag). The bottom ⻌, from 辵, has the meaning "to go forward." A child runs and moves forward while playing. The kanji 遊 means "to play; to have fun."

あそ
遊ぶ to play
ゆうえんち
遊園地 playground
ゆうえいきんし
遊泳禁止 no swimming allowed

あそ じかん
遊び時間 play time
がいゆう
外遊 trip abroad
ゆさん
遊山 picnic, excursion

丶 亠 う 方 方 斿 斿 斿 斿 游 游 遊   12

293

1029

ON-KUN READINGS: ユウ

HEADER: 阝

郵
to post

ORIGIN: The left side 垂 depicted a rice stalk drooping with a heavy head, that is, something that is dangling like a flag. The right side 阝 indicated a village. A flag hangs in a village where a long-distance imperial messenger stops by. The kanji 郵 means "to post."

ゆうびん
郵便 post, mail
ゆうびんきょく
郵便局 post office
ゆうびんばんごう
郵便番号 postal code; zip code

ゆうそう
郵送する to send by post

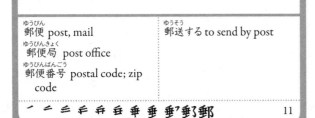 11

1030

ON-KUN READINGS: セキ・ゆう

HEADER: 夕

夕
early evening; dusk

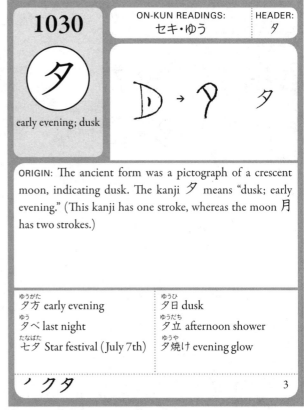

ORIGIN: The ancient form was a pictograph of a crescent moon, indicating dusk. The kanji 夕 means "dusk; early evening." (This kanji has one stroke, whereas the moon 月 has two strokes.)

ゆうがた
夕方 early evening
ゆう
夕べ last night
たなばた
七夕 Star festival (July 7th)

ゆうひ
夕日 dusk
ゆうだち
夕立 afternoon shower
ゆうや
夕焼け evening glow

ノ ク タ 3

1031

ON-KUN READINGS: ヨ・あらかじ(め)

HEADER: 亅

予
to prepare; preliminary

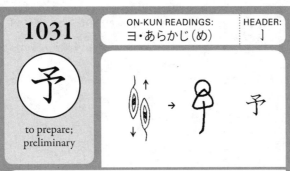

ORIGIN: The ancient form depicted something pushing another thing to make room, in preparation. Another interpretation is that it depicted a shuttle in weaving, which moves back and forth. The kanji came to mean allowing ample time in preparation. The kanji 予 means "to prepare," or "preliminary."

よてい
予定 plan, schedule
よやく
予約 reservation
あらかじ
予め in advance

よしゅう
予習 study in advance
よかん
予感 premonition
よせん
予選 preliminary game/round

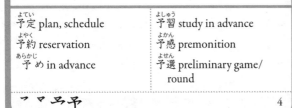 4

1032

ON-KUN READINGS: ヨ・あま(る)

HEADER: 人

余
excess; leftover

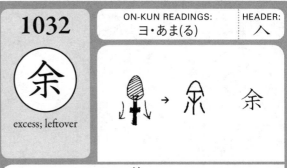

ORIGIN: The original form 餘 meant "plenty of food." The current form uses only the right side, which depicted a spade making a motion to divide something in two (making room in the middle). The kanji 余 means "excess; leftover."

あま
余り remainder, leftover
あま
余り〜ない not very
あま
余りにも too much

よぶん
余分な excess
よけい
余計な too many, uncalled for
よち
余地 room, space

ノ 人 △ 合 仐 余 余 7

294

1033

ヨ・あず(かる)

HEADER:
頁

預
to deposit

ORIGIN: The left side 予 depicted pushing something out of the way to make room. The right side 頁 was "head" with a ceremonial headdress. The form is believed to be a relatively new kanji; the origin of the use of "head" is not clear. The kanji 預 means "to deposit."

あず
預ける to deposit (in a bank), leave
いちじあず
一時預かり temporary checking

ぎんこうよきん
銀行預金 bank account
よげんしゃ
預言者 prophet

　マ　ユ　予　予　矛　矛　預　預　預　預　預　預　13

1034

ON-KUN READINGS:
ヨウ・おさな(い)

HEADER:
幺

幼
very young; immature

ORIGIN: The left side 幺 was derived from short threads (shorter than 糸 "thread"), signifying "minute; weak." The right side 力 is "strength; power." A person who is weak in body strength can be a very young child. The kanji 幼 means "very young; immature."

おさな
幼い young
ようちえん
幼稚園 preschool, kindergarten
ようじ
幼児 young child

ようち
幼稚な immature
ようちゅう
幼虫 larva
ようしょう
幼少 juvenile

く　幺　幺　幻　幼　5

1035

ON-KUN READINGS:
ヨウ

HEADER:
宀

容
to let in; to permit

ORIGIN: The top 宀 was a house. 谷 "valley" depicted deep mountains. Between the mountains is an opening or access (口). Together they indicated a house that had an opening to let someone in. The kanji 容 means "to let in; to permit."

ないよう
内容 content
きょよう
許容 allowance
びよういん
美容院 beauty parlor, hair salon

ようき
プラスチック容器 plastic container
じゅよう
受容する to accept
ようぎしゃ
容疑者 a suspect

　丶　宀　宀　灾　灾　灾　容　容　10

1036

ON-KUN READINGS:
ヨウ

HEADER:
日

曜
day of the week

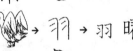

ORIGIN: This kanji was a composite of three pictographs: 日 "sun," 羽 "two wings," and 隹 "small bird." Together they indicated the sun flying like a bird, or the passing of the day. The kanji 曜 means "day of the week."

にちようび
日曜日 Sunday
ようび
曜日 day of the week

｜　П　A　日　日　日ヨ　日ヨ　日ヨ　日習　日習　日習　日習　日翟　日翟　日翟　日翟　曜　曜　18

295

1037

ON-KUN READINGS: ヨウ・さま

HEADER: 木

様

appearance; like; [honorific form of address]

ORIGIN: The older form 様 had 木 "tree," 羊 "sheep" or "something desirable," and 永 "long stream of water." How this form came to mean "appearance; like" or a form of address is not clear. The bottom 永 has been replaced by 氷, a reduced form. The kanji 様 means "appearance; like" or an honorific form of addressing someone.

いしかわさま
石川様 Mr./Mrs./Miss/Ms. Ishikawa
ようす
様子 appearance
さまざま
様々な various

よう
その様な something like that
ありさま
有様 condition
さま
その様 the way it appears

一 十 オ 木 オ オ 杉 栏 栏 样 样 栐 様 様　14

1038

ON-KUN READINGS: ヨウ

HEADER: 氵

洋

ocean; abroad

ORIGIN: The left side was 氵 "water." The right side, 羊, had the sound that meant "spacious and wide." The kanji 洋 means "ocean" and also refers to places beyond an ocean, that is, "abroad."

ようふく
洋服 Western clothes
とうよう
東洋 the East
ようふう
洋風 Western style

たいへいよう
太平洋 the Pacific Ocean
たいせいよう
大西洋 the Atlantic Ocean
ようこう
洋行 trip abroad

丶 丶 氵 氵 汁 汁 浒 洋 洋　9

1039

ON-KUN READINGS: ヨウ・もち(いる)

HEADER: 用

用

errand; to use

ORIGIN: The ancient form depicted a wooden fence, the kind used to confine sacrificial animals. Because animals were used for sacrifice, the kanji came to mean generally "to make use; to utilize." Using a person, one gets an errand done. The kanji 用 means "to make use; to utilize," or "errand."

よう　ようじ
用・用事 errand, engagement
りよう
利用する to use, to take advantage of
ようけん
用件 business

ふようひん
不用品 unnecessary thing
むよう
無用 no need
もち
用いる to make use of, to employ

丿 冂 月 月 用　5

1040

ON-KUN READINGS: ヨウ・ひつじ

HEADER: 羊

羊

sheep

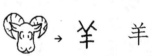

ORIGIN: The ancient form was a pictograph of a sheep's head. The kanji 羊 means "sheep." Because sheep produce wool, sheepskin, and meat and are attractive in appearance, when the kanji is used as a recurring component in other kanji, it often connotes goodness or desirability.

ひつじ
羊 sheep
ようもう
羊毛 lamb's wool
やぎ
山羊 goat

こひつじ
子羊 lamb
ひつじか
羊飼い shepherd
ようひし
羊皮紙 parchment, vellum

丶 丷 艹 兰 兰 羊　6

1041

ON-KUN READINGS: ヨウ・は

HEADER: 艹

葉
leaf

ORIGIN: The old form had 艸 "plants," and underneath was a "tree with three leaves or branches." The kanji 葉 means "leaf" and is used to indicate something that is flat and leaf-like.

木の葉 leaf
葉っぱ leaf
言葉 word
葉書 postcard

紅葉 autumn foliage
落ち葉 fallen leaf
葉緑素 chlorophyll

一 十 十 艹 节 苹 苹 苹 苹 華 葉 葉   12

1042

ON-KUN READINGS: ヨウ・い(る)・かなめ

HEADER: 西

要
important

ORIGIN: The top 襾 of the ancient form was a woman putting her hand on her waist and 女 "woman," which was added as emphasis (because a woman has more defined hips). One's waist is the center of one's body. The kanji 要 means "important; central." (The kanji for the original meaning of "waist" is 腰.)

要る to need
要するに in short
要約 summary

要 pivot
要人 VIP
要望 demand

一 一 一 一 西 西 要 要 要   9

297

1043

ON-KUN READINGS: ヨウ・ひ

HEADER: 阝

陽
sunny; positive

ORIGIN: The left side 阝 signified an earthen wall surrounding a house. The right side 昜 consisted of 日 "sun," 丅 "motion of raising something high," and 彡 "sun rays." Together they signified that the sun goes up and becomes bright—thus a sunny area. The kanji 陽 means "sunny" or "positive."

太陽 sun
陽性 positive
陽気に cheerfully

陰陽 yin-yang (the positive and negative)
陽だまり sunny spot
陽光 sunbeams

フ 了 阝 阝 阝 阝 阝 阝 阩 陽 陽 陽   12

1044

ON-KUN READINGS: ヨウ・やしな(う)

HEADER: 食

養
to support;
to foster

ORIGIN: The top was derived from a kanji form for sheep 羊, which provides good food. The bottom was food with a cover on top, from the kanji 食 "to eat." Together they indicated feeding someone well. The kanji 養 means "to foster; to support."

養う to feed, to foster
保養 recreation
養子 adopted child

休養 rest, relaxation
静養 rest, recuperation
養殖 farming, cultivation

丶 丷 丷 艹 兰 关 美 美 羔 養 養 養 養 養   15

1045

ON-KUN READINGS: ヨク・ほ(しい)・ほっ(する) HEADER: 欠

欲 — greed; wanting more

ORIGIN: The left side was 谷 "valley," which has a deep opening 口 into the mountain, signifying something deep. The right side was 欠, a person crouching with his mouth wide open to inhale. Together they indicated a person's deep desire or greed. The kanji 欲 means "greed," or "wanting more."

よく
欲 greed
よくば
欲張りな greedy
しょくよく
食欲 appetite

むよく
無欲な unselfish
ほ
欲しい want, a desire
にくよく
肉欲 sexual desire

ノ 八 グ グ グ 谷 谷 谷 谷 欲 欲 11

1046

ON-KUN READINGS: ヨク・あ(びる) HEADER: 氵

浴 — to bathe

ORIGIN: The left side 氵 indicated a stream of water. The right side was 谷 "valley," which has a deep opening 口 into the mountains, signifying something deep. Together they indicated immersion in deep water. The kanji 浴 means "to bathe."

あ
浴びる to bathe
にゅうよくじかん
入浴時間 bathing time
よくしつ
浴室 bathroom

にっこうよく
日光浴 sun bathing
かいすいよく
海水浴 bathing at the beach
ゆかた
浴衣 yukata (cotton summer kimono)

丶 冫 氵 汒 汖 浌 浴 浴 浴 浴 10

1047

ON-KUN READINGS: ヨク HEADER: 羽

翌 — next; following

ORIGIN: The top 羽 was a pictograph of two wings, signifying "to fly off." The bottom 立 depicted a person standing on the ground. Together they indicated flight or movement to the next action. The kanji 翌 means "next; following."

よくじつ
翌日 the next day
よくとし
翌年 the following year
よくじゅうににち
翌十二日に on the following 12th day

よくよくじつ
翌々日 the day after next

丁 刁 尹 羽 羽 羽 羽 羽 羽 翌 翌 翌 11

1048

ON-KUN READINGS: ライ・こ(ない)・く(る)・き(た)・きた(る) HEADER: 木

来 — to come; next; forthcoming

ORIGIN: The old form 來 originally depicted a barley plant. Over the years it came to switch meanings with a similar kanji, 麥 (a foot facing toward you and 夂, meaning "to come"). Now 来, from 來, means "to come" (and 麦, from 麥, means "barley plant"). The kanji 来 means "to come" or "next; forthcoming."

く
来る to come
こ
来ない not to come
きた
来る next, forthcoming
らいしゅう
来週 next week

しょうらい
将来 future
らいにち
来日 a visit to Japan
できごころ
出来心 impulse

一 ヒ 口 平 平 来 来 7

1049

ON-KUN READINGS: ラク・から(む)

HEADER: 糸

絡

to become entangled with

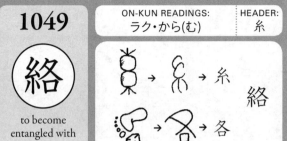

ORIGIN: The left side 糸 was a pictograph of thin silk threads being reeled out of silkworm cocoons, signifying threads in general. The right side 各 was used phonetically to express entanglement. The kanji 絡 means "to become entangled with."

連絡する to contact, to inform
連絡通路 connecting corridor

絡む to become entangled
脈絡のない incoherent

〈 〈 幺 幺 爷 糸 糸 紀 紋 紋 絡 絡　12

1050

ON-KUN READINGS: ラク・お(ちる)

HEADER: ⺾

落

to fall; to drop

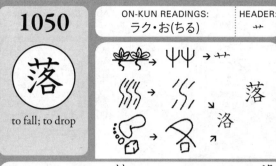

ORIGIN: The old form 艸 for ⺾ indicated "plants." 洛 /raku/, phonetically used here, was the name of a river in China that ran through a stony river bed; it was used to signify "(water) dripping down or falling." Together they described how leaves fall. The kanji 落 means "to fall; to drop" in general.

落ちる to fall
下落 fall
落雷 thunderbolt

落第 stay back a grade
落書き graffiti
落語 comedic narrative by a *rakugo* teller

一 十 艹 艹 芓 艾 莎 莎 落 落 落　12

1051

ON-KUN READINGS: ラン・みだ(れる)

HEADER: し

乱

to be out of order

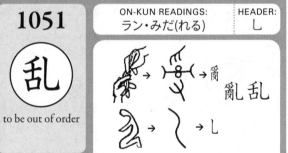

ORIGIN: The left side of the old form 亂 depicted two hands trying to untangle threads. The right side, し "spatula," signified an act of straightening something. Together they indicated something that needed to be straightened out because it was "out of order." Now with a simpler form 舌 on the left, the kanji 乱 means "to be out of order."

乱れる to become disorganized
混乱 confusion
乱暴な rough

乱雑な cluttered
乱闘 confused fight, affray
取り乱す to be disheveled

ノ 二 千 千 舌 舌 乱　7

1052

ON-KUN READINGS: ラン・たまご

HEADER: 卩

卵

egg

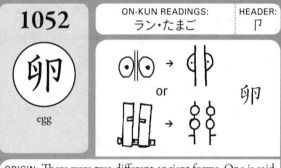

or

ORIGIN: There were two different ancient forms. One is said to have depicted eggs attached to leaves that faced each other. The other was a depiction of two foot pedals for weavers, whose origin is obscure. Today, the kanji 卵 means "egg."

卵 egg
卵黄 egg yolk
ゆで卵 boiled egg

産卵 laying an egg
鶏卵 hen's egg

ノ 亡 丘 丘 卯 卯 卵　7

299

1053

ON-KUN READINGS: ラン

HEADER: 見

覧

to view

ORIGIN: The ancient form was a combination of 監 and 見 on the bottom. The kanji 監 "scrutiny" depicted a person looking at his or her reflection in a basin of water. The kanji 見 also was a depiction of a person with an emphasis on the eye. The kanji 覧 means "to view."

ご覧になる [honorific] to view
展覧会 exhibition
閲覧室 viewing room

一覧表 table
天覧 emperor's viewing

ー广广尸尸尸臣臣臣臣臣臣臣臣臣臣臣覧覧 17

1054

ON-KUN READINGS: リ・き(く)

HEADER: リ

利

useful; sharp

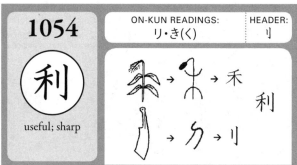

ORIGIN: The left side was 禾 "rice plant with ripe head" and リ "sharp knife," signifying cutting rice plants with a sharp knife. The kanji 利 means "sharp" and has also come to mean "useful."

便利な convenient
利用する to use
利子・利息 interest (on a loan or money)

有利な advantageous
不利 disadvantage
利益 profit

ノ一千千禾利利 7

1055

ON-KUN READINGS: リ

HEADER: 王

理

rational; reason

ORIGIN: The left side 王 was a "string of jewels." 里 "village" on the right had 田 "rice paddies arranged neatly" and 土 "soil or land," signifying "neatly divided land." Together they indicated splitting a gem neatly along the natural cleavage, which would be the rational way to do so. The kanji 理 means "rational" or "reason."

料理 cooking
理由 reason
無理 unreasonable

合理的 rational
理解する to understand
理屈っぽい argumentative

一丁千壬王玨玡珇理理理理 11

1056

ON-KUN READINGS: リ・うら

HEADER: 衣

裏

back; wrong side; inside; hidden

ORIGIN: 里 in the middle was used phonetically to indicate the "inside" of clothes. The outside of clothes was indicated by the depiction of the back of a collar 亠 and the bottom of the front portion of layered collars 衣. The kanji 裏 also indicated the interior of clothes in general. The kanji 裏 means "back; wrong side; inside" or "hidden."

裏 back, reverse side
裏面・裏面 back side
裏側 back side
表裏・表裏 both sides

裏返す to turn inside out
裏金 bribe, hidden money
裏話 an inside story
裏切る to betray

ー亠亠亠亠亩亩亩重重重裏裏裏 13

300

1057

ON-KUN READINGS: リ・さと

HEADER: 里

里

village; *ri*

ORIGIN: The ancient form consisted of 田 "rice paddies" and 土 "soil." If land had neatly divided rice paddies, people lived there. Also it was used as a unit of distance and other kinds of measurement. (In the old Japanese system, one *ri* was approximately 4 km.) The kanji 里 means "village" or "*ri* (distance)."

さと
里 village
さとがえ
里帰り return to one's
　　　parents' home
いちり
一里 one *ri*

きょうり
郷里 native town
ひとざと
人里 village
やまざと
山里 hamlet in the hills

ノ 口 戸 日 甲 里 里　　7

1058

ON-KUN READINGS: リ・はな(れる)

HEADER: 隹

離

to separate

ORIGIN: The left side depicted two worms stuck together, and the right side depicted a bird. Together they indicated a bird caught in birdlime (a sticky resin used to trap birds). The kanji came to signify not trapping a bird but rather detaching a bird from birdlime. The kanji 離 means "to separate."

はな
離れる to part
きょり
距離 distance
りりく
離陸する to take off, to leave
　　　the ground

はな
離れ detached house
かつじばなれ
活字離れ alliteration
りべつ
離別 separation

' 亠 ナ 广 卤 卤 离 离 离 离 离' 离' 离' 離 離 離　18

1059

ON-KUN READINGS: リク

HEADER: 阝

陸

land

ORIGIN: The left side 阝 signified an earthen wall or ladder for climbing. The right side consisted of two tent-like structures and a mound of earth. The structures signified places where gods alight on earth (土). The kanji 陸 means "land."

りく
陸 land
りくきょう
陸橋 overhead bridge
たいりく
ヨーロッパ大陸 European
　　　continent

ちゃくりく
着陸 landing
じょうりく
上陸 landing
りくじょうきょうぎ
陸上競技 track and field

' 3 阝 阝 阝 阼 陸 陸 陸 陸 陸　11

1060

ON-KUN READINGS: リツ・リチ

HEADER: 彳

律

law

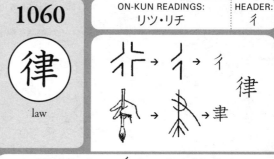

ORIGIN: The left side was 彳, from the left half of a crossroad, signifying "to conduct (an action)." The right side 聿 depicted a hand holding a brush upright. Together they indicated writing with a brush about the way one should live. The kanji 律 means "law."

ほうりつ
法律 law
きりつ
規律 discipline
りちぎ
律儀に honest

ふぶんりつ
不文律 unwritten
　　　constitution
せんりつ
旋律 melody
いちりつ
一律に across the board

' ク 夕 彳 彳 彳 彳 律 律 律　9

301

1061

ON-KUN READINGS: リツ・ソツ・ひき(いる)

HEADER: 亠

率
rate; to lead

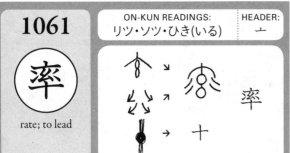

ORIGIN: The ancient form depicted a stick (亠 and 十) on each end of a skein of threads, to wring out water. The four short strokes on each side of 幺 were drops of sprinkled water. Pulling long threads is like uniting and leading people. The meaning of "rate" was added from borrowing. The kanji 率 means "to lead," or "rate."

そっせん
率先して take the lead
りつ
率 rate
のうりつ
能率 efficiency

ひゃくぶんりつ
百分率 percentage
いんそつ
引率する to lead (people on a trip)
ひき
率いる to lead

` ー ナ 玄 玄 玄 茲 淕 浐 淬 率   11

1062

ON-KUN READINGS: リツ・リュウ・た(つ)

HEADER: 立

立
to stand

ORIGIN: The ancient form was a pictograph of a person standing on the ground. The kanji 立 means "to stand."

た
立つ to stand
りっぱ
立派 impressive
きりつ
起立する to stand up

じりつ
自立 independence
りったいてき
立体的 three-dimensional
こくりつこうえん
国立公園 national park

` ー 亠 六 立   5

1063

ON-KUN READINGS: リャク

HEADER: 田

略
tactic; summary

ORIGIN: The left side 田 was "rice paddies" and the right side 各 was used phonetically. Together they indicated to conquer land, draw a boundary, and manage it. Doing this work successfully required "tactics." An abbreviated report on the work was called 略. The kanji 略 means "tactics" or "summary."

しょうりゃく
省略 omission
りゃく
略す to leave out, to abbreviate
りゃくれき
略歴 brief history

りゃくじ
略字 simplified character
せいりゃく
政略 political tactics
りゃくだつ
略奪 pillage, plunder

丨 冂 冂 冂 田 田 田' 畋 畋 略 略   11

1064

ON-KUN READINGS: リュウ・ル・なが(れる)

HEADER: 氵

流
a stream; to flow

ORIGIN: The left side 氵 was "water" and the right side was a depiction of an infant being born, head down, with amniotic fluid dripping. The kanji 流 means "stream," or "to flow."

なが
流れる to flow
りゅうこう
流行 popular
にほんかいりゅう
日本海流 the Japan Current
いちりゅう
一流の first-rate

ふうりゅう
風流 elegance, refinement
でんりゅう
電流 electric current
りゅうよう
流用する to misappropriate

丶 冫 氵 氵 浐 泸 泸 济 流 流   10

302

1065

ON-KUN READINGS: リュウ・ル・と(める)・とど(める)

HEADER: 田

留

to keep; to stop; to hold

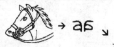

ORIGIN: The top came from a depiction of a bit in a horse's mouth that was viewed from the front. The bottom came from 由 and was used phonetically. One tied a horse to a tree or bar by the bridle to keep it in one place. From that it signified to stay in one place or to stop. The top of the old form was modified and the current kanji 留 means "to keep; to stay; to stop."

留め金 hook
留守 absence from home
留守番電話 answering machine
留める to hold
留学生 foreign student
在留届 resident registration

`, ℓ 幻 幻 丱 丱 留 留 留 留` 10

1066

ON-KUN READINGS: リョ・たび

HEADER: 方

旅

trip; to travel

ORIGIN: The ancient form consisted of a pole with a banner and 从, two people, which was used to signify many people. A group of people under a banner may travel together a long distance. The kanji 旅 means "to travel," or a "journey."

旅行 trip, travel
旅券 passport
旅 trip, travel
旅館 Japanese inn
旅立ち departure for a trip
旅客 passenger, traveler

`, ㇐ 方 方 方 㫃 㫃 旅 旅 旅` 10

1067

ON-KUN READINGS: リョウ

HEADER: 一

両

both; two

ORIGIN: The old form 兩 reflects the ancient form, which was a pictograph of a gourd split in two with dry seeds inside. The kanji 両 means "two; both."

両方 both
両名 both persons
両替 currency exchange, money changing
両親 both parents
両立 coexistence
両 *ryo* (an old unit of currency)

`一 ㄘ 币 両 両 両` 6

1068

ON-KUN READINGS: リョウ

HEADER: 宀

寮

dormitory

ORIGIN: The top 宀 was a house; the form underneath had 呂 "houses that were connected" and 火 "torches for guarding the premises." Together they indicated government offices where guards were present. Having the meaning of many rooms with someone who oversees them, the kanji 寮 means "dormitory."

寮 dormitory
学生寮 student dormitory
寮生 dormitory resident
母子寮 mother and child dormitory/shelter
独身寮 dormitory for single people

`, ハ 宀 宀 宀 穼 宨 宨 寏 寏 寏 寥 寥 寮 寮` 15

303

1069

ON-KUN READINGS: リョウ HEADER: 米

料
food; fee; provisions

ORIGIN: The left side was 米, rice scattered in all directions. The right side was 斗, a scoop with a long handle that was used to measure rice or other grains. Certain measured amounts of grain were established as fees. The kanji 料 means "food; fee; provisions."

りょうり
料理 cooking
りょうりや
料理屋 restaurant
にゅうじょうりょう
入場料 entrance fee

むりょう
無料 free of charge
ゆうりょう
有料 charged for
りょうきん
料金 fee

丶ソニ斗斗米米米米料料 10

1070

ON-KUN READINGS: リョウ・すず(しい) HEADER: 氵

涼
cool (to feel)

ORIGIN: The left side 氵 was derived from a depiction of water, and the right side 京 "capital" was used phonetically to indicate "cool." This kanji is used for a pleasant and cool feel in the air. The kanji 涼 means "cool" in temperature.

すず
涼しい cool
せいりょういんりょうすい
清涼飲料水 refreshing drink, soft drink
すず
涼しげな looking cool

こうりょう
荒涼 desolate, barren
のうりょう
納涼 cool summer breeze
りょうふう
涼風 cool breeze

丶ニシ氵氵浐浐浐浐涼涼涼 11

1071

良
good

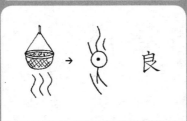

ORIGIN: The ancient form depicted a basket-like sieve to wash rice or other grains. Grain is washed to remove dust and make the rice good enough to eat. The kanji 良 means "good."

よ
良い good
りょうこう
良好な good
かいりょう
改良 improvement

りょうしん
良心 conscience
ふりょうひん
不良品 faulty goods
ふりょう
不良 bad lot, badness

丶コ彐ヨ自良良 7

1072

ON-KUN READINGS: リョウ・はか(る) HEADER: 里

量
mass; amount

ORIGIN: In the ancient form, the top 日 depicted a measure, viewed from above; underneath was a bag tied at the top and bottom, signifying something heavy. 土 "soil" emphasized the meaning of weight. The kanji 量 means "mass," or "amount."

りょう
量 amount
はか
量る to measure
りょうさん
量産 mass production

ぶんりょう
分量 measured amount
かんむりょう
感無量 immensely moved
うりょう
雨量 precipitation (rain)

丶口曰旦旦早昌昌昌量量量 12

1073

ON-KUN READINGS: リョウ

HEADER: 頁

head; chief; domain

ORIGIN: The left side 令 was used phonetically but has the meaning of humbly listening to an order. The right side was 頁 "head." Together they indicated a person who gives an order, and the "domain" or "territory" that the chief controls. The kanji 領 means "head; chief; domain; territory."

りょうど
領土 territory
だいとうりょう
大統領 (country's) president
せんりょう
占領 occupation, possession, capture

りょうしゅうしょ
領収書 receipt
りょうかい
領海 territorial waters
ようりょう　わる
要領が悪い do not get the hang of doing

ノ ⼈ ⼃ ⼿ ⼹ ⼹ ⼹ ⻌ 領 領 領 領 領 領　14

1074

力

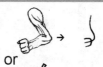

ON-KUN READINGS: リキ・リョク・ちから

HEADER: 力

strength; power

ORIGIN: There are two ancient forms for this kanji. One came from the depiction of a big hand with bulging muscles, which signified strength. Another was a plow, which also required manual strength. The kanji 力 means "power; strength."

ちから
力 strength
ちからしごと
力仕事 physical labor
ちからづよ
力強い powerful

りきさく
力作 masterpiece
じつりょく
実力 real ability
はくりょく
迫力 power, force, drive

フ力　2

1075

緑

ON-KUN READINGS: リョク・ロク・みどり

HEADER: 糸

green

ORIGIN: In the old form 綠 the left side was 糸 "threads." The right side was 彔, drilling a piece of wood for carving (and scattering sawdust), here used phonetically to indicate "green silk." Together they mean "green cloth." The kanji 緑 means "green."

みどり
緑 green
りょくち
緑地 green land
りょくちゃ
緑茶 green tea

しんりょく
新緑の fresh, green season
ろくしょう
緑青 green copper rust

く ⼷ ⼟ ⼿ 糸 糸 紀 絹 綁 綠 緑 緑 緑 緑　14

1076

林

ON-KUN READINGS: リン・はやし

HEADER: 木

woods

ORIGIN: Two (also signifying "many") trees standing side by side indicated woods. The kanji 林 means "woods." (Three trees, 森, is a "forest.")

はやし
林 woods
しんりん
森林 forest
みつりん
密林 jungle

まつばやし
松林 pine grove
りんりつ
林立する to stand close together
しょくりん
植林する to reforest

一 十 オ 木 村 材 林　8

1077

ON-KUN READINGS: リン・のぞ(む)

HEADER: 臣

臨

look out upon;
to be present at;
to deal with

ORIGIN: The left side 臣 was the wide-open eye of a person bowing deeply to serve a master, signifying "to keep a watchful eye." The right side had a person above 品 "three (many) items." Together they indicated "to look out upon," or "to be present at." Being at the scene enables one to deal with the matter at hand. The kanji 臨 means "to look out upon; to be present at; to deal with."

りんじ
臨時 temporary
のぞ
臨む to look upon
くんりん
君臨する to reign over

りんじゅう
臨終 dying hour
りんしょうい
臨床医 clinical doctor
りんせき
臨席 attendance of a
dignitary

丨 丨 厂 厂 F F E E 臣 臣 臣 臣 臣 臣 臣 臣 臨 臨 18

1078

ON-KUN READINGS: リン・わ

HEADER: 車

輪

wheel

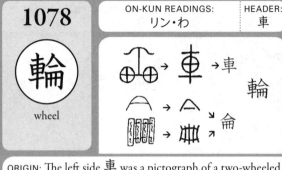

ORIGIN: The left side 車 was a pictograph of a two-wheeled chariot viewed from above. The right side 侖 indicated things that were connected 冊 as one 亼. On a wheel, all radii come to one point. The kanji 輪 means "wheel."

わ
輪 wheel, circle
しゃりん
車輪 wheel
わ
輪ゴム elastic band

さんりんしゃ
三輪車 tricycle
うちわ
内輪 private, inner circle
ねんりん
年輪 tree ring

一 丆 ㄅ 百 亘 車 車 軒 軒 軩 輪 輪 輪 輪 15

1079

ON-KUN READINGS: リン・となり

HEADER: 阝

隣

neighbor

ORIGIN: In the old form 鄰, the left side was a person surrounded by fires or lights (miscopied as 米), and his or her two feet 舛, and the right side was a village (a land with people). A neighborhood is a place where lights are lit and where there is a lot of foot traffic. The position of the two parts became reversed and the current kanji 隣 means "neighbor."

となり
隣 next door
りんじん
隣人 neighbor
きんりんしょこく
近隣諸国 neighboring
countries

となりきんじょ
隣近所 neighbors,
neighborhood
りょうどなり
両隣 neighbors on both
sides

丨 ⻖ ⻖ ⻖ ⻖' ⻖' ⻖' ⻖* ⻖* ⻖米 ⻖米 隣 隣 隣 隣 16

1080

ON-KUN READINGS: ルイ・たぐい

HEADER: 頁

類

sort; variety

ORIGIN: On the top left, 米 "rice" signified all kinds of grains; 大, from 犬 "dog," stood for animals in general. The right side 頁 is "head; person." Together they indicated a variety of things and groups. The kanji 類 means "sort; variety."

しゅるい
種類 kinds
じんるい
人類 human beings
ぶんるい
分類 classification
しょるい
書類 documents

いるい
衣類 clothes
どうるい
同類 same kinds
たぐい
類のない unique

丷 丷 丬 半 米 米 类 类 类 类 類 類 類 類 類 類 類 18

306

1081

ON-KUN READINGS: レイ

HEADER: 人

令
order

ORIGIN: The top 亼 indicated gathering things or people in one place. The bottom 卩 depicted a person kneeling in humility. Together they indicated people respectfully gathered to hear what a superior has to say. The kanji 令 means "order." (A mincho-style typeface looks like 令.)

めいれい
命令 order
ほうれい
法令 ordinance
ごうれい
号令 (voice) command

じれい
辞令 written appointment
れいじょう
令状 warrant
れいふじん
令夫人 wife [honorific]

ノ ㇒ 人 今 令　　5

1082

ON-KUN READINGS: レイ・たと(え)

HEADER: イ

例
example

ORIGIN: The ancient form consisted of イ "person," 歹 "beheaded head" with hair attached, and リ "knife; sword." After beheading enemies, their captors would display the heads in a row as a sign of victory, and as an example to others. The gruesome meaning was dropped. The kanji 例 means "example; row; line."

れい
例 example
たと
例えば for example
れいぶん
例文 example sentence

れいじ
例示する to show an example
じつれい
実例 actual example
れいねん
例年の annual, normal

ノ イ イ′ 仸 伤 歽 例 例　　8

307

1083

ON-KUN READINGS: レイ・つめ(たい)・ひ(やす)・さ(ます)

HEADER: 冫

冷
cool (to the touch)

ORIGIN: The left side 冫 depicted ice with a few cracks in it. The right side 令 was used phonetically to indicate "cool." The kanji 冷 means "cool (to the touch)." (冷 is also written as 冷 in a mincho-style typeface.)

つめ
冷たい cold (to the touch)
れいぞうこ
冷蔵庫 refrigerator
ひ
冷やす to cool

れいとうしょくひん
冷凍食品 frozen food
れいたん
冷淡 coldhearted, cold
ひ あせ
冷や汗 nervous sweat

丶 冫 冫′ 氿 冷 冷 冷　　7

1084

ON-KUN READINGS: レイ・ライ

HEADER: ネ

礼
to bow; propriety; a gift in token of gratitude

ORIGIN: An old form 禮 incorporated 示 "altar." The right side 豊 was stalks of freshly harvested broomcorn millet, signifying offerings. A religious ceremony requires a level of propriety. Even though the old form is seen occasionally in a festival, the kanji 礼 is used to indicate "to bow," "propriety," or "token of gratitude."

れい
礼 bowing, gratitude
しつれい
失礼 impolite
れいぎ
礼儀 etiquette
もくれい
目礼 silent bow

ぶれい
無礼な uncivil
ぶれいこう
無礼講 without formalities
れいふく
礼服 ceremonial outfit

丶 ラ ネ ネ 礼　　5

1085

ON-KUN READINGS:	HEADER:
レキ	止

歴

history; path

ORIGIN: In the ancient form, the top was 厤, depicting rice plants 禾, now 木, neatly hanging under a roof 厂 to dry. At the bottom 止 "foot" indicated that one walked a path of many stops in an orderly manner. Together the forms signified many seasons of harvest counted one by one. The kanji 歴 means "history; path."

れきし
歴史 history
しょくれき
職歴 work history
がくれき
学歴 educational history

りれきしょ
履歴書 curriculum vitae
けいれき
経歴 past career history
れきほう
歴訪 tour

一 厂 厂 厂 厤 厤 厤 厤 厤 麻 歴 歴 歴 歴 14

1086

ON-KUN READINGS:	HEADER:
レツ	リ

列

line; row

ORIGIN: The left side was 歹 "beheaded head," and the right was リ "knife; sword." After beheading, enemy heads were lined up in a display of victory. The gruesome meaning was dropped, and the kanji 列 now means "row; line."

れつ
列 line
ごれつめ
五列目 fifth line
れっきょう
列強 the world's (military) powers

ぎょうれつ
行列 procession
れっしゃ
列車 a train
れっき
列記する to list

一 ア 万 歹 列 列 6

1087

ON-KUN READINGS:	HEADER:
レン・こい・こ(う)	心

恋

to be in love

ORIGIN: The top of the old form 戀 had two skeins of threads and words, phonetically indicating "to yearn after." The bottom was 心, an anatomical heart. Someone with a heart tangled up with emotion, or yearning, is in love. Now with a reduced top 亦, the kanji 恋 means "to be in love."

こい
恋 love
こいびと
恋人 lover
れんあい
恋愛 love affairs

こい
恋しい to long for, to miss
しつれん
失恋 heartbreak
こいぶみ
恋文 love letter

` 一 亣 亣 亦 亦 恋 恋 恋 恋 10

1088

ON-KUN READINGS:	HEADER:
レン・ね(る)	糸

練

to refine; knead; train

ORIGIN: The left side 糸 "thread" came from thin silk filaments pulled out of silkworm cocoons. The right side 東 was from 束 "bundle" and 一 "tie"; the phonetic meaning was "to soften," referring to a process of boiling and refining silk. The kanji 練 means "to refine," "to knead."

ね
練る to knead
ね　　ある
練り歩く to parade
しれん
試練 trial, ordeal

せんれん
洗練 sophistication
れんたつ
練達した expert in, skilled in
れんにゅう
練乳 condensed milk

く 幺 幺 糸 糸 糸 紵 紵 紵 紳 練 練 練 14

308

1089

連

linking; accompanying

ORIGIN: The upper right was 車 "cart with a load of goods." The lower left 辶 had the earlier forms 辶 from 辵, the left half of a crossroad and a footprint, signifying "moving forward." Together they described a line of carts moving forward. The kanji 連 means "linking; accompanying."

つ
連れてくる to bring (person)
れんらく
連絡する to contact
れんりつせいけん
連立政権 coalition
　　government

つ
連れ accompanying person
こくれん
国連 the United Nations
れんぽう
連邦 federation

一 ⺁ ⺁ 盲 盲 亘 車 軎 連 連　10

1090

路

road

ORIGIN: The left side was 足 "leg; foot," which came from ロ "knee" and 止 "foot." The right side 各 "each" had 夂 "foot coming down" (with the toes pointed towards the bottom) on a rock ロ. Together they indicated alleys between blocks in town where one walks, or a road in general. The kanji 路 means "road."

どうろ
道路 road
つうろ
通路 passage
ろじょうちゅうしゃ
路上駐車 street parking

じゅうじろ
十字路 intersection
みち
路 road
ろじうら
路地裏 back alley

丶 口 口 口 ⻊ ⻊ ⻊ ⻊ ⻊ ⻊ 跁 跁 路 路　13

1091

労

to take trouble; hardship

ORIGIN: The old form 勞 had two burning torches (火) and a strong hand (力). It signified exerting all one's energy, as if burning a fire. Now reduced to 労, the kanji means "to take trouble" or "hardship."

くろう
苦労 hardship
ろうどう
労働 labor
いた
労わる to treat kindly

かろう
過労 overwork, exhaustion
ろうりょく
労力 trouble, effort
しんろう
心労 strain of grief or worry

丶 丷 ⺍ ⺌ 労 学 労　7

1092

朗

cheerful; bright

ORIGIN: The left side 良 depicted water running over rice in a basket to eliminate dust, but here it was used phonetically. The right side 月 "moon" signified "bright light" and also "cheerful." The kanji 朗 means "bright" or "cheerful."

ろうほう
朗報 good news
ほが
朗らか cheerful
めいろう
明朗な clear and transparent

ろうどく
朗読 recitation
ろうろう
朗朗たる clear, sonorous

丶 ⼇ ⺬ ⺬ 自 良 朗 朗 朗 朗　10

309

1093

ON-KUN READINGS: ロウ・お(いる)・ふ(ける)

HEADER: 耂

老

old

ORIGIN: The top 耂 depicted an elderly man with the long hair of age, and ヒ signified the body of a deceased person. An old person is close to death. The kanji 老 means "old."

ろうじん
老人 old people
けいろう ひ
敬老の日 senior citizens' day
お
老いた old

ろうか
老化 aging
ろうご
老後 one's old age
ろうれん
老練な experienced, veteran

一 十 土 耂 耂 老   6

1094

ON-KUN READINGS: ロク・リク・む(っつ)

HEADER: 八

六

six

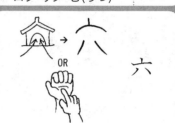

ORIGIN: When counting to six, one holds up a fist and an additional finger. The sound for "fist" is similar to the sound for "house," which may be why the kanji 六, which depicts an entrance to a house, means "six."

ろく
六 six
む
六つ six items
むいか
六日 six days, sixth day of the month

ろくにん
六人 six people
ろっかい
六回 six times
ろっぽう
六法 statute book, the six codes (of laws)

丶 一 六 六   4

1095

ON-KUN READINGS: ロク

HEADER: 金

録

to record

ORIGIN: In the old form 錄, the left side is metal. The right side 彔 depicted carving a piece of wood, with the sawdust dispersing. Together they indicated carving a piece of metal (such as bronze) to record an important event. The kanji 録 means "to record."

きろく
記録 record
ろくおん
録音 sound recording
ろくが
ビデオ録画 video recording

しゅうろく
収録 recording of video, sound, articles
じんめいろく
人名録 Who's Who
ぎじろく
議事録 meeting minutes

ノ ト ㇌ ㇌ 牟 牟 余 金 釒 釖 釾 鈩 鋳 鋳 録   16

1096

ON-KUN READINGS: ロン

HEADER: 言

論

logic; argument

ORIGIN: The left side was 言 "word" and the right side was 侖, consisting of 亼 "to collect in one place" and 冊 "bundle of bamboo sticks to write on." A neatly arranged set of ideas, or argument, is logical. The kanji 論 means "logic" or "argument."

ぎろん
議論 argument, discussion
ろんり
論理 logic
むろん
無論 beyond dispute

ろんがい
論外 out of the question
こうろん
口論 quarrel
もちろん
勿論 naturally

丶 亠 ㇟ ㇟ 言 言 言 訡 論 論 論 論 論 論   15

310

1097

ON-KUN READINGS: ワ・やわ(らぐ)・なご(やか)

HEADER: 口

和

harmony; Japanese

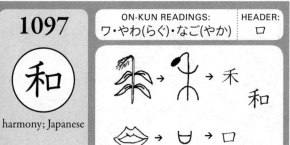

ORIGIN: In the ancient form the left side 禾 was rice plant, here used phonetically to indicate "to agree," and the right side 口 was "mouth." The kanji 和 indicated that people talk harmoniously, or just "harmony." From the old name of Japan, it also means "Japanese."

へいわ
平和 peace
しょうわ
昭和 Showa Era 1926–1989
かんわじてん
漢和辞典 Japanese kanji
　　　dictionary

やまと
大和 Yamato (Japan)
にゅうわ
柔和 gentle, meek
わか
和歌 Japanese poetry

一 二 千 千 禾 和 和 和　　8

1098

ON-KUN READINGS: ワ・はな(す)・はなし

HEADER: 言

話

to speak

ORIGIN: The left side 言 "word" consisted of a sharp needle over a mouth, signifying "to articulate sharply." The right side 舌 was used phonetically to indicate something good. Together they indicated "to speak well" or just "to converse." The kanji 話 means "to speak."

はな
話す to talk
はなし
話 story
かいわ
会話 conversation

はな
話しかける to accost
わだい
話題 topic of conversation
はな　あ
話し合い meeting

丶 二 ㇾ 言 言 言 言 訁 訐 訐 話 話 話　　13

1099

ON-KUN READINGS: ワク・まど(う)

HEADER: 心

惑

to confuse; bewilderment

ORIGIN: The top 或 indicated a certain piece of land that was protected with a weapon, or just "uncertain (that is, not specified)." The bottom was 心 "heart." A heart that is not certain is bewildered. The kanji 惑 means "to confuse," or "bewilderment."

とまど
戸惑う to be bewildered
まど
惑わされる to get confused
とうわく
当惑する to feel perplexed

ぎわく
疑惑 doubt, suspicion
ふわく
不惑 the age of forty
わくせい
惑星 planet

一 ㇆ 戸 币 玎 或 或 或 惑 惑 惑 惑　　12

1100

ON-KUN READINGS: (repeat mark)

々

(repeating the immediately preceding kanji)

ORIGIN: This kanji is a form for repeating the immediately preceding kanji, used like ditto marks in English. One theory holds that this kanji was derived from 仝, a variant form of 同 "same." The form 々 is generally not listed in kanji reference books.

らくらく
楽々と easily
ふかぶか
深々と deeply
ひとびと
人々 people, each person

ときどき
時々 sometimes, now and
　　　then

ノ 刀 々　　3

311

INDEX 1
Order of Appearance in *The Key to Kanji*
(本書所収の漢字)

Numbers refer to kanji numbers in this book.

#	漢字	#	漢字	#	漢字	#	漢字	#	漢字	#	漢字	#	漢字	#	漢字
721	段	770	程	819	銅	868	発	917	浮	966	訪	1015	野	1064	流
722	男	771	敵	820	得	869	髪	918	父	967	豊	1016	役	1065	留
723	談	772	的	821	徳	870	抜	919	符	968	亡	1017	約	1066	旅
724	値	773	笛	822	特	871	判	920	負	969	忘	1018	薬	1067	両
725	知	774	適	823	毒	872	半	921	武	970	忙	1019	訳	1068	寮
726	地	775	鉄	824	独	873	反	922	部	971	暴	1020	油	1069	料
727	池	776	典	825	読	874	板	923	風	972	望	1021	輸	1070	涼
728	置	777	天	826	突	875	版	924	副	973	棒	1022	優	1071	良
729	遅	778	展	827	届	876	犯	925	復	974	貿	1023	勇	1072	量
730	築	779	店	828	豚	877	班	926	服	975	防	1024	友	1073	領
731	竹	780	転	829	内	878	飯	927	福	976	北	1025	有	1074	力
732	茶	781	点	830	南	879	晩	928	腹	977	僕	1026	由	1075	緑
733	着	782	伝	831	難	880	番	929	複	978	牧	1027	誘	1076	林
734	中	783	殿	832	二	881	否	930	払	979	本	1028	遊	1077	臨
735	仲	784	田	833	肉	882	彼	931	仏	980	凡	1029	郵	1078	輪
736	宙	785	電	834	日	883	悲	932	物	981	妹	1030	夕	1079	隣
737	忠	786	徒	835	乳	884	批	933	分	982	枚	1031	予	1080	類
738	昼	787	渡	836	入	885	比	934	奮	983	毎	1032	余	1081	令
739	柱	788	登	837	任	886	疲	935	粉	984	又	1033	預	1082	例
740	注	789	都	838	認	887	皮	936	文	985	末	1034	幼	1083	冷
741	虫	790	努	839	熱	888	秘	937	聞	986	万	1035	容	1084	礼
742	駐	791	度	840	年	889	肥	938	兵	987	満	1036	曜	1085	歴
743	著	792	土	841	念	890	費	939	平	988	味	1037	様	1086	列
744	貯	793	怒	842	燃	891	非	940	並	989	未	1038	洋	1087	恋
745	丁	794	党	843	納	892	飛	941	閉	990	密	1039	用	1088	練
746	兆	795	冬	844	能	893	備	942	陛	991	脈	1040	羊	1089	連
747	帳	796	刀	845	脳	894	美	943	米	992	民	1041	葉	1090	路
748	庁	797	島	846	農	895	鼻	944	別	993	眠	1042	要	1091	労
749	張	798	投	847	波	896	必	945	変	994	務	1043	陽	1092	朗
750	朝	799	東	848	派	897	筆	946	片	995	夢	1044	養	1093	老
751	潮	800	湯	849	破	898	百	947	編	996	無	1045	欲	1094	六
752	町	801	灯	850	馬	899	俵	948	辺	997	娘	1046	浴	1095	録
753	腸	802	当	851	俳	900	標	949	返	998	名	1047	翌	1096	論
754	調	803	等	852	拝	901	氷	950	便	999	命	1048	来	1097	和
755	長	804	答	853	敗	902	票	951	勉	1000	明	1049	絡	1098	話
756	頂	805	糖	854	背	903	表	952	弁	1001	盟	1050	落	1099	惑
757	鳥	806	統	855	肺	904	評	953	保	1002	迷	1051	乱	1100	々
758	直	807	到	856	配	905	病	954	歩	1003	鳴	1052	卵		
759	賃	808	討	857	倍	906	秒	955	補	1004	免	1053	覧		
760	追	809	豆	858	梅	907	品	956	募	1005	綿	1054	利		
761	痛	810	逃	859	買	908	貧	957	墓	1006	面	1055	理		
762	通	811	頭	860	売	909	不	958	暮	1007	模	1056	裏		
763	低	812	働	861	博	910	付	959	母	1008	毛	1057	里		
764	停	813	動	862	泊	911	夫	960	包	1009	木	1058	離		
765	定	814	同	863	白	912	婦	961	報	1010	目	1059	陸		
766	底	815	堂	864	麦	913	富	962	宝	1011	問	1060	律		
767	庭	816	導	865	箱	914	布	963	放	1012	門	1061	率		
768	弟	817	童	866	畑	915	府	964	方	1013	夜	1062	立		
769	提	818	道	867	八	916	普	965	法	1014		1063	略		

INDEX 2
In Order of *On-* and *Kun*-Readings
(五十音順音訓読み)

Numbers refer to kanji numbers in this book.

読み	漢字	番号
	討	808
う(まれる)	生	601
う(む)	産	398
う(る)	得	820
	売	860
う(れる)	熟	503
うい	初	512
うえ	上	547
うお	魚	204
うけたまわ(る)	承	532
うご(く)	動	813
うし	牛	197
うじ	氏	424
うし(ろ)	後	304
うしな(う)	失	454
	亡	968
うた	歌	82
うたが(う)	疑	174
うち	家	79
	内	829
うつ(す)	写	459
うつ(る)	移	16
	映	38
うつく(しい)	美	894
うつわ	器	154
うぶ	産	398
	初	512
うま	馬	850
うみ	海	102
うめ	梅	858
うやま(う)	敬	250
うら	裏	1056
うわ	上	547
ウン	運	35
	雲	36

え

読み	漢字	番号
エ	会	95
	回	97
	絵	106
え	重	499
え(む)	笑	541
え(る)	得	820
エイ	営	37
	映	38
	栄	39
	永	40
	泳	41
	英	42
	衛	43

読み	漢字	番号
エキ	易	13
	液	44
	益	45
	駅	46
	役	1016
えだ	枝	421
エツ	越	47
えら(い)	偉	9
えら(ぶ)	選	640
エン	円	48
	園	49
	延	50
	沿	51
	演	52
	煙	53
	遠	54
	塩	55

お

読み	漢字	番号
オ	悪	2
	汚	56
お	御	305
	緒	515
	小	529
お(いる)	老	1093
お(う)	生	601
	追	760
	負	920
お(きる)	起	172
お(く)	置	728
お(す)	押	61
	推	584
お(ちる)	落	1050
お(びる)	帯	696
お(りる)	降	341
お(る)	居	199
	織	558
	折	621
お(ろす)	下	71
お(わる)	終	488
オウ	央	57
	奥	58
	往	59
	応	60
	押	61
	桜	62
	横	63
	王	64
	黄	65
	皇	330

読み	漢字	番号
おお(い)	多	691
おお(きい)	大	705
おおやけ	公	312
おか	丘	181
おか(す)	犯	876
おが(む)	拝	852
おぎな(う)	補	955
オク	億	66
	屋	67
おく	奥	58
おく(る)	送	666
	贈	671
おく(れる)	後	304
	遅	729
おこ(す)	興	217
おこ(る)	怒	793
おごそ(か)	厳	286
おこた(る)	怠	698
おこな(う)	行	336
おさ(める)	治	445
	収	480
	修	485
	納	843
おさな(い)	幼	1034
おし(える)	教	213
おそ(い)	遅	729
おそ(れる)	恐	212
おそ(わる)	教	213
おっと	夫	911
おと	音	70
おとうと	弟	768
おとこ	男	722
おとず(れる)	訪	966
おどろ(く)	驚	220
おな(じ)	同	814
おのおの	各	113
おのずか(ら)	自	449
おのれ	己	296
おび	帯	696
おぼ(える)	覚	118
おも	主	470
	面	1007
おも(い)	重	499
おも(う)	思	418
おもて	表	903
	面	1007
おや	親	572
およ(ぐ)	泳	41
およ(ぶ)	及	184
おり	折	621

読み	漢字	番号
オン	遠	54
	恩	68
	温	69
	音	70
	御	305
おん	女	520
おんな		

か

読み	漢字	番号
カ	下	71
	化	72
	仮	73
	何	74
	価	75
	加	76
	可	77
	夏	78
	家	79
	科	80
	果	81
	歌	82
	河	83
	火	84
	花	85
	荷	86
	課	87
	貨	88
	過	89
かが	日	834
ガ	我	90
	画	91
	芽	92
	賀	93
	飼	435
か(う)	買	859
か(く)	書	517
	欠	261
か(ける)	貸	700
か(す)	勝	524
か(つ)	兼	270
か(ねる)	借	466
か(りる)	交	309
か(わす)	代	703
か(わる)	変	945
	介	94
カイ	会	95
	解	96
	回	97
	快	98
	悔	99
	改	100

Reading	Kanji	No.
	械	101
	海	102
	灰	103
	界	104
	皆	105
	絵	106
	開	107
	階	108
	街	112
かい	貝	109
ガイ	外	110
	害	111
	街	112
かいこ	蚕	400
かえ(す)	返	949
かえ(る)	帰	164
かえり(みる)	省	539
かお	顔	150
かか(わる)	係	245
かがみ	鏡	219
かぎ(る)	限	291
カク	画	91
	各	113
	拡	114
	格	115
	確	116
	穫	117
	覚	118
	角	119
	閣	120
	革	121
	客	179
ガク	学	122
	楽	123
	額	124
かこ(む)	囲	10
かざ	風	923
かさ(ねる)	重	499
かしら	頭	811
かず	数	586
かぜ	風	923
かぞ(える)	数	586
かた	型	247
	形	248
	片	946
	方	964
かた(い)	固	295
	難	831
かた(る)	語	306
かたき	敵	771
かたち	形	248
かたな	刀	796
カッ	合	344
カツ	割	125
	活	126
ガッ	合	344
ガツ	月	267
かつ(ぐ)	担	713
かど	角	119
	門	1013
かな	金	232
かな(しい)	悲	883
かな(でる)	奏	652
かなめ	要	1042
かなら(ず)	必	896
かね	金	232
かの	彼	882
かばね	姓	592
かぶ	株	127
かま(う)	構	328
かみ	紙	427
	守	472
	上	547
	神	570
	髪	869
	通	762
かよ(う)	空	239
から	絡	1049
から(む)	体	694
からだ	仮	73
かり	軽	256
かる(い)	彼	882
かれ	軽	256
かろ(やか)	河	83
かわ	革	121
	川	632
	側	673
	皮	887
カン	寒	128
	刊	129
	巻	130
	完	131
	官	132
	干	133
	幹	134
	感	135
	慣	136
	漢	137
	環	138
	看	139
	管	140
	簡	141
	観	142
	間	143
	関	144
	館	145
かん	神	570
ガン	丸	146
	岸	147
	眼	148
	岩	149
	顔	150
	願	151
	元	284
かんが(える)	考	334

き

Reading	Kanji	No.
キ	危	152
	喜	153
	器	154
	基	155
	奇	156
	寄	157
	希	158
	揮	159
	机	160
	旗	161
	期	162
	機	163
	帰	164
	気	165
	汽	166
	季	167
	紀	168
	規	169
	記	170
	貴	171
	起	172
	己	296
き	黄	65
	樹	479
	生	601
	木	1010
ギ	技	173
	疑	174
	義	175
	議	176
き(える)	消	536
き(く)	効	314
	聞	937
	利	1054
き(た)	来	1048
き(める)	決	262
き(る)	切	619
	着	733
きざ(し)	兆	746
きざ(む)	刻	345
きさき	后	318
きし	岸	147
きず	傷	523
	創	650
きず(く)	築	730
きそ(う)	競	207
きた	北	976
きた(る)	来	1048
きたな(い)	汚	56
キチ	吉	177
キツ	吉	177
	喫	178
きぬ	衣	18
	絹	279
きび(しい)	厳	286
きみ	君	240
	公	312
キャク	客	179
ギャク	逆	180
キュウ	丘	181
	久	182
	休	183
	及	184
	吸	185
	宮	186
	弓	187
	急	188
	救	189
	求	190
	泣	191
	球	192
	究	193
	級	194
	給	195
	旧	196
	九	234
ギュウ	牛	197
キョ	去	198
	居	199
	巨	200
	挙	201
	許	202
ギョ	漁	203

	候	310
	光	311
	公	312
	功	313
	効	314
	厚	315
	口	316
	向	317
	后	318
	好	319
	孝	320
	工	321
	幸	322
	広	323
	康	324
	攻	325
	更	326
	校	327
	構	328
	港	329
	皇	330
	稿	331
	紅	332
	耕	333
	考	334
	航	335
	行	336
	講	337
	郊	338
	鉱	339
	鋼	340
	降	341
	高	342
こう	神	570
ゴウ	強	211
	郷	218
	業	221
	号	343
	合	344
こうべ	首	476
	頭	811
こえ	声	605
こおり	郡	244
	氷	901
コク	刻	345
	告	346
	谷	347
	国	348
	穀	349
	黒	350
	石	614
ゴク	極	224
ここの(つ)	九	234
こころ	心	564
こころ(みる)	試	432
こころざ(す)	志	417
こころざし	志	417
こころよ(い)	快	98
こた(える)	答	804
	応	60
コツ	骨	351
こと	言	290
	事	437
ごと	毎	983
こと(なる)	異	15
ことわ(る)	断	719
こな	粉	935
この(む)	好	319
こま(かい)	細	374
こま(る)	困	354
こめ	米	943
ころ(す)	殺	391
ころ(ぶ)	転	780
ころも	衣	18
こわ	声	605
コン	金	232
	建	273
	今	353
	困	354
	婚	355
	根	356
	混	357
ゴン	勤	226
	権	276
	厳	286
	言	290

さ

サ	佐	358
	左	359
	差	360
	査	361
	砂	362
	再	365
	作	383
	茶	732
ザ	座	363
さ(がる)	下	71
さ(く)	割	125
さ(げる)	提	769
さ(す)	差	360
	指	419
さ(ます)	冷	1083
さ(める)	覚	118
さ(る)	去	198
サイ	催	364
	再	365
	最	366
	妻	367
	才	368
	採	369
	歳	370
	済	371
	災	372
	祭	373
	細	374
	菜	375
	裁	376
	際	377
	財	381
	殺	391
	西	607
	切	619
ザイ	在	378
	材	379
	罪	380
	財	381
さいわ(い)	幸	322
さか	坂	382
	酒	475
さが	性	593
さか(える)	栄	39
さか(さ)	逆	180
さが(す)	探	714
さか(ん)	盛	602
さかい	境	210
さかな	魚	204
さき	先	628
サク	作	383
	昨	384
	策	385
	索	386
	冊	387
さぐ(る)	探	714
さくら	桜	62
さけ	酒	475
ささ(える)	支	420
さず(ける)	授	478
さそ(う)	誘	1027
さだ(める)	定	765
さち	幸	322
サッ	早	657
サツ	冊	387
	刷	388
	察	389
	札	390
	殺	391
ザツ	雑	392
さと	里	1057
さば(く)	裁	376
さま	様	1037
さむ(い)	寒	128
さら	更	326
	皿	393
さわ(る)	障	546
サン	三	394
	参	395
	山	396
	散	397
	産	398
	算	399
	蚕	400
	賛	401
	酸	402
ザン	残	403

し

シ	仕	404
	使	405
	司	406
	史	407
	四	408
	士	409
	始	410
	姉	411
	姿	412
	子	413
	市	414
	矢	415
	師	416
	志	417
	思	418
	指	419
	支	420
	枝	421
	止	422
	死	423
	氏	424
	私	425
	糸	426

シ
紙 427 / 至 428 / 視 429 / 詞 430 / 詩 431 / 試 432 / 誌 433 / 資 434 / 飼 435 / 歯 436 / 次 444 / 示 447 / 自 449

ジ
仕 404 / 事 437 / 似 438 / 児 439 / 字 440 / 寺 441 / 持 442 / 時 443 / 次 444 / 治 445 / 磁 446 / 示 447 / 耳 448 / 自 449 / 辞 450

じ
除 522 / 地 726 / 路 1090

し(いる) 強 211
し(ぬ) 死 423
し(み) 染 637
し(める) 閉 941
し(る) 知 725
しあわ(せ) 幸 322
しお 塩 55 / 潮 751
しか(し) 然 645
じか(に) 直 758
シキ 式 451 / 識 452 / 織 558 / 色 560
ジキ 食 561 / 直 758
しず(か) 静 610
した 下 71 / 舌 627

した(しい) 親 572
したが(う) 従 496
シチ 七 453 / 質 456
シツ 失 454 / 室 455 / 質 456
ジッ ジツ 十 495 / 実 457 / 日 834
しな 品 907
しま 島 797
しめ(す) 示 447
しも 下 71
シャ 砂 362 / 舎 458 / 写 459 / 射 460 / 捨 461 / 社 462 / 者 463 / 謝 464 / 車 465 / 借 466
シャク 尺 467 / 昔 613 / 石 614 / 赤 618
ジャク 若 468 / 弱 469 / 着 733
シュ 主 470 / 取 471 / 守 472 / 手 473 / 種 474 / 酒 475 / 首 476 / 修 485 / 衆 490
ジュ 受 477 / 授 478 / 樹 479 / 就 483 / 従 496
シュウ 収 480 / 周 481 / 宗 482 / 就 483 / 州 484 / 修 485 / 拾 486 / 秋 487 / 終 488 / 習 489 / 衆 490 / 週 491 / 集 492 / 祝 501

ジュウ 拾 486 / 住 493 / 充 494 / 十 495 / 従 496 / 汁 497 / 縦 498 / 重 499 / 宿 500 / 祝 501
シュク 縮 502
ジュク 熟 503
シュツ 出 504
ジュツ 術 505 / 述 506
シュン 春 507
ジュン 準 508 / 純 509 / 順 510
ショ 処 511 / 初 512 / 所 513 / 暑 514 / 緒 515 / 署 516 / 書 517 / 諸 518 / 助 519
ジョ 女 520 / 序 521 / 除 522 / 従 496
ショウ 傷 523 / 勝 524 / 召 525 / 商 526 / 唱 527 / 将 528 / 小 529 / 少 530 / 床 531 / 承 532 / 招 533 / 昭 534 / 松 535 / 消 536 / 焼 537 / 照 538 / 省 539 / 章 540 / 笑 541 / 紹 542 / 証 543 / 象 544 / 賞 545 / 障 546 / 上 547 / 姓 592 / 性 593 / 政 595 / 星 597 / 正 599 / 清 600 / 生 601 / 精 603 / 声 605 / 青 609 / 相 660 / 装 664

ジョウ 上 547 / 丈 548 / 乗 549 / 城 550 / 場 551 / 常 552 / 情 553 / 条 554 / 状 555 / 蒸 556 / 成 594 / 盛 602 / 静 610 / 定 765
ショク 植 557 / 織 558 / 職 559 / 色 560 / 食 561
しら 白 863
しら(べる) 調 754
しりぞ(く) 退 701

しる	汁	497					清	600	
しる(す)	記	170	す(る)	住	493		生	601	銭 641
しるし	印	25	スイ	刷	388		盛	602	鮮 642
しろ	城	550		出	504		精	603	ゼン 前 643
	代	703		吹	582		聖	604	善 644
	白	863		垂	583		声	605	然 645
シン	信	562		推	584		製	606	全 646
	寝	563	スウ	水	585		西	607	
	心	564	すえ	数	586		誠	608	**そ**
	新	565	すがた	末	986		青	609	ソ 祖 647
	森	566	すく(う)	姿	412		静	610	素 648
	深	567	すく(ない)	救	189		背	854	組 649
	申	568	すぐ(れる)	少	530	せい	税	611	想 654
	真	569	すけ	優	1022	ゼイ	説	624	そ(う) 沿 51
	神	570	すこ(し)	助	519	セキ	席	612	そ(める) 初 512
	臣	571	すこ(やか)	少	530		昔	613	染 637
	親	572	すじ	健	269		石	614	そ(る) 反 873
	身	573	すず(しい)	筋	229		積	615	ソウ 宗 482
	進	574	すす(む)	涼	1070		績	616	創 650
	針	575	すな	進	574		責	617	倉 651
	震	576	すべ	砂	362		赤	618	奏 652
ジン	神	570	すべ(て)	術	505		夕	1030	層 653
	臣	571		全	646	せき	関	144	想 654
	人	577	すみ	総	662	セチ	節	623	掃 655
	仁	578	すみ(やか)	炭	715	セツ	殺	391	操 656
	刃	579	すわ(る)	速	680		切	619	早 657
	尋	580	スン	座	363		接	620	巣 658
				寸	587		折	621	争 659
す							設	622	相 660
ス	子	413	**せ**				節	623	窓 661
	主	470	セ	世	588		説	624	総 662
	守	472	せ	背	854		雪	625	草 663
	数	586	ゼ	是	589		絶	626	装 664
	素	648	せ(く)	急	188	ゼツ	舌	627	走 665
す	州	484	せ(める)	攻	325		銭	641	送 666
	巣	658		責	617	ぜに	狭	215	ゾウ 贈 671
ズ	事	437	せ(る)	競	207	せば(める)	狭	215	雑 392
	図	581	セイ	歳	370	せま(い)	先	628	象 544
	豆	809		省	539	セン	千	629	像 667
	頭	811		情	553		宣	630	増 668
す(い)	酸	402		世	588		専	631	臓 669
す(う)	吸	185		制	590		川	632	蔵 670
す(き)	好	319		勢	591		戦	633	贈 671
す(ぎる)	過	89		姓	592		泉	634	造 672
す(ぐ)	直	758		性	593		浅	635	そうろう 候 310
す(てる)	捨	461		成	594		洗	636	ソク 側 673
す(べる)	総	662		政	595		染	637	則 674
	統	806		整	596		線	638	即 675
す(まう)	住	493		星	597		船	639	息 676
す(む)	済	371		晴	598		選	640	束 677
				正	599				測 678

読み	漢字	番号
ゾク	足	679
	速	680
	属	681
	族	682
	続	683
そこ	底	766
そこ(なう)	損	688
そそ(ぐ)	注	740
そだ(つ)	育	23
ソツ	卒	684
	率	1061
そと	外	110
そな(える)	供	206
	備	893
そな(わる)	具	238
その	園	49
そば	側	673
そむ(く)	背	854
そら	空	239
ソン	存	685
	孫	686
	尊	687
	損	688
	村	689
ゾン	存	685

た

読み	漢字	番号
タ	他	690
	多	691
	太	692
た	手	473
	田	784
ダ	打	693
た(える)	絶	626
だ(す)	出	504
た(つ)	経	253
	裁	376
	断	719
	発	868
	立	1062
た(てる)	建	273
た(べる)	食	561
た(める)	貯	744
た(りる)	足	679
た(れる)	垂	583
タイ	太	692
	体	694
	対	695
	帯	696
	待	697
	怠	698
	態	699
	貸	700
	退	701
	隊	702
	代	703
	台	704
	大	705
ダイ	代	703
	台	704
	大	705
	第	706
	題	707
	弟	768
	内	829
たい(ら)	平	939
たか(い)	高	342
たが(い)	互	302
たがや(す)	耕	333
たから	宝	962
タク	宅	708
	度	791
たぐい	類	1080
たくわ(える)	貯	744
たけ	丈	548
	竹	731
たし(か)	確	116
たす(ける)	助	519
たず(ねる)	尋	580
	訪	966
ただ(しい)	正	599
ただ(す)	質	456
ただ(ちに)	直	758
たたか(う)	戦	633
たち	達	709
タツ	達	709
ダツ	脱	710
たっと(い)	貴	171
	尊	687
たて	館	145
	縦	498
たと(え)	例	1082
たに	谷	347
たね	種	474
たの(しい)	楽	123
たば	束	677
たび	度	791
	旅	1066
たま	球	192
	玉	225
たま(う)	給	195
たまご	卵	1052
たみ	民	993
ため	為	14
ため(す)	試	432
たも(つ)	保	953
たよ(り)	便	950
だれ	誰	711
たわら	俵	899
タン	単	712
	担	713
	探	714
	炭	715
	短	716
	誕	717
	反	873
ダン	団	718
	断	719
	暖	720
	段	721
	男	722
	談	723

ち

読み	漢字	番号
チ	治	445
	質	456
	値	724
	知	725
	地	726
	池	727
	置	728
	遅	729
ち	血	266
	千	629
	乳	835
ち(る)	散	397
ちい(さい)	小	529
ちか(い)	近	231
ちが(う)	違	19
ちから	力	1074
チク	築	730
	竹	731
ちち	乳	835
	父	918
ちぢ(む)	縮	502
ちな(む)	因	27
チャ	茶	732
チャク	着	733
チュウ	中	734
	仲	735
	宙	736
	忠	737
	昼	738
	柱	739
	注	740
	虫	741
	駐	742
チョ	緒	515
	著	743
	貯	744
チョウ	重	499
	丁	745
	兆	746
	帳	747
	庁	748
	張	749
	朝	750
	潮	751
	町	752
	腸	753
	調	754
	長	755
	頂	756
	鳥	757
	直	758
チョク	直	758
チン	賃	759

つ

読み	漢字	番号
ツ	通	762
	都	789
つ(く)	就	483
	着	733
	突	826
	付	910
つ(ぐ)	次	444
	接	620
つ(ける)	点	781
つ(げる)	告	346
つ(もる)	積	615
つ(れる)	連	1089
ツイ	対	695
	追	760
つい(やす)	費	890
ツウ	痛	761
	通	762
つか(う)	使	405
つか(える)	仕	404
つか(れる)	疲	886
つかさ	司	406
つかさど(る)	司	406

つき	月	267		展	778		答	804	ともしび	友	1024
つぎ	次	444		店	779		糖	805		灯	801
つく(る)	作	383		転	780		統	806	とり	鳥	757
	創	650		点	781		到	807	トン	団	718
	造	672		殿	783		討	808		豚	828
つくえ	机	160	デン	伝	782		豆	809	とん	問	1012
つた(える)	伝	782		殿	783		逃	810			
つち	土	792		田	784		頭	811	**な**		
つづ(く)	続	683		電	785		道	818	ナ	南	830
つつ(む)	包	960					読	825		納	843
つど(う)	集	492	**と**				納	843	な	菜	375
つと(める)	勤	226	ト	図	581	ドウ	働	812		名	999
	努	790		徒	786		動	813	な(い)	無	997
	勉	951		渡	787		同	814	な(く)	泣	191
	務	995		登	788		堂	815		鳴	1004
つね	常	552		都	789		導	816	な(くなる)	亡	968
つの	角	119		度	791		童	817	な(げる)	投	798
つの(る)	募	956		土	792		道	818	な(す)	為	14
つま	妻	367		頭	811		銅	819	な(る)	成	594
つみ	罪	380	と	戸	298	とうと(い)	貴	171	な(れる)	慣	136
つめ(たい)	冷	1083		時	443		尊	687	ナイ	内	829
つよ(い)	強	211		十	495	とお	十	495	なお(す)	治	445
つら	面	1007		努	790	とお(い)	遠	54		直	758
つら(なる)	連	1089	ド	度	791	とお(る)	通	762	なか	中	734
つるぎ	剣	272		土	792	とき	時	443		仲	735
つわもの	兵	938		怒	793	トク	得	820	なが(い)	永	40
			と(い)	問	1012		徳	821		長	755
て			と(く)	解	96		特	822	なか(ば)	半	872
て	手	473		説	624		読	825	なが(れる)	流	1064
デ	弟	768	と(ぐ)	研	278	ドク	毒	823	なご(やか)	和	1097
て(る)	照	538	と(じる)	閉	941		独	824	なさ(け)	情	553
で(る)	出	504	と(ぶ)	飛	892		読	825	なつ	夏	78
テイ	体	694	と(まる)	泊	862	とこ	床	531	など	等	803
	丁	745	と(む)	富	913		常	552	なな	七	453
	低	763	と(める)	止	422	ところ	処	511	なに	何	74
	停	764		停	764		所	513	なの	七	453
	定	765		留	1065	とし	歳	370	なま	生	601
	底	766	と(る)	採	369		年	840	なま(ける)	怠	698
	庭	767		取	471	トツ	突	826	なみ	波	847
	弟	768	トウ	登	788	とど(く)	届	827		並	940
	提	769		党	794	とど(める)	留	1065	なら(う)	習	489
	程	770		冬	795	ととの(う)	調	754	なら(べる)	並	940
テキ	敵	771		刀	796	ととの(える)	整	596	ナン	男	722
	的	772		島	797	とな(える)	唱	527		南	830
	笛	773		投	798	となり	隣	1079		難	831
	適	774		東	799	との	殿	783		納	843
テツ	鉄	775		湯	800	どの	殿	783	なん	何	74
てら	寺	441		灯	801	とみ	富	913			
テン	典	776		当	802	とも	供	206			
	天	777		等	803		共	208			

に

ニ	児	439
	仁	578
	二	832
に	荷	86
に(げる)	逃	810
に(る)	似	438
にい	新	565
にが(い)	苦	237
ニク	肉	833
にし	西	607
ニチ	日	834
にな(う)	担	713
ニャク	若	468
ニュウ	乳	835
	入	836
ニョ	女	520
ニョウ	女	520
にわ	庭	767
ニン	人	577
	仁	578
	刃	579
	任	837
	認	838

ぬ

ヌ	怒	793
ぬ(く)	抜	870
ぬ(ぐ)	脱	710
ぬし	主	470
ぬの	布	914

ね

ね	音	70
	根	356
	値	724
ね(る)	寝	563
	練	1088
ねが(う)	願	151
ねぎら(う)	労	1091
ネツ	熱	839
ねむ(る)	眠	994
ネン	然	645
	年	840
	念	841
	燃	842

の

の	野	1015
の(ばす)	延	50

の(む)	飲	29
の(る)	乗	549
ノウ	納	843
	能	844
	脳	845
	農	846
のが(れる)	逃	810
のこ(る)	残	403
のぞ(く)	除	522
のぞ(む)	望	972
	臨	1077
のち	後	304
のべ(る)	述	506
のぼ(る)	上	547
	登	788
のり	法	965

は

ハ	波	847
	派	848
	破	849
は	羽	33
	歯	436
	刃	579
	葉	1041
バ	馬	850
ば	場	551
は(える)	映	38
	栄	39
	生	601
は(く)	掃	655
ば(ける)	化	72
は(たす)	果	81
は(る)	張	749
は(れる)	晴	598
ハイ	俳	851
	拝	852
	敗	853
	背	854
	肺	855
	配	856
はい	灰	103
バイ	倍	857
	梅	858
	買	859
	売	860
はい(る)	入	836
はか	墓	957
はか(る)	計	254
	図	581

	測	678
	量	1072
はがね	鋼	340
ハク	博	861
	泊	862
	白	863
バク	博	861
	麦	864
	暴	971
	幕	984
はぐく(む)	育	23
はげ(しい)	激	260
はこ	箱	865
はこ(ぶ)	運	35
はし	橋	214
はじ(めて)	初	512
はじ(める)	始	410
	創	650
はし(る)	走	665
はしら	柱	739
はず(す)	外	110
はた	旗	161
	機	163
	畑	866
はたけ	畑	866
はたら(く)	働	812
ハチ	八	867
ハッ	法	965
ハツ	発	868
	髪	869
はつ	初	512
バツ	抜	870
	末	986
はな	花	85
	鼻	895
はな(す)	放	963
	話	1098
はな(れる)	離	1058
はなし	話	1098
はね	羽	33
はは	母	959
はぶ(く)	省	539
はや(い)	早	657
	速	680
はやし	林	1076
はら	原	285
	腹	928
はら(う)	払	930
はり	針	575
はる	春	507

ハン	坂	382
	判	871
	半	872
	反	873
	板	874
	版	875
	犯	876
	班	877
	飯	878
	凡	980
バン	判	871
	板	874
	晩	879
	番	880
	万	987

ひ

ヒ	否	881
	彼	882
	悲	883
	批	884
	比	885
	疲	886
	皮	887
	秘	888
	肥	889
	費	890
	非	891
	飛	892
ひ	火	84
	灯	801
	日	834
	氷	901
	陽	1043
ビ	備	893
	美	894
	鼻	895
ひ(く)	引	28
ひ(める)	秘	888
ひ(やす)	冷	1083
ひ(る)	干	133
ひか(る)	光	311
ひがし	東	799
ひかり	光	311
ひき(いる)	率	1061
ひく(い)	低	763
ひさ(しい)	久	182
ひじり	聖	604
ひたい	額	124
ひだり	左	359

Reading	Kanji	No.
ヒツ	必	896
	筆	897
ひつじ	羊	1040
ひと	人	577
ひと(しい)	等	803
ひと(つ)	一	24
ひと(り)	独	824
ヒャク	百	898
ビャク	白	863
ヒョウ	俵	899
	標	900
	氷	901
	票	902
	表	903
	評	904
	兵	938
ビョウ	病	905
	秒	906
	平	939
ひら	平	939
ひら(く)	開	107
ひる	昼	738
ひろ(い)	広	323
ひろ(う)	拾	486
ひろ(げる)	拡	114
ヒン	品	907
	貧	908
ビン	便	950
ピン	貧	908

ふ

Reading	Kanji	No.
フ	不	909
	付	910
	夫	911
	婦	912
	富	913
	布	914
	府	915
	普	916
	浮	917
	父	918
	符	919
	負	920
	風	923
	歩	954
ブ	不	909
	武	921
	部	922
	分	933
	歩	954
	無	997
ふ(える)	増	668
ふ(かす)	更	326
ふ(く)	吹	582
ふ(ける)	老	1093
ふ(る)	降	341
フウ	夫	911
	富	913
	風	923
ふえ	笛	773
ふか(い)	深	567
フク	副	924
	復	925
	服	926
	福	927
	腹	928
	複	929
ふし	節	623
ふせ(ぐ)	防	975
ふだ	札	390
ぶた	豚	828
ふた(つ)	二	832
ふたた(び)	再	365
フツ	払	930
ブツ	仏	931
	物	932
ふで	筆	897
ふと(い)	太	692
ふな	船	639
ふね	船	639
ふみ	文	936
ふゆ	冬	795
ふる(い)	旧	196
	古	293
ふる(う)	奮	934
ふる(える)	震	576
フン	分	933
	奮	934
	粉	935
ブン	分	933
	文	936
	聞	937

へ

Reading	Kanji	No.
べ	部	922
	辺	948
べ(し)	可	77
へ(る)	経	253
	減	287
ヘイ	病	905
	兵	938
	平	939
	並	940
	閉	941
	陛	942
ベイ	米	943
ベツ	別	944
べに	紅	332
ヘン	変	945
	片	946
	編	947
	辺	948
	返	949
ベン	便	950
	勉	951
	弁	952

ほ

Reading	Kanji	No.
ホ	保	953
	歩	954
	補	955
ほ	火	84
ボ	募	956
	墓	957
	暮	958
	母	959
	模	1008
ほ(しい)	欲	1045
ほ(す)	干	133
ホウ	包	960
	報	961
	宝	962
	放	963
	方	964
	法	965
	訪	966
	豊	967
	亡	968
ボウ	忘	969
	忙	970
	暴	971
	望	972
	棒	973
	貿	974
	防	975
ほか	外	110
	他	690
ほが(らか)	朗	1092
ホク	北	976
ボク	僕	977
	牧	978
	木	1010
	目	1011
ほし	星	597
ほそ(い)	細	374
ホッ	発	868
	法	965
ほっ(する)	欲	1045
ほど	程	770
ほとけ	仏	931
ほね	骨	351
ほろ(びる)	亡	968
ホン	反	873
	本	979
ボン	凡	980

ま

Reading	Kanji	No.
ま	間	143
	真	569
	馬	850
	目	1011
ま(がる)	曲	223
ま(く)	巻	130
ま(ける)	負	920
ま(ざる)	交	309
ま(す)	増	668
ま(ず)	先	628
ま(ぜる)	混	357
ま(だ)	未	990
ま(つ)	待	697
マイ	米	943
	妹	981
	枚	982
	毎	983
まい(る)	参	395
まえ	前	643
まか(せる)	任	837
まき	巻	130
	牧	978
マク	幕	984
まご	孫	686
まこと	真	569
	誠	608
まさ	正	599
まさ(る)	勝	524
まじ(わる)	交	309
まず(しい)	貧	908
また	又	985
まち	街	112
	町	752

読み	漢字	番号
マツ	末	986
まつ	松	535
まつ(り)	祭	373
まった(く)	全	646
まつりごと	政	595
まと	的	772
まど	窓	661
まど(う)	惑	1099
まな	愛	1
まな(ぶ)	学	122
まなこ	眼	148
まぬか(れる)	免	1005
まね(く)	招	533
まめ	豆	809
まも(る)	守	472
まよ(う)	迷	1003
まる	丸	146
まる(い)	円	48
まわ(り)	周	481
まわ(る)	回	97
マン	万	987
	満	988

み

読み	漢字	番号
ミ	味	989
	未	990
み	三	394
	実	457
	身	573
み(ちる)	満	988
	充	494
み(る)	看	139
	観	142
	見	281
みき	幹	134
みぎ	右	31
みさお	操	656
みじか(い)	短	716
みず	水	585
みずうみ	湖	300
みずか(ら)	自	449
みせ	店	779
みだ(れる)	乱	1051
みち	道	818
みちび(く)	導	816
ミツ	密	991
みっ(つ)	三	394
みと(める)	認	838
みどり	緑	1075
みな	皆	105
みなと	港	329
みなみ	南	830
みなもと	源	288
みの(る)	実	457
みみ	耳	448
みや	宮	186
ミャク	脈	992
みやこ	京	205
	都	789
ミョウ	名	999
	命	1000
	明	1001
ミン	民	993
	眠	994

む

読み	漢字	番号
ム	武	921
	務	995
	夢	996
	無	997
む(こう)	向	317
む(す)	蒸	556
む(っつ)	六	1094
む(れる)	群	242
むか(える)	迎	258
むかし	昔	613
むぎ	麦	864
むく(いる)	報	961
むし	虫	741
むす(ぶ)	結	265
むずか(しい)	難	831
むすめ	娘	998
むな	胸	216
むね	胸	216
	宗	482
むら	村	689
むら(がる)	群	242
むろ	室	455

め

読み	漢字	番号
め	芽	92
	眼	148
	女	520
	目	1011
め(す)	召	525
メイ	名	999
	命	1000
	明	1001
	盟	1002
	迷	1003
	鳴	1004
めし	飯	878
メン	免	1005
	綿	1006
	面	1007

も

読み	漢字	番号
モ	模	1008
も(える)	燃	842
も(しくは)	若	468
も(つ)	持	442
も(り)	守	472
も(る)	盛	602
モウ	亡	968
	望	972
	毛	1009
もう(ける)	設	622
もう(す)	申	568
モク	木	1010
	目	1011
もち(いる)	用	1039
モツ	物	932
もっ(て)	以	7
もっと(も)	最	366
もっぱ(ら)	専	631
もと	下	71
	基	155
	元	284
	本	979
もと(める)	求	190
もとい	基	155
もの	者	463
	物	932
もよお(す)	催	364
もり	森	566
もろ	諸	518
モン	文	936
	聞	937
	問	1012
	門	1013

や

読み	漢字	番号
ヤ	夜	1014
	野	1015
や	屋	67
	家	79
	谷	347
	八	867
	矢	415
や(く)	焼	537
や(む)	病	905
や(める)	辞	450
やかた	館	145
ヤク	益	45
	役	1016
	約	1017
	薬	1018
	訳	1019
やさ(しい)	易	13
	優	1022
やしな(う)	養	1044
やしろ	社	462
やす(い)	安	4
	易	13
やす(む)	休	183
やっ(つ)	八	867
やど	宿	500
やぶ(る)	破	849
やぶ(れる)	敗	853
やま	山	396
やまい	病	905
やわ(らぐ)	和	1097

ゆ

読み	漢字	番号
ユ	油	1020
	輸	1021
	由	1026
	遊	1028
ゆ	湯	800
ゆ(う)	結	265
ゆ(く)	往	59
	行	336
ユイ	遺	20
	由	1026
ユウ	右	31
	優	1022
	勇	1023
	友	1024
	有	1025
	由	1026
	誘	1027
	遊	1028
	郵	1029
	夕	1030
ゆう	故	299
ゆえ	床	531
ゆか	雪	625
ゆき	豊	967
ゆた(か)	委	11
ゆだ(ねる)	指	419
ゆび		

ゆみ	弓	187		絡	1049	レツ	列	1086
ゆめ	夢	996		落	1050	レン	恋	1087
ゆる(す)	許	202	ラン	乱	1051		練	1088
				卵	1052		連	1089

よ

ヨ	予	1031		覧	1053	**ろ**		
	余	1032				ロ	路	1090
	預	1033	**り**			ロウ	労	1091
よ	四	408	リ	利	1054		朗	1092
	世	588		理	1055		老	1093
	代	703		裏	1056	ロク	緑	1075
	夜	1014		里	1057		六	1094
よ(い)	善	644		離	1058		録	1095
	良	1071	リキ	力	1074	ロン	論	1096
よ(ぶ)	呼	294	リク	陸	1059			
よ(む)	読	825		六	1094	**わ**		
よ(る)	因	27	リチ	律	1060	ワ	和	1097
	寄	157	リツ	律	1060		話	1098
ヨウ	幼	1034		率	1061	わ	我	90
	容	1035		立	1062		輪	1078
	曜	1036	リャク	略	1063	わ(かる)	分	933
	様	1037	リュウ	立	1062	わ(る)	割	125
	洋	1038		流	1064	わか(い)	若	468
	用	1039		留	1065	わか(れる)	別	944
	羊	1040	リョ	旅	1066	ワク	惑	1099
	葉	1041	リョウ	両	1067	わけ	訳	1019
	要	1042		寮	1068	わざ	技	173
	陽	1043		料	1069		業	221
	養	1044		涼	1070	わざわ(い)	災	372
よう	八	867		良	1071	わす(れる)	忘	969
ヨク	欲	1045		量	1072	わた	綿	1006
	浴	1046		領	1073	わた(る)	渡	787
	翌	1047		漁	203	わたくし	私	425
よこ	横	63	リョク	力	1074	わら(う)	笑	541
よご(す)	汚	56		緑	1075	わらべ	童	817
よし	義	175	リン	林	1076	わらわ	童	817
	吉	177		臨	1077	わり	割	125
	由	1026		輪	1078	わる(い)	悪	2
よそお(う)	装	664		隣	1079	われ	我	90
よる	夜	1014						
よろこ(ぶ)	喜	153	**る**			**（くりかえし）**		
よろず	万	987	ル	流	1064		々	1100
よわ(い)	弱	469		留	1065			
よん	四	408	ルイ	類	1080			

ら

			れ					
ら	等	803	レイ	令	1081			
ライ	来	1048		例	1082			
	礼	1084		冷	1083			
ラク	楽	123	レキ	礼	1084			
				歴	1085			

INDEX 3
On- and *Kun*-Readings in Rōmaji
(ローマ字による音訓読み)

Numbers refer to kanji numbers in this book.

A				A (cont.)				B				B (cont.)		
a(biru)	浴	1046		araso(u)	争	659		ba	場	551		boku	僕	977
a(garu)	上	547		arata	新	565			馬	850			牧	978
a(geru)	挙	201		arata(meru)	改	100		ba(keru)	化	72			木	1010
a(keru)	開	107		arawa(reru)	現	289		bai	倍	857			目	1011
a(ku)	空	239			表	903			梅	858		bon	凡	980
	明	1001		arawa(su)	著	743			買	859		bou	亡	968
a(mu)	編	947		aru(ku)	歩	954			売	860			忘	969
a(ru)	在	378		aruji	主	470		baku	博	861			忙	970
	有	1025		aruzi	主	470			麦	864			暴	971
a(shiki)	悪	2		asa	朝	750			暴	971			望	972
a(siki)	悪	2		asa(i)	浅	635			幕	984			棒	973
a(taru)	当	802		asa(ru)	漁	203		ban	判	871			貿	974
a(teru)	充	494		ashi	足	679			板	874			防	975
a(u)	会	95		ashita	朝	750			晩	879		bu	不	909
	合	344		asi	足	679			番	880			武	921
aba(ku)	暴	971		asita	朝	750			万	987			部	922
aba(reru)	暴	971		aso(bu)	遊	1028		batsu	抜	870			分	933
abu(nai)	危	152		ata(ri)	辺	948			末	986			歩	954
abura	油	1020		atai	価	75		batu	抜	870			無	997
ai	愛	1			値	724			末	986		bun	分	933
	相	660		atama	頭	811		be	部	922			文	936
aida	間	143		atara(shii)	新	565			辺	948			聞	937
aji	味	989		atara(sii)	新	565		bei	米	943		buta	豚	828
aka	赤	618		atata(kai)	温	69		ben	便	950		butsu	仏	931
aka(rui)	明	1001			暖	720			勉	951			物	932
akashi	証	543		ato	後	304			弁	952		butu	仏	931
akasi	証	543		atsu	圧	3		beni	紅	332			物	932
aki	秋	487		atsu(i)	厚	315		beshi	可	77		byaku	白	863
aki(raka)	明	1001			暑	514		besi	可	77		byō	病	905
akina(i)	商	526			熱	839		betsu	別	944			秒	906
aku	悪	2		atsu(maru)	集	492		betu	別	944			平	939
ama	雨	34		atu	圧	3		bi	備	893		byou	病	905
	天	777		atu(i)	厚	315			美	894			秒	906
ama(ru)	余	1032			暑	514			鼻	895			平	939
ame	雨	34			熱	839		bin	便	950		C		
	天	777		atu(maru)	集	492		bo	募	956		cha	茶	732
an	安	4		aya	文	936			墓	957		chaku	着	733
	暗	5		aya(bumu)	危	152			暮	958		chi	血	266
	案	6		ayama(chi)	過	89			母	959			治	445
	行	336		ayama(ru)	誤	307			模	1008			質	456
ana	穴	264			謝	464		bō	亡	968			千	629
ane	姉	411		ayama(ti)	過	89			忘	969			値	724
ani	兄	246		ayu(mu)	歩	954			忙	970			知	725
ao	青	609		aza	字	440			暴	971			地	726
ara(u)	洗	636		aza(yaka)	鮮	642			望	972			池	727
ara(zu)	非	891		azi	味	989			棒	973			置	728
arakaji(me)	予	1031		azu(karu)	預	1033			貿	974			遅	729
arakazi(me)	予	1031		azuma	東	799			防	975			乳	835

Reading	Kanji	No.
gen	激	260
	眼	148
	験	283
	元	284
	原	285
	厳	286
	減	287
	源	288
	現	289
	言	290
	限	291
getsu	月	267
getu	月	267
gi	技	173
	疑	174
	義	175
	議	176
gin	銀	233
go	期	162
	五	301
	互	302
	午	303
	後	304
	御	305
	語	306
	誤	307
	護	308
gō	強	211
	郷	218
	業	221
	号	343
	合	344
goku	極	224
gon	勤	226
	権	276
	厳	286
	言	290
goto	毎	983
gou	強	211
	郷	218
	業	221
	号	343
	合	344
gu	具	238
gū	宮	186
gun	群	242
	軍	243
	郡	244
guu	宮	186
gyaku	逆	180
gyo	漁	203
	魚	204
	御	305
gyō	業	221
	形	248
	行	336
gyoku	玉	225
gyou	業	221
	形	248
	行	336
gyū	牛	197
gyuu	牛	197

H

Reading	Kanji	No.
ha	羽	33
	歯	436
	刃	579
	波	847
	派	848
	破	849
	葉	1041
ha(eru)	映	38
	栄	39
	生	601
ha(ku)	掃	655
ha(reru)	晴	598
ha(ru)	張	749
ha(t)	法	965
ha(tasu)	果	81
habu(ku)	省	539
hachi	八	867
hagane	鋼	340
hage(shii)	激	260
hage(sii)	激	260
haguku(mu)	育	23
haha	母	959
hai	灰	103
	俳	851
	拝	852
	敗	853
	背	854
	肺	855
	配	856
hai(ru)	入	836
haji(meru)	始	410
	創	650
haji(mete)	初	512
haka	墓	957
haka(ru)	計	254
	図	581
	測	678
	量	1072
hako	箱	865
hako(bu)	運	35
haku	博	861
	泊	862
	白	863
han	坂	382
	判	871
	半	872
	反	873
	板	874
	版	875
	犯	876
	班	877
	飯	878
	凡	980
hana	花	85
	鼻	895
hana(reru)	離	1058
hana(su)	放	963
	話	1098
hanashi	話	1098
hanasi	話	1098
hane	羽	33
hara	原	285
	腹	928
hara(u)	払	930
hari	針	575
haru	春	507
hashi	橋	214
hashi(ru)	走	665
hashira	柱	739
hasi	橋	214
hasi(ru)	走	665
hasira	柱	739
hata	旗	161
	機	163
	畑	866
hatake	畑	866
hatara(ku)	働	812
hati	八	867
hatsu	初	512
	発	868
	髪	869
hatu	初	512
	発	868
	髪	869
haya(i)	早	657
	速	680
hayashi	林	1076
hayasi	林	1076
hazi(meru)	始	410
	創	650
hazi(mete)	初	512
hazu(su)	外	110
he(ru)	経	253
	減	287
hei	病	905
	兵	938
	平	939
	並	940
	閉	941
	陛	942
hen	変	945
	片	946
	編	947
	辺	948
	返	949
hi	火	84
	灯	801
	日	834
	否	881
	彼	882
	悲	883
	批	884
	比	885
	疲	886
	皮	887
	秘	888
	肥	889
	費	890
	非	891
	飛	892
	氷	901
	陽	1043
hi(ku)	引	28
hi(ru)	干	133
hi(yasu)	冷	1083
hidari	左	359
higashi	東	799
higasi	東	799
hijiri	聖	604
hika(ru)	光	311
hikari	光	311
hiki(iru)	率	1061
hiku(i)	低	763
hi(meru)	秘	888
hin	品	907
	貧	908
hira	平	939
hira(ku)	開	107
hiro(garu)	拡	114
hiro(i)	広	323
hiro(u)	拾	486
hiru	昼	738
hisa(shii)	久	182
hisa(sii)	久	182
hitai	額	124
hito	人	577
hito(ri)	独	824
hito(shii)	等	803
hito(sii)	等	803
hito(tsu)	一	24
hito(tu)	一	24
hitsu	必	896
	筆	897
hitsuji	羊	1040
hitu	必	896
	筆	897
hituzi	羊	1040
hiya(su)	冷	1083
hiziri	聖	604
ho	火	84
	保	953
	歩	954
	補	955
	包	960
hō		

Reading	Kanji	No.
	報	961
	宝	962
	放	963
	方	964
	法	965
	訪	966
	豊	967
ho(shii)	欲	1045
ho(sii)	欲	1045
ho(su)	干	133
hodo	程	770
hoga(raka)	朗	1092
hoka	外	110
	他	690
hoku	北	976
hon	反	873
	本	979
hone	骨	351
horo(biru)	亡	968
hos(suru)	欲	1045
hoshi	星	597
hosi	星	597
hoso(i)	細	374
hot-	発	868
	法	965
hotoke	仏	931
hou	包	960
	報	961
	宝	962
	放	963
	方	964
	法	965
	訪	966
	豊	967
hu	不	909
	付	910
	夫	911
	婦	912
	富	913
	布	914
	府	915
	普	916
	浮	917
	父	918
	符	919
	負	920
	風	923
	歩	954
huu	夫	911
	富	913
	風	923
hu(eru)	増	668
hu(kasu)	更	326
hu(keru)	老	1093
hu(ku)	吹	582
hu(ru)	降	341
huda	札	390
hude	筆	897
hue	笛	773
huka(i)	深	567
huku	副	924
	復	925
	服	926
	福	927
	腹	928
	複	929
humi	文	936
hun	分	933
	奮	934
	粉	935
huna	船	639
hune	船	639
huru(eru)	震	576
huru(i)	旧	196
	古	293
huru(u)	奮	934
huse(gu)	防	975
husi	節	623
hutata(bi)	再	365
huta(tu)	二	832
huto(i)	太	692
hutu	払	930
huu	夫	911
	富	913
	風	923
huyu	冬	795
hyaku	百	898
hyō	俵	899
	標	900
	氷	901
	票	902
	表	903
	評	904
	兵	938
hyou	俵	899
	標	900
	氷	901
	票	902
	表	903
	評	904
	兵	938

I

Reading	Kanji	No.
i	以	7
	位	8
	偉	9
	囲	10
	委	11
	意	12
	易	13
	為	14
	異	15
	移	16
	胃	17
	衣	18
	違	19
	遺	20
	医	21
i(kiru)	生	601
i(ku)	行	336
i(reru)	入	836
i(ru)	居	199
	射	460
	要	1042
i(u)	言	290
ichi	一	24
	市	414
ichijiru(shii)	著	743
ie	家	79
ika(ri)	怒	793
ika(su)	活	126
ike	池	727
iki	域	22
	息	676
ikio(i)	勢	591
iku	育	23
ikusa	軍	243
	戦	633
ima	今	353
ima(da)	未	990
imōto	妹	981
imouto	妹	981
in	印	25
	員	26
	因	27
	引	28
	飲	29
	院	30
	音	70
ina(mu)	否	881
inishie	古	293
inisie	古	293
inochi	命	1000
inoti	命	1000
inu	犬	277
iro	色	560
isa(mashii)	勇	1023
isa(masii)	勇	1023
isagiyo(i)	潔	263
ishi	石	614
isi	石	614
iso(gu)	急	188
isoga(shii)	忙	970
isoga(sii)	忙	970
ita	板	874
ita(i)	痛	761
ita(mu)	傷	523
ita(ru)	至	428
	到	807
itada(ku)	頂	756
itadaki	頂	756
itawa(ru)	労	1091
itazura(ni)	徒	786
iti	一	24
	市	414
itiziru(sii)	著	743
ito	糸	426
itona(mu)	営	37
itsu	一	24
itsutsu	五	301
itu	一	24
itutu	五	301
iwa	岩	149
iwa(u)	祝	501
izumi	泉	634

J

Reading	Kanji	No.
jaku	若	468
	弱	469
	着	733
ji	仕	404
	事	437
	似	438
	児	439
	字	440
	寺	441
	持	442
	時	443
	次	444
	治	445
	磁	446
	示	447
	耳	448
	自	449
	辞	450
	除	522
	地	726
	路	1090
jika(ni)	直	758
jiki	食	561
	直	758
jin	神	570
	臣	571
	人	577
	仁	578
	刃	579
	尋	580
jit-	十	495
jitsu	実	457
	日	834
jō	助	519
	女	520
	序	521
	除	522
	上	547
	丈	548
	乗	549
	城	550

	健	269
	兼	270
	券	271
	剣	272
	建	273
	憲	274
	検	275
	権	276
	犬	277
	研	278
	絹	279
	県	280
	見	281
	険	282
	験	283
ketsu	欠	261
	決	262
	潔	263
	穴	264
	結	265
	血	266
ketu	欠	261
	決	262
	潔	263
	穴	264
	結	265
	血	266
kewa(shii)	険	282
kewa(sii)	険	282
ki	黄	65
	危	152
	喜	153
	器	154
	基	155
	奇	156
	寄	157
	希	158
	揮	159
	机	160
	旗	161
	期	162
	機	163
	帰	164
	気	165
	汽	166
	季	167
	紀	168
	規	169
	記	170
	貴	171
	起	172
	己	296
	樹	479
	生	601
	木	1010
ki(eru)	消	536
ki(ku)	効	314
	聞	937
	利	1054
ki(meru)	決	262
ki(ru)	切	619
	着	733
ki(ta)	来	1048
kibi(shii)	厳	286
kibi(sii)	厳	286
kichi	吉	177
kimi	君	240
	公	312
kin	勤	226
	均	227
	禁	228
	筋	229
	緊	230
	近	231
	金	232
	今	353
kinu	衣	18
	絹	279
kisaki	后	318
kishi	岸	147
kisi	岸	147
kiso(u)	競	207
kita	北	976
kita(ru)	来	1048
kitana(i)	汚	56
kiti	吉	177
kitsu	吉	177
	喫	178
kitu	吉	177
	喫	178
kiwa	際	377
kiwa(meru)	究	193
	極	224
kiyo(i)	清	600
kiza(mu)	刻	345
kiza(shi)	兆	746
kiza(si)	兆	746
kizu	傷	523
	創	650
kizu(ku)	築	730
ko	黄	65
	去	198
	個	292
	古	293
	呼	294
	固	295
	己	296
	庫	297
	戸	298
	故	299
	湖	300
	子	413
	小	529
	神	570
	粉	935
	木	1010
kō	黄	65
	格	115
	興	217
	後	304
	交	309
	候	310
	光	311
	公	312
	功	313
	効	314
	厚	315
	口	316
	向	317
	后	318
	好	319
	孝	320
	工	321
	幸	322
	広	323
	康	324
	攻	325
	更	326
	校	327
	構	328
	港	329
	皇	330
	稿	331
	紅	332
	耕	333
	考	334
	航	335
	行	336
	講	337
	郊	338
	鉱	339
	鋼	340
	降	341
	高	342
	神	570
ko(eru)	越	47
	肥	889
ko(mu)	込	352
ko(nai)	来	1048
ko(re)	是	589
ko(u)	恋	1087
kōbe	首	476
	頭	811
koe	声	605
koi	恋	1087
kokono(tsu)	九	234
kokono(tu)	九	234
kokoro	心	564
kokoro(miru)	試	432
kokoroyo(i)	快	98
kokoroza(su)	志	417
kokorozashi	志	417
kokorozasi	志	417
koku	刻	345
	告	346
	谷	347
	国	348
	穀	349
	黒	350
	石	614
koma(kai)	細	374
koma(ru)	困	354
kome	米	943
kon	金	232
	建	273
	今	353
	困	354
	婚	355
	根	356
	混	357
kona	粉	935
kono(mu)	好	319
koori	郡	244
	氷	901
kōri	郡	244
	氷	901
koro(bu)	転	780
koro(su)	殺	391
koromo	衣	18
kota(eru)	応	60
	答	804
koto	言	290
	事	437
koto(naru)	異	15
kotowa(ru)	断	719
kotsu	骨	351
kotu	骨	351
kou	黄	65
	格	115
	興	217
	後	304
	交	309
	候	310
	光	311
	公	312
	功	313
	効	314
	厚	315
	口	316
	向	317
	后	318
	好	319
	孝	320
	工	321
	幸	322
	広	323
	康	324
	攻	325

Reading	Kanji	No.
	更	326
	校	327
	構	328
	港	329
	皇	330
	稿	331
	紅	332
	耕	333
	考	334
	航	335
	行	336
	講	337
	郊	338
	鉱	339
	鋼	340
	降	341
	高	342
koube	神	570
	首	476
	頭	811
kowa	声	605
ku	久	182
	宮	186
	供	206
	九	234
	句	235
	区	236
	苦	237
	空	239
	庫	297
	公	312
	功	313
	口	316
	工	321
	紅	332
kū	空	239
ku(mu)	組	649
ku(reru)	暮	958
ku(ru)	来	1048
ku(u)	食	561
ku(yamu)	悔	99
kuba(ru)	配	856
kubi	首	476
kuchi	口	316
kuda	管	140
kuda(ru)	下	71
kumi	組	649
kumo	雲	36
kun	君	240
	訓	241
kuni	国	348
kura	庫	297
	倉	651
	蔵	670
kura(beru)	比	885
kura(i)	暗	5
kurai	位	8
kurenai	紅	332
kuro	黒	350
kuru(shii)	苦	237
kuru(sii)	苦	237
kuruma	車	465
kusa	草	663
kusuri	薬	1018
kuti	口	316
kuu	空	239
kuwa(eru)	加	76
kuya(shii)	悔	99
kuya(sii)	悔	99
kyaku	客	179
kyo	去	198
	居	199
	巨	200
	挙	201
	許	202
kyō	京	205
	供	206
	競	207
	共	208
	協	209
	境	210
	強	211
	恐	212
	教	213
	橋	214
	狭	215
	胸	216
	興	217
	郷	218
	鏡	219
	驚	220
	兄	246
	経	253
kyoku	局	222
	曲	223
	極	224
kyou	京	205
	供	206
	競	207
	共	208
	協	209
	境	210
	強	211
	恐	212
	教	213
	橋	214
	狭	215
	胸	216
	興	217
	郷	218
	鏡	219
	驚	220
	兄	246
	経	253
kyū	丘	181
	久	182
	休	183
	及	184
	吸	185
	宮	186
	弓	187
	急	188
	救	189
	求	190
	泣	191
	球	192
	究	193
	級	194
	給	195
	旧	196
	九	234
kyuu	丘	181
	久	182
	休	183
	及	184
	吸	185
	宮	186
	弓	187
	急	188
	救	189
	求	190
	泣	191
	球	192
	究	193
	級	194
	給	195
	旧	196
	九	234

M

Reading	Kanji	No.
ma	間	143
	真	569
	馬	850
	目	1011
ma(da)	未	990
ma(garu)	曲	223
ma(keru)	負	920
ma(ku)	巻	130
ma(su)	増	668
ma(tsu)	待	697
ma(tu)	待	697
ma(zaru)	交	309
ma(zeru)	混	357
ma(zu)	先	628
machi	街	112
	町	752
mado	窓	661
mado(u)	惑	1099
mae	前	643
mago	孫	686
mai	米	943
	妹	981
	枚	982
	毎	983
mai(ru)	参	395
maji(waru)	交	309
maka(seru)	任	837
maki	巻	130
	牧	978
makoto	真	569
	誠	608
maku	幕	984
mame	豆	809
mamo(ru)	守	472
man	万	987
	満	988
mana	愛	1
mana(bu)	学	122
manako	眼	148
mane(ku)	招	533
manuka(reru)	免	1005
maru	丸	146
maru(i)	円	048
masa	正	599
masa(ru)	勝	524
mata	又	985
mati	街	112
	町	752
mato	的	772
matsu	松	535
	末	986
matsu(ri)	祭	373
matsurigoto	政	595
matta(ku)	全	646
matu	松	535
	末	986
matu(ri)	祭	373
maturigoto	政	595
mawa(ri)	周	481
mawa(ru)	回	97
mayo(u)	迷	1003
mazi(waru)	交	309
mazu(shii)	貧	908
mazu(sii)	貧	908
me	芽	92
	眼	148
	女	520
	目	1011
me(su)	召	525
mei	名	999
	命	1000
	明	1001
	盟	1002
	迷	1003
	鳴	1004
	免	1005
men	綿	1006
	面	1007

meshi	飯	878	mochi(iru)	用	1039
mesi	飯	878	moku	木	1010
mi	三	394		目	1011
	実	457	mon	文	936
	身	573		聞	937
	味	989		問	1012
	未	990		門	1013
mi(chiru)	満	988	mono	者	463
mi(ru)	看	139		物	932
	観	142	moppa(ra)	専	631
	見	281	mori	森	566
mi(tiru)	満	988	moro	諸	518
michi	道	818	moti(iru)	用	1039
michibi(ku)	導	816	moto	下	71
mida(reru)	乱	1051		基	155
midori	緑	1075		元	284
migi	右	31		本	979
mijika(i)	短	716	moto(meru)	求	190
miki	幹	134	motoi	基	155
mimi	耳	448	motsu	物	932
min	民	993	motte	以	7
	眠	994	motto(mo)	最	366
mina	皆	105	motu	物	932
minami	南	830	mou	亡	968
minamoto	源	288		望	972
minato	港	329		毛	1009
mino(ru)	実	457	mou(keru)	設	622
misao	操	656	mou(su)	申	568
mise	店	779	moyō(su)	催	364
mit-	三	394	moyoo(su)	催	364
miti	道	818	mu	武	921
mitibi(ku)	導	816		務	995
mi(tiru)	充	494		夢	996
	満	988		無	997
mito(meru)	認	838	mu(kō)	向	317
mitsu	密	991	mu(kou)	向	317
mitu	密	991	mu(reru)	群	242
miya	宮	186	mu(su)	蒸	556
miyako	京	205	mugi	麦	864
	都	789	muka(eru)	迎	258
mizika(i)	短	716	mukashi	昔	613
mizu	水	585	mukasi	昔	613
mizuka(ra)	自	449	muku(iru)	報	961
mizuumi	湖	300	muna	胸	216
mo	模	1008	mune	胸	216
mō	亡	968		宗	482
	望	972	mura	村	689
	毛	1009	mura(garu)	群	242
mo(eru)	燃	842	muro	室	455
mō(keru)	設	622	mushi	虫	741
mo(ri)	守	472	musi	虫	741
mo(ru)	盛	602	musu(bu)	結	265
mo(shikuwa)	若	468	musume	娘	998
mo(sikuwa)	若	468	mut-	六	1094
mō(su)	申	568	muzuka(shii)	難	831
mo(tsu)	持	442	muzuka(sii)	難	831
mo(tu)	持	442	myaku	脈	992

myō	名	999		年	840
	命	1000		念	841
	明	1001		燃	842
myou	名	999	netsu	熱	839
	命	1000	netu	熱	839
	明	1001	ni	荷	86

N

na	菜	375		児	439
	南	830		仁	578
	納	843		二	832
	名	999	ni(geru)	逃	810
na(geru)	投	798	ni(ru)	似	438
na(i)	無	997	nichi	日	834
na(ku)	泣	191	niga(i)	苦	237
	鳴	1004	nii	新	565
na(kunaru)	亡	968	niku	肉	833
na(reru)	慣	136	nin	人	577
na(ru)	成	594		仁	578
na(su)	為	14		刃	579
nado	等	803		任	837
naga(i)	永	40		認	838
	長	755	nina(u)	担	713
naga(reru)	流	1064	nishi	西	607
nago(yaka)	和	1097	nisi	西	607
nai	内	829	niti	日	834
naka	中	734	niwa	庭	767
	仲	735	no	野	1015
naka(ba)	半	872	nō	納	843
nama	生	601		能	844
nama(keru)	怠	698		脳	845
nami	波	847		農	846
	並	940	no(basu)	延	50
nan	何	74	no(mu)	飲	29
	男	722	no(ru)	乗	549
	南	830	nobe(ru)	述	506
	難	831	nobo(ru)	上	547
	納	843		登	788
nana	七	453	nochi	後	304
nani	何	74	noga(reru)	逃	810
nano	七	453	noko(ru)	残	403
nao(su)	治	445	nori	法	965
	直	758	noti	後	304
nara(beru)	並	940	nou	納	843
nara(u)	習	489		能	844
nasa(ke)	情	553		脳	845
natsu	夏	78		農	846
natu	夏	78	nozo(ku)	除	522
ne	音	70	nozo(mu)	望	972
	根	356		臨	1077
	値	724	nu	怒	793
ne(ru)	寝	563	nu(gu)	脱	710
	練	1088	nu(ku)	抜	870
nega(u)	願	151	nuno	布	914
negira(u)	労	1091	nushi	主	470
nemu(ru)	眠	994	nusi	主	470
nen	然	645	nyaku	若	468
			nyo	女	520
			nyō	女	520

Reading	Kanji	No.
nyou	女	520
nyū	乳	835
	入	836
nyuu	乳	835
	入	836

O

Reading	Kanji	No.
o	悪	2
	汚	56
	御	305
	緒	515
	小	529
ō	央	57
	奥	58
	往	59
	応	60
	押	61
	桜	62
	横	63
	王	64
	黄	65
	皇	330
o(biru)	帯	696
o(chiru)	落	1050
ō(i)	多	691
o(iru)	老	1093
ō(kii)	大	705
o(kiru)	起	172
o(ku)	置	728
o(riru)	降	341
o(rosu)	下	71
o(ru)	居	199
	織	558
	折	621
o(su)	押	61
	推	584
o(tiru)	落	1050
o(u)	生	601
	追	760
	負	920
o(waru)	終	488
obi	帯	696
obo(eru)	覚	118
odoro(ku)	驚	220
oga(mu)	拝	852
ogina(u)	補	955
ogoso(ka)	厳	286
oka	丘	181
oka(su)	犯	876
oko(ru)	怒	793
oko(su)	興	217
okona(u)	行	336
okota(ru)	怠	698
oku	奥	58
	億	66
	屋	67
oku(reru)	後	304
	遅	729
oku(ru)	送	666
	贈	671
omo	主	470
	面	1007
omo(i)	重	499
omo(u)	思	418
omote	表	903
	面	1007
on	遠	54
	恩	68
	温	69
	音	70
	御	305
ona(ji)	同	814
ona(zi)	同	814
onna	女	520
onoono	各	113
onore	己	296
onozuka(ra)	自	449
oo(i)	多	691
oo(kii)	大	705
ooyake	公	312
ori	折	621
osa(meru)	治	445
	収	480
	修	485
	納	843
osana(i)	幼	1034
oshi(eru)	教	213
osi(eru)	教	213
oso(i)	遅	729
oso(reru)	恐	212
oso(waru)	教	213
oto	音	70
otoko	男	722
otōto	弟	768
otouto	弟	768
otozu(reru)	訪	966
otto	夫	911
ou	央	57
	奥	58
	往	59
	応	60
	押	61
	桜	62
	横	63
	王	64
	黄	65
	皇	330
oya	親	572
ōyake	公	312
oyo(bu)	及	184
oyo(gu)	泳	41

R

Reading	Kanji	No.
ra	等	803
rai	来	1048
	礼	1084
raku	楽	123
	絡	1049
	落	1050
ran	乱	1051
	卵	1052
	覧	1053
rei	令	1081
	例	1082
	冷	1083
	礼	1084
reki	歴	1085
ren	恋	1087
	練	1088
	連	1089
retsu	列	1086
retu	列	1086
ri	利	1054
	理	1055
	裏	1056
	里	1057
	離	1058
	律	1060
richi	力	1074
riki	力	1074
riku	陸	1059
	六	1094
rin	林	1076
	臨	1077
	輪	1078
	隣	1079
riti	律	1060
ritsu	律	1060
	率	1061
	立	1062
ritu	律	1060
	率	1061
	立	1062
ro	路	1090
rō	労	1091
	朗	1092
	老	1093
roku	緑	1075
	六	1094
	録	1095
ron	論	1096
rou	労	1091
	朗	1092
	老	1093
ru	流	1064
	留	1065
rui	類	1080
ryaku	略	1063
ryo	旅	1066
ryō	漁	203
	両	1067
	寮	1068
	料	1069
	涼	1070
	良	1071
	量	1072
	領	1073
ryoku	力	1074
	緑	1075
ryou	漁	203
	両	1067
	寮	1068
	料	1069
	涼	1070
	良	1071
	量	1072
	領	1073
	立	1062
ryū	流	1064
	留	1065
ryuu	立	1062
	流	1064
	留	1065

S

Reading	Kanji	No.
sa	佐	358
	左	359
	差	360
	査	361
	砂	362
	再	365
	最	366
	作	383
	茶	732
sa(garu)	下	71
sa(geru)	提	769
sa(ku)	割	125
sa(masu)	冷	1083
sa(meru)	覚	118
sa(ru)	去	198
sa(su)	差	360
	指	419
saba(ku)	裁	376
sachi	幸	322
sada(meru)	定	765
	性	593
saga(su)	探	714
sagu(ru)	探	714
sai	催	364
	再	365
	最	366
	妻	367
	才	368
	採	369
	歳	370
	済	371
	災	372
	祭	373
	細	374

Reading	Kanji	No.
	菜	375
	裁	376
	際	377
	財	381
	殺	391
	西	607
	切	619
saiwa(i)	幸	322
saka	坂	382
	酒	475
saka(eru)	栄	039
saka(n)	盛	602
saka(sa)	逆	180
sakai	境	210
sakana	魚	204
sake	酒	475
saki	先	628
saku	作	383
	昨	384
	策	385
	索	386
sakura	桜	62
sama	様	1037
samu(i)	寒	128
san	三	394
	参	395
	山	396
	散	397
	産	398
	算	399
	蚕	400
	賛	401
	酸	402
sara	更	326
	皿	393
sasae(ru)	支	420
saso(u)	誘	1027
sat-	早	657
sati	幸	322
sato	里	1057
satsu	冊	387
	刷	388
	察	389
	札	390
	殺	391
satu	冊	387
	刷	388
	察	389
	札	390
	殺	391
sawa(ru)	障	546
sazu(keru)	授	478
se	世	588
	背	854
se(ku)	急	188
se(meru)	攻	325
	責	617
se(ru)	競	207
seba(meru)	狭	215
sechi	節	623
sei	歳	370
	省	539
	情	553
	世	588
	制	590
	勢	591
	姓	592
	性	593
	成	594
	政	595
	整	596
	星	597
	晴	598
	正	599
	清	600
	生	601
	盛	602
	精	603
	聖	604
	声	605
	製	606
	西	607
	誠	608
	青	609
	静	610
	背	854
seki	関	144
	席	612
	昔	613
	石	614
	積	615
	績	616
	責	617
	赤	618
	夕	1030
sema(i)	狭	215
sen	先	628
	千	629
	宣	630
	専	631
	川	632
	戦	633
	泉	634
	浅	635
	洗	636
	染	637
	線	638
	船	639
	選	640
	銭	641
	鮮	642
seti	節	623
setsu	殺	391
	切	619
	接	620
	折	621
	設	622
	節	623
	説	624
	雪	625
setu	殺	391
	切	619
	接	620
	折	621
	設	622
	節	623
	説	624
	雪	625
sha	砂	362
	舎	458
	写	459
	射	460
	捨	461
	社	462
	者	463
	謝	464
	車	465
	借	466
shaku	尺	467
	昔	613
	石	614
	赤	618
shi	仕	404
	使	405
	司	406
	史	407
	四	408
	士	409
	始	410
	姉	411
	姿	412
	子	413
	市	414
	矢	415
	師	416
	志	417
	思	418
	指	419
	支	420
	枝	421
	止	422
	死	423
	氏	424
	私	425
	糸	426
	紙	427
	至	428
	視	429
	詞	430
	詩	431
	試	432
	誌	433
	資	434
	飼	435
	歯	436
	次	444
	示	447
	自	449
shi(iru)	強	211
shi(meru)	閉	941
shi(mi)	染	637
shi(nu)	死	423
shi(ru)	知	725
shiawa(se)	幸	322
shichi	七	453
	質	456
shika(shi)	然	645
shiki	式	451
	識	452
	織	558
	色	560
shima	島	797
shime(su)	示	447
shimo	下	71
shin	信	562
	寝	563
	心	564
	新	565
	森	566
	深	567
	申	568
	真	569
	神	570
	臣	571
	親	572
	身	573
	進	574
	針	575
	震	576
shina	品	907
shio	塩	55
	潮	751
shira	白	863
shira(beru)	調	754
shirizo(ku)	退	701
shiro	城	550
	代	703
	白	863
shiru	汁	497
shiru(su)	記	170
shirushi	印	25
shita	下	71
	舌	627
shita(shii)	親	572
shitaga(u)	従	496
shitsu	失	454
	室	455
	質	456

Reading	Kanji	No.
	操	656
	早	657
	巣	658
	争	659
	相	660
	窓	661
	総	662
	草	663
	装	664
	走	665
	送	666
	贈	671
so(meru)	初	512
	染	637
so(ru)	反	873
so(u)	沿	51
soba	側	673
soda(tsu)	育	23
soda(tu)	育	23
soko	底	766
soko(nau)	損	688
soku	側	673
	則	674
	即	675
	息	676
	束	677
	測	678
	足	679
	速	680
somu(ku)	背	854
son	存	685
	孫	686
	尊	687
	損	688
	村	689
sona(eru)	供	206
	備	893
sona(waru)	具	238
sono	園	049
sora	空	239
sōrō	候	310
soso(gu)	注	740
soto	外	110
sotsu	卒	684
sotu	卒	684
sou	宗	482
	創	650
	倉	651
	奏	652
	層	653
	想	654
	掃	655
	操	656
	早	657
	巣	658
	争	659
	相	660
	窓	661
	総	662
	草	663
	装	664
	走	665
	送	666
	贈	671
sourou	候	310
su	子	413
	主	470
	守	472
	州	484
	素	648
	巣	658
	数	586
sū	数	586
su(beru)	総	662
	統	806
su(giru)	過	89
su(gu)	直	758
su(i)	酸	402
su(ki)	好	319
su(mu)	済	371
	住	493
su(ru)	刷	388
su(teru)	捨	461
su(u)	吸	185
sube	術	505
sube(te)	全	646
	総	662
sue	末	986
sugata	姿	412
sugu(reru)	優	1022
sui	出	504
	吹	582
	垂	583
	推	584
	水	585
	誰	711
suji	筋	229
suke	助	519
suko(shi)	少	530
suko(si)	少	530
suko(yaka)	健	269
suku(nai)	少	530
suku(u)	救	189
suma(u)	住	493
sumi	炭	715
sumi(yaka)	速	680
sun	寸	587
suna	砂	362
susu(mu)	進	574
suu	数	586
suwa(ru)	座	363
suzi	筋	229
suzu(shii)	涼	1070
suzu(sii)	涼	1070
sya	砂	362
	舎	458
	写	459
	射	460
	捨	461
	社	462
	者	463
	謝	464
	車	465
syaku	借	466
	尺	467
	昔	613
	石	614
	赤	618
syo	処	511
	初	512
	所	513
	署	514
	緒	515
	署	516
	書	517
	諸	518
syoku	植	557
	織	558
	職	559
	色	560
	食	561
syou	従	496
	傷	523
	勝	524
	召	525
	商	526
	唱	527
	将	528
	小	529
	少	530
	床	531
	承	532
	招	533
	昭	534
	松	535
	消	536
	焼	537
	照	538
	省	539
	章	540
	笑	541
	紹	542
	証	543
	象	544
	賞	545
	障	546
	上	547
	姓	592
	性	593
	政	595
	星	597
	正	599
	清	600
	生	601
	精	603
	声	605
	青	609
	相	660
	装	664
syu	主	470
	取	471
	守	472
	手	473
	種	474
	酒	475
	首	476
	衆	490
syuku	宿	500
	祝	501
	縮	502
syun	春	507
syutu	出	504
syuu	収	480
	周	481
	宗	482
	就	483
	州	484
	修	485
	拾	486
	秋	487
	終	488
	習	489
	衆	490
	週	491
	集	492
	祝	501

T

Reading	Kanji	No.
ta	手	473
	他	690
	多	691
	太	692
	田	784
ta(beru)	食	561
ta(eru)	絶	626
ta(meru)	貯	744
ta(reru)	垂	583
	足	679
ta(riru)	建	273
ta(teru)	経	253
ta(tsu)	裁	376
	断	719
	発	868
	立	1062
ta(tu)	経	253
	裁	376
	断	719
	発	868
	立	1062

Reading	Kanji	No.
taba	束	677
tabi	度	791
	旅	1066
tada(chini)	直	758
tada(shii)	正	599
tada(sii)	正	599
tada(su)	質	456
tada(tini)	直	758
taga(i)	互	302
tagaya(su)	耕	333
tagui	類	1080
tai	太	692
	体	694
	対	695
	帯	696
	待	697
	怠	698
	態	699
	貸	700
	退	701
	隊	702
	代	703
	台	704
	大	705
tai(ra)	平	939
taka(i)	高	342
takara	宝	962
take	丈	548
	竹	731
taku	宅	708
	度	791
takuwa(eru)	貯	744
tama	球	192
	玉	225
tama(u)	給	195
tamago	卵	1052
tame	為	14
tame(su)	試	432
tami	民	993
tamotsu	保	953
tamotu	保	953
tan	単	712
	担	713
	探	714
	炭	715
	短	716
	誕	717
	反	873
tane	種	474
tani	谷	347
tano(shii)	楽	123
tano(sii)	楽	123
tashi(ka)	確	116
tasi(ka)	確	116
tasu(keru)	助	519
tataka(u)	戦	633
tate	館	145
	縦	498
tato(e)	例	1082
tatsu	達	709
	貴	171
	尊	687
tatu	達	709
tawara	俵	899
tayo(ri)	便	950
tazu(neru)	尋	580
	訪	966
te	手	473
te(ru)	照	538
tei	体	694
	丁	745
	低	763
	停	764
	定	765
	底	766
	庭	767
	弟	768
	提	769
	程	770
	敵	771
teki	的	772
	笛	773
	適	774
	典	776
ten	天	777
	展	778
	店	779
	転	780
	点	781
	殿	783
tera	寺	441
tetsu	鉄	775
tetu	鉄	775
ti	血	266
	治	445
	質	456
	千	629
	値	724
	知	725
	地	726
	池	727
	置	728
	遅	729
	乳	835
ti(ru)	散	397
tidi(mu)	縮	502
tiga(u)	違	19
tii(sai)	小	529
tika(i)	近	231
tikara	力	1074
tiku	築	730
	竹	731
tin	賃	759
tina(mu)	因	27
titi	乳	835
	父	918
tizi(mu)	縮	502
to	戸	298
	時	443
	十	495
	図	581
	徒	786
	渡	787
	登	788
	都	789
	度	791
	土	792
	頭	811
tō	登	788
	党	794
	冬	795
	刀	796
	島	797
	投	798
	東	799
	湯	800
	灯	801
	当	802
	等	803
	答	804
	糖	805
	統	806
	到	807
	討	808
	豆	809
	逃	810
	頭	811
	道	818
	読	825
	納	843
to(bu)	飛	892
to(gu)	研	278
to(i)	問	1012
tō(i)	遠	54
to(ziru)	閉	941
to(ku)	解	96
	説	624
to(meru)	止	422
	停	764
	留	1065
to(mu)	富	913
to(ru)	採	369
	取	471
tō(ru)	通	762
todo(ku)	届	827
todo(meru)	留	1065
toji(ru)	閉	941
toki	時	443
toko	床	531
	常	552
tokoro	処	511
toku	所	513
	得	820
	徳	821
	特	822
	読	825
toma(ru)	泊	862
tomi	富	913
tomo	供	206
	共	208
	友	1024
tomoshibi	灯	801
tomosibi	灯	801
ton	団	718
	豚	828
	問	1012
tona(eru)	唱	527
tonari	隣	1079
tono	殿	783
too	十	495
too(i)	遠	54
too(ru)	通	762
tori	鳥	757
toshi	歳	370
	年	840
tosi	歳	370
	年	840
tōto(i)	貴	171
	尊	687
totono(eru)	整	596
totono(u)	調	754
totsu	突	826
totu	突	826
tou	登	788
	党	794
	冬	795
	刀	796
	島	797
	投	798
	東	799
	湯	800
	灯	801
	当	802
	等	803
	答	804
	糖	805
	統	806
	到	807
	討	808
	豆	809
	逃	810
	頭	811
	道	818
	読	825
	納	843
touto(i)	貴	171
	尊	687
tsu	通	762

	都 789	tu(moru)	積 615	鳥 757
tsū	痛 761	tu(reru)	連 1089	tyuu 中 734
	通 762	tudo(u)	集 492	仲 735
tsu(geru)	告 346	tudu(ku)	続 683	宙 736
tsu(gu)	次 444	tugi	次 444	忠 737
	接 620	tui	対 695	昼 738
tsu(keru)	点 781		追 760	柱 739
tsu(ku)	就 483	tui(yasu)	費 890	注 740
	着 733	tuka(eru)	仕 404	虫 741
	突 826	tuka(reru)	疲 886	駐 742
	付 910	tuka(u)	使 405	
tsu(moru)	積 615	tukasa	司 406	**U**
tsu(reru)	連 1089	tukasado(ru)	司 406	u 右 31
tsuchi	土 792	tuki	月 267	宇 32
tsudo(u)	集 492	tuku(ru)	作 383	羽 33
tsugi	次 444		創 650	雨 34
tsui	対 695		造 672	有 1025
	追 760	tukue	机 160	u(eru) 植 557
tsui(yasu)	費 890	tuma	妻 367	u(kabu) 浮 917
tsuka(eru)	仕 404	tume(tai)	冷 1083	u(keru) 受 477
tsuka(reru)	疲 886	tumi	罪 380	u(mareru) 生 601
tsuka(u)	使 405	tune	常 552	u(mu) 産 398
tsukasa	司 406	tuno	角 119	u(reru) 熟 503
tsukasado(ru)	司 406	tuno(ru)	募 956	u(ru) 得 820
tsuki	月 267	tura	面 1007	売 860
tsuku(ru)	作 383	tura(neru)	連 1089	u(seru) 失 454
	創 650	turugi	剣 272	u(tsu) 打 693
	造 672	tuta(eru)	伝 782	討 808
tsukue	机 160	tuti	土 792	u(tu) 打 693
tsuma	妻 367	tuto(meru)	勤 226	討 808
tsume(tai)	冷 1083		努 790	ubu 産 398
tsumi	罪 380		勉 951	uchi 初 512
tsune	常 552		務 995	家 79
tsuno	角 119	tutu(mu)	包 960	内 829
tsuno(ru)	募 956	tuu	痛 761	ue 上 547
tsura	面 1007		通 762	ugo(ku) 動 813
tsura(neru)	連 1089	tuwamono	兵 938	ui 初 512
tsurugi	剣 272	tuyo(i)	強 211	uji 氏 424
tsuta(eru)	伝 782	tya	茶 732	uketamawa(ru) 承 532
tsuto(meru)	勤 226	tyaku	着 733	uma 馬 850
	努 790	tyo	緒 515	ume 梅 858
	勉 951		著 743	umi 海 102
	務 995		貯 744	un 運 35
tsutsu(mu)	包 960	tyoku	直 758	雲 36
tsuwamono	兵 938	tyou	重 499	uo 魚 204
tsuyo(i)	強 211		丁 745	ura 裏 1056
tsuzu(ku)	続 683		兆 746	ushi 牛 197
tu	通 762		帳 747	ushi(ro) 後 304
	都 789		庁 748	ushina(u) 失 454
tu(geru)	告 346		張 749	亡 968
tu(gu)	次 444		朝 750	usi 牛 197
	接 620		潮 751	usi(ro) 後 304
tu(keru)	点 781		町 752	usina(u) 失 454
tu(ku)	就 483		腸 753	亡 968
	着 733		調 754	uta 歌 82
	突 826		長 755	utaga(u) 疑 174
	付 910		頂 756	uti 家 79

内 829	wa(karu) 分 933		
utsu(ru) 移 16	wa(ru) 割 125		
映 38	waka(i) 若 468		
utsu(su) 写 459	waka(re) 別 944		
utsuku(shii) 美 894	wake 訳 1019		
utsuwa 器 154	waku 惑 1099		
utu(ru) 移 16	wara(u) 笑 541		
映 38	warabe 童 817		
utu(su) 写 459	warawa 童 817		
utuku(sii) 美 894	ware 我 90		
utuwa 器 154	wari 割 125		
uwa 上 547	waru(i) 悪 2		
uyama(u) 敬 250	wasu(reru) 忘 969		
uzi 氏 424	wata 綿 1006		
	wata(ru) 渡 787		
W	watakushi 私 425		
wa 我 90	watakusi 私 425		
輪 1078	waza 技 173		
和 1097	業 221		
話 1098	wazawa(i) 災 372		

Y

ya 屋 67
家 79
谷 347
矢 415
八 867
夜 1014
野 1015
ya(ku) 焼 537
ya(meru) 辞 450
ya(mu) 病 905
yabu(reru) 敗 853
yabu(ru) 破 849
yado 宿 500
yakata 館 145
yaku 益 45

reading	kanji	no.
	役	1016
	約	1017
	薬	1018
	訳	1019
yama	山	396
yamai	病	905
yasa(shii)	易	13
	優	1022
yasa(sii)	易	13
	優	1022
yashina(u)	養	1044
yashiro	社	462
yasina(u)	養	1044
yasiro	社	462
yasu(i)	安	4
	易	13
yasu(mu)	休	183
yat-	八	867
yawa(ragu)	和	1097
yo	四	408
	世	588
	代	703
	夜	1014
	予	1031
	余	1032
	預	1033
yō	八	867
	幼	1034
	容	1035
	曜	1036
	様	1037
	洋	1038
	用	1039
	羊	1040
	葉	1041
	要	1042
	陽	1043
	養	1044
yo(bu)	呼	294
yo(i)	善	644
	良	1071
yo(mu)	読	825
yo(ru)	因	27
	寄	157
yogo(su)	汚	56
yoko	横	63
yoku	欲	1045
	浴	1046
	翌	1047
yon	四	408
yoroko(bu)	喜	153
yorozu	万	987
yoru	夜	1014
yoshi	義	175
	吉	177
	由	1026
yosi	義	175
	吉	177
	由	1026
yosoo(u)	装	664
yosō(u)	装	664
you	八	867
	幼	1034
	容	1035
	曜	1036
	様	1037
	洋	1038
	用	1039
	羊	1040
	葉	1041
	要	1042
	陽	1043
	養	1044
yowa(i)	弱	469
yu	湯	800
	油	1020
	輸	1021
	右	31
yū	優	1022
	勇	1023
	友	1024
	有	1025
	由	1026
	誘	1027
	遊	1028
	郵	1029
	夕	1030
yu(ku)	往	59
	行	336
yu(u)	結	265
yubi	指	419
yuda(neru)	委	11
yue	故	299
yui	遺	20
yuka	床	531
yuki	雪	625
yume	夢	996
yumi	弓	187
yuru(su)	許	202
yuta(ka)	豊	967
yuu	右	31
	優	1022
	勇	1023
	友	1024
	有	1025
	由	1026
	誘	1027
	遊	1028
	郵	1029
	夕	1030

Z

reading	kanji	no.
za	座	363
zai	在	378
	材	379
	罪	380
	財	381
	残	403
zan	雑	392
zatsu	雑	392
zatu	雑	392
ze	是	589
zei	税	611
	説	624
	前	643
zen	善	644
	然	645
	全	646
zeni	銭	641
zetsu	絶	626
	舌	627
zetu	絶	626
	舌	627
zi	仕	404
	事	437
	似	438
	児	439
	字	440
	寺	441
	持	442
	時	443
	次	444
	治	445
	磁	446
	示	447
	耳	448
	自	449
	辞	450
	除	522
	地	726
	路	1090
zika(ni)	直	758
ziki	食	561
	直	758
zin	神	570
	臣	571
	人	577
	仁	578
	刃	579
	尋	580
zit-	十	495
zitu	実	457
	日	834
zō	雑	392
	象	544
	像	667
	増	668
	臓	669
	蔵	670
	贈	671
	造	672
zoku	属	681
	族	682
	続	683
zon	存	685
zou	雑	392
	象	544
	像	667
	増	668
	臓	669
	蔵	670
	贈	671
	造	672
zu	事	437
	図	581
	豆	809
	頭	811
zyaku	若	468
	弱	469
	着	733
zyo	助	519
	女	520
	序	521
	除	522
zyou	上	547
	丈	548
	乗	549
	城	550
	場	551
	常	552
	情	553
	条	554
	状	555
	蒸	556
	成	594
	盛	602
	静	610
	定	765
zyu	受	477
	授	478
	樹	479
	就	483
zyuku	熟	503
zyun	準	508
	純	509
	順	510
zyutu	術	505
	述	506
zyuu	拾	486
	住	493
	充	494
	十	495
	従	496
	汁	497
	縦	498
	重	499

Repeat

reading	kanji	no.
(kurikaeshi)	々	1100

INDEX 4
Arranged by Total Number of Strokes
(総画数による索引)

How to use this index:

For an unfamiliar kanji, first count the number of strokes in the kanji, find the stroke count in this list, and then look for the section header.[1]

Numbers refer to kanji numbers in this book.

1-stroke kanji

Rad.	Kanji	No.
一	一	24

2-stroke kanji

Rad.	Kanji	No.
一	七	453
	丁	745
乙	九	234
二	二	832
人	人	577
入	入	836
八	八	867
刀	刀	796
力	力	1074
十	十	495
又	又	985

3-stroke kanji

Rad.	Kanji	No.
一	下	71
	三	394
	上	547
	丈	548
	万	987
、	丸	146
ノ	久	182
又	及	184
亠	亡	968
几	凡	980
刀	刃	579
十	千	629
口	口	316
土	土	792
	士	409
夕	夕	1030
大	大	705
	女	520
子	子	413
寸	寸	587
	小	529
山	山	396
	川	632
工	工	321
己	己	296
	干	133
弓	弓	187
	才	368

4-stroke kanji

Rad.	Kanji	No.
一	不	909
丨	中	734
	予	1031
二	五	301
	互	302
亻	仏	931
	仁	578
	化	72
	今	353
人	介	94
儿	元	284
	公	312
八	六	1094
冂	円	48
	内	829
刀	切	619
	分	933
匸	区	236
十	午	303
又	収	480
	反	873
	友	1024
大	太	692
	天	777
	夫	911
小	少	530
尸	尺	467
弓	引	28
心	心	564
戸	戸	298
手	手	473
支	支	420
文	文	936
方	方	964
日	日	834
月	月	267
木	木	1010
欠	欠	261
止	止	422
比	比	885
毛	毛	1009
氏	氏	424
水	水	585
火	火	84
父	父	918

5-stroke kanji

Rad.	Kanji	No.
一	丘	181
	世	588
丨	巨	200
、	主	470
人	以	7
亻	仕	404
	他	690
	代	703
	付	910
	令	1081
儿	兄	246
冂	冊	387
冖	写	459
冫	冬	795
几	処	511
凵	出	504
刂	刊	129
力	加	76
	功	313
勹	包	960
ヒ	北	976
十	半	872
厶	去	198
口	右	31
	可	77
	句	235
	古	293
	号	343
	司	406
	召	525
	台	704
	史	407
口	四	408
土	圧	3
夕	外	110
大	央	57
	失	454
工	左	359
巾	市	414
	布	914
干	平	939
幺	幼	1034
广	広	323
	庁	748
廾	弁	952
ネ	礼	1084
心	必	896
扌	打	693
	払	930
日	旧	196
木	札	390
	本	979
	末	986
	未	990
止	正	599
母	母	959
氏	民	993
水	永	40
	氷	901
氵	汁	497
犭	犯	876
玉	玉	225
生	生	601
用	用	1039
田	申	568
	田	784
	由	1026
白	白	863
	皮	887
皿	皿	393
目	目	1011
矢	矢	415
石	石	614
示	示	447
穴	穴	264
立	立	1062
辶	込	352
	辺	948

6-stroke kanji

Rad.	Kanji	No.
一	両	1067
亠	交	309
亻	仮	73
	休	183
	件	268
	仲	735
	伝	782
	任	837

[1]The section headers in Index 4 are arranged based on their old forms or origins. The following three-stroke headers are listed elsewhere: 氵:4 strokes (from 水); 辶:7 strokes (from 辵); 艹:6 strokes (from 艸); 犭:4 strokes (from 犬); 扌:4 strokes (from 手); 阝:7 strokes (from 邑.)

人	会	95
	全	646
夕	多	691
儿	光	311
	充	494
	先	628
	兆	746
八	共	208
冂	再	365
刂	列	1086
卩	印	25
	危	152
口	各	113
	吉	177
	吸	185
	向	317
	后	318
	合	344
	同	814
	名	999
囗	回	97
	因	27
	団	718
土	在	378
	地	726
女	好	319
ク	争	659
子	字	440
	存	685
宀	安	4
	宇	32
	守	472
	宅	708
寸	寺	441
川	州	484
干	年	840
弋	式	451
⺌	当	802
忄	忙	970
戈	成	594
日	早	657
曰	曲	223
月	有	1025
木	机	160
欠	次	444
歹	死	423
毋	毎	983
气	気	165
氵	汚	56
	池	727
火	灰	103
	灯	801
白	百	898
竹	竹	731
米	米	943
糸	糸	426
羊	羊	1040
羽	羽	33
耂	考	334
	老	1093
耳	耳	448
肉	肉	833
自	自	449
至	至	428
舌	舌	627
色	色	560
虫	虫	741
血	血	266
行	行	336
衣	衣	18
西	西	607

7-stroke kanji

亻	位	8
	何	74
	佐	358
	作	383
	似	438
	住	493
	体	694
	低	763
人	余	1032
乚	乱	1051
儿	児	439
八	兵	938
冫	冷	1083
刀	初	512
刂	判	871
	別	944
	利	1054
力	助	519
	努	790
	労	1091
匚	医	21
卩	即	675
	卵	1052
口	君	240
	告	346
	吹	582
	否	881
囗	囲	10
	困	354
	図	581
土	均	227
	坂	382
士	声	605
	売	860
子	孝	320
宀	完	131
寸	対	695
尸	局	222
巾	希	158
广	序	521
	床	531
弓	弟	768
彡	形	248
彳	役	1016
心	応	60
	志	417
	忘	969
忄	快	98
戈	我	90
扌	技	173
	折	621
	投	798
	抜	870
	批	884
攵	改	100
	攻	325
曰	更	326
木	材	379
	条	554
	束	677
	村	689
	来	1048
氵	汽	166
	決	262
氺	求	190
火	災	372
犬	状	555
ネ	社	462
田	男	722
	町	752
禾	私	425
穴	究	193
糸	系	252
臣	臣	571
艮	良	1071
艹	花	85
	芸	257
見	見	281
角	角	119
言	言	290
谷	谷	347
豆	豆	809
貝	貝	109
赤	赤	618
走	走	665
足	足	679
身	身	573
車	車	465
辶	近	231
	迎	258
	返	949
里	里	1057
阝	防	975
麦	麦	864

8-stroke kanji

一	並	940
乚	乳	835
亅	事	437
亠	京	205
亻	価	75
	供	206
	使	405
	例	1082
人	舎	458
	命	1000
儿	免	1005
八	具	238
	典	776
凵	画	91
刀	券	271
刂	刻	345
	刷	388
	制	590
	到	807
力	効	314
十	協	209
	卒	684
ム	参	395
又	取	471
	受	477
口	呼	294
	周	481
	味	989
	和	1097
囗	固	295
	国	348
土	垂	583
夕	夜	1014
大	奇	156
女	委	11
	妻	367
	始	410
	姉	411
	姓	592
	妹	981
子	学	122
	季	167
宀	官	132
	実	457
	宗	482
	宙	736
	定	765
	宝	962
尸	居	199
	届	827
山	岸	147
	岩	149
干	幸	322
广	底	766
	店	779
	府	915
廴	延	50
彳	往	59
	径	249
	彼	882
心	忠	737
	念	841
忄	性	593
戸	所	513
手	承	532
扌	押	61
	拡	114
	招	533
	担	713
	拝	852
攵	放	963
日	易	13
	昔	613
	明	1001
月	育	23
	肥	889
	服	926
木	果	81
	枝	421
	松	535
	東	799
	板	874
	枚	982
	林	1076
止	武	921
	歩	954
毋	毒	823
氵	泳	41
	沿	51
	河	83
	泣	191
	治	445
	注	740

波	847
泊	862
法	965
油	1020
版	875
物	932
牧	978
的	772
直	758
知	725
空	239
突	826
者	463
英	42
芽	92
苦	237
若	468
表	903
述	506
金	232
長	755
門	1013
雨	34
青	609
非	891

9-stroke kanji

乗	549
係	245
信	562
便	950
保	953
単	712
前	643
則	674
勇	1023
南	830
厚	315
品	907
型	247
城	550
変	945
奏	652

姿	412
客	179
室	455
宣	630
専	631
屋	67
巻	130
度	791
建	273
後	304
待	697
律	1060
急	188
思	418
怠	698
怒	793
悔	99
指	419
持	442
拾	486
故	299
政	595
映	38
昨	384
春	507
昭	534
是	589
星	597
昼	738
胃	17
背	854
肺	855
栄	39
査	361
染	637
柱	739
段	721
泉	634
海	102
浅	635
活	126
洗	636
派	848
洋	1038

炭	715
為	14
点	781
狭	215
独	824
祝	501
神	570
祖	647
界	104
畑	866
皆	105
皇	330
発	868
看	139
県	280
省	539
相	660
砂	362
科	80
秋	487
秒	906
紀	168
級	194
紅	332
約	1017
美	894
草	663
茶	732
要	1042
計	254
負	920
軍	243
逆	180
送	666
退	701
逃	810
迷	1003
重	499
限	291
郊	338
面	1007
革	121

音	70
風	923
飛	892
食	561
首	476

10-stroke kanji

個	292
候	310
借	466
修	485
値	724
俳	851
倍	857
倉	651
兼	270
剣	272
勉	951
原	285
員	26
夏	78
娘	998
孫	686
家	79
害	111
宮	186
容	1035
射	460
将	528
展	778
島	797
差	360
帰	164
師	416
席	612
帯	696
庫	297
座	363
庭	767
弱	469
従	496
徒	786

党	794
恩	68
恐	212
息	676
恋	1087
挙	201
旅	1066
時	443
書	517
胸	216
能	844
脈	992
朗	1092
案	6
桜	62
格	115
株	127
校	327
根	356
梅	858
残	403
殺	391
消	536
浮	917
浴	1046
流	1064
特	822
班	877
留	1065
疲	886
病	905
益	45
真	569
眠	994
破	849
秘	888
笑	541
粉	935
料	1069
索	386
紙	427
純	509
素	648
納	843

耕	333
航	335
荷	86
蚕	400
記	170
訓	241
討	808
財	381
起	172
造	672
速	680
通	762
連	1089
酒	475
配	856
針	575
院	30
郡	244
降	341
除	522
陛	942
馬	850
骨	351
高	342

11-stroke kanji

率	1061
側	673
健	269
停	764
副	924
動	813
務	995
商	526
唱	527
問	1012
域	22
基	155
堂	815
婚	355
婦	912
寄	157
宿	500

11-stroke kanji (continued)

Radical	Kanji	No.
	密	991
巾	常	552
	帳	747
广	康	324
弓	強	211
	張	749
彳	得	820
⺌心	巣	658
	悪	2
忄	情	553
扌	採	369
	捨	461
	授	478
	推	584
	接	620
	掃	655
	探	714
攵	救	189
	教	213
	敗	853
斤	断	719
方月	族	682
	脱	710
	脳	845
	望	972
木	械	101
欠	欲	1045
氵	液	44
	混	357
	済	371
	深	567
	清	600
	涼	1070
王	球	192
	現	289
	理	1055
生	産	398
田	異	15
	略	1063
皿	盛	602
目	眼	148
示	祭	373
	票	902
禾	移	16

Radical	Kanji	No.
宀立竹	窓	661
	章	540
	第	706
	笛	773
	符	919
糸	経	253
	細	374
	終	488
	紹	542
	組	649
羽	習	489
	翌	1047
舟艹	船	639
	菜	375
	著	743
行見	術	505
	規	169
	視	429
言	許	202
	設	622
	訪	966
	訳	1019
豕貝	豚	828
	貨	88
	責	617
	貧	908
車辶	転	780
	週	491
	進	574
里門阝	野	1015
	閉	941
	郷	218
	険	282
	都	789
	部	922
	郵	1029
	陸	1059
雨頁	雪	625
	頂	756
魚鳥	魚	204
	鳥	757
黄黒	黄	65
	黒	350

12-stroke kanji

Radical	Kanji	No.
イ	偉	9
	備	893
リ	創	650
	割	125
力	勤	226
	勝	524
	募	956
十口	博	861
	喜	153
	喫	178
	善	644
土	場	551
	報	961
大宀	奥	58
	寒	128
	富	913
寸	尋	580
	尊	687
尢尸彳	就	483
	属	681
	御	305
	復	925
忄心	営	37
	悲	883
	惑	1099
扌	揮	159
	提	769
攵	敬	250
	散	397
日	景	251
	暑	514
	晴	598
	晩	879
	普	916
	最	366
日月	期	750
	朝	224
木	極	275
	検	557
	植	566
	森	
	棒	973

Radical	Kanji	No.
止	歯	436
氵	温	69
	減	287
	湖	300
	港	329
	測	678
	渡	787
	湯	800
	満	988
火灬	焼	537
	然	645
	無	997
田广癶目矢禾	番	880
	痛	761
	登	788
	着	733
	短	716
	税	611
	程	770
	童	817
立竹	筋	229
	策	385
	等	803
	答	804
	筆	897
糸	絵	106
	給	195
	結	265
	統	806
	絡	1049
艹	葉	1041
	落	1050
血行衣	衆	490
	街	112
	裁	376
	装	664
	補	955
礻見言	覚	118
	詞	430
	証	543
	評	904
豕貝	象	544
	賀	93

Radical	Kanji	No.
貝	貴	171
	貸	700
	貯	744
	買	859
	費	890
	貿	974
走車辶	越	47
	軽	256
	運	35
	過	89
	達	709
	遅	729
	道	818
	遊	1028
里門阝	量	1072
	開	107
	間	143
	階	108
	隊	702
	陽	1043
隹雨頁食	集	492
	雲	36
	順	510
	飲	29
	飯	878

13-stroke kanji

Radical	Kanji	No.
イ	催	364
	傷	523
	働	812
力口土	勢	591
	園	49
	塩	55
	墓	957
夕宀巾干心	夢	996
	寝	563
	幕	984
	幹	134
	愛	1
	意	12
	感	135
	想	654
戈	戦	633

Radical	Kanji	No.
扌攵斤	損	688
	数	586
	新	565
日	暗	5
	暖	720
月	腸	753
	腹	928
	楽	123
木	業	221
止	歳	370
殳氵	殿	783
	漢	137
	源	288
	準	508
火灬	煙	53
	照	538
礻皿	福	927
	盟	1002
示	禁	228
竹糸	節	623
	絹	279
	続	683
四	罪	380
	署	516
	置	728
羊	義	175
	群	242
耳	聖	604
艹衣	蒸	556
	裏	1056
角言	解	96
	詩	431
	試	432
	誠	608
	話	1098
豆貝	豊	967
	資	434
	賃	759
足辛	路	1090
	辞	450
辰辶	農	846
	違	19
	遠	54
釒	鉱	339

	鉄	775
雨	電	785
頁	預	1033
食	飼	435

14-stroke kanji

亻	像	667
	僕	977
土	境	210
	増	668
宀	察	389
尸	層	653
彳	徳	821
忄	慣	136
心	態	699
方	旗	161
日	暮	958
木	構	328
	模	1008
	様	1037
欠	歌	82
止	歴	1085
氵	演	52
	漁	203
疋	疑	174
石	磁	446
禾	穀	349
	種	474
竹	管	140

	算	399
米	精	603
糸	緒	515
	総	662
	綿	1006
	緑	1075
	練	1088
耳	聞	937
衣	製	606
礻	複	929
言	語	306
	誤	307
	誌	433
	説	624
	読	825
	認	838
	誘	1027
辶	適	774
酉	酸	402
釒	銀	233
	銭	641
	銅	819
門	閣	120
	関	144
阝	際	377
	障	546
佳	雑	392
青	静	610
頁	領	1073
馬	駅	46

髟	影	869
鳥	鳴	1004
鼻	鼻	895

15-stroke kanji

亻	億	66
刂	劇	259
口	器	154
宀	寮	1068
寸	導	816
攵	敵	771
日	暴	971
木	横	63
	権	276
	標	900
氵	潔	263
	潮	751
灬	熟	503
	熱	839
石	確	116
禾	稿	331
竹	箱	865
糸	緊	230
	線	638
	編	947
艹	蔵	670
言	課	87
	諸	518
	誰	711

	誕	717
	談	723
	調	754
	論	1096
	賛	401
貝	質	456
	賞	545
車	輪	1078
辶	遺	20
	選	640
雨	震	576
食	養	1044
馬	駐	742

16-stroke kanji

大	奮	934
心	憲	274
扌	操	656
攵	整	596
木	機	163
	橋	214
	樹	479
氵	激	260
火	燃	842
禾	積	615
竹	築	730
米	糖	805
糸	縦	498
白	興	217

艹	薬	1018
行	衛	43
見	親	572
車	輸	1021
釒	鋼	340
	録	1095
阝	隣	1079
頁	頭	811
食	館	145

17-stroke kanji

亻	優	1022
灬	厳	286
王	環	138
糸	縮	502
	績	616
見	覧	1053
言	講	337
	謝	464
魚	鮮	642

18-stroke kanji

日	曜	1036
禾	穫	117
竹	簡	141
糸	織	558
耳	職	559
臣	臨	1077

見	観	142
貝	贈	671
佳	難	831
	離	1058
頁	額	124
	顔	150
	題	707
	類	1080
馬	験	283

19-stroke kanji

月	臓	669
言	警	255
	識	452
釒	鏡	219
頁	願	151

20-stroke kanji

立	競	207
言	議	176
	護	308

22-stroke kanji

馬	驚	220

INDEX 5
Arranged by Section Header
(部首による索引)

The gray number to the left of each kanji indicates the total number of strokes in the kanji excluding those in the section header itself. Numbers to the right refer to kanji numbers in this book.

1-stroke headers

Grp	Header	Strk	Kanji	No.
1	一	0	一	24
		1	七	453
		1	丁	745
		2	下	71
		2	三	395
		2	上	547
		2	丈	548
		2	万	987
		3	不	909
		4	丘	181
		4	世	588
		5	両	1067
2	丨	3	中	734
		4	巨	200
3	丶	2	丸	146
		4	主	470
4	ノ	2	久	182
		8	乗	549
5	乙 乚	1	九	234
		6	乱	1051
		7	乳	835
6	亅	3	予	1031
		7	事	437

2-stroke headers

Grp	Header	Strk	Kanji	No.
7	二	0	二	832
		2	五	301
		2	互	302
8	亠	1	亡	968
		4	交	309
		6	京	205
		9	率	1061
9	人 イ	0	人	577
		2	化	72
		2	仁	578
		2	仏	931
		3	以	7
		3	仕	405
		3	他	690
		3	代	703
		3	付	910
		4	仮	73
		4	休	183
		4	件	268
		4	仲	735
		4	伝	782
		4	任	837
		5	位	8
		5	何	74
		5	佐	358
		5	作	383
		5	似	438
		5	住	493
		5	体	694
		5	低	763
		6	価	75
		6	供	206
		6	使	406
		6	例	1082
		7	係	245
		7	信	562
		7	便	950
		7	保	953
		8	個	292
		8	候	310
		8	借	466
		8	修	485
		8	値	724
		8	俳	851
		8	倍	857
		8	俵	899
		9	健	269
		9	側	673
		9	停	764
		10	偉	9
		10	備	893
		11	催	364
		11	傷	523
		11	働	812
		12	像	667
		12	僕	977
		13	億	66
		15	優	1022
10	人 入	2	介	94
		2	今	353
		3	令	1081
		4	会	95
		4	全	646
		6	余	1032
		6	舎	458
		6	命	1000
		8	倉	651
11	儿	2	元	284
		3	兄	246
		4	光	311
		4	充	494
		4	先	628
		4	兆	746
		5	児	439
		6	免	1005
12	入	0	入	836
13	八	0	八	867
		2	公	312
		2	六	1094
		4	共	208
		5	兵	938
		6	具	238
		6	典	776
14	冂	2	円	48
		2	内	829
		3	冊	388
		4	再	365
15	冖	3	写	459
16	冫	3	冬	795
		5	冷	1083
17	几	1	凡	980
		3	処	511
18	凵	3	出	504
		6	画	91
19	刀	0	刀	796
		1	刃	579
		2	切	619
		2	分	933
		5	初	512
		6	券	271
20	刂	3	刊	129
		4	列	1086
		5	判	871
		5	別	944
		5	利	1054
		6	刷	389
		6	制	590
		6	到	807
		7	前	643
		7	則	674
		7	刻	345
		8	剣	272
		9	副	924
		10	割	125
		10	創	650
		13	劇	259
21	力	0	力	1074
		3	加	76
		3	功	313
		5	努	790
		5	労	1091
		5	助	519
		6	効	314
		7	勇	1023
		8	勉	951
		9	動	813
		9	務	995
		10	勤	226
		10	勝	524
		10	募	956
		11	勢	591
22	勹	3	包	960
23	匕	3	北	976
24	匚	2	区	236
		5	医	21
25	十	0	十	495
		1	千	629
		2	午	303
		3	半	872
		6	協	209
		6	卒	684
		7	南	830
		10	博	861
26	卩	4	印	25
		4	危	152
		5	即	675
		5	卵	1052
27	厂	7	厚	315
		8	原	285
28	厶	3	去	198
		6	参	396
29	又	0	又	985
		1	及	184
		2	収	480
		2	反	873
		2	友	1024
		6	取	471
		6	受	477
30	ク	4	争	659

3-stroke headers

Grp	Header	Strk	Kanji	No.
31	口	0	口	316
		2	右	31
		2	可	77
		2	句	235
		2	古	293
		2	号	343
		2	司	407
		2	史	408
		2	召	525
		2	台	704
		3	各	113
		3	吉	177
		3	吸	185
		3	向	317
		3	后	318
		3	合	344
		3	同	814
		3	名	999

No.	Radical	Strokes	Kanji	Index
		4	君	240
		4	告	346
		4	吹	582
		4	否	881
		5	呼	294
		5	周	481
		5	味	989
		5	和	1097
		6	品	907
		7	員	26
		8	商	526
		8	唱	527
		8	問	1012
		9	喜	153
		9	喫	178
		9	善	644
		12	器	154
32	囗	2	四	409
		3	因	27
		3	回	97
		3	団	718
		4	囲	10
		4	困	354
		4	図	581
		5	固	295
		5	国	348
		10	園	49
33	土	0	土	792
		2	圧	3
		3	在	378
		3	地	726
		4	均	227
		4	坂	382
		5	垂	583
		6	型	247
		6	城	550
		8	域	22
		8	基	155
		8	堂	815
		9	場	551
		9	報	961
		10	塩	55
		10	墓	957
		11	境	210
		11	増	668
34	士	0	士	410
		4	声	605
		4	売	860
35	夂	6	変	945
		7	夏	78

No.	Radical	Strokes	Kanji	Index
36	夕	0	夕	1030
		2	外	110
		3	多	691
		5	夜	1014
		10	夢	996
37	大	0	大	705
		1	太	692
		1	天	777
		1	夫	911
		2	央	57
		2	失	454
		5	奇	156
		6	奏	652
		9	奥	58
		13	奮	934
38	女	0	女	520
		3	好	319
		5	委	11
		5	妻	367
		5	始	411
		5	姉	412
		5	姓	592
		5	妹	981
		6	姿	413
		7	娘	998
		8	婚	355
		8	婦	912
39	子 子	0	子	414
		3	字	440
		3	存	685
		4	孝	320
		5	学	122
		5	季	167
		7	孫	686
40	宀	3	安	4
		3	宇	32
		3	完	131
		3	守	472
		3	宅	708
		5	官	132
		5	実	457
		5	宗	482
		5	宙	736
		5	定	765
		5	宝	962
		6	客	179
		6	室	455
		6	宣	630
		7	家	79
		7	害	111

No.	Radical	Strokes	Kanji	Index
		7	宮	186
		7	容	1035
		8	寄	157
		8	宿	500
		8	密	991
		9	寒	128
		9	富	913
		10	寝	563
		11	察	390
		12	寮	1068
41	寸	0	寸	587
		3	寺	441
		4	対	695
		6	専	631
		7	射	460
		7	将	528
		9	尋	580
		9	尊	687
		12	導	816
42	小	0	小	529
		1	少	530
43	尤	8	就	483
44	尸	1	尺	467
		4	局	222
		5	居	199
		5	届	827
		6	屋	67
		7	展	778
		9	属	681
		11	層	653
45	山	0	山	397
		5	岸	147
		5	岩	149
		7	島	797
46	川 巛	0	川	632
		3	州	484
47	工	0	工	321
		2	左	359
		7	差	360
48	己	0	己	296
		6	巻	130
49	巾	2	市	415
		2	布	914
		4	希	158
		7	帰	164
		7	師	416
		7	席	612
		7	帯	696
		8	常	552
		8	帳	747

No.	Radical	Strokes	Kanji	Index
		10	幕	984
50	干	0	干	133
		2	平	939
		3	年	840
		5	幸	322
		10	幹	134
51	幺	2	幼	1034
52	广	2	広	323
		2	庁	748
		4	序	521
		4	床	531
		5	底	766
		5	店	779
		5	府	915
		6	度	791
		7	庫	297
		7	座	363
		7	庭	767
		8	康	324
53	廴	4	延	50
		6	建	273
54	廾	2	弁	952
55	弋	3	式	451
56	弓	0	弓	187
		1	引	28
		4	弟	768
		7	弱	469
		8	強	211
		8	張	749
57	ヨ ⺕		no kanji entry	
58	彡	4	形	248
59	彳	4	役	1016
		5	往	59
		5	径	249
		5	彼	882
		6	後	304
		6	待	697
		6	律	1060
		7	従	496
		7	徒	786
		8	得	820
		9	御	305
		9	復	925
		11	徳	821
60	八	5	並	940
		7	兼	270
61	巛	6	単	712
		8	巣	658
		9	営	37

No.	Radical	Strokes	Kanji	Index
		14	厳	286
62	⺌	3	当	802
		7	党	794
63	忄	3	忙	970
		4	快	98
		5	性	593
		6	悔	99
		8	情	553
		11	慣	136
64	才 扌	0	才	368
		2	打	693
		2	払	930
		4	技	173
		4	折	621
		4	投	798
		4	抜	870
		4	批	884
		5	押	61
		5	拡	114
		5	招	533
		5	担	713
		5	拝	852
		6	指	419
		6	持	442
		6	拾	486
		8	採	369
		8	捨	461
		8	授	478
		8	推	584
		8	接	620
		8	掃	655
		8	探	714
		9	揮	159
		9	提	769
		10	損	688
		13	操	656
65	氵	2	汁	497
		3	汚	56
		3	池	727
		4	汽	166
		4	決	262
		5	波	847
		5	泳	41
		5	沿	51
		5	河	83
		5	泣	191
		5	治	445
		5	注	740
		5	泊	862
		5	法	965

#	Radical	Strokes	Kanji	No.
		5	油	1020
		6	海	102
		6	活	125
		6	浅	635
		6	洗	636
		6	派	848
		6	洋	1038
		7	消	536
		7	浮	917
		7	浴	1046
		7	流	1064
		8	液	44
		8	混	357
		8	済	371
		8	深	567
		8	清	600
		8	涼	1070
		9	温	69
		9	減	287
		9	湖	300
		9	港	329
		9	測	678
		9	渡	787
		9	湯	800
		9	満	988
		10	漢	137
		10	源	288
		10	準	508
		11	演	52
		11	漁	203
		12	潔	263
		12	潮	751
		13	激	260
66	犭	2	犯	876
		6	狭	215
		6	独	824
67	艹 艸	4	花	85
		4	芸	257
		5	英	42
		5	芽	92
		5	苦	237
		5	若	468
		6	草	663
		6	茶	732
		7	荷	86
		8	菜	375
		8	著	743
		9	葉	1041
		9	落	1050
		10	蒸	556

#	Radical	Strokes	Kanji	No.
		12	蔵	670
		13	薬	1018
68	辵 辶	2	込	352
		2	辺	948
		4	近	231
		4	迎	258
		4	返	949
		5	述	506
		6	逆	180
		6	送	666
		6	退	701
		6	追	760
		6	逃	810
		6	迷	1003
		7	造	672
		7	速	680
		7	通	762
		7	連	1089
		8	週	491
		8	進	574
		9	運	35
		9	過	89
		9	達	709
		9	遅	729
		9	道	818
		9	遊	1028
		10	違	19
		10	遠	54
		11	適	774
		12	遺	20
		12	選	640
69	邑 阝	6	郊	338
		7	郡	244
		8	郷	218
		8	都	789
		8	部	922
		8	郵	1029
70	阜 阝	4	防	975
		6	限	291
		7	院	30
		7	降	341
		7	除	522
		7	陛	942
		8	険	282
		8	陸	1059
		9	階	108
		9	隊	702
		9	陽	1043
		11	際	377
		11	障	546

#	Radical	Strokes	Kanji	No.
		13	隣	1079

4-stroke headers

#	Radical	Strokes	Kanji	No.
71	心	0	心	564
		1	必	896
		3	志	417
		3	忘	969
		3	応	60
		4	忠	737
		4	念	841
		5	急	188
		5	思	418
		5	怠	698
		5	怒	793
		6	恩	68
		6	息	676
		6	恋	1087
		7	悪	2
		8	悲	883
		8	惑	1099
		9	愛	1
		9	意	12
		9	感	135
		9	想	654
		10	態	699
		12	憲	274
72	戈	2	成	594
		3	我	90
		9	戦	633
73	戸	0	戸	298
		4	所	513
74	手	0	手	473
		4	承	532
		6	挙	201
75	支	0	支	420
76	攴 攵	3	改	100
		3	攻	325
		4	放	963
		5	故	299
		5	政	595
		7	救	189
		7	教	213
		7	敗	853
		8	敬	250
		8	散	398
		8	数	586
		11	敵	771
		12	整	596
77	文	0	文	936

#	Radical	Strokes	Kanji	No.
78	斤	7	断	719
		9	新	565
79	方	0	方	964
		6	旅	1066
		7	族	682
		10	旗	161
80	日	0	日	834
		1	旧	196
		2	早	657
		4	易	13
		4	昔	613
		4	明	1001
		5	映	38
		5	昨	385
		5	春	507
		5	昭	534
		5	是	589
		5	星	597
		5	昼	738
		6	時	443
		6	景	251
		8	暑	514
		8	晴	598
		8	晩	879
		8	普	916
		9	暗	5
		9	暖	720
		10	暮	958
		11	暴	971
		14	曜	1036
81	曰	2	曲	223
		3	更	326
		6	書	517
		8	最	366
82	月	0	月	267
		4	服	926
		6	朗	1092
		7	望	972
		8	期	162
		8	朝	750
83	月 肉	0	肉	833
		2	有	1025
		4	肥	889
		4	育	23
		5	胃	17
		5	背	854
		5	肺	855
		6	胸	216
		6	能	844
		6	脈	992

#	Radical	Strokes	Kanji	No.
		7	脱	710
		7	脳	845
		9	腸	753
		9	腹	928
		15	臓	669
84	木	0	木	1010
		1	札	391
		1	本	979
		1	末	986
		1	未	990
		2	机	160
		3	材	379
		3	条	554
		3	束	677
		3	村	689
		3	来	1048
		4	果	81
		4	枝	421
		4	松	535
		4	東	799
		4	板	874
		4	枚	982
		4	林	1076
		5	栄	39
		5	査	361
		5	染	637
		5	柱	739
		6	案	6
		6	桜	62
		6	格	115
		6	株	127
		6	校	327
		6	根	356
		6	梅	858
		7	械	101
		8	極	224
		8	検	275
		8	植	557
		8	森	566
		8	棒	973
		9	楽	123
		9	業	221
		10	構	328
		10	模	1008
		10	様	1037
		11	横	63
		11	権	276
		11	標	900
		12	機	163
		12	橋	214

No.	Radical	Strokes	Kanji	Page
		12	樹	479
85	欠	0	欠	261
		2	次	444
		7	欲	1045
		10	歌	82
86	止	0	止	422
		1	正	599
		4	武	921
		4	歩	954
		9	歳	370
		10	歴	1085
87	歹	2	死	423
		6	残	404
88	殳	5	段	721
		6	殺	392
		9	殿	783
89	母	1	母	959
		2	毎	983
		4	毒	823
90	比	0	比	885
91	毛	0	毛	1009
92	氏	0	氏	424
		1	民	993
93	气	2	気	165
94	水氵	0	水	585
		1	永	40
		1	氷	901
		2	求	190
		5	泉	634
95	火	0	火	84
		2	灰	103
		2	灯	801
		3	災	372
		5	炭	715
		8	焼	537
		9	煙	53
		12	燃	842
96	灬	5	為	14
		5	点	781
		8	然	645
		8	無	997
		9	照	538
		11	熟	503
		11	熱	839
97	父	0	父	918
98	片	0	片	946
		4	版	875

No.	Radical	Strokes	Kanji	Page
99	牛牜	0	牛	197
		4	物	932
		4	牧	978
		6	特	822
100	犬	0	犬	277
		3	状	555
101	王玉	0	王	64
		1	玉	225
		6	班	877
		7	球	192
		7	現	289
		7	理	1055
		13	環	138
102	ネ	1	礼	1084
		3	社	462
		5	祝	501
		5	神	570
		5	祖	647
		9	福	927
103	耂	2	考	334
		2	老	1093
		4	者	463

5-stroke headers

No.	Radical	Strokes	Kanji	Page
104	生	0	生	601
		6	産	399
105	用	0	用	1039
106	田	0	申	568
		0	田	784
		0	由	1026
		2	男	722
		2	町	752
		4	界	104
		4	畑	866
		5	留	1065
		6	異	15
		6	略	1063
		7	番	880
107	疋	9	疑	174
108	白	0	白	863
		1	百	898
		3	的	772
		4	皆	105
		4	皇	330
109	疒	5	病	905
		7	痛	761
		7	疲	886
110	癶	4	発	868
		7	登	788
111	皮	0	皮	887

No.	Radical	Strokes	Kanji	Page
112	皿	0	皿	394
		5	益	45
		6	盛	602
		8	盟	1002
113	目	0	目	1011
		3	直	758
		4	看	139
		4	県	280
		4	省	539
		4	相	660
		5	真	569
		5	眠	994
		6	眼	148
		7	着	733
114	矢	0	矢	415
		3	知	725
		7	短	716
115	石	0	石	614
		4	研	278
		4	砂	362
		5	破	849
		9	磁	446
		10	確	116
116	示	0	示	447
		6	祭	373
		6	票	902
		8	禁	228
117	禾	2	私	425
		4	科	80
		4	秋	487
		4	秒	906
		5	秘	888
		6	移	16
		7	税	611
		7	程	770
		9	穀	349
		9	種	474
		10	稿	331
		11	積	615
		13	穫	117
118	穴	0	穴	264
		2	究	193
		3	空	239
		3	突	826
		6	窓	661
119	立	0	立	1062
		6	章	540
		7	童	817
		15	競	207

No.	Radical	Strokes	Kanji	Page
120	四网	8	罪	380
		8	署	516
		8	置	728
121	ネ	7	補	955
		9	複	929

6-stroke headers

No.	Radical	Strokes	Kanji	Page
122	竹	0	竹	731
		4	笑	541
		5	第	706
		5	笛	773
		5	符	919
		6	筋	229
		6	策	386
		6	等	803
		6	答	804
		6	筆	897
		7	節	623
		8	管	140
		8	算	400
		9	箱	865
		10	築	730
		12	簡	141
123	米	0	米	943
		4	粉	935
		4	料	1069
		8	精	603
		10	糖	805
124	糸	0	糸	426
		1	系	252
		3	紀	168
		3	級	194
		3	紅	332
		3	約	1017
		4	索	387
		4	紙	427
		4	純	509
		4	素	648
		4	納	843
		5	経	253
		5	細	374
		5	終	488
		5	紹	542
		5	組	649
		6	絵	106
		6	給	195
		6	結	265
		6	絶	626
		6	統	806
		6	絡	1049

No.	Radical	Strokes	Kanji	Page
		7	絹	279
		7	続	683
		8	綿	1006
		8	緒	515
		8	総	662
		8	緑	1075
		8	練	1088
		9	線	638
		9	編	947
		9	緊	230
		10	縦	498
		11	縮	502
		11	績	616
		12	織	558
125	羽	0	羽	33
		5	習	489
		5	翌	1047
126	羊	0	羊	1040
		3	美	894
		7	義	175
		7	群	242
127	耒	4	耕	333
128	耳	0	耳	448
		7	聖	604
		8	聞	937
		12	職	559
129	自	0	自	449
130	至	0	至	428
131	臼	9	興	217
132	舌	0	舌	627
133	舟	0	航	335
		5	船	639
134	艮	1	良	1071
135	色	0	色	560
136	虫	0	虫	741
		4	蚕	401
137	血	0	血	266
		6	衆	490
138	行	0	行	336
		5	術	505
		6	街	112
		10	衛	43
139	衣	0	衣	18
		2	表	903
		6	裁	376
		6	装	664
		7	裏	1056
		8	製	606
140	西襾	0	西	607
		3	要	1042

7-stroke headers

#	Header	Str	Kanji	No.
141	見	0	見	281
		4	規	169
		4	視	429
		5	覚	118
		9	親	572
		10	覧	1053
		11	観	142
142	臣	0	臣	571
		11	臨	1077
143	角	0	角	119
		6	解	96
144	言	0	言	290
		2	記	170
		2	計	254
		3	許	202
		3	訓	241
		3	討	808
		4	設	622
		4	訪	966
		4	訳	1019
		5	詞	430
		5	証	543
		5	評	904
		6	詩	431
		6	試	432
		6	誠	608
		6	話	1098
		7	語	306
		7	誤	307
		7	誌	433
		7	説	624
		7	読	825
		7	認	838
		7	誘	1027
		8	課	87
		8	諸	518
		8	誰	711
		8	誕	717
		8	談	723
		8	調	754
		8	論	1096
		10	講	337
		10	謝	464
		12	警	255
		12	識	452
		13	議	176
		13	護	308
145	谷	0	谷	347
146	豆	0	豆	809
		6	豊	967
147	豕	4	豚	828
		5	象	544
148	貝	0	貝	109
		2	負	920
		3	財	381
		4	貨	88
		4	責	617
		4	貧	908
		5	賀	93
		5	貴	171
		5	貸	700
		5	貯	744
		5	買	859
		5	費	890
		5	貿	974
		6	資	434
		6	賃	759
		8	賛	402
		8	質	456
		8	賞	545
		11	贈	671
149	赤	0	赤	618
150	走	0	走	665
		3	起	172
		5	越	47
151	足	0	足	679
		6	路	1090
152	身	0	身	573
153	車	0	車	465
		2	軍	243
		4	転	780
		5	軽	256
		8	輪	1078
		9	輸	1021
154	辛	6	辞	450
155	辰	6	農	846
156	酉	3	酒	475
		3	配	856
		7	酸	403
157	里	0	里	1057
		2	重	499
		4	野	1015
		5	量	1072
158	麦 麥	0	麦	864

8-stroke headers

#	Header	Str	Kanji	No.
159	金 釒	0	金	232
		2	針	575
		5	鉱	339
		5	鉄	775
		6	銀	233
		6	銭	641
		6	銅	819
		8	鋼	340
		8	録	1095
		11	鏡	219
160	長	0	長	755
161	門	0	門	1013
		3	閉	941
		4	開	107
		4	間	143
		6	閣	120
		6	関	144
162	隹	4	集	492
		6	雑	393
		10	難	831
		10	離	1058
163	雨	0	雨	34
		3	雪	625
		4	雲	36
		5	電	785
		7	震	576
164	青 靑	0	青	609
		6	静	610
165	非	0	非	891
166	食	4	飲	29
		4	飯	878
		5	飼	435
		8	館	145

9-stroke headers

#	Header	Str	Kanji	No.
167	面	0	面	1007
168	革	0	革	121
169	音	0	音	70
170	頁	2	頂	756
		3	順	510
		4	預	1033
		5	領	1073
		7	頭	811
		9	額	124
		9	顔	150
		9	題	707
		9	類	1080
		10	願	151
171	風	0	風	923
172	飛	0	飛	892
173	食	0	食	561
		6	養	1044
174	首	0	首	476

10-stroke headers

#	Header	Str	Kanji	No.
175	馬	0	馬	850
		4	駅	46
		5	駐	742
		8	験	283
		12	驚	220
176	骨	0	骨	351
177	高	0	高	342
178	髟	4	髪	869

11-stroke headers

#	Header	Str	Kanji	No.
179	黄 黃	0	黄	65
180	魚	0	魚	204
		6	鮮	642
181	黒 黑	0	黒	350
182	鳥	0	鳥	757
		3	鳴	1004

12-stroke header

#	Header	Str	Kanji	No.
183	歯	0	歯	436

14-stroke header

#	Header	Str	Kanji	No.
184	鼻	0	鼻	895

INDEX 6

Arranged by the Educational Kanji Designation
(学年別学習漢字)[1]

Numbers refer to kanji numbers in this book.

Grade 1		Grade 2			Grade 3	
一 24	小 529	夕 1030	強 211	時 443	昼 738	毎 983	階 108
右 31	上 547	立 1062	教 213	自 449	朝 750	万 987	寒 128
雨 34	森 566	力 1074	近 231	室 455	長 755	明 1001	感 135
円 48	人 577	林 1076	兄 246	社 462	鳥 757	鳴 1004	漢 137
王 64	水 585	六 1094	形 248	弱 469	直 758	毛 1009	館 145
音 70	正 599		計 254	首 476	通 762	門 1013	岸 147
下 71	生 601	**Grade 2**	元 284	秋 487	弟 768	夜 1014	期 162
火 84	青 609	引 28	原 285	週 491	店 779	野 1015	起 172
花 85	石 614	羽 33	言 290	春 507	点 781	友 1024	客 179
貝 109	赤 618	雲 36	古 293	書 517	電 785	曜 1036	宮 186
学 122	先 628	園 49	戸 298	少 530	冬 795	用 1039	急 188
気 165	千 629	遠 54	午 303	場 551	刀 796	来 1048	球 192
休 183	川 632	黄 65	後 304	色 560	東 799	理 1055	究 193
玉 225	早 657	何 74	語 306	食 561	当 802	里 1057	級 194
金 232	草 663	夏 78	交 309	心 564	答 804	話 1098	去 198
九 234	足 679	家 79	光 311	新 565	頭 811		橋 214
空 239	村 689	科 80	公 312	親 572	同 814	**Grade 3**	業 221
月 267	大 705	歌 82	工 321	図 581	道 818	悪 2	局 222
犬 277	男 722	画 91	広 323	数 586	読 825	安 4	曲 223
見 281	竹 731	会 95	考 320	星 597	内 829	暗 5	銀 233
五 301	中 734	回 97	行 336	晴 598	南 830	委 11	区 236
口 316	虫 741	海 102	高 342	声 605	肉 833	意 12	苦 237
校 327	町 752	絵 106	合 344	西 607	馬 850	医 21	具 238
左 359	天 777	外 110	谷 347	切 619	買 859	育 23	君 240
三 394	田 784	角 119	国 348	雪 625	売 860	員 26	係 245
山 396	土 792	楽 123	黒 350	線 638	麦 864	飲 29	軽 256
四 408	二 832	活 126	今 353	船 639	半 872	院 30	決 262
子 413	日 834	間 143	才 368	前 643	番 880	運 35	血 266
糸 426	入 836	丸 146	細 374	組 649	父 918	泳 41	研 278
字 440	年 840	岩 149	作 383	走 665	風 923	駅 46	県 280
耳 448	白 863	顔 150	算 399	多 691	分 933	央 57	庫 297
七 453	八 867	帰 164	姉 411	太 692	聞 937	横 63	湖 300
車 465	百 898	汽 166	市 414	体 694	米 943	屋 67	向 317
手 473	文 936	記 170	矢 415	台 704	歩 954	温 69	幸 322
十 495	本 979	弓 187	思 418	知 725	母 959	化 72	港 329
出 504	名 999	牛 197	止 422	地 726	方 964	荷 86	号 343
女 520	木 1010	魚 204	紙 427	池 727	北 976	界 104	根 356
	目 1011	京 205	寺 441	茶 732	妹 981	開 107	祭 373

[1]Ministry of Education, Culture, Sports, Science and Technology–Japan. 1998.

坂	382	世	588	倍	857	緑	1075	救	189	士	409	達	709	望	972
皿	393	整	596	箱	865	礼	1084	求	190	氏	424	単	712	牧	978
仕	404	昔	613	畑	866	列	1086	泣	191	試	432	置	728	末	986
使	405	全	646	発	868	練	1088	給	195	児	439	仲	735	満	988
始	410	想	654	反	873	路	1090	挙	201	治	445	貯	744	未	990
指	419	相	660	板	874	和	1097	漁	203	辞	450	兆	746	脈	992
死	423	送	666	悲	883			競	207	失	454	腸	753	民	993
詩	431	息	676	皮	887	**Grade 4**		共	208	借	466	低	763	無	997
歯	436	速	680	美	894	愛	1	協	209	種	474	停	764	約	1017
事	437	族	682	鼻	895	案	6	鏡	219	周	481	底	766	勇	1023
持	442	他	690	筆	897	以	7	極	224	祝	501	的	772	要	1042
次	444	打	693	氷	901	位	8	訓	241	順	510	典	776	養	1044
式	451	対	695	表	903	囲	10	軍	243	初	512	伝	782	浴	1046
実	457	待	697	病	905	胃	17	郡	244	唱	527	徒	786	利	1054
写	459	代	703	秒	906	衣	18	型	247	松	535	努	790	陸	1059
者	463	第	706	品	907	印	25	径	249	焼	537	灯	801	料	1069
主	470	題	707	負	908	栄	39	景	251	照	538	働	812	良	1071
取	471	炭	715	部	922	英	42	芸	257	省	539	堂	815	量	1072
守	472	短	716	服	926	塩	55	欠	261	笑	541	得	820	輪	1078
酒	475	談	723	福	927	億	66	結	265	象	544	特	822	類	1080
受	477	着	733	物	932	加	76	健	269	賞	545	毒	823	令	1081
州	484	柱	739	平	939	果	81	建	273	信	562	熱	839	例	1082
拾	486	注	740	返	949	課	87	験	283	臣	571	念	841	冷	1083
終	488	丁	745	勉	951	貨	88	固	295	成	594	敗	853	歴	1085
習	489	帳	747	放	963	芽	92	候	310	清	600	梅	858	連	1089
集	492	調	754	味	989	改	100	功	313	静	610	博	861	労	1091
住	493	追	760	命	1000	械	101	好	319	席	612	飯	878	老	1093
重	499	定	765	面	1007	害	111	康	324	積	615	費	890	録	1095
宿	500	庭	767	問	1012	街	112	航	335	折	621	飛	892		
所	513	笛	773	役	1016	各	113	告	346	節	623	必	896	**Grade 5**	
暑	514	鉄	775	薬	1018	覚	118	差	360	説	624	標	900	圧	3
助	519	転	780	油	1020	完	131	最	366	戦	633	票	902	易	13
勝	524	登	788	有	1025	官	132	菜	375	浅	635	不	909	移	16
商	526	都	789	由	1026	管	140	材	379	選	640	付	910	因	27
昭	534	度	791	遊	1028	観	142	昨	384	然	645	夫	911	営	37
消	536	島	797	様	1037	関	144	刷	388	倉	651	府	915	永	40
章	540	投	798	洋	1038	願	151	察	389	巣	658	副	924	衛	43
乗	549	湯	800	羊	1040	喜	153	札	390	争	659	粉	935	液	44
植	557	等	803	葉	1041	器	154	殺	391	側	673	兵	938	益	45
深	567	豆	809	陽	1043	希	158	参	395	束	677	別	944	演	52
申	568	動	813	落	1050	旗	161	散	397	続	683	変	945	往	59
真	569	童	817	流	1064	機	163	産	398	卒	684	辺	948	応	60
神	570	農	846	旅	1066	季	167	残	403	孫	686	便	950	桜	62
身	573	波	847	両	1067	紀	168	司	406	帯	696	包	960	恩	68
進	574	配	856			議	176	史	407	隊	702	法	965	仮	73